*Mau Mau
from Below*

Eastern African Studies

Revealing Prophets
Prophecy in Eastern African History
Edited by DAVID M. ANDERSON
& DOUGLAS H. JOHNSON

Religion & Politics in East Africa
The Period Since Independence
Edited by HOLGER BERNT HANSEN
& MICHAEL TWADDLE

Swahili Origins
Swahili Culture
& the Shungwaya Phenomenon
JAMES DE VERE ALLEN

A History of Modern Ethiopia 1855–1974
BAHRU ZEWDE

*Ethnicity & Conflict
in the Horn of Africa*
Edited by KATSUYOSHI FUKUI
& JOHN MARKAKIS

Siaya
The Historical Anthropology
of an African Landscape
DAVID WILLIAM COHEN
& E. S. ATIENO ODHIAMBO

Control & Crisis in Colonial Kenya
The Dialectic of Domination
BRUCE BERMAN

Unhappy Valley
Book One: State & Class
Book Two: Violence & Ethnicity
BRUCE BERMAN
& JOHN LONSDALE

Mau Mau from Below
GREET KERSHAW

The Mau Mau War in Perspective
FRANK FUREDI

*Squatters & the Roots
of Mau Mau, 1905–63*
TABITHA KANOGO

*Economic & Social Origins
of Mau Mau 1945–53*
DAVID THROUP

Penetration & Protest in Tanzania
The Impact of the World Economy
on the Pare 1860–1960
ISARIA N. KIMAMBO

Custodians of the Land
Ecology & Culture
in the History of Tanzania
Edited by GREGORY MADDOX,
JAMES L. GIBLIN & ISARIA N. KIMAMBO

Jua Kali Kenya
Change & Development
in an Informal Economy 1970–95
KENNETH KING

The Second Economy in Tanzania
T.L. MALIYAMKONO
& M.S.D. BAGACHWA

Kampala Women Getting By
Wellbeing in the Time of AIDS
SANDRA WALLMAN

*Uganda Now
Changing Uganda
Developing Uganda*
From Chaos to Order*
Edited by HOLGER BERNT HANSEN
& MICHAEL TWADDLE

*Decolonization & Independence
in Kenya 1940–88*
Edited by B.A. OGOT
& WILLIAM OCHIENG'

Slaves, Spices & Ivory in Zanzibar
Integration of an East African
Commercial Empire into the
World Economy
ABDUL SHERIFF

Zanzibar Under Colonial Rule
Edited by ABDUL SHERIFF
& ED FERGUSON

*The History & Conservation
of Zanzibar Stone Town*
Edited by ABDUL SHERIFF

Being Maasai
Ethnicity & Identity in East Africa
Edited by THOMAS SPEAR
& RICHARD WALLER

*Kakungulu & the Creation
of Uganda 1868–1928*
MICHAEL TWADDLE

*Ecology Control & Economic
Development in East African History*
The Case of Tanganyika 1850–1950
HELGE KJEKSHUS

*Education in the Development
of Tanzania 1919–1990*
LENE BUCHERT

* forthcoming

Mau Mau from Below

Greet Kershaw

Formerly Professor of Anthropology
University of California
Long Beach

James Currey
OXFORD

E·A·E·P
NAIROBI

Ohio University Press
ATHENS

James Currey Ltd
73 Botley Rd
Oxford OX2 0BS

East African Educational Publishers
Kijabe Street, P.O. Box 45314
Nairobi, Kenya

Ohio University Press
Scott Quadrangle
Athens, Ohio 45701, USA

© Greet Kershaw 1997
First published 1997

1 2 3 4 5 01 00 99 98 97

British Library Cataloguing in Publication Data
Kershaw, Greet
   Mau Mau from Below. - (Eastern African studies)
   1. Mau Mau 2. Ethnology - Kenya 3. Revolutionaries - Kenya
   4. Kenya - History
   I. Title
   322.4'2'096762

ISBN 0-85255-732-9 (James Currey Cloth)
ISBN 0-85255-731-0 (James Currey Paper)

Library of Congress Cataloging-in-Publication Data
Kershaw, Greet.
   Mau Mau from below / Greet Kershaw.
   p. cm. – (Eastern African studies)
   Includes bibliographical references and index.
   ISBN 0-8214-1154-3. – ISBN 0-8214-1155-1 (pbk.). – ISBN 0-85255-732-9 (J. Currey cloth). – ISBN 0-85255-731-0 (J. Currey paper)
   1. Mau Mau–History. 2. Kenya–History–1895-1963. I. Title.
II. Series: Eastern African studies (London, England)
DT433.577.K47 1996
967.82'03–DC20
                             96-41339
                                CIP

Typeset in 10/11pt Baskerville
by Long House Publishing Services, St Vincent, West Indies

Contents

List of Tables	ix
Glossary	x
Acknowledgements	xiii
Foreword by John Lonsdale	xvi
Preface	1

One
The Settlement of Kiambu until the Kirika Famine of 1835

	13
The first months of fieldwork	13
Kikuyu ideology of history	15
Traditions of settlement and forest economies	18
The acquisition of land	20
Forest economies	21
The ideology of individual and gender	23
Women and men in a forest economy	25
Interpretations and traditions of land ownership	26
Mbari traditions from the days of the forest economies and mbari interpretations	28
Oral traditions of Thuita and Igi before Kirika	29
Wealth and poverty before Kirika	33
Fission of the Mbari	34
The Relationship with Murang'a and the Kirika famine	35

Two
From Kirika until the End of the Nineteenth Century

	43
Economic and Social development in the early post-Kirika decades	44
The ahoi system	46
The nineteenth-century post-Kirika mbari	48
Twentieth-century conflicts of Igi oral traditions	53
Conflicts based on interpretations of the mbari	54
Possible oral traditions before oral traditions?	56
Inheritance and inequality	58
The cost of the land	60
The last decades: wealth, concentration of power and dependence	61
The organization of the trade	63
The growth of social and political differentiation over time	65
The role of the anake and the mariika	68
Curbs on anake and mariika	69
Warfare and the disasters of the final decade	70

Three
Land Ownership in the Twentieth Century

	84
Immediate post-famine conditions	84
Local land alienation	85
Losses of land alienation	88
Immediate consequences of the loss of land	89
The opening of the Rift Valley	90
Consequences of the loss of land in the early decades	93
Monetization and land acquisitions	95
The position of the ahoi	96

v

Land holdings before the Carter Commission, early 1930s	98
The Carter Commission	101
The Carter Commission Report as colonial dividing line	102
Land ownership and acquisition after the Carter Report	104
Conflict about land	105
Litigation in Thuita and Igi: the thrust for land consolidation	106

Four
The Labour Market for the Local Population
116

Early labour markets	116
Clerical and administrative work in the local and settled area	118
Basic, semi-skilled and skilled work for men in the local and settled area	119
Work for women in the local and settled area	123
The Nairobi labour market before the Depression	127
The Nairobi labour market from the Depression to the 1940s	129
The labour market in Nairobi	130
Strategies for coping with Nairobi conditions in the 1940s	133
Strategies for coping with rural conditions	135
Employment immediately before the declaration of the Emergency	136

Five
Land, Labour & Living in the Colonial Era
144

Diet, crops and use of land in the early twentieth century	144
Factors of fertility: land and labour	146
Early land use of larger land owners and the changes of the 1920s	148
Early land use of smaller land owners and the changes of the 1920s	149
The use of land after the Carter Commission	157
Manure, government intervention and the larger land owners	157
Conditions in the late 1940s	165
The reform of education	169

Six
Resistance of the Elders until the Beginning of Mau Mau
175

The resistance of the elders	175
The ideology of the resistance of the elders	177
Pacification	177
Utilization	178
Direct protest, the land, and the Kikuyu Association	178
The weakening of direct protest by elders	184
The fight for rural unification through the Mbari	187
The battle for control of education	188
The female circumcision issue	189
Githunguri Teacher's Training College	193
The re-entry of the elders into the resistance	195
The return of the Rift Valley migrants	196
The return of Kenyatta	199

Seven
The Resistance of the Land Poor & Landless:
212
The Beginning of Mau Mau

The relationship between landless, land poor and the landed	213
The early Kenyatta years, 1946–50: myth and reality	216

The beginning of Mau Mau	219
The government's perspective	220
The probable beginning of urban Mau Mau	221
The possible beginning of Mau Mau in the rural area	226
1950, the year of anger and frustration	227
From 1951 until the declaration of the Emergency	236
Opposition to Mau Mau in 1952	237

Eight
The Emergency, Marige & the End of Mau Mau

	248
Screening	250
Marige	251
The end of Mau Mau	258

Appendices

Appendix 1
Data, Reliability & Analysis

	264
1. Method of work	264
2. Oral traditions	265
3. Oaths	265
4. Punishments for oaths	266
5. Time of oath taking	266
6. Dating of oaths and correlation with other factors	266
7. Where oaths were taken	267
8. Age	267
9. Data on domicile	268
10. Economic classifications	268
11. Information about the size of land holdings	269
12. Wages	269

Appendix II
Oral Traditions

	271
1. Oral traditions of Thuita	271
2. Statements about Kikuyu history from Igi	273

Appendix III
Notes on Kiambu Social Organization

	275
1. Kiambu personalities in the early colonial period	275
2. The Kikuyu as a tribe	276
3. Generation and handing over	277
4. Matuika and Mau Mau	280
5. Notes on colonial chiefs	280

Appendix IV
Economic data

	284
1. Currencies and taxes	284
2. Cost of goats	284
3. Cost of local land	285
4. Cost of clearing land	285
5. Minimum wages per day and per annum	286
6. Piece work	286
7. Brideprices	286
8. Production of basic foods, Grade 1, Grade 2, and DARD	286

9. Yield of three acres land	287
10. Cost of manure	288
11. Recommended sequence of crop rotation with minimal manure	289
12. Cost/yield of some auxiliary crops	289
13. Production one acre pineapples, 1950 prices	289
14. Production one acre onions, 1950 prices	290
15. Minimum wages in settled/local area; compared with general prices and productivity on one acre Grade 2 land	290
16. Mean wages Nairobi, before Emergency	291
17. Coffee in the settled area in the early twentieth century and its influence on the production of maize	291
18. Local coffee notes	291
19. Local coffee expectations and production	292
20. Cost of living, auxiliary foods and non-food items	293

Appendix V — 296
Notes on the Kenya Land Commission Report

Appendix VI — 299
Notes on the Rift Valley

1. Return from the Rift Valley	300
2. General data on the returnees	301
3. Mau Mau membership among Rift Valley repatriates	303
4. Violence and Nanyuki District	304

Appendix VII — 307
Notes on Local Education

Appendix VIII — 311
Late Nineteenth- and Twentieth-Century Oaths

1. Kunyua Muuma	311
2. Oaths which created, structured or restructured relationships	312
3. Cursing oaths	313
4. Commitment and structuring oaths in the twentieth century	315
5. Named twentieth-century oaths	315
6. Legitimacy and illegitimacy of Mau Mau oaths	317

Appendix IX — 321
Notes on Mau Mau

1. Relationship between KAU and Mau Mau	321
2. Initiation years and Mau Mau participation	322
3. Elders' rank and Mau Mau participation: Rift Valley, rural and Nairobi	323
4. Age and Mau Mau membership	323
5. Resistance and collaboration	323
6. Screening	325
7. Homeguards	327
8. Cleansing ritual	328
9. The unity of Mau Mau, Kiambu and the forest	329

Appendix X — 334
Land Consolidation & Villagization

1. Land consolidation	334
2. Villagization	336

Selected Bibliography	338
Index	348

List of Tables

Table 2.1	Approximate growth and decline of Igi households, population and land ownership between the Ruraya Famine and 1962	72
Table 2.2	Approximate growth and decline of Thuita households, population and land ownership between the Ruraya Famine and 1962	73
Table 3.1	Classification of Igi and Thuita households by land ownership before the Carter Commission and before the Emergency	99
Table 4.1	Profile local male population working in the local area before the declaration of the Emergency	124
Table 4.2	Profile local male population working in the settled area before declaration of the Emergency	125
Table 4.3	Profile local male population working in Nairobi before the declaration of the Emergency	131
Table 4.4	Employment (males) before the declaration of the Emergency	137
Table 4.5	Employment (females) before the declaration of the Emergency	138
Table 5.1	Approximate cost of production, yield and profit for maize and potatoes in shillings per acre	150
Table 7.1	Growth of Mau Mau in Nairobi (females between brackets)	225
Table 7.2	Development of Mau Mau oaths, males (multiple oaths between brackets)	228
Table 7.3	Development of Mau Mau oaths, females (multiple oaths between brackets)	229
Table 7.4	Composition of Mau Mau population (males) by period (excludes Rift Valley)	232
Table 7.5	Composition of Mau Mau population (females) by period (excludes Rift Valley)	234

Glossary

This glossary of Kikuyu and Swahili words reflects the orthography taught to me by my assistants in 1956. I make no claim for its scientific accuracy. Plural and singular forms, if needed, are given in brackets. – G. K.

askari	soldier, policeman
bangi	Indian hemp, *cannabis sativa*
bara	war; fight
baraza	meeting for public purposes
batuni	platoon, used to refer to an oath
bara bara	without ritual
boma	enclosure
bururi	Kikuyu land, often used to indicate land of all who claim descent from mythological ancestors Muumbi and Gikuyu
chocho	grandmother
fundi	craftsman
Gaki	Colonial Nyeri
gatego	syphilis
gichina mbangi	to burn the marigold: name of an initiation year around 1942 when young males used the marigold as a drug
gitati	obligatory labour, paid or unpaid
githaka (ithaka)	land which belongs to a person or *mbari*
githaku (ithaku)	subdivision of *mbari* land
githathi	sacred stones, bone of elephant used in ritual
Githunguri	small hill
gukuna	break virgin land, which becomes one's own because it was not claimed before
gutahikio	to cleanse, purify
guthathaya	to behave with mercy
gutwara	to carry, bring
igwima	the poorest of the poor
iregi	named ritual period, may be translated as those who resist, revolt
ita	war
itura (matura)	small group of homesteads
ituika (matuika)	rituals marking change from one ritual generation to another
kagilcha	scars from fire (late nineteenth-century initiation for girls only)
karinga	pure
kiama (ciama)	council
kienyeku	sores
kindu/indu	things
kipande	registration evidence, to be worn by males
kirege	girl who has remained uncircumcised past the appropriate time
Kirika	famine around 1835
kirira	knowledge given when reaching certain age and status, often refers to land and ritual matters
kirumi	curse, prohibition, used to warn against performing certain acts or punish such acts
koria	bush shelters in the late nineteenth and twentieth century
kuhoya	to pray, to ask
kuhuroria	to break a tie, a promise
kunyua	to drink
kunyua muuma	to take an oath
kurega	to refuse, reject (*Iregi*, those who reject or refuse)

Glossary

kuringa thenge	oathing ceremony in which a ram is beaten to death
kuigua tha	to give mercy
kuroga	bewitch, witchcraft
macamba	the settled area claimed by the Kikuyu; also *mashamba*: my land
magatha	land or stock given as bridal gift
Maina	one of a set of alternating ritual generations
Mandeleo ya Wanawake	Progess of Women
mbari	land and the descent group which owns it jointly and individually
mbaya	evil, the evil one
mburi	goats, livestock, excluding cows
miti	small, thin branches
mucii (micii)	the smallest family group or the homestead of a two/three generation family
mugendi (agendi)	sojourner
muhoi (ahoi)	user of land, often affinal kin
muhiriga (mihiriga)	clan
Muhimu	Central Committee of Nairobi Mau Mau
muka	wife
mundu (andu)	person
mundu mugo (andu aigu)	curer, ritual specialist
mundu umwe	ritually one person
mundu wa tha	man who is just, has mercy
muramati (arumati)	leader of *mbari* or *ithaku*
Muranga	Colonial Fort Hall
muratha (aratha)	friend
murica	ritual objects carried by traveller showing peaceful intent
muthami (athami)	man having his own land elsewhere, but living with another *mbari*
muthoni (athoni)	affinal relatives
muthamaki (athamaki)	leader, often of councils
mutherigu (mitherigo)	abusive songs
muthungu (athungu)	Europeans, Westerners
muthuri (athuri)	elder, can be followed by a number of goats paid for junior or senior eldership; husband
mutongoria (atongoria)	important person, stress on wealth, power
mutumia (atumia)	woman, married woman
muuma	oath
mwanake/anake	initiated youth, age of warriors
mwaki (miaki)	territorial division composed of several *micii*
Mwangi	one of a set of alternating ritual generations
mwathi (athi)	original owners, sellers of land
mwene (ene)	owners of land
nduka	local shop
ndundu	inner council
ndungata	underling, can be asked to marry daughter without paying brideprice
Ngai	God
Ng'aragu	distant, great
Ng'aragu ya Ruraya	Severe famine (*ng'aragu*) at end of nineteenth century (*ruraya* = distant, great). Depending on the informant or the person(s) addressed, can imply that its causes lay outside the Kikuyu
ngwatio	reciprocal aid between kin, age mates
njira-ini	in the road, without ritual
nyimbo (ruimbo)	songs

Glossary

nyumba	descent group
posho	ground maize
riika (mariika)	initiation year, regiment, ritual generation
rugongo (ngongo)	literally ridge, district, often largest cooperative political unit
ruguru	distant, Rift Valley
ruimbo (nyimbo)	song
ruracio	brideprice
ruraya	distant
safari	travel, often on foot
sufaria	tin cooking vessel
tatha	stomach content of animal, mixed with vegetable matter and medicinal or purifying herbs
tha	mercy, justice
thabari	robbers
thahu	state of ritual uncleanliness
thenge	ram
theru	state of ritual purity
thingira	man's hut
thirikari	Government
thukumu	slavers
tuhii (ihii)	uninitiated young boys
uhoro	matter
uhoro wa Ngai	matter which God decides
ukabi	ritual division of the Kikuyu
umoja	unity
unuthi	Nubians
weiyathi	freedom

The following mariika are frequently used in the text. Dates local and approximate.

Mburu	circ. 1886/1887	(yellow earth pigment)
Uhere	circ. 1888/1889	(scabies)
Ngigi	circ. 1890/1892	(locusts)
Mutungu	circ. 1892/1893	(smallpox)
Kienyeku	circ. 1896/1897/1898	(sores)
Kamande	1902/1903	(invasion of small, flat worms)
Gatiti	1903/1904	(tray)
Njege	1906/1907	(porcupines)
Nyaregi	1908/1909	(protesters)
Makio	1912/1913	
Kihiumweri	1916/1917	(popular song about a knife)
Kinyotoku	1919/1920	(disease)
Kibande	1920/1921	(introduction of *kipande*)
Chirringi/Nuthu	1923/1924	(shilling; 50 per cent previous rupia)
Ndege	1926/1927	(first observed aeroplane)
Kenya Bathi	1934/1935	(first local bus)
Hitler, Japan	1940/1941	(start of the Second World War)
Manjiniti	1952	(Emergency)
Kijiji, Gichagi	1953	(village)
Gatoro	1954	(homemade gun)

Dedication

To the Children
of Mbari ya Igi
& Thuita

Acknowledgements

If Stanley S. Morrison, Secretary of the Christian Council of Kenya during the Emergency, had not felt uneasy about the absence of Mau Mau voices in the understanding of the movement, I would not have been able to collect data. Access to a research area, permission and support from the District Commissioner of Kiambu, Mr D.J. Penwill and the Provincial Commissioner F.A. Lloyd, transformed the idea into reality. Chief Magugo Waweru allowed a stranger in his location. His courtesy, support, direct and indirect help, made the difference between being a tolerated guest who had to avoid controversies and someone free to ask questions.

I am grateful to Chief Kibathi and Mr Kiburi, the Chief Advisor on Law and Custom of Kiambu Court. Though 1956 and 1957 were still Emergency years and the population of four villages, *Igi, Nginduri, Thuita* and *Itara* had many more pressing matters on its mind, the people made

Acknowledgements

me feel welcome. I thank in particular the oldest elders of the community, Waweru Mahui and Kabogo Kangethe. Other elders, landowning or not, were ready to provide information, to instruct and answer questions. I knew that I was accepted when I was told – unceremoniously at times – that some of my questions were not acceptable and others too bothersome.

I owe a debt to all *arumati* and elders who met with me at regular and irregular times; Gathwe Kiramba, Murungu Kingara, Muchai Mugo, Nganga Ngechi, Njoroge Mathu, Kiburi Githagi, Karobo Muchunu, Mbirui Muchunu, Kuria Muraya, Kangethe Kabogo, Munyambo Kinuthia, Njuguna Kiarii, Kiigi Kiara, Njoroge Kirago, Mukabi Muhea, Njoroge Mwende, Makumi Njubi, Kinuthia Wakiawa, Wanyaikuru Kimani, Kihanya Njoroge, Thogo Kihanya, Wanganga Tutua, Mutiti Kanyingi. I also thank Wanyoike Kamawe and especially Mbiru Mare for their help; I am grateful to Waira Kamau for his visits after he returned from detention.

However grateful I am for what I learned from the elders, it was the acceptance of ordinary villagers and particularly the women which made me feel at home. I would have been the poorer without them. If I still do not understand or have misunderstood what it meant to be Kikuyu, they cannot be blamed for lack of teaching: thank you Wamucha, Ruth, Muumbi, Njambi, Esther, Wanjiru, Monica and Beatrice and the many others. Thank you for trying to teach me the elementary skills of daily life with good humour, though my clumsiness in things Kikuyu must have been exasperating. Above all, thank you for trying to teach me to 'think Kikuyu'.

No one deserves more thanks than my assistant, Beatrice Njoguna, my right hand, who eased my way into the community, who translated whenever necessary (which was often), who took a keen interest in the outcome of what became in consequence our data rather than mine. She used her empathy, knowledge and skill to teach me what to ask, where to stop, what to try to find out and where to draw the line. Without her there would have been neither data, nor might I at times have realized the meaning of the information and the appropriate follow-up questions. The Mbari ya Igi Advisory Committee (MAC), Chief Magugo Waweru, Peter Mahinyara, Mbiru Mare, Muumbi Mbiru and several others, helped me understand what factors were relevant in local land use; it is largely responsible for the wealth of agricultural data. The help of the Department of Agriculture through its Agricultural Officer Mr James Mburu in the 1962 research period was of considerable value. The medicines supplied regularly by Kiambu hospital and the food supplied by the Red Cross and the Christian Council of Kenya allowed me to help the community, but their largesse also helped my work.

There are many others who gave unstintingly of their time and knowledge. Among them were the erstwhile Moderator of the Church of Scotland, the Rev. R.G.M. Calderwood who knew the research area intimately and H.E. Lambert, who had been District Commissioner in

Acknowledgements

Kiambu and had extensive knowledge of Kikuyu land tenure. I pay tribute to Dr L.S.B. Leakey, his superior knowledge, his fluency in Kikuyu, the massive amount of data he collected in the Thirties. He kindly met with me a number of times, was generous with his advice, and allowed me to read several chapters of his then still unpublished manuscript. I regard it as a privilege to disagree with him on a number of points and I do so with the gratitude and respect I owe. I thank Mr Henry Muoria Mwaniki in London for his willingness to discuss certain matters pertaining to Mau Mau.

The East African Institute for Social Research under its Director Lloyd A. Fallers helped finance part of the fieldwork between 1955 and 1957; the 1962 fieldwork was entirely financed by the Institute. When visiting, I enjoyed its stimulating environment and hospitality and I probably would not have considered a career in anthropology without the support, if not proddings of Tom Fallers. He early on saw value in the data; he became my guide and mentor in the field and at the University of Chicago.

Clare Hall in Cambridge twice offered supportive hospitality; a grant from the Social Science Research Council allowed a semester's leave from teaching. The African Studies Centre in Leiden, where Dr Robert Buytenhuys was a stimulating colleague, made it possible to work there for a year.

In the years that it has taken me to produce the manuscript Dr John Lonsdale of Trinity College, Cambridge, has been my most patient and encouraging supporter. Were it not for his stimulating discussions, I might still hestitate to publish the data. I am particularly grateful for the way he and in the last years Dr Bruce Berman of Queen's University in Kingston have kept me abreast of what was happening in Mau Mau studies.

And there are the more personal thanks. I thank the Friends Service Council team in Kenya: John Starke, Mary and Walter Martin and Margarit Reed; I thank Stanley and Ann Booth Clibborn, all of them are always willing to agree and disagree with the data while providing hospitality to a weary fieldworker.

I thank my husband John, my co-worker in the field, my friend and companion; his work on litigation and the Great Famine has been invaluable for this publication. What little I know about the analysis of oral tradition I learned from him. I thank my sons, William and David, for their patience; though by now grown men, they may not have forgotten my plea 'Please give me five more minutes'.

I thank Mary Anne Patterson for learning to master possibly the most ancient programme on the most ancient word processor and becoming my hands. Without the professional skill and compassion of Dr Gary S. Rinzler, physiatrist, now of Honolulu, this publication would not have seen the light of day, and I thank him.

Foreword

JOHN LONSDALE

Past conflict between social movements and ruling powers has always attracted historians, and not just because it makes for a good story. It creates an abundance of evidence, often about the sort of ordinary people on whom the past is normally silent; it stimulates questions about the nature of social order as much as disorder; and its supposed lessons may often inform – or foreclose – the decisions of today.

Whatever its outcome, whether legal suppression, political reform, crushed rebellion or successful revolution, conflict generates competing – always partial, often mendacious – arguments at the time and thus enticingly controversial evidence for scholars to pick over thereafter. Because, too, it obliges the leaders of different social groups to define their constituencies more explicitly in order to defend their interests at a moment of danger, conflict also poses sharper questions about the more silent changes in social relations and the continuities of moral assumptions within which ruling authorities and their subordinates conduct and contain their political differences or social inequalities under more 'normal' conditions. Finally, the heroic or cursed memory of conflict constantly changes its meaning in the minds of later generations as people ask new questions of the past, looking for inspiration or warning in their own changing times.

For all these three reasons – its copious and contradictory evidence, its violent disclosure of colonial society's racial, ethnic and class hierarchies in the past and its contested memory in modern Kenya – there is a large and growing literature on the Mau Mau rising of the early 1950s, when tens of thousands of Kikuyu people felt impelled, for reasons which remain hotly disputed, to organize and bind together their loyalties in order to undertake possible civil disobedience and even political murder.

Under growing pressure from a government which only began to fathom the angry depths of African grievance in 1952, Mau Mau activists took to violence, as often to defend themselves from betrayal as to crush their enemies. These latter included, and most threateningly, their fellow Kikuyu in the African rural 'reserve', a few of them convinced supporters of the British regime but many more of them simply reluctant, on grounds of principle, to acknowledge any indigenous authority wider than their own sub-clan. The greater but less dangerous, because more ignorant, enemy were the white farmers on the so-called 'white highlands'. Some whites farmed land that had fifty years earlier been taken from Kikuyu; they, and other settlers further afield in the Rift Valley, also employed Kikuyu farmworkers, known as 'squatters', under conditions which the latter found increasingly insupportable. A third base of insurgent support was found among Nairobi townspeople, especially those whose enterprise in supplying the city with food, fuel, transport, housing, sexual and other domestic services was frustrated by colonial restrictions. Men and women were equally active in the movement in all three areas, the Kikuyu reserve, the Rift Valley squatter communities, and the slums of Nairobi.[1]

Kenya became independent in December 1963, barely eleven years after the Declaration of an Emergency had signalled a British determination to hang on to power by all possible means. For while they had defeated Mau Mau militarily by 1956, the British accepted that the huge political and financial costs of quelling the rising made African majority rule the only possible future for Kenya. However much the white minority protested against this betrayal of its own future, the imperial government had to come to terms with a largely new generation of nationalists whose chief entitlement to power, in British and indeed in many African eyes, was that they had had nothing to do with the violence of Mau Mau.

The many-sided Mau Mau movement and its place in the struggle for Kenya's independence has been examined from many different perspectives in the literature, internal and external, political, social and military. Why then do we need another book now and why this one in particular?

The general answer is that most academic studies of Mau Mau have been produced by scholars who know no Kikuyu, the language of almost all the insurgents. However attentive one's enquiry, this linguistic block must inhibit deep insight into rebel motivation. It is possible to make the theoretical case that such knowledge of motive and intention adds little to an understanding of violent social and political change.[2] For the rush of events inevitably outruns the power of leading actors to control them; eventual outcomes owe more therefore to the clash of blind political and economic structures than to the heroism of human wills. Most studies of Mau Mau have analysed the structural conditions of African resistance to colonial rule, on the assumption that the political activity of historical actors follows rather directly from their social and economic circumstances, as these are later interpreted by scholars. But real people in their own time seldom have the same sense of structural oppression as academics; historically, the commonest reaction to suffering is futilely to rail against one's fate. Politically creative anger, vision and a courage based on a culturally alert understanding of one's predicament, need a rare imaginative labour – what colonial rulers used to call agitation. We need to understand the magnetic field of discourse, for without fired-up human intention there can be no structural outcome, however unintended the latter may turn out to be.[3]

While some recruits were initiated into Mau Mau against their wills, as happens in all insurgencies, its many activists were by definition determined to resist, even to destroy, rather than merely to endure, their hardship and oppression; and if we are to understand Mau Mau's magnetic field at all we need to know how precisely, equipped with what historically informed view of the world, they construed their hardship and insecurity as a human injustice it was possible for them to redress, rather than mere blind mischance. But it is equally vital to grasp that they also felt constrained by their history in what range of counter-measures they could legitimately take. For Kikuyu criteria of moral agency and self-mastery governed both what they could do on their own account and, more stringently, what any one or group of them could properly do on behalf of their fellows, especially if members of other sub-clans or age-groups, without diminishing the responsibility which the latter owed to themselves. *Mau Mau from Below* allows us to enter more deeply into this moral world of Kikuyu responsibility and obligation at a time of crisis than scholarly enquiry has ever penetrated before.

This general reason to welcome Greet Kershaw's work stems from three more particular ones. First, her linguistic competence and participant observation enable her to bring new evidence to the task of explanation. This is the oral evidence of the Kikuyu villagers with whom she lived as an aid worker during the Mau Mau Emergency in the 1950s, and which is now irrecoverable in any form save her own field notes. The only other Kikuyu evidence of similarly contemporaneous immediacy is to be found in the proceedings of Mau Mau trials in the colonial courts, with defendants on trial for their lives: gruelling sources to which historians are only now beginning to turn.[4]

Second, Professor Kershaw has uncovered long local histories of social tension which could have been revealed by no other means than patient enquiry, of both her neighbours' memory and government archives. This remembered experience of a century and more of internal conflict was what decided how members of two small communities, Igi and Thuita, would act when the contrary demands of colonial regime and Kikuyu resistance at last forced them off the fence of canny or bewildered indecision.

Finally, nobody – not Kikuyu participant, neither Kenyan nor European scholar – has provided such startlingly authoritative ethnographic insights into the values, fears and expectations of Kikuyu society and thus of the motivation of Kikuyu action, insights which ring the more true the more they run counter to the assumptions of the liberally educated urban

Foreword

mind. Explanations of rebellious action based on intimate, culturally sensitive understandings of human decision, as here provided by Kershaw, can look utterly different from those inferred from the structural situation.

The people of the sub-clan settlements of Igi and Thuita, as Kershaw makes clear, were not typical of Kikuyu as a whole, not even of those others who lived, like them, in the southernmost Kikuyu district, Kiambu. Each settlement had its own particularities. Nonetheless, their arguments with their neighbours, between old and young, men and women, owners and dependants, touch on all the issues that have been raised elsewhere in the Mau Mau debate. Her readers, particularly those who think they know something about the movement, will be astonished how far she upsets their own supposed understandings on so many key issues. Not only does she call in question many previous findings, she points to entirely new avenues of enquiry.

Contested historiography ought to have that effect: to urge us who come after to redouble our efforts to make the dead live, to seek new ways of entering into the lives of human beings who in their own uncertain times were as ignorant of the next moment, but as fearfully hopeful of shaping it – or at least of escaping harm from it – as we are in our own day.

How then does Kershaw's new evidence, her grasp of deep local history and her ethnographic authority set *Mau Mau from Below* apart from the previous historiography and raise fresh questions about the dynamics of Kikuyu anti-colonial resistance? This introduction focuses on that question because the author herself is too faithful to the local knowledge – and thus to the wider ignorance – of her neighbours and informants of many years ago to venture a general assessment of Mau Mau. Her informants did not know what the movement was nor in any very precise way what it stood for, and were forever changing their prudential guesses about its likeliest opportunities and dangers. Her data suggest, as other scholars have also accepted, that there never was a single Mau Mau movement and that none of its members, even those who supposed themselves to be its leaders, ever saw it whole, not because they did not have a political aim, but because that agenda was contested within different political circles over which they had no control and of which they may scarcely have had any knowledge.[5] This, in the end, is one of the most important things that Greet Kershaw has to tell us.

A large degree of mutual Kikuyu ignorance, a deep parochial fragmentation that characterized all their previous history, henceforth has to be built into all our explanations of Mau Mau or, better, Mau Maus – a name, meaning 'the greedy eaters', in any case invented by their enemies. More than that, Kershaw shows that while Kikuyu may have shared a general sense of acute colonial injustice and a desire to recover lost land and freedom, they suffered, in the depths of their moral being, from a crippling sense of the particularity of the means with which they believed they could legitimately seek redress.

Foreword

And why is this finding important? It is because others, including almost all the movement's enemies, did see Mau Mau whole in order to try to comprehend it, a first step towards defeating it. They 'lumped' its various elements together, to make their analysis more intelligible to others; and it is their perspective, however much we may dispute it, which has shaped our subsequent understanding of what it is that needs to be explained. Perhaps the most extreme 'lumping' image in the published sources is to be found in the official British report on the origins of Mau Mau; this retrospectively pictured the movement, despite all its different ramifications, as fitting together 'as neatly as pieces of a jigsaw puzzle'.[6]

How hard the British had to push the pieces together to make them fit can be seen in the Colonial Office's character sketch of Mau Mau when justifying British policy in Kenya to other Commonwealth countries. 'What is Mau Mau? It is impossible to give a simple comprehensive answer to this question because Mau Mau is a complicated phenomenon embracing a number of seemingly contradictory characteristics.' That was a promisingly agnostic approach, but the officials in London went on to perform what they had just said was impossible. 'It is a movement', they explained,

> which has taken hold of one tribe, the Kikuyu, the largest and most advanced tribe in Kenya, and it produces its martyrs who are willing to die for their cause; it is equally an appalling development of bestiality and terror knowing no limits of shame or cruelty; it is in part an agitation against land policies and injustices real or imaginary; it is equally a perverted religion based on a misuse of the primitive superstitions of many of its adherents; it may even be a deep-seated and perhaps unconscious rejection of the whole Western way of life; finally it is a movement deliberately fostered and managed by a few clever men who are bent on securing control of the tribe and using it to serve their own ends and who know how to play on the primitive and irrational urges of the people. It has resulted in civil war within the tribe in which the loyal and sane elements assisted by the Gvt [*sic*] are arrayed against a campaign of intimidation, brutality and murder.[7]

Chief amongst the 'few clever men' was Jomo Kenyatta, then in his fifties, formerly general secretary of the Kikuyu Central Association, who had returned home in 1946 after sixteen years overseas, largely in Britain but with brief visits to Western Europe and Soviet Russia. While in London he had completed a diploma course in anthropology under Professor Malinowski, work which bore fruit in *Facing Mount Kenya*, a book of ethnographic nationalism which some whites later, improbably, claimed was a blueprint for revolution. In early 1953 he was convicted, on the thinnest of evidence, and imprisoned for 'managing' Mau Mau. 'Kenyatta and his henchmen' was a common British description of the movement's leadership. A later governor explained why he could not release him to public life: even when removed from the scene Kenyatta was still omnipotent. 'After his imprisonment Mau Mau, until it was defeated, grew in foulness. With his Communist and anthropological training, he knew his people and was directly responsible. Here was the African leader to darkness and death.'[8]

That was the British operational assessment of Mau Mau, what they thought they had defeated: a complex but nonetheless unified movement, whose foul strings of coordination were pulled ever tighter, even after the chief puppeteer, Kenyatta, had been put away. Historians are only now beginning to appreciate quite how radically this realization that our previously supposed 'knowledge' of Mau Mau was created for us by largely colonial – and hostile – evidence must cause us to revise the questions we should ask about its internal dynamics.

It is not enough simply to turn the colonial perspective upside down, to reverse the telescope, to re-describe villains as heroes, savagery as courage, subversion as patriotism, or even merely to 'split' elements that used to be 'lumped' together. There were more serious blindnesses in the colonial vision than we can allow for merely by reversing what we feel must be colonial prejudice. The movement's enemies were completely ignorant of, rather than simply opposed to some of its inner characteristics, with their ignorance not necessarily a mirror to those of Mau Mau's own participants. And Mau Mau's enemies in any case were divided in their interpretations of the movement's causes and character.

To begin now to discuss the historiography to which *Mau Mau from Below* comes as a breath of fresh air and robust, expertly informed common sense, this division within hostile white and African opinion is a matter to which historians have not always been sufficiently alert. Both dissidents and rulers tried to justify action and attract allegiance by contrasting the most compelling symbols of upright conduct in their own culture with the barbarity of their opponents; to explain why their world deserved to be either bloodily defended or bloodily destroyed. But neither side was united on what they most had to preserve or fear, what methods of combat were legitimate and to what future purpose.

Scholars are alert to such controversy, and therefore bias, in their sources. But what earlier students of Mau Mau did not sufficiently allow for was the way in which British disagreement about the movement's nature at the time accentuated the 'lumping' effect on its conflicting images. To hope to win an argument and therefore some say in policy, politicians and officials had to portray Mau Mau as either predominantly one thing or another; it could not, convincingly, be many parallel things at once. To 'split' Mau Mau in one's analysis, rather than 'lump' it, was to risk having one's advice ignored; for 'splitting' only confused policy and paralyzed action; and at moments of crisis rulers resist, above all else, the appearance of feebleness and indecision – failings of which the white settlers all too often accused the Kenya government.

The unequal nature of the Mau Mau war, between ill-armed guerillas with scarcely any external sympathisers, let alone allies, on the one hand, and the whole military and political apparatus of a modern state on the other, meant that the British published their evidence first. They had the information officers, the film crews, the capacity to lead the international press in its opinions or to exclude critics from privileged information. Mau Mau had none of these opportunities, although its own various competing leaders were well aware of their advantages. It was therefore conflict between different British views on Mau Mau, all lumpers rather than splitters, which both fuelled arguments between scholars and then determined how new evidence, retrieved later from Mau Mau memory and captured correspondence, would be received.

The British differed over Mau Mau on three related issues. The first was how far, if at all, it could be said to have a political agenda – and rulers, self-convinced of the beneficence, or at least necessity, of their own rule, never find it easy to admit that subversive movements can have some legitimate aim. If a justified goal is not admitted, then the motive and methods of leaders must also come in question. The second issue, therefore, was the relationship between leaders and followers, as this was revealed in initiatory oaths and murderous violence. Both questions arose from an underlying dispute on the effects of colonial rule and economic change on African tribal life – and no white observer doubted that Mau Mau was at bottom a tribal movement, characteristic of the Kikuyu people whom they stereotyped, in exasperated contradiction, as Kenya's most useful, sullen, progressive and yet unfathomable tribe.

These issues divided whites into conservative and liberal camps which were at times barely distinguishable. Settler farmers tended to be conservative; officials, civil and military, and larger businessmen were more often liberal. Missionaries were in both camps. Both schools of thought agreed that Mau Mau had a political aim: to expel the settlers, repossess African land and win 'independence'. Neither thought it legitimate, even if liberals accepted that it rested on a sense of grievance. Whites had brought the only progress Africans had ever known; there had already been ample compensation for lost Kikuyu land; and independence would scarcely bring freedom. Dictatorially sanctioned Kikuyu dominance over Kenya's other ethnic groups was more likely. The most generous white opinion held that Mau Mau was the militant wing of the nationalist Kenya African Union (KAU), 'a sort of Stern gang'; the most damning, that it was a primitive puppet of superior external forces, either Soviet communism or Indian nationalism, whose racial envy the settlers had long – and with reason – blamed for London's reluctance to devolve power on to Kenya's whites.[9]

The idea that Mau Mau was a communist conspiracy did not long survive the sceptical scrutiny of actual events.[10] And the legitimacy of its nationalism had been put in question from the moment that Mau Mau first came to whites' notice. It was not just its supposed programme but the nature of its organization and methods that disturbed them. If an African opposition there had to be – and liberals accepted that it was, if regrettable, nonetheless inevitable – then its most desired qualities were the moderate pursuit of gradualist progress, gratefully imitative of official British attitudes, by a legally constituted public body with audited accounts.

Mau Mau was, self-evidently, not a moderate movement; neither did it openly elect its leaders or debate policy. It worked in secret, by threats both physical and magical. All whites agreed that these features were totally unacceptable. 'This was no ordinary respectable rebellion', as the official historian of the Emergency put it (as if any rising could be, in the minds of those risen against).[11] But whites did not concur on the causes of disreputability, principally because they differed on the effects of colonial rule on native peoples – a difference which itself turned on the latter's supposed potential for progress. They therefore argued between themselves on how to 'explain' Mau Mau. We might now think that the British were 'explaining it away' as a cynical act of propaganda, to deny the movement any legitimacy; but that is not so. When rulers displace the causes of violent unrest from their own failings on to the faults of their subjects – their deluded ignorance, brute treachery or aberrant psychology – they often believe the explanation themselves, to the extent of using it as the foundation of their own strategy for political reconstruction. That was true of successive British diagnoses of Mau Mau. Was it a nativist religious revival, a recrudescence of long latent savagery, or something specifically modern; and how, in each case, should the British react?

What one might call the standard imperial view, instinctive in people who knew their schoolboy history of the Indian Mutiny and of countless border affrays since, wrote Mau Mau off as the sort of religious mania which so often gripped primitive peoples, whether in Asia or Africa, when they met the modern world: sudden, frantic frenzies against the brute fact of submission to external power, whose energies were soon spent when pathetically ignorant followers were let down, as they always were, by deluded prophets.[12] This habitually dismissive racism, which gave confidence to the habit of imperial command, was perhaps the main reason why the British were initially slow to take the subversive potential of Mau Mau seriously; it was sure to burn itself out, and soon.

When they did wake up to the threat, most settlers took a second racially conservative view, that of masters confronted with unruly servants. In an earlier generation they had held that for African men to work for white farmers was the moral equivalent of sending white children to school. Under the seemingly racist threat of Mau Mau such thoughts were once again thinkable, even after the Second World War. Mau Mau showed base ingratitude for all that whites had done to better African lives; its only possible explanation was that it had been stirred up by the liberal follies of a reforming government which had forgotten that mastery required firmness. The London *Times* agreed: there must be less 'loose talk about politics to people so manifestly immature in such affairs'.[13] Half-educated agitators were quick to exploit weakness by stirring up the black savagery that lurked under the sunny servant surface. Mau Mau was a bestial reversion to the unforgotten witch-ridden past to which Kikuyu seemed to be especially in thrall. Punitive suppression, without too much regard to legal niceties, was the only immediate solution and, in the longer term, an unapologetic reassertion of a white supremacy that must be stern in order to be kind. African fecklessness needed corrective white discipline for the foreseeable future.[14]

In some white circles in Nairobi there was, nonetheless, apologetic talk that the colour bar which operated in most spheres of life was really a 'culture bar'. Africans were not by nature inferior; only their history and environment had held them back from the advances in civilization of which an educated minority had already proved themselves capable. Such thinking informed a liberal interpretation of Mau Mau which came to inform policy – if not government statements. Although masked by a common determination to defeat armed rebellion, shared with the conservatives, the liberal view conceded that African violence was more a modern response to social change than a revival of ancient savagery. It was not that British policy had been wrong but that, however beneficent, it was bound to disturb and destroy the best elements in African society. This liberal view reflected, by and large, the official colonial mind. District officers saw much to admire in African society, its rural simplicity, its order, its solidarity; and much to abhor in their own, its urban anonymity, its industrial potential for mass destruction, its selfish individualism. Yet they knew that without appealing to largely individual African self-interest they could never themselves get anything done.[15]

Half doubting their cultural title to demand that Africans change their ways yet intent on engineering change nevertheless, many officials were persuaded that Mau Mau was in some appalling sense the product of modernity's own social dislocation and psychic bewilderment. Selfish agitators had exaggerated African grievances, yes, but the disorientation of the masses had given them a fertile field in which to sow their political lies, bedded in with murderous oaths. This liberal explanation of the causes of Mau Mau implied a solution in reform, too, but the relationship between interpretation and remedy was to some extent circular.

It was unthinkable for a post-war British government to meet the conservatives' demand for a merely punitive war in the cause of a reconstructed white supremacy; it had been so for years. Clearly on the path to decolonization under African majority rule in its West African possessions, British policy could not withstand that degree of contradiction in East Africa. In any case, Mau Mau could not be defeated without the acquiescence of other Africans in Kenya. The conservatives' demands not only risked setting the African powder-keg alight; they would also have amounted to a settler coup d'etat against the imperial government.[16] So it was essential that even while rebellion against white authority was being suppressed, Kenya's government should itself be reformed as a multi-racial coalition, if with a preponderance, still, of white power.

The idea that Mau Mau was an expression of the psychic trauma of transition between traditional communal security and modern individual responsibility conveniently removed from the reform of urban housing finance, industrial relations, land tenure, crop marketing, even political representation – all of them rational programmes for African advance – the crippling accusation that they were concessions to terrorism. Rather, they would, it was declared, cut away the uncertain transitional ground on which such insanity flourished.[17] All Kenya's peoples must become confidently modern, however much officials might regret the loss of traditional African innocence and their own paternal role.[18] There was no other way to preserve a future for its already modern minorities, the white and Indian settlers. But 'No African may say that Mau Mau has paid' was the saving principle behind all reform.[19] To go on ruling, if only with the objective of making it easier to beat an honourable retreat in the future, the British thus had to magnify the madness of an enemy one could not conceivably run the risk of being thought to appease. Mau Mau 'grew in foulness', as the Governor said, certainly in most (not all) British minds.

This British debate on the nature and causes of Mau Mau gave later historians their evidence and set their agenda. By the 1960s, when the first academics studied Mau Mau, no Western scholar saw any need to take on the racial conservatives; theirs was too palpably a lost cause. The imperial liberals were more of a challenge. Now that history had supplanted anthropology as the queen of the human sciences in the western study of Africa, scholars were less obsessed with the vulnerability of moral orders to social change and more excited by the capacity of political will to improve social conditions. Nationalism was also seen as an inevitable political expression of the wider social horizons imparted by colonial rule, literacy, and the market economy. Audiences had changed, too. The first historians wrote not to convince a colonial government but to educate a future Kenyan nation that had been born in bitter struggle.

That was why the first liberal historians, Rosberg and Nottingham and, later, Spencer and Tamarkin, set out to overturn the arguments of the last liberal colonialists. In these histories, the Kikuyu were not maddened by change; rather, they were the most modernized, the most politically adept of Kenya's African peoples, the obvious vanguard for a potential Kenyan nationality. Mau Mau oaths, the first of which had made no mention of violence, were necessary organizational tools amongst a largely unlettered populace, not cynical manipulations of the bewildered uncertainties of transitional men and women, grateful in crisis for the comforts of half-forgotten superstition. The growing violence was the entirely predictable outcome of the need for cash, secrecy and security.[20] In this last thesis liberal historians were unwittingly following the thinking of the British soldiers drafted in to Kenya, who were less interested in the supposed pathology of Mau Mau than the civil officials for whom the rising was both personal insult and professional failure. The generals were more coolly concerned to understand their enemy's mind – as they would any other enemy it was their job to defeat.[21]

Following an agenda of political education for the new nation, white

Foreword

liberal historians had to admit that Mau Mau's largely Kikuyu ethnicity made 'national integration' more difficult. But they argued that its cause lay in British repression rather than tribal pathology. The rising price of resistance had rocked an embryo liberation movement back on to its culturally most committed core.[22] The oaths, so disturbing to white colonial opinion, were merely culturally specific disciplinary sanctions, to combat the localism inherent in Kikuyu society; and as the pre-Emergency tempo of action mounted, so they had fallen into the hands of the most militant, often the younger and most urban, popular leaders who, far from being Kenyatta's 'henchmen', later confessed to a readiness to kill him.[23] And so the movement, battling against inherited fragmentation, itself split into moderate and militant factions under pressure. Here was a sophisticated analysis of structure and process, but one in which Mau Mau's 'splitting' remained a mark of failure: it became more narrowly ethnic; it also lost its moderate coherence to local militant gangs.

Some of Kenya's own liberal historians, Ogot, Kipkorir and Kanogo, in the first generation of African academics, went still further in deploring some aspects of Mau Mau. To them it represented an aroused populist ethnicity, a political tribalism that had outflanked the educated, pan-ethnic moderation of the KAU and, indeed, outraged Kikuyu elders – a point which Greet Kershaw elaborates. Far from being an inspiration to the new nation, its Rift Valley squatter supporters had indeed seen it as the tribally expansionist movement condemned in British propaganda.[24] It took an unrepentant, and much younger, British conservative historian, Throup, to ask 'so what?' Ethnicity was the strongest political base in a continent where class formation had scarcely begun to alter loyalties; there was no point in sentimentalizing pan-ethnic 'nation-building' and thus no need to be ashamed of a tribal Mau Mau.[25]

But, from the start, the 'radical' strand of Mau Mau historiography had always stressed the importance of class formation to its consciousness, both worker and peasant. Barnett, the editor of the Mau Mau general Karari Njama's memoirs, had thought that the experience of migrant labour had had a peculiarly unifying effect on Kikuyu,[26] and there is clearly much in the idea of an exile imagination of an ethnic 'home'.[27] Kenya's own radical academics, like their liberal counterparts more extreme than their closest white colleagues, would have none of that. Ethnicity was a 'false consciousness' manipulated by the bourgeoisie in their own class interest. Since Mau Mau's members were in economic terms workers and peasants, their class position must have inspired their political consciousness. This retrospectively imposed theoretical heroism stemmed from the radicals' view that only class struggle in their own day could create a patriotic nationhood which was proof against the corrupt and greedy wiles of tribalism; that then must be Mau Mau's message from the past.[28] The British radical historian Furedi took a similar view of the Rift Valley squatters, in contrast to the squatter's daughter Kanogo.[29] It took the more conventional Kenyan Marxist, Njonjo, using Cowen's findings on the differentiations of rural

Foreword

capitalism, to point out that class formation occurred within ethnic groups, as senior kin repudiated the land claims of their junior kin or their working dependents.[30] This is a finding that, without benefit of Marxist theory, Greet Kershaw's research amply corroborates. The separation of class from ethnicity is not so easy as the radicals supposed. It can indeed be argued that an awareness of impending class division makes the imagined solidarities of ethnicity all the more compelling.[31]

All these earlier studies were, in their different ways, 'lumping' analyses, whether of the failure of a moderate liberation movement to contain its variably militant ethnic pressures, or of the success of tribal loyalty in providing a firm base for wider political bargains, or of the betrayal of workers and peasants by compromising bourgeoisies, or of class struggle within an ethnic group. There was little room here for principled doubt, ignorance, even cultural and political debate within the insurgent ranks. This was left to the anthropologists, Buytenhuys and Kershaw.[32] And it was on their findings that I tried to build my own interpretation of what I called Mau Mau's 'moral economy'.[33] I argued that the internal agony of resistance emerged from a long debate, structured by clan, age-set and generational affiliation, about how it was possible to achieve the old ideal of productive and civic self-mastery in modern circumstances. Patrons had had to repudiate obligations to clients; the poor could not look even to industrious service for a patron as a laborious ladder to marriage, property, self-respecting adulthood. Neither, therefore, could easily establish their personal grounds for legitimate political action.

Hitherto Greet Kershaw has been a largely oracular presence in Mau Mau historiography, speaking to us in ways she could not fully control, through the mediumship of other people's footnotes, my own especially. It is good for scholarship and no less so, I believe, for the people of Kenya, now to have her speaking in her own voice. Judging, rightly, that we cannot get any further with our external structural assessments until we have a better grasp of the intimate delicacy of human judgment and action, she has been content to focus on the latter, but not without insisting on the constant and overwhelming impact of colonial rule and land alienation in shaping the issues over which divided Kikuyu opinion had to decide.

Kershaw makes demands on her readers' concentration, but they are valid and well-considered demands that we take people now dead as seriously now as they took each other when alive. She treats very literally of matters of life and death which were stirred up within small communities, which is the main reason why she has felt unable to tell us about them before now. She has allowed a long time to elapse before unravelling terrible secrets of dreadful events, secrets confided in her forty years ago and which she only now feels able to discuss without betrayal.[34]

Her local history of Igi and Thuita has a brutal beginning in the famine of *kirika*, back in the 1830s, a still worse experience than the Mau Mau emergency with which her story ends. Linking these two moral ordeals is

Foreword

a social history of peopling the land with men and women, two contrasted processes; an economic history of mobilizing the resources with which to buy land and reward labour, twin essentials of enterprising survival which first complemented each other and then fell apart into a mutual opposition; and a political history of reputation and honour between patrons and clients, seniors and juniors, land-rich and land-poor, which underwent the most agonizing changes under the pressures of alien rule, loss of land to white settlers and the development of rural capitalism among Kikuyu.

Greet Kershaw's informants felt that they and their forebears had exercised some moral agency, some self-mastery, in their local arenas. But they had no means of assessing the reputations of those, whether white or Kikuyu, who tried to wield power over them from afar and, in consequence, made the safest assumption about their motives, which was that they were selfish, evil. It was this ignorance and justified suspicion of a wider world, which had tremendous power to affect the locality for good or ill, that demanded the confusing switches of evidence and allegiance that Kershaw found among informants in the 1950s and 1960s. But in this still further complication in the search for usable evidence the historian learns another lesson about the conflicts which beset any locality that is subject to wider movements or to large regimes: the price of survival was constant vigilance towards both sorts of external power, incumbent and dissident, and relentless renegotiation of the terms of mistrust between themselves and outsiders. Just as arguments between whites had a 'lumping' effect on Mau Mau, so arguments between Kikuyu may also for this reason over-emphasize the 'splits'.

Greet Kershaw's work has made both the historical Mau Mau movements and the study of their evidence still more complex than they were before. But so they were for people at the time, for whom informed decision on inadequate and suspect evidence was just as difficult as it is for us and for whom the consequences of choosing one alternative assumption rather than another was not, as it is with us, merely intellectual confusion or enlightenment but, rather, death or life.

Notes

1. The role of women in Mau Mau, which both frightened and scandalized the British, has only recently attracted attention. See, especially, Tabitha Kanogo, *Squatters and the Roots of Mau Mau* (London, 1987), pp. 143–9; Cora Ann Presley, *Kikuyu Women, the Mau Mau Rebellion, and Social Change in Kenya* (Boulder, 1992). For the social context, Luise White, *The Comforts of Home: Prostitution in Colonial Nairobi* (Chicago, 1990), Chapter 8; and Claire C. Robertson, *Healing Together Gave Us Strength: Women, Men and Trade in the Nairobi Area* (forthcoming), Chapter 5.
2. Theda Scokpol, *States and Social Revolutions* (Cambridge, 1979).
3. John Dunn, 'Understanding revolutions', *Ethics*, 92 (Chicago, January 1982), pp. 312–13.
4. Here we await the findings of David Anderson whose sharp eye has uncovered a rich deposit of judicial proceedings of capital cases; and I hope myself to get closer to the fraught tensions of the every day in my own researches into the several 'Kenyatta trials'.

Foreword

5. The mutual ignorance and suspicion of the supposed leaders, all those detained on the night of 20 October 1952, is tellingly recorded in Gakaara wa Wanjau, *Mau Mau Author in Detention* (Nairobi, 1988), pp. 2–3.
6. Colonial Office, *Historical Survey of the Origins and Growth of Mau Mau* (Cmnd 1030, HMSO London, 1960), p. 65: generally referred to as the Corfield Report.
7. Draft memorandum, 'United Kingdom policy in Kenya', 14 October 1956. Public Record Office (PRO), CO 822/940.
8. Sir Patrick Renison, Draft statement, 20 April 1960. PRO, CO 822/1909/12. How little communism Kenyatta had learned in Moscow is vividly shown in Woodford McLellan, 'Africans and Black Americans in the Comintern schools, 1925–1934', *International Journal of African Historical Studies*, 26, 2 (1993), pp. 371–90.
9. Anthony Somerhough, Deputy Public Prosecutor, opening the Crown case against Kenyatta and others, 3 December 1952. Trial transcript, Vol. I, p.10: Kenya National Archives (KNA), RR 9/5. 'Interview of Secretary of State for the Colonies with Alfred Vincent', 31 October 1952. PRO, CO 822/461.
10. A. S. Cleary, 'The myth of Mau Mau in its international context', *African Affairs*, 89, 335 (1990), pp. 227–45. The communist connection existed not only in the British mind. For some Kikuyu ideas on 'Chinese' links, see Rawson Macaria to Noel Kennaway (DC Kiambu), 24 August 1952, enclosure in Baring to Secretary of State, 13 December 1958: PRO, CO 822/1848.
11. F. D. Corfield to J. L. Buist, 31 October 1958. PRO, CO 822/1221/8.
12. For this school of colonial thought see the first scholarly account of Mau Mau: Carl G. Rosberg, Jr. and John Nottingham, *The Myth of 'Mau Mau': Nationalism in Kenya* (New York and London, 1966), pp. 324–31. For a considered attempt at a religious explanation see, L. S. B. Leakey, *Defeating Mau Mau* (London, 1954), Chapter 4.
13. The *Times*, 9 October 1952; see also (amongst many others), report on 'Subversive native sects in Kenya', in *African World* (August 1950), p. 23.
14. This harsh summary is not unfair to such settler-authored books as C. J. Wilson, *Before the Dawn in Kenya* (Nairobi, 1952) and *Kenya's Warning* (Nairobi, 1954); Ione Leigh, *In the Shadow of Mau Mau: an Eyewitness Account of the Terror in Kenya* (London, 1954); C. T. Stoneham, *Out of Barbarism* (London, 1955).
15. The official mind and the official political predicament are analysed in depth in Bruce Berman, *Control and Crisis in Colonial Kenya: the Dialectics of Domination* (London, Nairobi and Athens, OH, 1990).
16. In the opinion of Kenya's Attorney General; see, Whyatt to Rogers, 2 September 1952. PRO, CO 822/437.
17. Two representative liberal statements, in their ambiguities, are L. S. B. Leakey, *Mau Mau and the Kikuyu* (London, 1952) and *Defeating Mau Mau* (London, 1954). For recent studies of the conflicting white constructions of Mau Mau, see John Lonsdale, 'Mau Maus of the mind: making Mau Mau and remaking Kenya', *Journal of African History* 31 (1990), pp. 393–421; Bruce Berman and John Lonsdale, 'Louis Leakey's Mau Mau: a study in the politics of knowledge', *History and Anthropology*, 5, 2 (1991), pp. 143–204; Dane Kennedy, 'Constructing the colonial myth of Mau Mau', *International Journal of African Historical Studies*, 25, 2 (1992), 241–60; Jock McCulloch, *Colonial Psychiatry and 'the African Mind'* (Cambridge, 1995), Chapter 5. And for the first, still useful, survey of the literature, Oliver Furley, 'The historiography of Mau Mau', pp. 105–33 in Bethwell A. Ogot (ed.), *Politics and Nationalism in Colonial Kenya: Hadith, 4* (Nairobi, 1972).
18. For the uphill struggle of official liberalism see, J. E. Lewis, 'The colonial politics of African welfare in Kenya, 1939–1952: a crisis in paternalism' (Cambridge PhD thesis, 1993).
19. Sir Evelyn Baring, Governor, to Secretary of State, 12 October 1953. PRO, CO 822/498/3.
20. Rosberg and Nottingham, *The Myth of 'Mau Mau'*; John Spencer, *KAU: the Kenya African Union* (London, 1985); M. Tamarkin, 'Mau Mau in Nakuru', *Journal African History* 17, 1 (1976), pp. 119–34.
21. General Sir George Erskine, despatch, 'The Kenya emergency June 1953–May 1955',

Foreword

2 May 1955. PRO, WO 236/18; for the best account of the security forces' Mau Mau war see, R. W. Heather, 'Counterinsurgency and intelligence in Kenya, 1952–56' (Cambridge PhD thesis, 1993).

22. An early expression of this view is found in Clyde Sanger (*Guardian* correspondent) to Mervyn Hill (editor, *Kenya Weekly News*), 24 March 1961. Enclosure in Coutts to Corfield, 29 March 1961. PRO, CO 822/1898/151.
23. Eliud Mutonyi, 'Mau Mau chairman' (n.d. typescript, *c.* 1970), pp. 78–85; Bildad Kaggia, *Roots of Freedom* (Nairobi, 1975), p. 114; Fred Kubai, in television interview for 'End of Empire' (London, Channel 4, screened 1 July 1985).
24. B. E. Kipkorir, '"Mau Mau" and the politics of the transfer of power in Kenya', *Kenya Historical Review*, 5, 2 (1977), pp. 313–28; B. A. Ogot, 'Politics, culture and music in central Kenya: a study of Mau Mau hymns', *ibid.*, pp. 275–86 and 'Revolt of the elders', Chapter 7 in B. A. Ogot (ed.), *Politics and Nationalism in Colonial Kenya* (Nairobi, 1972); Kanogo, *Squatters*, pp. 149–52.
25. David W. Throup, *Economic and Social Origins of Mau Mau* (London, 1987).
26. Donald L. Barnett and Karari Njama, *Mau Mau from Within* (London, 1966), p. 35.
27. Cf. Carola Lentz, 'Home, death and leadership: discourses of an educated elite from north-western Ghana', *Social Anthropology* 2, 2 (1994), pp. 149–69.
28. See, especially, Maina wa Kinyatti, 'Mau Mau: the peak of African political organization in colonial Kenya', *Kenya Historical Review*, 5, 2 (1977), pp. 287–310.
29. Frank Furedi, *The Mau Mau War in Perspective* (London, 1989).
30. Apollo Njonjo, 'The Africanization of the "white highlands": a study of agrarian class struggles in Kenya 1950–74' (Princeton PhD thesis, 1977); M. P. Cowen, 'Differentiation in a Kenya location' (University of East Africa Social Science Council conference paper, Nairobi, 1972).
31. John Lonsdale, 'Moral ethnicity and political tribalism', pp. 131–50 in Preben Kaarsholm and Jan Hultin (eds), *Inventions and Boundaries* (Roskilde, 1994).
32. Robert Buytenhuys, *Le mouvement 'Mau Mau': une revolte paysanne et anti coloniale en Afrique noire* (The Hague, 1971) and *Essays on Mau Mau* (Leiden, 1982); G. Kershaw, 'The land is the people: a study of social organization in historical perspective' (Chicago University PhD thesis, 1972).
33. John Lonsdale, 'The moral economy of Mau Mau', pp. 265–504 in Bruce Berman and John Lonsdale, *Unhappy Valley: Conflict in Kenya and Africa* (London and Athens, OH, 1992).
34. For her discussion of the morality of methodology see G. Kershaw, 'Mau Mau from below: fieldwork and experience, 1955–57 and 1962', *Canadian Journal of African Studies*, 25, 2 (1991), pp. 274–97.

Preface

When the government of Kenya declared a State of Emergency on 20 October 1952 it presumed, like many European and some African Kenyans, that Mau Mau was a seditious movement which through its oaths had made adherents morally unfit to live in society until they confessed and were rehabilitated. Kenya churches, including the Christian Council of Kenya (CCK), had offered assistance in this endeavour; in 1955 an international group of men and women was brought out to help design and execute rehabilitation programmes.

I have described elsewhere how almost all of us soon doubted the appropriateness of rehabilitation and shifted to literacy programmes and health care (Kershaw, 1991). I had asked permission for a study of why Mau Mau had occurred; CCK granted permission and the government approved study of four villages, Thuita and Itara, Mbari ya Igi and Nginduri in Kiambu. For brevity's sake I will use only the names of the main villages, Thuita and Mbari ya Igi.[1] The villages – an innovation imposed during Mau Mau – were chosen neither randomly nor because they were representative of animosity against Mau Mau or involvement in it. Rather, they were among the few Kiambu villages considered safe from Mau Mau attack at the time. Though the local population constituted roughly 1 per cent of the Kiambu population and I am reasonably certain that similar data could have been obtained in other Kiambu areas, my use of 'Kiambu' or 'Kikuyu' does not imply that I know this to be the case.[2]

The first fieldwork period ended in 1957; my husband, John Kershaw (a historian) and I did follow-up work in the summer of 1962. I had started work with scant background on the Kikuyu, colonial Kenya, or Mau Mau. I had read the few ethnographic and ethnological studies available (Hobley, 1938; Routledge, 1910; Kenyatta, 1938; Lambert, 1950; Middleton, 1953) and a number of articles in ethnological journals. During fieldwork Dr

Leakey generously allowed me to read some chapters of his then still unpublished major work on the Kikuyu (Leakey, 1977).

What little knowledge I had of colonial Kenya was dated (Dilley, 1935; Salvadori, 1938; Huxley, 1935). My knowledge of Mau Mau was restricted to some of the popular literature (Leakey, 1952; 1954). Soon after arrival I attended the last meeting of the Committee on the Sociological Causes underlying Mau Mau, and received a copy of its 1954 report. I had not seen Carothers's psychological analysis (Carothers, 1954); I was familiar with Bewes's *Kikuyu Conflict* (Bewes, 1953) and was aware that many churches presumed Mau Mau to be virulently anti-Christian; not until after 1957 did I see Wiseman's publication on this theme (Wiseman, 1953).

In the first fieldwork period general 'hard' data were difficult to come by although I occasionally received Press Office hand-outs from the Department of Information, some of which contained figures on the 'war'. I could read the *East African Standard*, the colony's principal newspaper, only the few times I was in Nairobi but the framework of its 'hard data' was so obviously one-sided and value-laden that its information raised more questions than it answered. The only local data I had been given were official lists of individuals who presumably had not taken the oaths characteristic of Mau Mau supporters. Those not mentioned were regarded as Mau Mau members.

Even by 1962 a bibliography of Mau Mau literature would not have filled two pages and local experience indicated that considerable information had been lost. By then the official history of Mau Mau with its anti-Mau Mau bias had been published (Corfield, 1960) and while a study on independent churches and schools was a good deal more sympathetic to the Kikuyu (Welbourn, 1961), most minor publications continued to emphasize the brutal, anti-colonial, anti-Western character of Mau Mau (Fazan, 1958; Lavers, 1955; Osmunson, 1959; Phillips, 1958). Josiah Mwangi Kariuki's defence of Mau Mau (Kariuki, 1963) was still a year away; the important study of Carl G. Rosberg, Jr. and John Nottingham (Rosberg and Nottingham, 1966) had not yet been published. By 1962 Kiambu District annual reports and the reports of the Kiambu Agricultural Department had become available; they contained some material pertaining to the local area and Mau Mau events.

Several reasons contributed to the long delay in publication of the fieldwork data. Given the localized character of the study which made informants and actors easily recognizable, sufficient time had to elapse to allow some anonymity and protection. By this time the principals have either died or are very old and the need for confidentiality is therefore less. I hope that the survivors are willing to accept that their story should be told, even if only to explain the thoughts and actions of the past to children and grandchildren.

My attitude to the data also played a role. Fieldwork was confined to a specific, delineated area and no comparable data were available from other areas. For a number of years I was of the opinion that a study which could not place the local population and its attitudes to Mau Mau within a wider context, and compare the findings with those of other areas, lacked sufficient validity. It has taken years to accept that one case study, with all its limitations, can nevertheless give insight, provided it does not claim to be representative without further evidence.

A third reason, which needs some explanation, discovered well after I had left the field, is that the analysis needed information which I did not have because my framework at the time had been too simplistic.

After arriving in Kenya, I had spent a few months in Kabare in Embu where observations led to the hypothesis that economic factors seemed to play a significant role in becoming involved in Mau Mau. Yet believing this to be the case did not automatically provide a guideline to the questions and their analysis which would be relevant to the economic life of twentieth-century Kikuyu. The literature did not provide guidance; almost all ethnological studies contained data on Kikuyu 'tribal' life as if it were an isolated social, political or economic entity and little or no allowance was made for internal differentiation. Whatever the validity of 'tribal studies', in the past, it was obvious by the 1950s that no study of the economics of local communities could ignore that they were inextricably integrated – within their areas, the white settler communities, and colonial and world markets – through production, labour, social and political relationships. Nor could studies ignore the stratification of the communities in which access to wealth and opportunity varied considerably.

Emergency regulations prohibited gathering data outside the four communities. Like other Kikuyu districts, Kiambu was a 'closed district'; access and travel within the district required permits. The research area had been carved out of a larger area; though I had a permit to travel to and from the four villages and for living in one of them, I had no permit to visit or do research in neighbouring Kikuyu areas, nor in Nairobi – which employed many males – nor the neighbouring settled area where white settlers employed many women.

This restricted information I would have liked to have had. While data about crops sold could be obtained from local sellers, buyers living beyond the villages were outside the scope of the study. Males who worked and lived a considerable part of the year in Nairobi could provide information about work and working conditions, but information from employers was not available. Women could talk about working conditions and wages on the plantations but the employing settlers could not be involved in the study. Moreover, economic information I did receive was often highly specific to the individual and varied considerably between individuals who ostensibly were in the same position.

The restrictions on gathering data also applied to the social and political relationships of the community with the wider world. While land outside the local community owned by local men could be taken into account, the kinsmen who lived on it were outside the scope of the study. Yet information about the relationships between kin, whether localized or not, about the role of social institutions in local life, and about the relationships between the local community and the wider area showed considerably less variation than the economic data. It is possible that the prohibitions on research affected the economic arena more than the social and political ones.

Problems with the economic data showed up in the first analysis of the data after I had left the field, when I also became aware that the primary orientation of the fieldwork had left much to be desired. The problems could not be solved without additional work; I am profoundly grateful that this was possible in 1962 when my husband and I could do the additional work required.

During the initial fieldwork I had followed the then accepted wisdom, possibly a result of the perception of the colonial government, that Mau Mau was a unitary movement in time and space. According to this perception Mau Mau might well be more prevalent in 1952 than in 1949, but it was the same Mau Mau. Similarly, Mau Mau in the Rift Valley was the same Mau Mau as Mau Mau in Kiambu. Interest in why or when individuals had decided to join Mau Mau was minimal; the real question was whether they had joined.

Though I had concentrated from the beginning on 'why' people had taken oaths, I had been guided by a similar approach. Even when volunteered, I had made only perfunctory notes on when and where oaths had been taken, partially because I did not want to inflame local antagonism. I had not made this information into a general question, which the analysis showed to have been a mistake. Quite a few informants 'explained' their oath with reference to place and time: 'I joined late', 'this was a Nairobi oath', or 'we lived in the Rift Valley' abounded and indicated that the local population perceived different Mau Maus, all of them in time perspective rather than one Mau Mau, constant in time and space.

The lack of time perspective had led to potentially serious flaws in the economic data. I had not looked at income in time perspective but erroneously presumed that oath takers and those who did not take the oath could be divided into economic groups on the basis of their 1956–7 economic situations. Not only were the economic conditions of the population highly variable in time, but the Emergency itself had given rise to profound economic changes. Higher productivity had brought increased income for some but many others had been deprived of income because Emergency regulations forbade giving work permits in Nairobi to those who had taken oaths. Knowing when individuals had taken oaths was needed together with their economic conditions at that time.

Many of these data were collected in the second period of fieldwork; they and earlier data will be discussed extensively in Appendices I and IV and in the text itself. The decision to drop the attempt to calculate individual income with all its inaccuracies and to place individuals in households which were grouped according to potential income will be discussed there too.[3] Here I need to point out that fieldwork was executed

Preface

in two periods which were materially different in terms of the population's approach to Mau Mau. In 1956–7 it was a movement which most would rather forget but which they could not escape due to the government's reprisals and relentless punishment. In 1962 it was a movement which an incoming government urged them to forget, but though membership sometimes led to preferment, it was no longer a cause for fear and discrimination. Non-membership had not become a cause for persecution: the official line was that Mau Mau was a thing of the past. The integration of the data from these different periods was as fraught with pitfalls as it was time-consuming; much of it had to be done during an academic career characterized by lack of time and resources.

One question which must be discussed is the reliability of data which lack outside corroboration, cannot be compared with other studies and rarely give the name or date of the contribution of individual informants. Appendix I deals with the reliability of the data in general; here I will only deal with the lack of attribution. Though I will give as much attribution as is compatible with protection of informants and my own knowledge, it will remain difficult to do so because of the collective nature of the information.

The study was executed when anthropological usage rarely mentioned individual respondents or gave time and place where specific information was obtained. At that time a researcher might well go into the field with specific questions, possibly even aimed at specific informants; yet this would take a back seat to understanding the culture. This was achieved by 'living' it, by accepting a learning role until the time was ready and more specific questions might be asked. During the learning period researchers often found that some of their questions had to be modified, while some might be dropped as immaterial and others had to be added. Researchers also might find that informants were more often groups of kin or associates than single individuals.

Although I had many specific questions, undoubtedly relevant from a European perspective, I needed to understand Kikuyu culture before I could judge whether these or other questions were appropriate and relevant. Information was often obtained without a question being asked: sitting together with villagers, who discussed their affairs with each other, I absorbed Kikuyu thinking and attitudes before and often without having framed specific questions. I have written this book from what I learned; the most relevant ideas, the Kikuyu approach to their lives, the events and the world, I learned not from questions but by sitting still and listening. The ideas and opinions in the book are a result of this listening, this absorption process.

Unless they were very senior elders, my teachers and informants were rarely single persons. Even when I had asked a question from one informant, or only one person had been invited to give information, kin, age-mates, friends and neighbours felt free to drop in on the conversation. I probably learned more from these informal meetings than from a more structured encounter. Informants and instructors were everywhere, be they women sitting together after work, selling their produce at the market, looking after their children, or cooking a meal in the evening. Instruction came from men who were looking for a cup of tea or medicine; they might be meeting in council, be on their way to work or sitting in the sun ready to enjoy a leisurely chat. Much of the information became public property; the villagers discussed their own and others' contribution and did not hesitate to make their comments known, leading to some of the most valuable information. While I take full responsibility for the data, most of them had passed the scrutiny of a village where a word spoken in one hut could be heard in the next.

Attribution is also made more difficult because a number of interviews might be needed before an adequate set of data would emerge. This can perhaps be illustrated by tracing the steps involved in my assertion in Chapter 2 of late nineteenth-century inequality. The idea might be born when asking about age of initiation: it became clear that several old and still wealthy elders had been initiated in their early teens, while others had waited till they were in their late teens if not their early twenties. While this could be due to the opening and closing of initiation years, it seemed worthwhile to look into the matter. In a discussion at another time – perhaps concerned with the breeding of stock – one informant might mention that a man in the late nineteenth century needed more stock than an earlier generation because the price of land had risen. The idea of inequality would get a boost, if another informant contributed that late nineteenth-century fathers also needed more stock because the price of eldership and initiation had risen also, while vegetable food could no longer be used as payment. It did not take much imagination to conclude that some would have more difficulty getting fees than others.

These data would lead to more specific discussions with *arumati* and elders; this would reveal that normally most *ahoi* sons were initiated late. When elders would also make clear that early initiation often meant earlier marriage, more wives and earlier entry into the councils – with the concomitant result that sons of wealthy parents reached council levels, mostly closed to poorer men – the data would allow me to make a statement about late nineteenth-century inequality. The information did not come from any specific person or group of persons; I drew a conclusion from statements by different persons, made at different times, in different contexts.

Though the conclusions I draw from the data are my responsibility, most of those reached before 1962 were discussed specifically with co-workers and local people excited by the study. Conclusions I arrived at after 1962 have been tested against the material as a whole within its emerging framework.

My original intent, which remains the same, had been to investigate why Mau Mau had occurred and what had motivated those who did or did not join. From that it was but one step to asking what joining or not joining meant. The justification of Mau Mau participation or non-participation

Preface

was of prime interest to informants; whether they had been motivated by a distant or a recent past, by their immediate circumstances or by fear for the future of sons. Mau Mau participation fitted within the framework of their lives; its study became a study of histories and history.

The study shows how ordinary women and men lived through a period of great change and – for many – suffering, and how they perceived their lot. Though they lived in small communities, members were in agreement neither about their history nor about the conclusions which should be drawn from it. Their knowledge of the past was limited to what they had been told and what they had observed and lived; this past dominated their perceptions and their images of the future. Few informants were motivated by other perceptions, of other pasts or other people.

Their knowledge of the colonial period and Mau Mau was not based on writings or opinions of others; it was largely limited to their own experience and affairs. Because they did not live by a 'wider' perspective, because their positions had differed and their experiences had not been the same, they also differed in what they thought important and relevant. They could no more provide a Kikuyu history than a history of colonialism or Mau Mau; in colonial affairs or in Mau Mau, they had not been the leaders whose knowledge was from above. Their knowledge was partial and from below.

The book contains eight chapters, all of which provide historical or modern material about relationships between the villagers. Footnotes provide additional historical or anthropological facts and are sometimes lengthy; they sometimes juxtapose local and published information. To avoid making the text and the footnotes too cumbersome, I have added appendices; they too provide additional data, sometimes basic to the conclusions in the text. Appendix I discusses the use of the data and their relative reliability. The tables which deal with early conditions are often based on calculations and assessments; the later ones are more precise and reliable.

Contents of the chapters

Chapter I begins with the discussion of early fieldwork conditions and introduces the thought world of the Kikuyu and its relevance for the ordering of their affairs. It also introduces, among others, a conflict over land which – to some – had not been solved since it arose in the nineteenth century. After a summary of the local Mau Mau experience, I describe how I concentrated on learning about Mau Mau membership and the primary source of local income: land. The population readily agreed that land had been a significant factor in Mau Mau membership. Being a Kikuyu meant having the right to own a share in Kikuyu land; status and position depended on the degree that one could assume such rights; being deprived of land and status had led to the protest of Mau Mau.[4]

It soon became clear that the relative agreement about why Mau Mau had occurred was not matched by similar agreement about land and land holdings. The location and size of the land available to each household were determined by the share each had received through inheritance: alienation of local land by white settlers in the early colonial period had frequently reduced what had been available before. Conflict often centred on the original acquisition; though the Kikuyu settlers were united by a common ideology of tradition and history, the conflicts represented different ideologies and oral traditions of specific tracts of land. Those conflicts played an important role in local relationships and therefore became part of the research. The end of Chapter 1 discusses the earliest acknowledged local Kikuyu settlements, possibly dating from the end of the eighteenth century when Kikuyu from Murang'a joined the local inhabitants, the Ndorobo. From that time until the *Kirika* famine around 1835, heavy forest and its Ndorobo owners restricted the number of Kikuyu settlements. Their subsistence was determined by how much land they had cleared and continued dependence on hunting and gathering; I have called this type of subsistence a forest economy.

The second chapter describes the role of the famine in the distribution of land and the expansion of the population by strong immigration, which in turn led to accelerated clearing of the forest. This set the stage for increasing differentiation within the population, with considerable wealth for some but increasing lack of resources for others.

Many Kikuyu settlers shifted from a forest economy to an agricultural economy combined with limited herding; by the last decades of the nineteenth century some would have moved to an economy which emphasized export of agricultural products and imports of cattle and goats. Where the pre-*Kirika* period provided few specific data, the later period was a gold mine of information about acquisition and division of land. The final part of this chapter shows that if egalitarian relationships had pertained in the early settlement period, they were giving way to a centralized political system in which access to land and decision making became restricted. Whether or not this was a return to conditions with which immigrants had been familiar in their areas of origin, protest against the restrictions seems to have been limited; the potential protesters needed the protection of those in control. Trade may have played a central role in this development; the period shows an expanding population, increasing socio-economic differentiation and cultural elaboration. This period ends with another famine, the *Ng'aragu ya Ruraya*, with heavy loss of life.

The colonial period in Kikuyu history, described in Chapter 3, started for the local population with the beginning of land alienation. The first years after the famine were devoted to the recovery of their nineteenth-century wealth. Europeans did not see nineteenth-century Kikuyu strength and losses: they saw small groups of primitives on empty land, which could become the base of their own wealth.

Though the famine was a recent event, population expansion through

Preface

polygyny and immigration had already started when alienation occurred; those who lost less land were able to provide some help to those whose land was alienated by the government until the post-famine generation of males needed land in the 1920s. As land remained the backbone of the domestic economy, unresolved old conflict and new tensions about its ownership and use created stressful relationships and bitter land litigation.

For many Kikuyu labour became a partial substitute for their lack of land and Chapter 4 discusses the contribution of wages and the division of labour. Whether or when men or women entered the labour market was largely determined by their land; where they would work, what they could do or earn and what their earnings would buy were equally a factor of their rights over land. While wages in some households made a significant contribution, in others they barely kept workers alive.

The fifth chapter uses land (the major determinant), its hypothetical productivity, and income from wages as the basis for a socio-economic stratification of the population in the late 1940s. Lack of land increased poverty and tension; additionally, government policies favoured the larger land owners, were punitive towards land poor and landless, and added significantly to the burdens of the poor, as did the flat-rate tax system. As a group, land poor and landless paid by far the largest share of the taxes which financed new opportunities; unable to afford the fees such improvements as schools, roads or clinics charged for use, they subsidized those wealthier who could do so.

The next three chapters deal with Kikuyu resistance to European colonialism, making clear that resistance followed Kikuyu ideas and used Kikuyu methods.

The sixth chapter deals with the resistance of the elders and those who controlled the land. Convinced that they, as guardians of the land, had a moral duty to resist the colonial government, their activities centred on the return of the land and a return to power of its owners. Not until their efforts failed did they recognize that those with little or no land had the right to mount their own protests, choose the means and yet remain entitled to the protection of the elders and those who controlled the land. Though this opened the field for their protests, landless and land poor who should have formed its natural base rarely became involved in organizations which tried to recruit them. They lacked the money the organizers needed, they were reluctant to get involved with movements opposed by the government – but, above all, they remained dependent on those who had land. Not until Mau Mau – for brevity's sake I will indicate it as one movement – with its promise that the Europeans would soon leave and abandon their land, would many dare to risk participation.

The seventh chapter deals with the resistance of the landless and the land poor and their growing involvement in Mau Mau, which they needed. It was locally seen as several different movements, which all recruited members through oaths. Prior to the Declaration of the Emergency on 21 October 1952 most oath takers had become involved because they saw in

Mau Mau the only organization which might rescue them from their dire poverty; overthrowing the colonial system and replacing it with a Kenyatta-led government was not their prime motivation.

Just before the Declaration of the Emergency 78.6 per cent of the male population lived in households which were either land poor or landless; by the Emergency more than half of them had taken an oath. They were neither part of the leaders nor party to their plans. Whether Mau Mau had their interests in mind is by no means certain; what is certain is that it appropriated their loyalty, allowing them to serve through oaths and contributions. Kikuyu with more land had remained aloof; where the poor and landless might need Mau Mau to force the government to do something about their grievances, the wealthier had different needs and could use other channels. Nevertheless, as long as local Mau Mau leaders saw to it that Mau Mau did not go beyond what was acceptable to Kikuyu morality, they, their movements and oath takers could count on local protection.

Kenyatta's political popularity had waned since he had returned from England after a long absence. His personal popularity had remained high; his ideas and demeanour had remained Kikuyu; he was a Kiambu man, committed to Kikuyu land and land ownership. He had not demonstrated political acumen, however, he had been unable to force concessions from the colonial government; in the eyes of most of the population, he was not a significant political leader. Contrary to these views the government considered Kenyatta the prime leader of Mau Mau, in its eyes a dangerous insurrectionist movement.

Local overall involvement had remained low; though Nairobi workers were more involved, the movement as a whole had not gained a strong foothold. Yet many Kikuyu, including local leadership, had become convinced that a number of Mau Mau activities violated the proper Kikuyu order. They therefore welcomed government plans to bring it under control, hoping that this would solve their problems at the same time. The arrest of Kenyatta as purported leader of Mau Mau was greeted with considerable surprise and drastically changed the view and the course of Mau Mau. Many who had feared the movement now welcomed and joined it because, if Kenyatta was behind it as the government charged, he was a more astute politician than he had been given credit for and Mau Mau, now openly under his leadership, would challenge their colonial subservience. He would be able to advance the cause of freedom; once he had openly been declared the leader he would be able to halt the undesirable actions of Mau Mau. Kikuyu needed to send Kenyatta a signal of support; the arrest turned into a festival of Mau Mau membership. Several members of households with larger land holdings joined the land poor and landless as members; where before the Emergency only 7 per cent of that group had been oathed, participation increased immediately after the Declaration of the Emergency to almost 20 per cent. Though a number of landless and land poor also joined at this time, in retrospect

Preface

the switch was damaging to the hopes of earlier members. Whatever Mau Mau's original intent, the arrest of Kenyatta, the joining of those with more land and government opposition all emphasized Mau Mau's political character, appropriating the Mau Mau of the dispossessed.

The eighth and final chapter discusses events after the Declaration of the Emergency and the arrest of Kenyatta, including the Marige massacre. Concerned with increasing Mau Mau support and violence, government mounted an aggressive, often virulent attack on Mau Mau. The choice of forced confessions, involving oaths which invoked the spirits as witness that the 'error' would not recur, led to the fatal violence of the local Marige massacre, a few days after the better known Lari massacre.

Policy had demanded that local authority ferret out oath takers, make them confess, and 'strongly encourage' that they go through a cleansing ceremony to prevent them from taking another oath. Some who were forcibly cleansed went to Nairobi and swore to take revenge; because their need coincided with the desire of the Nairobi Central Committee of Mau Mau's desire to kill at least one local man who aggressively pursued oathings and oath administrators, the Committee provided arms. It was up to local people to provide the manpower.

Leaders and members of the gang came from a broad economic spectrum; some prominent gang members represented different sides in severe conflict over land. Preparation for the attack involved heavy drinking and smoking *bangi* (Indian hemp) which played havoc with the plans of the attackers and destroyed the newly created unity.[5] Instead of attacking the intended victims, the drugged and inebriated gang engaged in several unplanned killings; the last ones killed were members of a household with which at least one member of the gang had recently had personal difficulties; this household was also part of one of the sides involved in long-standing conflict over land.

Shocked by its own actions into partial sobriety, the drunken gang tried to disperse and hide, but had little or no chance of escaping the Security Forces. Though informants allege that there was no armed encounter, the gang's death toll was heavy. A number of men were killed on the spot or – perhaps after a summary trial – executed within hours. Three members who were arrested later were brought eventually before the courts; others escaped with their lives, but were detained.[6]

In spite of untold suffering on both sides of the Mau Mau war, Kikuyu resistance to the colonial government ultimately carried the day. During the 1962 research the colonial regime was about to be replaced by an independent republic with Jomo Kenyatta as president; it was not clear at that time whether the landless and land poor would profit economically; what was certain was that the land and those who controlled it had triumphed with the coming of *weiyathi*, freedom.

Mau Mau from Below

Notes

1. The Kikuyu lived before the Emergency in homesteads on their land; first as punishment for Mau Mau involvement and later as general policy, government had imposed villagization. The four villages were two years old at the time of research. The district of Kiambu was divided into divisions, which were divided into sub-division and locations. The four villages formed the Gathiru sub-locations of Komothai location in the Githunguri division; Chief Magugo Waweru was Chief of the division and Komothai location. Sub-locations had headmen; Peter Mahinyara Waweru, a brother of the Chief, was the local headman during most of the research period. Political boundaries might cross land boundaries. The villages Mbari ya Igi and Nginduri contained the large *mbari* of Igi and their *ahoi*; *mbari* land was within Gathiru boundaries. Thuita and Itara contained a number of smaller *mbari*; they had few *ahoi*. The land of some *mbari* straddled the boundaries of two other sub-locations and was near the new villages Kibichoi and Kiratina, where another part of their *mbari* or close kin lived. Emergency conditions restricted my work to Gathiru; work in Kibichoi and Kiratina would have aided a fuller understanding of the Thuita and Itara *mbari*.
    1956. HOR 1954/1962 KBU 50 K.N. Githunguri Division, R. St. J. Mathews, Jan.
2. The 1955 census of Kiambu gave a total population of 59,454 adult males and 83,121 females; Komothai contained 3,070 men, 3,676 women and 8,082 children. Its land area was 18.82 square miles; it housed 20 villages, 4,369 huts, 3,731 cattle and 4,440 goats. The population of the four research villages was 702 adult males, 724 females and 2,051 children; the census did not indicate whether or not those numbers included the Rift Valley repatriates. According to these figures, the male research population represented 1.2 per cent, the female research population 0.88 per cent, of Kiambu District.

    I took a census for 1956/7; adjusted the period immediately preceding the Emergency, the adult male population (14 and over) would have been 734, the adult female population 868, exclusive of 125 males and 129 female Rift Valley repatriates. Children, less than 14 years old, were not counted. Given the lack of hard data, discrepancies are only to be expected; the various numbers are close enough to presume that the males represented roughly 1 per cent of the district population.
    1955. Census Kiambu District March 14 Ref. Adm: 15/6/1/1958 Office of the District Commissioner Kiambu to Provincial Commissioner, Central Province, Nyeri.
3. A household is a unit of people who use land together and are each other's basic economic support. They frequently live on the same plot where they may share several houses. A household may consist of a husband, wives and children; often it also contains other kin. Composition varies: where household and the unit of husband, wife and children was often identical for wealthier landowners, the composition of households with less land was more complex. Households where males were absent due to work often contained, apart from a female with her children, female kin of the woman, perhaps a married, widowed or deserted sister and her children and the wife's mother. Households may contain younger siblings of husband or wife. After 1962, when wives sought employment, they might leave their children with married sisters or aging parents. The size of the household depends on a number of factors. For this study the mean size has been set at five adults, with a child equal to one-half an adult.
4. Kenyatta expressed the unity of Kikuyu and their land as well as their grievance about land alienation when he declared 'You are the earth', adding 'and the earth is ours'.
    1952. Meeting of the Kenya African Union, Nyeri, 26 July.
5. *Cannabis sativa*.
6. Wanyoike, E. N., *An African Pastor* (Nairobi: East African Publishing House, 1974), pp. 200-3; *East African Standard*, 7 April and 9 April 1953; Supreme Court of Kenya, Nairobi, Emergency Assize Criminal Case No. 38 of 1953, 10 September 1953.

One

The Settlement of Kiambu until the Kirika Famine of 1835

The first months of fieldwork

That the histories of Thuita and Igi would probably differ, would be obvious to even a casual observer; after several walks it would be clear that most Thuita households had small holdings and were land poor, while Igi tracts were considerably larger.[1] This made an inquiry into the history of land a natural beginning of fieldwork.

Oral traditions about the settlements were initially readily available from *athuri*, elders, and members of the senior council or *kiama*, in both Thuita and Igi. They agreed that having land had depended on the decisions of ancestral forces; once given, decisions of the same forces would leave men to enjoy their land or take it back. According to Thuita informants, some men had acquired Thuita land before the *Kirika* famine, but only one, whose descendants were still living in Thuita, had survived it. After *Kirika*, land had been acquired by the ancestors of new arrivals; the present population had become owners through inheritance. The first division of land had occurred when fathers, during their lifetimes, parcelled out their land to sons who married, their remaining land being divided when they died. Even though they only got a share, most sons had initially sufficient land to share again with their sons. By the late nineteenth century some buyers or their descendants experienced scarcity, when they were unable to buy land for their expanding population. There was nevertheless little strife; those who had land helped their kinsmen as much as possible. When they were unable to continue this, landless and land poor had left to go elsewhere. Whatever the land position – and there *had* been some land poverty – men had lived in harmony; the poor were not envious of those who had more land, nor did they blame them.

The Settlement of Kiambu until the Kirika Famine, 1835

The *athuri* of Igi provided a similar picture: although the acquisition of the land had been both more gradual and complex and had not always been peaceful, once bought, the buyers had lived in peace with outsiders and each other. The land had initially been divided according to contributions to the land purchase each had made; it was sub-divided when sons married or fathers died. Whether wealthy or poor, men accepted their position and lived in harmony. *Tha*, the giving of mercy, often expressed in giving land in use, was able to make the lives of those with little or no land more comfortable; while it could contribute but little at bad times, any *tha* made life less harsh than it otherwise would have been.[2]

This ability to cooperate had changed with the coming of the Europeans and the theft of the land. As some lost land and others did not, the overall contribution changed significantly and could not be explained solely from how the land had been acquired. Unlike Thuita, Igi holdings could still be sizeable, but, as owners knew that they could no longer expand but needed to share what they had with their sons, *tha* was already curtailed before the First World War. This caused increasingly severe tensions, which elders laid at the door of the colonial government. Elders painted the past as a garden of Eden, in which all-knowing deities had provided according to just and righteous rules; the snake had entered with the European settlers and the colonial regime.

After the first few months of research the picture from Thuita did not notably change. Its histories of land buying did not paint a complex picture; beyond land alienation there was little room for alternative explanations of present-day holdings. Land scarcity was general and profound, inequality minor.

The holdings of *Igi* members differed significantly in size; explanations for this became more complex and contradictory with each interview. By no means did all share the positive image of nineteenth-century relationships: information from litigation showed that men had different views of what had happened in the past and what this had meant. Older women and some older men began to come forward with histories which conflicted with the authorized version of *kiama* elders. Neither they nor their information could be taken lightly; some were highly respected *athuri* even though they did not often attend the council. Other informants of lower status, perhaps *tuthuri* who were old enough to be elders but had not paid the requisite fees for council membership or had not been invited to join, needed to be heeded because they represented different strata of the population. The crux of their information was that men in 'early times' had differed in access to land, status and authority, and had not always lived together in peace. Igi land had neither been acquired nor distributed without strife and conflict; its present-day distribution could be linked as much to what had or should have happened then as to twentieth-century alienation.

Informants obviously believed in different pasts, yet were uniformly vague about what had happened before and during the *Kirika* famine,

The Settlement of Kiambu until the Kirika Famine, 1835

though quite a few older informants were grandsons of those who had lived through that time. The way in which those who had acquired the land had made it suitable for an agricultural lifestyle was barely remembered; what was recalled was selective. The explanation for this was contained in the ideology of history which the population shared; because they shared the same ideology, they had different histories and different oral traditions.

Kikuyu ideology of history

Kikuyu explained the world and their position in it as deriving primarily from decisions of supernatural forces embodied in *Ngai*, God, the ancestors and other spirits. Though his principal abode was on the high mountains, *Ngai* was not confined to specific places. Spiritual forces also were everywhere, but ancestors were present in and close to the land; they rewarded appropriate behaviour and punished wrongdoing. Such decisions were guided not only by the behaviour of the living and by that of their ancestors, but also by their conscious or unconscious thoughts and desires. Decisions were therefore beyond the understanding of mere humans; what mattered was that they formed the background of the realities of life and explained inequality and changes of fortune.

Spiritual blessings were expressed in land, fertile wives, a long life, wealth and authority. Though it might seem that land or wives were provided by one's older kinsmen, only those worthy would be able to profit from these gifts. The inheritance of land was worthless without the willingness to work it: only those who worked their land properly had large harvests; herds with idle herdsmen did not expand; authority flowed from one's achievements and was validated by payments and largesse.

No evidence of ancestral blessings was as convincing as land, the supreme source of wealth and authority. Owners of land were the guardians of the spirits who dwelt in it; they should protect them, honour and appease them through sacrifice and ritual. They should use the land properly. The larger the land, the greater the obligation to have male heirs and to give *tha* in land use to daughters or other relatives in need. Owners should protect those on the land and not treat them unjustly; those living on the land had a right to expect that owners would protect them from inside or outside danger and defend them when they were wronged. In return, land owners were owed obedience and allegiance.

A larger tract of land represented a greater concentration of spiritual powers; it made heavier demands for sacrifices and ritual; it was likely to shelter a larger group of dependents. Owners whose responsibilities were large had the right to demand that men with lesser responsibilities did not prevent them from exercising their duties and rights. As their needs should take precedence over those of smaller land owners, to the needs of all owners took precedence over those of users.

Because ancestral decisions were at the heart of each person's fate in life, the wealthy should remember and acknowledge that it was not

The Settlement of Kiambu until the Kirika Famine, 1835

necessarily given because they were more virtuous; what they had might be the consequence of the righteousness of kinsmen or those who had died. It could be lost quickly; it would not take long for spiritual wrath to reduce a herd of a hundred goats to one. Those who had limited land or perhaps none should not be downcast; their misfortune might originate in events long before they were born. They should live righteously; if this pleased the spiritual forces, they could transform one goat into a herd of a hundred.

One of the most important matters to remember was that evil created evil and good created good. This was as valid in history and what memories were kept alive as in daily life. It was important to recall blessings and the virtue which had brought them, but dangerous to recall punishments and their causes. Events which brought blessings should become part of history; they could be discussed freely and all might know them. Even then, important information should be withheld until the proper age: not until males reached senior elders' status would they be told the full oral traditions, shown the precise boundaries and receive the right to question matters of land.

Events which brought evil and their possible causes should be deleted from general memory. Ideology demanded that events indicative of lack of blessings were to be retained only in the memory of senior elders. They could decide whether or not to hand it down but it was not likely that they would do so, unless to other senior elders. This in itself could contribute to lack of history: if senior elders suffered a high rate of death in a disaster, their knowledge died with them.

The present could be a guide to judge whether an event had or had not 'occurred': if one oral history maintained that Marai did not have much land because he had been cursed by his father for wrongdoing, while Marai's oral history related that others had wrongly taken his land, Marai's flourishing descent group should be sufficient evidence to counteract rumours that he was cursed. Those who continued to recount the tale of a curse would do well to change their tune.

Lack of blessings, particularly if manifest in landlessness or death, should if possible neither be discussed nor told to the next generation. These beliefs profoundly influenced what informants knew about their own past. Not only would few twentieth-century landless men be able to give any information about landless grandfathers, let alone earlier generations, land owners equally had but scant information about their ancestors prior to the generation which bought land. Information about poverty was therefore hard to obtain even though it was – eventually – admitted that large sectors of the nineteenth-century population had been poor if not destitute.

Land buying might not suffice for history to begin: if a group suffered significant loss of life after having bought land, perhaps during the *Kirika* famine in which many died, the earlier history would be omitted and the survivors would date the acquisition of the land as occurring after *Kirika*, describing the survivors as the buyers. In this way the evil events of death and loss would not be recreated in speech and thought. While most elders

The Settlement of Kiambu until the Kirika Famine, 1835

were convinced that another disastrous famine at the end of the century had occurred because of evil at that time, pious elders could not escape the uneasy thought that incautious talk about the *Kirika* had also played a role.

Only limited information about the period before *Kirika* had survived and the famine itself was being removed from the historical record. The process was by no means simple and straightforward; not all had been affected equally, not all had the same need to protect the information. One sector of a land-owning group which had suffered few losses in the period might want to keep to the tradition that local land ownership had existed prior to the famine; others who had suffered severely might want to date its origin after the famine; those who had come after the famine and inherited land from members of a land-owning group who had died might date the buying of the land with their arrival. Though their oral traditions might show significant internal differences, those in power would at any time seek to determine the historical record, the official oral traditions. In spite of such attempts, unofficial oral traditions which might be equally diverse, held by those who lacked and sought power, continued to survive or were born, in their land-owning groups.[3]

Sometimes events were too recent to ignore: it was not possible to deny the late nineteenth-century famine, the *Ng'aragu ya Ruraya*. Yet one could profess ignorance of what had led up to or caused it and discuss the preceding years only in terms of their blessings. If questions about the famine could not be avoided, one might only give the bare outlines and use ritual speech reserved for recounting evil: slow, never loud or forceful. Elders refused to discuss the gangs which had roamed the area and lived from robbery during the famine; it was an evil within an evil. Information was restricted to those groups which had recovered; no information was forthcoming about those whose losses were so severe that they had died out or left.[4]

Given this perspective on history, it was not surprising that different people had different histories; it also explained the gap between elders and younger members in knowledge about land. As it was, though elders' knowledge about the distant past and its hardships had become limited and vague, younger males knew even less of the hardships of the past or of the past itself. Each generation would lose part of its history. Generalized lack of knowledge provided ammunition to those who, in the twentieth century, would alienate Kikuyu land, justifying it by pointing out the 'recent' settlement of Kiambu.

Contemporary events were subject to the rules of historical recall; Mau Mau information demonstrates that the processes of change started to operate within a short time. In 1956, when the government was still actively engaged in the defeat of Mau Mau, information was available which by 1962 should no longer be discussed. In the first research period, there was no objection to words such as Homeguard or Mau Mau member; in 1962 it was 'rude' to ask whether a man had belonged to either or both.

The Settlement of Kiambu until the Kirika Famine, *1835*

Complaints to the local KANU leader would result in a warning that such terms were no longer appropriate. If the offence was repeated, the District Officer could impose a fine. Mau Mau had brought evil and freedom: its latter role could be discussed because it had brought *weiyathi* and Kenyatta; its former aspect should be played down, forgotten, laid to rest.[5]

Traditions of settlement and forest economies

In the eighteenth and nineteenth centuries land could be bought by individuals – often in smaller parcels – or by a group of men, acquiring a larger tract. Such a land buyer or group of land buyers became a *mbari*, as did their heirs; the term *mbari* refers to men and their land. A specific group – mostly one buyer with his descendants – within a *mbari* formed a *githaku* (pl. *ithaku*) with its land.

Such groups need to be distinguished from descent groups without reference to land ownership – to which all Kikuyu belonged. A man with sons referred to his small group as a *mucii*, a home, but would use *nyumba*, house, for a larger group, perhaps himself, sons and grandsons. After his death, sons might continue to see themselves as part of his *nyumba*; they might also see themselves as the head of their own *mucii*, on the way to becoming a *nyumba*. I will reserve the word *nyumba* for the largest localized descent group; its subdivisions are segments, or if needed, sub-segments. *Nyumba* were named after their founders; inheritance of weapons, tools, clothing and ornaments, and sometimes offices, was based on this descent. Unless they owned land and were members of *mbari*, descent groups were often shallow.

Though they eventually would form different *ithaku*, joint buyers of land became a *mbari* regardless of previous relationships; they became 'one person' and 'one person' with the land itself. The relationship to the land was represented as a marriage between a land-wife and a human-husband consisting of the group of buyers, who became one with the land and each other. The descendants of buyers shared fathers who had become one; they shared a common mother in the land which had been acquired; as full 'brothers', they and their descendants were exogamous in perpetuity. The unity of men and land was symbolized by burying original buyers and senior elders of the *mbari* in the land; most others were deposited in the forest.[6]

Mbari could choose to be named for a real or putative ancestor of the most important buyer, or, more rarely, that of a cultural hero or a feature of the land. If only one or two men – perhaps with lineal descendants – bought, the *mbari* was likely to carry the name of the most senior male. *Mbari* names lapsed when *mbari* dissolved; if they fissioned peacefully the fissioned segment, which became a new *mbari*, continued to carry the original name.

Given the Kikuyu view of history, traditions have preserved little of the hardships under which individuals and *mbari* acquired Kiambu land, though genealogies hint at conflict and a high death toll. Though the

The Settlement of Kiambu until the Kirika Famine, 1835

acquisition involved transforming a heavily forested area owned by hunters and foragers into an agricultural-herding economy, oral traditions do not mention, unless specifically requested, the dangers, the back-breaking clearing, nor the hunting and foraging that maintained life during the process.

While some Kikuyu settlers had come from Maasai, Akamba or Northern areas, elders agreed that many Kikuyu settlers had originally come from Murang'a, though quite a few had already lived in northeastern Kiambu where they had taken possession of uninhabited land by right of *gukuna*, the 'breaking' of virgin land. These settlements had remained under Murang'a authority; there is no information on how this was exercised. It probably meant that the new settlers participated in Murang'a ritual and paid the appropriate fees to Murang'a elders.

Over time some individuals ventured into the Southern forests which belonged to Ndorobo hunters, beekeepers and gatherers. How early this started was unknown; no ancestors of local men were acknowledged to have been in the area before the middle or at the earliest the beginning of the eighteenth century. They came as individuals or small groups; their survival depended on the Ndorobo, who owned large tracts of land. How many intermarried and lived peacefully with the Ndorobo – hunting and gathering with them with perhaps a bit of agriculture on the side – is not known. Official oral history virtually denied that any time was involved; as far as it was concerned, arrival and buying of land were separated by no more than a few years, if any. It also asserts that ownership of land did not differ between Kiambu and Murang'a, yet acknowledged that, in Murang'a, all land sold could be redeemed. If it exceeded the needs of the owners, it could be given to someone in use for a period which did not exceed one 'generation'. Once some – and probably by no means all – incoming Kiambu settlers decided to abandon the hunting-gathering economy of their Ndorobo hosts, they had to buy the land; once bought, they could sell it. Kiambu tenure deviated from the Murang'a pattern.

Several factors make it unlikely that the Kikuyu bought soon after arrival. According to unauthorized oral traditions, intermarriage was common – many genealogies contained Ndorobo women – and undoubtedly a number of new arrivals continued to hunt with the Ndorobo, not interested in resuming agricultural pursuits. Even those who had come with this intent, would probably have regarded it only as a distant goal. They had to survive; there is no reason to presume that – though Ndorobo fathers gave land as dowry – they would have given their daughters to men who could not maintain them. While Ndorobo did not ask payments from those who hunted with them, they did demand payment as soon as men wanted to convert hunting land to agricultural land. It would take time to accumulate even a relatively small payment as it consisted of goats, which had to be bred under hunting-gathering conditions.

Before men could live from agriculture, they faced years of clearing the forest even if they had been able to do so full time. It is likely that the safety and survival of the future agriculturalists demanded they continue

The Settlement of Kiambu until the Kirika Famine, 1835

to spend a good deal of time hunting. Safety would have demanded their continued stay with the Ndorobo group; its migratory life style would have further cut down the time for clearing. It seems safe to assume that hunting would remain a major, if not the most significant, factor in survival, and that the Kikuyu lived for a considerable time in a manner not too differently from the Ndorobo.

For those who wanted to resume agriculture, the balance between hunting/foraging and agriculture would slowly change in favour of agriculture with some limited keeping of stock, perhaps a dozen goats. This would take years, probably decades, perhaps at least one generation, to achieve. The mode of subsistence in which agriculture expands as forest clearings grow, but hunting and gathering continue to be part of the economy, I have called a forest economy.

The acquisition of land

The following narrative is pieced together from scattered data from various elders, from genealogies and conflict over who had acquired what land. Local men and women thought of the forest as a place where legitimate owners hunted and trapped, but others, *thabari* or robbers, had lived a lawless existence. No one had a great interest in who they were: they might be men who had been banned or fled from their own people; they might be men who had wanted to live with the Ndorobo, but had been refused.

Some time after Kikuyu who were acceptable to the Ndorobo and allowed to live with them had arrived, the number of Kamba, Maasai and Embu, landless Ndorobo, and Kikuyu not accepted by the land owners increased significantly, perhaps as a result of a disaster. They hunted and trapped without permission, poached and robbed the game pits and honey barrels, and were not above abducting Ndorobo girls. At that time some Kikuyu who lived peacefully with the Ndorobo and wanted to revert to agriculture, but could not do so alone, proposed a diplomatic solution which served their aims: if the Ndorobo were willing to sell them land so that they could grow crops, they would ask kinsmen to come and help defend the Ndorobo. The Ndorobo would become *athi* (sing. *mwathi*), sellers of land.

If the Ndorobo consented, and after senior Kikuyu elders had arrived from Murang'a – as none were likely to be available locally – protracted ceremonial negotiations would start with the guardians of the land, the Ndorobo ancestors. The ritual was needed because informants presumed that acceptance by the living was not enough; the Kikuyu could only be sure in their assumption of the land if they knew that the ancestors had adopted the Kikuyu as descendants and owners. Though the arrangement was made for a specific pre-discussed part of the land, the adoption affected all the land of the selling Ndorobo; if he sold more land, neither the buyer nor he needed to go through another ritual of adoption. Sharing ancestors

The Settlement of Kiambu until the Kirika Famine, 1835

would make Kikuyu and Ndorobo kin, with rights to mutual aid and protection. While in other cases men who share a common ancestor became a descent group, the emphasis was not on the ancestors but on the land as the creator of the relationship.[7]

Though kin, the Ndorobo neither became a descent group together with the Kikuyu buyers nor became Kikuyu. The land had made them into affinal kin; the Ndorobo land as a whole had given a part – a land-daughter – to the Kikuyu. The Ndorobo thought of themselves and were regarded as Ndorobo as long as they hunted and gathered; the concept of belonging to a tribe seems to have been absent (Appendix III/2). Rather, people classified themselves and others in terms of subsistence patterns and allegiance; their daily lives were determined by kinship and interaction. Kikuyu can make land into Kikuyu land by taking possession of it; it then becomes a part of the large ancestral land, the *bururi* of the Kikuyu. The terms can also be used for smaller parts, such as Murang'a, Gaki and what was to become Kiambu. But there is no word to indicate the aggregate of those who are or become Kikuyu, though they might share significant cultural features and speak the same or almost the same language. Men might have distant kin but lived in a local area, in a specific setting, interacting with others perhaps because of proximity, kinship, formal or informal associations or mutual interests. What one called oneself or was called, whether Ndorobo, Maasai or Kikuyu, depended on one's primary mode of subsistence. Those who shared this and lived sufficiently close together were likely to share roughly similar organizational structures and ideologies.

The affiliation of males was determined by their subsistence pattern, that of women by that of fathers or husbands. With permission of the receiving group, men could change their affiliation: Ndorobo who became agriculturalists, became Kikuyu; Kikuyu men who wanted to live as herders, became Maasai; if hunters, they were Ndorobo. An interesting question would be how many of the Ndorobo who traditionally were said to have sold the land had in the preceding century or centuries become Ndorobo by sharing their lifestyle, though their origin had been Kikuyu.

Marriages across subsistence boundaries often set changes in motion. Kinsmen of the Ndorobo bride of a Kikuyu might ask her husband for agricultural land; if granted, they became Kikuyu like their kinswoman. If they brought some or all of their previous hunting land with them, a formal adoption was needed for the land. If kinsmen of the groom wanted to hunt rather than grow crops, they could go to the kin of their kinsman's wife and become Ndorobo. A young male who went to the Maasai and stayed there to remain a herder became Maasai.

Forest economies

During the adoption ritual, the Ndorobo gave the Kikuyu a piece of land called *magatha*, and received some goats in return.[8] Both were gifts; it was

The Settlement of Kiambu until the Kirika Famine, 1835

not a buying transaction. The Kikuyu would start clearing as much land as they could; they would also herd the Ndorobo goats if no one could be found to do so. The decision of the ancestors would become manifest in the fertility of goats and land. If favourable, buying would proceed; the buyers, most likely already local men, might be joined by others; it was not important that they had not been present at the adoption.

The facilitators of the adoption became the leaders of the new settlement; their authority rested on their relationship with the Ndorobo and on their wealth, which might consist of dowry land, *magatha*, and land which had been bought.[9] If the Ndorobo decided to leave the area, they asked such men to represent them in the sale of their remaining land; the service was likely to be rewarded with more land. Like the Ndorobo, these men became *athi* (sing. *mwathi*), sellers; later arrivals in Kiambu may well have bought predominantly through such men. Purchases were mostly for two hundred acres or more; an occasional buyer bought only one hundred acres.[10] Pre-*Kirika* Igi men purportedly bought larger tracts than Thuita. Small groups and small tract buyers paid more than strong groups buying large tracts; the latter could offer protection and important relationships as well as the price.

Buyers were sometimes described as one person, sometimes as a group made up mostly of (as many as ten) 'brothers'. It is probable that such a group either consisted of 'collapsed' generations – sometimes in response to disasters – or of men who had become 'brothers' by buying together.

Before *Kirika*, a hundred-acre tract of forest would be priced at about forty to fifty goats, depending on the nearness of a river. The payment would depend on the wishes of the seller and might well include a girl of the buying group; her value was half of the price of one hundred acres; brideprices were around twenty goats.[11]

Both sides preferred instalment payments. In the early days the Ndorobo – not dependent on payments as long as there was sufficient game – might ask for about a tenth of the price on settlement, followed by a third of the remaining price in the next decade; in some cases another payment was not asked until twenty-five years later. Payments commonly stretched over several generations; when clearing and agriculture increased and game became scarce, the Ndorobo might allow no more than a decade or two between a first and last payment.[12]

Using a conservative estimate, it would take the working life of the buying generation before a household could regard itself as settled, in the sense that crops would provide most of the food and hunting would be subsidiary, under normal circumstances more tied to the need for safety than for food. Vegetable food and medicines would still be gathered, and the forest would continue to provide firewood and building material. This 'settlement' would require about seven acres of cleared land; a beginning could probably be made as soon as four acres had been cleared.

Four acres would have provided space for an enclosed homestead and its few goats, a granary and a midden; a minimum of two to two-and-a-half acres – preferably three for a larger household – would be needed for cultivation. At least one acre would have to be cleared sufficiently of heavy tree growth for stock to use it for browsing and grazing; it would become the beginning of the first expansion when cultivation land needed to be fallowed and new land brought in use. Seven acres would provide for some additional auxiliary buildings, cultivation and fallowing land which could be used as browsing land for a dozen goats.

It is not known which crops the emigrants brought with them, and whether they had been tried while they were still living with the Ndorobo. The degree of continuity with their areas of origin is unknown; the complexity of crops cultivated by the end of the nineteenth century and the sophisticated use of land with crop rotation and fallowing presumes a lengthy period of experimentation.

As no fire was used in the earliest clearing, possibly because it might have scared the game in adjacent areas, clearing was slow and laborious. Fire was at times used for clearing lighter stands of trees and bush; there was a danger, however, that it might flare out of control and endanger isolated standing trees or groves which served as shelter for the spirits.[13]

The ideology of individual and gender

Individuals, unless they were so poor that they had no kin, were part of several relationships, some past, some present and some future. Men and women were regenerations of the alternating generation above, they promised that the alternating generation below would be born. A man was therefore his father's father, or father's father's brother; he was also his born or unborn grandson. A woman was her grandmother or mother's mother's sister; she was also her born or unborn granddaughter.[14] A good life was part of an unbroken chain of regeneration.

Gender, and expressing its implied sexual role, was crucial for men and women. Though a rare individual was allowed to refrain from marrying, the prime duty of males and females was to bring the next generation into the world and to provide for it so that this generation could do the same. Male and female roles were different, but as long as each fulfilled his proper role, they were essentially equal, each other's counterpart.

Men were identified with the land, they were its guardians, they represented its continuity.[15] They tended stock which acquired more land; their herding provided the sacrifices which gave thanks, implored for help and communicated with the ancestors who were buried in the land and brought blessing or punishment. Men cleared the land and made it ready for cultivation; as they maintained right relationships with the spiritual forces, so they maintained right relationships in household and community. Failure to do so would bring *thahu*, spiritual defilement of land and people; the task of men was to ensure *theru*, a state of righteousness. If they had performed their tasks properly and lived to a high age, if their lives were

The Settlement of Kiambu until the Kirika Famine, 1835

evidence of *theru* and closeness to the ancestors, they would be buried in the land, becoming one with it and the ancestors.

Women were neither ancestors nor land nor its guardians. Yet without them men could not fulfil their obligations and roles; women's agriculture enabled the land to bear fruit, women's sexuality and fecundity provided sons and daughters, without women, land and men would come to an end.

In marriage, through sons, a woman gave continuity to her husband and 'unlocked his life' and that of his land-owning group. By bearing daughters, she provided for her husband's kin group as the brideprices of daughters would provide wives for the sons. As her husband had sired their children, so he had to provide her with the cleared land from which she could feed those she had brought into the world.

Just as land continued to give, a woman continued to give through her sons and daughters and it was therefore right that, even when land and brideprice were fully paid, those who had provided them could come back again and again and ask for more: 'a brideprice never ends'. One obvious time to come back was when a woman's daughters received higher brideprices than had been paid for her.[16]

A woman's gifts were not confined to her husband and his kin; through marriage she brought and continued to bring gifts to her natal kin. Her brideprice enabled her father to acquire a wife for her brother – a common term of endearment from a brother to a sister was 'my *mburi*', my goats – and she 'unlocked her brother's life', continuing her father and mother in her brother's sons and daughters. If her husband had land to spare, a woman might pave the way for her brothers and father to use her husband's land.[17]

The brideprice, far from being a price paid for a chattel, marked the beginning of a relationship and rights for a man and a woman and their natal kin. Too much was involved to take risks: a man would think twice before marrying his son or daughter to partners they refused.

Within the context of Kikuyu ideology, women had high status; men with only sons would be poor men; a man with only daughters had no future. So strongly ingrained was the idea that the brideprice gave rights, that those who felt they were denied their appropriate roles after it had been paid and received, could demand legal redress. If a woman did not give a man sons or daughters, he and his kinsmen could bring a case to the elders of their land-owning group. They might accuse her or her relations of witchcraft; the elders might impose penalties and – if all else failed – decide that she should be sent back to her father or brother. If a woman felt wronged because her children died, she could bring a case against her husband and his kin before the council of her natal kin.[18] They might investigate, bring appropriate charges, demand compensation or – as a final judgment – advise the woman to return to her natal household.[19] Though there were unsatisfactory family and marital relationships among informants, nothing in Kikuyu ideology supported an inferior or superior position of either gender.[20]

The Settlement of Kiambu until the Kirika Famine, 1835

Women and men in a forest economy

Though based on restricted knowledge of the oldest informants, the following reconstruction reflects what information they had and were willing to share.

The Kikuyu frontier was not a society of men; men *and* women were needed if a settlement was to succeed and both were in short supply. Though large households had more labour, they were under more pressure to clear the forest, because sons who married would expect to get at least some cleared land. The work and the living conditions made life fragile, particularly so during early settlement: women – often isolated from other women – could die in childbirth; children and adults could be killed by animals; men could be maimed or killed when hunting or felling trees. In the pre-*Kirika* period, men needed if at all possible more than one wife; if one died there should be others to replace her. High child mortality made it imperative that there were sufficient women of childbearing and nourishing age to produce the next – working – generation. One man alone could not perform all the work; a household needed the help of more than one man to clear the forest, to hunt and provide.

Though early settlers may have returned to Murang'a for a first wife in accordance with the rule that she had to be taken from already affinal kin, settlers depended on local availability for replacements of the dead and for additional wives. Some were undoubtedly acquired from the Ndorobo or neighbouring Kikuyu, but new buyers of land might not have sufficient goats to pay for land and a wife at the same time.[21]

Raiding for Ndorobo girls might create lasting acrimony; raiding neighbouring Kikuyu settlements was too dangerous as the favour might be returned. Moreover, in both cases those captured could probably find their way home. This left the more distant Maasai: only a small party was needed for a raid; the raiders could withdraw quickly into the forest with their prey.[22] Maasai women occurred with regularity in genealogies.

It was as difficult to keep as to get wives. Non-Ndorobo women disliked the forest; males had difficulty convincing fathers and their daughters that marriage to a forest settler was an attractive proposition, even when they were able to raise a brideprice. The forest, though potentially arable land, was associated with the spirits of the dead; wild animals and renegade landless were potentially killers. Nevertheless, however difficult, the high 'normal' rate of death for women and children made polygyny highly desirable.[23]

Neither monogamy nor polygyny were certain to produce viable offspring; even the children who survived would not immediately provide the labour to maintain and expand the settlements. Incorporation of women through brideprices was not sufficient to ensure survival; men had to be incorporated as well.

The process for this was as simple as it was efficient. Under pioneer

The Settlement of Kiambu until the Kirika Famine, 1835

conditions it was not wise to buy land before one was familiar with the area. Kikuyu buyers therefore lived with men who had already bought, in much the same way as other Kikuyu had lived with Ndorobo before they bought or received land. To both Kikuyu and Ndorobo such men were *agendi* (sing. *mugendi*), sojourners; it is likely that Kikuyu in the past had been incorporated into the Ndorobo; it is virtually certain that a number of Kikuyu *agendi* were incorporated as *mbari* members into Kikuyu *mbari*.

Agendi who did not intend to become independent buyers were welcomed by Kikuyu settlers in need of manpower, as other labour would have been extremely scarce. Men living illegally in the forest would not have qualified; though not all might be *thabari*, robbers, they certainly would be *igwima*, destitute, and as such unwelcome. Settlements which failed or men who, while living with the Ndorobo or Kikuyu had had to conclude that they could not afford to buy independently, were probably the main source for suitable *agendi*.

If after working together land owners found that a *mugendi* would make a suitable partner, they would be loath to see him go. Offering continued use of land might not be attractive enough to men who knew the value of their services; to prevent a good *mugendi* from leaving, land owners might have to offer incorporation into the *mbari*. This had advantages for the *mugendi*: rather than facing the rigours of new settlement alone, he became a full member of an already existing group of men and shared in the ownership of land for which a first payment had already been made. In contrast to a later period, there is no evidence that contributing only to later payments at the time before *Kirika* restricted his rights to the land. The labour he had contributed before membership was likely to outweigh any payments he could have made.[24] Whatever his origin, whatever his *muhiriga*, clan, the incorporated member would over time assume the *muhiriga* of the *mbari* of which he had become part.[25]

As population strength in the early settlement years may have been a critical factor in success or failure, the punitive attitude towards members who left becomes understandable. They lost what contributions they had made; their 'goats stayed in the land'; if they returned, which they had the right to do for two – some say only one – generations, they could not reclaim the land once held unless it had remained unused; in other cases they could only be given land which no one used or needed.

Those incorporated were not excluded from leadership positions in the *mbari*, though members who had contributed earlier had preference. They also might have to compete with powerful sons of earlier buyers.

Interpretations and traditions of land ownership

The explanation that a *mbari* was formed by brothers, indicated the closeness of their relationship; it might be interpreted that the brothers had roughly identical rights over the land of the *mbari*. Nevertheless, as the section on inheritance will show, brothers did not have similar rights over their father's land and the expression indicates unity rather than equality.

This is also indicated in the even stronger expression that men who had become a *mbari* were 'as one person' and 'one with the land'. As with 'brothers', several interpretations are possible. They would be particularly significant in *mbari* such as Igi where men had joined at different times, had contributed or not contributed to all purchases, and contributed unequally when they did.

These symbolic statements would lead to two different interpretations Of *mbari* which would be of particular importance in the twentieth century.[26] In the first, the unity would mean equality in terms of possession of the land: all members had equal right to it, regardless of the varying contributions they had made to the purchase of the land. In the second, symbolic unity went hand in hand with economic inequality: the amount of each member's contribution determined the rights of *mbari* members in the land. The first interpretation tended towards communal, the second towards individual ownership of land.

Both interpretations shared a number of features. Both recognized that the *mbari* was the ritual owner of the land and that members of it shared obligations and rights. Both accepted that land once bought could only be sold in part or whole with the consent of the *mbari* council. Both accepted that the council decided whether new members could or could not join and that it represented the *mbari* in sacrifice and conflict. Both based their interpretation on the presumed will of the ancestors.

In the first interpretation higher contributions to the price did not give rights to more land, because being able to contribute more was a blessing for which men should give thanks rather than demand additional gifts from their fellow men. Once bought, need – the size and labour strength of the household – should determine access to the land. Some land should be kept in reserve – to be used by all for herding – until new or expanding households needed (more) land. As households had different numbers of sons, one *githaku* might over time 'own' more land than another. This was acceptable if based on its strength; if the *nyumba* lost this strength and others needed land, some of its land should revert to the *mbari* for redistribution.

The second interpretation saw a decision of the ancestral forces behind the capability and willingness to contribute. As land should reflect the blessings of the ancestors, it would be wrong to ignore what one could or could not contribute. Only when a contributor and all his heirs died without issue and no collateral relatives were members of the *mbari*, or if the buyer or his descendants violated the ritual unity of the *mbari* by witchcraft or murder, could *mbari* elders take the land.

Apart from these differences, the interpretations shared the belief that the rights of *mbari* members outweighed the obligations members might have to kinsmen who were not members. When *mbari* members died without issue, their land was inherited by kinsmen within the *mbari*; failing

The Settlement of Kiambu until the Kirika Famine, 1835

those, it reverted to the *mbari* as a whole. It could then decide to give a part of it to kinsmen from outside, but only if they became *mbari* members. Both interpretations accepted that the *mbari* as a whole could buy more land which became *mbari* land; opinions on how the new land should be divided varied with the degree to which they recognized communal or individual ownership. Land owned by an individual before he became a member of the *mbari* or bought afterwards was, according to those who held to individual ownership, his own. Those who gave more weight to communal ownership differed; sometimes they argued that it was *mbari* property, sometimes, in spite of their other ideas, they accepted that it was private land.

Mbari traditions from the days of the forest economies and *mbari* interpretations

The background to the buying of land and individual *mbari* histories are important in the conflict between the Kikuyu; they were equally important in that the Kikuyu were certain that they owned the land they had bought and/or inherited, while the colonial government and most Europeans who took part in land alienation, were convinced that the Kikuyu had at best 'owned' *usufruct* and held the land by communal tenure.[27] The different perspectives of the past on the side of the Kikuyu were important because rights to land in the present were based on what each believed to have occurred in the past. These differences sanctioned or ran contrary to the twentieth-century distribution of the land; inequality, poverty and landlessness were as much based on past history as on alienation. Different oral traditions had clashed in court; they had fuelled antagonism and some of this had spilled over in Mau Mau violence.

To understand the local community and its Mau Mau, one must understand their different perspectives and oral histories, as recounted in this and the following chapters as well as in Appendix I/2 and Appendix II. They must therefore be included, however complex, involved and contradictory. I will simplify as much possible and leave out any unnecessary minutiae; yet I am certain that the patience of readers will at times be sorely tried.

Given the nature of the material, it is not possible to declare that any specific version of the oral traditions is more factual than others. It would be foolhardy to make any such judgment, or to believe that one can make such a decision from sometimes as many as a dozen different versions. The versions included in the text were chosen because they explain twentieth-century conflicts; if these conflicts have relevance to Mau Mau, different versions of the tradition are included in the text. In other cases of conflict one version may be included in the text and another included in the notes. The oral traditions in Appendix II illustrate the events around the Thuita settlement of the area; they may have much wider relevance as well as explaining present-day relationships. To emphasize that no recorded tradition as a whole should be linked to any one *mbari* or *githaku*, and to protect their descendants, names are fictional.

Oral traditions of Thuita and Igi before *Kirika*

It is not known how many *mbari* had been established in the local area before *Kirika* and whether they survived *Kirika* only to leave or die out later. In the twentieth century two Thuita acknowledged that they had been formed prior to *Kirika*. The history of the two Thuita *mbari* shows that part of the land was not paid for, part was acquired in exchange for goats and a girl. It also shows that the *Kirika* famine probably wiped out part of even those *mbari* which did survive, with the subsequent difficulty in remembering what had been paid and when. As with Igi, the data for the traditions were provided by *arumati* and senior elders during several sessions; the information has been coordinated in a coherent narrative.

Thuita *Mbari*:
Before *Kirika* two 'brothers' bought land together, possibly in two parcels, part of it in Kibichoi and part of it in the lower south-eastern area. It may have been well over two hundred acres and was paid for with a girl and goats. Payments were not finished until the end of the nineteenth century. Losses during *Kirika* were severe, but some descendants of each brother survived.

A second group had started with land given to them by the Ndorobo, possibly as dowry; it may have bought more land, either before or after *Kirika*. Its land straddled the modern Thuita-Kibichoi boundaries, it probably also had land in the Kiratina area. The land may have been several hundred acres, the price was unknown and payments were finished well before the end of the nineteenth century.

*The pre-*Kirika *history of two* ithaku *of Igi*
Although an important senior elder asserted that Igi also had existed at this time, no further evidence or data were produced.[28] *Arumati* and senior elders of two of its later *ithaku*, Kungu and Chege, acknowledged that they antedated *Kirika* as independent *mbari* who would become *ithaku* of Igi after *Kirika*. This was confirmed by other elders of other *ithaku*. No agreement was reached whether a third, Njau, was still living with the Ndorobo or whether he had already bought land with his son Mwereri; even within Njau, evidence was conflicting. It is fairly certain that the ancestors of a fourth were Ndorobo, at that time living in the forest.

While the history of Njau is introduced to give some idea of the vicissitudes and internecine quarrels of forest life and living with the Ndorobo, the history of Chege is the most important on several grounds. It shows that not all settled down to agriculture or even wanted to do so; living with the Ndorobo may at times have been preferred. The Chege

The Settlement of Kiambu until the Kirika Famine, 1835

traditions also illustrate that founders, most likely a group of cooperating men, adopting each other, were perceived as 'brothers'. Most important, we find here the origin of a conflict which had remained unsolved well into the twentieth century, had become particularly virulent in the last years before the Emergency, and played a role in the Marige massacre. The conflict centres around the property of Gitau, a man presumed to have owned land before the creation of Igi. His descendants would assert that the first parcel of land Igi bought after *Kirika* included the Gitau land; Gitau people had not been present during the transactions and whatever compensation – if any – Igi had paid for the land, they had received nothing. Igi therefore owed Gitau men compensation when they returned. Others asserted that Gitau land was not part of the acquisition; if he had owned land in the area then it would have been part of the land of his 'brother' Chege. These men, not Igi, therefore owed compensation. The traditions of Kungu, Chege (with and without Gitau) and Njau follow.

Kungu Mbari
Little is known about Kungu and his *mbari* beyond that he had bought a large area of land. From whom and at what price is not known.

Chege Mbari (Version I – includes Gitau)
Between 1750 and 1775 a man called Mwaura and an adult son lived with the Ndorobo, where they were joined by 'his father and brothers', among them Chege and Gitau. Gitau, Chege and Mwaura had each received land, perhaps as dowry. They wanted to buy more land but the Ndorobo wanted to be adopted first. A senior brother of Mwaura, Thuo, started proceedings, probably between 1775 and 1800, but the ritual was broken off when a fight broke out between his son and a *mwathi* son; the *mwathi* fled to Mwaura, who eventually completed the ritual. Brother Chege was present at that time, but Gitau had left before the final ritual because his wife had died. He had cleared part of his land and built a homestead; he left his land in the care of Chege. By *Kirika* he had not yet returned. Mwaura and Chege acquired more land; it may have been *magatha* land, perhaps it was bought.

The Chege men and others of his kin who came later formed a *mbari* with their land which took the name Chege. It is not clear whether Mwaura and his land were in it, or whether Mwaura was a member who had a large private land outside the *mbari*. Whether the *mbari* or individuals acquired more land is not clear. Between 1800 and 1820, when even more kinsmen came, Mwaura decided to leave with the Ndorobo. He offered his land to Chege for three hundred goats. Chege could not afford it and approached Njau, 'a distant kinsman' who was living with other Ndorobo. Njau refused; Mwaura sold it to others instead. The Chege *mbari* was hit hard by *Kirika*; perhaps no more than five households survived.

Chege Mbari (Version II – excludes Gitau)
A long time ago Thuo, a man from Murang'a, lived with the Ndorobo; he had not bought land when the Ndorobo wanted to be adopted. In

the middle of the ritual some younger men got into a drunken fight. The Ndorobo took off Thuo's symbols of adoption and fled to a man called Mwaura who completed the ritual; Mwaura had at least one brother Chege and this Chege possibly was given *magatha* land. Some of Mwaura's people eventually formed a *mbari* with their land; it was eventually called the *mbari* of Chege. No one knows anything about a man called Gitau; he may have been a relation of Chege, but if he had land which he asked Chege to keep, any later problems would have been between those two men.

Njau Mbari
Njau belonged to a Murang'a *mbari*; he had land there and had cleared land in Makwa, which he claimed by *gukuna* because it was an uninhabited area of Kiambu. When he decided to go into the Ndorobo forest, his father disowned him; he lost his Murang'a land but retained his rights in Makwa. He went to Thuo, a distant kinsman who had initiated adoption but had not completed it, and who had continued to stay with the Ndorobo, with whom Njau was living also. Thuo's people fled to an area near present day Kiambu when a Thuo man killed a small brother of Njau; Njau stayed with the Ndorobo. He already had a married son Mwereri. He was joined by Mungai, a son of his brother who had died; Mungai brought his brother's wives; he also brought Kimani, a small son of another dead brother. Mungai returned to Murang'a for his initiation. Njau did not buy land before *Kirika*; he was nevertheless a powerful man. He too was hit hard by *Kirika*, which reduced him to possibly four or five households.[29]

The *mbari* histories do not provide much information about how the land had been shared or parcelled out, and its cost. This is not surprising considering the death toll of the *Kirika* famine which must have killed many persons who had bought land, which was inherited by those who had paid less or perhaps not at all. Nor do the traditions give much insight on whether land was individually or communally owned. The following ideas are therefore at best inferences and probabilities.

Though we do not know what kinds of trees and shrubs grew on uncleared land in the eighteenth and nineteenth centuries, we know that forest clearing involved heavy sustained labour.[30] It may have taken the largest part of a man's working life to cut out a basic holding for his household, if he had help and not too many hunting duties. The hard work, the dangers of pioneering, the uncertain outcome and the likelihood of an early death would have daunted anyone.

The ideal group to do the clearing would have included several males and we know that, if the group fell short, *agendi* were incorporated after the purchase. Whatever the earliest distribution, *agendi*, though paying to later installments, contributed in labour and less in goats than the original buyers.

A stronger case for individual and not communal ownership is made by inheritance, whether lineal, to one's sons or lateral, to *mbari* 'brothers'.

The Settlement of Kiambu until the Kirika Famine, 1835

There is abundant evidence that sons inherited their father's land, whatever the basis on which he had acquired it, and also inherited his debts to the purchase price. They did not inherit equal tracts; younger sons might get considerably less than older sons, presumably because older sons had contributed more labour to their father and his land. If a man died without heirs, his land did not revert to the *mbari* but was inherited by his *mbari* brothers, but I do not know what principles guided such division.

Given the incorporation of *agendi*, lineal and lateral inheritance, and a high rate of death, contributions made towards the purchase may well have become academic for later heirs. This does not invalidate the idea that contributions mattered. The following hypothetical case shows how death and inheritance most likely influenced the distribution of acquired land.

> Mwaura, a man in late middle age, came to the local area with two grown but still unmarried sons and two daughters. He lived for a short while with the Ndorobo, then decided – afraid that he would be too old if he waited longer – to buy land with Kabiru, a man who had stayed with the Ndorobo for at least a decade. They would be 'brothers'; Mwaura contributed one daughter, which was the total price for his share; Kabiru paid twenty goats and would have to pay thirty more over time. They got 100 acres and divided it in halves.
>
> When Mwaura's oldest son went looking for a wife, he was killed in the forest by *thabari*; however Mwaura's second son found a wife and helped his father clear their share of the land. During the clearing, a heavy branch of a tree fell on Mwaura's head; he was badly hurt and could no longer help with the clearing and died within the next year. Mwaura's second son, unable to continue alone, decided that he would have a better chance if he became a *mugendi* elsewhere. He took his small family and left.
>
> Mwaura's son's land was first used by Kabiru but when the 'owner' did not return, Kabiru, now old, left both shares to his own only surviving son. This young man, who had not helped pay the first instalment, got all the land but owed thirty goats to the original sellers. When he was pressed for a payment and had lost most of his goats to sickness, he made an agreement with a *mugendi* to be 'brothers', sharing the land and paying the outstanding debt together. This done during that generation, the *mugendi*'s sons in the *nyumba* eventually owned 50 acres of land for which their father had paid fifteen goats. The *nyumba* of Kabiru's second son retained the other 50 acres, for which their grandfather had paid twenty and their father fifteen goats. While both had an equal share in the land, they had contributed differently; the original distribution and price were of little importance to either.

The high death toll, lineal and lateral inheritance, and instalment payments changed the original intent of the buyers; the distribution of the land did not reflect the actual contributions. While this does give some evidence that individual land holdings may have little to do with the

The Settlement of Kiambu until the Kirika *Famine, 1835*

contributions made by ancestors, it does not show that land ownership was communal. It is likely nevertheless that, under conditions of high mortality, survivors had a fair chance to inherit ultimately land which had been paid for by others.

Wealth and poverty before *Kirika*

How early the first Kikuyu acquired local land and how many generations had been settled locally before *Kirika* cannot be established with certainty from *mbari* histories. Nor do we know whether local conditions approximated those in other areas of Kiambu when the famine struck. There were certainly differences between and within *mbari*: whether as a result of recent arrival or because of preference, some households lived predominantly from hunting and gathering; others were in the throes of change towards greater dependency on agriculture; some were able to keep a dozen goats; others could afford to keep thirty or more. Households with cleared land and larger herds probably – but by no means certainly – lived a somewhat easier life than those who were living within a forest economy.

It is not known how much land was needed to maintain a household by hunting and gathering; the first fairly reliable data come from agricultural endeavours. But, depending on the continued role of hunting, differences would be pronounced.

If a *mbari* retained about 10 per cent in forest for defence, gathering, bee keeping, firewood and building material, a hundred acre plot could at best support about thirteen monogamous households – each standardized in this study as five adults, with a child counted as half an adult. Each household could be given about seven acres, which would allow an agricultural base, fallowing of land and about a dozen goats. Males would have to divide their time between keeping the land cleared, defence, some supplementary hunting, and herding. Women would plant, tend crops, harvest, and take care of the dwellings and their households. Together husband and wife would prepare the land for the next planting and sowing.

Mbari with more than thirteen households on one hundred acres or even less would be hard pressed. It is likely that some members moved, that others became poor, that others joined other *mbari* as *agendi*. No histories of *mbari* with too little land for their population have survived *Kirika*; possibly because they would not have survived if they had been in that condition.

While some *mbari* may have been pressed for land, others may have had only a few monogamous or polygynous households on a hundred-acre tract and/or considerably more land. They could have afforded larger herds; once roughly cleared, one acre would maintain four or a maximum of five goats. With brideprices at about twenty goats, the extent of polygyny was determined by how much land a man could or was willing to clear.

33

The Settlement of Kiambu until the Kirika Famine, 1835

In addition to poorer or wealthier *mbari* and those who lived with the Ndorobo, about whom we do not know whether they were poor or not, there must have been men who were worse off. No record of them has survived; some certainly lived in the forest; some may eventually have returned to their areas of origin and been reabsorbed there or have been incorporated somewhere else within the Kikuyu, Maasai or Ndorobo. There is no way to assess the death toll in *Kirika* without knowing more of what precisely occurred and whether game was affected as much as crops and stock; it is nevertheless likely that – if no contagious diseases were involved – the wealthier had a better chance of survival.

Fission of the *mbari*

Even before *Kirika* some *mbari* expanded beyond their land and needed to buy more or undergo fission. Data from pre-*Kirika* fission in Chege and one Thuita *mbari* do not indicate that pre- and post-*Kirika* policies differed significantly.

If land became available, all *ithaku* or individuals within them could buy it, as could the *mbari* as a whole. All data indicate that the *mbari* did not become the owner of the land if it was bought individually by a *mbari* member. This procedure was accepted, it was not regarded as fission which the *mbari* had to approve. The new acquisition consequently did not become a fissioned part of the *mbari*.

If more distant land became available and was bought by an individual, or more likely by a group of *mbari* members – ideally senior men from a senior *githaku*, strengthened by younger men from less senior *ithaku* – they, unable to continue their responsibilities in their *mbari* of origin, might decide then or later that they would have to surrender their membership and fission would follow. The settlement of *Murang'a* men in Kiambu may well have been regarded initially as fission, even though it was unlikely to have included older males. They were unlikely to survive the dangers of the journey through forests with robbers and wild animals, and they might have balked at the hardships of pioneer living.

Yet new settlements ideally did contain older males or at a minimum males from the senior section of the *mbari* which was left: they would be buried in the new land, become the 'first' ancestor and perhaps give their names to the land. If those who left allowed their goats to 'stay in the land' – if they did not demand the goats an ancestor or *githaku* members had paid and left in peace – they could return to their *mbari* of origin for one or two generations; returnees could not expect to get their original tract.

If those they left behind had given them goats, they too acquired rights in the new land. The fissioned *githaku* was likely to retain the *mbari* name; new and old *mbari* remained exogamous, accepted common jural obligations, and assisted each other in aggression or defence as far as practicable. If the fissioned *githaku* had demanded its goats, it had no right

The Settlement of Kiambu until the Kirika Famine, 1835

to return and this fission indicated a greater separation.[31] It was likely to involve a change of *mbari* name; it could mean a refusal to recognize mutual judicial responsibilities or aid.

Witchcraft accusations or other malfaisance could lead to expulsions of an individual, his household, perhaps all his descendants or kinsmen. In serious cases he and they might lose all rights in local land; in less serious cases they only lost the right to live on local land. If wives were accused of witchcraft but husbands were innocent, the wives were banned. Husbands could keep the children; it was however preferred to leave them with their mother and, if possible, to buy land for them elsewhere.

The relationship with Murang'a and the *Kirika* famine

Early Kiambu life lacked the abundance of ritual events and celebrations, which, with its frequent sacrifices and large payments, its abundant meat and beer to celebrate every 'step' of life for those who could afford it, was yet to come.[32]

At the start of Kikuyu settlement, or as long as homesteads remained isolated and distances between them considerable, senior men would not have ventured to travel from Murang'a to Kiambu. Nor would Kiambu conditions have made for longevity and it is therefore likely that early Kiambu settlements lacked senior elders who could officiate at ceremonials. It is equally unlikely that it had abundant livestock for ritual and festivities. This goes some way to explain the continued ritual dependence on Murang'a, which was further strengthened because, though most who had left had lost their land rights and some had even been cursed, the stock they had left behind was still theirs. Though they had been unable to take it with them through the forest, *mbari* elders could not prevent their using it to pay for the rituals they needed.

Journeys to Murang'a for ritual purposes weakened the Kiambu settlements: males might be gone for extended periods; some might be killed on their journey; others might refuse to return altogether. However much resented, until Kiambu produced its own senior elders and the livestock situation improved when sufficient forest land was cleared, Kiambu remained a ritual outpost of Murang'a. When it finally did start its own rituals, the frugality learned in a forest economy continued for decades to permeate celebrations and ritual. Celebrations for initiations and advance in elders' status were short; a significant part of the payments consisted of vegetables and grains rather than meat.

Informants estimated that just before *Kirika*, at most forty to fifty households had lived in the research area, and about half to two-thirds of them were Kikuyu. *Mbari* ranged from first generation, which had barely broken sufficient land for agriculture, to some which had been here 'a long time' and had cleared much of their land. Some had 'hundreds of acres'; others may not have had fifty acres. Herding had become important for those who had cleared land.

The Settlement of Kiambu until the Kirika Famine, 1835

The famine was in the memory of informants linked to the break with Murang'a, a consequence of a curse of outraged Murang'a elders, punishing Kiambu men because they intended to conduct their own ritual in the future. Possibly because neither curses nor their consequences should be discussed, twentieth-century elders knew little about the events and were unwilling to discuss what little they did know; the separation can only be dated approximately.[33]

The ritual which caused the conflict was an *ituika* (pl. *matuika*), in which a new 'ruling generation' came 'to power' after having paid the old 'ruling generation' to release its power (Appendix III/3). 'Ruling' was probably predominantly concerned with ritual power, although political power was involved in that one of the prerogatives of 'ruling' elders was the right to organize or forbid the organizing of initiations, in which males and females became adults. Newly initiated males could get considerable power; those who controlled whether or not initiations would take place controlled the size of the groups of initiates, and could, by judicious planning, prevent any one group from getting too powerful.

Generations, called either *Maina* or *Mwangi*, alternated; one received one's generation through one's father. *Maina* fathers had *Mwangi* sons; their sons would again be *Maina*. Generations also had individual names; the *Mwangi* which broke with Murang'a was given the name *Iregi*, those who revolt. How many Kiambu elders were involved is unknown, but several local elders, including Njau and Chege, were said to have played a significant role.[34]

According to tradition, they and others had gone back to Murang'a for the *ituika*. They possibly participated in the ritual there, but became infuriated when Murang'a elders – who may well have regarded the Kiambu men as a fissioned segment, still under Murang'a authority – made more than the usual demands. Whether the Kiambu men decided on the break then and there, or not until they were back in Kiambu, is not clear. Either could have led to *Iregi*. There is no record that an *ituika* was held locally or an already started one, finished; what is certain is that on the return of those who had gone, an initiation was held in Njau's homestead. Its name was *Njoroge*; Kibui, the son of Njau's first wife, was among the initiates. It was an act of defiance; young males were supposed to return to Murang'a for initiation. *Njoroge* can roughly be dated between 1830 and 1835. If there is a connection between *Kirika* and Kiambu defiance of Murang'a, then an early date for *Kirika* would be 1835; a late date of 1840 is possible.[35] Though I shall use 1835, the reader should understand 'about 1835' or 'between 1835 and 1840'.

How the elders who engineered the break were able to convince others is not clear. What few general Kiambu data I have indicate a good deal of separate development. This would make it logical that breakaways occurred at different times. Even reaching local consensus may have taken time and have been achieved as a result of power: at least one local instigator belonged to a large *mbari*; they may have had stock; they may

The Settlement of Kiambu until the Kirika Famine, *1835*

have had enough authority to convince others that it was wise to go along. Murang'a elders were distant, local power was close. Some may have been attracted to the potential savings local ritual could offer. Though payment was still required, they would not suffer the absenteeism which going to Murang'a entailed. Nevertheless, not all were convinced and some continued to recognize the authority of Murang'a elders; during *Kirika* they could take refuge there while others could not.[36]

What caused *Kirika* is unknown; it is unknown whether the basic cause was crop failure or disease; nor is it known whether stock and game were equally affected. The human death toll was described as heavier than in the late nineteenth-century *Ng'aragu ya Ruraya* famine.

The general opinion was that a number of settlements had died out, leaving their land untenanted. Land was also left by other *mbari* who had fled to their areas of origin, including Murang'a, never to return, because they feared that they and their land were under a curse which could only be lifted by abandoning the land.[37] Others, in spite of devastating losses, stayed; they apparently trusted that the ancestors on the land they had acquired would eventually be able to overcome the evil intentions of Murang'a ancestors.

Notes

1. By the Emergency 272 Igi owner households supported 94 landless households in 2,200 acres of land. Mean ownership was 8.1 acres. In Thuita 190 owner households supported 13 landless households on 636 acres of land. Mean ownership was 3.3 acres.
2. *Tha* is derived from *guthathaya*, to behave with mercy and humility. A man who is merciful is *mundu wa tha*; to give mercy *kuigua tha*. Apart from use of land, *tha* could be expressed in gifts or loans of stock, help with the payment of fees for initiation for the daughters of the poor. There was theoretically no limit to the range of potential receivers; much depended on a man's wealth. Daughters – who had a right to inherit part of their mother's household goods, but only in exceptional cases could make a claim on their father's land – came first, if they had married men without land. The relatives of a man's mother and those of his wives would also rank high. A man might also give aid to members of his initiation year. Non-landowning artisans or curers could count on *tha* in land.
3. Shifts in the base of power would mean a shift in the acceptability of oral traditions; those which had been 'official', might trade places which those which had been 'unofficial'. Given the nature of oral traditions, there may be a time lag between internal adjustments and external knowledge of such adjustments. Local women would be aware what was and was not accepted in the group in which they had married; women coming from the outside, would have to be taught. Discussions among women were often revealing.
4. That evil should not be recounted affected individual genealogies. Members who were associated with evil were usually omitted, wives accused of sorcery were dropped with their offspring. Though contemporaries might remember her and recount that she was sent away, even that her husband had bought land for her elsewhere, and younger members might inadvertently hear about this later, she was not part of the history of the group.
5. This was one of the reasons why I left it to informants to decide whether they wanted to mention multiple (more than 2) oaths and their content. The Kikuyu perspective on history has made the post-Independence study of Mau Mau more difficult. Informants

might be torn between different perspectives; they might want to stress their loyalty to Kenyatta or their contribution in bringing freedom. They also might want to avoid 'bringing back evil' and be unable or willing to discuss features of Mau Mau which had caused or were still causing grief. Informants might prefer to ignore and forget the confusion of the time or its discord, in favour of a description which highlights Mau Mau or anti-Mau Mau actions as disciplined, focused and committed.

1973. Buytenhuys, Robert, *Mau Mau Twenty Years After*, The Hague: Mouton and Co., pp. 113ff.

6. Sellers and buyers of land entered into a kinship relationship. The land which was sold was a 'daughter' of the total land a man owned; men who acquired it became affinal kin. Buyers and sellers could not intermarry for three generations but after that they had to exchange daughters.
7. The most authoritative accounts of adoption and land acquisition in Kiambu are given by Leakey and Kenyatta. Both mention the change in subsistence patterns, both see it as an encounter between two discrete 'tribes' rather than an encounter between the hunting/gathering use of forest terrain and potential agricultural/herding use in which individuals made choices how they would live and on what subsistence they would base their future. They report it as a peaceful process and, though my data confirm this for much of the period after *Kirika*, some of my data point to at least some non-peaceful encounters before that time. They stress that the land was bought. I agree by and large that this is so for the post-*Kirika* period but even then some land was given and/or never paid (Appendix II). My analysis is based on numerous, often contradictory and mutually antagonistic accounts stretching over at least a century and a half of changing conditions. Their accounts assume constancy and continuance of a 'tribe' with change being forced by a destructive colonial government.

1938. Kenyatta, Jomo, *Facing Mount Kenya*, London, Secker and Warburg, pp. 20ff.
1977. Leakey, L. S. B., *The Southern Kikuyu before 1903*, Vols I–III, London: Academic Press, Vol. I, pp. 88ff.

8. The term *magatha* is used for goats given by a man to his daughter on marriage as the nucleus of a herd for her household and children. Goats were probably the first Kiambu livestock; when the forest economy waned, sheep and later cattle were added. I will use goats to indicate livestock whatever the composition of the herd.
9. Although Kiambu Kikuyu in general acquired their land by buying and payment, some land was acquired as dowry land. Such land could only be inherited by sons of the woman; should she die without male issue or should her husband leave her, the land reverted to her father. *Magatha* land could be inherited by sons of all wives. While circumstances are not entirely clear, after *Kirika* the Ndorobo no longer gave dowries but demanded brideprices. They then also had to pay them, and consequently pressured the Kikuyu who had bought land from them to pay more rapidly, and if they had paid, to provide additional 'gifts'.
10. Well into the twentieth century, Kikuyu bought land not in acres but in specific tracts, named sometimes after previous owners, events, or a natural feature. Boundaries were based on natural features and after *Kirika*, it was customary to bury boulders in the land as boundaries. When the population increased, the planting of fire-resistance *itoka* lilies became customary. Boundaries might be protected by *kirumi* or curses from tampering.

1977. Leakey, L. S. B., *op. cit.*, Vol. I, p. 107.

11. Male informants claimed that Kikuyu girls willingly accepted such exchanges: 'they would go with the Ndorobo gladly, knowing that they had helped their father and brothers'. This might well have been an important factor if the groom had been Kikuyu. It is doubtful whether a girl would have relished to be married to someone whose language she might not understand and whose lifestyle was not hers.
12. Ultimately the selling of land destroyed the Ndorobo way of life; they lost the forest and its game. To what degree the Ndorobo themselves survived is a matter of speculation. According to some, selling Ndorobo were given the rights of *ahoi* in the land they had sold; according to others, some became Kikuyu agriculturalists, a *mbari* on their own land, having asked a Kikuyu to go through the land adoption for them. Others joined existing

The Settlement of Kiambu until the Kirika Famine, 1835

mbari with their land. The same processes which merged Kikuyu and Ndorobo also applied to Maasai–Ndorobo relationships.

13. I am indebted to Dr J. Lonsdale for drawing my attention to the use of fire in clearing land. The earliest clearing involved stands of heavy trees, later clearing involved lighter tree growth and bush. Thin branches and leaves became green manure. To make it ready for crops, the land was dug twice; between the first and second digging and afterwards, clumps of soil were beaten with sticks. Ideally women only helped with the last beating. After each harvest, men were expected to dig any remaining green manure into the land. The use of fire is described by

    1910. Routledge, W. S. and K., *With a Prehistoric People*, London: Edward Arnold, p. 5.
    1913. Stigand, C. H., *The Land of Zinj*, London: Cass, p. 239.
    1933. Cmnd 4556 *Kenya Land Commission Report. Evidence and Memoranda*, Vols I–IV. Hereafter called the Carter Report, after its Chairman, Sir Morris Carter, CBE, Vol. I, p. 591. This is denied in the testimony of H. E. Lambert, Vol. I, pp. 551–2.
    1977. Leakey, L. S. B., *op. cit.*, Vol. I, p. 168.

14. Kinship terminology expressed the relationship between generations. When a man, A, sired a son, he could rightly assume that he had given his father a new life. In times of stress, therefore, he could address this child as father. Similarly, when this child sired a son, he brought back A, who had sired him. This child, A's grandson, was therefore grandson A and A's grandfather. A similar regenerational picture can be drawn up for A's daughter.

15. Under special circumstances, perhaps if a man had sons but they had offended him, if he had no sons and did not want to take another wife, if he had daughters or a daughter who had a son without having married, he might leave all or part of his land to women. The women did not become guardians of the land: the closest acceptable male performed this function.

16. Selling Ndorobo, affinal kin, because they had sold part of their land to the Kikuyu, frequently exercised the rights of kin by asking for additional goats or other items, even when the land price was paid. Neither a brideprice nor land was ever regarded as fully paid.

17. Brothers were beholden to sisters for their wives, and thus for the children wives would bear; under certain circumstances a sister was instrumental in providing him with land, if she inherited from her husband. A son had a special relationship with his mother's brother, who was expected to indulge him: 'A sister's son cannot be refused'. This relationship may well have originated in the ability of a sister to provide for her brother.

18. Cases in which women accused husbands of causing the death of their children were on a level of cases of witchcraft. Only the most senior elders would sit in on such cases.

19. The deep involvement of kin on each side might make it harder to break the bond if matters were wrong after the start of a marriage. I have no cases of men resorting to desperate measures, but women did resort to suicide 'to punish the husband' if he did not 'let her go'.

20. When economic factors prevented many males from providing their wives with land, the repercussions were felt throughout the relationships.

    1975–6. Kershaw, G., 'The changing roles of men and women in the Kikuyu family by sociological strata', *Rural Africana*, No. 29, African Studies Center, Michigan State University, pp. 173–95.

21. Marriage to Ndorobo women whose fathers still hunted had all but stopped by the late nineteenth century. By that time women who came from Ndorobo or Maasai might well be called Kikuyu because their fathers had changed to agriculture.

22. Given the complementary nature of the aggressive Kikuyu–Maasai interaction, the use of raiding may at times give too much the impression of endemic warfare. What the victims experienced is not known. Male informants felt that Maasai girls did not mind being raided 'because they got a better life'; old Maasai women, acquired in the late nineteenth century, said that they initially missed their mothers but could not escape. Having their own children had cured the hurt.

23. There is an inherent contradiction in the early data between the oft-repeated complaints

The Settlement of Kiambu until the Kirika Famine, 1835

about lack of goats and the relatively high report of polygyny. It is one of the many sets of data which point to the tendency to collapse generations and to let 'history begin' after a disaster. A partial explanation is the high death toll of males in which spouses were inherited by other males, thus giving an image of polygyny for the receivers. Still another explanation may be that the incidence of marrying Ndorobo women and receiving dowry land may have been higher than admitted; a fourth explanation may be that raiding for women was more prevalent.

24. Like any other *mbari* members, if incorporated men were the sole survivors after a disaster, they inherited all the land regardless of how little or how much they had paid. Kinsmen of the dead who were not members of the *mbari* could try to claim; though they had no right, it would be advisable to give them a – small – share.

25. All Kikuyu regard themselves as descendants of Gikuyu and his wife Muumbi. This descent group is divided into dispersed clans or *mihiriga* (sing. *muhiriga*), based on their legendary daughters. Some clans have special functions, such as the working of iron or salt; others are associated with curing and witchcraft. Landless, non-Kikuyu who were incorporated into Kikuyu land-owning groups, took the clan of their new kin; non-Kikuyu who bought land adopted the Munjiru clan. *Mihiriga* are not land-owning groups; the *bururi wa Agikuyu* refers to the land of all Kikuyu, it is divided among land-owning *mbari*. In *mbari* formed by men of different clans, or non-Kikuyu, all eventually assumed the clan of the most powerful group. The information about Kikuyu mythological descent was so well ingrained that I received no other myths of origin during fieldwork. I do not know where the version I received originated but am grateful to Dr J. Lonsdale for drawing my attention to different myths of origin as recounted by Muriuki. There are many sources for Kikuyu history, among them versions taught in schools. The printed word had a strong tendency to create history as well. When I inquired into initiation years, I realized after some time that Cagnolo, not local experience, provided the answers from some educated informants.

1933. Cagnolo, C., *The Akikuyu: Their Customs, Traditions and Folklore*, Nyeri: Mission Printing School.

1974. Muriuki, Godfrey. *A History of the Kikuyu 1500–1900*, London: Oxford University Press.

26. As my accounts of adoption and land buying, so my accounts about the concept of the *mbari* differ from those of Leakey and Kenyatta. They, and many others, saw homogeneity and consensus. My data emphasize the varying ideas struggling for control over other versions.

27. The colonial administration's conviction that the nature of pre-colonial Kikuyu society had been 'communal' is clear in Lambert's description of their presumed legal system which he compares with colonial tribunals: 'A tribunal stops squabbles once and for all – with luck – by dividing up the land between the litigants; the old clan courts would have divided only the cultivation rights and would have regarded finality as anti-social. The tribunal says: 'Stop the argument. Here is a bit of land for each of you. Go and sell it and buy a lorry and when that wears out go and tell the government you are penniless and have nowhere to live'. The Clan court would have said: 'The land belongs to neither of you. We divide the cultivation rights according to your needs but subject to review because those needs may change. How do we know how many mouths your progeny will have to feed in the distant years to come? No, there is no appeal. The land is ours, not yours. We will always do what we believe is the best for you, you are our own flesh and blood and on your well-being depends the continuity of the clan.'
1942. AR/314 KBU/33.

28. Version from an important senior elder: Igi was formed before *Kirika* by eight men who bought land. Chege was a brother of one of them, Gitau may have been another. One of the eight adopted the *mwathi*; they sold their land to others after *Kirika*. The buyers also became Igi, although the sellers left. During the nineteenth century others joined Igi when the *mbari* bought additional land. Some were however lost as they and their *nyumba* left. Kinsmen who came to *mbari* members who had land were, before *Kirika*, given as much land as the owners could spare [because they were wanted]. After *Kirika* those who

The Settlement of Kiambu until the Kirika Famine, 1835

wanted to become *mbari* had to buy their own land or wait until someone might ask them to buy with him.
29. Alternate version: Njau had bought land before *Kirika* with his son Mwereri.
30. The only data we have are from an adjacent area and date from 1910 when the original forest had long since been removed. Based on information from the Forest Service and informants, I have assumed heavy tree growth with a low level of underbrush.
    1960. 3 October. Chief Conservator of Forests FOR 212/1/6/31.
31. At that time he had to be given the number of goats he or an ancestor had contributed; whether he would also receive their natural increase to compensate for labour which had been contributed depended on the *mbari* and their resources.
    1962. 6 August. Mr Kiburi, Senior Member and Chief Adviser on Law and Custom of Kiambu Court.
32. Information on 'traditional' Kikuyu society is available in many older sources. Unfortunately, some of them, like my own, have a tendency to generalize to all Kikuyu from a too small area. Moreover, conditions in the late nineteenth century are sometimes taken to be representative for a much longer timespan.
    1933. Kenyatta, J. *op. cit.*
    1950. Lambert, H. E., *Systems of Land Tenure in the Kikuyu Land Unit*, Cape Town: University of Cape Town, Communications of School of African Studies, No. 22.
    1956. Lambert, H. E., *Kikuyu Social and Political Institutions*, London: Oxford University Press.
    1972. Middleton, John, and Greet Kershaw, *The Kikuyu and Kamba of Kenya*, Ethnographic Survey of Africa, East Central Africa, Part V. London: International African Institute.
    1974. Muriuki, Godfrey, *op. cit.*
    1960. Sluiter, G., *The Kikuyu Concepts of Land and Land Kin*, University of Chicago: unpublished M.A. thesis.
    1972. Kershaw, Gretha, *The Land is the People*, University of Chicago: unpublished PhD thesis.
    1977. Leakey, L. S. B., *op. cit.*
    Leakey was an authority on Kikuyu culture; in the late 1930s, he wrote a significant monograph for which the bulk of the data were provided by selected Kiambu (?) senior elders. During my discussions with him in 1956, he stressed that the data, with but minor variations, were applicable to Murang'a and Gaki. The 1977 publication prepared after his death does not make this claim. It is a gold mine for data which now would be irretrievably lost, but tends to dwell on the minutiae of Kikuyu cultural actions to the neglect of the meaning of custom and ritual. Leakey admired the 'traditional' Kikuyu and their elders; his anthropological background was acquired in a time which accepted the homogeneity of 'tribal' culture, lacking history or change until 'the West' caused 'cultural breakdown' and disintegration. Within this framework it is possible to accept the world of selected elders as the world of all, the ideal they may present as the real, in which there is neither strife nor conflict, in which the elaboration and wealth of some nineteenth-century men becomes the norm. His deep love for the Kikuyu made him a strong opponent of colonial land alienation but his distress about twentieth-century changes among the Kikuyu stem from a preoccupation with a society that never was. His informants were elders; Leakey apparently remained unaware of nineteenth-century conflicts; even twentieth-century conflict over land which by the time of his writing was widespread, was not included and his elders apparently did not represent different, let alone conflicting perspectives on past or present. They created an image of an unchanging tribe, which had been disturbed – or changed – only by European intrusion. Although Dr Leakey was unfailingly helpful and willing to discuss Kikuyu matters and I was allowed to read several chapters of his manuscript, he expected that my findings would parallel his. This was often not the case; many of my informants, outside the ranks of power and authority had a different view of past and present. I gratefully acknowledge Leakey's insights but my findings differ from his in crucial areas.
33. Kenyatta, who gives an evolutionary history of the Kikuyu, sees the name *Iregi* linked to

The Settlement of Kiambu until the Kirika Famine, 1835

the males who revolted against the oligarchy imposed by their elders. Murikuki links Iregi to the defeat of invaders, particularly the Barabiu.
1938. Kenyatta, J., *op cit.*, p. 187.
1974. Muriuki, G., *op cit.*, p. 65.

34. It is unlikely that Chege would have been alive after or even during *Kirika* or the separation from Murang'a. According to some traditions, Njau was still living with the Ndorobo at that time; the first initiations after the separation from Murang'a would not likely have been held in a Ndorobo homestead. Yet the inclusion of both men is important Kikuyu history: Chege's inclusion would sanction the revolt; Njau's inclusion the independent new Kiambu settlement.

35. A recent theory about the need for *matuika* was put forward by Lonsdale. He suggests that *matuika* might signify the transfer of ritual authority from one generation to another, but more interestingly, that an *ituika* might be called when disaster struck to cleanse the land and appease the forces which had brought the disasters. Local informants remembered two *matuika* clearly, and one was barely recalled. Given that all history is oral tradition, what evidence I have indicates that the *ituika* of the 1830s was planned before *Kirika*; Kiambu elders saw it as a consequence of curses of Murang'a elders because they had decided to go their own way. The *ituika* of 1858/1865 was only remembered as a change from *Mwangi* to *Maina*. The *ituika* of the late nineteenth century took place when disasters had started although the famine itself had not. The theory is nevertheless attractive for two reasons. It would explain the extreme reluctance of Kikuyu elders to discuss *matuika* because this would mean discussing disasters, something to avoid as they brought *thahu*, disturbing the desired state of ritual purity, *theru*. One might speculate that *matuika* were called when disasters seemed imminent or had already started, in the hope that the spiritual forces would change their decisions (Appendix III/3).
1992. Berman, Bruce, and John Lonsdale, *Unhappy Valley. Conflict in Kenya and Africa*, Book II, pp. 346, 349.

36. That some went back to Murang'a does not suggest that the famine was localized; we do not know whether they arrived safely and survived there.

37. Curses, oaths, witchcraft are connected with *thahu*, a state of ritual pollution of human beings, who should be *theru*, ritually pure. The strength of the *thahu* depends on the status of those who use these means and the ritual involved. Curses of old men and women of high status, and those of ritual specialists, had great power; the curses of young males were only dangerous if they used elements, such as blood, which only senior elders could use, or elements of witchcraft, which no one could use (Appendix VIII/3).

Two

From Kirika *until the End of the Nineteenth Century*

Though *Kirika* ended the lives of a large number of settlers, the land they left behind was the start of intensive local development. At the heart of this were local survivors, *mbari* members who, perhaps together with *agendi*, reconstituted the *mbari* and took possession of cleared and uncleared land. As soon as possible they put a major effort into herding; they also used the land of abandoned *mbari* until it was reclaimed. Even *athi* who repossessed it, perhaps because it was not fully paid, would turn a blind eye to continued herding of legitimate neigbouring settlers; unused land was an invitation to *thabari*.

The thinly populated land created a wave of land seekers; kinsmen of *mbari* which had died out might come to claim the land; others came because they heard rumours about cheap, partially cleared land. The image of Kiambu as pioneer country was changing to land of opportunity.

Understandably, no evidence has survived that land was taken by men who had no rights at all; the risks, that those who had bought it or their descendants might return, or that angry ancestors would vent their ire on the new occupants, were too great. These encumbrances kept the price low; land with at least one clearing was resold by the *athi* for one goat an acre.

Sometimes it was bought by survivors, sometimes by Kikuyu or Ndorobo *agendi*, sometimes by newcomers. The land had the prime advantage that herds could expand rapidly; this enabled the buyer to pay for his land quickly, paving the way to acquire more.

Not all emigrants from Gaki, Murang'a and Maasai country could afford even this price; they had to buy bought forest land, at the same price as before *Kirika*. Similarly, when about a decade after *Kirika* the only remaining partially cleared land was held under option by powerful *mbari*, the common purchase was forest land.

From Kirika *until the End of the Nineteenth Century*

Original settlers had bought land at about 4,500 to 5,000 feet. Around 1865, land at this altitude became scarce and expensive.[1] It was then rare to find a tract larger than seventy acres; around 1870 men were lucky if they could acquire thirty acres in one piece at two or three goats per acre.

This was too steep for many landless who were herding towards land ownership and for men who sought land for sons. They settled for cheaper land, probably at around 4,300 feet, to the south-east of existing settlements. These lands were also in Ndorobo hands; we will probably never know the extent of Ndorobo ownership. Many died during *Kirika* and the famine of the last decade of the nineteenth century. Others had merged into Kikuyu or Maasai, yet others had left the area; the history of their land is obscured by Kikuyu buying but also by European alienation.

The lower land provided good herding, but had shorter rainy seasons and was more susceptible to droughts. It had the added disadvantage that it was closer to Maasai and Akamba and more subject to their raids, although if one's settlement was strong enough, this could be turned into advantage by raiding them, either in return or without provocation. Wealthier land owners also began to extend their holdings into the lower land; its price of one goat per acre was attractive. Settlers with only lower elevation land used it for all purposes; those who had both used the higher land for crops and light grazing and the lower land for more intensive grazing with only a few crops.

By 1880 even small tracts of virgin land at 5,000 feet elevations were only available in the rare case that original buyers wanted to sell. Land still in Ndorobo hands was not for sale; the remaining Ndorobo had taken up agriculture and become Kikuyu.

Economic and social development in the early post-*Kirika* decades

Because empty land gave more herding opportunities, the position of *Kirika* survivors had improved. Fortunate newcomers might start with at least a cleared homestead area and grazing over unused land; those who came still later often had to start clearing the forest. Even they were probably in a better position than pre-*Kirika* settlers since they could profit from pre-*Kirika* experiences with weather, rainfall, crops and agricultural methods. The higher population density had reduced the danger from wild animals and *thabari*; in accident or sickness men and women could come to each other's aid. There is little doubt that post-*Kirika* life, but for those who were completely isolated, was easier than it had been.

There was a high demand for women as men wanted to replace wives who had died and young immigrants wanted to start their own families. There were somewhat more girls available because there were more settlers. Yet brideprices had risen; between early settlement and the first

From Kirika until the End of the Nineteenth Century

decade after *Kirika*, they doubled to forty and sometimes fifty goats. The powerful surviving settlers often paid less; fathers of girls they married accepted that the power of their new affinal relations was part of their recompense.

One of the lessons of pre-*Kirika* life reinforced by *Kirika* had been that monogamy was fragile and polygyny gave better survival chances. Monogamy's wry consolation had been that it put less pressure on forest clearing; it was nevertheless better to have more survivors, even if that created pressure to clear more land. The move towards extensive polygyny is apparent in the genealogies of first post-*Kirika* survivors; later settlers were not always polygynous and, if they were, they had fewer wives.[2]

After *Kirika*, Kiambu no longer required male incorporation, in which, before *Kirika*, suitable males had become members of the *mbari* after it had been formed, sharing rights over land which had already been bought.[3] In the later period, this was no longer part of tradition; *mbari* strength becomes based on marriage and descent. Rather than dilute one's property by sharing with 'brothers', one should keep it for one's offspring. If men need additional support, they should obtain it without paying by a share in the land.

After *Kirika* men no longer record that their ancestors who bought land were a group of 'brothers' whose age differences stretch across an unconsciously large span of years. Instead, they report that land was bought by a man alone or with sons. If land was bought by two brothers, they formed one *mbari* but the two *ithaku* were clearly delineated. *Ithaku* and *mbari* continued to incorporate individuals, but the rights of these men were severely limited and they are no longer described as 'brothers' or 'sons' but as distant kin, 'too far to be linked' to other members of the *mbari*, or as men with no relationship to *mbari* members at all. They received a small, bounded tract of land from a particular sponsor; it did not become a separate *githaku* but remained within the *githaku* of the donor. Owners of such small tracts, like other *mbari* members, could ask to use the land of larger owners; they were, like all *mbari* members, bound by *mbari* rules, including exogamy. If they ever got wealthy, they might on their own accord participate in more acquisitions. When a kinsman of a *mbari* member wanted to become a member but was refused because he could not contribute a sufficient number of goats, his kinsman might give him a small tract of land out of *tha* and so incorporate him into his own tract.[4] It also sometimes happened that a *mbari* member in a *mbari* which could not sell land had not enough stock to pay a fine. He could circumvent the problem by asking a *muhoi* for a gift of stock, giving him a gift of land in return.[5]

After *Kirika* not many men found *ithaku* or *mbari* which were willing to incorporate them. Few *mbari* needed their work; survivors and buyers had enough cleared land to start. If they lacked herding land, they did not immediately need to clear more because their herds could graze the clearings of others who had abundant land. This kept brush low and fertilized the land. It also meant that the owners did not have to pay the high price of incorporation and lose the land, which would be guarded by the users.

After *Kirika*, many men had come to the area who lacked the goats to buy land. They were quite willing to provide help to *mbari* in exchange for long-term use of land so that they could accumulate stock. Buying land remained the ideal but had become more difficult. The price of the land itself had increased only slightly, but Ndorobo sellers demanded larger down-payments and less time between instalments because game, their principal source of food, was declining under the influx and expansion of an agricultural population.

This combination of needs soon after Kirika created the institution of *ahoi* (sing. *muhoi*). It may have been an innovation, or it may have originated in Murang'a.[6]

The *ahoi* system

Where Thuita in the twentieth century would have many land poor, Igi would have many landless, because in the nineteenth century it had depended strongly on *ahoi*. *Muhoi* is derived from *kuhoya*, to petition, make a request, mainly for land. A potential *muhoi* asked a *mwene* or owner for the right to use land; he would be accepted if he could offer services – curing, for example – and sufficient land was available.[7] While the *mbari* as a whole had to accept him, the particular *mwene* became the sponsor.[8] Such gifts of land were regarded as the highest expression of *tha*. The initial relationship was formalized by a ritual meal with senior *mbari* members; the goat was provided by the *muhoi*. A *muhoi* with extensive herding rights provided each season a male goat for such a ceremony; all *ahoi* who shifted their homestead to another area did the same. *Ene* and *ahoi* invited each other to ritual and celebrations; each could abrogate the relationship but only after due notice, and no *mwene* could evict a *muhoi* while he was using his services.[9] Some *ahoi*, particularly if they owned land elsewhere, remained only for a time; others left when they had accumulated enough stock to buy their own land; again others might stay with the *mbari* during their lifetime, even if their sons would later leave.

It is possible that *ahoi* were used during the forest period for labour and mutual defence, but it is more likely that men at that time would have demanded *agendi* positions. Until the end of the nineteenth century, when some *ahoi* occupied a special position, *ahoi* were probably at no time important for labour. They occupied and kept safe from intruders land a *mwene* did not use at the time; they also improved the land against the time the owner would need it. Their most important service – restricted to those who were desirable kinsmen – was the creation of affinal relationships between groups who themselves were barred from doing so. Large land owners could marry their daughters to *ahoi* and so keep control over them and their households.

From Kirika until the End of the Nineteenth Century

In Thuita different *mbari* had either bought from the same *mbari* or from each other; they could therefore not intermarry for three generations. Cooperation during this time would have depended on land affinity alone, had not *ahoi* given and taken wives from different *mbari*, which created links of human affinity between the *mbari* involved. By the third generation the *mbari* were obliged to replace affinal land relationships by human affinity and had to intermarry; *ahoi* were no longer needed and by this time many Thuita *mbari* would have lacked sufficient land to maintain *mbari* households and *ahoi*. This was the more so as intermarriage, as land affinity had done, gave those involved *ahoi* rights; the wife giving *mbari* expected at least some herding rights in the land of the wife taking *mbari*. If the *mbari* involved had not been able to expand because adjacent land was already sold or was too expensive, if *mbari* males were unwilling to leave – by the late nineteenth century land in Kabete was expensive, and only Limuru land was still cheap – such *mbari* frequently needed to ask Igi for herding land while cultivating and living on their own land. This in time might provide the necessary goats to buy, if at all possible, close to their *mbari* of origin.[10]

Ahoi performed a similar but more enduring role in Igi; in consequence they there made up 25 per cent or more of the population well into colonial times. Their importance originated in the nature of Igi, which had become a *mbari* by joint buying of land; few of its constituent *ithaku* were related by human kinship. They were barred from intermarriage; solidarity depended on their acknowledgement of being one person through land. Though they had taken a *mbari* oath to that effect, promising not to sell, their solidarity was weak because of internal differences; some *ithaku* or individuals within them had a great deal of land and large descent groups, others had little land and few descendants. Some had participated in all acquisitions, others in some, others again had been admitted late and had participated only in the last acquistions. *Ahoi* who gave or took wives from different *ithaku* were vital to the survival of the *mbari*; those who were able to link important *ithaku* were a force to be reckoned with. The importance of women stands out: the land owner who had married a daughter was unlikely to refuse his request for the use of land; the father of a *mbari* daughter who had married a *muhoi* would not deny him or his children.

Igi *ahoi* often had more land for herding than Thuita *ahoi* and sometimes Thuita *mbari*. They could build up sizeable herds which enabled them to act as lenders to *mbari* members. If the *mbari* member failed to repay the loan, *ahoi* had the right to ask for a part of their land in ownership, becoming *mbari* members who owned a small share of land. Livestock also enabled *ahoi* to become full members of a *mbari*; if the *mbari* had insufficient goats to buy land, *ahoi* could make their stock available in return for membership and a share commensurate to their payment.[11] In Igi, in all but possibly one acquisition, wealthy *ahoi* were important contributors to territorial expansion. Whether they remained *ahoi* or became *mbari* members, some *ahoi* could well outweigh less wealthy *mbari* members in importance.

From Kirika *until the End of the Nineteenth Century*

The status of *ahoi* varied throughout the nineteenth century; by the end of the nineteenth century some *ahoi* were powerful and wealthy, others were little more than labourers with few rights. Most were not a permanent population even then; they might stay perhaps two or three generations, then buy their own land for themselves or their sons. In the twentieth century, their position would become hazardous. They could not afford to buy land and their continued usefulness as marriage partners had to be weighed against the inability of *mbari* members to give them land. Though *ahoi* continued to link different *ithaku*, men bent on commodity production became more inclined to trust their ability to prevent marriages between *ithaku* members and the power of the oath of unity.[12]

The nineteenth-century post-*Kirika mbari*

Thuita

Although informants, whenever asked, would spend an immense amount of time on discussing their *mbari* traditions, there is no guarantee that the information given in the preceding chapter, here, or in Appendix II recounts what actually occurred. Two devastating famines almost certainly 'screened out' part of history and *ithaku* which had died out were unlikely to be mentioned. Those who had been expelled for violations against the proper order might not be mentioned by those most intimately concerned, though information about them sometimes came from outside their ranks. Where Thuita *mbari* did not give their traditions to explain twentieth-century strife, Igi traditions were the subject of intense conflict. *Ithaku* and *mbari* members had fought each other in twentieth-century courts, using oral traditions to bolster their positions. I am fairly sure that the actual history of any settlement cannot be found, nor will all informants agree to one version.

The traditions of Thuita for two pre-*Kirika*, seven post-*Kirika* and two twentieth-century *mbari*, all extant in the 1950s, are collected in Appendix II, which also contains a few notes on early Igi traditions.[13] Histories of two Thuita *mbari* which survived the late nineteenth-century disasters but sold their land in the twentieth century, were not available.[14] The history of one small nineteenth-century Igi *githaku* which did die out at that time was not available either, and the background of heirs from outside the *mbari* which inherited a share of their land, was sketchy in the extreme.[15] If there were more *mbari* in Thuita or more *ithaku* in Igi in the nineteenth century, they were not mentioned. Yet it is highly likely that some sold their land, merged with others, were expelled or died.

Igi and Thuita traditions make clear that the origin of *mbari* and *ithaku* varied widely, but whether Kikuyu, Kamba, Maasai or Ndorobo, they became Kikuyu agriculturalists. Local traditions stressed whether those who joined *mbari*, or created their own, had been wealthy or poor, though informants carefully screened their information to conform to conditions

From Kirika until the End of the Nineteenth Century

in the twentieth century. Whether factual or not, it was not advisable to describe powerful twentieth-century elders as coming from poor Ndorobo backgrounds.

Around the 1890s, nine *mbari* of Thuita probably owned close to 1,100 acres. They were unequal in terms of population and the size of the land they owned; the smallest *mbari* may not have had more than fifteen, the largest several hundred acres, still well below Igi tracts. By the late nineteenth century, a significant number of households owned no more than ten acres.

As in Igi, Thuita oral traditions show that the pre-*Kirika* buying of 'brothers' had given way to buying by one or two men and that *mbari* ties took precedence over kinship ties: a man did not have rights over his brother's land; an adult son who had not contributed to the price of the land normally would not inherit part or all of that tract.

Both Thuita and Igi spread slowly from land at higher elevations into lower-lying areas which were cheaper; even so, the increase in cost of both higher and lower land had forced Thuita buyers to acquire smaller tracts. This, together with twentieth-century colonial land alienation and population expansion would destine Thuita for land poverty.

In Igi and Thuita, the influence of strong personalities stood out and – far from this being a golden age of peace and security – conflict, if not violence, was common. Lawbreakers in Thuita who were expelled sometimes became *ahoi* of Igi; others, whose offences were less severe, retained the right to use their *mbari* land but could no longer live on it and became Igi *athami*, living on Igi land. Igi offenders may have been absorbed in other *mbari* or have become *ahoi* elsewhere.

Igi

Igi originated in the aspirations of one or several men for regional control; they, together with others, neither of them related to each other, formed a *mbari* by buying land together.[16] Over time, its founders formed *nyumba*, descent groups, who laid claim to their own *githaku* in *mbari* land; when *nyumba* split into segments, they claimed their part of the *githaku* land.[17] The *mbari* thus consisted of *ithaku* whose owners were related to other *ithaku* owners by common descent and *ithaku* who were related only by the common buying of land. All, having obtained land together, were one in land and therefore with each other, but, as it was recognized that such solidarity was relatively weak, it was reinforced by a *mbari* oath (Appendix VIII/2).

After an initial acquisition, additional land was bought at least four more times; some *ithaku* participated in all acquisitions, others in few. Wealth acquired by the caravan trade of the last part of the nineteenth century fuelled some of the later expansion; several larger land owners who engaged in it – sometimes devoting up to 100 acres to commodities – were by then the principal buyers but some smaller land owners or landless men saw their chance and participated as well. By 1890 Igi's total area, including land bought privately by individuals but 'ritually made

From Kirika until the End of the Nineteenth Century

part' of the *mbari*, was at least 2,700 acres.[18] At that time there were probably 11 *ithaku*; if one of the largest *nyumba* had already split into different *nyumba*, each with their own land, there would have been more. In the twentieth century Igi would recognize 18 distinct *ithaku*.

Ithaku differed in population and in claims to land: by 1890 some may have owned as many as a thousand acres, others no more than fifty. Similar differences existed within *ithaku*, though those who had little land used the land of other *mbari* members with their permission. Igi also had a large population of *ahoi* who neither owned land nor were *mbari* members. Some *ahoi* used a great deal of land; others no more than poorer *mbari* members, or less. Loss of land to colonial land alienation, population expansion and a change in use of land, would make the *ahoi* into the twentieth-century landless. In the nineteenth century many of them, like the general population including members of Thuita *mbari*, would herd on the land of Igi's larger land owners. They were welcome; stock fertilized the land and kept bush down.

Even a simplified history of the development of Igi is complex, colourful and controversial; the oral traditions in the text are confined to accounts which clarify twentieth-century relationships or conflicts over land. To dispel the notion that all land conflicts led to Mau Mau violence, I discuss several which all led to protracted litigation. They fed an atmosphere of uncertainty and contributed to the need for a change in land tenure, but only one played a role in Mau Mau. I follow the method outlined in Chapter 1: all relevant versions of a tradition are included in the text; other disagreements are mentioned in the notes.

The story starts with joint acquisition of land by two founders of the pre-*Kirika mbari*, Kungu and Chege, which had survived *Kirika*. A third man, Njau, who may have owned land and/or was still living with the Ndorobo, had also survived and was persuaded to join them.[19] While several others claim to have been settled by that time, and to have joined in the first acquisition with the 'founding fathers', there is no definite proof. Others, again, including a Kamba man who would become part of the *githaku* of one of the members, admit that they were not yet local men. It is highly likely that the ancestors of a Ndorobo who became part of Igi, were living in the forest. How many of the later *ahoi* – some of whom became *mbari* members and joined in buying land – were already in the local area is unknown.

Either before or after the first joint acquisition of land, Chege would sell his private land, but buy another private tract.[20] While a member of Igi, Njau would buy privately at least 300 acres; much of his tract was still under forest and the price was therefore only one hundred and ten goats and ten rams. Kungu also had private land from before *Kirika*; all would ritually make their private land a part of the land of the *mbari*.[21] Kungu would lose most of his private land when a member of his house sold a large part, in spite of an injunction. The perpetrators were expelled but Kungu's status declined as it had depended on the size of his private land.

From Kirika until the End of the Nineteenth Century

Some Igi members would aver that the first acquisition was not bought, but acquired by *kuna*, or the right of first clearing (Appendix II/2).

Igi oral traditions
After *Kirika*, Chege and Kungu had small populations, which they and their adult sons strenghtened by extensive polygyny. They had large tracts of land; by any standard they would have had abundant agricultural and herding land for the next few generations.

Both had been powerful local *mbari*; they were determined to reestablish their leadership which would demand a stronger population and consequently almost immediately more land. They also needed to make sure that others did not get the land before they did; they needed options over it until they could afford it. If they did not get this, the *athi* might increase the price of land, or worse, sell to higher bidders or unacceptable neighbours.

Chege had important links to the *athi* as had Njau, who was probably still living with the *athi*; Chege asked Njau to join in acquiring land: he had potentially a strong descent group as among his survivors were three wives. After initially refusing, Njau decided to join Chege and Kungu and to become one *mbari* by acquiring land. Its price was not remembered; in the twentieth century it would be a matter of dispute whether Chege gave the land, sold it to the founders or whether it was acquired by *kuna*. The parcel was well over four hundred acres; it was situated north of Chege's earliest private land and east of Kungu's land. Each founder became the head of his independent *mbari* which carried his name; each formed his own descent group or *nyumba*. They, and all who joined later took a *mbari* oath which forbade the selling of the land and became one; violators of the injunction not to sell the land would be subject to a *kirumi*.

Chege became the first *muramati*, but because he was quite old, he soon shared it with Njau, whose descendants retained the position. Chege, Kungu and Njau, after he bought private land, brought their private land into the *mbari* for ritual purposes.

Either before or after the first Igi land had been bought, Njau inherited sons and probably wives from two of his brothers who had stayed in Gatang'a and had died there at an early age. Mungai and Kimani were among these sons, Kimani was almost certainly still a small boy. When Njau bought his private land, they were already part of his household. In the twentieth century their relationship to Njau would become a source of conflict: Mungai's descendants would argue that their ancestor should have received a son's share in Njau's private land as inheritance; he had been a young boy at the time of purchase, as was Kimani who had received part of the land as inheritance. The descendants of Njau rebutted this contention; according to them, Mungai had been old enough to contribute to the purchase. He had refused to do so which abrogated any inheritance rights. Mungai's descendants did not deny that their ancestor had not paid and might have done so, had he not been obliged to return to Murang'a for ritual purposes.

The following traditions bring Gitau, mentioned in Chapter 1, back on

From Kirika until the End of the Nineteenth Century

the scene in his grandsons. They claimed that the first land acquired by the new *mbari* contained the land their grandfather had left behind when he had to leave to return to his natal area. They claimed compensation and asserted that they were *mbari* members by virtue of the land their grandfather had left. Descendants in the twentieth century would assert that the *mbari* at that time had accepted their claims, had given them a token tract and asked them to wait for full settlement until land became available. The land they claimed was occupied by descendants of Njau's son, Mwereri. This would be denied by other *mbari* members: *Gitau* descendants were given a small tract out of *tha;* they had no rights to the land and no promises were made.

The matter was not resolved and became a source of twentieth-century conflict when land scarcity added fuel to the fire. Until the 1930s relationships had remained cordial; when descendants of Mwereri went to the Rift Valley, they asked Gitau descendants to take care of their land. When they returned, they expected their land back, but Gitau members refused to comply. The issue festered and became a source of continuous litigation; during Mau Mau, under the influence of beer and drugs, it turned deadly.

Version I
The first tract Igi acquired contained the land Gitau had owned when he had to return to Murang'a and asked Chege to take care of it. When *mbari* members took possession, it was still clearly visible where he had cleared and built; even in the twentieth century it still carried his name.

Several decades after *Kirika* Gitau's descendants came back and demanded their land from Chege and from Igi. Chege gave them some of his private land, but Igi gave them only a small part in the land it had obtained, asking for patience. The land was used by Mwereri, the son of Njau, a man with seven wives. (He was eventually killed by the Maasai, with one of his sons). Gitau's descendants were few; they would get compensation for what they could not be given now, as soon as possible. This was acceptable to the Gitau people; they participated in several subsequent acquisitions as *mbari* members but, as they remained small, they did not contribute heavily until the last ones.

Version II
This excludes Gitau in part or totally. The story which Gitau's descendants tell is untrue. They did not own any land in the first Igi acquistion; who says that he lived here? If Gitau had lived here before *Kirika* and owned land, it must have been in the land Chege sold or in the private land Chege bought later and had brought ritually into the *mbari* but remained his alone. That may well be the case, which explains why Gitau descendants were given a small part of that land by Chege descendants.

When Gitau's descendants came, they were welcomed as kinsmen of Chege, an important *mbari* member; to please Chege they gave the Gitau people land in the first *mbari* acquisition as *ahoi*. Gitau's people eventually became *mbari* members, when they participated in acquiring more *mbari* land.

From Kirika *until the End of the Nineteenth Century*

In addition to the claims of Mungai's descendants over Njau's private land, the same land would become subject to claims from a section of Chege; their claim opened the protracted land litigation after the 1930s. According to them, Njau had not been able to meet a sudden demand for payment from the *mwathi* and had to borrow goats from three people, including Chege. Chege descendants claim that their goats were not paid back and that they therefore owned part of the Njau land; Njau descendants claim the goats were paid back.[22] Whatever cultivation Chege members had in that land were *ahoi*, not owner rights.

The acquisition of Igi land was not always peaceful; but no problems were encountered with the expansion fuelled by trading wealth − into the lower-lying lands, which probably were under Kamba or perhaps Maasai control.[23] Where the price of the first acquisition was not recalled, it was stated that all who contributed to the second acquisition paid two goats for a first payment. The price of the last three, possibly four acquisitions was less controversial.

Ithaku participated unevenly in buying land; even when a *githaku* did contribute, some of its members might not have paid their share, perhaps because they did not need land or faced other expenses. When contributions lagged, *ahoi* with sufficient stock and acceptable as *mbari* members, might get a chance to buy into the *mbari* by participating in a particular acquisition; they formed a *githaku* on the new land. Only Njau's descendants claimed to have participated in all acquisitions and paid half of the purchase price.[24] That they paid more than others, was not disputed in the twentieth century; it was frequently invoked to explain why their holdings were − as a whole − larger than those of most *mbari* members.

The complexity of Igi oral histories, the size of its land and its internal inequality would make it particularly vulnerable to twentieth-century litigation based on conflicting oral traditions. Differences in the interpretation of what it meant that members had 'become as one person' by buying land together and taking the *mbari* oath were equally divisive. Thuita had its own complement of conflicts, but they rarely dealt with disputed history or images of the *mbari*: *mbari* were too shallow, too close to the 'founding fathers' to have doubts on how the land was acquired, and *mbari* members did not doubt that they held their land individually. Its small holdings did not encourage opportunistic litigation; conflict over and between specific holdings could be solved by strong *arumati* and councils of elders.

Twentieth-century conflicts of Igi oral traditions

In twentieth-century litigation before colonial courts, three conflicts of oral traditions would be persistent. Highly simplified, the questions were whether Njau had bought his private land when his brother's son Mungai was still a child and could not participate or when Mungai was an adult who for whatever reason did not participate. In the first case, his descendants should share in the ownership of the land – because Mungai had been accepted by Njau as a child – like Kimani, who definitely was a child at that time. In the second case, they had no rights.

A second question affecting the same land was whether Njau had returned the goats he had borrowed from Chege to satisfy the seller. If he had, then Chege's descendants had no rights in the land; they could perhaps use it, as *ahoi*. If he had not returned the goats, they had rights to a share.

The third, most complex question concerned the position of Gitau and his descendants. Had he been an original owner of part of the first Igi acquisition and, if so, what rights had his descendants retained after he left this land? Did they have a claim on Chege, on all of Igi, on both or on neither? Were the small tracts the descendants received from Igi given in ownership or use? If given in ownership, were they fair settlements of his claims?

Conflicts based on interpretations of the *mbari*

Though Thuita had two pre-*Kirika mbari*, their members claimed common descent as well as *mbari* membership. Igi was not based on common descent but only on joint *mbari* membership; within its confines were at least three, possibly more, pre-*Kirika ithaku*, which also had private land. During its formation *ahoi* had become members; some *ithaku* which had been powerful had become land poor. Small wonder that in Igi rather than Thuita questions about the nature of the *mbari* would come to the fore; two opposing perspectives were of importance. Evidence shows that the second view dominated the post-*Kirika* period; how strong the first view was in the past, cannot be known. It persisted into the twentieth century as the background to certain land litigation cases; it would be defended until the divisions of land in mid-twentieth-century land consolidation.[25]

The first perspective held that *mbari* land in the final analysis was communally owned; some would also include private land which had been 'ritually brought into the *mbari*'. In this view, contributions to the price of any land might be relevant when all members had sufficiencies, but they became largely irrelevant if one *mbari* member had more than 'he needed' and another *mbari* member was in need.

In a second perspective, the *mbari* was ritually one, but the land was divided according to the contributions to the price. Private land was private; it could ritually be part of *mbari* land while being wholly separate and individual. Those who had more land than they could use were beholden to aid fellow members, but were not obliged to share ownership.

The different interpretations agreed that *mbari* members were one with the land and 'one person' to each other, which demanded exogamy. They also agreed that *mbari* which were not composed of one descent group, needed oaths to stress solidarity and unity. Whether composed of one descent group or created by joint buying, *mbari* members should use for each other terms of reference and address, modelled on those of kinsmen through descent. *Mbari* were responsible for the actions of their members versus outsiders; they had one ritual leader who officiated at rituals for fertility and rain and performed all other ceremonials which affected the land and the population as a whole.

Supporters of the second view relied heavily on indirect evidence as they could not demonstrate that their view had prevailed in allocating or dividing land. They alleged that this had not occurred because strong and wealthy elders had 'deviated' from the ancestral path in the nineteenth century.

They pointed out that *mbari* members with unused land could refuse it to *ahoi* even when these men needed it, but would be censured by the elders if they refused fellow *mbari* members in need. Those who got such land were allowed to leave such usage to their sons; this was common and could continue over the generations.

There was a contradiction in speaking of *mbari* members as if they were using land – that is, as if they were *ahoi*. Those who used land should be prepared to exchange wives with the *mbari* which gave the land: land users were actual or at least potential affinal relations for whom affinal terms had to be used. *Mbari* members should use the terminology of (patrilineal) descent for each other; using affinal terminology to members of one's descent group implied that an offence against the rule of exogamy had occurred. Whether in fact or in word, it created *thahu* of such magnitude that one Igi *githaku* had instituted a *kirumi* against violators. A *mbari* member who used the land of another did not become a *muhoi*; the user had at the very least the right not to be disturbed in his use until he no longer needed the land, but proper terminology implied ownership.

Factual post-*Kirika* evidence strongly supports the first, not the second perspective. Oral traditions show clearly that land was paid for and that contributions differed; there is no evidence, nor is it logical to assume that this would be ignored in the division. Igi traditions make it clear that those who joined late got ownership rights only over that part to which they contributed, commensurate with their contribution.

Data do indeed show that members – with permission – could use the land of other *mbari* members if it was not needed by the owners. Though *mbari* members with little land were 'one' with those who had large tracts, their small tracts did not merge with the larger tracts. There is no evidence that the moral oneness of the *mbari* translated into economic oneness and equality with regard to the land.

As for private land, the available evidence shows that it was regarded as private to the buyer even when one ritual for purity or harvest was sufficient to cover both *mbari* land and private land. The land was paid for by the buyer, not by others, and, if the buyer did not have sufficient stock, he borrowed to meet his payments. Only if he did not return what had been given did the lenders receive ownership rights commensurate to what they had provided. Non-contributors did not get such rights. That

From Kirika until the End of the Nineteenth Century

privately owned land did not become *mbari* land can be seen in the case of Kungu, whose son sold part of his private land. Kungu's request to the elders of Igi for help in redeeming it was refused: the land was his responsibility, not that of the *mbari*.

Use by *ahoi* or other *mbari* members was common as land owners did not like to leave their land uninhabited and covered by bush which might hide *thabari* and wild animals which threatened men, herds and harvests. No one would argue that *ahoi* became owners of the land they used by virtue of use, even when use became entrenched and sons inherited it from their fathers.[26] If use of land did not constitute ownership for one category of men, there seemed to be no reason to presume that it did so for others. When owners provided *tha* for other *mbari* members, they should not be penalized by losing land they might need for sons and grandsons.

Possible oral traditions before oral traditions?

Where early Kikuyu history in Kiambu was filtered through the lens of two disasters, *Kirika* and the *Ng'aragu ya Ruraya*, nineteenth-century colonial land alienation was probably another force which shaped Kikuyu history in Kiambu. The approved European version of Kikuyu history, sanctioned and supported by the colonial government, would deny that the Kikuyu had bought their land, owned it and held it within *mbari* which knew individual tenure. The very need of the Kikuyu to protest land alienation and versions of history which relegated them to the ranks of 'primitives who had no knowledge of ownership of land' could have affected vitally what little could be told – and handed down to the next generation – about pre-*Kirika* times.

The history the Kikuyu needed to defend themselves against the European version seems to have become *the* history of the Kikuyu in Kiambu. Kiambu settlement was ages old; land had been acquired through purchase; Ndorobo had been only too willing to sell; amicable relationships had been the rule; land had always been held by *mbari* but members of the *mbari* had individual rights to their land.

This version of history glosses over many realities, not least the significantly different conditions of life before and after the Kikuyu started to use the area for agriculture, to a large extent destroying the Ndorobo way of life. Admittedly, information is scarce, disparate and inconclusive; much of what follows must therefore remain tentative. Data come from genealogies, from isolated remarks made by elders in conversations and from land litigation (Appendix II/2).[27] Most of this information deals with the rights to land and settlement before *Kirika*. The genealogies are not reproduced; though they provided a rich amalgamation of fathers, brothers and sons, they are as such not germane to the subject.

Oral traditions dealing with the post-*Kirika* period frequently mentioned that the Kikuyu practised agriculture in Kiambu before *Kirika*; yet further

From Kirika until the End of the Nineteenth Century

information about acquisition or buyers is notably absent. The land in question may well have been dowry land or land which continued to belong to the Ndorobo, with Kikuyu, living with them, using some of it.[28] It is also possible that land – if all forest land did indeed belong to the Ndorobo – was taken by Kikuyu, Maasai or Kamba and used on the basis of *kuna*, first rights based on clearing the forest. There are indications that land which did belong to the Ndorobo was not paid for until the Ndorobo discovered the intrusion.

The information indicates a long pre-*Kirika* period, in which individuals from different ethnic groups apparently tried to make inroads in the forest, hunting for basic survival but exploring agricultural pursuits to the degree possible, later enhanced by limited herding.

It is not possible to estimate how long this period lasted, but the second period of Kiambu history may have started when the invaders became numerous and the Ndorobo felt beleaguered; their livelihood endangered by intruders on their borders or within forests which could not be expected to maintain a sizeable population. Perhaps they resisted, perhaps they tried to repel the invaders, perhaps they tried to incorporate some of them within their own ranks. This probably did not stem the flood; unauthorized settlements continued to be a threat; if they did not take up land, they swelled the ranks of *thabari*.

Life for the intruders was not much easier; in addition to the dangers of the forest, they could become victims of the feared curse of the Ndorobo, the more potent if the Ndorobo ancestors had indeed owned the land the would-be settlers had taken. Whether the Ndorobo or the Kikuyu broke through the impasse of fear is unknown, but in time it must have become imperative that Ndorobo and Kikuyu reach a more peaceable and cooperative relationship, even if only for protection against each other and newcomers. What may have started when Ndorobo allowed a few Kikuyu to practise agriculture on dowry land may have ended with selling land to those Kikuyu who were willing to defend the Ndorobo and pay for acquisitions and disturbance of game. In this hypothetical version of history, mutual adoption – at the start of peaceful settlement – may have been as much a Ndorobo device to obtain greater safety as a Kikuyu device to legitimize acquisitions, live in greater peace and avoid Ndorobo curses. The Ndorobo initially did gain time; when Kikuyu immigration increased, a number of them joined the Kikuyu in their agricultural pursuits. Others may have joined Kamba or Maasai, or moved.

Adoptions heralded the beginning of a new period in Kiambu history, in which Ndorobo land slowly became Kikuyu land. The long, unacknowledged history of Kikuyu settlement came to an end and the period of acceptable oral histories could start, as would many genealogies.[29]

The right of Kikuyu to buy the forest did not end the hardships; given the conditions of early agricultural settlement, it is highly unlikely that individuals, or even men with sons, could clear large areas. Even if fire were used, the clearing of stumps and secondary growth would have taken most of the settlers' time. Clearing demanded a stronger group, in its formation 'ethnic origin' would have been of far less importance than cooperation and the work of 'brothers'. Though valuable, one brother's gift of a daughter to pay for the land would soon be eclipsed by the value of the work provided by the others. If the multiple brothers and long-living fathers of genealogies can indeed be interpreted as a time of *agendi* integration, then this must have been common.

In early frontier settlements, life expectancies must have remained dangerously low. It is not likely that many males old enough to start breaking the forest would live long enough to leave mature sons who could successfully continue the work. Under such circumstances, lineal inheritance, from father to son – whether he had provided a girl or not – must have been much more rare than lateral inheritance, from a man to his *mbari* 'brothers'. The dying man could only hope that the *mbari* brothers would care as well as provide for his sons. With lineal inheritance problematic, 'communal' rather than individual ownership would have characterized early settlements.

While some *mbari* in some areas remained at the level of forest settlements with all that entailed, others who had cleared a large part of their land for agricultural use eventually underwent new changes. There was less need for *agendi* and incorporation; newcomers would find land only if they were able to buy the land Ndorobo were still willing to sell. By about 1860 the latter no longer allowed payments by instalment: this may have meant that some of them intended to join Maasai with their herds; others became Kikuyu settlers.

For *mbari* which could devote most of their time to agriculture, the most dangerous times were over. Clearing more forest land would become an occasional rather than a daily labour; wild animals could be kept at bay on open land. Some herding might be possible; diets might have improved. More men might live long enough to see sons grow to maturity before they themselves died; their rights in the land could be perpetuated by lineal inheritance. Contributions to the price would become relevant if land had been bought jointly; communal tenure would give way to individual tenure.

Inheritance and inequality

In addition to differences in contributions, members became unequal as land was divided differently between heirs. Land was divided during a man's lifetime according to the conviction that all descendants should have land, but land should not be cut up into too small parcels. Rather, it was better, if necessary, that most of it should go to one or two sons while others only received a token parcel to confirm their *mbari* membership. This would allow a man to keep his land together; those who received too little would perhaps become *ahoi* and eventually buy elsewhere. Behind this division stood hard economic reality and the ideology of male regeneration.

Each man was the regeneration of his father's father; his grandson would regenerate him. Grandfathers were therefore grandsons; grandsons, grandfathers: it was common to hear an old man address his grandson as *guka*, grandfather. Because the desire for regeneration was strong, fathers paid the brideprice for the first wife of their sons and gave them land and herds so that the sons could provide for their sons, who were one with their grandfathers.

Fathers therefore liked to give at least one or two sons a 'sufficiency': as much land as was needed to continue or even improve upon their lifestyle.[30] The one receiving it was more likely to be an older son who had produced sons during his father's lifetime, than a younger son. Sons of younger wives were less favoured; serial polygyny, practised by the wealthy, made it likely that the youngest sons would be only small boys when their father died and would receive little land.

Few if any Kikuyu rules were set in stone; perhaps the only absolute rule was that no rule was absolute. Human decisions were always regarded as better than rules; there was therefore no strict rule which son should receive at least a sufficiency if there was not enough to give to all. It all depended 'on what a man wanted to do'. In some *mbari* and *nyumba*, primogeniture seems to have been common, in others it was not. Genealogies give only limited help, because men with more land often claimed to be descendants of senior sons whether they had assumed this position or had been born to it. Broadly speaking, senior sons often had more land than younger ones, sons of senior wives more than sons of junior wives. There are plenty of exceptions to this rule; some men gave larger shares only to the first-born son of a senior wife, others to all senior sons of all wives; some might give as much as possible to all sons of a senior wife and little to sons of junior wives. In some cases, men who had reached a high age had favoured young wives and sons over older wives and their sons.

Inheritance became more complex when men died young. By that time, some of his land was used by his wives; this was given on marriage and at the birth of each child. A strong-willed woman might refuse to be inherited; if her own *mbari* was strong enough, she might be able to hold on to the land her husband had given her until her last child was married. Most women, however, would be inherited by a brother of the husband, or – particularly if she were a younger wife in a polygynous marriage – by an older son of another wife. The land was inherited with her, supposedly in trust for her sons, but whoever inherited her could defray the cost of the upbringing of her children from the land. Land of men who died without sons was inherited by their senior – or, if they were senior themselves, their junior brother. Fathers with daughters could try to avoid this, by providing an unmarried daughter with a *ndungata*, a man who was beholden to the land owner, possibly because of debts or as a

From Kirika *until the End of the Nineteenth Century*

captive of war, to sire 'sons for the land'.[31] The *ndungata* did not pay a brideprice and did not have rights over the children. Instead, because the daughter belonged to her father and was not transferred by a brideprice, the children ranked as her father's children. A small piece of land might be left to a daughter who had not married for physical reasons; when she died it returned to her senior brother. In a few cases, women did inherit land outright; when a man had no sons or when his sons had offended him, he could leave all or most of his land to a daughter.[32]

When, possibly as the result of a disaster, one *mbari* died out altogether, or left because the *muramati* was convinced that the land was cursed, the land remained technically the property of the dead and most definitely the property of the ancestors. It was not wise to buy or use such land immediately without the appropriate sacrifices. If members of one *githaku* died out, the first heirs were *ithaku* kinsmen in the *mbari*; lacking these, it was divided among all *ithaku* who had bought land with those who had died.

The cost of the land

Though it was obvious that contributions had mattered, what had been paid and by whom was often lost; given the high death toll in disasters, it would have been more surprising if precise knowledge about what had been paid, by whom, to whom, had been preserved meticulously. Nor could the divisions of land in the twentieth century be used as indicative of who had paid what in the past. In Thuita, where land mostly had been acquired by one man, the price of the whole land might be known but not which sons had contributed and how much. Igi land had been acquired in at least five parcels; informants did not know the price of all tracts, nor could they indicate the size of each instalment and the contributors. Even Njau's descendants could not go beyond claiming to have paid half of what was due. They did, however, know the price of their private land, while neither Chege nor Kungu knew what their ancestors had paid for theirs. Yet such memories were not necessarily accurate; when the descendant of a *mwathi* seller of Igi land demanded more goats and elders refused, he brought a case before Kinyanyui wa Gathirimu who had become powerful in colonial times (Appendix III/1).[33] His assessment differed considerably from what elders had surmised.

Oral tradition of Igi
Early in the twentieth century Kioi, a grandson of the Ndorobo *mwathi*, demanded another payment. The *mbari* countered that they did not owe anything but, concerned about a Ndorobo curse, it brought a case before Kinyanyui wa Gathirimu, the government-appointed chief for the area. He sided with the *mbari*, but ruled that it owed Kioi – as kinsman through land – fifty goats for a wife. Kinyanyui declared that the *mbari* had paid 10,700 goats for its land, as well as the usual sacrificial

From Kirika until the End of the Nineteenth Century

animals, barrels of honey and iron tools. It is not clear whether this included the land bought before the formation of Igi which was private to the buyers, though ritually *mbari* land.[34]

Given the estimated acreage by 1900, the date of acquisitions and comparative prices, the estimate of elders seems low, but 10,700 excessively high. Elders declared that all the land had been paid before the *Ng'aragu ya Ruraya*; the judgment declared that four generations had contributed. If land was not bought until after *Kirika*, then only three generations could have contributed: a fourth would have been too young. Unless the *mbari* lost far more land than it acknowledged in 1956 – which is unlikely – the judgment may have reflected primarily political realities.

The influence of disasters can be illustrated from the following composite case:

> Soon after *Kirika*, Njehia bought seventy-five acres of land for one hundred goats with his married son and Mwarai, his brother. Fifty goats were paid immediately: no one knows who paid what. When, twenty years later, the *mwathi* demanded the final payment, Njehia had five contributing households. Mwarai with two sons had been killed in an attack by the Maasai; he left four households of which three contributed.
>
> Ten years later all households together bought an adjacent piece of twenty-five acres for fifty goats; it was paid for immediately, all contributed equally. By 1890 Njehia's descendants had sixty acres but only four households. His descendants had suffered severely: two males had been killed in wars with the Maasai; the wives of two others had been captured by the Akamba, their husbands followed their tracks and were never heard of again. Marai's descendants used forty acres and had five households.
>
> The *mbari* suffered severe losses in the *Ruraya*; Njehia's descendants were wiped out but for one wife and two small boys, who were inherited by Marai's one surviving adult male who also inherited two younger, unmarried brothers. He brought them up and provided for their initiation and first wives.
>
> In 1956 all had sons with their own households; no land was lost in alienation. The descendants of the two Njehia boys owned twenty acres together; the Marai descendants eighty acres, but in that group the descendants of the married male who had survived owned fifty acres. The males in this *mbari* did not know the contributions of their ancestors.

The last decades:
wealth, concentration of power and dependence

While trade with Kamba and Maasai had been important at least since *Kirika*, the expansion of Kikuyu lands had brought an increase in trade goods and stock. In the early 1870s, the caravan trade became significant.

From Kirika until the End of the Nineteenth Century

Instead of selling to the Kamba, who only bought when they did not have enough for sale themselves, Kikuyu began to sell their cereals and legumes directly to the caravans or their search parties.

Many were excluded from the trade because of lack of land. As fathers or grandfathers had perhaps bought a hundred-acre tract, and subdivided for sons, the number of small estates, with no more than perhaps ten acres, had grown sharply; they had insufficient herding land. Only when Igi allowed them to use the lands it obtained with the profit from trade could they raise goats to finance their own expansion, although that would remove them from the local area where land had become more expensive.

In Igi, large land owners and perhaps one or two *ahoi* started to produce for the caravan trade, stimulating the acquisition of more land, more wives and more stock for the bridewealth of sons.[35] Though their domestic groups expanded, they lacked sufficient labour to grow the trade crops. Sons set up their own households, daughters either moved away or married *ahoi* who, when they had accumulated sufficient goats or when they felt that too much was expected from them, would move. Adjacent small land owners did not have labour; they were engaged on their own land, herding their own stock on the land of others.

The prosperity of the traders and their expanding lands had stimulated immigration. Some were potentially new *ahoi*; others were too poor to qualify for *muhoi* status. This latter group was willing to settle for cultivation and minimal herding rights; they became the tributary *ahoi*; in exchange for sufficient land to ensure survival, they provided labour. Most of them had little chance to work themselves out of this position. They would only be accepted if their households were small enough not to need too much cultivation land; yet they had to be large enough for several members to work, whether at herding, clearing land, cultivation, building granaries, or drying and pounding grain.[36] They received enough herding land to take care of daily needs but not enough to accumulate the goats needed to pay for participation in social and political life. They could rarely provide for their sons, who tended to seek refuge among the Maasai, where they were initiated in exchange for labour; they might even be given a wife. Daughters might be initiated as the recipients of their labour paid the fees; the presence of a *kirege*, a big uncircumcised girl, was a danger to the community. As a group these *ahoi*, though able to survive physically, were *igwima*, the poor.[37]

According to one – unsupported – informant, the name Igi derived from the general relationship of landowners to *ahoi:* Igi came from *Oigi*, those who demand. This was contradicted by the fact that Igi had existed long before the trading period; it was also denied by the twentieth-century descendants of nineteenth-century *ahoi*. It is however quite possible that young men were sent to raid tributary *ahoi*, who had accumulated more than they were allowed to keep.

From Kirika *until the End of the Nineteenth Century*

The organization of the trade

Until the 1850s, local trade with Ndorobo, Maasai and Kamba was based on barter; rather than this being a specialized occupation for some, most people participated in it to obtain basic necessities.

When the Kamba, already involved in the caravan trade, began to buy Kikuyu produce to trade it to the caravans, Kikuyu production first tried to meet the Kamba demands, mainly for non-perishable goods such as grain and beans.[38] They received trade goods, mainly wire, cloth, beads and cowries in return, which they again exchanged with other Kikuyu outside the ambience of the caravan trails, mainly for stock which was used to procure wives and more land.[39]

The attempt to exclude the Kamba probably started in the late 1860s; though the local area was not on a major caravan route, local men wanted the increased profits and more trade goods which were rapidly becoming popular enough to be included in brideprices. Local men also wanted to prevent the slave raids of Kamba *thukumu*, slavers, who used the trade as cover for their activities.[40] They succeeded in their first objective, but only partially in the second. Although caravans as such rarely engaged in slaving, small Kamba parties continued to raid until the turn of the century, and many genealogies show losses of men, women and children.

By the mid-1870s, trading had expanded and included durable goods such as millet and beans as well as perishable goods bought to last the buyers for a few days. Caravan representatives came frequently from an area close to modern Nairobi or Dagoretti; local men would be warned of their impending arrival when they reached Wangengi, close to present-day Kiambu. There they would buy at Ng'waro's, an elder whose homestead was half-way between Kiambu and what became Komothai, after which some of the porters would be sent back to their camps. Others continued to Mahui, the son of one of Igi's founders' second wife, who had been entrusted by his father, the *muramati* of Igi, with control of the trade. From Igi they proceeded to Kibichoi and Githunguri; as they then 'had as much as they could carry', they probably returned to their base camp, which in the early years they sometimes had been allowed to erect in Igi herding lands.[41] This route was followed for almost twenty-five years, until lack of food and the railway, begun in 1896, put an end to the local caravan trade.

The first European – whom I have been unable to identify – came to the local area in the early 1880s; he may have been an explorer because he brought only few porters and bought little food, though he did want to buy a sheep for his porters, which was refused. *Anake* made it their occupation to watch for caravans or porters, ostensibly to prevent theft and rape – but according to elders their looting was as likely to be the problem.

Around 1870, Unuthi (Nubians) and Swahili traders might come with around twenty porters; by the 1880s and 1890s, elders had to restrict groups which wanted to traverse the area and buy to forty men. Elders

From Kirika *until the End of the Nineteenth Century*

felt forced into the restriction because of the lawlessness of both sides; they recalled that whenever elders had not been watchful, problems had been severe. Some looting and burning had taken place not too far away at Thika; none however, as serious as near Fort Smith. The story of Waiyaki wa Hinga, whose conflict with an officer of the IBEAC led to his death, the tales of roving caravan bands, looting, burning and raping, served as examples of what could have happened (Appendix III/1).[42] Local problems were minor in comparison. Around the time of the death of Waiyaki, local *anake* had followed a small caravan to present-day Kambui and caravan leaders, suspecting hostilities, took hostages. One local *muhoi* threw a spear, which 'went through the hat of a European'; caravan leaders opened fire and killed two *anake*.

In spite of problems, trade had increased rapidly; early caravans had not come more often than about four times a year. In the early 1880s, they might come every other or even every month. By this time, Mahui was *muramati* of his own *githaku* and of Igi as a whole, and one of the major traders in the region. In this capacity, he had put some of his sons in charge of gathering surplus. He directed the sale negotiations and mounted his own expeditions if caravans stayed away and too much surplus accumulated. He was well known to the caravans; in turn, he and other local inhabitants were familiar, by the 1880s with the Europeans of the trading stations.[43] The IBEAC was for them the European counterpart of their own trading efforts; when, after some years, the IBEAC became the Protectorate government, called *thirikari* by its agents, they regarded the change a European affair.[44] The only difference was that one of its agents, most likely C. W. R. Lane, came more frequently than before.

Mahui's influence grew with the trade; by the 1890s he was a recognized *muthamaki*, a weighty man with influence well beyond his *mbari* and territorial area.[45] It was not surprising that in 1896-7 the Assistant Controller for the Protectorate government – presumably C. W. R. Lane – asked him to appoint a representative to the *thirikari*. Mahui, thinking in terms of trade and control of the *anake*, appointed his brother's son, Kimama wa Macharuga, whom he had raised when his brother died and who was a leader in his *riika*. Mahui undoubtedly hoped that Kimama's appointment would help control his restless age-mates, who failed to see that peace might be more profitable than raiding and warfare. He worked together with Lane to get this message across. To Mahui the *thirikari* was an organization, interested in peace and trade; its interests and that of the local population were identical. To maintain the peace was of paramount importance; the local population should be willing to pay a small tribute so that the *thirikari* could pay its soldiers to guard it.

When Lane returned in 1898-9, he announced that he had divided Kiambu into 'divisions' under 'headmen' such as Kimama: they were to collect trade goods, recruit 'friendlies' and, with the help of the elders, collect one goat every other season from all adult males so that the 'friendlies' could be paid.[46] This coincided with the drying up of the flow of trade goods as a result of bad harvests; sickness among stock was another disaster and, though the elders agreed to the payments, it was agreed to postpone collections to better times.

Though only large land owners were involved in trade, that they put their profit into land expansion made the trade of importance to *ahoi* and small land owners who needed to use the land. In so far as they had *anake* or were still young enough to be involved in raiding, the demand for peace by large land owners was not to their advantage. They could not afford it; raiding represented a principal source of wealth for initiations, wives and stock to pay for land and elders' councils. Though the large land owners, who could claim that their lands were the principal dwelling places of the spiritual forces, carried the day, trade as well as internal conflict, particularly with the *anake*, characterized the last decades of the nineteenth century.[47] During that period, large *mbari* and important trading *ithaku* within them established themselves as the true authority which was made visible by costly and time-consuming ritual, both in the organization of the *mbari* themselves and in the territory where they lived.[48] If Kiambu Kikuyu had ever enjoyed equal access to decision making, this was now coming to an end.[49]

The growth of social and political differentiation over time

The mbari *and its councils*

Ultimate authority in *mbari* was vested in the spiritual forces which dwelt in the land. Owners of large tracts were more obviously blessed than owners of small tracts; they were therefore the principal guardians of the spirits and the land. They were the executors of the wishes of the spiritual forces; they therefore had the right – and obligation – to exercise worldly authority; they had the right to dominant positions in the *kiama* (councils).

Data on *mbari* organization in the time of the forest economy or immediately after *Kirika* are contradictory and incomplete; informants stress that 'in the past' all men who wanted to had been able to become members of the *kiama* and that 'almost everyone' had been able to pay the fees 'needed to make decisions'. Only the more wealthy men in the research area would contend that this had remained the same, though they could give little in the way of hard data and descendants of poorer *mbari* and *ahoi* disagreed strongly. They pointed out that only large *mbari* could afford to pay all the fees and reach the higher ranks. This led to a division of the *kiama*, the councils, into junior and senior. By the 1880s this however affected all *mbari*, even the poorer ones. Whatever earlier and possibly 'democratic' organization had been like, in the 1870s larger land owners and important *ithaku* had considerably more influence than small land owners and unimportant *ithaku*.

Mbari had a junior and a senior *kiama*; the latter had an inner or secret council, the *ndundu*, in which only the most senior elders could deal with matters of *thahu*, witchcraft or murder. The principal *ithaku* of the *mbari* had mirror organizations; admission to the different levels in the councils was based on admissions to the *ithaku* councils. All access depended on payment of fees.

Soon after marriage young males paid one goat for membership in the junior council, which entitled them to make decisions in meetings of the junior council and to attend meetings of the senior council without participation in the deliberations.[50] A second goat gave admission to this council, but one could only speak after the older members had finished. The first step in becoming members of the *ndundu* cost another goat, but only candidates who were invited could attend or speak. Those who desired to officiate at sacrifices and to hold initiation rituals at their homestead owed still another goat.

Even if they had paid the requisite goats, poorer land owners and members of smaller *ithaku* were less likely to be consulted or have a chance to voice their opinion. Though the senior council as a whole dealt with accusations of adultery and set the date for agricultural ritual, the *ndundu* would adjudicate conflict over land, and only the most senior men in the *ndundu* would deal with behaviour which might bring *thahu*. Poorer men might not be important enough to sit in judgment; the gravity of a case determined whether it was handled by the senior council as a whole, its *ndundu*, or the most senior elders within the *ndundu*. Poorer men had less access to history and tradition; like all elders, they had received basic information about the past when they were *anake* and junior elders, but as they would not advance enough, they would not receive information – notably about disasters and matters of *thahu* – which was only shared with those who were members of the *ndundu*.

The territory and its councils

Territorial units, and therefore territorial councils which consisted of *mbari* and *ahoi*, were not fixed political entities; their size depended on their constituent members, who might decide to join, become independent, form their own territory or join another territory.

Whether territorial councils existed prior to *Kirika* and if so how they were formed, is not certain; it is likely that cooperation between *mbari* remained informal as long as they were isolated and had few if any *ahoi*. Data on how and when they came into being are unreliable; some elders maintained that the territorial councils came into being when the number of small *mbari* proliferated, looking towards each other for protection from the large *mbari*; others stressed that the councils were an outcome of the large number of *ahoi*, some powerful and wealthy, in the large *mbari* who wanted a say in the affairs of their locality.

Like the *mbari* councils, the territorial councils put a premium on wealth, favoured large *mbari* over small ones, strong *ithaku* and their members over weaker ones, strong *ahoi* over weak ones.

Informants described a complex, hierarchical set of councils on three spacial levels between five to ten homesteads, often inhabited by patrilineal

From Kirika until the End of the Nineteenth Century

kin and perhaps *ahoi*, would live in an *itura* (pl. *matura*); several *matura* could form a *mwaki* (pl. *miaki*); several *miaki*, a *rugongo* (pl. *ngongo*). Though formal councils started at the *mwaki* level, the *rugongo* was the largest unit of decision making. Several *ngongo* might cooperate on a more or less regular though informal basis; local information does not record formal councils and regular cooperation beyond the *ngongo*.[51] The smallest *mbari* might live in one *itura*; all Thuita *mbari* were however large enough to be *miaki*, who formed together one *rugongo*. Igi with its many *ahoi* was large enough to have three *miaki*, who formed one *rugongo* together.

Little was known about councils below or above the *rugongo* level. In Thuita, with few *ahoi*, the *miaki* corresponded to the *mbari* and most business could be handled through its councils. In Igi, *miaki* – which cross-cut the divisions of the *mbari* – did have councils, each with their own leader, but again little is known about their functions. Some information indicates that the *rugongo* council was a delegate council from the *miaki*. Delegates had to pay additional fees.

The *rugongo kiama*, like the *mbari* councils, was divided into a junior and senior council, the latter having a *ndundu*. All men had to become members of both councils; one goat paid for membership in the junior council, which was little more than a service organization for the senior council. 'Elders of the first goat' could attend joint meetings of the councils but were barred from taking part in deliberations. They could wear certain insignia, however, and should be addressed as *muthuri*, elder. Payment of a second goat gave the right to speak in joint sessions; those who had children who needed to be initiated were obliged to pay a third goat, which made them into members of the senior council. They were again expected to be silent; after a few seasons they might be invited to speak. Significant decisions were however made in the *ndundu*, restricted to invited males who paid another goat; invitations were significantly influenced by one's own status, the wealth and power of one's immediate kinsmen and one's *githaku*. Members of the *ndundu*, when advanced in years and invited by those already involved in ritual decisions, could pay several more goats for specific ritual rights and information about the past.

Leadership was theoretically open to all, but, as it demanded payments and largesse, only large land owners and wealthy men could aspire to *rugongo* leadership; wealthy *ahoi* might become leaders of constituent *miaki*. The *ndundu* of the senior *rugongo* council had jurisdiction over administrative and judicial matters. It decided the opening or closure of initiations and where and when they would be held; it decided whether raiding would be allowed or prohibited; it might decide whether to go to war or not; it adjudicated matters of conflict between *mbari* in the *rugongo*, while the senior council as a whole dealt with conflict between *ahoi* and *mbari* members. Depending on the seriousness of the accusation, the senior council or the *ndundu* dealt with criminal matters across *mbari* lines. Only the most senior members would deal with accusations of witchcraft or murder; since in such cases judicial authority needed to be strong enough

From Kirika until the End of the Nineteenth Century

to protect itself against curses from the accused, senior elders from *ngongo* as far as Githunguri might be called in to help adjudicate the case and decide what compensation had to be paid.

Though the Thuita *rugongo* was independent of Igi, the economic dependence of a number of its constituent *mbari* on Igi and the latter's economic and political power encouraged Igi's political leadership. By the 1880s, Igi's decisions about raiding, closure and opening of initiations were followed by Thuita and possibly other neighbouring *ngongo*. Igi was the prime political power in the area; within it, trade had allowed power to accumulate in the hands of a relatively small number of *mbari* members and *ahoi*.

In the last decades of the century, authority, whether in *mbari* or *rugongo*, was clearly a factor of wealth; land poor and landless had little chance to advance to significant decision-making levels. In a typical Kikuyu play on words, leaders of territorial councils, officially *athamaki*, can be referred to as *atongoria* (sing. *mutongoria*), as could leaders of *mbari*. It is an honourable title, indicating wealth and high status, but it can also indicate 'fatness' with the implied suggestion that the fat was not due to one's own achievements.

There is little evidence that Kikuyu then or in the twentieth century disagreed with the ideology which linked authority and wealth, nor is it possible to say whether this ideology was old or a more recent development. The land poor and landless of the late nineteenth century had sound economic reasons to accept the political authority of the wealthy; they needed to use their land for their immediate needs and as a gateway to owning their own land. Though disenfranchised politically, they were enfranchised economically. Land poor and landless may therefore have acquiesced in the concentration of power in the hands of the wealthy, yet the *anake* and their *mariika* seem to have been less complacent and may have invoked curbs on their power.

The role of the *anake* and the *mariika*

Males and females reached adult status through initiation which included circumcision; after initiation girls could be married, males became *anake* (sing. *mwanake*), initiates of roughly the same period formed a *riika* (pl. *mariika*), and a number of *mariika* formed a regiment, also called *riika*.[52] In the first post-*Kirika* decades, payments for females – who were initiated before the menarche – and males – who, depending on wealth and status, might be initiated as early as sixteen or as late as their early twenties – were at most two goats with gifts of vegetable food and honey.

At that time *anake* were expected to herd and protect the community; they also had the right – with permission of *rugongo* elders – to raid in small groups for livestock and girls. Avoiding *mbari* with which their own had peaceful relationships, raiding of other Kikuyu, Akamba and Maasai was

From Kirika *until the End of the Nineteenth Century*

permitted. In the early post-*Kirika* decades raiding had not been important and only occasionally brought significant wealth; the population was still too sparse and dispersed, most herds still small. Even though at that time younger *anake* were obliged to give gifts of their booty to more senior *anake* and elders, a lucky raid might yield enough livestock to acquire a wife or land. Girls who were brought back would be raised as Kikuyu girls; they might be married by those who had captured them or by their relatives. Raiding provided poorer young males with stock for wives, if not the wives themselves; landless or land poor fathers, who lacked stock to provide for all their sons, welcomed the contribution the young could make, even though not always pleased with their show of independence.

As settlements increased, *mbari* expanded, and more land was bought, local land came closer to Maasai and other Kikuyu. While this increased the profitability of raiding, it also provoked more counter-attacks and hostilities.[53] As this ran counter to the interest of trade, larger land owners sought to curb the aggression of the *anake* by restricting access to the *mariika* and reducing the profits of raiding.

Curbs on *anake* and *mariika*

By the middle 1870s, fees for female initiation, still predominantly paid in agricultural produce which almost all parents could afford, had increased only slightly, but senior *rugongo* elders had decreed that male fees were to be paid in stock instead of agricultural produce. They increased to as much as seven goats; the protracted ceremonial and numerous sacrifices might take several months; fathers also had to provide suitable clothing, ornaments and weapons. All this was a heavy burden on smaller land owners and *ahoi*; even if they had access to herding land they still might have to delay the initiation of sons. Sons of the wealthy could be initiated early, with the result that they had an advantage over other young males of the same age. Poorer men might lose their disgruntled sons who ran away to the Maasai for initiation, where they might stay and marry.

These costs were only the beginning; *anake* were expected to pay older initiates for any right which previously had been theirs as a matter of course. They had to pay before they could dance or have access to girls; though they became immediately an initiation year within a junior regiment – *anake* were divided into junior and senior regiments, each with a number of initiation years – they had little or no rights beyond serving the senior regiment, whose members could fine them for the most minor infractions. It took a number of years before junior regiments became senior regiments; in the meantime, the senior regiments would restrict the raiding of the juniors. If they could raid at all, senior regiment members and elders demanded their share of the booty. Acceptance of all the restrictions of the elders gave some return to senior *anake*; junior regiments had to wait before they got any advantages.

From Kirika *until the End of the Nineteenth Century*

The measures taken by the elders did not contribute to solidarity between junior and senior *anake*, nor could the solidarity of an initiation year be taken for granted. Splits were likely to follow *mbari* lines; sons of fathers with sufficient land to provide their sons with brideprices and land could afford to obey their elders; sons of fathers who could not do so had less incentive to comply. Strain between elders and *anake* and expressions of anger became common; some of the violence earlier directed outside was directed inside. Genealogies show a number of cases of serious injuries and death, because the orders of elders not to engage in mock fights in homestead enclosures and to stop the brandishing of swords or throwing of spears had been ignored. When elders during the 1880s put a ban on dancing in punishment for some infraction, the *anake* invaded the homestead of one elder and killed his son, who came to his father's aid.[54] Elders had serious difficulty keeping the *anake* from attacking caravans; that caravans had superior arms was more an incentive than a deterrent. In the early 1890s attacks ended in death; some *anake* attacked a small European-led caravan near Kambui and were killed. That no members of the caravan party were injured saved the local area from a punitive raid.

Anake, disgusted with the restrictions, sometimes took to roaming the countryside; others went to areas where trade was less dominant. Some found an outlet by going to trading centres of the IBEAC and the Protectorate government; they enlisted as caravan porters or became 'friendlies'. This option was so appealing that when C. W. R. Lane came in about 1896 to recruit, a whole initiation year wanted to enlist; Lane, aware of the volatile presence of a complete local *riika*, sided with the elders and refused.

While no one sided openly with the *anake*, the sympathy of smaller land owners may well have been on their side; successful raiding of sons would have made it easier to provide them with land and wives. Their dependence on larger land owners won out, however; there is no record that they joined the defiance of *anake*; they may well have widened the gulf between their sons and themselves by the political realities of their position or telling the young that the time of the pioneers was past. Their arguments failed to impress; genealogies indicate that sons left for Kabete or Limuru. Many more would have become 'friendlies', with its chance for loot, had the caravans or the incoming Europeans accepted them.

Warfare and the disasters of the final decade

In spite of the growing trading interests, skirmishes between local Kikuyu, Akamba and Maasai had intensified. From the 1870s onwards, attacks had become more frequent. In the early 1880s skirmishes acquired characteristics of warfare, as greater population density, the desire for stock and women, conflict over control of herding land, and access to the

From Kirika until the End of the Nineteenth Century

caravan trade became issues. Skirmishes became more lethal as population density made it possible to combine the forces of several *ngongo*; among those killed or enslaved were *anake* as well as the non-combatant population. Around 1880 Mahui's older brother was among those killed; the efforts of elders to curb warfare in the interest of trade had had little success as these interests were not sufficiently shared by their own young males and by neighbouring peoples; peace treaties had been as frequent as breaches of the peace, although informants were sure that their opponents, not they, were the guilty party.[55] Elders' interests in trade made Europeans their natural allies; apart from being profit-bringing buyers, their arms and power could be used to threaten the *anake* and their proclivity for raids.

Around 1884 Maasai affected by rinderpest successfully attacked the Kikuyu to recoup losses; the Kikuyu counter-attacked in 1886-7 in a fierce battle 'of many men' at the confluence of the Komathi and Ruiru rivers, the boundary of Igi land. Newly initiated Mburu *riika*, under Mahui's son Waweru, was in the front line They routed the Maasai and pursued them deep into Maasai country, bringing back girls and a large amount of livestock. Delighted with its victory, Mburu refused to give most of it, as was customary, to elders and older warriors; it strengthened its commitment not to yield by an oath (Appendix I). The elders used their customary method of resistance by losing the war but winning the peace: they accepted a smaller payment, but broke the solidarity of the *anake* by coopting the more prominent leaders into junior eldership well before they could have aspired to this. By the 1890s, several Mburu males were polygynous.

Rinderpest was not confined to Maasai country and may have spread by trading and raiding as caravans bought and transported infected cattle. In the 1880s Kikuyu herds twice suffered some losses but suffered worse in the 1890s, when smaller and larger disasters struck, sometimes affecting stock, sometimes people, sometimes both.[56] In the beginning, the disasters were sufficiently separated to allow recovery. Whether or not the *ituika* held at that time was an attempt to 'cleanse the land' to avoid further disasters, as Lonsdale has suggested, it is certain that the years between 1894 and 1897-8 continued to bring smaller or larger plagues such as *ndutu* or jiggers and *kagicha* or scars from fire or sickness (Appendix II/I). The years afterwards were even more disastrous: neither population nor livestock could withstand three successive seasonal droughts which started in 1898 and brought the *Ng'aragu ya Ruraya*, the great famine.[57] Many died of hunger and digestive disorders from eating bark or other 'foods'; others died of minor diseases they otherwise might have survived; again others died of smallpox, which reappeared.[58] Estimates of the death toll are dependent on the less than reliable estimates and calculations from genealogies for the last decade of the nineteenth century, and on specific information about persons who died. No information was available about the death toll among those who had left the local area after the disasters; nor is there information about the significantly large number of refugees

From Kirika until the End of the Nineteenth Century

Table 2.1. *Approximate growth and decline of Igi households, population and land ownership between the Ruraya famine and 1962.*

Period	Total	Households			Ahoi households	Adult population[b]			Land ownership		
		Owner Households				Total	Male	Female	Total	Mbari	Private
		Total	Mbari	Athami							
Before *Ruraya* famine	245	120	120	?	125[c]	?	?	?	2,700	1,700	1,000
Kamande, 1902/3	113	69	69	?	44	?	?	?	2,700	1,700	1,000
Alienation											
Before Makio, 1912/13	106	65	65	?	41	?	?	?	1,700	1,100	600
Kinyotoku, 1919/20	148	99	76	23	49	?	?	?	1,800	1,100	700
Before Carter, 1931/33	204	145	118	27	59	?	?	?	1,900	1,100	800
Hitler or Bote, 1940	291	215	181	34	76	?	?	?	1,960	1,100	860
Before the Emergency 1952	366	272	228	44	94	1,036	470[d]	566[e]	2,200	1,100	1,100
1955/56	409	298	253	45	111	1,113[f]	?	?	2,360	1,100	1,260
1962	405	345	314	31	60	1,203[f]	?	?	2,540	1,100	1,440

a Until 1952 figures are low estimates based on elders' information, genealogies and calculations.
b Fourteen years and older.
c Includes 50 tributary households.
d Male population: owners 334, *ahoi* 136.
e Female population: owners 403, *ahoi* 163.
f Approximate.

From Kirika until the End of the Nineteenth Century

Table 2.2. Approximate growth and decline of Thuita households, population and land ownership between the Ruraya famine and 1962.

Period	Households					Adult population[b]			Land ownership		
	Total	Owner households			Ahoi households	Total	Male	Female	Total	Mbari	Private
		Total	Mbari	Athami							
Before *Ruraya* famine	89	74	74	?	15	?	?	?	1,100	?	?
Kamande, 1902/3	61	55	55	?	6	?	?	?	1,100	?	?
Alienation											
Before Makio, 1912/13	58	52	52	?	6	?	?	?	700	700	—
Kinyotoku, 1919/20	71	61	58	3	10	?	?	?	600	600	—
Before Carter, 1931/33	110	96	92	4	14	?	?	?	586	580	6
Hitler or Bote, 1940	151	138	135	3	13	?	?	?	605[e]	580	25
Before the Emergency 1952	203	190	184	6	13	566	264[c]	302[d]	636[e]	570	30
1955/56	241	228	222	6	13	626[e]	?	?	646[e]	520	70
1962	252	246	242	4	60	685[e]	?	?	666[e]	510	100

a Until 1952 figures are low estimates based on elders' information, genealogies and calculations.
b Fourteen years and older.
c Male population: owners 250, *ahoi* 14.
d Female population: owners 284, *ahoi* 14.
e After the Carter Commission several *mbari* members sold and others bought. Buying outweighed selling for the *mbari*.

who had come to Igi from other areas during the last years of the disasters and then left immediately afterwards. Information is also less reliable as all deaths between 1890 and 1900 were lumped together as famine deaths, regardless of age or circumstance.

Based on information of surviving members and the geneaologies they provided, around 1890 the Thuita population would have consisted of at least 74 *mbari* and ten affinal *ahoi* households; the number of tributary *ahoi* was probably no more than five. As in Igi, all tributary *ahoi* are said to have died, although it is possible that some of them fled, and how many of these would have survived is unknown. The *mbari* which were extant in 1956 may have lost as much as 30 per cent; *nyumba* losses ranged from 10 to 90 per cent.

Based on similar data, Igi had about 120 member households, at least 75 affinal and more than 50 tributary *ahoi*. While it had much larger herds than Thuita, there is no evidence that this gave Igi a better chance for survival. Its losses were in the area of 50 per cent if all tributary *ahoi* indeed died (Table 2.1).[59]

The data do not give insight into who did and did not die. Although wealth, particularly stock, may have given protection from starvation in the early years, it also increased the likelihood of attack. Economic position did not protect against virulent diseases, though anyone would try to shun homesteads where smallpox had broken out. The *igwima*, the poorest of the poor, died out unless they all reached safety elsewhere; but one *githaku* in Igi which was by no means poor died out too. Roaming or leaving the area did not give more protection; some of the highest death rates are found among the roaming *anake*. Well over half of males initiated in *Ngigi*, around 1891, died in the disaster years, even though they were armed and there is evidence that they did not shun using their weapons to obtain food. Some survived because they attached themselves to posts of the Protectorate government or to camps of European hunters or missionaries.[60] Some became 'friendlies'; some of them were killed in the next few years while executing retaliatory raids.

Again other young males formed gangs which scoured the countryside for food for their families or themselves. They might get as far as Embu or Gaki or the Coast; a number were never heard of again. At least one such gang was holed up close to the local forest near Kamiti; they preyed on those who returned with food from mission stations or trading; they attacked homesteads rumoured to have hidden food. They earned the sobriquet *Mau Mau*, indicating the sound made by a hyena devouring his ill-gotten catch, for their greed. The name implies anger as well as understanding that the men resorted to their actions; the name would be applied again in the twentieth century.[61]

There were similarities and differences between *Kirika* and the *Ng'aragu ya Ruraya*. Both took an enormous death toll, but because the population by the end of the nineteenth century was more numerous, depopulation of territory in general was less extensive. During the *Kirika* the death or departure of whole groups was common and resulted in much completely abandoned land. During the *Ruraya* the *mbari* and *nyumba* were larger, some people almost always survived and land was rarely abandoned.

While little is known about women and children who survived *Kirika*, one of the first actions after *Ruraya* was the incorporation of widows and immature children into the households of survivors; the rebuilding of descent groups had high priority, as it did after *Kirika*. *Mbari* members might have inherited wives and incorporated surviving young girls without protectors into their households; they nevertheless tried as soon as possible to get wives of their own choice. *Ahoi* were less inclined to take on the burden of additional wives and would wait until the situation stabilized.

Loss of *mbari* land was not a factor in the famine; surviving individuals often had much more land than before. One case of *mbari* loss occurred when only one older wife of a member survived, and she and her land were inherited by an older kinsmen who was not a *mbari* member. When he died, he left the land to her; at her death she left it to her brother. Within *mbari*, men inherited land from their collateral relatives who died, though they might have to provide, and eventually give, some of the land to sons and widows their kin had left behind. *Ahoi* might become land owners when kinsmen who had bought land and formed a *mbari* died and no acceptable heirs in the *mbari* had survived beyond the kinsmen who were *ahoi*.

The high death toll sometimes dramatically changed land relationships within a *githaku* or *mbari*, if a man with little land who survived inherited the land of a wealthy member who died with all his descendants. It was not for anyone to ask why this was so, or to judge whether the man who lost relatives but gained land was more severely punished than the man who kept his relatives but did not gain land. That was tantamount to speculating why the famine had occurred: whether it had to do with the way some men had left Murang'a or whether some had refused to give *tha* they should have provided. The famine was *uhoro wa Ngai*, a matter for God. The consequences of the famine for land are illustrated by the following hypothetical case:

> Around 1850, Ichau and Bari each received about 200 acres from their father. By 1895 both men had five households. In Ichau's *nyumba*, one household had seventy acres, one had fifty, the other three had about 26 acres each. In Bari's *nyumba* two households had sixty acres, the other three also about 26 acres. After the famine, all but one of Bari's households died; it inherited two hundred acres. In Ichau's *nyumba* three households were formed from those who had survived. One had 120 acres, the other two each had thirty.

A significant number of men had more land than they could use immediately, a situation which also had prevailed immediately after *Kirika*. It was to be kept in trust for future generations; any present surplus could be used for herding, surplus production or *ahoi*. *Ahoi* positions were therefore

From Kirika *until the End of the Nineteenth Century*

strengthened; *mbari* members and *ahoi* had survived and were surviving because they had helped each other. After the *Ruraya*, affinal *ahoi* no longer had to pay a goat from the increase of their herds. The *mbari* did accept some new *ahoi* from the refugees, and exchanged surviving daughters with them and older *ahoi*. Some of the refugees however returned to their *mbari* of origin, others did not reclaim their land because they thought it cursed. There were still local residents in 1956 who intended to reclaim their land in the future. Tables 2.1 and 2.2 give some approximations about population strength and composition in the late nineteenth and twentieth century.

There were important differences. *Kirika* occurred when the area was thinly populated, some men living in a forest economy, others in an agricultural-herding economy. By the time of the late nineteenth-century famine, population density was high, forest economies had been abandoned in the local area, and agricultural economies with herding predominated. In addition, a small, powerful group of surplus producers, traders and large-scale herders who were part of an extensive network were dependent on links well beyond those in their area. *Kirika* had occurred when no major differences in wealth divided an isolated population; *Ruraya* occurred when populations where stratified and economic, social and political ties and differentiation in and between settlements were strongly developed and developing. Rebuilding after *Kirika* involved individual decisions; rebuilding after *Ruraya* meant recreating complex sets of relationships.

Notes

1. The local area which remained after land alienation, corresponded to Fisher's 'middle zone' with a long rainy season between March and June and a short one between October and December. In the twentieth century, rainfall of land between 5,000 and 6,000 feet varied from a low 36 to a high 64 inches. I made no measurements; I do not know whether these data are valid for the nineteenth century, nor do I know the effect of rapid local deforestation in the eighteenth and nineteenth century. Harvests depended not only on the amount of rainfall, but also on regularity and predictability; growers complained that both were wanting.
   1955. Fisher, Jeanne, *The Anatomy of Kikuyu Domesticity and Husbandry*, Cambridge: Department of Technical Cooperation, pp. 2ff. The four villages were in Fisher's 'middle zone'; her research area included Mbari ya Igi.
2. Because of the inheritance of wives, monogamy can mask as polygyny and polygyny can look more extensive than it is.
3. Informants tended to see *Kirika* as a sharp dividing line. This may have been fostered because so little was known about the time before *Kirika* and so much of that was negative. However, it is likely that developments were gradual rather than sharp. Also, while some land owners were adding rapidly to their wealth, others were still clearing the forest for a homestead space.
4. Larger land owners might allow impoverished kinsmen to use land; those who were 'men of *tha*' might give them a small piece.
5. In order to strengthen a decision, elders might put a curse or *kirumi* on disobedience.

From Kirika until the End of the Nineteenth Century

When unrelated men bought land together, they might take a *mbari* oath not to sell the land. This would be reinforced by a *kirumi* on those who did. One frequent complaint of elders was that 'Kikuyu find it difficult to have unity' and that they therefore had to have so many oaths and *kirumi*.

1962. 6 August, Mr Kiburi, Senior Member and Chief Adviser on Law and Custom, Kiambu Court.
1962. August, Charles Karugu Koinange.

6. *Ahoi* must be distinguished from *athami*. The former use the land of their hosts for all purposes; the latter use their own land, but live on the land of others. There is a discrepancy between my data and Leakey; According to Leakey, *athami* were men who used the land of their hosts and had affinal relationships with them while *ahoi* used the land, but had to provide gifts on demand. According to my data, both could have affinal relationships, and only one kind of *ahoi*, the tributary *ahoi*, could be subjected to demands. Many other *ahoi* were powerful wealthy men, whom no one would subject to such treatment.
1977. Leakey, L. S. B., *op. cit.*, pp. 115ff.
7. There probably were men who asked for such places but were refused. What happened to them is – as with all the poor – unknown. The enigmatic statement 'there were always *igwima* in the forest who were often robbers' can mean that the forest was the only refuge of those poor who were not acceptable anywhere.
8. The early Bible translators unwittingly fostered the image that *ahoi* were without rights, when they translated 'to pray' with *kuhoya* and missionaries stressed that men had no rights before God.
9. Providing wives was one of the most permanent services, and some *ahoi* would claim that as long as such relationships continued, they had a right to use the land.
10. If land elsewhere was bought with herds which had grazed on its land, Igi might ask for a gift. Igi's political influence expanded when men who had used its land created new *mbari*.
11. One question I should have asked, but did not, was how elders handled the situation if *ahoi* who had married into the *mbari* became members. The two relationships were not compatible.
12. When land consolidation had ended and individuals had received title deeds, many younger *mbari* members thought that this absolved them from *mbari* exogamy and quite a few married within the *mbari* to the dismay of the elders. This became one reason to reimpose the *mbari* oath.
13. Thuita got its present name around 1870 with the arrival of a large buyer, who originally had come from a Murang'a ridge of that name (Appendix II/1). Thuita men owned land in Kibichoi as Igi men owned land in Kiratina.
14. One sold to an Igi *mbari* leader; the other, a Ndorobo who had created his own Kikuyu *mbari* on land he had not sold in the nineteenth century, sold it in the 1930s to a *muhoi*. As neither Thuita nor Igi recounted the histories of those who had sold all their local land or died out, there is no certainty about the number of nineteenth-century *mbari* or *ithaku*. At least one *githaku* of Igi was lost in the late nineteenth-century famine.
15. Such inheritance was rare; this case was used to demonstrate the unsettled, confused conditions after the late nineteenth-century famine.
16. According to elders, by 1890 Igi land was located between the confluence of the Karia and the Katamayu rivers in the north-west and the Karia, Komathi and Ruiru rivers in the south-east.
17. When *nyumba* became too large, they separated into segments. If a *nyumba* had land and was thus a *githaku*, each segment took its own land with it in the separation; each would choose its own *muramati*.
18. Alternate version: there was no distinction between ritual and other ownership in the past. All land was *mbari* land.
19. Alternate version: Njau was the owner of a large tract of land which he had bought with his son Mwereri. He approached Kungu and Chege; it was he who planned the *mbari*.
20. How much history is lost can be illustrated by an undisputed account that Chege, before

From Kirika *until the End of the Nineteenth Century*

Kirika, had a 'large land', for which he had paid '1500 goats'. It is likely that the price was expressed rather than paid in goats and that time and number of participants were highly truncated.
21. Njau's private land was situated between Chege's private land and the first Igi acquisition.
22. Njau's descendants claim that he had paid a first instalment when the *mwathi* almost immediately demanded a subsequent payment. Njau therefore had to borrow stock; he was given some by Chege, by another *githaku* founder and by a *muhoi*; he returned the goats to Chege but not to the other two. The *muhoi* became an owner within Njau's private land; he became a *mbari* member when he participated in later *mbari* acquisition, founding his own *githaku*. Some of Chege's descendants would maintain that the goats were not returned, or that, if they had been returned, they were returned to a part of Chege which had fissioned or would fission. If that was the case, it had been a mistake on Njau's part and Chege's people still owned rights in Njau's private land.
23. In one situation the *mwathi* had sold land to someone else while Igi claimed to hold an option on the land, and that it had already made one payment. Igi attacked the 'intruders' and killed at least one of them. Afraid of the *mwathi* forest curse and the curse of the buyers, Igi negotiated and was allowed to take possession. Because the *mwathi* denied having received a payment, 'we paid twice'.
24. As some of Njau's descendants were active in the caravan trade, this statement could have validity. Others would deny it; some would state that even if they had, they paid with stock raised on *mbari* land and their contributions were not individual but *mbari* ones. Nevertheless, one of Njau's sons was sufficiently powerful to become *muramati* of all of Igi.
25. When discussing land consolidation, a number of males and females — mostly land poor — would assert that the land should have been divided equally among *mbari* members at that time.
26. *Ahoi*, whose sons assumed the land, provided a meat feast for the owner, who needed to confirm their right to use the land.
27. One story referred to a *mbari* in the vicinity which had 'never paid for its land'. It had 'lived with the Ndorobo for generations', the Ndorobo had become agriculturalists and their Kikuyu had continued to share the land. In the 1956 land consolidation, the Ndorobo, now Kikuyu, and the sojourning Kikuyu received deeds to separate tracts of the land; the Kikuyu (Ndorobo) tract was larger than the Kikuyu tract.
28. Dowry land is not secure until the children of the woman involved claim it. Land paid for with a daughter is secure when she has produced offspring for the sellers.
29. Leakey provides an extensive description of adoption. Though he discusses the Kikuyu acquisition of the *Ndorobo* forest, the ritual clearly describes the acquisition of bush land. The higher regions remained forest until cleared; even in fallowing they were not allowed to revert to the kind of bush which characterized virgin land. Local Kikuyu did not take possession of the lower bush lands until around 1865-70.
1977. Leakey, L. S. B., *op. cit.*, pp. 92ff.
30. What constitutes a sufficiency is determined by the economy as a whole and the particular position of the land owner. In a forest economy, a man with one wife and seven acres might have a sufficiency but, if more than one son survived, he could not give sufficiencies to all. In the post-*Kirika* period a monogamous household would have needed about eleven acres, which would allow for thirty goats but again was insufficient land for more than one son. The larger the land, the greater the need for labour. Wives and daughters were an important labour force; polygyny gave a larger labour force but also more obligations. By 1870 polygyny was more difficult to achieve; brideprices ranged between forty and fifty goats. Larger land owners and important *ahoi* were polygynous; the maximum number of wives was probably around six or seven. The sufficiency of one individual or generation was the poverty of another, or of the next generation.
31. A *ndungata* could be a Kikuyu or a non-Kikuyu; some had become *ndungata* because of poverty, others because of crimes. They could become sexual consorts for daughters of their owners or were taken by widows who did not want to be inherited by their husband's kin. Children born in such unions belonged to the owner of the *ndungata*. The term is

From Kirika until the End of the Nineteenth Century

derogatory, on the same level as *igwima*, poor landless or poor hunters. Men who had acquired a young boy, perhaps while hunting or raiding, could bring him up and make him into a *ndungata*. A young male caught in a criminal act could be made into a *ndungata* of the man he had offended. Some men would allow a *ndungata* to herd and keep part of the increase; a successful *ndungata* could then redeem himself and pay a brideprice retroactively if he had received a wife or become her consort. He could become a *mbari* member in his own right, if he participated in buying land.

32. Another way to get [more] sons would be to ask one's wife to marry another woman for which she paid the brideprice, possibly from offspring of her *magatha* goats. This woman was given a *ndungata*; her children belonged to the woman who had paid the brideprice and so to her husband, who had paid hers. Women could, but rarely did, inherit land.
33. A man who was accused of not having paid for the land could defend himself by 'showing the goats' in the land. He had to describe the goats given, with all their markings; he had to indicate the circumstances and the witnesses.
34. According to some Igi informants, the case was brought around 1895; the plaintiff, Kioi, was a Ndorobo, he was not the same Kioi wa Nagi who became a headman in the Dagoretti area in early colonial times. It is unlikely that the case was heard around 1895 because the arbiter, Kinyanyui, had barely begun his rise to power when after 1892 his services to officers of the Imperial British East Africa Company (IBEAC) and later to the Protectorate government were rewarded with official appointments. He was gazetted under the Village Headman Ordinance of 1902 and on 18 March 1908 gazetted chief over the area south of the Rui Raka, later the Chania river. This included the local area; Kinyanyui had no other local ties. He became paramount chief after the First World War, a position he held until his death in 1929. His father, a man called Mugo, was neither a large land owner nor a member of an important *mbari* (Appendix III/1).

1909. AR/15 *Ukamba Province Quarterly and Special Report*, October–December, C. W. Hobley.
1909. *Ukamba Province Quarterly Report, Machakos District Political Record Book*, Vol. I (up to 1910), Part I, p. 4.
1970. Thuku, Harry, *An Autobiography*, Nairobi: Oxford University Press, pp. 25–7.
1974. Muriuki, Godfrey, *op. cit.*, pp. 72ff *passim*.
1974. Wanyoike, E. N., *An African Pastor*, Nairobi: East African Publishing House. p. 96.

35. Agricultural crops for family use were planned by women, those for export, by males, who also had some specific crops which were grown for 'male use' in a social or ritual context. Whatever the crop, men prepared the land and helped with harvesting; harvested trade crops were owned by males. Women could be asked but not be forced to work such land or any other land under 'male crops'.

1975–6. Kershaw, Greet, *op. cit.*, pp. 173–95.

36. In the twentieth century, some people asserted that these *ahoi* had used land which had not been allocated; individual ownership of such land could only be presumed. It should have been decided after the famine who had right to it; even better, it should have been equally divided between surviving *mbari* members. Others asserted that the land had belonged to specific *mbari* members.
37. From a material perspective, these men and women probably lived no worse than the early Kiambu settlers and did not have to face some of the hazards they had faced. Yet the society in which they lived demanded greater resources, which they lacked and were unlikely to gain.
38. 1972. Kershaw, Gretha, *op. cit.*, pp. 146ff.
    1974. Muriuki, Godfrey, *op. cit.*, pp. 136ff. If I have correctly identified the Kamba area with which local Kikuyu interacted as *mweia*, then important data are available in
    1988. Ambler, Charles Hart. *Kenya Communities in the Age of Imperialism*, New Haven: Yale University Press.
39. Men who had land on which to produce agricultural surplus, but had not yet been able to buy enough land to graze livestock received in trade, could ask other *mbari* for herding land; they also might send it to the Maasai. They provided herdboys and paid their hosts

79

From Kirika until the End of the Nineteenth Century

part of the increase. If Kikuyu received trade goods, they exchanged most of them with Kamba and Maasai or Kikuyu who lived further from trade routes. Maasai were occasionally willing to give a girl in exchange.

40. Thukumu 'wore long white cloth', sometimes they engaged in legitimate trade as well as raiding for slaves.
41. The normal load for a porter was between 50 and 60 lbs.
42. How much elders at that time knew in detail is open to question. They maintain that they had been aware of the founding and burning of Dagoretti and the building of Fort Smith. According to them, Waiyaki was a trader who tried to keep the caravans and his own *anake* under control but got into a fight with a European when he was drunk and unable to control himself or the European. Because of the fight Waiyaki was deported and died at Kibwezi; the European got the nickname *Mbaya*, the evil one. According to legend, Waiyaki gave the order that the *anake* should not attempt to liberate him. This decision would make him during Mau Mau into a hero of younger males, who would herald him as one of the fathers of the resistance. Older elders were more prosaic; they interpreted Waiyaki's order as the wise decision of a nineteenth-century elder and trader who knew that once the *anake* entered the fray, trade contacts built over decades would be lost, as well as lives. The image of Waiyaki as a resistance leader was nevertheless pervasive and may have played a role in the abduction of Mr and Mrs Gray Arundel Leakey by a Mau Mau gang. They died on or about October 1954; some thought that their deaths had taken the form of a sacrifice; at least one person saw a connection between the manner of Arundel Leakey's death and the death of Waiyaki.

    1966. Rosberg, Carl G., Jr., and John Nottingham, *The Myth of Mau Mau, Nationalism in Kenya*, Hoover Institute on War, Revolution and Peace, London: Stanford Praeger, pp. 13, 14.
    1974. Muriuki, Godfrey, *A History of the Kikuyu before 1903*, Vol. I, London: Oxford University Press, pp. 150–2.
    1977. Leakey, L. S. B., *The Southern Kikuyu before 1903*, Vols I–III, London: Academic Press, pp. 30, 31; 72–83.
    1980. Kinyatti, Maina wa, *op. cit.*, pp. 13, 25, 29.
    1994. Anderson, David M. and Douglas Johnson, eds, *Revealing Prophets, Perspectives in East African History*.
    Lonsdale, John, *The Prayers of Waiyaki*, forthcoming, James Currey, Oxford.
    Rhodes House Documents MSS Afric. s. 742 (3) Colchester, Trevor Charles, 'Note on the association between the death of Chief Waiyaki in 1893 and the Leakey sacrifice during the Mau Mau Emergency'.

43. Some of the traders and early administrators were given Kikuyu names. *Tayari* (always in a hurry) was George Wilson; *Njue-ini* (newly arrived or demanding) was John D. Ainsworth; *Mbaya* (the wrong, the bad one) was G. Perkiss; and *Wanyahoro* (the man of many things or the man of peace) was Francis Hall.
44. The Imperial British East African Company (IBEAC) was formed in 1888; a British Protectorate was declared to exist by June 1895; in April 1905 the Protectorate was transferred from the Foreign to the Colonial Office; Kenya became a colony in 1920. Histories of pre-colonial Kenya are scarce; the most important are cited in Chapter 1, note 32. Histories of colonial Kenya with reference to the Kikuyu are numerous.

    1929. Hobley, C. W., *Kenya from Chartered Company to Crown Colony*, London: H. F. & G. Witherby.
    1966. Dilley, M., *British Policy in Kenya Colony*, Second Edition, London: Frank Cass.
    1963. Bennett, George, *Kenya, A Political History*, London: Oxford University Press.
    1965. Bennett, George, 'Settlers and politics in Kenya up to 1945' in V. Harlow *et al.* (eds), *The History of East Africa*, Vol. II, Oxford: Clarendon Press, pp. 265–332.
    1966. Mungeam, G. H., *British Rule in Kenya, 1895–1912*, Oxford: Clarendon Press.
    1974. Clayton, Anthony, and Donald C. Savage, *Government and Labour in Kenya 1985–1963*, London: Frank Cass.
    1976. Tignor, Robert L., *The Colonial Transformation of Kenya*, Princeton, NJ: Princeton University Press.

From Kirika *until the End of the Nineteenth Century*

1990. Berman, Bruce, *Control and Crisis in Colonial Kenya*, London: James Currey.

1992. Berman, Bruce, and John Lonsdale, *Unhappy Valley*, Books I and II, Eastern African Studies, London: James Currey.

45. Leaders of councils could be given the honorific *muthamaki*; the word implies a man of status, a ruler. In the late nineteenth century, it was applied to the principal land owners in an area, men who were also frequently the main traders. They were expected to have sufficient land so that they could make it liberally available to *ahoi*; a man who refused to give *tha* in accordance with his status would not be regarded as a *muthamaki*.

46. 'Friendlies', though a Eurocentric designation, is used for want of a better word. Men who enlisted with caravans, the IBEAC and the Protectorate government were not necessarily friendly to any of these institutions; they exploited a resource, in this case work opportunities. That the early and most consistent contact of the local area was with C. W. R. Lane is supported by the record. His attempt to divide Kiambu into divisions and appoint unpaid headmen is reported in

    1909. October–December. *Ukamba Province Quarterly Report, Machakos District Political Record Book*, Vol. I (up to 1910), Part I.

47. I follow local tradition which regarded the concentration of power in the hands of wealthy men as a post-*Kirika* development. It is certain that the forest economy with its dispersed, isolated homesteads would not have supported this; the boundaries of each *mbari* would have been the boundaries of its power. Yet immediately before or after *Kirika* certain men wielded power beyond their *mbari*; they were able to orchestrate the break with Murang'a for ritual purposes. Though probably new to the local area, it may have indicated a continuance or revival of Murang'a conditions. It may also indicate that the development of the local area was a much longer, slower process, that the forest economy had ended well before *Kirika*, perhaps before another famine, and that oral traditions have 'collapsed' a much larger time-frame or ignored pre-*Kirika* events.

48. Cultural elaboration is apparent in the multiple sacrifices and the ornaments of wealthier men and women. The complexity of the political system indicates a large population and evidence shows that only those who had considerable wealth could fully participate. Leakey's description of Kikuyu economic, social, political and religious life, and his emphasis on cultural elaboration and sacrifices, is valid for the local area only for the last decades of the nineteenth century. It describes the life of the wealthy, who could meet the demands.

    1977. Leakey, L. S. B., *op. cit.*, Vols I, II, III.

49. The limited data in my possession indicate that, although the caravan trade was a motor of much of the late nineteenth-century change, the growth of small *mbari* was equally a factor. The number of large land owners had declined sharply, and their interests often ran counter to those of the small land owners. They needed greater power if they were to retain or obtain the right to direct their *mbari* and territories to their greatest advantage.

50. Payment was always made to a group which was senior to that of the payers; this group shared it again with those above them. At least part of it should be consumed, with the givers receiving a small share. Those who received goats sometimes shared the meat with the females of their households; often it was eaten only by males. This made the diet of older males heavy in meat; eating meat was associated with wealth in the twentieth century. Diets of women and children were oriented towards vegetable foods.

    1956. Leakey, L. S. B., 'The economics of Kikuyu tribal Life', in *East African Economics Review*, Vol. 3, No. 1, 1956, pp. 158–80.

51. Leakey refers to a unit above the *rugongo*, the *bururi*; he describes a highly organized system of delegated councils from the *matura* to the *bururi* and beyond. I am unable to confirm this; organization was different when seen from the perspective of large or small *mbari*; size of land, population and dependence all influenced participation. Elders used *bururi* not in reference to a specific, defined territory but in reference to unity beyond such boundaries. It was used frequently in songs and appeals to unity like *bururi witu*, this our land, or *bururi wa Agikuyu*, the land given to the Kikuyu by the ancestors. Though there was a sizeable population of Maasai origin, many local Kikuyu had come from a territory called Murang'a, some had come from Gaki. The area where they arrived was at that

From Kirika until the End of the Nineteenth Century

time not known as Kiambu. In the nineteenth century, an area near Kiambu township belonged to the *mbari kia Mbu*. In colonial times, three defined Kikuyu districts were created, Murang'a, Kiambu and Gaki; I do not know to what degree nineteenth-century boundaries of Murang'a and Gaki were the same as colonial Murang'a and Gaki.
1952. Leakey, L. S. B., *Mau Mau and the Kikuyu*, London: Methuen, p. 35.
1977. Leakey, L. S. B., *op. cit.*, pp. 8ff.

52. Initiation years and regiments were named after significant events; it might take several seasons for local names to be superseded by one name which was valid for a larger area. Leakey provides a rich description of the ceremonial involved in becoming *anake*; he also provides a wealth of detail about the relationships between junior and senior regiments and the generation set system. Research into initiation years and regiments for the nineteenth century, using genealogies and information of males born in the nineteenth but surviving into the twentieth century, does not indicate that initiation years and regiments were always formed according to precise timespans. Much depended on the number of those to be initiated, the ability of fathers to pay and the willingness of elders to allow initiations. The years can be used only for a rough dating system, which gets more reliable closer to the twentieth century. Given that until a few decades after *Kirika*, the Kiambu population was relatively small and dispersed, the organization into regiments, including the division into junior and senior sectors – which may have existed in Murang'a – must have taken time to develop.
1956. Lambert. H. E., *op. cit.*, pp. 40ff.
1972. Kershaw, Gretha, *op. cit.*, pp. 128ff.
1974. Muriuki, Godfrey, *op. cit.*, pp. 15ff.
1977. Leakey, L. S. B., *op. cit.*, Vol. II, pp. 587ff.

53. Before *Kirika*, *anake* returning from Murang'a initiations sought hospitality at homesteads of other initiates. Normally, travellers, whatever the reason for their journey, were advised to carry the *murica*, objects which symbolized that they were harmless travellers. They nevertheless might get out of hand and prey on the areas they traversed. Bands of *anake*, certainly by the late nineteenth century, were not trusted because – unless they were close to home – they were likely to get out of hand and prey on those they encountered. At least two reports of deaths in the genealogies were attributed to that cause. Whether the 'ceremonial rape' of a woman living outside the territory of the initiates by the *anake* was a reminder of this, or whether it developed independently, is unknown; it did continue for some time after the separation from Murang'a. The rape was by no means ceremonial for the woman, who could be seriously injured and might die. The consequence was likely to be raids and warfare; opposition to this may have contributed to the demise of the custom.

54. The initiation year was cursed and not cleansed until their fathers had paid heavy compensation.

55. Genealogical information rarely distinguishes whether death is due to warfare or raids. Both, when inflicted on the local community, killed women, children and other non-combatants, and defenders might lose their lives as genealogies show. Local males engaged in warfare or raids who took on a braver, larger or better-led enemy ran significant risks: one initiation year in about 1886 had by 1890 lost close to 10 per cent of its manpower. It fought one aggressive 'war'; smaller groups raided at least four times.

56. The various disasters are dated according to local events. Between 1870 and the end of the nineteenth century a margin of error of one to two years is quite possible; in the twentieth century the margin is more likely to be around one year. Although some disasters occurred in a wide area, some were more localized. Even if they had a wide distribution, fatalities differed. In some areas, contagious diseases were rigorously controlled by isolation; diseases which struck an area during the cold rainy season might have a much higher toll there than in a area where they occurred during the dry season. After particularly successful raids on the Maasai between 1886 and 1887, the local area suffered in 1889 an outbreak of *unere*, scabies, which was blamed on the Maasai who, having lost their herds to raids and rinderpest, came to the local area to exchange cattle for grain. According to elders, the local area at that time 'had too many people and

From Kirika until the End of the Nineteenth Century

cattle' because 'people kept coming from all over'. By 1891 'friendlies' from the caravan brought a new disease, *gatego*, syphilis. The food supply for men and animals was affected between 1890 and 1892 when several attacks of *ngigi*, locusts, depleted grazing land and harvests. In about 1892–3 endemic smallpox, *mutungu*, became particularly virulent and caused a number of deaths. Women could not plant on time and the next harvest suffered. Around that time sheep began to suffer a disease, which I have not been able to identify: 'their feet rotted and their tail, then they died'. This disease struck several times; some said it was contagious, others said that land where the animals had grazed could not be used for at least one season. After *mutungu*, only girls were initiated for several years because an *ituika* was held. Of the four female initiations, one was called after a severe outbreak of *ndutu*, jiggers which affected feet and hands; some died of gangrene, others were maimed. Another female initiation was *kagicha*, when at least some initiates suffered from burns. By 1897–8 male initiations resumed, but initiates were affected with *kienyeku*, sores, and smallpox broke out again. During 1897–8 the rains failed almost completely and millet was scarce; they failed again in the next two seasons and smallpox returned.
1988. Ambler, Charles Hart, *op. cit.*, Chapter 6.

57. *Ruraya* has several meanings, depending on what the speaker wants to convey. At its simplest it means large or far. The famine was large, and therefore *ruraya*. Some have linked the famine to European demands for food; although this may have been a factor in a few areas, the famine struck a much larger area than the one to which Europeans had access. If one wanted to attribute the famine to European machinations, however, *ruraya* could be interpreted this way. On the other hand, Wanyoike, the pastor of the local area in the twentieth century, attributed *ruraya* to the food which Europeans made available; the food came from afar, and the famine was called *ruraya* because of it.
1974. Wanyoike, E. N., *op. cit.* pp. 20ff.

58. Data cannot be regarded as highly reliable; they probably underestimate the real toll. If the famine was seen as a curse, many of those who died, particularly if a man and all his descendants died, would not be mentioned. Survivors might not mention husbands, wives or children who had died. Some information is available in
1972. Kershaw, Gretha, *op. cit.*, pp. 176ff.
1988. Ambler, Charles Hart, *op cit.*, Chapter 6.

59. Population data in the tables for the final years of the nineteenth century are calculations; from 1930 onwards data are somewhat more precise; data from genealogies are supplemented from then onwards with the recollections of a large number of the living. *Ahoi* are more likely to be underestimated than *mbari* members. Unless otherwise indicated, 1955 and 1962 data are based on a field census.

60. One missionary, T. N. Krieger, had set up camp at Thimbigua, not too far from the local area; he loved hunting and became known as *muratha*, friend, because he distributed meat on a regular basis. Other mission aid is described in
1970. Macpherson, R. *The Presbyterian Church in Kenya*, Nairobi: Kenya Litho Ltd., pp. 28ff.

61. During the nineteenth century less land was under forest than before, though most *mbari* maintained forest on the boundaries of their land even when all land had been cleared. New buyers, who could not afford cleared land, might have to buy land that was still covered by forest. *Anake* used these forests as their lair, they built *koria*, shelters, and raided homesteads which still had food, or ambushed those returning with relief food from trading or mission stations. Of particular notoriety were ambushes near Ngenda and Kamiti. According to elders, none of the attackers were local men; they belonged to the *mariika* of Ngigi, Mutungu, and Kienyeku. As late as 1956 elders refused to go into detail: when I asked questions, I was told in no uncertain terms to change the subject. Elders did admit that the behaviour had been evil, that the young men had been called Mau Mau, and that this was a general term to indicate anger with wrong behaviour. However, the term can also be used to explain why people behave wrongly and where the ultimate guilt should be placed. A child who eats greedily can be admonished to eat properly by using Mau Mau, but it can also indicate that the mother is at fault for starving the child.
1974. Muriuki, Godfrey, *op. cit.*, pp. 94, 95, 155.

Three

Land Ownership in the Twentieth Century

Earlier chapters have dealt with the acquisition of local land and highlighted the differences between large and small land owners, land poor and landless. Conflict over acquisitions dating from the nineteenth century would play a role in Mau Mau conflict. The next three chapters will continue the history of conflict but concentrate on the determinants of ordinary membership.

This chapter deals with access to land and its consequences; the next discusses to what degree wages could substitute for lack of land. Chapter 5 pulls these data together, indicating why Mau Mau, for a large sector of land poor or landless, became the only hope. The final two chapters deal with political factors which affected local households and Mau Mau itself.

Immediate post-famine conditions

Because of the high death toll in the disasters, most men had inherited land and had larger tracts than before; there was more than enough for surviving *ahoi* as well. Restoration of the food supply and the herds had high priority; many needed help from *ngwatio*, the exchange of labour within a descent group and between kin.[1] There was little trade, the railway had reached Nairobi and there was no need for tributary *ahoi*; some of the refugees who had sought shelter in the area became new and affinal *ahoi*.[2] By 1900 surviving and new *ahoi* constituted probably close to 40 per cent of the Igi and 10 per cent of the Thuita population.

The *thirikari* remained important as a potential employer and source of adventure for young males; older males with large holdings hoped soon to produce sufficiently to renew trade connections. They consented in about 1901 to begin the collection of tribute they had agreed to earlier for the protection of the trade which had been postponed because of the disasters. Kimama wa Macharuga was the main collector; elders helped and sometimes drove goats to the collection centres or confiscated goats from those who did not pay. Tribute could also be paid in coin; in the first years collectors were lenient because goats and coin were in short supply. People often paid out of fear, wanting to avoid the retaliatory raids of the *thirikari* or its servants, like Kinyanyui wa Gathirimu who would become paramount chief (Appendix III/1). Because Kimama was killed in 1902 in a *thirikari*-sponsored raid, Waweru Mahui, a son of the same father but a different mother, took over his work, including the collection of tribute.[3]

Local land alienation

Elders were aware that in the last decade of the nineteenth century Kikuyu land had been taken by Europeans and that Kikuyu had sold or given land under threat or in exchange for trade privileges. Local opinion held that, because these transactions had not followed proper ritual, Europeans would fail to prosper and eventually leave; elders nevertheless had no intention of selling any part of their land. They trusted that the *thirikari*, their partners in trade, would back them in keeping Europeans out.[4] That they occasionally camped for a few months in the south-eastern area of *mbari* land caused little concern. It had not been allowed before, but had certain advantages.

> Around Kamande (1902–3) a *muthungu* had built close to where ... was cultivating. He lived with another *muthungu* who hunted a great deal. That was good, because game had become very bold during *Ruraya*. He was like a Ndorobo, only better because he had guns to protect the goats. He gave the meat to the Kamba who were with him. I do not know when they went or why they went but one day they left and soon another one came. Before *Gatiti* (1903–4) there had been at least three others. I do not know why this was....

The temporary settlers sometimes hired local men as gunbearers or guards; they might buy food for their retainers.

One arrival during *Gatiti* (1903–4) created more concern as he was accompanied by a woman and children, built a more substantial hut and permitted his retinue to break the ground in an area which he had demarcated with pegs. Though he offered work to local young males and was willing to pay in cash or the highly desired seed potatoes, his behaviour suggested that he regarded the land as his.[5]

The land was covered with bush; part of it belonged to Thuita and Igi, most of it had undergone first and subsequent clearings before the famine, but by *Gatiti* only part had been recleared. It was not empty land: some of the new *ahoi* cultivated and herded in it; younger males used it for herding. Homesteads – probably no more than fifteen Igi and Thuita *mbari* members and six *ahoi* – were still small: most of the owners and their older *ahoi* lived in the higher, agricultural holdings.

The protest of the elders and Waweru was rebuffed; the angry settler demanded that those who already resided on the land leave or pay tribute in stock, food and labour. The *anake* wanted to drive him out; elders, while anxious to regain control of the land, were determined to prevent exploits which could only end disastrously. The number of seasoned *anake* who had survived the famine or returned to the community was small, so was the number of new recruits. Only 16 males, well below half the number of the last pre-famine years, had been old enough for initiation in *Kamande* (1902–3). Better that the *thirikari* take care of the settler; its action would also teach the *anake* who were already again chafing under restrictions that the elders and Waweru had strong backing.

Waweru and several senior elders went to see *Njue-ini*, J. D. Ainsworth, who lived 'close to where the Coryndon Museum is today' and asked for a punitive expedition against the settler.

The gist of their interview was that the *thirikari* backed the European; the Kikuyu should understand that conditions had changed. The *thirikari* remained interested in trade, but its prime objective was now 'development' for which it needed Europeans; because they came from countries where people owned their land, they had the right to own it here. They would get 'papers' which proved their rights; the *thirikari* would protect anyone with 'papers', if necessary by force. It would tolerate neither raiding nor theft which would be punished with forfeiture of stock.[6]

The Kikuyu protest that they owned the land was countered by the statement that they did not and never had; if they had paid at all, they had paid at most for temporary occupation and usufruct. They could not get 'papers' to protect what was left after the Europeans had taken what they wanted. The *thirikari* would protect Kikuyu rights to use the land as long as they worked it properly.[7] They would eventually learn what ownership was all about; when they reached the appropriate stage, they would be able to apply for 'papers'.[8]

The interview turned friendship and cooperation into enmity; land alienation marked the beginning of the colonial era and the resistance.

By 1908–9, the time of the *Nyaregi* initiation, significant appropriations had ceased, but smaller tracts continued to be taken until the end of the First World War for 'boundary adjustment', 'right of way' or 'the common good.' Between the First and Second World Wars land was taken for public services – often outside Kikuyu reach – though some compensation was paid.[9]

Alienation was not a definitive, clear-cut process; Kikuyu did not always know whether, how much and by whom land had been taken. The erratic behaviour of Europeans made life insecure; alienation was sometimes only temporary; settlers paid a visit, declared a certain area to be theirs, disappeared and the Kikuyu could continue as before. Sometimes land remained alienated, but 'owned' by a succession of men; each might declare a boundary, do some desultory clearing and leave to be followed – sometimes several seasons later – by someone else. In the midst of this a surveyor would come out, measure and 'draw a line' but the boundaries drawn for the sitting might be different from those drawn for previous owners. If the land were sold, the next owner might claim other boundaries; a new surveyor might well follow this lead.

Some settlers did little with their land; others cultivated a variety of crops and had stock. Until settlers started to grow coffee in about 1904–5, Kikuyu and Akamba hired by the settlers, outnumbered the Europeans on alienated land.[10] Over time the Kikuyu would feel forced to leave. Individual stories may differ, but they end alike.

> It was land of my grandfather they took. He belonged to *Mburu* and his father had died in *Ruraya*. So he had a lot of land which he shared with others who survived. The Europeans took about half of it and the line went straight through a plot which had bananas around it and maize, beans, potatoes [?] and sweet potatoes on it. The *muthungu* had a wife who would send a servant to buy food. Sometimes she came herself and then she would tell my mother how clever she was that she could grow such good food. When my father talked with the *muthungu* and told him that he was on his land, the European would say that there had been no one on it. His wife had just gotten food from that same land; if there had been no one, who had cleared the land....

> [He] had cultivated for a long time and a *muthungu* had sometimes been there for a few seasons. Then another *muthungu* settled on the land which had been used for grazing ... went and worked for the *muthungu* for three moons. Then the *muthungu* started to plow over [his] cultivated land with a plough until the door of his hut. Then [he] left because there was no place for his goats and his children....

> [He] was living on the land and a *muthungu* came and employed [him] for some years. Then [he] saw that the European paid him badly. Later when the land was drawn over [his] land, the *muthungu* said it was all his and [he] moved to the other side of the line because he would have to pay for grazing his cows and not have any more payment for his labour....

> [He] worked for a *muthungu* for a season. When he came to get his money, the *muthungu* told him to bring five female goats the next day, the *muthungu* took the goats and did not give [him] money, because he said [he] had used the land of the *muthungu* for grazing. But [he] knew that the land was his....

The government had developed some rules for compensation, through a fee system; in the hands of poor and greedy settlers it opened the door to severe abuse. Settlers needed to pay government for 'unused' and used land; they needed Kikuyu permission and had to pay them for used, but not for unused or under-used land.[11] It was in the interest of settlers to declare the land unused or under-used; owners with fallow land or land which was not yet or only partially cleared after the famine, ran the greatest risk. Such land was a bargain for the settler who could start planting without costly heavy clearing.

Settlers had little difficulty finding 'under-used' or unused land; though post-famine clearing was in progress, homesteads, cultivation and herds were still thin on the ground, particularly in the lower lands, which the settlers coveted.

Although government inspectors were supposed to protect Kikuyu land which was already cleared and used, ruthless settlers could make used land look under-used by the time a surveyor came out: it did not take much persuasion to get the Kikuyu to move if their stock was chased away, their homesteads demolished and their crops uprooted. If the surveyor discovered foul play, the worst which could happen to the settler was that he was denied permission to buy that particular tract. If it was discovered later the settler would be fined, but he did not need to vacate the land.

Stories abounded of flagrant abuse of those Kikuyu who had stayed on the land after it had been taken over; yet few informants had personal experiences of severe abuse. They believed that they were treated more leniently because settlers had come to depend on them and their kinsmen, who provided labour and food.[12]

Settler demand for labour from those who stayed on the land was limited initially to some hours of clearing each day in exchange for settling and grazing rights. The burden became more onerous when settlers imported their own stock, often demanding that Kikuyu reduce their herds.[13] When settlers started to plant coffee, goats and sheep were no longer welcome, but cows could be kept, if penned at night, as long as the settlers got the manure. At that time demands for labour also increased; households which did not provide several members were apt to be evicted.

Yet a number of Kikuyu stayed; recent *ahoi*, who had come during the famine but whose protectors had lost land, feared that they would not be offered other land. They needed time to accumulate goats to buy land elsewhere.[14] Owners were afraid to leave as the settler was sure to bring in other Kikuyu or *Akamba* who would regard themselves as owners when the Europeans left. Eventually, most were nevertheless forced out; the final straw was that the settlers allowed each household only a few acres of land, and increased the hours of work, demanding that more household members made themselves available. Some returned to the Kikuyu areas; a number of them became wage labourers in the settled area; not infrequently, they worked for the same settler from whose land they had been evicted.

Losses through land alienation

The standard amount the Kikuyu could claim as compensation for some alienated land (shs 2/50 per acre, sometimes increased to shs 4/–) was more a reward for peaceful abandonment than compensation. Money was inadequate in every sense of the word: Kikuyu thought that a productive item – be it land, stock or women – should be exchanged for other productive items, and they looked down on the Ndorobo who ate goats instead of breeding them.

Local land prices can give some idea of Kikuyu losses. The cost of the higher elevation land had varied from 1 to 4 goats per acre depending on when and by whom it was bought; the cost of lower elevation land in 1870 was about 1 goat; by 1890 it might be as much as 2 goats. Using the cash value of goats for 1902–3, one acre of virgin higher elevation land could have cost between shs 4/20 and shs 16/80; the cost of lower elevation land would have been between shs 4/20 and shs 8/40 (Appendix IV/2).[15]

If Europeans took partially or fully cleared land, they saved a great deal of back-breaking labour. In 1956 men calculated that it would take 500 days of male labour to clear one acre of heavy bush, including trees, by hand. In 1902 Kambui Mission paid adult males shs 6/– for 24 days of work. Clearing one acre of land would therefore have cost more than shs 120/–. Perhaps the most telling statistic is that every grant of 640 acres of lower land would have provided basic food for 150 households, year after year.

Immediate consequences of the loss of land

An educated estimate would be that the *mbari* which lived in Thuita in 1956 lost at least 400 out of 1,100 acres; if some *mbari* were wiped out completely, and went elsewhere without leaving a local history, it lost more. Igi lost roughly 600 acres from perhaps 1,700 acres *mbari* land and 400 acres of private land out of a possible 1,000 acres. The losses were unequally divided between *ithaku* in both; some lost little, some 30 per cent, some 70 per cent of their land. As the losses had mainly concerned land at lower elevations, those whose land had been predominantly there lost most. This included those who had asked for their inheritance in herding land and those who had come to Thuita late in the nineteenth century or in Igi had participated mainly in the last acquisitions. Two versions from Igi *arumati* indicate the losses:

Version I
Kungu lost most of the private land he had left, it may have been over 200 acres. Chege and Njau also lost, Chege more than Njau.[16] Within *mbari* land, the large number of descendants of Mwereri lost most; the losses of all those who had joined in the last acquisitions were severe. Gitau, who had joined late, lost most of his land.

Version II
Mwereri and Gitau owned land in the higher elevations. Gitau owned land there on the basis of earlier purchases.[17] Although he lost much

of his lower land, he retained the rights to the higher area land and should have received it.

The Kikuyu belief that the European occupation would be short-lived was a factor in the relatively peaceful abandonment of the land; even those who had lost significantly did not regard this loss as final. Most apparently did not move – or could not afford to move – to areas where land was still available.

That the *mbari* itself did not own the land but that individuals within it did, was demonstrated amply after alienation. However severe the losses, no *githaku* and no individual apparently claimed land from others; redistribution of the remaining land was considered neither in Igi nor in Thuita. Some would later claim that their fathers or grandfathers at that time should have demanded it, but did not do so because they expected the stolen lands to be returned.

Whether members who had lost would receive help from their immediate kin, their *ithaku* or the *mbari*, depended on various factors. Losers whose fathers still had undistributed land were at an advantage as they might receive a new inheritance. Others got some land from one source or another – but as users, not owners. All *mbari* members who had lost were given priority in user rights over any land within their *githaku* and *mbari*; some got all the land they needed, some got only cultivation land with little fallowing or herding land.

The exercise of their user rights worsened the position of *ahoi*; although there is no record that established *ahoi* were dispossessed for them, sons of *ahoi* could, from this period onwards, no longer be certain that they would inherit all the user rights of their father. They had the right to ask for land from other *ithaku* or *mbari* than those who had given land to their fathers, but only land owners with exceptionally large tracts could provide what they needed. The most secure *ahoi* in the past had been men who had married daughters or mother's sisters of members; after alienation owners were less inclined to give their daughters or younger sisters to *ahoi*.

Land alienation aggravated inequality within *mbari* and in *ithaku* between close kinsmen: a man might have been unaffected by alienation and retained close to fifty acres, while his brother, whose land had been taken, had only five acres left. The wealthier man might allow his brother to use his land, but this would make one brother the *muhoi* of another.[18] This inequality was deeply felt and resented: caused by land alienation, it was not the result of decisions of the spiritual forces but of men who, by taking the land, opposed what the ancestors had intended.

The opening of the Rift Valley

The immediate consequences of alienation were softened because of government-promoted European settlement in the Rift Valley. As did a number of newcomers, local settlers who had alienated land decided around *Njege* (1906–7) to try their luck there; they invited their resident labour to join them with other *mbari* members and their herds. Those who accompanied them would be free to use any land not needed by the settler in exchange for a number of days of work.

The majority of the local population strongly opposed the move as inappropriate fission. Although eventually more land would be needed and many had lost land, *mbari* members who left the settled area could still be accommodated; herds were still small and new settlers might well allow the population to use the alienated land for herding. By the time more land was urgently needed, the stolen lands would have come back as settlers went home.

The *mbari* should stay together and wait out the disaster of human wickedness; leaving would only provoke more alienation because the government would declare more land under-used. The present was admittedly difficult, but the land would return, the encirclement which prevented expansion would be broken, and the *mbari* would buy more land. It was foolish to trust the promises of Europeans; once Kikuyu labour and Kikuyu herds had made the land fertile, the Europeans would expel them and their herds.

The counter-arguments of those who wanted to go was that local alienation would continue whether they went or not, because no settlers were ever content with what they had; new settlers would not only come but also want even more land than the earlier ones. The land which was still in *mbari* hands might become endangered; ideas of expanding herds and buying land were dreams. The warning that the Kikuyu in the Rift Valley would become little more than tributary *ahoi* ignored that tributary *ahoi* could not herd, while they would be able to use as much land as they wanted. If anything, those who had stayed on alienated land had been tributary *ahoi*; they had provided the settler with labour, food and manure, and all they got in return was the use of a little bit of land.

European promises could not be trusted, wherever they were; Rift Valley Europeans would certainly not honour their promises to the Kikuyu when they needed the land the Kikuyu would be using. But this was not likely to come soon; Europeans in the Rift Valley had much more land than local settlers; and long before the land ran out, the returning strength of the Kikuyu would have forced them to leave. Those who had settled with them could then take the land by rights of *kuna* or first clearing. The Maasai had left of their own free will; the Europeans had never owned the land legitimately and so the land would count as abandoned.[19]

Neither side convinced the other; some elders were so dismayed that they put a *kirumi* on their departing kinsmen forbidding them to return.[20]

Some Thuita *mbari* which had lost all their land may have gone; no other *mbari* or *githaku* went as a whole. That those who went treated it as fission to new land is evident in that the rules of fission were followed: those who departed belonged predominantly to senior segments of *mbari* and *ithaku*; they were accompanied by their senior elders and also by some men, including *anake*, from junior *ithaku*. Most took at least a sector of their *ahoi*; local *ahoi* did not go alone. Quite a few of those who stayed behind sent some of their stock with those who went to the Rift Valley.

Based on the data – probably not too unreliable data – provided by Kikuyu who returned from the Rift Valley before and during the Emergency – Igi lost at least ten *mbari* and eight *ahoi* households between *Njege* (1906/7) and the year before *Makio* (1912/13); the corresponding losses for Thuita were eleven and three.[21] About half of the *mbari* members who went before 1912 had lost land; yet none would be landless in their generation. Most left between ten and twelve acres behind; the smallest tracts were about eight acres, the largest fifty. None, it seems, sold their land.

After the First World War individuals and their households might join kin settlements in the Rift Valley if these allowed them to come; asking them to take local stock, passing it off as their own, was no exception either. Rift Valley Kikuyu had large herds early on; it was their herds, not their use of land for agriculture, that sparked the first restrictions by the 1920s. Rift Valley Kikuyu dealt with this by demanding that Kiambu kin take their stock back.

Initially, local Kikuyu went predominantly to the Nakuru-Naivasha area; most seem to have stayed there although they did 'change Europeans'. Others moved between Rift Valley areas. It was not uncommon for those who did to leave at least a small section behind to guard their *kuna* rights, in order to be in a position to claim the land when the time came. The same was done when Kikuyu repatriated themselves or were repatriated during the Emergency (Appendix VI).

Until the 1920s the local population maintained a good deal of contact with the Rift Valley kinsmen when they visited to discuss kinship affairs and matters of stock. As the development of the local population and their Rift Valley relatives diverged, contact declined; those who had left were increasingly seen as a fissioned segment which had left against the will of the *mbari* elders, retaining only few rights. Those who had stayed behind did not get rights in the new land; stock they had sent with those who went had continued to belong to those who stayed at home. Rift Valley men no longer sought wives from the local population but from other Rift Valley settlers; legal obligations, such as help with paying fines or indemnities, were less and less recognized. When the Rift Valley relatives – often a second generation – at last came back before or during the Emergency, problems were frequent because they were thought to have gone for the duration and their land had been put to other use. According to elders:

Oral traditions of Igi: Version I
A senior segment of Mwereri went to the Rift Valley and gave part of its land to Gitau in use; some was bush. Gitau did not clear much of it, because several of their households had also gone to the Rift Valley. In the 1930s a Government official demanded that it be cleared. The *mbari* then asked the remaining – and returning – Gitau members to

clear it with their *ahoi*; Gitau considered that the land had been given to them in part compensation for what they had lost in the nineteenth century.

Version II
Mwereri gave the land to Gitau only in use; it was not meant to compensate Gitau; there was no reason that they should do so.

Consequences of the loss of land in the early decades

Whether they owned the land or only used it, all land owners and *ahoi* had lost a great deal of herding land in alienation. This made it difficult to rebuild the herds; need for herding land became pressing when the herds expanded and many could no longer breed sufficient stock for bridewealths, nor receive them.[22] The refugee population was affected earliest; they had rarely been given enough herding land beyond what was needed for a maintenance herd.[23] In the early years men could send stock to Rift Valley relatives, to Ndeia, to Kamba, Embu, Maasai or Kikuyu in other areas, but this would not last and required supervision and care. Initially the refugees pinned their hopes on the return of the land, pressuring the government to restore their rights, but by 1915 they knew that, even if the land was returned, it would take years before it could again be used for herding as it had been terraced and planted to coffee.

Between *Makio* (1912/13) and *Kihiumweri* (1916/17) the government's *barazas* which Waweru and elders had to attend often focused on Kikuyu demands for the return of the land and the issue of title; *barazas* were also places where the government provided information about its policies. One of the most important *barazas* was held in 1915; it dealt with new and clarified older policies concerning the 'reserves' and introduced the 1915 Crown Lands Ordinance.[24]

An earlier *baraza* had announced that the *thirikari* had 'drawn a line' around Kikuyu country; this *baraza* explained that the Kikuyu within the line did not own the land but were to be 'tenants at will of the Crown'.[25] Land lost to alienation would not be returned but no more land would be taken and Kikuyu would have exclusive rights within 'the lines'.[26] As they were not owners, they would not get 'papers'; but government would protect the integrity of the reserve and the 'tribe' within the lines against further alienation, though this meant neither protection of individual boundaries nor recognition of individual ownership (Appendix III/2).

Loss of herding land, monetization and bridewealth
This forced the Kikuyu to seek other solutions, and monetization became one answer to lack of herding land. When smaller land owners and *ahoi* had insufficient land to raise or receive stock, they could no longer give or receive stock in payment. Larger land owners were therefore similarly

Land Ownership in the Twentieth Century

restricted: in a relatively short time most land owners reduced the emphasis on stock and herding. By the 1920s smaller land owners had reduced their flocks to perhaps a dozen goats; only the wealthier had more than a maintenance herd and were changing from goats to cattle. Money was beginning to replace stock when payments had to be made, with far reaching consequences.

Because of the reproductive capability of goats, any man with sufficient herding land and labour could over time produce a herd which would provide for his household's needs. A father, knowing that he would have to pay a brideprice for a son, might set one fertile goat aside when the boy was five or six years old; by the time the boy was in his twenties, careful breeding would allow him to pay a brideprice of ninety goats.

Bridewealth

The shift from stock to cash meant a shift from a productive medium to an unproductive one: cash. If the father had only limited herding land and needed to pay a brideprice of shs 1,000/- in cash, he had two equally impossible options. He could sell six goats each year from his maintenance herd at shs 11/- for 15 years, impossible because he could not replace them by breeding the few who remained. Or he could – assuming that he was an unskilled agricultural labourer – save three months' wages at shs 22/- a month for 15 years, which was equally impossible.

Monetization was probably the major factor in the increase in brideprices, as recipients tried to compensate for the lower value of cash: goats they could have bred into more goats, cash could not be bred into more cash, unless one had enough of it to buy land. By the First World War payments ranged between 60 and 65 goats; by the early 1920s brideprices were rarely below 70 and slowly climbing.[27] In 1917 livestock accounted for 90 to 100 per cent of the brideprice; by 1925 it was down to between 30 and 40 per cent. By 1935 at least 80 to 90 per cent was expected in cash (Appendix IV/7).

Payment in cash changed the relationship and cooperative patterns between many fathers and their sons as well as marriage patterns in general. When a large part of the brideprice had to be paid in cash, only the wealthiest fathers continued to pay for their sons' brideprice; other fathers decreased constantly what they paid, ultimately paying at best the ceremonial goats which would be eaten as a token of the new alliance. When the burden was shifted to the sons, they, knowing that they would be old before they had accumulated a brideprice, married before the brideprice had been paid, then paid it slowly over the first 20 years of marriage. Fathers of daughters could not object: it was the best they could expect. Fathers of sons could not object either; their nominal contribution took the matter out of their hands. Left in the hands of younger males who accepted that they would pay over time, when they could, the age of marriage slowly dropped. By the 1940s it was not uncommon for an 18-year-old male – not in school – to have a wife.

Indebtedness often haunted marital relationships; wives knew that they were not legal members of their husband's *mbari* until the brideprice had been paid; they were in limbo: no longer full members of their own *mbari*. but not yet members of their husband's *mbari*. When children were born, they were members of the husband's *mbari;* but because the wife was not a full member of that *mbari*, her interests in the children could be ignored, if conflicts arose. Conversely, the husband's interest in the children could be ignored: if the brideprice was not fully paid, it could be argued that the children did not – yet – belong to their father's *mbari* and – in conflict – the mother could take them to her *mbari* of origin. Husbands and wives were held hostage to the unpaid brideprice; any unexpected bonus a father earned or gained was likely to go to pay the brideprice without direct benefit to his family. By the 1950s the instalments paid to the brideprice might well finance the education of the son of a man's affines, while he was hard-pressed to pay the education of his own son at the same time.

Monetization and land acquisitions

Because insufficient land was available to breed larger herds, buying land became more difficult because accumulating sufficient cash was outside the reach of most. Fathers with small holdings, unable to acquire more, could not provide sons with sufficiencies. Sons often had to share already small tracts, leading to increased fragmentation.

Whether in response to monetization or not, prices of land had also risen; after the 1930s the increased productivity of land was certainly a factor. Higher prices restricted transactions to small tracts; only the wealthier could buy larger tracts. Prices of land continued to be expressed in goats, though cash payments had taken over: before the First World War land was paid in goats; by 1920 goats were still important though 20 per cent of the price was expected in cash. By 1926 this had risen to 70 per cent. By 1930 cash would become still more important and payments in stock would amount to no more than 10 per cent of the price. Ceremonial payments would continue to be paid in stock if at all possible, whether they accompanied brideprices or land.[28]

Land prices were not only determined by size and fertility; the status of the parties involved was equally important. Men with high status and good connections paid less because the seller – in addition to the price – had the right to expect future support from the buyer, with whom he had entered into a kinship relationship through land.

The influence of high and low status on prices of land can be seen in the few transactions which took place before the Carter Commission Report.[29] The first, large local acquisition was paid in goats; the buyer was an important local office holder (Appendix IV/2). *Arumati* and senior elders provided the following data:

Land Ownership in the Twentieth Century

Oral traditions of Igi
One nineteenth-century Igi member had been an important trader who contributed heavily to all buying of land.[30] After the famine, few male descendants were alive; one son, who had lost at least one wife and her children, inherited a large area of land. Industrious and hardworking, he soon resumed trade and inherited the position of headman when a close kinsman died. He married many wives, had many sons and gave *tha* to his daughter's husbands and their relatives. During *Kihiumweri* (around 1916–17) he bought a hundred-acre plot from a Thuita *mbari*. The seller left. Some said he went to Kiambu where his sons inherited, some that he had other land in Thuita, others that he had no Thuita land with the result that his sons locally became *ahoi*. They had the right to expect *tha* from the buyer, possibly as *ahoi*. The price of the land was about one goat per acre; with ceremonial payments it worked out to roughly shs 1100/–.

Three other Igi men bought; one in about 1920 and two in about 1925. They belonged to important *ithaku* but were as yet too young to reap much benefit from this. One got about seven acres, two about 16 acres. All paid cash; the 1920 buyer paid at a rate of shs 75/– per acre, the others shs 125/– per acre (Appendix III/2).

In Thuita three small transactions took place; in one half an acre changed hands between equals for shs 75/–. Another transaction took place between a Thuita *mbari* member and someone who was probably a – new Igi *muhoi*. The third sale was to a man for whom the acquisition would mark the start of a *mbari*; the high price reflected that he was an outsider.

Oral traditions of Thuita
Two *anake* had come during the famine, they stayed in the Igi lower lands where they lived from trapping. Later they became Igi *ahoi* and exchanged wives with them. While with Igi, they were visited by kinsmen, two brothers who bought between two and three acres of land in Thuita. The price was unknown, but it was 'many goats'. At a later date the brothers quarrelled because one took the other's wife. He fled, sold his land and became a *muhoi* to his wife's father. The other brother continued, had children and by 1962 had begun to call his small descent group a *mbari*.[31]

Before the famine a man in Murang'a suffered great misfortunes from the Maasai; in the famine he also lost badly. He cursed his land, left and became a resident worker on alienated land. The European allowed him to herd but after his death the sons were obliged to sell. They bought land, somewhat more than two acres; the 'goat' price was 120 for the whole land; the cash price close to shs 500/– per acre.

The position of the *ahoi*

Before colonial times, a number of owners had sufficient land to attract and hold *ahoi*; they had provided marriage partners for each other, complex patterns of affinity cemented the relationships. This had been true to a lesser extent in the land-poor Thuita *mbari* than in land-rich Igi. Most Thuita men had bought smaller acreages; when their descent groups expanded in the nineteenth century they needed all their land. Their *ahoi* – and they themselves – might ask Igi for help. The population reduction of the famine again left some land for *ahoi*; but they had to give way again when the *mbari* expanded anew.[32]

In the nineteenth century some *ahoi* of Igi, through multiple ties of affinity with *ithaku*, had built a network of security that increased rather than diminished through the famine. So much land was left untenanted at that time, that Igi attracted new *ahoi*; by the time of alienation, these men had not yet built strong ties with the *mbari*.

After the famine, sufficient land had been available for owners and *ahoi*; *ahoi* who, with owners, lost land to alienation, were accommodated in what *mbari* land remained. The newer *ahoi* were at a disadvantage: because their affinal ties with *mbari* members were limited, they had greater difficulty in finding new sponsors and, when they got land, they were apt to get less than those who could claim extensive kinship ties. Judging from the Rift Valley Emergency repatriates, more newer than older *ahoi* had accompanied the land owners to the Rift Valley.

It is evident from genealogies that *ahoi*, even the oldest and most established ones, had engaged to a lesser extent in polygyny than members of *ithaku* with a great deal of land. These men had – after the famine – immediately increased the number of their wives but not so the *ahoi*: in the early twentieth century their level of polygyny was significantly lower than that of senior *mbari* members.[33]

Though the *ahoi* population expanded at a lower rate and continued to lose younger members who found wives and land elsewhere, they occupied enough land for land owners, who in the 1920s felt pressure from marriageable sons, to seek to reduce their acreage. Newer *ahoi* and sons of older *ahoi* found *mbari* members less eager to provide them with land or daughters, as this often meant providing land as well. Most *ahoi* fathers were encouraged to share with their sons; but no new land was made available. This worsened in the 1930s and 1940s; in addition to having to share what they had, *ahoi* could not hold on to what they 'always' had used. Moreover, *ahoi* sons grew up with the fair certainty that they would not inherit their fathers' user rights. They sought to leave; over the decades the *ahoi* population in Thuita would decline, as would Igi *ahoi* households in relation to *mbari* members. Overall, *ahoi* households were likely to be older.[34]

When *ahoi* married from outside the *mbari*, they, like members of poorer *ithaku*, could no longer bring their wife's kin on the land. The marriage of *ahoi* daughters into the *mbari* no longer meant the certainty of land rights for their kin.

The luckiest got small pieces of land from a number of land-owning kinsmen instead of one or two larger tracts from one; those *ahoi* whose kinship ties were limited were at a disadvantage. As early as the late 1920s, *mbari* members with small acreages could no longer provide their sons with sufficiencies; by the time of the Carter Commission, even the most established *ahoi* could no longer count on sufficient land.

Land holdings before the Carter Commission, early 1930s

After the famine a larger than usual number of *mbari* males had engaged in extensive polygyny; initiations of the second and the beginning of the third decade showed the result. Close to fifty males born after the famine were initiated with *Kinyotoku* (1919/20). They were followed by the even larger initiations of *Chirringi* (1923/4) and *Ndege* (1926/7), and from then onwards – with a few smaller years in between – the number of males reaching adulthood rarely abated.[35] By the 1940s the last sons born to the last wives of adult famine survivors were joined by the first-born sons of sons of first wives. A few years after initiation these males wanted to marry and needed land; after the 1920s the demand for land would relentlessly cut down what men had saved from land alienation. Many fathers had difficulty in giving even one son a sufficiency.[36]

Tables 2.1 and 2.2 in Chapter 2 showed the approximate growth in households; Table 3.1 in this chapter gives a calculation of the probable distribution of land ownership around the time of the Carter Commission and just before the Emergency.[37] The data gain in reliability as they come closer to the Emergency.

By the 1930s *ahoi* as well as small land owners might well use land of larger land owners: a man with twenty acres and as yet no sons, who claimed land, might use land for domestic production, fallowing, herding and some cash crops, but still have five acres for others, less favoured. By the 1950s correspondence between ownership and use was closer.

Table 3.1 shows the legal distribution of land before the Carter Commission and before the Emergency. Chapter 5 will discuss the close relationship between size of land and well-being; here it is important to remember that size of land is an imperfect measure of what a particular tract can produce. Similar-sized tracts may vary widely; factors of location, rainfall, maintenance, labour and size of household all play a role in what is possible.

Land ownership was divided into several categories; the terms used do not follow particular theories; the designation 'peasant', for instance, is used without prejudice; the many definitions extant do not come sufficiently close to this particular local population.[38] All the land claimed was taken into account; no consideration was given to the potential of the land, such as whether it was too steep, too stony or too wet.

Land owners were first divided into small and larger land owners; small holders were subdivided into subsistence plot owners and small peasants. The subsistence plot owners are often identified as land poor;

Land Ownership in the Twentieth Century

Table 3.1 Classification of Igi and Thuita households by land ownership before the Carter Commission and before the Emergency

Categories of households by land ownership	Igi				Thuita			
	Before Carter 1931/3		Before Declaration of the Emergency, 1952		Before Carter 1931/3		Before Declaration of the Emergency, 1952	
Ahoi	59	28.9%	94	25.7%	14	12.7%	13	6.4%
Ownership								
Subsistence plot owners[a]	23	11.3%	110	30.1%	42	38.2%	133	65.5%
Small peasants[b]	26	12.7%	44	12.0%	28	25.5%	38	18.7%
Peasants[c]	63	30.9%	95	26.0%	25	22.7%	19	9.4%
Small farmers[d]	27	13.2%	20	5.5%	1	0.9%	—	—
Farmers[e]	6	2.9%	3	0.8%	—	—	—	—
TOTALS	204	99.9%	366	100.1%	110	100.0%	203	100.0%

a Owning less than 3.99 acres.
b Owning 4–6.99 acres.
c Owning 7–19.99 acres.
d Owning 20–59.99 acres.
e Owning 60 acres and over.

they had at most 3.99 acres, but by the Emergency men in this group more often had less than 2.5 acres than more. Under favourable conditions, such as small households, they could grow basic food and herd a few goats. Those with less than 2.5 acres could neither grow sufficient basic food nor graze stock on their land. Small peasants had between 4 and 6.99 acres; ideally, they could grow basic food and have some surplus for barter or a few more goats. All smallholders – and the landless *ahoi* – as early as the Carter Commission would be dependent on larger land owners and on wage income; as a group they could not provide sons with sufficient land, nor with wives.

Larger land owners were subdivided into three groups. Peasants owned between 7 and 19.99 acres; they were able to grow basic food and surplus. The small farmers (20 – 59.99 acres) and the farmers (over 60 acres) had often developed their land along modern production lines. They were involved in commodity production well before the Carter Commission, though at that time income from cash crops was low. Herding, therefore, had remained important; these men also strengthened their social and political position by providing *tha* in land to *ahoi* and small holders. Peasants might be able to provide a modest holding for sons and make a goodly contribution to their brideprice, as could small farmers and farmers who were likely to be able to provide their sons with full brideprices. Even the small farmers were concerned that they, if they had numerous descendants – perhaps the consequence of polygyny – could give no more than small peasant holdings to their sons. Those who could, would still be concerned about what would happen to grandsons.

Table 3.1 indicates that *mbari* members in Igi owned in general more land than those in Thuita, but that Igi was responsible for a large group of *ahoi*. While most of them would not use more than the smallest land owners, until the Carter Commission some used a good deal more. The *ahoi* would decline with the availability of land; their needs would decline with the aging of a population which was losing its sons. Just before the Declaration of the Emergency, it was a rare *muhoi* who had more than two acres.

The decline of land for *mbari* members is also obvious. By the Carter Commission only 11.3 per cent had subsistence plots; it would grow to 30.1 per cent before the Emergency. While the number of small peasants remained stable as a percentage of the whole, the number of farmers and small farmers – the former were most likely to support several *ahoi* households – had declined dramatically. Thuita already had a large percentage of subsistence households by the Carter Commission; by the Emergency, almost two thirds of the population fell into that category. It had no farmers, and by the Emergency the small farmers had disappeared as well.

The Carter Commission took place against the background that a significant part of the population already needed help, either in the form of land or wages. Larger land owners could predict that in the future their sons would be in the same position.

The Carter Commission

Local memory retained no trace of several earlier commissions concerned with Kikuyu land claims, though memories of the Crown Lands Ordinance and the Kenya Land Commission were keen. The Kikuyu prepared their testimony for the Commission against the backdrop of rapidly rising prices, affinal kin – often daughters – who needed land and pressure from sons who had or were reaching maturity.

The Commission accepted written and oral statements, as long as an English translation was available. Elders received a good deal of help with translation from sympathetic missionaries and their own literate younger members, but were given no other aid. Many of the poorer or less well-known land owners received no help at all.

The task of preparing a *mbari* claim was difficult because ideally it meant a high degree of unity within the *mbari* about its origin, the subsequent divisions of land and what had happened during and after alienation. This revealed conflicts: *ahoi* might claim ownership of land they had used for generations and come to regard as their own, *mbari* members might be told that they had used land which belonged to another *githaku* or someone in that *githaku*. The conflicts thus revealed resulted sometimes in rival claims; some would be serious enough to mark the beginning of land litigation.

When even members of a *mbari* could not settle their problems, the help from outsiders, such as the Kikuyu Association (KA), an organization especially concerned with the rights of the larger land owners, was unlikely to help. Its most significant contribution was the preparation of a memorandum detailing the history of the land in general.

Many, even when there was no internal division, felt unable to press their rights and – with the KA unable to help – sought help from the Kikuyu Central Association (KCA), a rival organization of the KA, even less equipped to give the needed assistance.[39] The KCA was not fazed by lack of local knowledge, because it treated the matter as a dispute between the government and settlers, on the one hand, and Kikuyu rights on the other. In this context there was no need for specific knowledge; what mattered was to get the land back. Sorting out claims and settling internal matters or contradictions could be left to local elders once the land had been returned. It therefore sold pre-printed forms on which a *mbari* or individuals could state their claims; the KCA would submit them as their representative (Appendix V).

Amid the genuine claims reaching the Commission, phantom claims abounded, as did many contradictory ones reflecting internal problems or problems with neighbouring *mbari* that had not been settled. Some originated in the idea that *any* Kikuyu had more right to the land than any European. Others claimed land of distant relatives, using the numerous ways in which Kikuyu could claim kinship. Yet others operated from the belief that the Europeans would not be able to check claims and that they might as well take advantage of it as Europeans had taken advantage of the Kikuyu. Unfortunately, whatever the intent and attitude of the Commission, the false claims made it all too easy for the Commission to reject much of Kikuyu testimony, doing so moreover while impugning the integrity and veracity of the Kikuyu as a whole. Even where it accepted that land had been alienated wrongly, true to its view of the Kikuyu as a tribal entity with largely communal ownership – if not use only – of land, the Commission recommended that any compensation should take the form of adding land to the 'tribal reserve'. The government responded accordingly; it allowed Europeans to keep land, even if it could be proved that it had been taken wrongly; the government, not the Europeans, would give restitution. As the Commission had not decreed that compensation should entail land of comparable worth, it was possible for the government to offer virtually worthless land; as the idea of communal land property persisted and the image that all land was owned by the Crown continued, the government could treat even the land which was given as its land and impose restrictions on its use and those who settled on it.

The Carter Commission Report as colonial dividing line

Because a number of important events occurred around that time, the Carter Commission Report is used as a dividing line between two periods of colonial rule. While it ended the first, and seemed to have been planned as the foundation for continued colonial rule, it heralded the coming of the second, final period of colonialism. Not all the events are related causally to the Carter report or to each other.

The subdivisions of the 1920s had preceded the Report but, because of them, hopes that the land would be returned had been high. When this did not occur, most land owners thought it a final decision and felt forced to turn their attention to their land, to coax maximum fertility out of what was left. The idea that protest and resistance without economic strength were doomed to failure gained ground; using the economic possibilities opened up by Europeans and the government might help provide what their protest had not.

It was time to accept the realities; it was time to recognize that their sons, not the fathers who had protested in *baraza* after *baraza*, were the future leaders. At the time of the Carter Commission a number of land-owning fathers who had survived the famine abdicated, leaving the affairs of their *mbari* and its councils to their older sons.

In the same spirit of preserving one's land, the Carter Commission marked the start of serious land litigation to regain or defend land one had thought to be one's own but others had claimed. Many of the cases which in the late 1940s wound their slow way through the courts found their origin in the surprise, fears and anger of the early 1930s.

Land Ownership in the Twentieth Century

With the development of their land as prime concern, those with sufficient land were quite prepared to accept whatever the government could provide in the pursuit of agricultural improvements, particularly if it worked through the Local Native Council (LNC), in which they themselves were seated. Its involvement in stimulating commodity production and soil preservation were welcomed at a time when manure was revolutionizing Kikuyu agriculture. The land owners continued to view the government with distrust; but they were more than ever inclined to use it to advantage, particularly if it worked through the LNC, which they – and many who were not land owners – perceived as the organization of the large land owners. They would only protest when their rights were threatened, as when the government demanded that land owners – whose right to their land had been confirmed by the Carter Commission, but who had been asked to vacate it for Europeans – leave before they had been offered compensation. LNC members, like all land owners, continued to honour their fathers' perspective that no one could make decisions over land but its owners: it refused to accept the government's proposals for land conservation and terracing which did not honour *mbari* sovereignty.

Until the Carter Report Kikuyu protest had been muted, its prime objective the return of the stolen lands. Elders firmly believed that sufficient pressure on this would automatically force the Europeans to leave; the time of freedom could not be far away. After the Carter Report, both hopes seemed to belong to a distant future; the prime Kikuyu task was to strengthen themselves, replace the stolen lands with higher yields from what was left, become the equals of the Europeans and convince them, if not to leave, at least to yield to Kikuyu strength. The time was more likely to be distant.

Neither these sentiments nor the Carter Report gave much attention to the problems facing men and women with little land, little access to education and even less chance to parlay what they had into strength. Where the return of the land might have provided them with at least some land for the near future, the move to strengthen those who still had land, did little for them. While they had been willing to accept the leadership of those who agitated for the return of the land – which at this time would have benefited them – they were much less inclined to leave resistance to the government in the hands of those whose plans did not seem to consider the plight of landless and land poor. They could only conclude, reluctantly, that the salvation of the latter was increasingly in their own hands.

The Carter Report meant that the landless and the land poor would not be able to provide the necessary fees for themselves and their sons; nor would they be able to provide their sons with wives and land. This ultimately meant social and ritual death: their generations would come to an end as had happened to the nineteenth-century poor who could not buy land and found no one who would give them land in use.

Their fears were not unknown to the larger land owners who, however, were still at least one generation removed from the same realities. It strengthened their will to develop their land; if this were properly done, they might never have to face what the poor already faced. But even they might not be able to give to all sons if these sons did not contribute enough themselves. If they did not help sufficiently, they would not be able to give land and wives to their sons: the regeneration of their father's father. Then their generations would also come to an end; their time would run out. What separated the landed from the land poor might be no more than one generation.

While the decades before the Carter Commission were filled with anger, hope and the protest of elders, the later decades have an extraordinary sense of anger and urgency. Leadership is passing out of the hands of the elders; landless and land poor are struggling to find their own protest in an increasingly hopeless and bleak situation. Yet landed and landless do not form opposite camps; they are too closely linked by kinship, residence and fear. The woman trying to save school fees for at least one son, living on maize in order to buy some manure for her land; the man doing without shoes for the same reason, agitating for higher wages and joining political action; the land owner bringing more land under cash crops and joining a cooperative; the men and women who would take Mau Mau oaths – all would in their way fight the same fight: the right to exist for their fathers, themselves and their sons.

Land ownership and acquisition after the Carter Report

In the two decades between the Carter Report and the Declaration of the Emergency, more and more households needed land – and pressure, as well as prices of land, increased.[40]

Larger land owners still bought land, but cautiously: traditional methods of buying had lost protective power, and as long as the government did not recognize Kikuyu land ownership and provided title deeds, no transaction was secure. Though no *mbari* purchases took place, 28 individuals from Igi bought, between the Carter Report and the Declaration of the Emergency, close to 300 acres, partially for sons, partially for expanded commodity production. Seven peasants bought peasant holdings; one small farmer bought a small farm and two farmers bought another farm holding. Thirteen Thuita *mbari* members bought thirty acres, though some *mbari* land was sold. Poor land owners often bought small parcels from even poorer sellers, though one *muhoi*, a government official, bought all the land of a Thuita Ndorobo *mbari*, close to twenty acres. *Ahoi* began cautiously to buy small tracts outside Igi; sometimes a small tract was available in Thuita. Nine individuals bought a total of 20 acres. *Ahoi* buying was stimulated by lack of land; they, more than any others, would fear land consolidation, which became a topic of discussion after the Second World War. It would end their right to use land; many feared that it also would end their right to live on the land of others.[41]

Land Ownership in the Twentieth Century

Conflict about land

In the late nineteenth century *mbari* councils had far-reaching authority to settle conflicts, including those over land. Within each *githaku* senior elders adjudicated; conflict between *ithaku* could be settled by the elders of the *ithaku* involved; and, if they failed to bring a solution, conflicts were brought before *mbari* elders. Conflicts between members of different *mbari* were handled either by the senior elders of the *mbari* involved or the senior members of the *rugongo* to which the *mbari* belonged. Proceedings started with sacrifices and oaths, their severity depending on the gravity of the matter under discussion.

Although they would deal with the complaint which was brought, the elders – not the complaint, nor the litigants – determined the extent of the case. Elders would look for underlying problems and make these part of the matter at hand; they would look at the position of the litigants, the social fabric of which they were part, and – with all these factors in mind – give their decisions. If litigants brought a case over a small boundary or if goats had strayed in land someone claimed as his, elders might well give judgment about all their property. No decision was based on precedent; elders made their decision on what they regarded as truth within the appropriate social context.

Verdicts were binding; litigants who refused to accept the decisions could only appeal by embarking on ritual containing potentially dangerous oaths which invoked the ancestors and their wrath. In such cases elders were likely to impose an ordeal; its cost was high enough to deter many. Some ordeals involved the castration of all animals and sexual abstinence for humans until such time as a death established the decision of the ancestors.

Twentieth-century elders felt that – however harsh – the past system had been realistic and preferable to what the government had imposed; all relevant factors could then be considered; the process restored proper relationships for all. That the government demanded 'uniformity' and 'evenhandedness' seemed nothing short of impossible; no human beings, no cases were ever the same.

In early colonial times litigants could take their case to a government-instituted *kiama* although they should not do so until they had brought the matter before their local council. Kikuyu had little interest in abstract justice; that the government *kiama* did not know local conditions was to them a disadvantage. That they had little power to enforce decisions, moreover, made them even less effective.

In 1924 the government, concerned at what it regarded as the arbitrariness of decisions and the actual or potential corruption of local elders, widened its attempts at reforms by increasing opportunities for appeal, though elders retained the right to hear and mediate disputes if litigants were willing to accept their verdicts. Contrary to the government's hope that the majority of claims could be settled at the local level and that appeals would only be lodged with a Tribunal in exceptional cases, litigants swamped the appeal process. Whether a claimant had a justified case or not, it was likely to be disputed as any loss of land meant greater poverty in the present and less land for sons in the future. Local decisions were only accepted when the contested tract was small and not part of a potential wider claim, which meant in reality that only the land poor, who had difficulty in producing the court fees and whatever witnesses expected for donating their time, accepted the decisions. Tribunals were soon so overloaded that they had to be expanded in 1943, when several levels of appeal were added.[42]

There is little or no evidence that larger land owners used the inability of the land poor to finance a defence, as an opportunity to prey on their land. It would have created too much hostility in areas where land poor outnumbered larger land owners by far; the land of land poor was rarely worth the cost of litigation, as it was likely to be under-manured and under-worked.

Tribunals and appeals could only deal with the case before them and verdicts could be appealed virtually endlessly, leading to an unending series of cases. If Njoroge brought a case over a small part of Mungai's land and lost, nothing prevented him from filing another case over another part of Mungai's land. Nothing prevented Mungai, perhaps to warn Njoroge against further litigation, from responding by bringing a case over a part of Njoroge's land; nothing prevented either man from continuing this process right up to the Provincial Commissioner's Court, then starting all over again with a case over another parcel of land. Litigation became a self-perpetuation process; cases started in the 1930s were still winding their weary way through the courts by the late 1940s.

Tribunals lacked proper assistance; until the 1940s they had neither court reporters nor clerks, and records of arguments and decisions were kept badly, if at all. Judges and arbiters changed frequently; it was possible to file in 1944 a case already decided in 1936; if there was a record that it had been filed, there might not be a record of its disposition. Tribunals did not have an investigative staff; neither did District Officers, District Commissioners or Provincial Commissioners.

The process of litigation was long and costly. There were clerks to be paid to get the case down on paper; there were filing and court costs at the different levels of appeal; costs for days spent in court, costs for finding and reimbursing witnesses. Litigation costs outran all other costs of production; some informants claimed that they had spent by the late 1940s over shs 10,000/- a year. That all this produced no more than temporary security, until the next case was filed, made it an extraordinarily unproductive investment.

Litigation in Thuita and Igi:
the thrust for land consolidation

Litigation in Thuita was limited; land poverty was general and few would gain from changes of boundaries. *Mbari* were relatively shallow, and older men continued to carry a good deal of authority which enabled them to settle conflicts between their – close – descendants.

The opposite was the case in Igi, where the complexity of the acquisition of Igi land, and different perspectives on the *mbari*, made grounds for litigation easy to find. Many issues had already emerged during the preparation for the Carter Commission. Litigation was also more worthwhile: inequality between members in access to land was pronounced. Rights of members were based not only on inheritance – which could be the cause of dispute given the losses in the famine – but also on the way Igi had been formed over time. Different *ithaku* had joined at different times and had made different contributions to the buying of separate tracts of land; some land was bought as much as four to five generations ago, if not more. Even though *githaku* elders might continue to exercise authority over their descendants, *mbari* elders had less authority than in Thuita because of the strain between and in the different *ithaku*. Their relationships – though some were also related by descent – were mainly based on land kinship strengthened by the *mbari* oath. Where in the past powerful *ahoi nyumba* had linked *ahoi* and *ithaku* through affinity, after the Carter Commission the influence of *ahoi* had declined. History did not help either; while Thuita had fewer illusions about its past and its previous greatness, in Igi those who had lost most would often have a pervasive sense of having lost a past of power and prosperity, however unlikely this would have been for some.

Igi had – compared to Thuita – considerable private tracts which also provided plenty of grounds for dispute, with potentially considerable gains at stake. Conflicts in the nineteenth century had been buffered by an abundance of land; *tha* could be given, those who could or would not accept the decisions of elders could go elsewhere, join others or start anew. The situation in the twentieth century was profoundly different.

Almost all Igi *ithaku* were at one time or another involved in litigation. And although as a rule the larger land owners suffered more from litigation than smaller ones, smaller ones became involved when their hopes for additional land at the death of a father were dashed because the father lost the land. Smaller land owners, who had no unused land, also suffered considerably more than larger ones when Rift Valley repatriates in the late 1940s began to return to the local area and those who had thought that they now owned the land were asked to leave.[43]

Litigation was a psychological drain: it created a climate of distrust between kinsmen and between kinsmen and their affinal *ahoi*. It was an economic impediment: insecurity, not knowing whether one would have a tract several seasons hence, inhibited development. Even winners did not feel secure enough to plant cash crops on land which had been a source of dispute. The litigious atmosphere did not encourage buying or selling land; more than anything else, development needed official sanction for a system which would end litigation and strengthen ownership by title deeds.

Land Ownership in the Twentieth Century

This became still more important when it was learned, several years after the Second World War, that Kiambu Kikuyu would be allowed to grow coffee, a crop until that time reserved for Kiambu Europeans. The administration was unlikely to give coffee permits, however, while it was burdened by appeals and well aware that the higher the value of the land the more it was likely to be the subject of litigation. Local land owners, also, were unlikely to make the costly investment if they could not be certain that their ownership would be protected.

All this gave an impetus to a change in land tenure. It had to serve several objectives. It would aid development, and stimulate better farming. Moreover, it was bound to overrule the 1915 Crown Lands Ordinance, which had defined the status of the Kikuyu as 'tenants at will of the Crown'. Finally, it would provide title deeds, allow bank loans and counteract the extensive fragmentation.

In 1948 Chief Magugo Waweru sought government approval to consolidate Igi *mbari* land, but the government demanded evidence that the move had general approval and that the *mbari* agree to settle the outstanding cases (Appendix X/1).

Mbari members and elders met a number of times; no records have been kept. Land consolidation found general favour; it would give owners title to a tract of land equal to the fragments owned now and *githaku* members would have adjoining land. Consolidation would not overrule *kirumi* against sales; the *mbari* would remain ritually one and bound by exogamy, thereby following the ancestral rules. The land would be safe from litigation, would be easier to work, to develop and manure; members would be able to get loans and plant coffee. None of the potentially serious problems – such as the right of *ahoi* and restrictions on growing coffee or not dividing land after death unless one had seven acres – were apparently known or considered; within a year they would be one of the factors which drove men into Mau Mau.

Agreement on how to solve the outstanding cases proved elusive. Some were worried that it might lead to claims that the land should be divided equally; the government might even support such views. Before the Carter Commission it had often propagated the idea that 'traditionally' land was held communally by a 'clan' or even a 'tribe' and that each member received equally, according to his needs: such ideas were still very much alive (Appendix III/2).

Although the overwhelming majority argued that contributions had mattered and should matter, there was much less agreement on who had paid what and when. Disputes about what rights for descendants stemmed from such payments were equally difficult to solve. Those who had argued that private land, brought ritually into the *mbari*, remained private land, found overwhelming support. There was agreement that *mbari* members and *ahoi* had the right to use the land of other *mbari* members with consent of the actual owner.

No agreement could be reached on some nineteenth-century events nor on their twentieth-century interpretation. Had Mungai been a child when Njau bought his private land and should he therefore have received a child's portion like Kimani, another adopted child of Njau? Or was he already an adult who could have participated but had not done so, and therefore had no ownership rights in Njau's private land? Had Njau returned the goats he borrowed from Chege to finance his private land and were those men of Chege who now lived in that land therefore *ahoi*? Or had he not returned the goats and did the men have ownership rights over part of the land?

The position of Gitau was open to many interpretations. That he had lost a great deal of land in alienation did not give him rights in the land of others, but did he or did he not have rights in land acquired by the *mbari* earlier, as he claimed? Was the land, used by *Mwereri* before they went to the Rift Valley, given to Gitau as compensation for what had not been returned to them, when they at last came back? Or had they never owned land at all, at least not land which later had become *mbari* land? Instead, had he owned land within what Chege owned at that time? Was the twentieth-century quarrel over land between him and Mwereri's *githaku*, between him and Chege, or between him and all those who had been involved in the first acquisition of *mbari* land? No one doubted that many Gitau households needed land, but so did those of Mwereri. Need might lead to *tha* if it could be given; it did not give rights of ownership.

The following court cases make clear that at least the courts were certain that tenure was going to be changed well before it was approved by the administration. The court's question was when, not whether. This was also the sense among local *mbari* members and *ahoi*; among the local population this knowledge intensified rather than abated litigation as the population was striving for a position which they could accept when land consolidation came. It was small wonder that litigation in the last few years before the Emergency reached an all-time high.

The first case cited – all data were obtained from court records to the extent that they existed – is of 1948; Gitau's descendants had won a case against Kimani, the small boy adopted by Njau who had received some of Njau's land as an inheritance. They had been allotted the land in dispute. Kimani brought a counter-claim against Gitau descendants, but the court refused to consider the case.

> Both parties present ... CNT elders having heard all available evidence, they dismissed the case....
>
> *Remarks*
> The portion claimed is in the enclosure of *mbari* land. The portion will remain at status quo and every one will follow his garden till such time who will decide why the land will be shared according to what one paid goats *mwathi* [seller].[44]

Another case involved Gitau and returning members of Mwereri, Njau's oldest son. They demanded the land they had left when they went to the

Rift Valley. Gitau members claimed that it had been given to them in part compensation for what the *mbari* owed them. Mwereri's descendants maintained that they had given it to Gitau as *ahoi*. This case is from 1949; the court again refused to consider the case and, while not giving Gitau ownership rights, did not evict him:

> ... will stay with his small shamba in *mbari ya Igi* land until the whole *mbari* land shall be divided between members of the *mbari*.⁴⁵

Both these decisions had favoured Gitau: neither had declared them to be *ahoi* in the specific tract of land, both had declared them *mbari* members. They felt equally vindicated when the appeal of Mwereri's descendants to the District Officer, the District Commissioner and the Provincial Commissioner was turned down on similar grounds.

It seemed at that time that the Gitau position, if not favoured in the courts, was at least not denied. This increased litigation; all involved would later complain that they could have done little else. Mwereri's descendants would complain that Gitau's refusal to return their land was condemning them to perpetual poverty; Gitau would claim that they were already poor and that Mwereri's people had no right to ask that the land be returned. Njau's descendants were embattled in litigation over their private land, particularly with Mungai; they had litigation with Gitau and Kimani and were constantly in court to defend themselves against Chege.

The pervasive atmosphere of litigation had several consequences, which reached a climax when Gitau, a sector of Chege and a sector of Mungai filed a case in 1951 against most other *ithaku*, aimed at dividing all *mbari* land. The case was dismissed, and so was an appeal to the District Officer's court in 1952: 'status quo to be observed until *mbari* members will jointly decide the land in dispute'.⁴⁶ Clearly, the danger of the idea of communal ownership had come back to haunt many who owned land.

The *ahoi* had known for years that litigation threatened their position: they might be the first to be evicted if their patron lost in court. They were deeply disturbed by the 1948 discussions of possible changes in tenure. Whatever the decision, they would lose as *mbari* members would use all the land themselves. The new tenurial system was a European one; it did not enshrine the traditional rights to *tha* in land for close or affinal kin into law; any *tha* they still might receive would be a matter of charity which could be revoked at any time. If the new tenure system was consistent, they might even lose a place to live.⁴⁷ This would mean the misery and hardship of Nairobi or any other urban ghetto.

A second, less tangible but very real consequence of the stepped-up litigation was its influence on the Nairobi workers. After the Second World War conditions in the Nairobi locations had worsened. Where in the past only the wealthier workers had had the shs 5/- needed for the bus ride home, the abundance of taxis made it possible for six to eight men to hire a taxi together for a week-end ride and escape the depradations of Nairobi for home. But wives could no longer welcome them with white bread and

Land Ownership in the Twentieth Century

tea, and men saw at first-hand the poverty conditions of their wives and children. Their frequent presence made them more part of the land conflict than ever before; fear of losing the land they still had accompanied them on their way back to Nairobi. Litigation pervaded relationships: events which normally would have been seen as unfortunate incidents, such as the death of a child in a bicycle accident, were now coloured by mutual suspicion.

Notes

1. *Ngwatio* was a right by which members of the same descent group, men and women connected through affinity, or members of the same *riika* could ask for help from each other. It was expected to be reciprocal; *ngwatio* rarely provided sufficient help for wealthy men who therefore paid for additional labour.
2. 1967. Morgan, W. T. W., *Nairobi, City and Region*, Nairobi: Oxford University Press, pp. 100ff. The railway reached Nairobi June 1899.
3. Waweru and other old elders claimed that Kimama had been killed in a raid of the *thirikari* against *Akamba*. According to Wanyoike he was killed by neigbouring Kikuyu who did not recognize his authority.
   1974. Wanyoike, E. N., *op. cit.* pp. 34, 35.
   1978. Clough, M. S., 'Chiefs and politicians: local politics and social change in Kiambu, Kenya, 1918-1936', PhD thesis, Standford University, p. 73, footnote 18.
4. The Kikuyu called the neighbouring settled area *macamba*, literally 'settled area' but, in a play of words, 'my land'. The Rift Valley was called *ruguru*, distant.
   1968. Sorrenson, M. P. K., *Origins of European Settlement in Kenya*, Nairobi: Oxford University Press.
   1988. Overton, John, 'The origins of the Kikuyu land problem, land alienation and land use in Kiambu, Kenya, 1895-1920', *African Studies Review*, Vol. 31, No. 2, September, pp. 109-26.
5. Kikuyu dating and naming recalled Kikuyu events. Colonial events were only used if important to the Kikuyu. *Kibande* commemorated the introduction of the *kipande* (1920-1), *Chirringi* or *Nuthu* (1923-4) the introduction of the shilling and the perception that wages were being halved. *Ndege* (1926) honoured the first aeroplane observed, *Kenya Bathi* (1934-5) the first local bus. The start of the Second World War was indicated by *Hitler* or *Japan* (1940-1). How widespread names were in the nineteenth and early twentieth century is not certain; the same name does not indicate the same year. Names adopted in one area might reach another area years after they had arisen. After the 1930s names are and remain increasingly local. The Declaration of the Emergency gave *Manjiniti* or *Mwehigo* (1952), villagization was remembered as *Kijiji* or *Gicagi* (1953); *Gatoro* (1954) indicated a homemade gun.
6. Informants insisted that the *thirikari* had been at pains to explain that it took prime responsibility for alienation. Although they often did not separate the settlers from the government, or, for that matter, any whites, they did not blame the individuals for taking the land as no one was expected to refuse land which was offered. This may explain the low level of hostility to European settlers during Mau Mau. In Kiambu district losses were minor and late; the settled area lost two civilians in 1954; Nairobi lost 4, Kabete 1 and Ruaraka 2 persons.
   1958. *1956/7 Statistical Abstract*. Nairobi: Government Printer, p. 15.
7. Ainsworth was more familiar than anyone else with the high productivity of Kikuyu land, on which he had relied during the days of the caravans and the IBEAC. Nevertheless, as a Protectorate official, while arguing for protection of the 'natives', he chided them

for their wasteful and unacceptable agricultural practices, which warranted that at least part of their land be given to others. 'Therefore tribes like the Wakikuyu who are blessed with a very fertile land and who, in their own state, cultivate in the most reckless manner scattering their shambas all over the country and allowing land, which has perhaps only borne two or three crops, to run fallow for one or two years, require shewing that their just and ample requirements can be met by their being restricted to much more limited areas....'

- 1903. Land file, Office of the DC, Machakos, J. D. Ainsworth to H. H. Horne, 30 November 1903, 236/3/6.
- 1904. J. D. Ainsworth, *Memorandum to the Land Committee of 1904*, 30 November, Reply to the Land Committee's Circular dd. November 1904 236/3/6.
- 1955. Goldsmith, F. H., *John Ainsworth, Pioneer Kenya Administrator 1864-1946*, London: Macmillan and Co. The various Ukamba Province land files, 1903-11, contain information about land alienation, surveys and attitudes of J. Ainsworth, J. A. W. Hope, Collector Maasai land and C. F. Elliott, Conservator of Forests.

8. In this as in other memories, such as the Maasai treaties which opened up the Rift Valley, informants probably collapsed several interviews and sources of information into one event, chosing a date depending on circumstances. As early as 1912 some administrators were willing to concede that the Kikuyu had bought their land and were familiar with the difference between ownership and usufruct. They were not in positions of authority and it is unlikely that they, even if they had been, would have been able to undo alienation.

- 1967. Sorrenson, M. P. K., Oxford: Oxford University Press, pp. 3-35.
- 1988. Overton, John, *op. cit.*

9. Demands of land for public utilities or government dictates about terracing of the remaining land, its policies for the use of land given as compensation for what was taken, such as in *Olenguruone*, were all experienced as continued alienation.

- 1968. Sorrenson, M. P. K., *Origins of European Settlement in Kenya*, Oxford: Oxford University Press. Late alienation is described by
- 1975. Dutto, Carl, A., *Nyeri Townsmen, Kenya*, Nairobi: East Africa Literature Bureau.
- 1988. Overton, John, *op. cit.*

10. Early settler agricultural activities and wages are chronicled in

- 1904. 'Report of the Agricultural Conditions obtaining at Various Homesteads in the Kikuyu District', *East African Quarterly*, July/September 1904. It is reproduced in
- 1956. Hill, M. F., *Planters' Progress*, Nairobi: Coffee Board of Kenya, pp. 17ff. Sorrenson, 1968, p. 105 gives statistics on the rate of absentee land ownship among European settlers. Early productivity is discussed in
- 1938. Salvadori, Max, *La Colonisation Européene au Kenya*, Paris: La Rose Editeurs.

Studies dealing with later periods and wider areas are

- 1965. Anderson, David and David Throup, 'Africans and agricultural production in colonial Africa: the myth of the war as watershed', *Journal of African History*, 26 (1985) pp. 327-45.
- 1973. Brett, E. A., *Colonialism and Underdevelopment in East Africa: The Policies of Economic Change 1919 - 1939*. London: Heinemann.
- 1980. Kitching, Gavin, *Class and Economic Change in Kenya*, New Haven: Yale University Press.
- 1983 Mosley P., *The Settler Economies: Studies in the Economic History of Kenya and Southern Rhodesia*, 1900-1963, Cambridge: Cambridge University Press.
- 1983. Overton, J. D., 'Spatial differentiation in the colonial economy of Kenya: Africans, settlers and the state', unpublished PhD thesis, University of Cambridge.
- 1980. Spencer, I. R. G., 'Settler dominance, agricultural production and the Second World War in Kenya', *Journal of African History* 21 (1980) pp. 497-514.

11. European surveyors who might have little or no knowledge of Kikuyu agriculture or herding did not regard fallowed land as land in full use. According to Ainsworth's instructions, land which was used less than 30 per cent of its agricultural or less than 20 per cent of its grazing capacity, was under-used and available for alienation.

Land Ownership in the Twentieth Century

1903. Land file, Office of the DC, Machakos, J. D. Ainsworth to H. H. Horne, 30 November.

1904. [n.d.] Ainsworth, J. D., *Memorandum to the Land Committee of 1904*. Reply to the Land Committee's Circular dd. November, 236/3/6.

12. Only two informants claimed that they were removed by physical force or threats. Two men complained that they were driven away when the settler plowed their cultivated land. One of the oldest early settlers, still alive in 1962, who with another male had bought 640 acres from a European in 1910 and had played an important role in the production of coffee, explained that *bona fide* settlers disapproved of force or trickery. It was counter-productive, moreover, and was likely to result in problems with labour. He asserted that, though 'alienation was historically unavoidable', settlers who wanted to make their home in the area strongly discouraged 'playing rough'; 'brutality only destroyed relationships' and 'those who alienated their labour force rarely made a go of it'.

1956. Hill, M.F., *Planters' Progress*, Nairobi: Coffee Board of Kenya.

1962. Interview with P. J. H. Coldham, July.

13. By making neighbouring headmen responsible for security on alienated land, settlers could expropriate livestock in 'fines'. Such animals did not constitute a threat to their stock.

14. When relationships between a settler and a Kikuyu were relatively positive, working on the land of a settler might enable a man to accumulate a sizable herd. Sons might not inherit this right and would have to sell the stock when their father died. Even short-time grazing on settlers' land might accumulate a brideprice or pay for new land unless settlers demanded a hefty share of the increase.

15. 1970. Thuku, Harry, *An Autobiography*, Nairobi: Oxford University Press, p. 7.

1974. Wanyoike, E. N., *op. cit.* p. 23.

16. Alternative version: all the land was *mbari* land, there was no private land in the past.

17. I have no information on *mbari* and their *ahoi* who lost all their land; informants said that it had happened to one Thuita *mbari*, but outside the area of modern Thuita. They had left, and no one knew where they were now.

18. Alternative version: 'no *mbari* member can be a *muhoi* in his own *mbari*; the returnees kept their rights. It was perhaps impossible to redistribute the land at that time because it would have been seen by Europeans as acceptance of alienation; whatever land they got should at least temporarily have been regarded as theirs, until they got their own land back. It is wrong to call *mbari* members *ahoi*'.

19. 1968. Sorrenson, M. P. K., *op. cit.* pp. 190ff.

1977. Njonjo, A., 'The Africanization of the "White Highlands" of Kenya: a study in agrarian class struggles in Kenya, 1950–1974', unpublished PhD thesis, Princeton University.

1977. Osolo-Nasubo, Ng'weno, *A Socio-Economic Study of the Kenya Highlands from 1900–1970. A Case Study in Uhuru Government*, Washington DC: University Press of America.

1987. Kanogo, Tabitha, *Squatters and the Roots of Mau Mau*, London: James Currey.

It seems unlikely that by 1906 the Kikuyu were aware of all the details of the Maasai treaties which opened the Rift Valley for European settlement.

20. *Kirumi*, a special type of cursing oaths spoken over those who went to the Rift Valley, were similar to the ones Murang'a elders put on descendants who migrated to Kiambu. A number of Rift Valley *kirumi* were eventually removed. Those who remained under a curse did not return during the Emergency but went to other relatives.

21. Whenever *kirumi* are involved, data on descendants are likely to be inaccurate as sons, kinsmen and others subject to the curse might be omitted from genealogies.

22. The brideprice for the wife of a young male was paid from his father's stock, with gifts from his father's father and his father's senior brothers. Some of the goats were taken from his mother's herd, which orginally had come from her father.

23. The growth of herds of goats was calculated according to the numbers sequence of Fibonacci. According to this model, a small herd can expand rapidly. A herd derived

from one pregnant female may reach 21 goats in its seventh year, 34 goats in its eighth, 56 goats in its ninth and 90 goats in its tenth year.

24. A detailed discussion of colonial land policy and the drafting of the 1915 Crown Lands Ordinance, with some of the consequences, is provided by
    1968. Sorrenson, M. P. K., *op. cit.* Chapters 7-10.
25. One discussion of the 'reserves' probably dealt with the boundaries established in 1912. *Barazas* brought together elders and headmen from larger areas than had cooperated through the *ngongo* of the past.
    1968. Sorrenson, M. P. K., *op. cit.* pp. 184ff.
    1974. Wanyoike, E. N., *op. cit.* pp. 95ff.
26. Before *Kirika* and for a time afterwards, boundaries of land were defined by natural features. With higher density, destruction of the forest and selling of smaller parcels, boundaries might be created by burying boulders, and stengthened by ritual or the planting of *matoka* lilies. The *matoka* lilies in the settled area were not removed; elders offered to show me where they were if we could get permission from settlers to come on their land. This was refused. The Kikuyu did not accept the boundaries recognized by settlers and the government; they did not plant *matoka* on the new boundaries delineated during alienation.
27. At the beginning of the Emergency brideprices were between eighty or ninety goats at shs 20/- each. By that time some Christian parents no longer accepted or demanded brideprices.
28. Ritual payments continued to be paid in goats; they were consumed by the parties involved to seal the contract.
29. 1933. Kenya Land Commission Report, Evidence and Memoranda, Vols 1-4, *op. cit.*
30. Alternative version: there is no evidence that his ancestor paid more than others. All land was *mbari* land and his ancestors asked for a large part of it because they wanted many *ahoi*. When the *ahoi* died or left, they kept the land as if it was their own.
31. The areas bought were so small that the buyer did not call himself a *mbari* until 1962. By that time his *muhoi* brother had also bought but had given his *mbari* another name.
32. In Thuita *ahoi* households had probably constituted about 10 per cent of the population after the famine; by 1920 it had reached a high of almost 15 per cent. By 1930 it had dropped to about 13 per cent; by 1940 to 8.6 per cent; by 1950 to 6.4 per cent; by 1962 to 2.4 per cent. The corresponding figures for Igi were 38.9 per cent, 33.1 per cent; 28.9 per cent; 25.7 per cent.
33. In 1956, 23.9 per cent of Igi and 12.4 per cent of Thuita *mbari* males had been or were still living in polygynous marriages. The rate for *ahoi* was 9.7 per cent.
34. In 1956, 27.5 per cent of *ahoi* households were headed by a person over 60 years of age; only 14.2 per cent of *mbari* households were.
35. In the early twentieth century initiations were still a community matter though closures and the formation of official regiments were no longer observed. *Kinyotoku* was possibly followed by a closure of two years; after *Chirringi* no closures were observed; they were not ordered after the large years *Ndege* (1926-7) and *Japan* (1941-2). Many were initiated without explicit ceremonial, *bara bara* or *njira-ini*. Kinsmen might organize initiations together, and simplify the ritual as they saw fit.
36. Given the diversity of lifestyle, sufficiencies were hard to define; men might or might not be content with what their fathers could provide; what would have been a sufficiency for a man in a forest economy would not be so in another economy.
37. Early data are based on some direct information but largely on calculations and probabilities based on information. Later data depend more on the information and calculations. Genealogies, interviews with heads of households, leaders of *mbari*, *ithaku* and *nyumba* were all used. Dates have been organized around important Kikuyu events.
38. A summary of the recent status of the discussion concerning peasants and peasantry with particular reference to Africa is found in
    1990. Isaacman, Allen, 'Peasants and social protest in Africa', *African Studies Review*, Vol. 33, No. 2 (September).
39. Political parties are discussed in Chapter 6.

Land Ownership in the Twentieth Century

40. Land consolidation, and the expectation of coffee incomes, caused another rise in the prices of land. By 1956 the price of one acre was shs 1500/-. By 1962 shs 2500/- per acre was common.
41. *Ahoi* who bought small tracts of land which they cultivated, though continuing to reside with those whose land they had used, became *athami*. If the land remained unused, they remained *ahoi*.
42. After initially putting their support behind chiefs and headmen, the Protectorate government in 1907 recognized the jurisdiction of the judicial and administrative powers of the the senior councils of elders, and confirmed this with the 1912 Native Authority Ordinance, even though the councils were given little executive power. In 1924 the Native Councils Ordinance broke the reliance on local councils and substituted government bodies with authority over wider areas. Administrative matters were entrusted to African District Councils; judicial affairs came under the authority of paid magistrates, appointed by District Commissioners. They had authority over several locations. Local Councils were expected to act as mediators in local affairs but, if they failed, cases had to be brought to the new tribunals. A major reform was introduced in 1943 by the then District Commissioner of Kiambu, H. E. Lambert. He created a system of Native Divisional Tribunals, with several levels of appeal. One of the objectives of the reform was improved record keeping, greater uniformity and avoidance of corruption.
 1945. Philips, Arthur, *Report on Native Tribunals*, Nairobi.
43. The era of protracted litigation was opened in 1931 with a dispute over whether or not Njau had returned the goats he had borrowed from Chege to pay for his land. If not, then Chege's descendants would be part owners; if paid, Chege's descendants had user rights by virtue of *tha* as long as Njau's descendants were willing to grant it. That a Chege man who lived in the land, gave his daughter's husband the right of use, started the case. In spite of many appeals, suits and counter-suits, the case was not yet finally decided at the start of land consolidation.
44. Precise dating and exact references for litigation were difficult to obtain. In 1956/7 access to court records was denied because officials claimed that they were needed for land consolidation. In 1962 they were not available and a senior land consolidation officer told us that they had been destroyed to avoid litigation after consolidation. Litigants relied on memory and witnesses of what was important to them; even if they had documents, they had only certain decisions but not others; they might have copies or part copies only. Written evidence might have only limited value; dates could refer to the time the case was filed for the first time, when it was heard first or decided first. They might also concern a case which had been heard before, perhaps before the same or before another court. It was also possible that the place or date where the case had been heard and to which the decision referred, was missing from the available documentation. References are therefore at best of limited use. This particular case had as reference number
 1948. L 81/48 and *Chief Native Tribunal, Githunguri*, S/S/08/12/48.
45. This case was probably filed in 1949; a first decision was made on 13 April 1950; the case was appealed and the decision mentioned here was probably Githunguri L 52/49/MRN0 208526.
46. The case, 17/1951, was probably filed before the Chief Native Tribunal in Githunguri and appealed as case 107/52 in the District Officer's court in Kiambu.
47. Land consolidation gave a number of long-term *ahoi* a quarter acre of land in ownership.

Four

The Labour Market for the Local Population

The preceding chapter demonstrated that fewer and fewer households were adequately supported by land; this chapter will show that employment did not compensate for the losses, though the households of landless and land poor often contained several wage earners. Local and settled area work was by and large confined to women; they rarely earned more than a minimum wage. The higher wages of males in migrant labour were offset by the cost of living away from their households. Many of these households could not afford education for more than one son, if that; the younger members of these households could only look forward to less land, less education and continued low-wage employment as long as it could be found. The doors to the future were closing; unless someone or something miraculously brought the spiralling impoverishment to a halt, sons would find only closed doors.

Early labour markets

Labour for pay was well known in the nineteenth century; males received gifts or use of land for significant services such as driving goats to a seller through hostile territory; curers, circumcisers and artisans were rewarded with goats. The herding of *anake* and others was rewarded with part of the increase; in raids and warfare part of the loot in girls and stock was theirs. Smaller items were exchanged or bartered: pots, stools, spears and tools were regularly exchanged. In the twentieth century when the range of work expanded considerably for males and to some extent for females, the colonial economy rewarded work with food and cash or cash alone, and the local economy followed suit.

The Labour Market for the Local Population

The range of jobs broadened considerably over time, but wages, which will be discussed extensively in the next chapter, continued to compare unfavourably with the yield of even one acre of land (Appendix IV/15). Trading, clerical and administrative, and sometimes domestic work paid better, but clerical and administrative work demanded sufficient schooling, which only landed fathers could afford. For most workers wages were at best a supplement to land; households which had to subsist on wages alone faced rank poverty, if not starvation.

Land-poor males and females entered the wage economy early; wealthier land owners and older males entered later; by 1956 most women of wealthier households were not yet involved. Gender expectations affected the place of work: few women could work outside the local or settled area, or accept work if it was not supervised by older women or male kinsmen; they also had to return home each evening.[1] Males had greater freedom; after initiation they might roam for several years; when their working years started they could stay away as long as their work demanded.

In the early years most males preferred to work in Nairobi, which offered a variety of jobs and, when education became available, different levels of pay. The predominant work for males and females in the local and settled area, which included Kiambu, were low-paying agricultural jobs with little opportunity for advance; the later, more skilled jobs which demanded training or education, went to males. They could live near the jobs or, if they had bicycles, return home in the evening. Because until just before the Emergency women lagged behind men in education, few had acquired skilled or clerical employment; they were also held back because they were not expected to compete with males.[2]

Employment of the local population is divided into basic or unskilled labour, semi-skilled and skilled labour, and clerical or administrative work; it will be discussed separately for males and females in the local and settled area and for males in Nairobi.[3] In the early decades basic labour dominated the labour market everywhere; it remained the most common employment for women. It did not require education and was predominantly day or seasonal, paid by the day or the job. It was available for males in all areas, for women only in the local and settled area.[4]

During the Depression semi-skilled and skilled labour was concentrated in Nairobi; afterwards the settled area also offered opportunities but the rural area lagged. Most workers were trained on the job; after the Depression formal and vocational education was an asset.

Clerical work demanded education, as did administrative jobs in the later decades.[5] In the first decades the local area had a headman or Chief as well as an evangelist-teacher; while the first chief was not literate, the evangelist-teacher performed his clerical duties when needed. Until the 1930s most other clerical jobs were limited to Nairobi; in the 1930s the settled area, including Kiambu, became important but Nairobi continued to absorb more clerical workers than other areas. Clerical jobs in Nairobi went to males; by the end of the Second World War employers were willing to accept females with sufficient education as clerks or teachers. No local men occupied administrative jobs outside the rural area.

Clerical and administrative work in the local and settled area

The local area saw the early appointments of Waweru wa Mahui as headman and of Wanyoike wa Kamawe as evangelist-teacher. Before Waweru became headman, his father's brother's son, Kimama wa Macharuga, had been the local representative of the trading interests; he had become an unpaid headman during the Protectorate government but, as far as the local population was concerned, he was their man. When he died in 1902 the local *kiama* encouraged his close relative, Waweru Mahui, to take over his work: it wanted local interests − land − represented by a member of its largest *githaku*. Through him the population would have access to the incoming powers (Appendix III//5).

In the eyes of the Protectorate government such men belonged to the unpaid 'friendlies'; when its rule became more firmly established some were appointed 'headmen' to serve at its pleasure. They collected taxes and were paid a share: sometimes 5 per cent, sometimes 10 per cent (Appendix IV/1).

Revenue sharing was abolished in 1910; by 1912 Waweru was gazetted and for the first time paid a wage.[6] For the local population nothing changed; he remained their representative, their buffer between colonial and settler demands. They owed him loyalty; in turn, he was to learn as much as possible about what had made the government and Europeans strong enough to take Kikuyu land. As long as he protected them and shared what he learned, they would protect him (Appendix III/6, 7). Wanyoike Kamawe, the teacher-evangelist, was a graduate of the neighbouring Kiambu mission of the Gospel Missionary Society, only a few miles away. Though the local *kiama*, eager for the innovations missionaries could bring, had hoped that the mission would build on its land, the *mbari ya Gathirimu* to which Wanyoike belonged, had made a too-attractive offer; relationships had remained cooperative, however.

The mission's prime objective was conversion; it hoped to reach this through a literate indigenous clergy while converts would avoid 'backsliding' by being sufficiently literate to read the Bible. Its literacy goals were high and because it believed that its clergy should be able to understand and live in the world in which they had to work, they were given training in numeracy, technical skills and English. Early students lived at the mission where, as missionaries were still learning Kikuyu, English was the daily language. Students helped in the building of the mission, learning technical skills. Three or four years of such education gave considerable expertise.

Waweru needed these skills for his and other elders' expanding trade;

he also wanted them for his sons. In 1913 Wanyoike became the first evangelist-teacher of a local 'outschool'; Waweru had donated the land. Their cooperation involved not only the school; together they planned the roads and bridges demanded by trade; Wanyoike, providing the literacy and English which Waweru lacked, became his political ally.

Although neither the local nor the settled area could absorb highly trained personnel, some students became mission evangelists and teachers elsewhere; several trained men from neighbouring *mbari* found clerical employment in Nairobi. What they received in salaries stimulated enrolment; outschools provided basic instruction, Kambui more advanced education.[7]

Until well into the 1930s clerical work in the settled area was scarce. The owners of smaller plantations or their wives kept the books; some employed an Indian or Goan clerk, as did the government centre at Kiambu. In the 1930s large plantations and the expanding District Office, the Department of Agriculture, the Kiambu LNC, the courts and the hospital began to use mainly African labour, but until wages warranted buying bicycles local men were not involved. Most had land and wanted to come home every evening. Plantations preferred resident clerks who would also oversee labour; few local men sought this employment.

Wanyoike had remained in charge of the local church and many smaller churches around the area, but had given up teaching at the local and other outlying schools when they opened. By the 1940s the local school employed a headmaster, teachers and aides; one teacher was a woman. Wanyoike continued to be the crucial link between church and school and between schools and Kambui. Waweru retired in 1935 and was succeeded by his son, Magugo.[8] He had several headmen under him and his father's location, Kibichoi, was renamed Komothai in 1943. More administrative appointments were made when many locations, including Komothai, got their own tax collectors.

When Kambui Mission had to disband, partially because of lack of funds and internal conflicts but principally because parents, Christian or not, disagreed with the heavy emphasis on conversion in the curriculum, Wanyoike successfully directed the local hierarchy to the Presbyterian Church of East Africa, which was known to have a stronger academic programme in their schools. In 1945 he became Moderator of the Chania Presbytery.[9]

Basic, semi-skilled and skilled work for men in the local and settled area

Although later data indicate land scarcity as an overriding factor in seeking wage employment, for the early period evidence is less clear. Those who lost most of their land were either helped by kin where they lived or moved to kin who had not lost land. Low-paid wage labour would hardly have been attractive: it would not have been sufficient even for basic necessities. There is little evidence that taxation played a role; in most periods a single male – less than one goat – could be met more cheaply by breeding a female goat than from wages (Appendix III/1, 2).

While by the 1930s men as old as fifty worked for wages, in the early years *anake* predominated, particularly in Nairobi. Much of their involvement was a response to the attempts of settlers, government or local officials to impose *gitati*, compulsory paid or unpaid labour, which was essentially a tax in labour.

Soon after the turn of the century government had sought workers for road construction; by 1906/7 settlers pressured Waweru Mahui for young males as – mostly temporary – labour to start to clear their land and plant coffee. By 1910 local officials would discover the value of such labour for roads, needed for the expanding trade.

If land owners were to break the hold of Indian merchants on the trade, they would need oxcarts and roads by which to take their crops to buying centres or settlers. This demanded far more labour than *ngwatio*, the exchange of labour between close kin, could produce. Tributary *ahoi*, used in the nineteenth century, were not available or practical; during alienation few men wanted to invite more people to live on their land. They did not have sufficient stock or cash with which to pay; government did not return any part of the taxes for local development.

The traders, mostly land-wealthy elders, therefore sought government permission to use *gitati*, with the argument that roads would benefit not just the local population but the government as well.[10] The government accepted the reasoning, promised technical aid and allowed the use of *gitati*.[11] The conditions under which it could be used were laid down, in addition to some basic exemptions: all who worked for three months – with pay – for Europeans, could be excused.[12] Those who would profit immediately from the roads were mostly exempt from the work involved; those who would not profit for a considerable time had to perform the work. The main work force consisted of the land poor and landless, their wives, and the younger population, including the *anake*.[13]

To escape the onerous work, males and females sought paid labour; because females lacked mobility, they depended on the local and settled area. Males rejected these areas: they wanted to be more distant from parental pressure.

While fathers were often opposed to *gitati*, at least for government or settlers, they were irritated by the general disinclination of the young to contribute work or wages to the household. *Anake*, on the other hand, felt that they had a time-honoured right to roam in the early years after initiation; deprived of raiding, they were not inclined to do more work at home. Settlers would only pay them a pittance; if they had to work, then Nairobi was their preferred territory.

Though fathers had initially opposed their departure, by the First World War resistance in poorer households had declined as fathers no longer needed the work of the *anake* for their reduced herds but expected their sons to do other work instead. When fathers had been *anake*, they had

The Labour Market for the Local Population

deserved the appropriate domestic privileges and rewards: they would have contributed by raiding and eventually herding. That sons could not do either, did not absolve them from making other contributions. It was time they started to earn some money, pay their own taxes, buy their own cloth and provide the slaughtered goat to eat with friends; they should not expect that fathers, without their help, would be able to pay a brideprice when the time came.

The rule that three months' paid work for a settler provided an exemption from *gitati* became a powerful method of labour recruitment, yet did not provide much labour for the local or settled area.[14] Locally, a few younger males were used to clear land or to herd for owners of sizeable herds; some took herds to Ndeia or the Rift Valley until overcrowding put an end to this. Few were employed in the settled area; employers there regarded the young males as 'unreliable', 'lazy' and 'cheeky'.

The local area had some semi-skilled and skilled work available. *Askari*, often employed by the headman, did some of his work; they were frequently paid from his own resources or, if they were asked to collect taxes, from part of the revenue. Local producers needed oxcarts and drivers – the first lorry was probably bought just after the First World War – to transport surplus to centres where – until the middle 1920s – it continued to be bought by Indian merchants. Peddlers might buy second-hand clothes in Nairobi; men working in Nairobi might bring greatcoats and blankets for sale.

In the early decades there may have been a few *fundis* who repaired carts and yokes; a roof of kerosene tins may have been installed as early as the 1920s. Though by and large repair and building was done by domestic labour, traditional craftsmen, makers of stools, ornaments, pots or basketry continued to furnish their goods; medical help was available from curers, some of them experienced herbalists. Kambui provided medical help as well. Ritual specialists continued to operate as before.

The government centre at Kiambu – small through lack of government support – needed little labour and what was needed was provided by prisoners. Paid work was available for 'runners', 'messenger boys', sweepers and night watchmen; Indian *ndukas* needed cleaners and loaders.[15] They might also need oxcarts and drivers.

Until after the First World War, government officials who went 'on safari' had needed porters and a few *askari* as guards. Settlers and officials had from the beginning needed domestic personnel. But though it was paid as semi-skilled work, it was only attractive if it provided housing.

By the late 1920s opportunities increased; the District Office had a car and driver, and there were undoubtedly several private cars, probably with drivers.[16] There was certainly one garage and the usual complement of small businesses, including tailors, though what evidence I have indicates that there were more openings for Indians than Africans. Whether the skilled personnel of the small hospital – opened in 1916 – was European, Indian or African, is not clear.

The Labour Market for the Local Population

For reasons not quite clear, semi-skilled and skilled jobs on the plantations passed by the 1920s from Indians to local men. The early oxcarts had given way after the First World War to lorries and drivers; quite a few plantations had their own *fundi*. As labour was mainly Kikuyu, labour supervisors were Kikuyu; older local men also supervised the nurseries and the processing of coffee. As more settlers had arrived, the demand for domestic personnel service had increased slightly as well.

Marige, the old four-day market place, was changing. One or two shops opened; at least one had a 'teahouse' as well. Here oxcarts also gave way to a few lorries which, like the bus which in the middle 1930s would open a regular connection with Nairobi, were often stationed at the market because of the lack of local roads. There were a few drivers, and certainly four or five *fundis*; there was more trade and, while most larger surplus producers still sold their produce to Indian merchants, some had started to cut out this middleman and sell directly to Nairobi.

When from the 1930s onwards more local land was brought into production to take advantage of rising commodity prices, more landless and land poor had to enter the labour market. Younger men were likely to go into Nairobi but older men, often without education and unable to withstand the rigours, were restricted to the settled or local area.

Innovations provided some male local employment, though paid at the unskilled rate. Some work was available as surplus producers experimented with different types of planting material and growing conditions; others were experimenting with labour-intensive crops such as vegetables, onions, fruits and pineapples. High-grade dairy cattle had been introduced, demanding capable herders.

Certain new jobs paid more than the minimum wage, some paid twice as much. As more land was put to cash crops, larger producers needed supervisors for labour. Wives, who had undertaken this task in the past, could no longer do all the work; they also wanted greater independence to develop their own interests – notably poultry keeping. More semi-skilled and skilled work was created when lorries and drivers were needed to transport and distribute the imported manure and to take local produce back to processing or buying centres. More employment meant more income; the greater wealth of larger land owners and successful merchants meant more tin roofs and more building. Marige brought employment for masons; *fundis* made tables, chairs and beds as well as door and window frames. School uniforms and clothing had to be sewn and tailors at the market centre were kept busy.

By the early 1940s the surge and Kikuyu-ization of trade and business elicited the entrepreneurial spirit of local men with sufficient land income to make modest investments. Brothers might combine and buy a lorry or sewing machines; they might open local shops or expand their one shop to several over a wider area, employing most of their kin. Lorries went further away to buy surplus and resell it in the larger centres; shops, taking advantage of the greater amount of cash available, sold retail goods for

The Labour Market for the Local Population

which one earlier had had to go to Kiambu or Nairobi. Marige was rapidly becoming a regional trading centre, though it also continued to operate as a place for barter and social interaction.

Traditional occupations were declining as younger men lacked interest and needed more income than such occupations provided. Some of the famed ritual workers had died; traditional knowledge was becoming the property of a small group of older men. Traditional crafts were in low demand; a stool could not be used to sit at a table; *sufarias* were quicker and easier to handle than cooking pots.

By the 1940s local men were also profiting from the expansion of semi-skilled or skilled work in the settled area, if wages warranted buying a bicycle. Dressers, medical orderlies and dispensers were needed at Kiambu hospital; European car owners needed maintenance, and some needed drivers. Semi-skilled and skilled work was available for *fundis* and mechanics, plumbers, electricians and other specialized workers.

Although they could have found low-paying local jobs or gone into Nairobi, a number of younger males regarded themselves as frequently unemployed and tended to congregate. They were not willing to take the available low-paying jobs; quite a few had education and sometimes specific skills; but where others ultimately accepted that they could not get the work they wanted or the wage they deserved, these young men had not accepted this verity.

As they lived at home, they had food and shelter, though the attitude of their kin was mixed. The Kikuyu work ethic held by most parents was that not working was no answer to the common difficulties everyone faced. Because they were relatively free to go when and where they wanted, they often went on extensive visits to kinsmen in the Rift Valley and Nairobi, serving as important nodes in a communication system between the local and other areas.

Table 4.1 indicates that the oldest male workers before the Emergency stayed in the local area; over 40 per cent were over forty. Table 4.2 shows that settled area workers were a somewhat younger group. Older men could rarely go too far afield; Kiambu was too far to walk; they would not be able to ride bicycles; the wages they could command even for supervisory labour did not warrant buying them. About 50 per cent of local workers and 65 per cent of those who worked in the settled area were involved in semi-skilled or skilled work.

Work for women in the local and settled area

Unlike young males who expected to roam several years after initiation, young females were expected to work the land of their mothers. They were married young to older males and were then expected to work their own land. Some of these young women became an early paid labour force.

Alienation did not bring immediate and dire scarcity of food land,

The Labour Market for the Local Population

Table 4.1 *Profile local male population working in local area before the Declaration of the Emergency*

No.: 164
Marital Status: Married 82.7%
Landless or less than 3.99 acres: 57.3%
Age: 25 or under: 21.9%; 26–40: 36.0%; 41–60: 38.7%; 61 and over: 3.4%.

Education:
Illiterate: 41.5% 2 or more but less than 4 years: 14.0%
Semi-literate: 17.7% 4 or more but less than 8 years: 19.5%
    8 or more years: 7.3%

Workforce:	Ahoi	Subsistence plot owners	Small peasants	Peasants	Small farmers	Farmers	Total
BASIC LABOUR							
Agricultural	17	21	10	–	–	–	48
Casual, pool and informal sector	6	7	4	2	–	–	19
SEMI-SKILLED AND SKILLED LABOUR							
Supervisors labour	–	5	2	8	–	–	15
Military, police, *askaris*	–	3	3	5	–	–	11
Fundis, artisans, tailors	2	6	2	1	–	–	11
Mechanics, drivers, technical labour	–	5	2	1	–	–	8
Domestic personnel	1	3	–	–	–	–	4
Traditional workers, curers	3	–	–	1	–	–	4
Self-employed traders, shopkeepers	2	9	4	8	4	–	27
CLERICAL AND ADMINISTRATIVE LABOUR	–	4	2	8	1	2	17
Total	31	63	29	34	5	2	164
Total (per cent)	18.9	38.4	17.7	20.7	3.0	1.2	99.9

40.9% Basic labour
48.8% Semi-skilled or skilled labour
10.4% Clerical and administrative labour

The Labour Market for the Local Population

Table 4.2 *Profile local male population working in the settled area before the Declaration of the Emergency*

No.: 124
Marital Status: Married 89.1%
Landless or less than 3.99 acres: 71.8%
Age: 25 or under: 35.5%; 26–40: 44.4%; 41–60: 20.2%; 61 and over: 0%.

Education:
Illiterate: 20.2%   2 or more but less than 4 years: 35.5%
Semi-literate: 26.6%   4 or more but less than 8 years: 16.1%
                        8 or more years: 1.6%

Workforce:	Ahoi	Subsistence plot owners	Small peasants	Peasants	Small farmers	Farmers	Total
BASIC LABOUR							
Agricultural	10	15	2	–	–	–	27
Casual, pool and informal sector	5	1	5	1	–	–	12
SEMI-SKILLED AND SKILLED LABOUR							
Supervisor labour	9	13	4	10	–	–	36
Military, police, *askaris*	–	–	–	–	–	–	–
Fundis, artisans, tailors	3	14	3	2	–	–	22
Mechanics, drivers, technical labour	–	6	–	–	–	–	6
Domestic personnel	2	9	4	1	–	–	16
Self-employed traders, shopkeepers	1	–	–	–	–	–	1
CLERICAL AND ADMINISTRATIVE LABOUR	–	1	1	2	–	–	4
Total	30	59	19	16	–	–	124
Total (per cent)	24.2	47.6	15.3	12.9	–	–	100.0

31.5% Basic labour
65.3% Semi-skilled or skilled labour
3.2% Clerical and administrative labour

because larger owners who were unaffected provided *tha*, but many women did lose a traditional right to excess cultivation land, which was of particular importance to young women with small families.

Husbands owed their wives sufficient fertile land for basic and auxiliary food for their households; women owed the labour necessary to produce enough food and were obliged to maintain the fertility of the land by proper cultivation methods.[17] How much land the household needed depended on its size and the condition of the land; in the mid-twentieth century about two and a half acres staple and half an acre auxiliary food would barely suffice for a larger than normal household, but be too much for a small one. As any labour not needed to care for their children or grow food was their own, ambitious women, with small households or with help from kinswomen, habitually asked for extra land.[18] Though they needed to give part of the harvest to their husbands for clearing additional land, the remainder belonged to them as the labour to produce it had been theirs. Women could use this as they chose: they could give *tha* to visitors and guests, or they could barter it to provide luxuries for themselves, their household and their helpers. When households started to develop additional needs, they looked to their women to satisfy what they needed and the extra harvests might have to pay for salt, sugar and fat as well as cloth or soap, a manufactured garment or a blanket. When hospitality demanded tea, bread and tinned milk, women were expected to provide.

By the First World War husbands – strapped for herding land – became reluctant or unable to provide extra land; households had become accustomed to the 'extras' and women began to see wage labour as a possible alternative, to provide what was expected. They could choose between working in the local or settled area.

Local work was not easy to find as land owners did not like to employ kinswomen for wages. Employers found it difficult to escape the notion that they – in the spirit of *tha* – should have given them more land rather than ask them to work for pay. Even in later years local employers relied to a considerable extent on women from neighbouring areas who were at most distant kin. Women found local work when growers expanded their land under maize and sold it for *posho* – ground maize – to the settled area which was expanding its coffee (Appendix III/17).[19] Yet such work was, before the expansion of commodity crops in the 1930s, only intermittently available, which made local women subject to *gitati*. A further disadvantage was that employers paid in food, which did not give women a choice how to spend their earnings; an advantage was that they could look after their children during their work and were in a familar environment.

Women who had to work preferred the settled area; it could be reached in at most an hour's walk because local land abutted alienated land. One advantage of working for settlers was that settlers paid at least some cash, though supplemented with food, and women had some choice on how to spend the money. 'Good employers' rarely had difficulty in attracting labour; they soon paid through a 'ticket' system. In its early form a ticket consisted of thirty tasks of five to six hours; bad employers did not pay even if a woman had almost completed a ticket before becoming ill. Good employers allowed several workers to work a ticket together and and did not fix a time when it had to be completed. This made it easier for women to work; a household with several adult females could work together on one ticket, earn a full wage and still care for their land and children.

Over time the settled area provided some male employment as well, because settlers did not regard women, for whom household and land came first, as a stable enough labour force to entrust them with tasks which had to be done at specific times of the year or under specific climatic conditions. Plantation labour was consequently gender-linked, with weeding – an ungoing task – set down as women's work, as was planting, preparing trenches, picking coffee and some pruning. Women did not share in the more responsible jobs or even in supervision; yet by the 1930s women probably outnumbered men five to one. By that time some older males, who had already given land to their sons, were looking for supplementary income; they worked as supervisors, planted coffee, and were in charge of disease control and pruning.[20]

There were no semi-skilled and skilled openings for women; when they became available in the local and settled areas they went to males. By 1956 granddaughters performed the same tasks which their grandmothers had done.

By the late 1940s the majority of women still worked in coffee, while the local area often relied on women from outside. Wages remained low; producers were convinced that the cost of commodity production had become too high as manure had risen in price and labour was abundant.

The settled area remained the prime area for local basic female labour. Just before the Emergency 212 local females had worked 'in coffee' in the last twelve-month period; the majority came from landless or land-poor households and worked out of economic necessity. Women with small tracts of land had to tend their land as well as their households; the maximum number of tickets any woman could work – if she could find as many – had remained at eight. Some women, with help from other female members of their household, worked the year round, dividing their time between the settled area and local land. None of the women working in coffee, however long they had worked, were employed in supervisory, semi-skilled or skilled coffee jobs; men with less experience took precedence. Some women still engaged in traditional craft: five were potters but only part-time. The work of the female circumciser had been reduced as some parents no longer circumcised daughters.

The Nairobi labour market before the Depression

Already before the First World War a significant number of local, mostly unmarried, males from households with less or no land, spent at least five or six months a year in some kind of paid Nairobi employment. Though they tended to stay at home after marriage, early male urban work consisted of a series of jobs. It was customary to spend time at home 'resting' between jobs; they expected and wanted short-time employment. Only males in domestic service and those in jobs which demanded some schooling remained in the same job for longer periods. Although some local males, often from economic necessity, tried to emulate this, not until the 1930s, when land scarcity became serious, did most workers seek more permanent jobs. Whether married men stayed in Nairobi after marriage became a function of how much land they could give to their wives.

The Nairobi labour market absorbed in the early decades an increasingly large number of males as temporary, basic labourers. They were needed by Indian contractors, on roads or in shops; workers could dig foundations and haul building materials; they could be water carriers or loaders of carts and freight trains. There was work for streetcleaners, sweepers and night watchmen.

Almost all this work – which could be done by short-time employees, easily replaced – continued during the colonial period. Possibly because employers began to need workers who would be more reliable, some time after the First World War, and perhaps as early as the early 1920s, workers who had gone home 'to rest' often found it difficult to find jobs when they returned. Males from areas more distant from Nairobi – who could not go home so easily – were entering the labour market at this time. Local men therefore sought more stable employment, which often meant seeking semi-skilled or skilled jobs which demanded training or extensive directions. Semi-skilled earned twice the wages of unskilled men; skilled men were sometimes paid as much as five times the unskilled wage. *Dhobis* – laundrymen – gardeners or watchmen were semi-skilled, as were oxcart and cattle drivers. Personal servants, cooks and houseboys in families or hotels were skilled and ranked socially above other skilled workers such as bricklayers, carpenters and those who repaired harnesses and carriages. Helpers of these men, or those who cleaned their premises, could be unskilled or semi-skilled. Most work was piecework; skilled workers might be employed on a more regular basis but semi-skilled and unskilled workers continued to be employed on an on–off basis. Personal and domestic personnel were engaged by the month with the expectation that employment would be continuous until the employer 'went home'. They lived segregated from other workers; housing, clothing and food were part of their wage.

By the middle and late 1920s those seeking clerical work were at an increasing disadvantage. Though they had remained in school for six or seven years and their expectations were high, their skills and competence had declined compared to earlier candidates. Their training in mission outschools where teachers had multiple demands on their time, including preaching and visiting outlying districts, not to speak of demands from local authorities and the care of their own land, no longer achieved what training on mission stations had achieved.

As the vernacular had been used in daily interaction and as the medium of instruction, their skills in English were low. It might have taken them twice as long to finish the basic curriculum compared to earlier entrants, yet they were unqualified for the jobs these men had been able to fill. Due to low educational attainments and oversupply, someone with four years' education could at best find a job as 'runner'; someone with six years might qualify as an 'office boy' if he could find a vacancy (Appendix VII).

The Nairobi labour market from the Depression to the 1940s

After the first significant post-famine subdivision of land, the late 1920s saw a rural exodus of young and married younger males who had received only subsistence tracts. They were joined by males from areas more distant from Nairobi. The majority sought work for economic reasons; they wanted full employment to maintain themselves, accumulate (in part) their brideprices, contribute to their households and, if possible, participate in Nairobi life. Their arrival was inopportune; they arrived in the Depression, when the labour market was shrinking, wages were dropping and employers were devaluing the available jobs.

The influx of work seekers from areas outside Kiambu brought men who were willing to work for lower wages, which allowed employers to reduce pay for basic, semi-skilled and some skilled labour. This was particularly hard on well-established Nairobi workers from Kiambu, who might well suffer a double loss. They had to work for less money, and, if they were senior sons, the divisions had probably cost them the land their father had given them in temporary use, but which they now needed to share with younger brothers. They could, in consequence, provide less help for their households, so that wives or daughters had to work or work longer. As many new arrivals had low skills, previous Nairobi workers tried to break into categories of work for which pressure was less: semi-skilled and skilled work. As unskilled workers attempted to break into the ranks of semi-skilled workers, and semi-skilled workers tried to find skilled jobs, there was increasing pressure on the available jobs in those categories.

Most of these efforts were in vain because the over supply of workers at all levels allowed employers to continue downgrading jobs and wages. As they could get a semi-skilled worker for the wage of an unskilled one, so they could get a skilled worker for what they earlier would have paid a semi-skilled worker.

Whether or not a worker was literate, increasingly determined job classifications and wages. Where men with seven or eight years' education might still find clerical jobs, men with five or six years' of education were shut out; they had to settle for skilled jobs. Men who sought skilled jobs on the basis of on-the-job training were no longer acceptable; they had to give way to men with several years' education who, no longer clerks, quickly cornered the market in some of the more technical or artisan fields.

These trends, set during and immediately after the Depression, continued even when more jobs became available, because the supply of labour from Kiambu, other Kikuyu areas and increasingly from non-Kikuyu areas continued to increase. Unskilled men, even with one or two years' education, had difficulty getting work; employers would hire literate rather than illiterate men for semi-skilled jobs. As workers knew that they could be replaced many times over, they had to accept the job classification of their employers and the concommitant pay. These trends continued during the Second World War and immediately afterwards: though the number of jobs kept growing, the number of applicants increased even more, and wages lagged.

The labour market in Nairobi

Table 4.3 presents an overview of the conditions and work done in Nairobi by 203 local men who were still in Nairobi when the Emergency started.[21] Though young, their marriage rate of 70 per cent shows that males married early. More than 80 per cent were landless or land poor, with only a subsistence holding; their dependence on wages was high. The 17 female workers were too small a group to warrant a special table.

Though Nairobi had increasingly less employment for unskilled workers, more than one in five workers are so classified, and divided into three distinct groups: workers in the informal sector, casual workers and 'pool' workers. Far from being unskilled, the men in this category had a variety of skills.

No more than eight or ten described activities which fitted the usual 'informal sector' criteria. They described their life as poverty-stricken; in contrast, four of the seven *nyanya*, female prostitutes, who were classified in the same category, 'had no complaint'. There were not too many casual workers; the few whose description fitted that category were there by choice; they emphasized that a number of short, basic jobs paid better than a more permanent job. They tended to be unskilled, uneducated and older than the average Nairobi worker.

The largest number of unskilled workers were part of a labour pool. They differed from casual workers in that they had not willingly chosen a situation in which they had to keep body and soul together by casual jobs. Many had credentials for semi-skilled, skilled or even clerical jobs, but had no employment at the moment. Yet they did not dare to be unemployed, and would take any job which came their way until they found work commensurate with their skills. The stringent Nairobi rules against unemployed workers in the locations, the strictness of the various 'vagrancy' laws, which allowed the deportation of the unemployed after a

The Labour Market for the Local Population

Table 4.3 *Profile local male population working in Nairobi before the Declaration of the Emergency*

No.: 203
Marital status: Married 70.0%
Landless or less than 3.99 acres: 82.2%
Age: 25 or under: 55.7%; 26–40: 38.9%; 41–60: 5.4%; 61 and over: 0%.

Education:
Illiterate: 35.0%   2 or more but less than 4 years: 14.8%
Semi-literate: 19.7%   4 or more but less than 8 years: 25.6%
                                       8 or more years: 4.9%

Workforce:	Ahoi	Subsistence plot owners	Small peasants	Peasants	Small farmers	Farmers	Total
BASIC LABOUR							
Agricultural	–	–	–	–	–	–	–
Casual, pool and informal sector	11	25	4	5	–	–	45
SEMI-SKILLED AND SKILLED LABOUR							
Supervisor labour	–	–	–	–	–	–	–
Military, police, *askaris*	–	3	–	–	–	–	3
Fundis, artisans, tailors	10	23	2	2	–	–	37
Mechanics, drivers, technical labour	8	21	5	2	–	–	36
Domestic personnel	19	30	3	–	–	–	52
Self-employed traders, shopkeepers	1	4	4	3	–	–	12
CLERICAL AND ADMINISTRATIVE LABOUR	–	12	4	2	–	–	18
Total	49	118	22	14	–	–	203
Total (per cent)	24.1	58.1	10.8	6.9	–	–	99.9

22.2% Basic labour
69.0% Semi-skilled or skilled labour
8.9% Clerical and administrative labour

---

short time, the all too frequent inability of their land to support them, let alone finding another Nairobi job from there, forced them into this.[22]

The labour pool contained men new to Nairobi and men who had been in Nairobi for years but were between jobs. New arrivals almost always started their careers from the pool. How long they stayed in the pool depended on why they were there, the ability of their network of kin to find a first or new job, their qualifications and the economy. The images conjured up by informants about the Depression was that at that time more people were in than outside the pool. Before the Emergency – and possibly throughout the history of Nairobi labour – the pool fluctuated in size but was a safety valve for workers and a source of cheap labour.

Close to 70 per cent of Nairobi workers were employed in semi-skilled or skilled work. Though domestic workers – largely older – remained by and large illiterate, literacy among other workers was growing; some had attended vocational schools.[23] Employment was available in a wide array of occupations: work might be found in hotels, printing and engineering plants or the transportation and communication industry. Some work was available in private homes and in smaller businesses such as bakeries or dairies; government departments or semi-government organizations employed large numbers of workers: in this category were a number of young veterans who had received their training in military service during the Second World War; some had extensive technical experience.[24] They joined the more educated workers in technical jobs or started their own businesses.

In the late 1940s skilled work in Nairobi was affected by three important developments. African-owned businesses had become visible when the veterans pooled knowledge and gratuities, bought buses and taxis, and opened garages and workshops for painting and carpentry, for the first time offering serious competition to Asian-owned establishments. Not all were successful; those who bought taxis and buses did better than others; many failed because of lack of business experience.

The building industry and other enterprises expanded rapidly and began to emulate government and semi-government employers by hiring a core of permanent employees.[25] While many remained pieceworkers, the more educated and skilled workers profited from the trend; they joined the large Asian workforce in the building and manufacturing industry. A third development was the – hesitant – growth in employment for women, who until this time had only been able to find employment in the informal sector. Although seven of the 17 female workers in Nairobi remained in that occupation, three were employed by relatives who had vegetable stalls, six were in domestic service at the same place as their brothers or husbands, and one had a clerical position.

Clerical workers constituted less than 10 per cent of the Nairobi population. They were employed mainly in government and semi-government service or worked in banks; about one third had a High School education. They continued to demonstrate the economic value of sufficient education; salaries of men with education and experience compared favourably to earnings of – female – European secretaries.[26] Business or government offices might employ some higher-paid clerical workers; less educated, or less experienced clerical workers might work for the same employers at lower wages.

The Labour Market for the Local Population

If they did not already know it, as soon as they started to look for work all Nairobi men learned that education was capital: those without it should not expect anything, those with only a few years could only expect a minimal return, those with most education had the highest returns. The lower the educational achievements, the greater the chance that their years in school had been spent dealing with matters irrelevant to the Nairobi labour market. They would not have been taught English or clerical skills; they would have been taught 'Scripture' and agriculture, though they had no land. Nairobi men, from the highest level of employment to the lowest, in consequence opposed mission control of education.

Strategies for coping with Nairobi conditions in the 1940s

Nairobi conditions were harsh throughout the colonial period; 'locations' built for housing labour were no more safe than the 'shanty towns' earlier workers had erected, though men who had space, even if it was only a 'bedspace', were better off than those who had no housing at all.[27]

Crime was rampant; a major Nairobi need for all workers was to find a group which would support and protect them. In the 1920s Nairobi had developed an institution which can best be called an informal reference group. Such groups did not rely on kinship or even geographical proximity, but were composed of men who in Nairobi worked or lived close together. There was no official membership, men moved in and out of the group as their jobs and location allowed. Such groups were likely to contain several *mariika*: that they often spent recreational and free time together, exchanging information and news from rural and Nairobi areas, created the sense of belonging to large generalized *rūka*. Groups had neither leaders, dues nor sharply defined boundaries; one belonged because one's belonging was taken for granted. Because members had relationships outside their own group, reference groups were linked into a large informal network through which information could be disseminated rapidly. Moreover, a significant number of 'members' would be literate enough to read at least the vernacular press and the information so obtained was equally passed on through these channels.[28]

When by the mid-1940s Nairobi conditions worsened because of the high influx of unemployed males and the return of veterans of the Second World War, the reference groups gave birth to smaller self-help groups. In these groups, men, living close together, protected each other's lives and property against locational banditry and crime. Members of such groups functioned as an 'early warning system', against government raids under the May 1949 Nairobi Vagrancy (Amendment) Bill, which allowed the arrest and repatriation of anyone who had been in Nairobi for three months without a job. By 1950, when mere suspicion was sufficient to be deported, warnings were needed even more; the Voluntary Unemployed

The Labour Market for the Local Population

Persons Ordinance gave police permission to arrest anyone suspected of being unemployed.[29]

The second strategy was probably as old as Nairobi itself and involved Nairobi kinsmen. They might be few; if so, kinsmen who would have been regarded as distant in the rural area might assume the status of close kinsmen in town. While a man interacted daily with at least some members of his reference group, he might not see his kinsmen for days or weeks. The role of the kin group was specific and restricted; its prime obligation was to give aid in need – perhaps a meal, a bed space for a night – and to find jobs through each kinsman's contacts. The length of time a kin group had been in Nairobi could be surmised from the number of kinsmen in the same occupation.

The third, and least successful, strategy as far as individual workers was concerned, was to support the Kenya African Union (KAU) and the unions, hoping that they would agitate on behalf of the workers. The influence of KAU – in the sense of a political party created in 1944 and working within constitutional bounds – cannot be assessed because, although 32 of the 203 Nairobi workers were members of KAU, I do not know whether they became members of KAU soon after it was formed, or later, when it had to all intents and purposes become indistinguishable from Mau Mau (Appendix IX/1).

According to informants, Nairobi men appreciated the work of the unions for higher wages and better conditions, though this did not translate into membership. Lower-paid workers by and large did not join: wage increases, mostly given as a percentage of wages, affected the wages of the lower-paid workers only minimally. Even those who received a larger increase did not think it significant enough: it was absorbed by the rising cost of living in Nairobi. Measured against their real standards, it contributed little or nothing to rural costs, land, manure, school fees and brideprices.

Thus calculations show that just before the Emergency, even after wage increases, 68 per cent of the Nairobi men earned less than three acres of well-manured land could produce. An increase of 5 per cent in wages would have been absorbed by the rising cost of basic foods in Nairobi and would not have benefited the land. Set against rural costs, it would have provided no more than the cost of manuring one tenth of an acre of land.[30]

Wage increases did not affect most businessmen, but for most clerical workers, and perhaps one or two other categories of worker, this same increase of 5 per cent brought sufficient extra income to provide a small surplus after rising living costs in Nairobi had been met. Their earnings before the Emergency surpassed the income from three acres of land. While most Nairobi workers were in a different position, they might well be Union members (Table 4.3; Appendix IV/9).

Where KAU and its president, Jomo Kenyatta, had shown little inclination to challenge the government, the unions and their leaders were willing to do so. The 1947 Mombasa strike, the agitation against the March 1950 celebration of Nairobi cityhood, and the May 1950 Nairobi strike neither drastically changed working conditions nor resulted in a flood of new members, but it did foster the political awareness of Nairobi men.[31]

The indirect effect of the strikes was consequently far greater than the immediate result; men like Fred Kubai or Bildad Kaggia could openly disassociate themselves from KAU policies and substitute their political agenda without fearing a backlash.

Strategies for coping with rural conditions

In the rural area and for workers in the settled area, traditional institutions remained paramount. Inhabitants continued to rely on the bonds of *mbari* rights and *tha*, even when this could rarely be honoured in the form of land. *Tha* continued to be acknowledged in speech, kinship terminology and attitude.

Information flowed through these channels; they were the most important source of jobs. Not all could provide equally; as in the past, those who had important resources were expected to provide more than others. The higher a man's job, the more senior his position, the greater his knowledge to be shared, and the more binding the obligation to extend *tha*. While each should help the other to use the colonial government to the fullest extent possible, one of the most important obligations was to provide protection from it. The colonial government had to be kept distant from any criminal and civil conflicts; only when local elders could not settle conflicts or were powerless in dealing with flagrant breaches of the moral code, would they ask the government to intervene. Even then they would try to use the colonial powers for their own ends, rather than for the government's ends.

The *mariika* had retained some importance in the rural area as opportunities for young males; the organizational forms were dying, however, through the loss of overt functions. Fewer and fewer young males were initiated together; circumcision continued with only a vestige of its previous ritual as most young males were either circumcised in hospitals or without ceremony.

Protests against labour conditions were not among the defence mechanisms of the rural and settled workers; unions did not take root. The only known instance of protest against working conditions was some marginal involvement of women coffee pickers and male unskilled settled area workers in small strikes organized by union members from outside the area in 1947 and 1951.[32] They floundered as strikers were too easily replaced and blacklisted and workers could not afford this risk.

Organizations to use new conditions to greater advantage came in the form of cooperatives. They were intended to cross *mbari* lines and deal with specific commodities, such as potatoes or, for women, poultry and eggs. Although economically successful, few managed to cross *mbari* lines or to overcome internal conflicts.

More successful in this respect were organizations in which women from the households of larger land owners played a dominant or sole role. Their activities were reminiscent of *tha*; though they worked through two modern organizations, a Revival which involved members of the Presbyterian Church and the *Mandeleo ya Wanawake* (Women's Progress) organization, they were an outcome of Western developmental ideas.[33] The Revival, originating in Uganda in the late 1930s, was a reaction against a Christianity which could be learned in schools but did not involve emotions or behaviour, and stressed neither conversion, nor personal commitment and faith. Though it was predominantly a women's movement, men who 'had seen the light', and were prepared to confess their sins and make reparations, had the right to participate in the regular meetings, which were given to much singing of hymns and confession of sins.

All were enjoined to a lifestyle which eschewed laziness or deceit; they should not be involved in polygyny or other 'heathen' practices; they should not drink alcohol or eat food contaminated by blood.[34] Believers regarded themselves as strongly committed to preserving life; most refused to carry arms or to support revolt or violence in any way. Mutual aid was stressed; providing *tha* went well beyond the traditional bounds of kin but embraced, to the degree that the women were able, all those in need. As women did not have land and men had little land to give, *tha* was given in the form of the second most important resource of the community: school fees, clothing and food for children who otherwise could not have attended.

There was a good deal of overlap between the membership of the Revival group and the *Mandeleo ya Wanawake*, although the latter was exclusively female. Both groups came predominantly from the larger land owners, met during the day and charged membership fees, which reduced the participation of working women. Most members were educated, meetings were oriented towards increasing 'women's skills' and instruction of less fortunate others. They stressed mutual aid and help to the poor; they provided help during sickness and birth; they helped with clothing and school fees when able.

Employment immediately before the Declaration of the Emergency

According to Table 4.4, close to 70 per cent of the male population roughly 14 years old and older was employed. Landless, land poor and small peasants had the highest rate of employment; larger land owners had lower employment rates because they only accepted employment which was compatible with the care of their land. Their participation was further reduced because their sons, unlike those of small land owners or landless, entered the labour force late as they stayed in school.

Landless and land poor produced a significant part of the labour force;

Table 4.4 Employment (males) before the Declaration of the Emergency

Type of household	Individuals in household	Not employed		Employed							
				Total		Basic labour		Semi-skilled & skilled labour		Clerical & admin. labour	
		No.	%	No.	%	No.	%	No.	%	No.	%
Ahoi	150	40	26.7	110	73.3	49	44.5	61	55.5	–	–
Ownership											
Subsistence plot owners[a]	331	91	27.5	240	72.7	69	28.8	154	64.2	17	7.1
Small peasants[b]	96	26	27.1	70	72.9	25	35.7	38	54.3	7	10.0
Peasants[c]	122	58	47.5	64	52.5	8	12.5	44	68.8	12	18.8
Small farmers[d]	29	24	82.8	5	17.2	–	–	4	80.0	1	20.0
Farmers[e]	6	4	66.7	2	33.3	–	–	–	–	2	100.0
Totals	734	243	33.1	491	66.9	151	30.8	301	61.3	39	7.9

a Owning less than 3.99 acres.   c Owning 7–19.99 acres.   e Owning 60 acres and over.
b Owning 4–6.99 acres.   d Owning 20–59.99 acres.

Table 4.5 *Employment (females) before the Declaration of the Emergency*

Type of household	Individuals in household	Not employed No.	Not employed %	Employed Total No.	Employed Total %	Employed Basic labour No.	Employed Basic labour %	Employed Semi-skilled & skilled labour No.	Employed Semi-skilled & skilled labour %	Employed Clerical & admin. labour No.	Employed Clerical & admin. labour %
Ahoi	181	57	31.5	124	68.5	122	98.4	2	1.6	—	—
Ownership											
Subsistence plot owners[a]	400	251	62.8	149	37.3	140	94.0	9	6.0	—	—
Small peasants[b]	99	78	78.8	21	21.2	13	61.9	6	28.6	2	9.5
Peasants[c]	152	152	100.0	—	—	—	—	—	—	—	—
Small farmers[d]	32	32	100.0	—	—	—	—	—	—	—	—
Farmers[e]	4	4	100.0	—	—	—	—	—	—	—	—
Totals	868	574	66.1	294	33.9	275	93.5	17	5.8	2	0.7

a Owning less than 3.99 acres.   c Owning 7–19.99 acres.   e Owning 60 acres and over.
b Owning 4–6.99 acres.   d Owning 20–59.99 acres.

they also had the largest number of unskilled workers. Land poor and small peasants, though employed at the same high rate, had to a significant degree been able to leave basic work behind. Farmers had only clerical employment. All other categories, *ahoi* as well as land owners, had more semi-skilled and skilled workers than basic ones. Landless or *ahoi* had no clerical workers; clerical employment increased with land holding and the two administrative appointments were in the hands of the largest land owners.

The land holding, education and job of an individual should not be linked without considering that education is likely to be the result of the land position of the father, not of the son himself. A man with a subsistence holding may have had a father with a peasant holding; he may have been educated because of this and therefore hold a clerical position. That the landless did not have clerical jobs is not so much caused by their own, as by their fathers' lack of land.

Table 4.5 stresses the economic importance of women in commodity production, in the labour market and in the development of their own land. They were confined by and large to low-paid, basic work; women with sufficient land did not work for wages but maintained and developed their own land. The contributions of women to their households will be discussed in the next chapter.

Notes

1. Eleven males and two females who worked in then Tanganyika and one male who worked in Embu have been classified as local workers to avoid too-small categories. All had local land and at least one local spouse.
2. Information about work, wages and work conditions in wider areas is available in
   1974. Clayton, Anthony, and Donald C. Savage, *Government and Labour in Kenya 1895–1963*, London: Frank Cass.
   1976. Tignor, Robert L., *The Colonial Transformation of Kenya*, Princeton: Princeton University Press.
   1979. Lonsdale, John, and Bruce Berman, 'Coping with the contradictions of the colonial state in Kenya 1895–1914', *Journal of African History*, Vol. 20 (1979), pp. 487–505.
   1980. Kitching, Gavin, *Class and Economic Change in Kenya*, New Haven: Yale University Press.
   1980. Swainson, Nicola, *The Development of Corporate Capitalism in Kenya 1918–1977*, London: Heinemann.
   1986. Lonsdale, John, 'The Depression and the Second World War in the transformation of Kenya', in David Killingray and Richard Rathbone (eds), *Africa and the Second World War*, London: Macmillan.
3. Statistical data are based on local information, much of it unchecked. Work categories are based on the descriptions of informants; regional differences are not corrected for uniformity. A man who described himself as the local carpenter might do the same work in Nairobi and regard himself as a carpenter's helper. An office boy in Nairobi might do similar work as a local man who described himself as a clerical worker. Early employment is not quantified; data were often shaky. The denotation 'unskilled' for agricultural work is used reluctantly; agricultural labour was often highly skilled.

The Labour Market for the Local Population

4. A few women had gone to Nairobi to escape parental or marital control or the onus of childlessness. They tended to drift into the informal sector, selling sexual favours or beer.
   1990. White, Luise, *The Comforts of Home, Prostitution in Colonial Kenya*, Chicago: University of Chicago Press.
5. Administrative appointments were often appointments by the colonial administration or one of its departments.
6. Waweru was first gazetted as president of the Native Council of Marigi Locality (OG 1911, p. 142) under the Native Tribunal Rules, 1911. He was gazetted as headman under the Native Authority Ordinance, 1912. Later he became chief; others served as headmen under him. He held this position until 1935, when he was succeeded by his son Magugo. Waweru's initial location as chief was Kibichoi, which was renamed Komothai on 17 July 1943. In Kiambu District Annual Reports Waweru is habitually praised as a 'progressive headman' with a keen interest in agricultural innovations.
   1924. Confidential Records, DC Kiambu, *Chiefs and Headmen* (OG 1924, p. 478), Government Notice No. 176 of 1 May 1924.
7. It is not useful to compare rural and urban wages for clerical workers. Rural government or mission wages were so low that only relatively wealthy land owners could afford such jobs, which, however, gave a good deal of freedom to spend time on their land; employees would consider that the low wage, which would not keep their households, entitled them to put their land first.

   It is common for administrative offices to assume the venality of chiefs; little evidence is given, however, beyond that they were and became wealthy. What is sometimes forgotten is that Kikuyu were well aware that twentieth-century Europeans presumed that they all had been equally poor in the past and were predisposed to ascribe wealth to malfaisance. Complaints to the administration were the supreme weapon of the Kikuyu; if a headman or chief did not do their bidding and they had enough local support, neither headmen nor chiefs lasted long. This does not deny that corruption was probably rife, but while we have data about corrupt chiefs and headmen, we lack the most elementary data about those who complained. What wealth chiefs and headmen acquired came often from inheritance and from having a cash income to invest earlier than most, while they could oversee the land themselves.

   Once headmen began to be paid, their pay depended on the size of their locations. Until 1920 Waweru's location was about 17 square miles and had a population of about 4,500. His pay was shs 34/− a month. Wages increased in the 1920s but by 1948 few headmen earned more than shs 150/−. Wanoike's starting salary, after at least eight years of training, was shs 8/− a month; in 1920 he earned shs 21/−. Thuku s/o Kairianja, a 16-year-old who had left the mission after four years, earned in his first Nairobi job shs 20/− a month. Three years later he earned shs 64/−; in 1918 shs 87/− and in 1921 shs 140/−.
   1918–1919. AR/26, Ukamba Province Annual Report.
   1970. Thuku, Harry, *op. cit.*, pp. 12ff.
   1974. Wanyoike, E. N., *op. cit.*, p. 142.
   1978. Clough, Marshall Sander, *op. cit.*, pp. 76ff.
8. Magugo was gazetted by Government Notice No. 65, 19 January 1935, OG p. 79. He eventually became chief of North Githunguri Division; after the death of Waruhiu wa Kungu on 7 October 1952 he inherited the honorary title of divisional chief. Like his father, he was lauded for progressive attitudes in agriculture; like his father he was reported to be liked and respected by the population.
   1952. AR/325 KBU/43.
9. 1970 MacPherson, R., *op. cit.*, pp. 84ff.
   1974. Wanyoike, E. N., *op. cit.*, 129ff.
10. 1974. Wanyoike, E. N., *op. cit.*, pp. 36, 37ff.
11. *Gitati* is demanded by authority and not reciprocal; *ngwatio* is requested and reciprocal. Unpaid *gitati* meant loss of wages; paid *gitati* paid no more than the lowest local wage. Using this as a guideline for potential wages the labour tax of a man performing unpaid *gitati* for 24 days would have been shs 7/84d in 1913/14; shs 11/20d in 1921; shs 22/−

The Labour Market for the Local Population

in 1935 and shs 21/- in 1940. This is higher than a year's regular tax of that year, which would have been shs 4/20d; shs 16/-; shs 18/- and shs 20/50d.

12. *Askari*, who supervised the work, were exempt, as were men and women over 45 or employed. Husbands and wives were exempt if the husband was in church or government service or self-employed, raising stock or surplus for the market. Wives whose husbands were otherwise employed were not. Men and women who had worked for Europeans for three months were exempt that year. In 1920 the government curbed local power by restricting *gitati* to 24 days, still later to 10 days of unpaid labour. Instead, the government used prison labour or low-paid workers to build bridges and to construct or maintain roads or housing.

The Kiambu LNC used it extensively for rural roads until 1932; until 1950 it was used to build clinics, schools and demonstration farms. It carried the brunt of terracing. The LNC stopped using the term *gitati*, projects were 'communal', the new term for obligatory paid or unpaid labour. During the Emergency it was used extensively.
1974. Clayton, Anthony, and Donald C. Savage, *op. cit.*, pp. 135ff; 190ff.
1932. AR/303 KBU/24.
1938. AR/310 KBU/29.

13. It was common during the colonial period that taxes and labour were used to finance projects which those who provided the principal part of labour and taxes could not afford to use. Some could use the innovation immediately, most could not. They might profit at a later time, but the bitterness was immediate.

14. When a District Annual Report states that an area is 'a good one for labour' or that the 'headman is progressive' one is likely to be dealing with an area where leading men are trade-oriented, *gitati* is rife, and young men and women prefer working for wages to escape it.
1910. KBU/2/KNA/DC HOR, Kiambu.
1915-16. AR/281 KBU/9, Ukamba Provincial Annual Report.

15. The designation 'Indian' follows local usage; it does not distinguish between the people of the Indian Continent.

16. The district had only one car in the early 1920s; funds were so scarce that when it needed extensive repairs, it was withdrawn; in 1923 it was withdrawn altogether for a time. When it was out of action, part of government came to a halt. Lack of transport prohibited officials from knowing their districts; transfers moreover were frequent. In 1925 not one officer had worked for a full year in the district.
1922. AR/289 KBU/15.
1925. AR/292 KBU/18.

17. Twentieth-century staple foods were millet, beans, peas and sweet potatoes with some maize. By the 1920s millet was declining in importance; the basic diet was changing to maize, European potatoes and beans, with a large number of other foods of lesser importance. Kikuyu women followed a complex agricultural calendar, they grew a great variety of crops.
1955. Fisher, Jeanne, *op. cit.*, pp. 228ff.

18. One adult without other obligations could work four acres of land; a work day would be about five to six hours, longer during planting or harvesting. There was little work on the land for about two months of the year. Men or women working their own land, having other domestic obligations, could work at most three acres, five to six hours a day.

19. 1956. Hill, M. F., *op. cit.*, 22ff.

20. When the Kikuyu were allowed to grow coffee they could draw on decades of male and female experience with the actual work; they would use a much lower labour force than the settlers; they had, however, little experience with or data on marketing and the fluctuations of the world market.

21. Workers were classified according to their own job description.

22. 1990. Throup, David W., *op. cit.*, p. 193.

23. In 1924 the Native Industrial Training Depot was opened at Kabete and a technical school at Machakos, both for industrial training; the Jeanes School at Kabete, opened

in 1925, was to teach rural and community development. In 1950 several local males had attended the schools; some females had taken courses at the Jeanes School.
1925. AR/292 KBU/18.

24. By 1943 between 12,000 and 15,000 motor-car and lorry drivers had been trained, nearly 50 per cent of whom had passed the first and second class test. They sought work in Nairobi industry, which kept many who otherwise would have returned to rural areas in town. They also set up repair shops and garages as the number of private cars doubled between 1945 and 1950.

    1943. *The Post-War Employment of Africans*, Report of the Post-War Employment Committee and Report of the Sub-Committee on Post-War Employment of Africans, Nairobi: Government Printer.

    1961. *Commerce and Industry in Kenya*. Colony and Protectorate of Kenya, Nairobi: Government Printer, p. 34.

25. Between 1945 and 1950 the total monthly average of completed buildings rose from 23,000 square feet to 82,000 square feet.

    1961. *Commerce and Industry in Kenya*, Colony and Protectorate of Kenya. Nairobi: Government Printer.

26. An *East African Standard* report of August 1952 gives the data from an income survey of the East African Women's League on European incomes and expenditures; its date is close enough to be useful. Out of 1,000, 181 responded, of whom slightly more than half lived in Nairobi. They were divided into several income classes; 125 answers were analysed; ten belonged to the lowest, eighteen to the highest income groups. Two wage earners were common, as in the poorer Kikuyu households. As in the Kikuyu households the women had less prestigious jobs. The survey and data itself were no longer available; information is based on

    1952. *East African Standard*, 29 August, pp. 27ff.

27. Conditions in Nairobi for African workers are documented in literature and government reports.

    1941. *On the Housing of Africans*, Report by the Senior Medical Officer of Health and Municipal Native Affairs Officer, submitted to the Native Affairs Committee of the Municipal Council of Nairobi, 30 April.

    1950. *Cost of Living Commission Report*, 11 November, Colony and Protectorate of Kenya, Nairobi: Government Printer.

    1950. *African Population of Kenya Colony and Protectorate*, Geographical and Tribal Studies, East African Population Census 1948, The East African Statistical Department, 15 September.

    1954. *Report of the Committee on African Wages* (Carpenter Report), Colony and Protectorate of Kenya, Nairobi: Government Printer.

    1957. Walmsley, R. W., *Nairobi, the Geography of a New City*, Nairobi: Eagle Press.

    1961. *Reported Employment and Wages in Kenya*, 1948–60, East African Statistical Department, Colony and Protectorate of Kenya, August, Nairobi: Government Printer.

    1961. *Reported Employment and Wages in Kenya*, 1948–60, East African Statistical Department, Colony and Protectorate of Kenya, Nairobi.

    1961. *Commerce and Industry in Kenya*, Colony and Protectorate of Kenya, Nairobi: Government Printer.

    1962. Forrester, Marion Wallace, *Kenya To-day*, 's Gravenhage: Mouton and Co.

    1967. Morgan, W. T. W., *Nairobi, City and Region*, Nairobi: Oxford University Press.

    1973. Furedi, Frank, 'The African crowd in Nairobi', *Journal of African History*, Vol. 14, No. 2.

    1974. Werlin, Herbert H., *Governing an African City*, New York: Africana Publishing Co.

    1975. Stichter, Sharon, 'Workers, trade unions and the Mau Mau Rebellion', *Canadian Journal of African Studies*, Vol. 9, No. 2.

    1975. Stichter, Sharon, 'The formation of a working class in Kenya', in Sandbrook, Richard and Robin Cohen, eds, *The Development of an African Working Class*, Toronto: University of Toronto Press.

1977. Hake, Andrew, *African Metropolis*, New York: St. Martin's Press.
1990. White, Luise, *op. cit.*
1990. Throup, David, *Economic and Social Origins of Mau Mau 1945–53*, London: James Currey, pp. 172–96.
28. 1980. Gadsden, Fay, 'The African Press in Kenya 1945–1952', *Journal of African History*, Vol. 21, pp. 515–35.
29. n.d. Throup, David A., 'Kenyatta and the Kenya African Union 1944–1952', unpublished manuscript.
1976. Berman, Bruce J., 'Bureaucracy and incumbent violence; administration and the origin of Mau Mau', *British Journal of Political Science*, No. 6 (April), pp. 143–75.
30. 1954. Carpenter Report, *op. cit.*
31. 1957. Mboya, Tom, 'Trade Unions in Kenya', *Africa South*, Vol. 1, No. 2 (January–March), pp. 77–86.
1969. Singh, M., *History of Kenya's Trade Union Movement to 1952*, Nairobi: East African Publishing House, pp. 82ff; pp. 140ff.
1975. Sandbrook, Richard, and Robin Cohen, eds, *The Development of an African Working Class*, Toronto: University of Toronto Press.
1975. Stichter, Sharon B., 'Workers, trade unions and the Mau Mau rebellion', *Canadian Journal of African Studies*, Vol. 9, No. 2.
1985. Spencer, John, *op. cit.*, pp. 208ff.
32. 1947. AR/320 KBU/38.
1951. AR/324 KBU/42.
33. 1975–76. Wipper, Audrey, 'The Maendeleo ya Wanawake movement in the colonial period', *Rural Africana*, African Studies Center, Michigan State University, pp. 195ff.
34. Wanyoike, E.N., *op. cit.*, pp. 152ff.

Five

Land, Labour & Living in the Colonial Era

Diet, crops and use of land in the early twentieth century

Little is known about possible nineteenth-century differences in cultivation practices and diet between the land poor and the wealthier who produced for their domestic needs and the caravan trade. The ethnological literature does not provide information for the early or later decades of the colonial period, though it provides extensive descriptions of soil types, crops, planting and harvesting. According to the available literature, which does not indicate differences between rich and poor, the late nineteenth- and early twentieth-century basic diet of a variety of cereals, legumes, root crops and a host of auxiliary crops was augmented by gathered foods and honey.[1] Meat consumption by the general population was low; even when the household demanded regular sacrifices, women and children received little meat. Young males were at times allowed to drink the blood of cattle they herded, mixed with cereal; however, older wealthy males who habitually took part in ritual and sacrifice had a heavy meat diet.[2]

The literature provides little information why some basic nineteenth-century foods – particularly millet – became auxiliary foods in the twentieth century. This process was well advanced in the mid-1930s; European potatoes and maize had become basic foods, supplemented with beans for the wealthier. Sweet potatoes were not edged out by the European potato, but often grown side by side with them: they provided excellent ground cover.

These crops demanded less labour than millet, of importance when women sought work and children went to school; they could be interplanted and so saved land. Millet had demanded heavy weeding and monoculture; growing it had demanded frequent crop rotation. Interplanted maize, beans, and sweet potatoes (with some Europeans potatoes at intervals) not only reduced the burden of weeding, but made less demands on the soil, so that the intervals between rotation could be lengthened. Unlike millet, potatoes and maize were also in demand for commodity trading: Europeans bought potatoes for their own use and maize or maize meal, to pay labour.[3]

European potatoes were an innovation, introduced in the local area around 1901, when a *mwanake* brought some back from Dagoretti; an occasional local settler might pay women with seed potatoes as part of their wage. Maize and beans were known, but profited from the introduction of improved seeds with increased yields and quality. Gathering of vegetables and medicinal herbs depended on forest or bush land, and declined after alienation; the higher density of habitation made the production of honey impractical. Most other auxiliary foods continued in the twentieth century as before; banana trees were planted on the edges of flat-land plots; others were planted close to water or on steep hills, not suitable for main crops, which preferred flat land or land with only a small incline. The orange tree, introduced well into the colonial period, did not become a success; on the other hand, pineapples – grown for trade – were beginning to make an impact in the 1940s. Vegetables such as carrots, cabbage, tomatoes, and onions were already grown at that time, but price restricted their use to the wealthier.

While chickens and eggs were commercially available soon after the First World War, that they could be sold to advantage prevented them from becoming part of the diet until after the Second World War, when the wealthier started to use them. Milk was always used sparingly; after the 1930s it was used sometimes in maize porridge. On the whole, elderly males got less meat, whether from goats, cows, or sheep, as the number of sacrifices and payments for initiation and council membership declined. It became a luxury item for women and children in land-poor and landless households, where even males might go without it for weeks. Males, and gradually females too, in wealthier households were eating meat several times a week by the 1940s; it was normally prepared on charcoal braziers.

Innovations in agricultural tools were early and major; Kikuyu migrants to the Rift Valley borrowed the use of a sharper and shorter cultivation knife from Boer settlers. A short-handled hoe was introduced around 1910, as was the *panga*, a broad digging, cutting and weeding knife, not unlike a cutlass. For wealthy land owners the plough started to cut the time needed to bring unused or fallowed land back into production; they also began to use wire to pen up some of their cattle at night. By 1920 the most intrepid land owner and trader had exchanged his team of oxen for a motorcar.[4]

Traditional cultivation methods used a variety of land and soil types: hill, valley, and flat land gardens all had their own crops. Main foods were grown in different areas; agricultural practices were naturally fragmenting. Women received from their husbands an array of different types of land, and only 'lazy women' would avoid the work involved in dispersed gardens. Together with herding, the variety of crops utilized most of the land. The new basic crops used a more restricted range of land, preferring land which was flat or had only a limited incline; cultivation of auxiliary foods continued on other land.[5] Land poverty would eventually force people to plant crops suitable only for moderate slopes and flat land on hill gardens.

Factors of fertility: land and labour

Fertility of Kikuyu land depended on abundant land and labour; it was essential that all land be fallowed after a period of use. Basic cultivation of most crops was women's work; though women might help, preparing land for cultivation was predominanty in the hands of males, who also were expected to clear land after harvests and fallowing. Clearing involved digging out any stalks which could be used to feed stock; unusable stocks, together with any greens remaining after the harvest, were dug into the land.

Fallowed land reverted to bush; the length of fallowing depended on how long it had been used and the crops it had carried. In 'traditional time', different crops had different use–fallow cycles; most seasons some land would have to be brought back into cultivation. As a rough rule, the longer the use of land, the longer the fallowing; the longer the fallowing, the more fertile the land. Ideally, certain crops demanded that a woman use one tract for four to six growing cycles; after that she would return to a previously used, but fallowed piece of land. Some crops allowed land to be used longer and rotation might prolong the period of use; other crops needed to be shifted more quickly.

Fallowing land was used for herding until it was returned to agricultural use. It might be left to return to bush for one or two seasons; when bush reached a certain level, young boys old enough to keep goats away from cultivated land took their goats into the bush which was unsuitable for sheep or cows. After a time the goats would be shifted to another area, allowing the bush to grow back.[6] After a number of cycles of bush and browse, the land would be cleared by *ngwatio* of males, perhaps helped by females; the work involved was heavy. The fertility of fallowed land was mainly due to its restorative powers combined with green manure; animal manure provided at best some help. The loss of goats in the first decades of the century was not so much a loss of manure as a loss of labour: goats cut down on brush.

Even when in the early years males worked for wages, they used their frequent 'resting' periods for help with the crops and for clearing fallowed land. Wages were low, and the hold on most jobs tenuous compared to the security of land. In the rare instance that men in Nairobi had a secure

Land, Labour & Living in the Colonial Era

job – perhaps domestic employment in a European household – workers counted on a mixture of furlough, hired labour, and *ngwatio*. Yet repeated absence could diminish one's hold on good jobs; this may have been a factor in the shift away from millet.

After alienation, *ahoi* and others who had lost land but had strong ties with *mbari* which had retained land did not necessarily suffer loss of cultivation land. *Mbari* provided when they could: solidarity was sound policy as a larger population on the land might deter alienation. The reward of giving *tha* in land was allegiance; those who gave it gained power and authority.[7]

The exodus to the Rift Valley masked for a time the extent of the loss; over time the effects of alienation were felt more sharply. Local losses in land were predominantly in the lower lands, often used for herding; sharing the remaining land with kinsmen, using the land of kin, all meant a reduction in the availability of herding land. If kinsmen with remaining land were increasing their cash crops, or planned to do so – if they had sons who would marry within the next few years, say – one might use their land for agriculture, but not for herding. Herding, involving breeding of stock, was not a seasonal, but a long-term activity.

Those who lost herding land did not immediately lose their herds: they could use Rift Valley kinsmen and their abundant land, and some could take stock to Ndeia. This meant loss of control and often loss of the increase of the herd – which was demanded in payment by the owners of the land. When by the mid-1920s use of Rift Valley land or Ndeia became more problematic, most had already reduced their stock to no more than a maintenance herd of ten or twelve goats, which they herded around the local area (Appendix VI/1). Not all lost their herding land; those who had lost less and had fewer demands for *tha* or inheritances could continue to herd. They would by the 1920s follow the general trend of replacing goats with cattle. When larger land owners converted more land to cash crops, they and all who had depended on them for herding land had to reduce their stock. Larger land owners often kept only a few goats; the trend towards replacing goats and sheep with cattle continued.

Monetization, discussed earlier, de-emphasized herding, and freed more land for cultivation; by the end of the First World War, with more demand for commodities, larger land owners could bring more land under cash crops, though they sometimes had to reduce the number of households which depended on their *tha*. Matters notably worsened in the mid-1920s when sons demanded land. If fathers were to fallow as needed, then smaller land owners could only provide for sons – giving them enough land for cultivation and fallowing – by sharply restricting the number of kinsmen who received *tha*, reducing the size of the tracts of those who still got land to a few acres, if that. Larger land owners could continue to fallow and could provide sufficiencies, including fallowing land, for sons, but they too needed to reduce their *tha*. By the 1920s those who provided *tha* were often unable to provide land for cultivation and fallowing, though providing the one without the other was tantamount to accepting the deterioration of the land.

The problem of fallowing, which took much land out of production for extended periods, would engage smaller and larger land owners in the late 1920s and the 1930s. After the divisions of land for sons from the mid-1920s onwards, only the largest land owners could continue to fallow their own land for long periods; smaller land owners had to reduce their period of fallowing. Small owners and *ahoi* had no fallowing land. Large land owners had to provide fallowing land for small land owners, while *ahoi* needed cultivation and fallowing land. In the struggle to provide, *ahoi* began to lose out; owners did not want their land destroyed by cultivation without fallowing.

Early land use of larger land owners and the changes of the 1920s

The larger land owners' group contained peasants with at least seven acres, and small and large farmers; under ordinary circumstances none of them needed to use the land of others for land maintenance or subsistence.

After the famine, when survivors knew that it was incumbent on them to restore the descent group as well as the fertility of the land, the rate of marriages – including multiple marriages – was high. The incorporation of young women had resulted in strong population expansion; by the mid-1920s a large number of males in all households were reaching marriageable age. Until this time the limited number of young males who had survived the famine had received land, and large land owners had tended to have a surfeit of land. This land had been used for herding, but when herding began to lose its lustre, it was used to give *tha* to *mbari* members and kinsmen, with commodity crops a distant third.

In the early decades large land owners had started to put land into commodity production in the hope that it would restore the prosperity of the late nineteenth century, but the commodity acreage had remained limited even though white settlement brought increased demands.[8] While local growers had been the moving force behind the road-building programme, hoping to displace the Indian middlemen, they had met with only limited success. Commodity production had increased in part because Indian merchants came to buy in the local area, but more because settlers, who also bought potatoes, needed ground maize, *posho*, to pay workers as part of their wages. In the Kiambu area, the growth of the coffee plantations had gone hand in hand with the expansion of land under maize (Appendix IV/17).

A true revival of trade had not – yet – occurred; maize and potatoes remained the main crops; beans were not grown for the market as local rainfall was unreliable. Though the cost of production, given the low cost of labour, was ostensibly low, so were the profits as Indian merchants paid only low prices. Table 5.1 shows that before the Carter Commission one acre of maize would have netted shs 42/88*d*; one acre of potatoes shs 99/50*d*. Only an exceptional land owner would have allotted twenty acres to each; his profit would have been close to shs 2848/- per year. These estimates are inflated, moreover, as they do not subtract the cost of fallowing, the cost of labour to bring the land into production and other costs (Appendix IV/4).[9] With this in mind, a senior clerk in Nairobi, working for the postal service or a para-government institution, earned a higher annual income than a farmer with forty acres under cash crops.

When sons, born after the famine, began to ask for brideprices and land in the 1920s, few fathers were prepared: they had been unable to save by adding land and breeding stock during the years that sons were growing up.

The number of claimants was large: between the mid-1920s and mid-1930s a monogamously married father might have to provide for several sons; fathers with a number of wives faced more claims. If they had engaged in serial polygyny, claims might continue for decades. The first-born son of a first-born son would already make a claim on his father, while the grandfather was still trying to provide for his last-born son. If men had inherited land from brothers who had died in the famine, they also might have to provide for their brothers' sons.[10]

The subdivision of a father's land meant more small estates, threatening continued *tha*. Farming estates became peasant holdings; peasant holdings, subsistence tracts. Sons who had received land, could rarely provide the level of *tha* a father had been able to give; a man with 60 acres could perhaps provide 10 acres for *ahoi*. If he kept 10 acres for himself and divided the remainder between 6 sons, neither they nor the father were likely to be able to support the *ahoi*.

Providing brideprices was no easier than providing land. By the mid-1920s monetization of brideprices was well advanced: while a few larger land owners had cash income from better-paying jobs, others had to sell stock. Others again could only help their sons because - in the early 1920s - they had extended their cash crops, to the disadvantage of *ahoi*. Few large land owners paid the whole bridewealth for all their sons; men who married had to contribute themselves and might well start out with debts.

Early land use of smaller land owners and the changes of the 1920s

The smaller land owners' group consisted of small peasants who owned at most 6.99 acres and subsistence tract owners with at most 3.99 acres. The latter are usually called land poor in this study. The term landless is reserved for those without land; most were *ahoi*; at this time only a few would be *mbari* members whose fathers or brothers were too poor to give

Table 5.1 *Approximate cost of production, yield and profit for maize and potatoes, in shillings per acre*

Crop	Cost of production per acre				Yield per acre			Profit	
Type of Land and approx. period	Manure costs	Labour costs	Bagging and transport	Total cost	Bags per acre	Market value per bag	Gross yield per acre	Net profit per bag	Net profit per acre
Maize									
Fallowed land before Carter	–	37.50	11.–	48.50	10¾	8.50	91.38	3.99	42.88
Manured land, 1939	64.–	45.–	15.–	124.–	14¾	18.–	265.50	9.59	141.50
Manured land before Emergency	150.–	60.–	30.–	240.–	14¾	30.–	442.50	13.73	202.50
Potatoes									
Fallowed land before Carter	–	37.50	13.–	50.50	25	6.–	150.–	3.98	99.50
Manured land, 1939	96.–	45.–	34.–	175.–	34	8.50	289.–	3.35	114.–
Manured land before Emergency	225.–	60.–	60.–	345.–	34	20.–	680.–	9.85	335.–

them a share. Many had inherited their tracts in the mid-1920s from peasant or small peasant fathers.

Small peasants and subsistence tract owners used their land for food production; small peasants might occasionally sell surplus for barter or cash at the local market; a few might sell their surplus to larger farmers, who sold it together with their own in the commodity market.

Until the divisions of the 1920s, the land poor and even some subsistence tract owners had relied on the larger land owners for fallowing, herding a maintenance herd and – particularly land poor – for supplemental cultivation land.

The rate of polygyny in this group had been lower than the rate for larger land owners: except for the unlucky few who had inherited several wives or taken them immediately after the famine, they had fewer sons who claimed land on marriage. Yet the subdivision of their tracts created quite small estates and resulted often in significant fragmentation, as sons were entitled to a share in all the types of land in their father's estate. Table 3.1 (page 99) gives an indication of ownership of land around the Carter period; it does not indicate how many households used a holding. Taking this as base, it can be shown that, between the Carter Commission and the Declaration of the Emergency, the number of households steadily increased and the size of their land decreased.

After the divisions of the 1920s, many more households needed help from larger land owners. Though the tracts of the latter were reduced as well, they might still be willing to give fallowing land, perhaps in dispersed tracts, as this had a natural time limit when users returned to their own land. They were more reluctant to give basic cultivation land which could easily become a permanent burden. Giving basic cultivation land logically meant providing users with fallowing land as well, to avoid over-use and destruction of the cultivation land.

Large and small land owners and *ahoi* were kin, rather than distinct, separate groups. Those needing land might be *mbari* members; they could be daughters who had married landless or land poor men, or else the kinsmen of these men, who might also have married into the *mbari*. Those who had received such help before, continued to expect it; they were now joined by many who, after the divisions, also found themselves with insufficient land. New claims, perhaps from *ahoi* or subsistence tract owners who had married daughters of larger land owners, added to the burden. Giving the newcomers land came dangerously close to recognizing them as *ahoi* at a time when larger land owners were trying to shed responsibility for the sons of their established *ahoi*. The needs of sons not yet married, and the desire to plant more cash crops, also mitigated against making more land available.

Larger land owners were often torn between the desire to help and conflicts about whom to help and whom to refuse. They knew also that – unless they accepted that land users would destroy the land – they had to offer cultivation and fallow land to a substantial number of aid seekers, or, if they had only offered cultivation land, face the task of refusing further help when what they had given needed fallowing. As early as the Carter Report, larger land owners found that they might still be able to aid kin with subsistence plots; they owned at least part of what they needed. *Ahoi* on the contrary, became a heavier, sometimes a too-heavy burden.

The Department of Agriculture and production of the DARD

The government had shown little interest in encouraging Kikuyu commodity production, possibly out of fear that it would undermine European monopolies, and that stimulation of local productivity would interfere with the flow of cheap labour.[11] Nor had it shown much interest in the Kikuyu landless and land poor; it was a colonial article of faith that the Kikuyu had sufficient land for domestic purposes, if they only used it properly. Government concern was therefore directed towards persuading the Kikuyu to grow basic food.

Directing the production of an adequate supply of basic food became one of the primary tasks of the Department of Agriculture, created in Kiambu in 1923. It could not do much; it had only one officer, stationed at the Scott Agricultural Laboratory which was primarily concerned with European commodity production. Nevertheless, it came up with suggestions for land use which headmen or chiefs were supposed to enforce.[12]

According to the Department, the basic needs of staple food for a mean-sized household of five adults could be satisfied with about 13¾ bags of maize, 4½ bags of beans and 10¼ bags of potatoes. These recommendations will be called the Department of Agriculture Recommended Diet or DARD; it was supposed to assure a minimal but sufficient basic diet (Appendix IV/8). Though it might be a sufficient basic diet, the Agricultural Department did not concern itself with whether it was a basic adequate diet; it was not concerned with auxiliary foods, such as vegatables, millet or even sweet potatoes; it also ignored foods such as meat, milk, eggs or other protein foods.

I asked the local Mbari ya Igi Agricultural Committee (MAC) to consider how much land a local household would need, whether owned or used, to produce the DARD; the Committee was also asked to consider the consequences of not having enough land, or land of inferior quality. The Committee played an indispensable advisory role in this phase of the research. It was well equipped to do so: members were familiar with local cultivation; they had holdings of different sizes; some had been adults when herding and fallowing were still generally practised; they had all witnessed the changes brought by the introduction of manure in the early 1930s, which had put an end to large-scale fallowing.

The Committee was not concerned with the lower elevation land, which the community had by and large lost in alienation; it concentrated on the different ways in which higher elevation land could be used. Although, for comparative reasons, I would have welcomed more specific information about earlier years, the Committee could describe those decades only in general terms; for later decades it could be considerably more precise. What other information I needed I obtained in 1962 through the Department of Agriculture and the sources mentioned in Appendix IV/8.

The Committee warned that their findings could only be used as guides; it was impossible to standardize the productivity of any acreage across the board: no two tracts, no two seasons, no two cultivators sowed or worked the same way. Productivity depended on the location of the plot, on its rainfall, the type and condition of land and its elevation. Important factors were the skill and industry of the cultivators, whether crops were planted together – intercropped – or monocropped, and a host of other factors.

Monocropping had become popular in the early twentieth century with those who produced for the market: it gave somewhat higher yields and allowed the grower to avoid products for which there was little demand in favour of those which were popular. It did require more weeding, but most early monocroppers used cheap paid labour.

The majority of cultivators intercropped, which allowed a woman to decide which crop to emphasize of those she planted together. When land was scarce, she could emphasize maize; it was hardy and tended to grow even when rainfall was lower than expected, and potatoes and particularly beans failed. Intercropping also demanded less work; if sweet potatoes – which grew under most conditions – were interplanted, weeding was reduced to a minimum and the greens provided fodder for goats.

The Committee estimated that after the famine and for the first decades three monocropped acres, one of beans, one of maize and one of potatoes, on adequately fallowed land – standardized as five years' use, followed by three years' fallowing – would have come close to producing the DARD, as would three acres of intercropped land if crops were well balanced.[13] Even the few who monocropped would still plant some sweet potatoes under at least one crop, probably maize. Intercropping cultivators would grow sweet potatoes wherever possible. A hypothetical cultivator would plant bananas along the edge of the land; if she was close to the river or had low lying land, she would grow some famine crops there. She probably would need some extra land for additional crops; space was also needed for an enclosed homestead, granaries, and a place of safety for stock. Stock would be herded on fallowed land which needed to be about the same size as the land in use, even though different crops would be fallowed at different times. All in all, a household would need to own or have the use of a basic acreage of about seven acres. A small peasant would have barely enough land for cultivation and fallowing; subsistence land owners would need help with fallowing land, landless would need cultivation and fallowing land.

In the opinion of the MAC, before the subdivisions of the 1920s, the overwhelming majority of inhabitants had owned or been able to use enough good cultivation land to reach the DARD, some relying entirely on their own land, others with the help of larger land owners. The main factor in failing to do so would have been lack of labour, particularly male labour. Men who had good jobs in Nairobi did not like to leave them frequently to help with the land. This undermined *ngwatio*, because reciprocity became doubtful, and though women could take over some of the work of men, they could not do all the work involved in fallowing.

Use of land around the time of the Carter Commission

While there were undoubtedly as many ways to use land as there were cultivators, the MAC recognized two broad hypothetical types for the late pre-Carter period. Most larger land owners fallowed as before and monocropped; a sizeable group of small land owners, lacking sufficient land, fallowed at about half the customary rate and intercropped with an increasing emphasis on maize. The two types of cultivation resulted in different size harvests and quality of produce: high quality produce will be called Grade 1, lesser quality, Grade 2. All things being equal, one might expect large land owners to produce Grade 1 products while smaller land owners, with insufficient fallowing, would produce Grade 2; they fetched different prices in the market.[14] Grade 1 producers were more likely to use paid labour; Grade 2 producers relied more on domestic labour. Labour was cheap at that time; domestic labour might not turn out to be much cheaper than hired labour (Appendix IV/5).

Using the memory of Committee members, and information from district annual reports and the Department of Agriculture, I established cost of production and prices for three periods: just before the Carter Commission, around 1939/40, and just before the Declaration of the Emergency. I used the crops of the DARD: maize, beans and potatoes; prices were for bulk sales, and prices fetched by small quantities in Marige market were ignored. If written or oral information differed for the same period and crop, I usually – unless the discrepancies were too great – averaged the prices. This made sense: producers did not sell their harvest at one time to one buyer; crops might get higher prices at the end of the season than at the beginning. As beans were not often sold commercially, and written information about them was consequently scarce, I adhered to the local dictum 'beans are twice as costly as maize'.

Just before the Carter Commission, larger land owners with one acre maize, one acre potatoes, and one acre beans would have, according to the DARD, a surplus of potatoes, but a lack of beans and maize. If the potatoes were sold, and maize and beans bought at Grade 1 prices, they would have a cash surplus of shs 50/25d. To buy the DARD in grade 1 produce would have cost shs 254/88d (Appendix IV/9).

In the unlikely event that smaller land owners or users could not get sufficient land, or if they lacked labour, they would have intercropped with an emphasis on maize. This would have given a maize surplus according to DARD standards. If they sold this and bought beans and potatoes up to DARD standards in Grade 2 produce, they would be shs 6/25d short. This would have to come from other sources. The cost of buying the DARD in second grade produce would have been shs 188/88*d* (Appendix IV/9).

The difference in price between Grades 1 and 2 was already significant, but was even greater later, when the difference in quality became more pronounced. Marige market sold predominantly Grade 2 produce in small quantities, though the shops might buy bulk and Grade 1, as did Indian merchants. Producers complained about the low prices given by Indian merchants; buyers complained about their high prices and avoided their shops. They would buy or barter from local kinsmen, in Marige shops or market; at times they bought quantities no larger than a half calabash, Grade 2 produce.

Social changes after the subdivisions and the Carter Commission

When the Carter Commission made it clear that the Kikuyu could not expect to get their land back, all land owners and users were faced with using what they had to best advantage. For some this would mean intensifying the use of the land; for others, finding alternative sources of income; some would do both.

Larger land owners started to put more land under cash crops in spite of the relatively low return – though it meant that land for *tha*, already diminished by the sub-divisions, was even more reduced. They might try to get a local job which did not interfere with the care of their land, but as most were still illiterate, it was more advantageous to send younger sons to school and help other sons to start a local or regional business or trade. Several shops were opened at Marige; some lorries were bought. These moves made some inroads on Indian control of local production.

For smaller land owners or users, wage labour would become increasingly important, even though most could only demand basic wages as they too were illiterate. More of their wives and daughters would start working 'in coffee'. Smaller land owners also started to use hillsides, initially intending this to be only temporary to fallow their cultivation land, but often continuing to do so permanently. Some women with a few acres practised wage labour together with internal fallowing. They divided the land into parts, 'resting' one part for several seasons and using the other parts. After a few seasons they would switch. Maize would be a prime crop, sweet potatoes would be interplanted. Under favourable conditions, one acre might produce as much as eight bags of maize.[15] The heavy maize diet, however stodgy and inadequate, had the advantage that maize could be cooked quickly after a day 'in coffee' or in the fields.

When a household had so little land that most basic food needed to be bought, several wage earners would be needed. A husband's wage might go to his maintenance in Nairobi, taxes, payments towards the brideprice, and other social expenditures. A woman alone could not sufficiently feed her family from basic labour. Before the Carter Commission, a woman who worked 300 days of the year and bought Grade 2 DARD would still have provided a heavy maize diet; when maize prices went up but wages did not, her work was insufficient (Appendix IV/15). It would then be necessary to augment the female workers of the household; the new recruits might come from unmarried or divorced daughters, a divorced sister, or an elderly mother. Together the women might tend what land they owned or could use and share wage labour.[16]

Between the time of the subdivisions, the Carter Commission and the late 1940s, when the size of holdings and availability of *tha* affected all, kin and marital relationships changed, as did the relationship between large and small land owners. The changes would not affect all at the same time, nor would they affect all equally. Some changes had started before the Carter Commission, some occurred in the first decade afterwards, some emerged slowly in the 1940s.

Women in poor households, with husbands in migrant labour, became more dependent on their female kin, and, as they did so, they created a (probably new) female social and economic group. It provided care of children and land, in *ngwatio* and sickness. It provided more labour, more income, and companionship when husbands were absent. It gave a psychological refuge: though aging women had the right to live in the homestead of their sons, they often would rather depend on and receive help from daughters than be beholden to daughters-in-law. Women who, for whatever reason, did not or could not stay with a husband, might have found their sisters more accepting of their presence than their fathers and brothers, who had to return the brideprice.[17]

Poorer men lost status in their households and with their wife's kin for not paying the brideprice or paying too slowly. They lost status with their children, who saw that 'their mother's, not their father's labour fed them'. Even if they led an impoverished life in Nairobi to pay taxes and pay towards the brideprice, and perhaps fees for education of a son, their absence counted against them: growing children in poor households were surrounded by women and were beholden to them.

Households which had relied on their wealthier kinsmen realized that the needs of their kin began to outstrip their ability and desire to give *tha*. That a man asked his kinsmen to leave his land or be satisfied with a small tract was sad, but understandable. He could not do otherwise if he needed to increase the land under cash crops, because sons needed to be sent to school, he needed to help with bridewealths, and he had to provide sufficiencies. There was no enmity between those who had left and those who had asked them to leave; there was a greater sense that the land poor and landless were less beholden to those with land than before.

Among larger land owners some opposite trends could be discerned, as husbands took over the care of all the land and women no longer had their food land but took what they needed from the crops. Males therefore increased their influence in the domestic sphere: as they controlled income, they increased their influence on domestic decisions in areas such as clothing, furniture and education. Women's status and influence were enhanced, however, in land poor or landless households when men were absent; wealthier women, whose husbands had local jobs and entrusted the supervision of labour to their wives, equally gained. If they started their own enterprise, such as keeping chickens, they also gained. Women also gained influence through new institutions: wives of larger land owners were likely to be church members; there they, not men, made many decisions even though officials tended to be male.

Where the decision-making rights of all women had been relatively high before the colonial era, many women regained some of this after the Carter Commission, though poorer women paid an exceedingly high price.

The use of land after the Carter Commission

Beginning with the 1930s, local agriculture underwent an almost revolutionary change with the introduction of manure, the active intervention of the government in agricultural affairs, and rising prices for commodities.

Commodity production of the larger land owners increased significantly when manuring replaced fallowing and more land therefore became available for constant use. Most of it went into increased commodity production rather than *tha*. Yields from manured land were higher in quantity and quality; prices rose rapidly as the result of greater government intervention. Through the Native Crops Ordinance of 1935 and the Marketing Boards, the government enforced regulations by which certain commodities such as maize were inspected, graded in official centres, and sold only to licensed traders at set prices which, in spite of some chicanery, were by and large considerably better than what commodity producers had been able to get before. What the Boards rejected continued to be sold at Marige, and growers dissatisfied with grades or prices offered by the Boards also sold through their 'own channels', mostly to settlers or to African middlemen who resold to more distant areas.[18]

The new interest of the government provided Kiambu in 1934 with its first permanent agricultural officer.[19] Whether one of his first activities included the promotion of manure over fallowing is not clear. The MAC thought that local initiative had been most important; some land owners were already using some manure while they cut down on fallowing – with its 'hidden costs' in land – before M.H. Grieve had been appointed.

Manure, government intervention and the larger land owners

The use of animal manure was not an innovation, but the extent to which it came to be used, was. In the nineteenth and early twentieth century, specific crops were manured from time to time when the domestic midden, which contained manure of animals kept within the homestead at night, was dug in. Fallowing, though strongly relying on green manure, had a component of animal manure through grazing and browsing of stock. Kikuyu, however, relied strongly on green manure and fallowing, even selling their manure to settlers for grazing rights on settler land until land scarcity forced them to change.[20]

Once started, demand for manure was such that in 1935 the Kiambu LNC forbade sales to settlers.[21] When this did not produce enough, the Maasai became the main suppliers. It was shipped to Nairobi; transportation to the local area would double the cost.

The Department of Agriculture at around this time had produced general guidelines for the manure needs of various cash crops, but even the best local farmers used only 80 per cent of what was recommended, though they acknowledged that heavier manuring might have increased their yields. The amount they used I have called the local standard of excellence, leading to Grade 1 produce. As a result of the high demand, the cost of manure at Nairobi rose from shs 8/- per ton in 1939 to shs 12/- in 1945, with the local area price doubled due to transportation. At that time the LNC decided to pay half of the cost of transportation; whether this set off the new, more rapid rise in prices which more than doubled the cost by 1950 was not clear (Appendix IV/10).

Before the extensive use of manure, even without taking the hidden costs of fallowing into account, growers had complained that their cost of production was too high for the returns. Though their yields increased considerably with manure, the cost of production remained high and commodity producers retained a sense of vulnerability, which depressed wages – or did not help to increase them to any extent. Bad harvests due to drought or a drop in prices could destroy producers, a concern shared by the Department, particularly when the cost of manure reached shs 37/50d a ton.[22] It advocated greater use of mixed farming, which would both reduce the need for manure and produce part of what a cultivator needed; it remained adamantly opposed to fertilizers, except for isolated crops such as pineapples.

Yet incomes rose sharply as producers could pass the cost of manure on to the consumers. Table 5.1 shows that in 1939 the profits of one acre of maize had risen to shs 141/50d although profits for potatoes had only slightly increased to shs 114/-. Before the Emergency a producer would make on average shs 202/50d from one acre of maize and shs 335/- from an acre of potatoes. A producer who had twenty acres each of maize and potatoes in production would have netted shs 5,110/- in 1939; just before the Emergency, when there were fewer who could afford to use forty acres for cash crops, it would have been shs 10,750/-. This was a higher income than any clerical worker or chief earned. Only successful traders might come close to or surpass it.

Larger land owners also benefited materially from the Department's demonstration farms, which had started as early as 1926 but increased in importance by the Second World War.[23] While owners of larger holdings

Land, Labour & Living in the Colonial Era

could imitate what was done, the demonstrations were of little use to men who had well below seven acres of land.[24] The successful plans emphasized mixed farming – including penning up cattle at night – with its potential saving on the cost of manure. After initial opposition out of fear that cattle dips would poison lifestock, some large land owners, intrigued with the possibility of high-grade cattle for dairy production, were willing to pay out of their own pockets for the first dip to combat East Coast Fever.[25]

All these improvements did not quiet the demand for crops which gave better returns. Moreover, the farm plans presumed a relatively high level of initial capital, hidden though this was by the Department's use of 'communal': the old *gitati*, in other words, and its generosity in providing manure and – some say – young stock. Land owners who considered copying the plans rarely did so; they were aware that the plans gave a much rosier image than the reality. Local men would not have access to free labour, manure or stock; if they had to carry these costs then the increase in the yield of demonstration farms did not warrant the investment. Larger land owners were no longer looking for small improvements; they wanted higher-yielding crops which would allow them to buy land, educate sons and daughters, and provide sufficiencies when sons married.

The influence of manure on small holders

Though a number of cultivators in this category until well into the 1950s would be unable to afford manure or do the hard work manuring required, it was initially a boon for all land owners, even the subsistence tract owners. In the early years it was relatively cheap; any large or small land owner who manured to the local standard of excellence and monocropped could have met the DARD and sold surplus from all three crops. In 1939 a three-acre plot would have produced a surplus of shs 288/88*d*; if owners continued to manure at the same level, three acres just before the Emergency would have produced a surplus of shs 530/–. In 1939 buying the DARD would have cost shs 496/63*d*; just before the Emergency shs 887/50*d* (Appendix IV/9).

Land poor and landless had so many claims on their small incomes that they could not afford to reinvest adequately in increasingly costly manure; they gradually lowered how much they bought, until the luckier ones reached the 25 per cent level; they could not decrease their investment further if they wanted to get a reasonable price for their produce. Yet at that level of manure their land was better used, their diets possibly improved, and they did get some cash income. If they continued to intercrop and emphasized maize, they would have a Grade 2 crop, but a large surplus of maize. If they sold this and bought beans and potatoes to DARD standards, they would have made a profit of shs 155/– in 1939, and shs 232/50*d* just before the Emergency. In 1939 the Grade 2 DARD would have cost shs 357/25*d*; just before the Emergency, shs 598/50*d* (Appendix IV/9).

Compared with those who could use manure, even if only at the 25 per cent level, crops of households with less than three acres, whether in one tract or in fragments, not manured, perhaps because they were too poor or because they were *ahoi*, deteriorated year by year. They were caught in a spiral of poverty as food prices rose but wages increased only fractionally. In 1930 the wages of a woman working full-time, partially in the settled area and partially in local land, would have paid for 83.7 per cent of the DARD in Grade 2 produce. In 1939 this had dropped to 54.9 per cent; just before the Emergency it paid for only 44.1 per cent (Appendix IV/15).

Lack of productive land increased the tendency to sow maize at high density and/or to use wages to buy maize over other food. They bought less and less, however; just before the Carter Commission a minimum wage would have bought about 24 bags of maize; by 1939 the buying power had dropped to 15 bags; by the Declaration of the Emergency it had dropped still further (Appendix IV/15).

The influence of government on small holders: terracing and soil conservation
While government intervention in the affairs of larger land owners might be onerous, it was also profitable. Small owners would have been hard put to see a beneficial aspect. They received little if any help, and though they agreed with the Department that some of the practices which had grown up in the last decades were detrimental to the land, they could not afford the Department's remedies, which were geared towards saving the land for the future. This was in particular the case with terracing and soil conservation, which came down heavily on small holders.

The Department had started its operation at a time of world-wide heightened awareness of soil and land destruction. The central government saw this exemplified in Kikuyu country and it expected a cure from terracing of land, although experts were not yet certain about the best way to implement this.[26] That there had been neither sufficient field trials nor wholehearted approval from the Kiambu Administration was lost in the fervour;[27] the Department of Agriculture was charged with its implementation.

There were also political motivations. It was important to demonstrate that the Kikuyu were not short of land; that alienation had mainly taken land the Kikuyu never owned and did not need; and that deterioration and shortage were caused by bad agriculturalists, and also by 'individualist' or downright greedy acts of men who increasingly used their position and wealth to enrich themselves rather than sharing, as tribal men should. The latter explanation was relatively new.

In 1941 a District Commissioner wrote with obvious disapproval about 'influential land grabbers'; a few years later another would be more blunt and blame 'Chiefs and other influential men'; a third would echo this and accuse the 'richer Kikuyu of increasing their land holdings by purchasing from poorer ones'.[28] As late as 1947, the same popular accusation that Kikuyu land poverty was caused by the Kikuyu 'rich' would be part of the administrative stock in trade.[29] It did not go beyond rhetoric: no brake was put on the government's attempt to encourage larger land owners to plant more commodities; nor is there any evidence that it made the Department of Agriculture more compassionate towards the alleged victims, the land poor.

The Department could not have started its soil conservation programmes at a worse time. The Kiambu Local Native Council was still profoundly angry about having been 'deceived' and forced to donate the moneys it had collected for its own Kiambu High School at Githunguri, free of mission control, for a primary school in Kagumo outside Kiambu. The slights of the Report of the Kenya Land Commission were fresh in its members' minds and it saw in the Department's attempt to halt soil erosion a not-so-subtle attempt to force Kikuyu to acknowledge that any land scarcity was due to 'primitive' and wasteful use of land. It refused cooperation.[30]

By 1937 its anger would take shape in turning down the government's land conservation rules; it passed its own rules, which the government turned down. The LNC tacitly supported those who refused agricultural officers access to their land; visits of any agricultural officer were felt as attacks on *mbari* autonomy as well.[31] When the government started to extinguish Kikuyu claims which had been accepted by the Carter Commission, before claimants had received acceptable compensation, the LNC continued its defiance.[32]

Even when agreeing that the land was deteriorating badly, the LNC, large land owners, and particularly land poor and landless refused to be cast in the role of the guilty, ignorant cause of the damage. The real culprit was not the Kikuyu, but alienation condoned and encouraged by the government.

Traditionally, neglect constituted one of the few situations in which *mbari* leaders could deprive people of land; Kikuyu were worried that the accusations of the Department could be interpreted as harbingers and threats of more alienation to come. For this reason, and to keep agricultural officers at bay, they ultimately complied with the order that they terrace the land. Yet small land owners, who held most of the land which needed terracing, remained angry.

The LNC passed the government ordinances, and made terracing a communal responsibility suitable for *gitati*, now called communal labour. It was supposed to be paid, but could be demanded without pay if no money was available.[33] In its hurry to get started, narrow-based terraces were imposed; when they disintegrated with crops and rain, the work had to be repeated for the construction of broad-based terraces.[34]

The work took up relatively little of the time of the agricultural officers themselves. African assistants who had operated in the district as early as 1936 could do the inspections, as obedience and disobedience were clearly visible. If agricultural assistants were sure that the officer would not visit the area, they, like chiefs and headmen, could help the population by passing or signing off as many jobs as they could. Though the population knew that they occasionally had to impose fines if they were to keep their jobs, as long as they worked with *tha* and accepted that the population would do as much as it could, there was no quarrel. Unfortunately, agricultural officers often did visit: assistants therefore applied the rules harshly and became the most visible image of government repression.

Communal labour put a heavier burden on those who had little land than on large land owners, who had less land which needed terracing, were often excused from the actual work because the usual exceptions prevailed, and could hire labour to do the necessary work. It came down much heavier on women at home than on men, absent in migrant labour. Women had their own work, their households and their land to do; they often had to start terracing as well: it was not a foregone conclusion that 'communal' would get to their land before sowing time or before one would be fined for being in default.

To the degree that 'communal' helped small land owners with terracing, it was useful; to the degree that small land owners had to help others – a seemingly unending task – it was a burden carried angrily and reluctantly, as poverty did not allow this *tha*. There were many other reasons to oppose it. The work would disturb the fragile top soil and reduce fertility; the size of the land available for food would be reduced as terracing, even contour terracing, reduced land for planting. Poor women with no alternative land were likely to lose a harvest while terracing the land; if little help was available or the work was done badly – because of anger over 'communal' labour – they might well lose a second harvest while they tried to repair the damage. And after it was all done, they might have more work in the future; early terraces were unstable and needed repair after every harvest; heavy rains could destroy a crop and create havoc.

Resistance to terracing or 'communal' labour was rarely expressed in open defiance. It was the quality of the work performed that made the attitudes of the people crystal clear: obedience and loyalty, as well as political soundness, could be measured in feet.[35]

Because so many opposed it, the *gitati* aspect was ultimately dropped in favour of owner's responsibility.[36] Yet the pressure tactics which had been used by the Department fostered an attitude in which a large part of the population came to see the agricultural department and its employees as the most repressive and abusive part of the colonial government. This attitude was not confined to those who suffered; even if they had received their share of departmental benefits, chiefs and headmen who took their jobs seriously chafed under a situation in which they had to deal with a restive population which they could not protect.

While not all small land owners were living in abject misery, many did and others were at risk. They shared certain hopes and needs; however small their holding, they wanted a crop which would give a high enough yield for food and other necessities which had to be bought. They shared a deep concern about sons; they had already lost the hope that they could give them sufficiencies in land, let alone brideprices. What remained was education; if parents could provide that, sons might get some compensation for all they had not been able to give. Even the landless lived by the hope that education might make up for all they could not provide. Two case histories of land poor can give a glimpse of their lives and worries.

The case of Rerei and Wamaitha: land poor with wages

When they married in 1929, Rerei was given about one and a half acres of land by his father, which Wamaitha cultivated while Rerei worked in Nairobi. He was in and out of the labour pool, and Wamaitha took every other month a small bag of maize flour to him so that he would not be hungry. She had difficulty conceiving; she also lost her first three pregnancies. However, in 1936 she had a son and in 1937 a daughter, followed in quick succession by three more children, so that she had five children in 1940. Pregnancies and young children had worn her out; she worked her own land but managed only three tickets in coffee each year. In 1939 she had spent it on medicine and Rerei insisted they sacrifice a goat because the last pregnancy had been extraordinarily difficult.

By 1940 Rerei was a helper on a building site in Nairobi, learning to be a mason and earning shs 37/50*d*. He had started paying the brideprice and fees for the lowest elders' grade, and could not help the household financially beyond about shs 5/- each quarter. He fell behind with his taxes, was caught, and served time in a labour gang. When he came out, he went back into the Nairobi pool.

Wamaitha knew that she badly needed to buy manure, because her land produced less and less and her youngest two children had 'the disease of children', *kwashiorkor*. She could rarely work more than three tickets, however. The wife of a larger land owner had given *tha* by convincing her husband to let Wamaitha use some land so that her land could rest.

Rerei was lucky: he found a Nairobi job for shs 45/- and now regularly contributed shs 10/- each quarter when he came home. In 1945 Wamaitha bought manure for the first time, but the bus fare for Rerei, who had to dig it in, had to be paid from the money he otherwise would have contributed. Fortunately he did bring some badly needed second-hand clothes; they celebrated by buying tea, sugar, milk, and one loaf of bread, and two buns which the children shared. Unfortunately, Rerei became ill, had to stay home beyond his leave and lost his job. He went back into the labour pool, but when the two youngest children became very ill, Wamaitha sent for him. He took them to the clinic in Kiambu, where the dresser charged shs 8/- for medicine and said that the children would die unless they got better food. They died in 1946.

That year Wamaitha worked four tickets in coffee, but Rerei, only a night watchman, had to make a choice between paying for a bus ticket to come home or sending money home. He alternated between the two, but once a man lost the money he had given him to take to Wamaitha.

In 1948, the land was manured to 10 per cent; the remainder of the money was needed for food. In 1949 one of the 'Revival women' gave them each month some maize flour and potatoes, and Wamaitha manured that year to 25 per cent. In 1950, Rerei was hit by a car in Nairobi and lost much of the use of his right leg; he could no longer work and came home. Wamaitha worked five tickets and her land; for a few years they had sufficient food. When money for manure was no longer available, their food supply became precarious.

Because they were so poor, the boys could get a partial remission of school fees, and over the years they had gone, depending on whether their parents could afford the uniforms and the remainder of the fees. None had finished more than standard three.

Small peasant with wage labour: Munai and Maria

Munai received five acres of land when he married Maria in 1932; he had to pay his own brideprice, which was high because Maria was literate. He worked in a garage in Nairobi and earned only shs 30/–; she however managed to work four acres of the land, while a small brother herded a few goats over the other acre. The land was no more than adequate quality. Maria rotated the crops and fallowed internally as much as possible; Munai, who knew several men with lorries, could come home more frequently than usual, and helped with the conversion of fallow land to agricultural use. Internal fallowing, however, was always too short; they received no help.

In 1937 they had bought a little manure, only 5 per cent of what was locally regarded as a standard of excellence. They had produced more food which had allowed Maria to barter at Marige, but their real chance came in 1939, when Munai got work in Kiambu for shs 45/–. They managed to save most of his income by offering to take the son of a Kiambu kinsman in their house so that he could attend local schools, purported to be excellent. Munai lived for free with the Kiambu kinsman. As Maria's father and brothers were pressing for payment of the brideprice, three quarters of Munai's money went for that purpose but one quarter was used to manure two acres to 40 per cent and three acres to 25 per cent. Maria – who eventually would have seven children, four of them boys – worked the three acres and sold her surplus at Marige; they also employed an old woman part-time for the other two acres. That produce was also sold at Marige.

In 1945 a settler whose car Munai had repaired, offered him the job of labour supervisor and *fundi* at the unusually high wage of shs 70/– a month. They had been saving to buy more land, but pressure of Maria's relatives forced them to use all of it for her brideprice, which was paid by 1947. They continued manuring at the previous level and selling their surplus, living very frugally because they wanted to buy two acres of land adjacent to their own. In 1949 they got the land for shs 1,200/–. They resumed manuring, hired a full-time labourer and by 1952 for the first time started to increase the level of manure and buy new instead of second-hand clothes for the family. By 1952 Munai sold the produce of his first 80 per cent manured acre of maize to a local buyer.

However frugally the family had lived, education was regarded as a prime need, and as soon as the boys reached five, they were sent to school. Though Munai and Maria hoped that they would be able to buy two more acres, the increasing price of land was of concern. They had seven acres of good land, but if divided between the four sons it would not give them much. They had tried to provide them with education; the eldest had stayed in school for almost ten years and now had a well-paying job in Embu, but the next son had failed and was in Nairobi refusing to tell them what he did and where his money came from. Two other ones were still in school; maybe one would be able to go far enough to get a paying job. There was little chance that the parents could do more than make a token contribution to the bride-price. There was a very real chance that, in spite of all their hard work, their old age would be as poor as their sons would be.

Conditions in the late 1940s

By this time, regardless of whether they belonged to the same *mbari* or were close kin, households differed considerably in access to resources and opportunities. Some had good incomes from cash crops and salaries, and could provide adequately for their food and whatever else they needed; their taxes were low; they could afford schools and medical aid. Others could meet the DARD from land and/or income; they could afford to satisfy some needs beyond food. Others again were hard pushed to provide sufficient food from land and wages, let alone other expenditures; because taxes were based on a flat rate, those with the lowest income paid the highest taxes (Appendix IV/1).

To better understand the economic and social conditions in the late 1940s, I attempted to get some idea of spending patterns in the different households within the land categories. I asked adults in one household within each land category what their income had been during the year just before the Emergency from land and/or wages; and what – if applicable – they had used from their land or bought with cash during the month after the main harvest in 1956. After analysing these answers, I included five more households in each land category; some prices were obtained from local merchants and *ndukas*. The data are rough indeed: no control was possible, and the gap between 1950 and 1956 was considerable. Reliability is therefore low, but the data are the best I can get. Households were divided into those who lived below and those who lived above the poverty line. I established the poverty line as sufficient income or land to satisfy the DARD requirements in Grade 2 food, and an additional income of shs 400/- for all other expenses.

Households below the poverty line

Households below the poverty line were those which had less than one acre of land in use, whether they were *ahoi* or owned subsistence tracts. To make up for lack of land they generally needed to have three adult wage earners; after having paid for basic food, they would have on average no more than shs 200/- for all expenditures beyond the DARD each year (Appendix IV/20). The wage of the male, often in Nairobi, was used to provide for himself, to pay taxes, make contributions to the brideprice – most of these households still faced many payments – and for some incidental contributions to his household. If he made these, they were likely to be school fees, uniforms or second-hand clothes. Food would be mainly maize or maize porridge; auxiliary food would concentrate on sweet potatoes, sugar – a surprisingly high amount of sugar was consumed, probably to make the porridge more palatable – salt, fat, soap and matches. These households lacked clothing, and could not repair dwellings or replace worn-out tools. While circumcisers would be paid, no celebratory gathering would take place, and no fees were available for advance in eldership. Medical aid, whether from the clinic or the medicine man, would be used only in extreme cases if at all. Education was highly prized, and parents would do whatever they could to send a son, even if it was only intermittently. I would estimate that by 1950 as many as 40 per cent of the households belonged to this category.

A second category, also below the poverty line, had at least two acres of land but still needed two wage earners, if it were to pay for the DARD and some auxiliary needs. A husband might work in Nairobi or the settled area; he might make a regular contribution of shs 10/- a month when he worked. Employment was irregular; a male might go for months without a job. Wives worked; at least one other female would live with the working woman. A mother and sisters worked what land the woman had; they jointly cared for the children. After food had been bought, the household had no more than shs 400/- available. The diet, though still heavily maize-dependent, would include sweet potatoes, European potatoes and root crops, but no meat, eggs, milk or other protein foods. Like the first households, they bought second-hand clothing, but did repair tools or the homestead if possible. School fees ranked high on the list of needs, even if at the expense of food; only one son could go to school at a time. Medical aid might be sought somewhat earlier, and contributions to the brideprice were made more regularly than in the first group. This group comprised about 30 per cent of the households; even small peasants whose land was exhausted might belong to this group.

The lives of both groups were fragile. Rising prices of food and lack of sufficient land, lack of education, low wages, and frequent unemployment pushed their backs to the wall. All dreaded the time when sons would need land; rarely had they been able to provide more than one with basic education.

Households above the poverty line

All other households, about 30 per cent, were above the line, mainly because they had more land, income from cash crops, and better-paying jobs because of education. There was still a significant difference between them; while the lower group would have at least shs 800/-, besides the

DARD, the top-income group might have the DARD and an additional shs 10,000/- a year. In these households women rarely worked for wages; in the lower-income group a woman worked her own land together with labour; in the higher-income group she might have her own business.

The lower-income group above the poverty line remained tied to the basic local diet of maize, potatoes, beans and sweet potatoes; it bought carrots and tomatoes. Higher-income households used more European foods. Significant differences in use of auxiliary foods remained; what would be a luxury for the lower group would be a regular item on the menu of the others, whether milk, eggs, tea, meat, vegetables, bread, or rice. Even the lower-income category regarded kerosene lamps as a necessity, though to be used sparingly; the higher-income category would use them daily. Where soap had been a scarce item among the households below the poverty line, in these households it was common; they had also sufficient clothes, blankets and furniture.

Food was cooked on charcoal in braziers which provided heat in different rooms; collecting firewood was a thing of the past. The brideprice was mostly paid – but for an occasional present – in cash; and fees for medical treatment, elders' rank, school and – if they were members – church were accepted as normal expenses. Education was of high importance, and daughters and sons attended school regularly. While the lower-income households from those above the poverty line might find it difficult sending a son or daughter to high school, the others would not, though they would hope for help if a college opportunity opened up.

Cash crops were important to higher-income households; the highest-income groups had significant incomes from the basic cash crops, potatoes and maize. Households with less land might have more labour-intensive cashcrops, such as onions, vegetables or pineapples (Appendix IV/13). They were highly in favour of a change in land tenure and of growing coffee; they had suffered a great deal from litigation. While the lower group was concerned about the cost of planting coffee, all were saving towards the time that permission would be given.

Kikuyu solutions: coffee and education

Kikuyu saw coffee through rose-tinted spectacles; though aware that the coffee market could show considerable fluctuations, they believed that good years far outnumbered the bad, and that the profits of those years would provide a hedge against losses in others. They were also convinced that they would be able to invest their profits more wisely than Europeans, who 'ate what they earned and did not buy land'.

In 1948 it was widely known that at least some local men would soon be allowed to grow coffee, and it was probably one of the strong arguments used in that year's abortive attempt to bring about a change in land tenure. In 1951, when Githunguri District including the local area was gazetted for coffee, or during 1956 when some larger land owners were ready to market their first crop the next year, the image of coffee was of bumper crops and markets eager for Kenya coffee.[37] In 1956 the MAC illustrated the hopes and expectations, using members' 1955 data (Appendix IV/19).

MAC members were convinced that the high cost of the first four years after planting would have been recovered by the end of the fifth year, which would provide an additional small profit. In the following years, the profits for one acre of 540 trees were estimated at shs 4,480/–; each tree would yield about shs 8/30d. One acre of coffee in 1956 prices would produce nine times as much as an acre of maize. Their ideas about the coffee market and their expectations would turn out to be unrealistic.

Large land owners wanted coffee and its high yields; they did not want to rely on coffee alone but intended to continue to grow other commodities as well. Smaller land owners hoped to grow some coffee; even the landless hoped that their kinsmen would allow them to use a quarter of an acre until their gains would allow them to buy land. The high cost of investment could be reduced by using domestic labour; in the first four years when husband and wife needed to continue in wage labour, they would rely on *ngwatio*. Small land owners thought a quarter of an acre, or about 135 trees, would be well within their capabilities: to begin with it would pay for basic food and leave a surplus of around shs 500/–. Soon a wife might be able to stay at home and look after the coffee, instead of working for a settler; sons might be sent to school. In time more land might be brought under coffee; slowly a household would bring up its number of trees; in ten years they might have as much as an acre of coffee. Even if they had to subdivide their land for sons, each would get a sufficiency.[38]

The conditions for coffee licences

It was not until late 1949, perhaps early 1950, that the local population learned that, although coffee licences would become available, neither landless nor land poor would get them.

Charged with drawing up the rules, the Department of Agriculture kept to the principle that an adequate food supply should be a priority. It did not share the small holders' belief that good coffee harvests would buy food, more food than the land could produce. The Department insisted that the land be preserved for future generations: innovations – such as coffee – should be introduced slowly under stringent control by those who had sufficient land and could care for it as demanded by the Department. In its opinion, households which had four acres of land or less could not provide sufficient food, mulch and manure and therefore should not be given licences.[39] Licences should only be given to men who had undisputed private, not *mbari*, land; the Department must have been convinced that a change in land tenure was imminent.[40]

Even the largest land owners would only get 100 trees to start with; subject to Department approval, they might get more. Small peasants and peasants had to show evidence that they produced sufficient food; small farmers and farmers did not need to do so. Yet, in addition to excluding many from growing coffee, the Department insisted that those who did grow it, entered some type of mixed farming; growers needed to pen their cattle at night so that they produced sufficient manure.

The reform of education

Parents, well aware of the low return of education, blamed the structure of the school system and the refusal of government and missions to give the same education as European children received for the low value of the education of their children (Appendix VII). In reality, the way many parents used education, the way missions saw it as a means to introduce the Gospel, and the endeavours of those who saw African education as a means to create a docile workforce, often inadvertently worked together to make education slow, inefficient, and inferior by any standard.

Because they could not afford to continue paying the fees, many parents had to take their children out of school long before students could use education in jobs or were ready for the scholastic hurdles of examinations. Children who stayed in school – theoretically after four or five but more likely after eight years – would sit the Common Entrance Exam. As passes were given on the basis of openings in Intermediate classes, the rate of failure was 90 per cent. If a child passed, he might sit the Kenya African Preliminary Exam (KAPE) at the end of the 8th (official) year; failure rate here was between 80 and 90 per cent. Those who continued to pass might get one of the scarce places in secondary schools, or could apply for places in Teacher Training Colleges or Trade Schools.

Parents across the board supported the idea of a drastic reform; poorer parents wanted affordable education, which taught literacy, numeracy and, particularly, English. Wealthier parents wanted stress on academic subjects, less mission control, greater access to post-primary and secondary education, and parity with European education.

The reforms eventually proposed were the result of extensive studies. *A Ten Year Plan for the Development of Education* outlined a number of goals in 1948; the *African Education in Kenya: Report* of 1949 – called, after its Chairman, the *Beecher Report* – gathered extensive data on the condition of education and proposed structural changes and a possible timetable. It was adopted by the Legislative Council in 1950 (Appendix VII).[41]

The Report acknowledged the sorry state of African education and made it clear that the African District Councils – the old LNCs – could not carry the burden of education alone; there was no possibility of reform without strong financial backing from the government. Teacher training at all levels needed to be extended; more junior and senior secondary schools needed to be opened for the qualified. Parents came in for a good deal of blame for stagnation and problems in elementary education; what was at fault was not their poverty or the low value of instruction, but their 'tribal' attitudes, and child labour in agriculture and pastoral economies. If left unchecked, the first years of education would remain a bottleneck of pupils who would remain or return to school again and again, without profit for themselves, to the detriment of others and quality education.

While at the time of the Carter Commission many Kikuyu would have been unable to read English, the *Beecher Report* was accessible, and its conclusions about the Kikuyu and their capabilities were scathing and negative. It had little good to say about the moral content of modern African child rearing; proper moral behaviour was rooted in Christian values which the Western child received even if neither he, his parents nor his teachers were church members. Only missions and the Church could make up what African children lacked; continued mission influence in school and curriculum was vital. As far as African aspirations were concerned, Africans should understand that the demand for universal education was premature; the labour market did not yet encourage such demands.[42] In the foreseeable future many young men would not earn a living from 'white collar jobs', but only from agricultural, pastoral, and manual labour.

Children should enter school at around seven years of age and leave at eleven, unless they could pass an examination which allowed them to enter the next years of schooling; neither repeating, nor the drop-in, drop-out method of attendance should be allowed any longer. Since so few could expect to be qualified, the government should plan for only one place in standard five for every three children who entered standard one. In the higher grades attrition would be even more marked: for each sixteen pupils entering standard one, only one place would be needed in standard seven.[43]

There was enough in the Report to anger most Kikuyu. There was the condescending attitude that Africans were not ready for better instruction, and that African children at home did not receive training in moral values; there was the self-congratulatory mission attitude that missionaries were the proper instructors in values and could use the schools for this purpose. Kikuyu resented the Report's conclusion that even with mission guidance the curriculum should reflect that most Africans would be able to perform only manual work for a long time to come. Even the few who would be able to go to high school and beyond would by no means have had an education which would allow parity with Europeans.

Nevertheless, large land owners, who could send their children to school at the right time and keep them there, were promised greater access and better education. Many teachers, too, saw advantages in not having to struggle with large classes of diverse ability, with students who might have been 'in school' for six years but had actually attended less than one.

The real victims of the *Beecher Report* were the children of the poor, who were no longer allowed to use the methods which had allowed some access to education. Others would determine what the poor, regardless of their ability, would have to do: they *had* to send their children when they were seven, *had* to take them out when they were eleven unless they gained entrance to Intermediate School by passing the Common Entrance Exam

(CEE); few parents expected that their children would be among the lucky, and most could not afford to find out. Though about 10 per cent of parents might apply for remission of part of the fees through the African District Council (ADC), fees would rise to shs 22/- for each of the first four years. With uniform and obligatory Bible, the fees came close to 15 per cent of the annual minimum wage. For the next four years fees would be shs 45/-; with the usual additions, it could amount then to about 25 per cent of the annual minimum wage.

By the end of the 1940s, economic conditions of larger land owners were improving; they could compensate for rising prices and increased needs with higher cash crop yields. If they worked, their wages were likely to have risen more than those of poorer men. Coffee was within their reach. Their sons were likely to get more education in the future than had been available before.

Yet economic improvement was bought at a high price of self-respect and expectations. Improvements were introduced for them but without them; they were small boys who, under the tutelage of European masters, would be shown how to bring up their children, and how to handle stock or crops.

The smaller land owners, the land poor and landless suffered the patronizing attitudes without compensation. They were required to accept peacefully that they had no other rights than to obey and let the government make its decisions for them and their sons. If the government decided that they could not improve their situation by growing coffee, they should accept this; if the government decided that there was no need to plan education which parents could afford, then that was the end of the matter. Their fears of the past were now enshrined in rules and laws; there was to be no reprieve for them or their sons, who could only look forward to greater destitution and poverty.

Notes

1. 1885. Thomson, Joseph, *Through Masai Land*, London: Sampson, Low, Marston, Searle and Rivington, p. 307.
   1893. Lugard, F. J. D., *The Rise of Our East African Empire*, Edinburgh: Blackwood, p. 328.
   1955. Fisher, Jeanne, *op. cit.*, pp. 174ff.
   1977. Leakey, L. S. B., *op. cit.*, Vol. I, pp. 168ff.
2. This chapter gives only a restricted overview of Kikuyu agricultural and veterinary practices to indicate changes and attitudes of the colonial period. Much more complete and detailed information is available in Fisher and Leakey.
   1955. Fisher, Jeanne, *op. cit.*
   1977. Leakey, L. S. B., *op. cit.*, pp. 168ff.
3. The first dietary change was the reduced use of honey, many vegetables, and herbs, including medicinal bark, when the forest disappeared and women had less time for gathering. Some products became commercially available but prices were outside the reach of most. A small barrel of honey, for instance, cost shs 30/- in about 1922.

4. Kinyanyui wa Gathirimu had a motor-car well before most administrators.
   1916–1917. AR/278 KBU/10, Dagoretti sub-district annual report.
   1974. Miracle, Marvin P., *Economic Change among the Kikuyu 1895–1905*, Nairobi: Institute for Development Studies, University of Nairobi.
5. Traditionally flat land and hill land had both been valuable; during the early decades of colonialism, flat land became premium land. When coffee was introduced as a local crop, terraced hillsides became important.
6. Three to four goats could browse several months on one well-overgrown acre. Neither sheep nor cows were browsers, one cow needed between three quarters and a single acre of well-cleared land. Labour depended on terrain and flock. If animals were docile, the land flat, and cultivation at a distance, small boys could handle about a dozen goats, older boys up to forty sheep or goats. Adults could handle twenty to twenty-five cows or sixty to seventy goats. Highly fertile land could accommodate more stock, but such land was in the past returned to agriculture.
7. Perhaps the earliest victims -- after those who lost all land -- of land alienation were ambitious women who had relied on additional land and whose husbands were willing to ask wealthier men for fallowing and herding land.
8. Beyond an increase in maize production for settlers who used it as *posho*, little is known about the organization of trade in the first decades of the twentieth century. It involved more products, certainly; buyers wanted the staples but also a regular supply of foods which earlier had been of only marginal interest. Some wanted fowl or goat meat (one dressed goat produced 20 lbs of meat); other buyers wanted charcoal, firewood and building materials. A few settlers wanted ewes to mate with imported rams. Indian merchants first paid with goods such as bread, tea, matches or cigarettes. Later they also paid cash.
9. Not only was land prepared for each sowing, but it also needed periodic fallowing for a number of seasons to keep it fertile; after a number of seasons it would be brought back into production (Appendix IV/4).
10. The unusually large 1919/20 initiation year showed the post-famine population recovery. Initiations a few years later were even larger. Under nineteenth-century conditions a ten-year gap between initiation and marriage would have been normal; during colonial times the age of male initiation dropped, as did the age of marriage.
11. 1980 Spencer, I.R.G., *op. cit.*
    1985. Anderson, David, and David Throup, *op. cit.*
12. Duties of headmen were defined loosely; much depended on the district administrator. When an agricultural show was badly attended, the then District Commissioner felt that he had grounds to complain about the 'utter inefficiency and uselessness of most of the Headmen'.
    1923. AR/298 KBU/16.
13. In the hypothetical cases fallowing was standardized. Under actual conditions the length of fallowing depended on the crop and the rotation which had been used on the land.
14. Many other less obvious and less easily quantifiable factors make differences in yield or quality. To do justice to the variety of grades of produce, the MAC would have had to establish many more classes and taken seasonal variation as well as availability of labour into account.
15. The estimate for before the Carter Commission may be on the low side. Not long before that time land had probably still been fallowed. It might be too high ten years later, if in the interim the land had neither been manured nor fallowed.
16. While it is often thought that the use of domestic labour constitutes 'free labour', women made it quite clear that domestic labour could be costly. In addition to food and shelter those who helped on the land expected their share of 'presents' and privileges. In some cases women complained that using hired labour would have cost less.
17. In modern times many men and women from low-income households started marriage before the brideprice was paid. If all went well, both had emotional security, but if conflicts arose, the woman had greater problems. She could lose her children, or could be left with the children without right to support. As no bridewealth had been received

by father or brothers, her welcome home with or without children was not secured.
18. 1976. Tignor, Robert L., *op. cit.*, pp. 293ff.
    1980. Kitching, Gavin, *Class and Economic Change in Kenya*, New Haven: Yale University Press, pp. 57ff.
    1980. Spencer, I.R.G., *op. cit.*
    1985. Anderson, David, and David Throup, *op. cit.*
    1990. Berman, Bruce, *Control and Crisis in Colonial Kenya*, London: James Currey, pp. 235ff.
19. 1934. AR/306 KBU/26 appended agricultural report M.H. Grieve, p. 1.
20. High-grade cattle produced more manure than native animals, but, unless given supplementary food, their pasture would demand more manure than the cattle produced.
21. The LNC in Kiambu had started to meet in July 1925. The DC had opposed the sale of manure as early as 1933 but he was unable to prevent it until 1935.
    1933. AR/305 KBU/25.
    1935. AR/307 KBU/27.
22. 1954–1962. HOR/194 KBU/50.
23. The objective was to show that small acreages could provide an adequate diet, based on the DARD and additional protein-rich food, by mixed farming without the need to buy expensive manure. They would use domestic labour and provide a small cash income. In the local area such small acreages could not sustain sufficient cattle.
    1926. AR/293 KBU/19.
    1976. Tignor, Robert L., *op. cit.*, p. 306.
24. At least ten land owners had planned holdings; kinsmen of office holders apparently had priority rights. Holdings were owned by peasants, small farmers, and at least one farmer; as their land was fragmented, only part of the holdings of small farmers and farmers was planned. The cost of the plans was shs 10/– per acre; by 1962 there was no evidence that the Department had demanded payment.
25. In 1947 permission was obtained for the building of local dips; by 1949 three dips had been built.
    1947. AR/320 KBU/38.
    1949. AR/322 KBU/40.
26. 1937. Maher, A. Colin, 'Soil erosion and land utilisation in the Kamasia, Njemps and East Suk', mimeo, Agricultural Department, Nairobi; also Manuscripts, Rhodes House, Afric.S. 1741.
    1984. Anderson, David, and David Throup, *Africans and Agricultural Production in Colonial Kenya: The Myth of the Year as Watershed*, Cambridge: Cambridge University Press, pp. 2ff.
    1984. Anderson, D. M., 'Depression, dust bowl, demography and drought, state attitudes to soil conservation in East Africa 1920–1939', *African Affairs*, Vol. 83, No. 334, pp. 321–43. Though an enthusiastic defender of terracing, Maher did not push terracing as the government would do eventually. He was convinced that important problems such as drainage remained to be solved.
27. 1935. AR/307 KBU/27.
    J.G. Hopkins pointed out the high cost, the need for heavy manuring afterwards, and the overall reduction in harvests because of the disturbance of the top soil. It is not clear whether he voiced his own concerns, those of the LNC, or those of officials in the Department of Agriculture.
28. 1941. AR/313 KBU/32, addendum H. E. Lambert.
    1945. AR/317 KBU/36.
    1947–1953. (1947) AR/319 KBU/38–44.
29. 1947. AR/320 KBU/38. Local 'rich' men did not buy from 'poor' men. Land of the poor was relatively expensive, as reimbursement for improvements did not take labour into account, and paid little for non-permanent improvements, even manure. Poor owners also had only small plots; buyers of such land needed to invest a great deal in improvements at a high cost of labour due to the dispersal of the plots.
30. 1934. AR/306 KBU/26.

31. 1938. AR/310 KBU/29.
32. The Carter Commission Report brought a strong revival of the notion that no one had the right to enter *mbari* land or the right to tell the owner how to use it, as this implied less than full ownership.
   1938. AR/310 KBU/29.
33. 1942. AR/314 KBU/33.
34. 1954. Penwill, D. J. *Provisional Development Policy Kiambu District, Appendix A*. While leaving no doubt about the need for soil conservation, it indicates the numerous mistakes made in the early period, before sufficient trials and observations had been made.
35. 1947. AR/320 KBU/38.
   1949. AR/322 KBU/40.
36. 1950. HOR/1950 KBU/194.
37. 1951. AR/324 KBU/42.
38. These dreams were unrealistic. By 1962, prices were much lower and wages had risen; in that year, one minimum wage would be higher than the yield of a quarter acre of coffee.
39. Despite strongly held local beliefs, my only documentary evidence is indirect. By 1956 all 24 men with coffee licences owned more than four acres of land. Local demonstration farms of four acres were regarded as uneconomic; they could not provide a sufficiently high level of animal and green manure to maintain fertility for food production. Given that this was a Departmental priority, it is unlikely that it would have permitted taking land from food production and using it for coffee, which would make high demands for manure and mulch. Several documents make it clear that coffee licences should be given only to those with enough land to grow food, mulch, and provide sufficient green and animal manure. In 1962 the four-acre rule had been relaxed to two acres.
   1953. 14 November, Assistant Agricultural Officer to District Agricultural Officer, Kiambu, re *African Coffee Growing in Kiambu District*. JDB/SMT.
   1954. Penwill, D. J., *Provisional Development Policy Kiambu District, Appendix A*.
40. The Department of Agriculture was in 1953 certain that consolidation would take place even though it was not approved until 1954. According to one of its documents a licence should only be given if requested by a man who could show that 'It is his own *shamba* and not a *"Mbari"* shamba which will be divided up in the future with the probable dividing up of the coffee *shamba*....'
   1953. 14 November, Assistant Agricultural Officer, Kiambu to District Agricultural Officer, Kiambu re *African Coffee Growing in Kiambu District*. JDB/SMT.
41. 1948. *A Ten-Year Plan for the Development of African Education*, Nairobi: Government Printer.
   1949. *African Education in Kenya: Report of a Committee Appointed to Enquire into the Scope, Content, and Methods of African Education, its Administration and Finance, and to Make Recommendations (Beecher Report)*, (Rev. L. J. Beecher), Colony and Protectorate of Kenya, Nairobi: Government Printer. Adopted by Legislative Council in 1950. Though he was vilified for the Report, Bishop Leonard J. Beecher had spent years representing African interests in the Legislative Council, often against considerable European opposition.
   1985. Spencer, John, *op. cit.*, pp. 119ff.
42. 1949. *Beecher Report*, pp. 36, 55, 56.
43. At least three of the eight members of the Commission were missonaries.

Six

Resistance of the Elders until the Beginning of Mau Mau[1]

Local resistance can be divided into two periods. In the first, elders were the dominant force; they expected younger men, landless and land poor to follow their lead. The end of this period started with the creation of the Kiambu LNC and was completed after the Carter Report. In the second period, younger, landless and land-poor men came to the fore; during that period elders protected them and remained watchful that their resistance did not contaminate the land or violate the Kikuyu moral order. When it did, the elders tried to regain control of the resistance, but they failed to do so; instead, the government used them to take action against all resistance. This chapter deals with the resistance of the elders.

Resistance may have taken a different form in other Kikuyu areas; though the Kikuyu shared common pressures such as the appointment of headmen, imposition of taxes, and probably *gitati*, many matters, including land alienation, were specific to certain areas.[2] The resistance of local elders was rooted in land alienation; elders in other areas may have been reacting to different events and circumstances (Appendix III/4; 5; 6).[3] In the period which started with the Carter Commission, and culminated in Mau Mau, there was probably more unity. The root causes – exclusion from land, education, decent wages and opportunities to participate – were more widespread than alienation had been.[4]

The resistance of the elders

In Kikuyu ideology, *mbari* and their elders were in proportion to the land they owned the guardians of the ancestral land of Muumbi and Gikuyu, with specific responsibility towards their own land and its spiritual forces.

Resistance of the Elders until the Beginning of Mau Mau

Within each *mbari*, members of the senior council of elders, likely to be the owners of the largest tracts, carried major responsibility. The most senior elders performed sacrifices on behalf of the *mbari* and all who lived on the land to its ancestors and to Muumbi and Gikuyu.

Concerned that the famine had been caused by ancestral displeasure, elders had hoped that its end signalled the return of blessings. When land alienation occurred, elders were sure spirits had again been provoked and would not give peace until their land was returned. The resistance of the elders was therefore grounded as much in spiritual duty as in political anger and economic need. It started when J. D. Ainsworth refused to help elders and headman Waweru Mahui evict a European settler from *mbari* property and thereby made land alienation a reality.

Waweru had succeeded his father's brother's son Kimama wa Macharuga, who had been killed in the earliest colonial years, possibly because he was not accepted as headman outside Igi and its allies.[5] To what degree Kimama had worked with and through the elders is not known; his primary task had been to ensure the peace and facilitate trade. That the taxes ostensibly imposed to protect the trade were not collected until the early twentieth century may have made cooperation with the elders less imperative.

Waweru, like most other local land owners, had lost a considerable tract of land in alienation and, like them, regarded the *thirikari* as an unwanted presence and the Europeans, though soon to be again trading partners, as enemies nevertheless. By status, land position, and appointment he was a logical ally and partner of the senior elders, united with them in their desire for the return of the land. As he was their man, he could rely on their protection and aid; they eased his access to councils of other *mbari* within his territory.[6] They aided in the collection of taxes, recruitment of labour for settlers, and *gitati* for government and local interests. When necessary, they would help stonewall the demands of settlers who did not pay or mistreated their labour. In return the council expected that he would be their executive arm; they and the population expected protection from the government, which was to be kept out of local affairs.

As Waweru did not disappoint them, the *kiama* supported Waweru's innovations; it therefore protected those interested in the Kambui Mission and its educational and medical work. Waweru's concern with technical development, roads and bridges brought trading advantages for surplus producers; his desire for English and an education for his sons brought Wanyoike wa Kamawe and one of the first regional outschools, from which *kiama* members and the population could profit.

School and roads increased Igi's status and influence among other *mbari*, as did its 'ownership' of the headman. Yet, for all its influence, neither its councils nor its headmen could speak for other *mbari* and their land. *Mbari* remained separate, sovereign entities; the *mbari* council of each was the final authority within its land.

The ideology of the resistance of the elders

Bringing about the return of the land and resistance against further alienation was the most important task of the elders. Though alienation was comparable to a physical attack and elders would not have incurred *thahu* had they responded in kind, the idea was rejected because of European superior power. The *anake* were therefore excluded and their desire for battle had to be controlled. Elders tended to agree with Waiyaki wa Hinga, that *anake* were more a danger than an asset when dealing with highly armed and trigger-happy Europeans (Appendix III/1). Aggression by *anake* would cost lives and jeopardize the newly expanding herds, as Europeans could use the attacks as an excuse for punitive raids and further alienation.

Elders opted instead for resistance which would bring gain rather than loss. Whether they knew the advice of Chege wa Kibiru or not, elders believed that the strategy of pacification and utilization, which closely resembled his advice, had a better chance (Appendix VII). They followed his advice to 'establish friendly relations with the coming strangers', to 'keep aloof, neither resist nor welcome ... but learn from them', slowly adding direct, though non-aggressive, muted protest.[7] In this way elders hoped to learn the secret of their enemies' strength, become part of it, and ultimately defeat the enemy from inside.

Pacification

Pacification involved drawing attention away from local affairs by obeying settlers and government as much as possible. Settlers should be provided with labour, food or stock; if necessary, local authorities should even maintain the peace on alienated land. Government should receive its share of *gitati*; taxes should be paid; its officials should be kept out of internal conflict or tension; relationships should be presented as peaceful and free from strife. Faithfully followed, this would create conditions which could be used to Kikuyu advantage, building their strength.

Settlers might return the favours rendered by not seeking alienation of land which provided essential resources; they might allow access to salt licks and water, or permit Kikuyu herds on alienated land. Settler land might provide refuge from government *gitati*; when theft or mayhem occurred, settlers would not automatically accuse 'friendly' Kikuyu and force them to pay fines.

The government's power should be used when conflict with settlers was unavoidable, as in repeated shifting of boundaries, encroachment of settler labour on unalienated land, or interference with Kikuyu women. Other matters of tension such as non-payment of labour or physical abuse might also create conflict; only if they could not be solved on the local level should the government be brought in to make a settler see reason. If complaints were rare, the government might take the side of the Kikuyu.

Utilization

Utilization of Europeans and their resources similarly built strength by providing economic advantages and learning opportunities; at its most basic level, it gave some compensation for the loss of the land. Any innovations brought by the government should be used; settlers could provide access to new tools and crops; using government or settlers to learn new methods of agriculture or herding was good. When eventually the Europeans returned the land, it would be important to know how they had made it productive with crops which fetched good prices. The men who had moved with them to the Rift Valley would learn their skills and inherit their land when the Europeans left.[8] Missions were able to give access to education and medical aid; education brought immediate results; even a few years of schooling could result in good wages; the knowledge of English brought better jobs, and one could understand conversations among officials and settlers and read government documents.

Kikuyu should achieve as much control over the relationship with government, settlers, and mission as possible by infiltration and Kikuyuization of the chain of command from the bottom up. Jobs as labour supervisors or foremen were important, but none more so than those of headmen, chiefs, clerical workers or teachers. Jobs which gave access to authority went as of right to those who carried authority in the Kikuyu community. They were uniquely able to fill them; they could accept low pay because they had land. They could use their colonial authority to provide information and protection to the Kikuyu community.[9]

Direct protest, the land, and the Kikuyu Association

While pacification and sometimes utilization involved and used the land poor and landless, whether or not to use direct protest was the sole province of the elders. They might do so to foster the return of the land and to get access to the highest possible level of education for their sons. This would enable these sons to infiltrate and slowly take possession of the European power structure. The needs of landless and land poor were secondary in all respects; they would be served by the return of the land and the return of the proper authority of elders. Then elders in their turn could help the landless and land poor and open ways for their empowerment.

There is no evidence that *mbari* elders sought out other *mbari* for more effective protest until the end of the second colonial decade. When they did so they involved *mbari* which had lost land as well as those which had not; the larger rather than the smaller *mbari* participated.

Resistance of the Elders until the Beginning of Mau Mau

Efforts originated in *barazas*, which were ordered by the government and held on a more or less regular basis on the dancing grounds of large *mbari*. The objective of *barazas* was to inform headmen and the population of administrative decisions and to hear complaints; though small *mbari* attended, larger ones and those with a headman would turn out with a retinue of senior elders. *Barazas* were often regional affairs which Kikuyu used for informal encounters and exchange of information; they learned about the host of matters which united and divided them. Opponents of missions might meet those who used them for medical aid and education. The new elites of the city came to translate the English or Swahili of administrators into Kikuyu, and incidentally met some of the most important rural men.

Elders from land wealthy *mbari* met some who were relatively land poor; those who had lost a great deal of land to alienation encountered those who had lost little or nothing. They differed in many other aspects: some were land providers with many *ahoi*, also providing herding land to neighbouring *mbari*; others were land takers, who were dependent on such *mbari*. There were already differences in orientation between the oldest senior elders and younger attenders; where land was a central, ideological concern of older males, younger ones tended to be more pragmatic, concerned with the productivity of land but also with urban affairs and colonial policies in general.

They varied in their obeisance to Paramount Chief Kinyanyui wa Gathirimu; though all would observe the civilities because of his government position, some sought his active cooperation, and would not oppose him; others would – if at all possible – go their own way, particularly on the divisive issue of missions and education which Kinyanyui had opposed.[10]

It may be that these encounters helped change his mind; by the end of the First World War, he no longer discriminated against Christians when it came to finding areas to live; he accepted that most chiefs wanted at least some education for their sons. Supported by missionaries, these chiefs convinced Kinyanyui in 1919 to appoint an educated male to each of the four government *kiama*.[11]

While *mbari* undoubtedly cooperated in this, there is little evidence of other organized cooperation or even of a great deal of unity between *mbari* whose land had been alienated and those which had retained their land. Without Wanyoike's explanation, the formation of the Kikuyu Association (KA) by the end of that year or by the first few months of the following year would remain puzzling.[12]

In Wanyoike's explanation, the KA was not so much a party as an interest group which was born from the efforts of some elders to protect the land against attempts at internal alienation. This was a matter which potentially concerned all *mbari*; land owners, familiar with each other through *barazas*, threw their support behind a land owner, whose *ahoi* claimed that the Crown Lands Ordinance of 1915 had abolished ownership of land, giving all *ahoi* equal rights to the land with those who 'owned' it. Fearful that such notions might spread and be supported by the government, owners approached the Administration to confirm ownership rights; they were not successful, as the government could not afford to be seen recognizing Kikuyu rights of land ownership. Yet the *ahoi* were stopped; that owners won the right to arbitrate land cases in their own areas was a tacit confirmation that their land rights went beyond those of *ahoi*.

The men involved in creating the KA belonged to the younger senior elders, they were men over 50; most had been senior *anake* or junior elders during the famine. Their experience that concerted action could bring results where individual *mbari* failed became the driving force behind the formation and maintenance of the KA. Though they continued to show deference to the older senior elders and were in no way prepared to compromise *mbari* sovereignty, they broke new ground by asking Koinange wa Mbiu, who had reached maturity in the famine, had some education, and belonged to a *mbari* which had lost a great deal of land, to become chairman.[13] They chose neither the most senior, nor the wealthiest elder; they avoided Kinyanyui, whose claim to wealth and status was ambiguous to say the least. Other younger senior elders also held office; Waweru Mahui was a vice president; Wanyoike Kamawe was treasurer for a few months.

To all intents and purposes, the KA was a council of elders; because its members were legitimized through their land, it needed neither oaths nor dues. The KA thought of itself as representing the land as a whole, the *Mbari* of Muumbi and Gikuyu, one of the many names for the land and the people who had a right to call themselves Kikuyu. Being the *Mbari* did not interfere with the sovereignity of elders over their specific *mbari* land.[14]

In spite of the choice of Koinange and his co-workers, Kinyanyui often dominated the KA's public persona. He officially accepted Koinange's leadership, but expected to officiate whenever matters involving the administration were discussed. As he had recently become an advocate for the return of the stolen lands, he could be helpful, though he took little active part in more mundane affairs. Earlier Kinyanyui had taken the name of the powerful Gathirimu *mbari* which had sold land to the Gospel Missionary Society at Kambui. One of its members, Harry Thuku, who worked in Nairobi, often acted as Kinyanyui's interpreter, gaining rural recognition.[15]

The actual work for the KA was handled by Koinange and the *ndundu* formed by him and other office holders. Like Koinange, several men in the *ndundu* had strong personal ties with missionaries, quite a few of whom spoke fluent Kikuyu. Missionary influence in the KA was consequently pronounced, and missionaries frequently helped with the preparation of petitions and the planning of strategy.[16] Koinange and the *ndundu* had missionary backing when they asked government permission to give evidence in England about the land and Kikuyu relations with the Indian population.[17]

Resistance of the Elders until the Beginning of Mau Mau

Missionary influence was also behind the growth of the KA from being an assembly of elders, meeting when matters of land were at stake, to the hesitant beginning of a 'party' concerned with a larger number of issues. Strong opposition of older elders, for whom land was the only cause, prevented this from developing fully. Many younger elders also hesitated to 'dilute' the land issue; they feared that taking on more issues would demand more meeting time, taking them away from their herds, land, and *mbari* affairs, which only the wealthiest with many adult kinsmen could afford. Some *ndundu* members, particularly Koinange, were in favour of this development, which got a boost when in 1921 Thuku formed the Young Kikuyu Association (YKA) which soon became the East African Association (EAA).[18] Many elders regarded this as a challenge to their hegemony over protest.

The issues Thuku and his EAA introduced were not too different from those the missionaries and the *ndundu* were – slowly – trying to incorporate in the KA list of grievances: *gitati*, taxes, low wages, deplorable urban conditions, and the *kipande*.[19] Some who were in favour of incorporating the issues were in favour of coopting him and so neutralizing the EAA, though they were put off by his arrogance and afraid that his stridency would rebound on the KA. They were also concerned about his contacts outside Kiambu; they did not want to bring Murang'a men into Kiambu affairs, let alone deal with 'Indians' who were regarded as being as much a threat to the land as Europeans.

While they were deliberating, Thuku was strengthening his position. He had little to gain from cooption or cooperation, nor did he intend to become a junior KA member under the authority of senior elders, who would tell him with whom he was allowed to associate. All nascent attempts to find a way of bringing Thuku within the fold failed when he made it crystal clear that, rather than being used by the elders, he would use them; rather than follow their agenda, he would advance his own.

Attempts to broaden the base of the KA had continued; Koinange and the *ndundu*, with the active help of the Rev. A. R. Barlow, were testing the willingness of the KA to get involved in more active protest when they prepared a memorandum for a discusssion with the Chief Native Commissioner. Besides matters of land, it included many of the Thuku and EAA issues. Thuku, present at the meeting, absconded with the memo and sent it with some changes directly to the Colonial Office as a Thuku-EAA manifesto. This ended the possibilities for rapprochement; it also fatally damaged Kinyanyui's already fragile position among the KA members. Thuku was not concerned; he continued to recruit for the EAA, and to attack government policies, settlers, the KA, elders, and headmen.[20]

The EAA was not a council of elders with members qualifying because they were landed. Like later colonial organizations, such as the Kikuyu Central Association (KCA) and the Kenya African Union (KAU), it was based on fee-paying members pledging allegiance to a leader or leaders, whose programme they supported. Such organizations contained at least two, sometimes more, levels of membership.

Resistance of the Elders until the Beginning of Mau Mau

At the bottom was the largest group, whose main function was to provide support by paying dues. They might have to meet certain criteria – in Thuku's EAA they needed to be at least junior elders; they might have to be initiated males – but all had to be able to pay.

In a small organization, members might be recruited by the leader himself; more often recruitment was left to some prominent men who were already involved; they recruited in their local area and were rewarded with a percentage of the fees collected. They had – and to maximize their income were wont to use – considerable latitude in their interpretation of the organization. Members in different areas might perceive or hope for quite different things from the same organization. Few members would have felt responsible for the declarations or acts of their organization elsewhere.

While the loyalty of ordinary members to organizations was low and membership could vary considerably from one area to another and from one year to the next, ordinary members did not expect leaders of organizations to spell out their plans. As 'men of one goat' – lowly contributors – their rights to know were limited.

Because of the differences between recruiters, their strategies, and relative ignorance of the leaders' plans or ideas, movements which had been in existence for some time were likely to acquire local or regional characteristics. Like the KCA later, Thuku's EAA had a different face in Kiambu than in Nairobi, and probably in Murang'a and elsewhere.

A second, much smaller tier was made up of men with a greater interest in the movement, willing to make larger contributions or give other help. Some of them might have been recruiters, others might be tied to the leader by bonds of initiation, kinship or common interests. They had rights to more information and expected face-to-face relationships with the leader. Yet they were not equal; how much a leader would share depended on his and the supporters' personalities, the degree to which they trusted each other and shared ideas, and the ease with which they could be reached. These few people within the small group acquired the characteristics of a *ndundu*.

While this type of organization provided some security in colonial times and allowed recruitment in widely diverse areas among diverse groups, it was essentially unstable and became more so over time. To gain greater stability, leaders of organizations were pressured to enlarge the number of their closer supporters, adding in essence a fairly large second tier of members. Closer associates became a third tier; the *ndundu* might well become more distinct from the third, let alone the second tier. While this may have contributed greater stability – though probably not among ordinary members – it had its own problems. Even second-tier members might be separated from the followers at the bottom; several layers of men might separate the common followers from the leader. As they were the largest source of money, yet remained essentially a volatile group, leaders could not rely on a steady supply of money. The increase of higher-level

Resistance of the Elders until the Beginning of Mau Mau

supporters was a two-edged sword: a leader might have to spend a disproportionate amount of time solving conflicts between these men and his local followers or between higher-echelon followers in different areas. These men, aware of the 'flexibility' of their leader and the inherent weakness and dependency of his position, would vie with each other, sometimes for the trust of the leader, sometimes for maximum control over him if not the movement as a whole.

Though Thuku's EAA did not live long enough to reach this elaboration, from the beginning he too struggled with the problem of stabilizing cash flow and membership. One method used selectively was to offer the recruiters among the basic members and the members who were closer to Thuku himself, a commitment oath from the *kunyua muuma* group, a traditional means for creating temporary alliances for specific purposes. Many of the later twentieth-century oaths belonged to the same group: they were easily taken and equally easily dissolved; ritual was kept to a minimum. They were difficult to enforce: perhaps for this reason, *muuma* frequently invoked a symbolic witness, perhaps soil, taken in one's hand, or a Bible for the more educated. What was used, depended on the purpose, the oath administrator and the oath taker. In the *muuma*, the witness was no more than an observer, he/it was not a party to the promise as in the more serious, structuring oaths. Eating of a ritually slaughtered goat and drinking beer were common in the *muuma*; in the most basic ones, meat was eaten after the oath, if participants could afford this. In oaths for more important members, ritual was more elaborate; a clause might stress the need to support the leader, and meat was eaten during the oath. These *muuma* I have called amended commitment oaths (Appendix VIII).

Although not in the time of the EAA, but early in the rise of its successor, the KCA, amended commitment oaths would be offered to all more important supporters; they would be solicited through an invitation to kill – or eat – 'a goat together' (AppendixVIII/1).[21]

Thuku kept within the proper moral and ritual boundaries, until he allowed his associates to threaten the wives of those who refused to become members with the curse of barrenness.[22] Punishment was swift; he and his EAA were banned from *mbari* land. Local membership had been low. Four males, probably all with peasant holdings, and two of whom worked in Nairobi in semi-skilled jobs, were said to have been members.[23] Thuku had little to offer those who were dependent on land of kinsmen or patrons who did not want them to become involved. Moreover, the annual fee in 1922 of shs 5/– was equivalent to five months of a single hut tax, more than a week's income of a rural unskilled worker, and a week's wage for an unskilled urban worker. Thuku's spending patterns and his inability to reward his followers did not make many willing to underwrite his endeavours.[24]

Thuku's political youth was short; his increasingly vitriolic attacks on all but his own supporters created fear among KA members that the government would ban all expressions of opposition and discontent. His self-aggrandizing dismayed even his own supporters. When the government sought grounds to ban him, it did not lack assistance. Though his arrest provoked an urban disturbance, there was no local reaction. Whether the movement of the Mita ya Kenya was connected with his arrest or not, local males were not involved.[25]

The weakening of direct protest by elders

By the mid-1920s the most senior elders rarely attended KA meetings because of age and infirmity. Younger elders also had begun to attend less; they were beginning to be preoccupied with finding brideprices for sons, allocating them land, and finding land for the few daughters they allowed to marry men without land. The KA therefore reacted with less hostility to the founding of the KCA, which in turn seemed less hostile and more willing to confer and consult than the EAA. It recruited in much the same manner as the EAA had done, but was somewhat more liberal with its oaths. Members paid a fee of shs 5/-; some ordinary members, who paid a higher than normal fee, might be oathed with an amended commitment oath of the *kunyua muuma* type (Appendix VIII/1).[26]

Recruiters came from among the higher paying members; it was left up to them and those they recruited whether they would give an oath. Information indicates that this was not often the case because both sides tried to avoid it. By and large, oaths were reserved for the recruiters themselves and for those who paid higher fees. Almost always those oaths were administered by somebody close to a leader, if not by the leader himself. A *thenge* – a male goat – might be slaughtered before the ceremony; its blood and raw meat might be used by the oathing leader and those to be oathed, to touch each other. The blood was not ingested; the meat was cooked before it was eaten during the ceremony. Ingesting the blood would have lifted the oath out of the *kunyua muuma* category.

Because there were fewer, it is possible that the oaths given by leaders had a relatively standard content; oaths given to ordinary members varied from place to place, depending on circumstances. None of these oaths were of particular concern to the elders, though most preferred, as with any oath, that they were taken in the *thingira* of a member of another *mbari*. They were inclined to give the KCA men leeway, provided they confined themselves to matters which did not affect Kiambu land.

Though the KCA initially avoided Thuku's confrontational approach, relationships soured when the KCA refused to accept the KA's belief in separate spheres of protest. Like the EAA, it demanded access if not control of the whole field; it demanded untrammelled access to the rural areas without permission of headmen or chiefs. It demanded freedom to recruit and collect money, and the right to speak about the land when and how it saw fit. When elders protested, the KCA revived the

Resistance of the Elders until the Beginning of Mau Mau

aggressive policies of its predecessor, attacking headmen, chiefs, KA members, and the later LNC, as enemies on a par with government, settlers, or missions.

The oldest elders refused to yield; they, not younger males, were the proper representatives of ancestors and land. But they did not attend many KA meetings, nor did the somewhat younger elders who, though no less concerned about the land, were preoccupied with the economic problems caused by the division of land as their sons married. They were not eager to deal with 'KCA threats'; their economic problems were at least as important. Koinange and the *ndundu* could continue to do what was needed; they supported them but did not need to be physically present.[27] The LNC could do more for them than the KA.[28]

Koinange continued to work from the platform of the KA and the LNC; the feisty KCA lost no opportunity to reward him with attacks, depicting him, the KA and the new LNC as nothing but a collection of government stooges.

In spite of Koinange the KA might well have died around 1930 had it not been given a new lease of life when it was advised that a British Commission would come to settle Kikuyu land grievances. The promise brought older and younger men back to the meetings; it even opened the door for cooperation between the KA and the KCA.

Members of the KA whose land had been taken had their hands full with their own claims; they could give but little assistance to *mbari* which lacked older members, or *mbari* in which conflict and confusion were rife. They therefore welcomed, perhaps not wholeheartedly, the help offered by the KCA. The KA and the KCA approached their testimony from opposite sides: the KA wanted to demonstrate Kikuyu losses through a number of documented claims of *mbari*. The KCA wanted to proclaim Kikuyu losses; individual claims were important, but not the basis of their assertions. The help they provided to those who wanted to claim consisted of pre-printed forms, which left little space for the complex history or development of ownership. Both organizations wanted to demonstrate the wrongness and the hardship loss of land had caused; only its return would satisfy (Appendix V).

The outcome, the rejection of most Kikuyu claims, is well known; when the Commission Report appeared, the anger of the people was not only directed at the colonial Administration and Britain, but also at the KCA and the KA. They accused the KCA that their expensive forms were as hollow as the promises of the government; what goodwill it had gained by providing help was locally lost. The KA came in for its share of blame: elders had concentrated on their own land; the KA did not represent anyone but themselves.

After the Carter Report, the KA virtually ceased to function but even then Koinange continued.[29] Elders lost interest in participation; the oldest elders saw the Carter decisions as evidence that they had failed the land.[30] Not only was there little reason to continue the fight through the KA; they should withdraw in favour of their sons; maybe the ancestors would be merciful and allow them to bring back the land.

In 1956 few senior elders who had participated in the preparation of the testimony before the Commission were still alive or accessible. Those who were alive were unwilling to discuss the experience; although the subject was less 'closed' than the causes and loss of life in the famine, the Report was a reminder of the loss of land. Men who then had been younger elders, as well as sons of the older men – now often advanced in years as well – freely discussed certain reactions to the Report. A number of them had at about that time become important in their *githaku, mbari* or community; when asked when and how fathers had given them control, they would point to the Carter Report. Fathers, weighed down by their sense of failure, had given them the right to make decisions. The fight had to continue, but in ways which promised eventually greater success; the younger men were better equipped to deal with a future in which the return of the land could no longer be taken for granted.

These younger men accepted the decisions of the Commission with anger, yet were free of the sense of failure older men had felt. The fight for land would continue but it would take economic strength to make Europeans listen; once this was achieved, political strength would naturally follow. They agreed with the older men that the KA had not proven its mettle; Europeans could ignore it because it had been weak. The LNC and its economic and social endeavours would bring strength; economic strength, not words, would convince the government. Any Kikuyu knew that a clever but poor man could sometimes get the better of a rich man, but it was more certain that the poor man would be defeated. Old and younger elders shared the belief that gaining economic strength was in itself resistance; it should take precedence over other resistance, whether covert or overt.

Resistance from land owners would not notably benefit their restless *ahoi*, nor provide for land-poor sons and kin. Those deprived had the right to point their finger at those who caused their misery: Europeans and government. Even if the resistance of the elders had to be muted for the time being, *ahoi*, landless and land poor were justified in starting what protest they could muster. Elders should not stand in the way; they should support the expression of anger, even if their own task was different at this time. Yet, one task could not be laid down; though their fathers retained responsibility as long as they lived, the younger land owners also were increasingly the guardians of the land. It was their obligation to see to it, that the land, the ancestors and the living were protected from *thahu*. Resistance, however justified, which defiled the land and the people, would bring doom rather than freedom. While all men had the right to protest and resist, the ultimate rule was vested in the sanctity of the land.[31]

This broadening of the idea of resistance went a long way to legitimize the protest and resistance of the KCA. The KA had related indirectly to landless and land poor in its agitation for the return of the land; because this had failed and the KA was no longer of importance, land poor and landless no longer had a spokesman. The KCA had been important to small peasants and peasants, and to men in the Rift Valley; its leaders were often urbanized. Yet, it might in time become the spokesman of landless and land poor; sons of small peasants and peasants were in danger of becoming just that.

The KCA slowly acquired the right to hold meetings and recruit on *mbari* land; the protection of *mbari* elders could keep it secret from the government. Yet, though hostility softened and some local KCA leaders actually sought rapprochement with the old leaders of the KA, the KCA of the Rift Valley and Murang'a remained hostile, Kiambu elders never trusted them, either.[32]

Koinange, though by no means rejecting the endeavours of the LNC to bring greater economic power, continued to carry the political fight. His creation of the *Mbari* and Githunguri Teachers Training College were only a few years apart; he had started recruitment for Githunguri two years after the founding of the *Mbari*. Both carry the Koinange imprint; although I have less material than I like, I think it sufficient to suggest that the creations were the two sides of the same coin: a rallying cry of Koinange to prepare for the future.

The fight for rural unification through the *Mbari*

Local images support the idea that the *Mbari* was not so much a political party, a rival of the KCA or the KA, as an organization which had the moral objective of reminding the Kikuyu of the need for unity in their search for freedom.[33] Discord and disunity had been demonstrated amply during the Carter Commission; the *Mbari* was to remind all Kikuyu and all political activists that divisiveness would only harm the cause. Centered at Kiambaa or Banana Hill, the *Mbari* was probably the first organization which was intended to bridge the gap between Kiambu, Murang'a and Gaki on one side and owners and *ahoi* on the other. It operated from a spiritual and moral statement of *umoja*, unity, which Koinange hoped would grow into economic and political reality. The name, *Mbari*, was a reminder of what the Kikuyu should strive for: the *Mbari* of Muumbi and Gikuyu, included all Kikuyu, young and old, rich and poor. As the *Mbari* of Muumbi and Gikuyu was one, so the Kikuyu should have *umoja*, unity. The *Mbari* should fight for the stolen lands and see to it that no new land was taken; it should be as concerned with the conditions of the landless and the land poor as with those of the landed; it should not leave protest to the LNC only.[34]

The *Mbari* would remain largely symbolic, with perhaps seven members locally; among the Rift Valley repatriates – a male population of 125 – ten had been *Mbari* members, indicating higher Rift Valley, than rural support.[35] Koinange had recruited extensively in other Kikuyu areas than the Rift Valley; he did not recruit in Nairobi, because the migrant labourers did not live there permanently.

The *Mbari* oath was likely to mention the *Bururi wa Agikuyu*; its ritual used soil to symbolize *umoja* (unity) because all shared the land of Muumbi and Gikuyu. Though there would be more *umoja* oaths later, the *Mbari* oath was their prototype. It was based on the land; it was also based on the myth of joint origin and was therefore one of the few oaths which had the right to call itself a *Muumbi na Gikuyu* oath. Like all *umoja* oaths, it was pacific; it asked men to work for the return of the land. It was an exclusively male oath, because males owned the land. While I have no data about the oath in the Rift Valley, all evidence indicates that it was a *kunyua muuma* oath; in the more important homesteads, it might have been an amended *muuma* (Appendix VIII, page 319).

The *Mbari* was not seen as a threat to *mbari* sovereignty; it did not seek to replace individual *mbari*. Yet, while it was not often taken, the conviction seems to have grown over time that those who wanted to speak for Kikuyu land could only do so if they had taken the *Mbari* oath. Mathu, the nominated African member of the Legislative Council between 1944 and 1957, took it in 1951/52 after having been in office for several years; Kenyatta took it immediately on his return.[36]

In the early years of the *Mbari*, Koinange was the link between the *Mbari* and his other creation, Githunguri Teachers' Training College. When his son Mbiu became its headmaster, he maintained the relationship and Koinange's son-in-law Kenyatta was to do the same when he took over. Both institutions aimed at creating unity; the *Mbari* was aimed at all Kikuyu, the College at a future cadre of leaders.

The battle for control of education

Where the *Mbari* reminded the Kikuyu that the future demanded that they become one, Githunguri Teachers' Training College was concerned with the preparation of those who would lead the people during and after the struggle. That it was built at Githunguri was no accident; the legendary prophet, Chege wa Kibiru had warned the Kikuyu to learn from the Europeans until they had achieved the strength to manage their own affairs. The sign would be the building of a *thingira* – a man's hut – at Githunguri; when that was done, freedom would be close. The 1939 initiates, who chose the name College, sang about this freedom:

Cege wa Kibiru ni oigire	It was once foretold by Cege wa Kibiru
Thingira uria wi kia wairera	That a man's house will be built at Githunguri
Riria ugakuo na urika	And when it has been built and finished
Niguo tukena weiyathi.[37]	It will be our time to get freedom

Resistance of the Elders until the Beginning of Mau Mau

The building of Githunguri climaxed decades of struggle between Kikuyu, missionaries and the government about the content of education.

The earliest education had been provided by missions; but though education at stations had carried significant rewards, 'outschools' which soon reached a wider population were considerably less successful. Already in the second decade of the twentieth century, those who had spent more years in school than those educated earlier at mission stations and reached the highest level of education available could not hope for jobs which gave access to European power or provided high wages (Appendix VII). Even the best educated could hope for no more than being clerks, rural pastors or teachers in rural schools.

Many parents used the schools not because they wanted their children to adopt Christianity, but because they wanted them to learn Western skills and thus get jobs which compensated for the loss of land. Even Christian Kikuyu parents, a minority, wanted schools to concentrate on academic subjects, giving less attention to Christianity. All blamed the school curriculum for low achievement; the missions should spend less time on religion and conversion, on vocational and practical subjects. The time should instead be used on academic subjects, particularly English.

By 1917 a group of men had requested, without result, that the government provide a College of Higher Education under direct government, not mission, control.[38] Interest in education beyond what missions offered remained high among landed elders, and, though it seriously strained the relationships with individual missionaries, in 1926 proponents managed to push a plan through the LNC to build a high school at Githunguri. That Protestant Missions were opening Alliance High School that year did not satisfy parents; they expected that the school would continue the missionary 'anti-African bias', offering courses which prepared for teaching positions in African schools, African agriculture and vocations.[39] The Githunguri school was to concentrate on academic subjects; it would be financed from a special cess on all adult males.[40] After collecting this for three years, in sight of their goal, the government refused to approve the school; in a bitter 'compromise', the LNC eventually gave two thirds of the money for a Gaki elementary school. Kiambu, with Koinange in the lead, felt deceived; that their mission associates had actively agitated against the school was a humiliating reminder of their subject status. In the name of control over the Christianization of its converts' children, it demanded control over education for all.

The female circumcision issue

Informants linked the female circumcision issue to the Githunguri controversy as further efforts of the missions to assert and reassert its control over education, and to stifle what was seen as incipient rebellion.

Early missions had allowed their adult converts a certain latitude in

Kikuyu practices. The local mission with its fundamentalist clergy had soon become stricter, particularly opposing polygyny and female circumcision. It interpreted Western monogamy and male circumcision as compatible, but polygyny and female circumcision as incompatible, with Christian doctrine.[41]

Polygyny was important in Kikuyu economic and socio-political organization, and the mission's stance created hardship for women and made polygynously married women converts into second-class Christians. Polygynously married women who converted could not become full members of the church unless they left or no longer cohabited with their husbands. If polygynously married males converted, they were expected to separate themselves from all but one of their wives; though they were expected to provide for them and any children, the wives felt abandoned. In the case that a wife left or would no longer maintain marital relationships with her husband and give him children, he – in Kikuyu law and custom – could demand a return of the brideprice, which her infuriated kin would refuse. In that case, she remained polygynously married, even if she managed to live alone, and was barred from communion.[42] Males had somewhat more choice; theoretically they could provide for all wives and live with only one; they could remain monogamous. In practice males left the church when faced with these demands.

The mission position on female circumcision ostensibly affected only girls and their parents who had become Christians, but ultimately it threatened to affect all parents, their sons and daughters, Kikuyu-Christian and Christian alike.

Missions had initially hoped that the government would take action against the circumcision of all female children on medical and moral grounds. It would have had some settler support; settlers were already concerned that the extensive rituals of male and female circumcision interfered with the flow of labour; they had not been satisfied with decisions of a 1922 *baraza* to confine initiations to two months a year.[43]

Missions became more convinced than ever that female circumcision had to cease when the KCA made mission and any other opposition to female circumcision evidence of colonial interference. Continuance of the custom became one cornerstone of a KCA campaign against missions, educated Kikuyu, elders of the KA, and LNC members, singling out men like Koinange and fundamentalist missions like Kambui. Where the KCA had made continued female circumcision a touchstone of Kikuyu purity, Kambui made opposition to female circumcision and refusal to participate, a touchstone of Christian purity.[44]

The administration, seeking to pacify the missions without driving those who wanted to retain circumcision into the arms of the KCA, did not want to be seen as taking sides; it wanted any response to come – at least officially – from the Kikuyu themselves through the LNC. Equally inclined to avoid antagonism, the LNC tried pacification by eventually passing a resolution which restricted the operation to clitorodectomy by a qualified, registered circumciser with paternal consent required. This should give all parents the right to circumcise or not; the mission might be satisfied with that solution as it could influence convert parents; if other Kikuyu accepted a few restrictions, they could go on as before. The LNC ordinance did not incorporate measures to enfore the ruling, nor did it impose significant penalties.[45]

The KCA had not counted on the anger of parents who wanted education and circumcision, but were afraid that because missions controlled education they could not have both.[46] The KCA was not willing to leave the choice to parents; their demand for *karinga*, purity, demanded that no girl remain uncircumcised in Kikuyu country; it threatened to promote mass circumcisions for uninitiated girls. The mission was not prepared to give parents a choice either; it demanded obedience to the 'no female circumcision' rule. Between the two intransigent attitudes, those like Wanyoike and Koinange, who sought a middle way, lost an opportunity for pacification.[47]

Kambui, convinced that its interpretation of the Gospel did not allow any exceptions, started concentrating on its converts, and threatened those who allowed their daughters to be circumcised with excommunication. It also continued its campaign to influence the decisions of other parents by demanding that the LNC decisions be monitored and offenders severely punished. This gave more ammunition to the KCA, which redoubled its efforts, concentrating its attacks on Koinange.[48] It used the common method of shaming by abusive songs, *mitherigu* (sing. *mutherigu*), sometimes well known, sometimes specially composed, attacked favourite targets.[49]

Kambui's ban on female circumcision for the daughters of its converts had been greeted with loud approval but low compliance. Mission problems were exacerbated because – although there were not that many girls in mission schools – they often had parents who had not converted. Matters came to a head in early 1929, when a gang forcibly circumcised a girl in one of the Kambui dormitories and the government imposed only a light fine. Not able to impose their will on the LNC or the administration, some missions, including Kambui, made the decision that Christians and non-Christians had feared all along: girls in Kambui schools could not be circumcised; parents had to promise to refrain from doing so, on pain of being refused access to education. From the side of the mission, it meant living up to what it regarded as its duty according to the Gospel; from the side of parents, it stated that education was controlled by the mission, which had the right to demand compliance with its conditions.

Kambui teachers were forced to sign a declaration not to circumcise their daughters, then a similar statement was demanded from Church elders. Although as yet this concerned a small group of fathers, the population thought this only the beginning; eventually the mission would enforce its decision on all parents who sought education.

For many parents, whether Christians or not, circumcision was tied to marriage and the ability to bear children. The fear was high that a non-circumcised daughter would not be able to find a husband and would remain a burden for her father, not bringing in a brideprice which could ensure a wife for her brother. Even greater was the fear that the control of access which the mission wanted to exercise over a man's daughters would soon also be extended to sons: if daughters were denied access to schools because parents refused to sign the no-circumcision declaration, it seemed unlikely that the mission would allow sons of the same family to continue.

The declaration not only threatened access to one of the most sought-after colonial resources, education; its phrasing could not have been worse. With its different clauses, it resembled oaths; though each clause did not end with invoking the wrath of spiritual forces on offenders, the mission made it clear that the Christian God was party to the declaration. It also contained a clause forbidding membership in what was rapidly becoming the mission nemesis, the KCA, until the mission gave permission, though there was little or no evidence that the forces opposed to mission absolutism had drawn their strength from the KCA.

Resistance became unavoidable: Kikuyu parents, Christian or not, refused to accept that the mission could hold education to ransom and removed their children from school. It was a symbolic rather than a permanent statement; as soon as the missions officially stopped demanding declarations, the children returned. How much government pressure against linking 'Christian practices' to educational access was a factor is an open question. While the local mission remained strongly opposed to female circumcision, it could no longer legally use this view to deny access. Parents may well have felt that their victory did not go far enough; they might have gained some control over access, but not over the content of education.[50]

There is no evidence that any students transferred to independent schools. While the female circumcision issue may have stimulated the creation of these schools, organized in the Kikuyu Independent Schools Association (KISA) and the Kikuyu Karing'a Educational Association (KKEA), local data do not support the contention that the issue became a recruitment advantage for independent schools, then or later: it was a rare pupil, who had had access to mission schools, but went to an independent school.[51] Independent schools were proprietary and more expensive; their examination results were lower than the already low mission school achievements; they could not attract properly trained teachers any more easily than the missions could.

The Kikuyu had demonstrated how far they were willing to go to get education. Men like Koinange were well aware that, although one battle was won, a more important battle loomed about control over the curriculum and the academicization of the schools.

The early Githunguri school fiasco and the female circumcision issue ended the close relationship between Kikuyu and mission politicians. Though personal relationships often survived, Kikuyu no longer used missionaries as primary advisers. Nor did they accept that missionaries, however fluent in Kikuyu, were more suitable representatives than their own men. When early missions needed land, large *mbari* had willingly provided it. When in 1927 Canon Leakey needed land for a school, neither Christian nor other land owners were willing to provide; that he argued that the land he wanted should be alienated shows how far they had grown apart.[52]

Githunguri Teachers' Training College

The idea for a private, fee-charging college originated with Koinange in 1934; it is not far-fetched to think that it was a response to the humiliations of the Carter report, the Githunguri failure and the Kikuyu need to get control over the curriculum of schools.

He started a personal campaign among larger land owners; those who contributed at least shs 50/– were invited to 'eat a goat together', the first College oath (Appendix VIII). Contributors were not sworn to secrecy; they did not become a group, nor did they become Koinange's advisers. Like the *Mbari*, the College might eventually have a board of directors chosen from such contributors, but it would have little or no influence on decisions.

The school did not become a reality for several years, but the site at Githunguri which the LNC had intended to use was still available. It had some rudimentary buildings which dated from 1922, when it had been used for one of the first independent schools under a teacher-evangelist who had broken with Kambui.[53] Academically oriented teachers were regarded as crucial; a headmaster was not found until 1938, when Peter Mbiu Koinange returned from abroad and, when seeking a teaching post, was told by the colonial Department of Education that, regardless of qualifications, he could only be paid an 'African wage'.

Elders would declare in 1956 that they had doubted his ability to make a success of the school from the beginning; they were impressed by his education, but he had been away too long. They doubted his capability to deal with people; he was 'a man of the head', who lacked his father's easy charm and 'heart to make people do things'.

Nevertheless, by 1939 the school was ready to make a modest start, though it still lacked virtually everything it would need. The event became an unrivalled demonstration of Kikuyu resistance and unity.[54] Attenders ranged from senior elders to urban politicians, from large land owners to landless and land poor. Not all believed that the college would be a place of peaceful learning; some had other ideas in mind when they called that year's initiation publicly 'College', but privately *micuthi wa Mbiu*, Mbiu's little snakes.[55] Prominent Kikuyu would later regard the start of the college as the opening salvo of a more public resistance, later to become Mau Mau.[56]

The College ran into problems almost immediately. Fees, for boarders and day boys, though high, did not cover salaries and equipment, let alone the cost of building. Fund raising proved difficult: Peter Mbiu's appeal to larger land owners did not bring success; appeals to smaller land owners were equally unproductive. The idea of an appeal to the *mariika* was rejected; only those *mariika* below Mbiu's own could be approached, and, as he was young, so were the men in the initiation years below him. Whatever contribution they could make would be outweighed by the effort of collection.

Mbiu was therefore thrown back on the support of already existing organizations. They wanted a secure meeting place and the use of the Koinange name; if they could create the image that support for their organization was support for Koinange, they would stand stronger.[57] In return they offered Mbiu access to their network of supporters, and sometimes accompanied him when he approached these resources. He was linked to two of the more powerful organizations: the KCA and KISA; both provided names of possible supporters. This help, however, demanded constant travelling and attention to the maintenance of multiple relationships; while it did bring in some money, income remained well below what was needed. Informants would blame his and later Kenyatta's long absence on his lack of success; neither man was sufficiently attuned to the factionalist and sometimes byzantine character of Kikuyu politics; both men overestimated their ability to bring the opposing forces together. Yet the college depended on the support of other organizations and individuals whose objectives might have little to do with education; it was in many ways mortgaged from the beginning.

As early as 1940 those who contributed significant amounts, either singly or in groups, and more frequently in the Rift Valley than elsewhere, were offered an oath. In the planning years it had been called a 'College' oath, only offered to large contributors. In the Mbiu years the oath became also known as a *Githunguri* and sometimes an *Umoja* oath. Mbiu did not often allow College oaths to be given at Githunguri; in earlier days they had been given at the homesteads of contributors, or at Koinange's homestead.[58] Now they might be given at places where several contributors lived or worked; this added safety and security but also added to their diversity. Though College oaths at Githunguri where therefore relatively few, organizations such as the KCA, which met at and supported Githunguri, gave their more important oaths at the college. These oaths should carry the name of the organizations, but the organizers might have a vested interest in calling them Githunguri or College oaths. It helped create an image of strength; Githunguri profited to the degree that Kikuyu perceived it as the hub of Kikuyu activity and leadership. The KCA in particular had been wont to use Githunguri; as late as 1956 a number of informants were convinced that Githunguri had been the KCA and vice versa.

While I have virtually no information about oaths from other organizations, Mbiu's College oaths were quite similar to his father's *Mbari*

Resistance of the Elders until the Beginning of Mau Mau

oaths, though oriented towards education rather than the land.[59] Like all pre-Second World War oaths, they were broad and described categories of behaviour rather than specific acts. Although elders would not encourage any oaths, they were not regarded as particularly dangerous because they were perceived as commitment oaths, having but limited purpose and duration (Appendix VIII/1). These oaths mentioned the organization which gave the oath; they frequently involved promises to follow – not to obey – a named leader.

Until Thuku in 1933, after his detention, formed the Kikuyu Provincial Organization, women had not been allowed to take oaths; they remained barred from *Mbari* oaths because they dealt with the land.[60] Yet by this time all but the most conservative elders felt that little danger could come to women or their households from taking ordinary commitment oaths such as the College or Githunguri oath, though these oaths in general were oriented towards males. Under colonial circumstances, oaths, or the homily preceding or following them, did stress the need for caution, but not until 1940 do oaths for the proscribed KCA have specific clauses enjoining secrecy (Appendix VIII/5).[61]

After the proscription of the KCA in 1940 and the detention of its leaders, Mbiu's access to KCA networks became restricted; deprived of the company of some of KCA's best orators, Mbiu had more problems raising money than ever before. In spite of his devotion, the school languished; it did not have the facilities nor did Mbiu feel impelled, to transform it into a co-educational boarding school. Difficulties multiplied; there were frequent problems with paying and holding staff. Though Murang'a or Gaki students kept coming, parents of Kiambu students who had mission education available and could live at home, did not feel that the examination results of the school warranted the expense.

The re-entry of the elders into the resistance

The Second World War period provided for many elders and land owners extended opportunities; they could sell their produce at prices higher than before. A significant number of young males from among the land poor and landless were in the army; sons of land owners found places in school or as clerks in Nairobi. This period of comparative quiet came to an end with the return of the veterans, who wanted to find work in Nairobi or open shops in the rural area. Whether they wanted to or not, elders had to concern themselves with the post-war world.

The post-war elders were a very different group of men from the elders of the days before the Carter Report. A few among them might still be of 'the old order', yet they were likely to be so senior that they were mainly concerned with ritual and with serious infractions of the Kikuyu moral and legal order.

There were fewer elders of high senior status than before; the scarcity of land, the increasing number of small peasants, and the decline in the number of larger land owners had reduced the numbers who paid the fees and qualified for the inner council, the *ndundu* of the *mbari*. Payment of fees for *ithaku* councils or small *mbari* were often postponed.

As elders, as land owners, perhaps also as shopkeepers and rural clerical workers and officials, they were busy with their economic affairs, and as fewer men became elders of high status, meetings were no longer held with the same regularity; members of *mbari* and *githaka* meetings came when called for special occasions. As a body they were less powerful than before; large *mbari* or *nyongo* councils were further weakened by constant land litigation. Several, though not all, were Christians; some had become involved in the Revival movement; others were 'resting' from church membership, again others had never converted. Like most Kikuyu Christians, those who were church members did not regard Kikuyu ethics as incompatible with Christianity. They continued to hold that they should protect all Kikuyu land from *thahu*, defilement; that they held their land in trust for their descendants and should maximize its yield.

They were aware of the post-war unrest, the conditions in Nairobi, and the plight of land poor and landless, many of them kin – though more remote than before, as marriages between *ahoi* and *mbari* daughters had been discouraged after the late 1920s. Though often either members of the LNC or close to someone who was, they were aware of the political activities of KAU; some were even members.[62]

Many urban events and conditions, though important, remained peripheral to their real cares, which centred around land litigation and productivity of the land. Elders and land owners had taken a great deal of interest in the contest for appointment between Eliud Mathu and Mbiu for a seat on Legislative Council. They had hoped that the latter would win; his ties to the land were strong.[63] Rumours about a comeback of the KCA, or that it was gaining members in the Rift Valley, seemed to be just that; the KCA had never played a significant role in their lives, and the Kenya African Union (KAU) could deal with the KCA if this was needed. Unions were only important in the sense that Nairobi workers brought information about their actions and demands; there was no reaction of local labour. Unrest in the settled area was equally rare; however much elders might sympathize with the plight of landless and land poor, their own lives were hardly affected. The return of Rift Valley migrants, starting in 1946 but soon increasing in numbers, and the return of Kenyatta, also in 1946, would bring the economic and political changes home.

The return of the Rift Valley migrants

Women and men who had gone to the Rift Valley had from time to time returned home, if not prohibited by a curse; local men had at times joined the Rift Valley migrants. Some returnees had stayed only a few years in the Rift Valley; others had lived there for decades. Their children had been born there, had married and had again had children; the original migrants might have lived in one or in several areas, with one or several Europeans. Over the years, the use they could make of the settlers' land had well outstripped what they earned in wages. Their families had been large due to a high level of polygyny. Some sons might have followed their footsteps, perhaps becoming tractor drivers or work supervisors; other sons had tried to find urban jobs, often with difficulty because their educational level was low (Appendix VI/2).

In spite of sometimes having had to move when employers demanded too much or imposed too many restrictions, the original emigrants had learned to put their security in Rift Valley land. Against this background they had raised their children; without them, European settlers could not survive. They had broken the land; they had created wealth where there was only shrub and bush before; they would be the legitimate heirs of the land when the Europeans had to go. Until the Second World War, Rift Valley Kikuyu, though frustrated by European attempts to limit Kikuyu access to land or herds, had almost always been able to respond to too onerous restrictions by 'waiting it out' or by moving to another Rift Valley area. The restrictions after the Second World War were not only much harsher than before; the pressure on individual Europeans to tow the line was strong and reinforced by the government. Safe areas, away from the pressure, became virtually non-existent.

This evoked all the memories of early twentieth-century land alienation in Kiambu; adult sons and daughters of the early Kikuyu settlers experienced themselves the trauma which had brought their fathers to the Rift Valley. They lost not only a livelihood; their right to live in the Rift Valley was undermined. When they attested to being labourers, they implicitly accepted that their right to live on the farm – perhaps to use some land – was for the duration of the contract only.[64]

The older Kikuyu settlers rarely found a voice of protest, but as early as 1945 some of the young males asserted that they had been empowered by KCA leaders to fight the restrictions. Far from surrendering the land to the Kikuyu, the Europeans were becoming more entrenched than ever. The young men should make it clear to the Europeans that they had outstayed their welcome and should leave.

A fight demanded weapons: non-combatants should provide for those who did. They should contribute money; many Rift Valley Kikuyu had more money than usual because they had been forced to sell stock. Leadership should come from the KCA; the KAU, which should have promoted the KCA, had not done so. Men and women should declare their loyalty to the KCA through an oath. Because the KCA remained banned, it had to be given under different names, among them the 'Kenya', or the 'United Natives' oath.[65] The oaths were administered by the young males; while previously men or women might have been asked whether they wanted to take an oath, refusal was no longer an option. Those who refused were forced: well before the return of Kenyatta, quite independent from other oaths, certain farms in the Rift Valley, particularly near Nakuru and Naivasha, became centres of oath taking. The essence of the oaths – taking into account that my information is limited – seems to have been that a reborn KCA would drive out the Europeans. Ritual was minimal and the clauses of the oath varied widely but the demand for secrecy was certainly present in some of the oaths, as were threats – which may have involved ritual – against those who betrayed the cause (that is, did not obey the young men). My information is too limited to judge whether these oaths had gone over the edge of what could be done with an oath of the *kunyua muuma* type. Elders' opposition to them indicates at least some doubt; the lack of action by elders against Rift Valley oath takers indicates that they may just have been acceptable.

The European demands on one side, the loss or threatened loss of their livelihood and the pressure of the young males on the other, left many without protection against Europeans or over-eager Kikuyu. Being forced from their homesteads into 'labour lines', open to attack, they started an exodus back to the rural area to await easier times. By 1946, eight once-local households had already returned; this trickle would increase over the years.

Elders were concerned; the returnees increased land conflict. When they demanded land which they had left and those using it – often thinking it their own – would not yield, litigation followed. Whatever the outcome, the number of land poor increased; those who were deprived of the land were joined by those who got it back: a tract of 30 acres left originally by 2 households might have to be shared by 10, with all the confusion and anger involved.

Oaths taken by the returnees, caused concern as well. However much elders were beholden to protect the reviving KCA, they thought KAU a good deal more attractive. The aggressive tone of the oath, the rumours of forced oathing and the use of threats in the ritual, were unwelcome. They had certain dangerous characteristics, and, though they had been taken on what was – still – European land, they should definitely not be used on Kikuyu land.

If Rift Valley returnees did not find the welcome mat spread for them, there is no evidence that they had intended to spread the oath locally. Those who had taken the oath held that it did not refer to Kiambu Europeans or Kiambu land, but to Rift Valley Europeans and Rift Valley land. Outside the Rift Valley the oath would have been moot. Of prime importance for them in Kiambu was their lack of land and jobs; they did not ask for oaths but for work. A number of the females sought work in the settled area; males might go into Nairobi. Some, together with several local males, joined the large Kikuyu settlement in Arusha. It is possible that they spread an oath there; the few Arusha oaths I have are early.[66] During the Emergency local Mau Mau members did not accept the Rift Valley oath as compatible; those who 'wanted to eat and drink with them' had to take the local oath.

The return of Kenyatta

The attitude of local elders to the return of Kenyatta in September 1946 was guarded. Elders felt no personal antagonism towards him; even as a KCA man he had been conciliatory rather than belligerent.[67] As son-in-law of Koinange he would more likely be on the side of the land as President of KAU and, as it soon appeared, in search of his own land, he would most likely be on the side of the landed in matters which counted. That he had come back to seek political power, starting with a seat in the Legislative Council, was certain. That he chose to make his headquarters in Githunguri was all to the good; it showed that he knew that Kiambu, not Nairobi or other Kikuyu districts, was the centre of power.[68] That he took the *Mbari* oath was logical and understandable; that he was rumoured to have taken an aggressive KCA oath was one of the few signs of activism and understandable once he had to deal with – covert – KCA leadership at Githunguri.

Neither they, nor other local men, had a clear understanding of the reasons why Kenyatta had come back; that Mbiu had often referred to him as the one man who could bring help to the Kikuyu did not seem to be reason enough. Even those who knew him personally had no more information: several local men had close contacts with Githunguri and one local man, Waira Kamau, was his close co-worker and aide.[69]

What they did know was that one of Kenyatta's early concerns had been how to make an – appropriate – living, given that he did not have much land to fall back on. He may have hoped for a government job, but when this did not materialize, and knowing that he could not expect help from the covert KCA, he may have had little choice but to accept in 1947 the headmastership of Githunguri when Mbiu wanted to go abroad. The position carried some status, but not much else; Kenyatta inherited a poverty-stricken school, which was a meeting place of movements and organizations which his predecessor had tried in vain to bring together.

That he was elected to the presidency of KAU that year when Gichuru stepped down for him was a step in the right direction: it gave broader exposure and a political platform; it may have given a sufficient income. Though KAU was more an urban than a rural organization, and though contact with other ethnic groups, an avowed interest of KAU, was virtually limited to urban areas, Kenyatta made it clear that he was first and foremost a rural Kikuyu. He did not move to Nairobi, but moved KAU affairs to Githunguri. This was reassuring to the elders; it added to their conviction that Kenyatta was one of them.

Kenyatta may well have shared the image of Githunguri's significance as a *thingira*; the distance between dream and reality cannot have escaped him, living at the delapidated, poorly maintained school. He needed money; his political aspirations – let alone the school – demanded an environment which validated his ambition to become a man who had the right to a large following, who could dispense power and *tha*.

All the evidence points to the fact that Kenyatta in England retained the image of himself as a Kikuyu elder and leader. As such he cannot have failed to realize within the first months of his return that power could not be found in the fragmented, prohibited KCA, nor in the fledgling KAU, nor in a college which still lacked elementary equipment, let alone an acceptable level of examination results. Power could only come from whence it had always come: land. He could claim a small farm holding; it was not sufficiently developed and had been – and probably would be again – subject to litigation from his father's younger brother.[70] If he ever were to be an important Kikuyu leader, he needed more; nor would it do for him to live in a mud and wattle homestead while many Kiambu land owners were already building stone houses. Land and house needed to declare his status, his authority.

Raising funds for the college and raising funds for Kenyatta were therefore a dire and inseparable necessity and in terms of priorities, laying the base for Kenyatta power had to take precedence.[71] Kenyatta's speeches were in high demand; while many organizations liked to ask him to be guest speaker, elders did not often hear anything which upset them. Accused by KCA members of having abandoned the KCA, he would tell his audience that KAU was a reborn KCA, had incorporated all KCA demands and would serve them better, because the government did not distrust KAU as it had the KCA. Confronted with angry women who wanted him to take a stand against *gitati* and terracing, he pointed out that *gitati* was wrong if a woman could not do her own work and men found an excuse not to participate. *Ngwatio* instead of *gitati* was needed: however hard, terracing could save the land. What did concern elders to some extent was that his speeches ended so often in oath taking, though these seemed simple commitment oaths and were not given on their land. The oaths stressed the *umoja* theme of the *Mbari*; they incorporated features of Githunguri oaths and – as elders knew – stayed clear of the aggression of the KCA Rift Valley oaths. But when Kenyatta had been back for some time, these certainties became doubts: according to rumour Kenyatta and Mbiu had at least been present when a small group of men were oathed in the Rift Valley with a much more aggressive KCA-type oath.

It was somewhat disturbing that the oaths so often heralded Kenyatta and Mbiu as leaders. Though Mbiu was not likely to entertain such ideas, elders were concerned that Kenyatta might have larger ideas, aspirations which might at one time or another come too close to ideas that Githunguri – or Kenyatta – had, or could gain, authority which might supplant *mbari* sovereignty. This old fear, easily awakened, was fuelled by the actions of Kenyatta's aides.

Already before his return but definitely afterwards, elders feared the proliferation of oaths, earning them the sobriquet of *muuma wa kindu na kindu*, the oaths for/of many things. Oaths with the same name, might not

Resistance of the Elders until the Beginning of Mau Mau

have similar clauses; the one safeguard elders had was to keep oaths which pertained in general to their land and to watch for other actions which might run counter to their ideas of good order. Elders felt that Kenyatta had not sufficient control over his followers; elders' concern became anger when in 1947/48 he – or his aides – made a major mistake, which violated the Kikuyu order.

In the eagerness to find sources of income, Kenyatta allowed his aides, Waira Kamau and Dedan Mugo, to offer advancement in eldership to suitable candidates in exchange for a sizeable contribution.[72] Gifts should be at least shs 60/−; donors were offered a *Githunguri* oath if they so desired, administered by one of the aides at the college. Those accepting the offer were young, and most had only a small peasant holding.[73]

Advancement in eldership, a matter of payment, was virtually automatic until a man reached the level of senior eldership; even then, few would be refused permission to pay the first goat which marked the entry into senior status. The decision was a local decision; if permission was asked for entry into the *mbari* council, it was made by *mbari* elders. If permission was sought for entry into the *ngongo* council, elders, *mbari* members and *ahoi* made the decision. Allowing Waira and Dedan to solicit men and convince them that Githunguri now could take a decision in a supremely local affair, confirmed the worst fear of elders: Githunguri, Kenyatta, were attempting to make inroads, to supplant *mbari* authority.

Their response was quick; Mbiu, Kenyatta's usual collaborator, and James Gichuru were deputized to express the displeasure of the elders. The choice of these men was in itself a harsh rebuke: though both ranked high in modern political terms, they were considerably junior to Kenyatta in age and therefore well below him in status. That they were to discuss his lack of control over his aides, his and his aides' lifestyle, his concentration on acquiring the trappings of authority while KAU got no attention and the affairs of the college suffered, made it into a stinging rebuke.

Elders were not only furious that their rights had been invaded; they began to look at other Kenyatta actions with greater mistrust. Kenyatta seemed to be oblivious of the many oaths; oathing had started in Nairobi and reached local workers there. What they had joined seemed innocuous, but seven local migrant workers had taken a second oath, which older elders thought to be only barely legitimate. Dedan Mugo was actively oathing in the rural area; some of his oaths were equally dubious. The watchfulness of elders was being stretched to the limit.

Kenyatta had lost their confidence; it was no use asking him to intervene; it was widely believed that he, though not a party to many oaths, profited from oathing. Though he seemed to keep unacceptable oaths away from Githunguri, it was increasingly apparent that he was barely in control of the school and those who met there, let alone their and his own assistant's oathing. If elders wanted to avoid *thahu*, they should become more involved. The resistance was being abused; the land was in danger, the more so if government took action.

Notes

1. I gratefully acknowledge the origin of the title, a variant of the one used by Dr B. Ogot. 1972. Ogot, Bethwell A., 'Revolt of the elders', *Hadith*, Vol. 4 (1972), pp. 134–48.
2. As long as taxes were paid, labour supplied, alienation suffered without aggression and the peace maintained, the government, in the early years, left the local area alone. Influence of outsiders like Paramount Chief Kinyanyui wa Gathirimu was minimal because of distance, though he was feared. His power was used by Igi, when it asked him to arbitrate between them and a descendant of the original owners who claimed that the full price of the land had not been paid in full.
3. Though the Protectorate government had been declared in 1895, local Kikuyu dated the start of colonialism from alienation, which in their mind was akin to, if not worse than, having been defeated in battle. It is likely that research would show that different areas dated colonialism and the start of their resistance, differently.
4. The literature on Mau Mau reflects several historical and sociological approaches. The most recent discussion of these can be found in:
    1986. Atieno Odhiambo, 'The production of history in Kenya: the Mau Mau debate.' Paper presented at the Fifth International Round Table in Anthropology and History, Paris, July.
    1990. Lonsdale, John M., 'Mau Maus of the mind: making Mau Mau and remaking Kenya', *Journal of African History*, Vol. 31, No. 3, pp. 393ff.
    1992. Lonsdale, John M., 'The moral economy of Mau Mau: the problem', in Bruce Berman and John M. Lonsdale, *Unhappy Valley*, Vol. 2, London: James Currey, pp. 265–314.
    1992. Lonsdale, John M., 'The moral economy of Mau Mau: wealth, poverty & civic virtue in Kikuyu political thought', in Bruce Berman and John Lonsdale, *Unhappy Valley*, Vol. 2, London: James Currey, pp. 315–504.
5. According to Wanyoike, Kimama was killed by hostile members of another *mbari* in his territory; other versions disagree. If Wanyoike is right it would illustrate that colonial appointees, who worked without the consent of those they administered, had little chance to succeed.
    1974. Wanyoike, E. N., *op. cit.*, p. 34.
6. Waweru had lost at least one wife and children in the famine as well as other members of his *ithaku*. Like other young males, he would be coopted early in the senior council of elders which in the first decades of the twentieth century therefore had a wider than usual age range. A *muramati* of his *githaku*, Waweru became eventually *muramati* of Igi. His location was large and its size and boundaries changed several times. It was divided eventually into sub-locations under headmen and extended at all times beyond Igi and Thuita. Until the Emergency, when some headmen became leaders of the Homeguard, sub-locational headmen played only minor roles; they were dependent on the chief. That they were often kinsmen gave a chief additional authority.
    1978. Clough, M. S., *op. cit.*, p. 68ff.
7. Such strategies, but for direct protest, had been used in the past to deal with strong enemies; exchanging daughters was frequently used to ensure the peace. There are a number of variations on the predictions of Chege wa Kibiru; they began to be important in the late 1930s.
    Forthcoming. Lonsdale, John M., *The Prayers of Waiyaki: Political Uses of the Kikuyu Past*. James Currey: Oxford.
8. That the Maasai, the earlier occupants of the Rift Valley, might at that time claim the land, was not considered relevant. If the Maasai had been deprived unjustly, the

Resistance of the Elders until the Beginning of Mau Mau

Europeans should pay compensation. The Kikuyu had 'broken' the land and made it fertile; it should become theirs when the Europeans left.

9. 1915/1916. AR/273; April/December 1921. AR/288;
   1916/1917. AR/277 KBU/8; 1923. AR/290 KBU/16;
   1918-1919. AR/284 KBU/12; 1926. AR/293 KBU/19;
   1919-1920. AR/285 KBU/13; 1927. AR/296 KBU/20.
   1920-1921. AR/286 KBU/14;
   1974. Wanyoike, E. N., *op. cit.*, pp. 142ff.

10. Hostility to missions and education was by no means rare; some chiefs and councils tried to evict *ahoi* who became Christians or refused to admit Christians to eldership. Land poor or landless Christian converts who had run into problems with their *mbari* might ask missions for the use of their surplus land, though *mbari* who had provided the land did not recognize the right of the mission to dispose of it in this way. Even those who opposed giving land for missions used the services of educated men. Kinyanyui, who did not send his children to school until 1919 used Harry Thuku; Chief Kioi used Jomo Kenyatta when his English attorneys needed an explanation of Kikuyu land tenure.
    1915/1916. AR/273;
    1918/1919. AR/284 KBU/12;
    1919/1920. AR/285 KBU/13;
    1970. Thuku, Harry, *op. cit.*, p. 21.
    1978. Clough, M. S., *op. cit.*, p. 152, footnote 98.

11. Of the four appointees, Canon Harry Leakey proposed Koinange Mbiu and Josiah Njonjo. James Karanja and Waruhiu wa Kungu were supported by Kinyanyui. All were rural men; they soon became chiefs.
    1978. Clough, M. S., *op. cit.*, p. 142.
    1985. Spencer, John, *op. cit.*, pp. 26, 27.

12. Where Wanyoike stressed the limited, land-linked objectives of the KA, Clough and Spencer see wider political objectives. The information in this chapter builds on the information and opinions of Wanyoike, the local pastor.
    1921. AR 287 KBU/14.
    1968. Sorrenson, M. P. K., *op. cit.*, pp. 189ff.
    1970. Thuku, Harry, *op. cit.*, pp. 20ff.
    1974. Wanyoike, E. N., *op. cit.*, pp. 94ff.
    1978. Clough, M. S., *op. cit.*, pp. 148ff.
    1985. Spencer, John, *op. cit.*, pp. 26ff.

13. Koinange's date of birth is unknown. He had become a *mwanake* during the disasters preceding the great famine. Like Waweru Mahui he owed his government office to the trading of senior kinsmen with Europeans in the last part of the nineteenth century. He succeeded his father as chief in 1908, and when he took over the KA he was probably in his forties. He would become senior chief in 1929 after the death of Kinyanyui; he was president of the Central Native Tribunal for Kiambu, member and vice president of the Kiambu LNC; he fulfilled many other official functions and retired in 1949.
    1980. Clough, Marshall S., 'Koinange wa Mbiu, mediator and patriot', in B. E. Kipkorir (ed.), *Biographical Essays on Imperialism and Collaboration in Colonial Kenya*, Nairobi: KLB, pp. 57-86.

14. The KA cannot be adequately described as a party of chiefs. In 1921 some of the 22 Kiambu headmen were members, others were not. Those who were may have been more motivated by being larger land owners than by being chiefs. Other land owners, not chiefs, far outnumbered chiefs. Antagonism to chiefs was often to the person more than the institution, which has shown great resilience. Though headmen and chiefs were killed during Mau Mau, so were teachers. Whether they were killed because they were chiefs or teachers, cannot be established.
    1922. AR/289 KBU/15.
    1978. Clough, M. S., *op. cit.*, p. 17.

Resistance of the Elders until the Beginning of Mau Mau

      1985. Spencer, John, *op. cit.*, p. 27.
15. 1970. Thuku, Harry, *op. cit*, pp. 15ff.
16. In Kabete, Canon Leakey, Dr J. W. Arthur and the Rev. A. R. Barlow played significant roles; locally Rev. W. P. Knapp, though less sympathetic to political aspirations, was important.
17. 1923. AR/290 KBU/16.
      1966. Rosberg, Carl G., Jr., and John Nottingham, *The Myth of Mau Mau, Nationalism in Kenya*, Hoover Institute on War, Revolution and Peace, London: Stanford Praeger, pp. 38ff.
18. 1970. Thuku, Harry, *op. cit.*, pp. 19ff.
19. The *kipande* was a documentation system introduced in July 1916 to facilitate recruitment for the Carrier Corps. It became a method for controlling workers and the free flow of labour. The name is derived from the Swahili *kibande* and referred to a container which held registration papers. As most men lacked clothing with pockets, it had to be carried on a string around the neck. It was abolished in 1949.
      1960. Cmnd 1030 *Historical Survey of the Origins and Growth of Mau Mau* (Corfield Report) (F. D. Corfield), London: HMSO, pp. 25–6.
      1966. Savage, D. C., and J. Forbes Munro, 'Carrier Corps recruitment in the British East African Protectorate 1914–1918', *Journal of African History*, Vol. 7, No. 2, pp. 313–42.
      1970. Thuku, Harry, *op. cit.*, pp. 18ff.
      1974. Clayton, Anthony, and Donald C. Savage, *op. cit.*, pp. 83, 296.
      1978. Clough, M. S., *op. cit.*, pp. 154ff.
20. Thuku and his extensive land holdings abutted the local area. His selective account of the political events highlights the ambivalent relationship between him and Kinyanyui. That he had become one of the wealthiest men in the area, inhibited the gathering of information. Official local information made him out to have been a somewhat unruly and ambitious *mwanake* who, like many other *anake*, had not always obeyed the elders. As to be expected, he had changed when he grew older and wealthier. Wanyoike, who belonged to the same *mbari*, describes him primarily as a victim of colonialism.
      1970. Thuku, Harry, *op. cit.*, pp. 19ff.
      1974. Wanyoike E. N., *op. cit.*, p. 96.
      1985. Spencer, John, *op. cit.*, pp. 37ff, 42ff.
21. While the Kikuyu until the 1940s avoided the use of more serious oaths outside their traditional context, the government imposed structuring oaths on members of the tribunals and the LNC.
      1926. AR/294 KBU/19.
      1927. HOR/192 KBU/20.
      1950. AR/323 KBU/41.
22. He had set up an office in the land of his *mbari*, close to the local area. Curses of barrenness, acted out by putting *gitugi* sticks in front of women's huts, demanded cleansing and a sacrifice.
23. To judge an Association by an official's information is fraught with danger. Membership varied widely from year to year; hard data are scarce. Sympathy for a movement is quite different from support of a movement.
24. Thuku reports that he once paid Rps 1,300/– (about shs 1,750/–) to hire a taxi. Around 1922 this would have been close to three years' wages for a headman, four and a half years' income for a full-time employed urban semi-skilled worker, or six years' income for a similarly employed unskilled worker. Soliciting money and contributions by those aspiring to power was acceptable if they showed that they had power and 'mercy'; conspicuous consumption, though evidence of power, was condemned if it was not used to bring *tha*.
      1970. Thuku, Harry, *op. cit.*, p. 32.
25. Miti could refer to the male initiation ritual in which young males competed by throwing

Resistance of the Elders until the Beginning of Mau Mau

sticks, *miti*, provided by kinsmen, over a tree. Against that background, the organization was possibly one of *anake*, who were to become defenders of Mount Kenya, the dwelling place of Ng'ai. Members might have come from Kinyotoku and Chiringi; no local men admitted to have been party to the Miti. If one of its aims was the restoration of female circumcision, then its relationship to Thuku is not clear. Although missions at that time frequently preached about its evil, the actual battle about it was was still several years away.

1961. Welbourn, F. B., *East African Rebels*, London: SCM Press p. 130.
1985. Spencer, John, *op. cit.*, p. 58.

26. The Miti apparently had taken similar oaths. An extensive discussion of different oaths is available in Appendix VIII.
27. Elders did not believe that lack of active participation in the KA jeopardized its decisions; they could always attend the next meeting and protest decisions they did not accept.
1921. April-December ASR/288.
1924. AR/291 KBU/16.
1927. AR/296 KBU/20.
1967. Sorrenson, M. P. K., *op. cit.*, pp. 15ff.
1968. Sorrenson, M. P. K., *op. cit.*, pp. 176ff.
1974. Wanyoike, E. N., *op. cit.*, pp. 94 ff.
1978. Clough, M. S., *op. cit.*, pp. 148ff.
1985. Spencer, John, *op. cit.*, p. 261.
28. The LNC held its first meeting on 17 July 1925. Waweru was an elected, Wanyoike a nominated member. It was and remained, in keeping with the prevailing ethos, an organization which, though oriented towards the needs of all, was more attuned to the well-to-do than the poor. Health care is a case in point. The government had, for decades, left the provision of health care to missions and settlers' wives. Kambui had saved many lives in the smallpox epidemics of 1912, 1913 and 1915; it was lauded for its work during the outbreak of cerebrospinal meningitis and the 1915 outbreak of malarial influenza. By 1927 the Kiambu LNC had used its funds to open a dispensary at Dagoretti and was planning a second one. In 1930 a native hospital was opened at Kiambu and dispensaries provided basic aid in Mutunyi, Githunguri and Wangigi. But patients had to pay, sometimes for visits, sometimes for medication, or for both. By 1956 the patients with contagious diseases, such as tuberculosis, still had to pay for medication. The cost for wealthier men was negligible; for the poor it constituted a barrier. Other LNC work also was of limited use for the landless and land poor. After the Carter Commission the LNC would be particularly successful in introducing agricultural improvements; before that time it had midwifed the Kiambu Native Produce Cooperative Society and instituted standing Educational and Agricultural Committees.

1915–1916. AR/273 KBU/9;   1928. AR/297 KBU/21;
1926. AR/293, 294 KBU/19; 1929. AR/301 KBU/22;
1927. AR/296 KBU/20;   1931. AR/302 KBU/24.

29. Koinange, member and President of the LNC, used not only the weak KA but also the LNC as a platform for protest. He used the KA to agitate against a KCA-supported plan to replace the aging Kinyanyui with another paramount chief, a potential threat to *mbari* independence. He lead the LNC in its fight against government soil conservation rules.
1935. AR/307 KBU/27.
1938. AR/310 KBU/29.
30. As late as 1956, very old elders would recount how government actions had prevented them from acting as proper Kikuyu should. They used this argument to defend leniency even for those who had taken unacceptable oaths; the government had interfered with proper morality.
31. This was the gist of the information, provided in 1956 about the Carter Commission Report and its consequences. Two remarks may be in order: though a number of prominent elders were undoubtedly convinced that they should become wealthy to bring

freedom to the people, there is little doubt that for others wealth was a goal in itself. Given the approbation of wealth, this was not something for disapproval: the only question about wealth would be whether those so blessed gave *tha* as they should. Though it is true that larger land owners were by and large absent from Mau Mau, neither in 1956 nor in 1962 were they faulted for this. Mau Mau remained a questionable, extremely painful episode in the life of the people. Many land poor and landless had not been able to escape becoming involved. Many landed had been able to remain outside. As long as they had protected and shielded those who were inside, their wealth was immaterial.

32. Organizations which had suffered the brunt of illegitimacy encountered more difficulty with their legitimacy than new organizations. The KCA is a case in point; it continued to distrust and often vilified rural authority, which often responded in kind if it had not distrusted the KCA itself first.

33. The literature tends to see the *Mbari* as the Kikuyu Land Board, apparently a brainchild of Kenyatta, conceived during the KCA efforts to gather testimony for the Carter Commission. Koinange was supposed to have left the KA for the KCA, as its head. The *Mbari* is supposed to have remained powerful, though it was not banned with the KCA, playing a pivotal role in rural and eventually urban Mau Mau. My data are limited: informants did not mention this. Oaths for the *Mbari* were few, and informants did not call them Mau Mau oaths, nor oaths for a Land Board. Only one informant took an oath at Bananahill (which he did not call a *Mbari* oath). No one in Nairobi took an oath for the *Mbari*.

1966. Rosberg, Carl G., Jr., and John Notttingham, *op. cit.*, pp. 145ff.
1972. Murray-Brown, Jeremy, *Kenyatta*, London: Allen & Unwin, pp. 107ff.
1985. Spencer, John, *op. cit.*, pp. 86, 94, 203, 208.

34. The evictions from Tigoni, when men whose rights had been recognized by the Land Commission were forced to leave before compensation had been paid, and the imposition of conservation rules brought strong LNC reactions.

1938. AR/310 KBU/29.
1966. Rosberg, Carl G., Jr., and John Nottingham, *op. cit.*, p. 287.

35. Koinange was identified with Kikuyu land and recognized as such, certainly by part of the Rift Valley population, which expected him to take timely action when their rights were endangered. Samuel Koina Gitebe would come to him for help in the matter of the land at Olenguruone, where he had administered an oath, essentially a localized, aggressive oath about the land, to men, women and children. Though Koinange's *Mbari* oath was pacific, he recognized that what was occurring at Olenguruone violated the ownership of Kikuyu land and amounted to new alienation. An aggressive response was therefore appropriate. Koinange offered to pay for legal assistance and provided shelter to some of the dispossessed on his land. Koinange's stature in Murang'a and Gaki may have been different.

1987. Kanogo, Tabitha, *op. cit.*, pp. 105ff.

36. Like Kenyatta on his return in 1946, Mathu was oathed in Koinange's *thingira* by Koinange, but not until years after he had become a Legislative Council member, and Kenyatta had come back. According to chiefs Kibathi and Magugo, Kenyatta was instrumental in making him take the *Gikuyu na Muumbi* oath, another name for the *Mbari* oath, late in 1951 or early in 1952. Mbiu and Kenyatta were present; Gichuru had taken the same oath. The objective was to make sure that both men remained 'true to the land'. According to Amos Wagacha, Mathu took an oath, normally associated with lower cadre Mau Mau leaders, the following year in the house of Stefano Wangei (Appendix VIII/6). When the District Commissioner of Kiambu wanted to deny Mathu's right to register for the first African elections to the Legislative Council in 1957, Mathu angrily denied that he had taken any oaths.

37. It is common for Kikuyu to attribute ideas to a public person to emphasize and teach the message which should be conveyed. The modern spelling for freedom is *wiathi*; in 1956 *weiyathi* was used, as was *wiyathi*.

38. 1917. AR/281 KBU/11.
39. The curriculum of Alliance High School, which opened in 1926, was oriented towards the positions Africans were presumed to occupy. First-year students had to choose between clerical skills, teaching, and agricultural training presuming that they later would be clerks, native teachers, or agricultural instructors. The curriculum was somewhat more demanding than that of mission schools for students who had finished their elementary training. Among the first students were Eliud Mathu and the local chief, Magugo. Peter Mbiu, the son of Koinange, attended for a short time; when his father realized the type of curriculum his son was offered, he sent him to the USA for further schooling.
40. The cess was to yield eventually £10,000; about one third was collected in the first, the remainder in the next two years.
    1927. AR/296 KBU/20;
    1927–28. AR/297 KBU/21;
    1928. AR/299;
    1929. KBU/301 AR/22.
    1976. Tignor, Robert L., *op. cit.*, pp. 255ff.
41. Although some missions believed in a more gradual policy than Kambui, their insistence that Christianity demanded conformity to Western cultural practices disrupted the social fabric. While some educated males desired uncircumcised wives, and such women could reach high status, other males desired circumcised wives because marrying an uncircumcised wife would enrage their parents. Fathers might claim that their sons deprived their mother of continuity and disinherit them. Monogamy is also hard on women in a society with high infant and child mortality; they may have multiple pregnancies to respond to the demand that each generation reproduce her husband's and her parents.
    1925. R/292 KBU/18.
    1931. Leakey, L. S. B., 'The Kikuyu problem of the initiation of girls', *JRAI*, Vol. 90, pp. 277–85.
    1974. Murray, Jocelyn M., 'The Kikuyu female circumcision controversy with special reference to the Church Missionary Society's sphere of influence', PhD thesis, University of California, Los Angeles.
    1974. Wanyoike, E. N., *op. cit.*, pp. 91ff.
    1978. Clough, M. S., *op. cit.*, pp. 305ff.
    1979. Hoskin, Fran P., *The Hoskin Report*, Lexington, Mass.: Women's International Network News.
    1985. Spencer, John, *op. cit.*, pp. 72ff.
42. 1974. Wanyoike, E. N., *op. cit.*, p. 55.
43. 1923. AR/290 KBU/16.
44. 1974. Wanyoike, E. N., *op. cit.*, p. 97.
45. 1974. Wanyoike, E. N., *op. cit.*, p. 93.
46. Though no hard data exist, that the KCA did not campaign on the need to reinstate male circumcision with all attendant ritual may be because the KCA men, like many leaders, had been to mission schools, and had participated in mission-organized initiations, with circumcisions in hospital and no (or only partial) participation in Kikuyu rites. They would nevertheless claim the *riika* of the year in which they were circumcised. Thuku and Wanyoike were circumcised at Kambui by Dr J. E. Henderson; while Thuku did not participate in ritual, Wanyoike is somewhat vague. Both claimed *Matiba*. That female circumcision could be equated with purity did not convince parents. The KCA did not notably benefit; the best local estimate is that it gained perhaps four members during the circumcision issue.
    1970. Thuku, Harry, *op. cit.*, p. 8.
    1974. Wanyoike, E. N., *op. cit.*, p. 30.
47. Pacification only worked as a strategy when those who were subjected to it were ignorant or willing to comply with its rules. Cooperation might mean that a missionary or District

Resistance of the Elders until the Beginning of Mau Mau

Officer could demand that his directions be laid down in orders or memoranda; however, checking that they were executed would go too far.

48. Koinange was caught between KCA and mission anger. He had voted with the LNC, but opposed heavy fines for non-compliance as wanted by the mission. He equally opposed that missions made non-circumcision a criterion for admission to education. Some of the *mithirigu* attacked him for sending his son to America; they also attacked the son.

49. *Mithirigu* are related to the mocking and insulting songs of young males the night before initiation. They mock authority, and are frequently sexually explicit. They can be directed against women of their mothers' generation, which means that they are directed at their future mothers-in-law. In time, females will demand compensation: a male must pay a fee 'for the abuse' to his future wife's mother during bridewealth negotiations.
    1974. Wanyoike, E. N., *op. cit.*, pp. 102ff.

50. An added problem was that, while male circumcision could, if needed, be delayed till schooling was finished, female circumcision had to take place within the short period that girls were no longer children but had not yet menstruated or developed secondary sex characteristics. The number of girls who were reaching that age and in school can only have been small. According to government documents Kambui together with its outschools had in 1926 95 students on its rolls. In almost all years for which government data are available, girls account at most for 25 per cent of the number. They were concentrated in the two lowest grades.
    1926. AR/292 KBU/19.

51. 1961. Welbourn, F. B., *op. cit.*, pp. 145ff.
    1970. Kovar, M., 'The Kikuyu Independent Schools Association', PhD thesis, University of California, Los Angeles.

52. 1927-28. AR/297 KBU/21.

53. During caravan days Githunguri had been a collecting and trading post. The early independent school there had been a founding member of the Kikuyu Karinga Independent Schools Association.
    1974. Wanyoike, E. N., *op. cit.*, p. 43.

54. The government had allowed the school to open, provided it adhered to the government syllabus and allowed inspection.
    1939. AR/311 KBU/30.

55. Small snakes, hidden in the grass, which jump up when trod upon. Their bite causes a painful swelling and can be deadly to children.

56. There are many extant explanations for the name Mau Mau; there was no agreement among informants, though the following explanation was promoted by men willing to accept that some men from the initiation years *Ngigi, Kienyeku* and *Mutungu* had preyed upon the population during the famine. These men had been given the name Mau Mau. It had a dual meaning: children and badly brought up adults might take food which was not theirs, or eat it noisily. They acted wrongly, but if they were so hungry that they had to steal food or eat greedily, their mothers might have deprived them of food, or not taught them manners. The mothers were therefore the real culprits. This explanation was used for Mau Mau, but with a colonial slant. The Europeans and the government were ultimately the guilty party, they had taken the land and people were Mau Mau because they were poor. Note 61, Chapter 2 enlarges on this. While this is a pleasant enough explanation, and widely accepted, most researchers even today would have found that most Kikuyu were quite unwilling to discuss Mau Mau in any detail. I cannot shed much light on the origin of the term. That Kikuyu are reluctant to recall the experiences of the Mau Mau years, is undoubtedly due to the suffering they endured, which they do not want to bring back by words.

57. One of the striking aspects of Mbiu's campaign in the Rift Valley was his stress on Kenyatta as the needed 'helper'. Whether he did this to give Kenyatta an incentive to return, whether some men in the KCA prompted him to do so, or whether this was a

Resistance of the Elders until the Beginning of Mau Mau

decision made by Kenyatta and Mbiu at one or another time to prepare the population for Kenyatta's return and increase his appeal, I do not know.

58. Githunguri oaths would become the most expensive oaths, reserved for anyone who paid at least shs 60/–. By the time of Kenyatta they would almost certainly be given at the college.
59. The local screening team, in contrast to screening teams elsewhere, did not classify college oaths taken before 1950 as Mau Mau in contrast to screening teams from other areas. Nor did they classify the *Mbari* oath as Mau Mau, while the Rift Valley certainly did so. Perhaps this is why I found only a few local *Mbari* oaths, but counted 10 among the 125 Rift Valley males. It may be but is not likely that the *Mbari* had more followers in the Rift Valley.
60. No local women had joined. After Olenguruone, membership and oathing of women became standard.

    1966. Rosberg, Carl G. Jr., and John Nottingham, *op. cit.*, p. 139.
    1987. Kanogo, Tabitha, *op. cit.*, pp. 105ff.
61. Parts of oathing clauses may emerge in *nyimbo* (sing. *ruimbo*) and vice versa. According to legend, Chege wa Kibiru had promised that the Kikuyu would get freedom when a *thingira* had been built at Githunguri. This could be interpreted as the time that the college was built; it could also mean the time when Kenyatta took up residence. Because *Mbiu* had asked Kenyatta to take charge of the college, it was interpreted that he was the kingmaker, who made Kenyatta understand that he had a legitimate right to rule. In a Mau Mau song, the promise of freedom is taken up again; whites must leave all Kikuyu land on pain of being thrown out:

Na inyui mbari ya Nyakeru	You of the *mbari* of whites
Inyuothe mwakiti bururi-ini witu	You will all have to sneak out of our country
Ngai yaigua Gikuyu na Muumbi	God gave Gikuyu and Muumbi
Mukagira magenda mbia	or you will leave through the hole of pierced ears.

    It takes little imagination to realize that only those who are pulverized can be driven through small openings.
62. KAU had more local members than the KCA had had. Wages had risen slowly, but KAU charged the same fee as the KCA and it was therefore more affordable. Where the KCA had been combative and aggressive to other Kikuyu, KAU reserved what aggression it did display for the government. Members were therefore not likely to run into conflicts with non-members. Whether the slogan 'KAU is KCA' brought in more members, would have to be studied in the Rift Valley. It may have worked for the rank and file there, but was probably less than convincing for Nairobi KAU leaders.
63. Mbiu suffered political damage because of his long absence and inability to relate easily to the elders. For some, his presumed ties with the KCA were a factor. He did not get the Legislative Council appointment nor become president of KAU. Though Gichuru was younger and had less education, he had not been absent.

    1985. Spencer, John, *op. cit.*, pp. 115ff.
64. 1987. Kanogo, Tabitha, *op. cit.*, pp. 96ff.
65. Among the 125 Rift Valley males were two, among the females three, 'Kenia' oaths. Each had one 'United Natives' oath. The content of the oaths shows some of the characteristics of the later Mau Mau oaths, particularly in their threat to the taker should he fail to perform according to the promises. They had been screened in the Rift Valley; they had been declared there to be Mau Mau.
66. Little is known about Mau Mau involvement of Kikuyu in Northern Tanganyika. By December 1953 those who had not repatriated themselves were expelled and many were detained. Twelve males and six females from the local area worked in Arusha; most had initially come from the Rift Valley and taken an oath in 1946/7 which they did not acknowledge as a Mau Mau oath, even though their screening teams in Tanganyika regarded them as such. Probably for that reason their rate of (male) second oath taking

Resistance of the Elders until the Beginning of Mau Mau

is higher and earlier than elsewhere. By the end of 1949 ten of the twelve males and one of the females had taken another oath. They did not engage in violence though some held Mau Mau office in Tanganyika.

67. Kenyatta had been a member of Thuku's Young Kikuyu Association, but had not shown an overriding interest in politics until he became the general secretary of the KCA in 1928 and editor of *Muigwithania*, the KCA newspaper. The KCA sent him to England in 1929 (after having asked him to take an oath that he would be faithful and return). He reluctantly returned in 1930, only to leave again as a KCA delegate in 1931, staying abroad until 1946.

68. Githunguri was an employer of local men. By 1956 local men had worked there as teachers; one had been a headmaster, others had helped with building or been volunteers. They would remark on Kenyatta's friendliness and ease, his willingness to listen and to attend the many meetings which were held there, of which they or kinsmen were often part. He rarely committed himself to a particular course of action, but kept his own counsel. In 1962 the political climate made it important to have been a close Kenyatta associate, working even during his absence for the goal of his return and rule. Yet, even though some Githunguri aides who had returned from detention boasted of their closeness, evidence was scant. Kenyatta did not want to alienate any group, yet confided in none.

69. Waira was a Thuita man whose father had sold his local land to Waweru Mahui; though he had retained land near Kiambu, Waira became a local *muhoi*. He attended Githunguri school but remained close friends with young local males, including a member of the *githaku* of Gitau. As he had a shop at Marige he was closely affiliated with the young males who used the market as a gathering place. He and Dedan Mugo, about whom little is known, regarded themselves as members of the KCA, but it is unlikely that Waira had joined before it had been prohibited. After his return from the war he became a clerk at the information office in Kiambu and served on the District Council, the old LNC. He joined Githunguri in 1947, with the special assignment of raising funds. Both he and Dedan Mugo maintained strong Nairobi contacts, but there is no evidence that either was connected with the *Muhimu*. Waira was arrested on 7 October 1953, as one of those accused in the Waruhiu murder. He was freed because of lack of evidence but rearrested under the Emergency regulations. He returned to the local area and his shop in 1962, where he was greeted with many 'tea parties'. Mugo administered oaths outside Githunguri and operated particularly in and around Kiambu. By 1950 his oaths had characteristics elders could not condone; the oaths also attracted the attention of the administration. He was arrested and convicted in July 1950.

   1960. Corfield Report, *op. cit.*, p. 85.
   1967. Itote, W., *'Mau Mau' General*, Nairobi: East African Publishing House.
   1973. Furedi, Frank, *op. cit.*, 275ff.
   1975. Kaggia, Bildad, *Roots of Freedom*, Nairobi: East African Literature Bureau.
   1977. Spencer, John, 'KAU and Mau Mau: some connections', *KHR*, Vol. 5, No. 2, pp. 201–24.
   1975. Wachanga, H. K., *The Swords of Kirinyaga*, Kampala: East African Literature Bureau.
   1977. Spencer, John, 'The Kenya African Union 1944–1953, a party in search of a constituency', PhD thesis, Columbia University, pp. 212ff, 280.
   1982. Buytenhuys, Rob, *Essays on Mau Mau Contributions to Mau Mau Historiography* (Research Reports No. 17), Leiden, the Netherlands: African Studies Center, pp. 12ff.

70. There is no agreement whether Kenyatta owned the land on the basis of inheritance, or bought it almost immediately after he returned to Kenya, using contributions made by the population. At that time, land in the Ngenda would have cost roughly shs 700/– per acre, unimproved. Kenyatta as an important person might have paid less. The problem would have been finding a large enough tract to satisfy his status.

1972. Murray-Brown, Jeremy, *op. cit.*, p. 230.
71. A recurrent complaint of the administration would be that Kenyatta did not keep his financial affairs separate from those of the college. Given Kenyatta's conviction that he had a right to authority and the resources for it, he was not obliged to do so.
1960. Corfield Report, *op. cit.*, p. 182ff.
72. Whether Kenyatta was fully informed about this breach of customary behaviour cannot be separated from ideas about how Kikuyu officials use co-workers. Traditionally kinsmen were expected to shore up the power of the most powerful among them, and they would expect appropriate rewards for doing so. This remained the same under colonialism. During that time and in the past, high officials should be perceived as fully obeying the law and keeping to the rules; when it was not advisable to do so, kinsmen were expected to act in his stead, so that the image of the official remained unsullied. If problems arose, the kinsmen could be blamed, receiving appropriate rewards for the unpleasantness at a later time. Kikuyu were convinced that 'no men can rule without kinsmen'.
73. Six local men at least sought advancement at Githunguri; one paid shs 140/- to become a second-grade junior elder. They took an oath, but the local screening team did not count it as a Mau Mau oath.

Seven

The Resistance of the Land Poor & Landless

The Beginning of Mau Mau[1]

It is not likely that *mbari* members, who had survived the famine, were land poor; as heirs of the dead, they probably owned more land than before. *Ahoi* could – within limits – use as much land as they wanted; some had lived with the *mbari* before the famine; others had come during or immediately after it. *Ahoi*, never important in Thuita, had always constituted a sizeable population in Igi. By 1902 38 per cent of Igi and 10 per cent of Thuita households were *ahoi*; owners provided land for cultivation, fallowing and herding (Tables 2.1, 2.2, pp. 72, 73). Being landless was not necessarily a stigma, if it was used as an opportunity to breed stock with which eventually to buy land.

Land alienation affected landed and landless. Some who lost all or most moved away with their *ahoi*; those who had retained basic holdings stayed with their *ahoi* and were aided by those who had lost less or none. They rarely got back what they had owned or used; some *mbari* members and *ahoi* immediately, others gradually, lost surplus cultivation, fallowing and herding land. In the first decades of alienation, landlessness of *ahoi* and land poverty of *mbari* members developed for many into pronounced shortage of land. In the 1920s, when user rights had to yield to the needs of *mbari* sons and owner investment in cash crops, similar conditions developed into poverty, necessitating wage labour by one or more members of the household.

The number of land poor households increased over time as land poor *mbari* members tended to stay with the *mbari* where they had rights. The number of *ahoi* households decreased, as *ahoi* sons, who no longer could count on inheriting the user rights of their fathers, and were less welcome as husbands for *mbari* daughters, moved away. By the time of the Carter Commission, *ahoi* or landless households had dropped in Igi to 29 per cent;

just before the Emergency they made up 26 per cent of the population. The corresponding figures for Thuita were 12.7 per cent and 6.4 per cent. *Ahoi* households tended to contain a smaller and older population.

By the mid-1920s land-poor *mbari* households increased considerably as small peasants and peasants, with several heirs, could provide only subsistence holdings for their sons. No reliable figures exist for the pre-Carter growth in land poverty; calculations indicate that by the time of the Carter Commission, about 11.3 per cent of Igi and more than a third of Thuita *mbari* members were land poor. The corresponding figures just before the Emergency were 38.2 per cent of Igi and 65.5 per cent of Thuita households. Though both *ahoi* and land poor relied on wage income and some use of land, *ahoi* tended to be poorer than the land poor: many of the latter still owned perhaps an acre and might get another acre in use; the *ahoi* got about as much land in use but could not shore this up with land of their own.

The relationship between landless, land poor and landed

Throughout the colonial period, the landless and land poor were viewed somewhat differently, by the landed and by themselves, if their poverty had occurred before the period of land alienation and colonial occupation. The Kikuyu viewed poverty, though not landlessness, as a stigma, a lack of blessings; the man with property was more blessed because the spiritual forces seemed to favour him. Being poor was a sign from the spiritual forces; those who were poor, or their ancestors, had failed somewhere spiritually. While the good poor man knew that poverty could be removed by hard work, he could not know when it would please the spiritual forces to favour him.[2]

During the colonial regime this harsh perspective was softened, not least because it was inherently untenable when those who were poor could be joined in the next generation by the sons of the landed. In the face of land alienation, colonial restrictions and European control, even those who judged by the strictest interpretation of their ethical world could hardly maintain that moral shortcomings were the main cause of poverty.

Yet, the lingering feeling of landless and land poor of having somehow failed, the fear of those who had land that their sons might well be blamed if they became land poor, created the necessity to keep the evil of colonial control in the foreground of thought. This brought wealthy and poor closer together; those who still had land felt less certain that this was a reward for moral purity; those who lacked land did not see this as a moral judgment which demanded submissiveness. In the early years of the colonial occupation, landed and landless were probably closer than under normal conditions.

Ahoi and land owners shared the ethos that land was the ultimate authority; those who owned it were its guardians and protectors. In the early decades of the twentieth century, they accepted that the elders, the proper authority, should make decisions, including whether and how to resist European occupation and to bring back the land. The prime obligation of *ahoi*, and all who lived under the protection of the land, was to follow.

The land poor, as *mbari* members, had more rights than the landless, but were not likely to belong to senior elders or be part of the *ndundu* of the elders' councils, where decisions were made. Like the *ahoi*, they were expected to obey. If elders accepted a headman or Chief, it was up to landless and land poor to pay the taxes levied upon them. If, in the interests of pacification, elders or chiefs demanded labour for settlers, if they and the government demanded *gitati*, *ahoi* and land poor might grumble, but did turn out.[3]

The rewards for compliance could be significant: a landed chief or headman could allow the use of his land and share tools or seeds he received for his own compliance. He could find well-paying rather than unfair employers. Also, wages could supplement what the land produced: they could buy cloth, a *panga*, sugar or tea. Cash might mean school fees for a son. That poverty was pervasive could not be blamed on chiefs or elders; Europeans were to blame for lack of land, low wages, abuse, or the *kipande*.

As guardians of the land, large land owners had more rights than small owners, who had more rights than those who used the land. Large land owners, as intermediaries and protectors of the population, as men who sought strength which eventually would drive the Europeans out, had the right to use the colonial power to advantage. If they asked for a central college for higher education, landless and land poor should pay; it was immaterial that opportunities for the sons of landless and land poor were few.

Whether land poor and landless would have protested in earlier decades, cannot be answered. Yet some of the protests against demands by the landed found their origin in the greater awareness of landless and land poor that their poverty was not a sign of moral failings. Throughout the colonial period, they mostly responded positively to demands of the landed, though refusal occurred. When the LNC imposed a cess of shs 6/- on each male for a Kikuyu high school at Githunguri, not likely to be of benefit to land poor or landless, opposition against this subsidy for the education of sons of larger land owners was widespread, and the LNC was forced to reduce the cess in subsequent years. *Gitati* was similarly attacked when the LNC used it in the 1920s and 1930s for demonstration farms, which were mainly for land owners. Later, when terracing and soil conservation brought little immediate benefit and took too much time from wage labour, vocal and widespread opposition forced the LNC to pay minimum wages.[4]

In spite of occasional conflict, land owners, landless and land poor remained linked by interdependence, kinship and a common ethos. Landless and land poor wanted to steer clear of organizations which attacked chiefs or headmen, on whom their security depended, as if these men, and not the government, were the cause of misery. They were well aware that the landed derived more profit from the European presence, yet their world view accepted inequality as normal; it stemmed ultimately from spiritual decisions. Men could not redress the balance; the spiritual forces would take action when it pleased them to do so. However much wage workers might agree with the EAA and the later KCA's attack on the *kipande*, this was not a sufficient reason to align oneself with their organizations. Rather than pay hefty fees to Thuku's EAA or the later KCA, land poor and landless counted on their kinsmen's obligation to provide *tha*.

After the Carter Commission, land owners concentrated on the development of their land, hoping to achieve sufficiencies for sons. *Ahoi* and land poor regretfully accepted this; when their own allocations became steadily smaller and more dispersed, they did not blame land owners. The less they got, the more important the small tracts they did get; land, whether owned or used, was their security net. Though land poor and landless realized, after Carter, that they had gained greater freedom to join opposition against the government, little changed for decades; nor did their opinion of the KCA, the one organization which could be regarded as openly resistant to the government.

The fees it charged were beyond most landless and land poor; around 1935 KCA annual fees would have paid six months' schooling. The KCA platform became increasingly irrelevant for land poor and landless; when it agitated for the return of the stolen lands, landless knew that it would go to land owners, who, one generation and many sons after alienation, would have little to share.[5] Moreover, the return of the land would not be accompanied by the capital needed to develop it.

The KCA came closer to the interest of the land poor and landless when it spoke about wages and conditions of labour, which were central to their existence. Yet its demands, like those of the later unions, would have little effect on the most needy: the mass of unskilled workers whose fathers had been too poor to provide education because, even then, they had little or no land. Improvement in working conditions became an unrealistic idea in a work climate in which a hundred men stood ready to take one's job in worse conditions. No wonder that, where the KCA blamed the government for wages and working conditions, workers tended to blame the competition.

The post-Carter political enfranchisement of landless and land poor by the landed did not translate into political power, which both landed and landless perceived in economic terms. Rather than being empowered, landless and land poor bore the brunt of the improvements for the landed: they built the roads, the school and the clinics, yet the fees charged by these institutions often put them outside their reach. Githunguri College might symbolize the coming of higher education, but, given its cost, it was unlikely that their sons would become 'Mbiu's little snakes'. Government interest in agriculture and development was a boon for land owners, but meant terracing and *gitati* for landless and land poor. Similarly with LNC decisions: it might decide to pay part of the cost of manure, but this benefit was paid from the taxes of those who had little or no land.

That landless and land poor neither could nor did participate in political life was nothing new: their nineteenth-century sociological ancestors had not done so either. They had accepted this in exchange for economic security in the present and hope for a future in which they would buy their own land.[6] Yet, twentieth-century land poor and landless had neither economic security nor hope for a future in which they would be able to buy land.

The early Kenyatta years, 1946–50: myth and reality

Few politicians would have survived an absence of fifteen years, during which constituents received no tangible benefits. That so many Kikuyu were convinced that Kenyatta was all the while busy accumulating power in their interest was a tribute to the impression he left behind, the relentless admiration and promises of *Mumenyerere*, Mbiu Koinange and the KCA. How successful they were was apparent when Kenyatta returned in 1946.

His welcome was overwhelming, yet many in the crowds had their own expectations. Though hoping that he would break the European control over the Highlands and lucrative crops, older land owners were cautiously delighted but intended to keep to a wait-and-see policy. The KCA hoped that his return would force the government to lift its proscription: Kenyatta would rebuild its political base, forcing the withdrawal of KAU while restraining the restive young, who used the KCA name for their predatory forays in the Rift Valley. KAU hoped that Kenyatta would see the need for a more accommodating Kenyan party, which, through cooperation, would be allowed greater freedom and participation in the colonial political processes. The unions may have expected an ally.

The greatest local enthusiasm came from the younger landless and land poor who had not shown much interest in the KCA, and whose second-hand knowledge of Kenyatta was derived from the information put out by various sources. He had been described as the one man who could bring deliverance, the embodiment of new Kikuyu power. His return was a triumph over the colonial government which had opposed it. He had come back with the authority of the British government behind him: he carried secret British agreements which would abolish the 'White Highlands'. Cheap land would soon become available. Their enthusiasm showed how much they wanted and needed to believe that Kenyatta could solve their problems without attacking their kinsmen who still had land.[7]

Kenyatta's reception underscored his perceived authority and expected roles. He was provided with services and homage: his passage was paid with help from KCA members and contributions from independent schools; he was driven by J. M. Mungai, president of the then Nairobi African Taxi Drivers Union. He was feasted and fêted in different districts; local chiefs came to greet him, and local KCA chapters paid the bills and provided tribute. He was offered and took the *Mbari* oath administered by Koinange Mbiu himself; he retook the KCA oath, which during his absence had become a 'goat oath', an oath in which the killing of a goat and eating the meat were an integral part of the ritual (Appendix VIII/5). Soon Koinange would offer him one of his daughters as a wife.

While organizations vied with each other for his attention and some KCA men acted as if they owned him, ordinary Kikuyu were delighted to see that Kenyatta, by refusing to let others decide with whom and where he should spend his time, made it clear that he was his own man. This could only mean that he was more than a KCA man; he would see their need and they eagerly awaited evidence of his authority. They were disturbed that the government seemed to have sufficient power to ignore Kenyatta's mandate, and did not throw the Highlands open to Kikuyu, did not lift the ban on the KCA, and did not offer Kenyatta a seat in the Legislative Council. The Kikuyu seemed to be the only ones who recognized his position, but, having no power, how could they give it? Although of symbolic importance, the offer from Mbiu Koinange of a Githunguri position was still less than they had expected. Kenyatta's prestige was somewhat restored when James Gichuru, shortly afterwards, made way for him by stepping down as President of KAU.

After the excitement of the first years wore off, landless and land poor took stock. There were favourable signs: Kenyatta had supported the *Mbari* and Koinange's efforts to help the dispossessed of the Rift Valley; he obviously had Koinange support. Whether it was positive or negative that he – having failed to regain legal status for the KCA – did his utmost to lead it into KAU, under the slogan that they were one anyway, depended on one's point of view. It was not a major concern for the Nairobi or Kiambu landless and land poor, few of whom expected solutions from either. That he had urged the government to help the Rift Valley squatters and visited Olenguruone was all to the good; that he had not offered them financial support or land use like Koinange, made sense: he had no land to offer. That he lived at Githunguri rather than Nairobi was potentially positive; freedom would ultimately come from the *thingira* at Githunguri, as Chege wa Kibiru had foretold. Living at Githunguri, moreover, indicated that Kenyatta was a Kiambu man who knew that power and authority derived from the land. His preoccupation with getting land, a house, and transportation demonstrated his Kikuyu-ness and determination to obtain authority. As long as he was poor and lived in a humble dwelling, others would direct him, and his claim to authority would remain hollow.

Negative signs unfortunately prevailed. As president of Githunguri, he had not lowered fees nor offered free places for sons of those who could not pay. KAU had shown no particular interest in land for landless and land poor, and Kenyatta as president did not do so either; there was no sign that Kikuyu would be able to buy land in the Rift Valley. He had not directed KAU to take a stand on Rift Valley re-attestation, and those who had refused continued to be evicted, coming back to Kiambu to claim their land or hope for *tha*. Neither he nor KAU had shown strong support for the January 1947 strike in Mombasa. He rarely went to Nairobi; neither he nor KAU did much to protest Nairobi conditions and its lack of police protection. Though he wanted Nairobi men to oppose crime, he left in the evening for safer areas and did not speak against the Forty Group, which some saw as a contributory factor to urban unrest. Its violence, intimidation, and occasional vitriolic speeches were likely to lead to government raids which many undocumented workers could not afford. Kenyatta did not help the veterans, nor did he tell them to tone down their agitation. He did not direct the unions to do more for the lowest wage earners; he had not spoken for Chege Kibachia nor visited and given signs of support for the 1947 Uplands strike. He was all in favour of hard work but had little to say about not being able to find it or live from its wage: no amount of hard work changed a basic wage into a living one, let alone into riches.

That he stressed the need for unity was understandable; but what had happened to the power he was supposed to have brought back? Kenyatta's attitude towards the agricultural endeavours of land-poor households, with small scattered pieces and all able-bodied adults working for wages, was too close to the Department of Agriculture. The Department and Kenyatta failed to understand that lack of land and inability to afford manure, not laziness or ignorance, caused land deterioration. The adage that land conservation rules and terracing were going to improve the land and agriculture did not solve the problem of those who lacked land, or who could not afford to take the land out of production for the time it took to improve it. Advocating *ngwatio* – cooperation between kin – instead of *gitati* – recruited labour – sounded fine until one remembered that able-bodied males were absent in migrant labour and could not come home when needed, any more than women could give up working in coffee. Advocacy of modern animal husbandry sounded hollow to men whose sons, instead of going to school, herded their few goats on the side of the road.[8]

Therefore, although initially they had flocked to his speeches – and would continue to do so because they loved his oratory – land poor and landless no longer believed that Kenyatta would be able to help in the short run. He might in the long run provide a chance, because by buying land he had at least acknowledged that having land was security and that land poverty or landlessness crippled any man.

When Kenyatta and his aides imposed the 'Kenyatta tax' to help the college and pay for Kenyatta's trappings of authority, they responded, though cautiously, because their initial high hopes had not endured.[9] That rumours were soon rife that the money, ostensibly for the college, was diverted, was a minor point and expected, as landless and land poor were

Resistance of the Land Poor & Landless

more interested in building Kenyatta's power than in building the school. The tax was a voluntary levy on all *mariika*, or initiation years. Each member was to pay their leader, who would take it to Githunguri where it would be offered at 'tea parties' and where the carriers might or might not be offered an oath for *umoja*, for the college, *Muumbi na Gikuyu* or *Githunguri* – all commitment oaths, or sometimes amended commitment oaths (Appendix VIII/5). Contributors were not oathed; those who took the money to Githunguri were free to refuse.

After the first collection, subsequent assessments did not become the outpouring of support Kenyatta had hoped for, in spite of the strong support from at least one vernacular paper, *Mumenyerere*.[10] As time went on, they produced less and less; by 1948/49 demands for money were increasingly refused, and pressure from Kenyatta's aides resulted in complaints to chiefs or headmen about harassment.[11]

There were several reasons for the decreased support. Kenyatta had not involved himself in land tenure reform, an issue which, by this time, was uppermost in the minds of local landless and land poor. It was rumoured that *ahoi* would no longer have the right to ask for land, neither on the basis of kinship nor because of *tha*. Local men were angry; Kenyatta had not demanded land in the Rift Valley for the landless who were dismissed; he apparently did not intend to take the case of the landless who would be disenfranchised within Kiambu either.

Though elders had not forbidden the collections, and many wanted Githunguri to succeed, they were less than enthusiastic about the way in which Kenyatta was building his power base. A levy from one *riika* on another was common enough; a levy, which came down to a levy from one man in one *riika* on all *mariika* below his, even if force was not used, indicated that this particular man seemed to think that he had the right to become the beneficiary, the centre of Kikuyu social and political organization. This, like the selling of eldership, betrayed a desire for a dangerous level of centralization; saying that it was necessary for the resistance, did not make it any less problematic.

Githunguri had not become a symbol of successful resistance: Kenyatta had not created the *umoja* of rich and poor so often referred to in his or Koinange's speeches. He had not even been able to unite the groups with which he had most contact; they met at Githunguri, they continued to administer their separate oaths, whether they called them *umoja* or something else. Elders continued their wait-and-see position, but by 1948/49 the landless and land poor, who had expected so much, feared that whatever was coming from the *thingira* at Githunguri was neither the leadership Chege wa Kibiru had promised nor the land they had hoped for.

The beginning of Mau Mau

Though a fair number of oaths were taken in 1948 and 1949, the questions of whether, why and how they became Mau Mau oaths is difficult to answer. The absence of an accepted definition makes it difficult to compare the various movements; it impedes discussion about the beginning and end of Mau Mau.

The local population recognized different Mau Maus, named after the areas where they 'belonged'. It recognized the existence of a Rift Valley Mau Mau in late 1947 or early 1948, because Rift Valley repatriates talked about it. It was certain that by the end of 1948 a Mau Mau had appeared in Nairobi and by 1949 there were Mau Mau in some Kiambu areas, created by Githunguri men. It is, however, quite possible, particularly for Nairobi and Githunguri, that hindsight played a role in this information. Until 1950, the various Mau Maus kept to their territory; most rural men working in Nairobi were oathed there with a Nairobi oath. The few rural men who took an oath took a Githunguri oath. Apart from the Nairobi oaths the population, as a whole, was oriented towards Githunguri.

This changed in 1950 when Nairobi Mau Mau began an aggressive recruitment campaign in the rural area; oaths taken in the rural area may then indicate allegiance either to Nairobi or to Githunguri. There is no evidence that Githunguri recruiters ventured into Nairobi, nor that Rift Valley men reached out beyond their territory. To all intents and purposes, local Mau Mau involvement ended in the early summer of 1953, though the government would continue to punish membership as late as 1960.

The government's perspective

In August 1950, the government condemned a unitary Mau Mau movement, whose main characteristic was that it enlisted members through – what the government judged to be – illegal oathing. Every oath taken after August 1950 was unlawful and Mau Mau. The condemnation was *de facto* retroactive; persons who had taken an oath, or been present at an oathing in earlier years, could be arrested and prosecuted under the provisions of the Penal Code. The Penal Code had been used to proscribe the KCA in 1940; and, convinced that it had continued underground, the government used the same articles to punish not only those who had taken the aggressive KCA oath of 1946, but also all movements and men it thought to be KCA or Mau Mau fronts.[12] This brought a large number of oaths for different organizations under one broad umbrella.

When the government, after the Declaration of the Emergency, demanded that the population be screened for oaths, it demanded that local screening teams follow its 'definition'; whether or not persons regarded the oaths they had taken as Mau Mau is immaterial in this part of the study. They – and I – follow the judgments of local screening teams (Appendix IX/6).

Every person over 14 had to appear before the local screening team and was regarded as guilty until proved innocent. Until they had been screened and found 'not guilty', their movements were restricted. The screening team expected self-incrimination and used information from others; those appearing were either declared Mau Mau or loyal; in the first case the team imposed punishment, depending on the number of oaths and their circumstances; in the latter case it recommended that the District Officer issue a 'loyalty certificate'.

The early teams worked under strict control of a District Officer and could not follow their own judgment – within reason – until supervision slowed down. Some early teams then regarded 1948, others 1949 or 1950 as the cut-off line, after which oaths taken for independent schools, Githunguri or KAU were deemed to be Mau Mau. Involvement in the underground KCA – of importance to Rift Valley repatriates – after 1948 was Mau Mau. Most oaths taken after 1950 were likely to be Mau Mau.

Due to differences of opinion between local areas, judgments of screening teams differed over time and by region. The local team would designate oaths taken in Nairobi from 1948 onwards as Mau Mau but, unless they had special characteristics, oaths taken at Githunguri before 1950 were probably not Mau Mau; *Mbari* oaths would rarely be Mau Mau. In the Rift Valley, where settlers saw much of the opposition against their economic measures as evidence of underground KCA activity, oaths – whether *Mbari* or Githunguri ones, or administered by Kenyatta or KCA men – were regarded as subversive as early as 1947. The local settled area had one of the most 'liberal' classifications.[13]

The probable beginning of urban Mau Mau

In the years following the Second World War, the urban and rural areas had more contact than before, because males came home more often. The wealthier ones used public transport, the poorer ones would band together and hire an – often ramshackle – taxi. Males shared more of the life of their households; females were more influenced by urban events. The fears around land litigation and possible reform of tenure would remain with urban workers when they returned to town, as would anger at the lack of involvement of KAU or Kenyatta. Females would become party to urban vicissitudes, low wages, lack of housing, and crime.

Second World War veterans were a particularly discontented group. They had come mainly from the landless, land poor and a sprinkling of small peasants; most had some schooling, but the military had provided more education and technical training. They had high hopes that their separation pay and savings would allow them to open a business, preferably in Kiambu and Nairobi, but the administration and chiefs refused the necessary permits. According to the administration, the area was saturated with small businesses; licences would only waste the money of the applicants. Few would be able to comply immediately with all the existing regulations, whether ultimately they would have succeeded or not.

There was little chiefs could have done to help; they neither could nor would overrule the district inspectors who controlled the permits. Even so, chiefs had no interest in having more struggling establishments; the existing ones were often far from healthy, and their owners strongly opposed more competition. The veterans could not vent their anger on the administration, but, succeeding where the KCA had failed, they put the blame squarely on the chiefs and local officials. They used a traditional way to hit back at them: by 1947 the district government was inundated with complaints about local corruption.[14]

While some artisans were able to establish themselves in the local area, replacing Indian carpenters in market centres, most veterans with technical training ended up in Nairobi. They sometimes banded together and opened their own workshops; more often they worked for Indian – and a growing number of African – garage and taxi owners. They were an involved, volatile and restive group; they chafed under their post-war exclusion, their lack of land, and the privation of their wives and children. More than those who had not been in the services, they were inclined to become members of organizations and take part in local and district politics. By 1946 thirteen men, mostly veterans who were KAU and union members who worked in Nairobi but lived in Kiambu, were elected with KAU support to the Kiambu LNC, at that time still predominantly a stronghold of the rural landed interest, occupied with rural issues.

Though they did shake the complacency of LNC members, they had little lasting impact because, rather than following the KAU policy not to fight on too many fronts at once, they followed the time-honoured KCA method of attacking colonialism and Kikuyu authority simultaneously. They not only put the government on the alert, but also alienated elders, land owners, and large numbers of those who remained dependent and were not yet ready to blame their land-owning kin. Though they, too, were more critical of local authority than before, the veterans were too strident, too negative for their taste. They also alienated the rural population by ignoring the achievements of Koinange, then vice-president of the Council, and ridiculed his lack of education and traditional style. They sought confrontation at every point; ignoring their own participation in British wars, they accused the older members of having sold out to the enemy and having failed to use their position for protest.[15]

Yet, partially as a result of their endeavours, many ordinary workers in the rural area, as well as in Nairobi, began to pay more attention to the political processes of the day. They had been empowered by the landed to do so for decades; yet the actions of the veterans, sons of the land poor and landless, opened the doors to making it a reality.

The Kikuyu political establishment, KAU as well as unions, began to realize the latent power of the rural area: Nairobi political leaders started to include the rural area in their programmes of speeches and forays. As no self-respecting politician would drive himself or arrive without taxis and buses of supporters, they hired Nairobi taxis and buses and recruited men from the labour pool, always in need of employment. They came at a bargain; they could protect the speaker and drown out the opposition; they could stir up the crowd, watch out for dissidents, and collect money. Pool labour was always available: whether for a minor strike, a speech or a disturbance, hundreds of men could be mobilized at a moment's notice, at a cost of a few shillings each. If such men were arrested, they were 'safe' because they knew little or nothing about the organization or sponsors who paid them; after they had done their job, they would disappear into Nairobi anonymity, but when they went home to the rural area, they could tell of their exploits and the speeches they had heard.

Urban men had few sources of information and outlets for anger, but did carry information back to the rural area. When, from 1947 onwards, the unions had aggressively 'moved in on' KAU, the ensuing conflict between Kenyatta's KAU and union KAU had been played out at the leadership level, and ordinary members had not been asked to take sides.[16] Nevertheless, the alignments and realignments formed a topic of conversation in the informal reference groups. Though few if any Nairobi men expected that much would change, by 1948 a number of Nairobi men expected more from the unions and men like Kaggia and Kubai than from Kenyatta.

The earliest oath associated with, but not officially organized by KAU, took place in Nairobi during 1948; it was also associated with the unions because it was probably arranged by Kubai and possibly by Kaggia, who were closely connected to the unions. Yet those who took it regarded it as a KAU oath; it was offered and taken by some of the veterans and their friends. Three of them were KAU members without having taken an oath (Appendix IX/1).[17] Soon several others, not KAU members, were offered the new oath as well; it is not known how many took it at that time. The offer of oaths may have been an attempt to test the strength and control of KAU or of one or more unions.[18] It was thought that 'a Mau Mau' had started in Nairobi in 1948; yet not until 1949 did oath takers recognize that their oaths belonged to Mau Mau, possibly because the separation between Mau Mau, KAU and the unions was by no means clear.

Some informants declared that they too had taken this oath in 1948/9 when the Kenya Houseboys Organization and the Kenya African Road Transport and Mechanics Union ordered its members to take it.[19] It cost shs 30/-, asked loyalty to KAU and secrecy, but did not mention Kenyatta. By 1950, 17 Nairobi men had taken the oath; the oaths were probably simple commitment oaths (Table 7.1).

Of these 17, seven were almost immediately asked to take another oath, which was again introduced as a KAU oath which would make them members of a 'core group'. In fact, the oath was different rather than similar; instead of support, it asked for obedience and willingness to perform unspecified tasks assigned by 'the leaders' of 'the movement' on pain of punishment. According to elders, such oaths were 'more advanced' commitment oaths and broadly legitimate (Appendix VII/6). Even when they were not, elders did not regard these oaths as their concern: they were taken in Nairobi. Had the organizers asked whether they could administer them in *mbari* land, which would mean slaughtering a goat there, most elders would have refused unless they could have officiated themselves. The government would later call these oaths second oaths. Even those who would have refused to perform the rites on *mbari* land were well aware that second oaths were far less dangerous than oaths the government called third or fourth oaths. They, and the *batuni* oath, would crop up several years later. The *batuni* oath was thought to belong in the Rift Valley and the Forest (Appendix IX/6).[20]

Those who took the second oath were more or less aware that they had joined 'Nairobi Mau Mau', though the name would not be part of the oath.[21] They did not greatly object; they associated them with the resistance, though not with armed conflict or violence. Thinking the oath to be part of the plans of KAU, they had been told instead that they now belonged to a new society or movement and should obey its leaders, though they were not told who these men were. They were promised that the movement would soon be strong enough for Kikuyu to demand land from Europeans; when it became available, members of the 'Society' would have 'more rights' than those who had not joined or had only taken one oath.[22] In the immediate future they were to act as guards and organizers for new inductions. They did not get the right to administer oaths but could make likely candidates known to the person who had invited them; they knew the persons with whom they had taken the second oath. They were supposed to help each other and first oath takers when they were attacked or suffered from crime in the locations. Oath takers averred that they had used little violence and then only for defensive purposes. That some Mau Mau leaders had used violence in a power struggle with other leaders as early as 1949 had nothing to do with them. During the Emergency they were at pains to point out that they had joined before 'Mau Mau became violent'.

It was a boon for Nairobi Kikuyu to have a man who had taken a second oath in their informal reference group, because he could call in the help of other such men when needed in cases of robbery and assault. Their ability to mobilize and fight back made for a somewhat more protected life.[23] It did give Kikuyu locations a reputation for violence but helped to keep crime to some extent within bounds.[24]

Though all Nairobi work categories, but for the police, were represented among those who took an oath in 1948/9, the labour pool and taxi drivers – needed by politicians – were, with four each, better represented than others (Table 7.1). Landless and land poor formed the majority with four and eight each; an additional four were small peasants, one was a peasant. The second oath takers came from a wide range of occupations, though clerical workers and police were not represented: four were land poor, three were small peasants; all had more education than those who only took a first oath.

Subsequent history shows that early first oath taking in Nairobi might,

Table 7.1 *Growth of Mau Mau in Nairobi (females between brackets)*

Period	Total	Basic labour	Semi-skilled and skilled labour						Clerical and admin.
			Total	MPA	FAT	MDTL	DL	SETS	
Before Becher Report	17	4	12	–	4	4	3	1	1
Becher Report	31 (12)	8 (7)	20 (5)	–	3	7	7 (3)	3 (2)	3
After Becher Report until Declaration of Emergency	51 (3)	18	29 (3)	–	9	8	12 (2)	– (1)	4
Total before Declaration of Emergency	99 (15)	30 (7)	61 (8)	–	16	19	22 (5)	4 (3)	8
After Declaration until May 1953	53 (1)	8	42 (1)	1	17	10	12 (1)	2	3
June 1953 and later	12	3	9	–	3	2	3	1	–
Total after Declaration of Emergency	65 (1)	11	51 (1)	1	20	12	15 (1)	3	3
Unknown when oathed	3	1	2	–	–	1	–	1	–
Total involved	167 (16)	42 (7)	114 (9)	1	36	32	37 (6)	8 (3)	11
Total uninvolved	36 (1)	3 (–)	26 (–)	2	1	4	15 (–)	4 (–)	7 (1)
Total population	203 (17)	45 (7)	140 (9)	3	37	36	52 (6)	12 (3)	18 (1)

Semi-skilled and skilled labour abbreviations:
MPA = Military, police and *askaris*;
FAT = *Fundis*, artisans and tailors;
MDTL = Mechanics, drivers and technical labour;
DL = Domestic labour
SETS = Self-employed traders and shopkeepers

but usually did not, mean subsequent deep involvement. Though one of the first 17 oath takers would become a victim in the counter-attack of the security forces at Marige, he had not enlisted in the gang because of his oath but because he was angry over having been cleansed against his will (Appendix IX/8).

The men who took early second oaths were more likely to become more deeply involved: of the seven, three eventually took a third oath; one was detained at the start of the Emergency, one became a Mau Mau organizer in the settled area. One, however, 'never did anything with his oaths' and another followed his example.

In 1953, the screening team would regard the Nairobi first and second oaths as Mau Mau. Had the team been left to its own judgment, it probably would have excused all but some of the second oaths, which had aroused the anger of a number of elders, though they were not serious enough to demand cleansing.

Early Nairobi Mau Mau seemed to have been oriented towards a broad-based membership which included the poor and the illiterate. It provided, perhaps unintentionally, some badly needed protection in the locations. Its internal power struggles with a slower-moving KAU did not involve the early members, who remained separated from the higher echelons and their aims.

The possible beginning of Mau Mau in the rural area

In 1948 and 1949, rural unrest increased: husbands and sons brought tales about urban crime back from Nairobi; the attempts to change land tenure rules were a source of unrest at the same time that the failure to change them was also a source of concern. If one could no longer use the land of others and if the status of *muhoi* was abolished, Thuita and Igi *ahoi* and land poor would no longer be able to use the small tracts of Igi land on which they depended. Igi elders had, in 1948, turned down a proposal to change the system of land tenure, but landless and land poor knew that this was at best a delay. *Ahoi* knew that change might abolish user rights and their right to live on *muhoi* land. Land poor realized by 1949/50 that they would not be allowed to grow coffee any more than the landless.

Neither Kenyatta nor KAU took up their cause; they were too busy trying to enlist landed elders and local leaders through a new oath. That the disillusioned poor paid even less into the *marüka* collection was at this moment no longer their prime concern. Yet, though Kenyatta travelled far and wide making highly applauded speeches and more and more openly declared the right of the Kikuyu to freedom and independence from British oppression, the finances remained low, and too few of the landed elders were taking the oath of *umoja*, now widely offered by Githunguri and on Kenyatta's travels.

The screening team decided that in 1948/9 ten males and eight females had taken Mau Mau first oaths, while two males and one female had taken Mau Mau second oaths. The males were almost all landless or land poor; five were *ahoi*, four had subsistence tracts, and one was a small peasant.[25] Several of them protested that their oaths had been taken for Githunguri and before 1950, and so should not have been called Mau Mau (Tables 7.2 and 7.3).

None of the ten males had taken the oath locally. Three men and two women took their oaths at Arusha which was an early, active oathing centre.[26] Four had been oathed in Nairobi, when they were visiting a kinsman; they neither worked nor sought work in Nairobi, and could not be classified as Nairobi men. One young man had taken the oath at an independent school; some oathed their senior students as early as 1948, possibly under the influence of Peter Gatabaki, president of the Kikuyu Independent School Association, who spent a great deal of time at Githunguri.

Two males and five women took their oath at Kiambu; both men and one of the women took an additional, second oath. The oath administrator was Dedan Mugo Kimani, a senior Githunguri aide; the oaths were called college oaths. Their clauses asked for support of Kenyatta, Mbiu, and the college; they stressed secrecy. Because those who took the early oaths were angry about having been classified as Mau Mau, they refused to give more information about the content of either oath.[27]

I can only speculate whether perhaps one Githunguri aide was beginning to involve ordinary men and women outside the local area. One argument against it is that, after these oathings, Dedan Mugo rarely oathed at Githunguri itself but mostly at places like Thika, Ruiru, and Kiambu, and there is no evidence that Kenyatta supported this. It is also possible that Dedan Mugo, who had extensive Nairobi contacts, realized more than other Githunguri functionaries the need for and potential of a grass roots in addition to a leadership movement.[28]

1950, the year of anger and frustration

Probably no year before the Emergency was so significant for the involvement in Mau Mau of landless and land poor as 1950. For many it was a year of desperation: their land use was already threatened. Now the educational chances of their children took a significant step backwards. Under these circumstances, Mau Mau became their last hope. At the same time, the landed learned that many – though land tenure had not yet changed – would be able to plant coffee, while the educational opportunities of their children would take a significant step forward. Though concerned with the need to invest more than ever, doors were slowly opening for them.

The population was aware of Mau Mau, but by the beginning of 1950, was not yet convinced that it would solve their problems. Local Mau Mau barely existed; the two other Mau Maus they recognized were localized

Table 7.2 Development of Mau Mau oaths, males (multiple oaths between brackets)

Period	Totals			Nairobi			Rural and Tanganyika		
	First oaths	Multiple oaths	% of pop.	First oaths	Multiple oaths	% of pop.	First oaths	Multiple oaths	% of pop.
Before Beecher Report	27	(9)	3.7%	17	(7)	8.4%	10	(2)	1.9%
Beecher Report	62	(24)	8.4%	31	(15)	15.3%	31	(9)	5.8%
After Beecher Report until Declaration of the Emergency	101	(14)	13.8%	51	(10)	25.1%	50	(4)	9.4%
Total before Declaration of the Emergency	190	(47)	25.9%	99	(32)	48.8%	91	(15)	17.1%
After Declaration of the Emergency until May 1953	170	(13)	23.2%	53	(7)	26.1%	117	(6)	22.0%
June 1953 and later	26	(3)	3.5%	12	(3)	5.9%	14	–	2.6%
Total after Declaration of the Emergency	196	(16)	26.7%	65	(10)	32.0%	131	(6)	24.7%
Unknown when oathed	35	(39)	4.8%	3	(16)	1.5%	32	(23)	6.0%
Total involved	421	(102)	57.4%	167	(58)	82.3%	254	(44)	47.8%
Total uninvolved	313	–	42.6%	36	–	17.7%	277	–	52.2%
Total population	734	–	100%	203	–	100%	531	–	100%

Table 7.3 *Development of Mau Mau oaths, females (multiple oaths between brackets)*

Period	Totals			Nairobi			Rural and Tanganyika		
	First oaths	Multiple oaths	% of pop.	First oaths	Multiple oaths	% of pop.	First oaths	Multiple oaths	% of pop.
Before Beecher Report	8	(1)	0.9%	–	–	–	8	(1)	.9%
Beecher Report	42	(4)	4.8%	12	–	70.6%	30	(4)	3.5%
After Beecher Report until Declaration of the Emergency	94	(4)	10.8%	3	(1)	17.6%	91	(3)	10.7%
Total before Declaration of the Emergency	144	(9)	16.5%	15	(1)	88.2%	129	(8)	15.1%
After Declaration of the Emergency until May 1953	275	(1)	31.7%	1	–	5.9%	274	(1)	32.2%
June 1953 and later	15	(4)	1.7%	–	–	–	15	(4)	1.8%
Total after Declaration of the Emergency	290	(5)	33.4%	1	–	5.9%	289	(5)	34.0%
Unknown when oathed	12	(11)	1.4%	–	(3)	–	12	(8)	1.4%
Total involved	446	(25)	51.4%	16	(4)	94.1%	430	(21)	50.5%
Total uninvolved	422	–	48.6%	1	–	5.9%	421	–	49.5%
Total population	868	–	99.9%	17	–	100%	851	–	100%

with – probably – local objectives. According to them, Rift Valley Mau Mau had come about by alienation and reduction of stock; it was led by the old KCA. Nairobi Mau Mau, led by unions and a sector of KAU, promised land in the future but was for the moment involved in internal struggles. A few rural people had taken other oaths, but it was dubious whether they should be counted as Mau Mau.[29] Neither Mau Mau was led by Kenyatta who, though using oaths, opposed the more advanced ones. Moreover, while Rift Valley Mau Mau was almost certainly violent and the leadership of Nairobi Mau Mau could be violent, Kenyatta neither used nor wanted to use violence. It ran counter to the role of landed elder; he wanted to lead but on his terms in which old and new movements should come together through *umoja*.

Several events happened in 1950. The exclusion of land poor from coffee, which became firm, excluded roughly two thirds of the Thuita and close to one third of Igi households. Together with landless households, more than 70 per cent of the Thuita and well over 50 per cent of the Igi households were barred: more than 80 per cent of the Nairobi workers would not get coffee (Tables 3.1, 4.3, pages 99, 131).

Around this time Nairobi workers were informed that they, like other 'natives' would get a day's leave if they were willing to form the cheering throngs celebrating the granting of Nairobi's charter to become a city. It rubbed salt into their wounds, and unions and KAU activists asked them to stay away. The decision was easy. Where Europeans celebrated city-hood, Kikuyu saw the potential for more land alienation for the services the Europeans would need. They had little interest in cheering a parade of Europeans, some of whom had grown 'fat on our land'.

Strengthened by this response, smaller unions started to flex their muscles by calling strikes to underline their demands and disrupt Nairobi routines. Nairobi meetings became more belligerent, leading to the arrest of union leaders and a strike of eight days. Though successful to a certain extent, the strikes also stretched the resources and the willingness of Nairobi workers to respond to the unions; many found themselves disenchanted and unemployed when the strike ended.

Had not the Beecher Report been accepted that year, Nairobi men might have sacrificed their anger to the need for wages, and Nairobi recruiters might have realized that they did not have sufficient strength to increase urban recruitment, let alone penetrate the rural area. Kenyatta and his aides would not have feared that their rural hegemony was threatened, and might not have been propelled into broadening their own appeal.

The landless and land poor, by far the majority of the Nairobi workers, viewed the Beecher report as an attack on their children's future. Because they might well be unable to send their children to school at the age of seven, and keep them there consistently until they could sit their first exam at 11, sons might not become literate, would not learn English and be condemned to the poverty of basic labour.

Resistance of the Land Poor & Landless

Nairobi activists were quick to respond, attending and calling protest meetings in Nairobi and – for the first time – in the rural area where the women, many of whom worked to pay school fees, lived. Githunguri was shocked into action; it was not far behind.

The Nairobi men organized meetings which often ended in oathing; parents who attended were persuaded to take an oath even if they had not intended to. Women as well as men were offered an oath, by now openly called an oath for 'the Movement' or Mau Mau. Githunguri threw its – much weaker – forces into the recruitment campaign, offering first oaths to men and women. Some men, who had already taken a Nairobi oath, were offered a Githunguri first oath which the screening team would count as a second oath; others were offered a Githunguri second oath which asked for obedience, financial support and acceptance of Kenyatta's leadership and orders.

It gained 31 males, of whom nine took a second oath (Table 7.2) and 30 females, of whom four took a second oath (Table 7.3). Nairobi was not far behind; it gained 31 males and asked 15 men, some oathed in earlier years, some in 1950, to take a second oath (Table 7.2). Of the 17 rural females who worked in Nairobi, 15 were oathed that year (Table 7.3).

The entry of Nairobi Mau Mau into the rural area did not go peacefully. Its representatives might come to meetings when they were not invited; they campaigned with their successful strike, hoping to demonstrate that they, rather than Githunguri, could obtain results. Githunguri men argued – to little avail – that Kenyatta had many more Kikuyu leaders behind him, that he stood for *umoja* and peaceful solutions, and demanded that Nairobi leaders go back to Nairobi. Fist fights followed all too often; a Githunguri supporter might call the police on Nairobi 'unauthorized meetings'; Nairobi did the same when its meetings were disturbed by Githunguri men. Both sides would be hauled off to jail; some were fined and released; others were detained. Some did not come back until well into the Emergency.

There was little doubt in the minds of those who took the oath that it was a Mau Mau oath. Though they did not necessarily regret this, in hindsight they would have preferred to keep the territorial separation between the Mau Mau: rural (Githunguri) Mau Mau was quite different from Nairobi Mau Mau; interests of Nairobi men were different, as were their leaders.

The conflicts between administrators from Githunguri and Nairobi undermined both places, because many did not feel 'at home' with the oath taken in the other place. The oaths blurred the distinction between Nairobi and Githunguri: Githunguri oaths continued to ask support for Kenyatta; Nairobi oaths did not. Oaths could no longer be divided along territorial lines; a rural man may have taken a Nairobi oath and vice versa. This might lead some to seek a second oath to clarify their positions. Some second oaths were taken at the request of the oath taker, perhaps on the instigation of others. Some, because of the organization they had previously supported, demanded that they 'set the record straight', and take the 'proper' oath.

Resistance of the Land Poor & Landless

Table 7.4 *Composition of Mau Mau population (males) by period (excludes Rift Valley)*

Period	Total	Ahoi	Subsistence plot owners	Small peasants	Peasants	Small farmers	Farmers
Before Beecher Report	27 3.7%	9 6.0%	12 3.6%	5 5.2%	1 0.8%	–	–
Beecher Report	62 8.5%	24 16.0%	25 7.6%	8 8.3%	4 3.3%	1 3.4%	–
After Beecher Report until Declaration of the Emergency	101 13.8%	29 19.3%	50 15.1%	17 17.7%	5 4.1%	–	–
Total before Declaration of the Emergency	190 25.9%	62 41.3%	87 26.3%	30 31.2%	10 8.2%	1 3.4%	–
After Declaration of the Emergency until May 1953	170 23.2%	31 20.7%	93 28.1%	20 20.9%	22 18.0%	2 6.9%.	2 33.3%
June 1953 and later	26 3.6%	1 0.7%	17 5.1%	3 3.1%	5 4.1%	–	–
Total after Declaration of the Emergency	196 26.8%	32 21.4%	110 33.2%	23 24.0%	27 22.1%	2 6.9%	2 33.3%
Unknown when oathed	35 4.7%	5 3.3%	18 5.4%	6 6.3%	6 4.9%	–	–
Total involved	421 57.4%	99 66.0%.	215 65.0%	59 61.5%	43 35.3%	3 10.3%.	2 33.3%
Total uninvolved	313 42.6%	51 34.0%	116 35.0%	37 38.5%	79 64.7%	26 89.7%.	4 66.7%
Total population	734 100%	150 100%	331 100%	96 100%	122 100%	29 100%.	6 100%

Githunguri got, for the first time, a sizeable number of second oaths, some because its supporters, oathed in the heat of the moment for Nairobi, desired to 'come back'. Yet as far as analysis is concerned, as early as 1950 it becomes difficult to deduce the side an oath taker supported, from the place where he took the oath or the person who administered it (Table 7.2).

Many older people continued to reject oathing; the few who accepted oaths were more inclined to seek a Githunguri than a Nairobi oath. Many younger people sought an oath; there is little if any evidence that they became members by force. The Beecher oaths clearly showed the anger of landless and land poor; of the 62 new members 49, or 79 per cent, belonged to the landless or land poor (Table 7.4). They are not the only ones involved; some with more land and at least junior elder status, afraid of what the Beecher Report might mean to their relatives, also became involved.

Some of the Beecher oaths had been administered by Dedan Mugo, ostensibly for Githunguri. By this time it was widely reported that his oaths used human blood and that men and women were oathed together using blood. This violated moral rules and was not acceptable. Though rumours about bawdy behaviour of aides at Githunguri were widespread, they had tried to avoid a breach of the moral code. Perhaps Dedan Mugo had already broken with Githunguri at an earlier time; perhaps he had gone too far this time; there is no record that he could or did call for help from Githunguri when he was arrested by the administration and convicted of administering unlawful oaths.[30] The Githunguri oath had become more aggressive after the Beecher Report: though Githunguri men would claim that the word was used metaphorically, clauses asked those oathed to *fight* for Githunguri and Kikuyu education. They mentioned Kenyatta as 'our leader' who should be obeyed. KAU/union oaths in Nairobi mentioned neither him nor Koinange. Nairobi oaths, particularly the second oath which began to detail hypothetical acts, also seem to have become more aggressive at this time. Several Nairobi workers who had taken a Nairobi first oath without questions and now could afford to return to the rural area, did so because they felt increasing pressure to take the more violent Nairobi second oath. They returned, though they had to take an additional, rural Githunguri first oath; the screening team judged that they had taken two oaths.[31]

Perhaps to avoid confrontation between men who did not know each other, perhaps to consolidate the inroads it had made, by the end of 1950 Nairobi Mau Mau had asked several sympathizers for the use of a homestead or at least a *thingira*, man's hut, for occasional oathing ceremonies, and a few men responded. Githunguri did the same, and from 1950 onwards several local centres occasionally organized oath taking for small groups.[32]

By the Declaration of the Emergency there were possibly four local places where Nairobi men and sympathizers could take a Nairobi oath and contribute to Nairobi; there were possibly three locations which took

Table 7.5 *Composition of Mau Mau population (females) by period (excludes Rift Valley)*

Period	Total		Ahoi		Subsistence plot owners		Small peasants		Peasants		Small farmers		Farmers	
Before Beecher Report	8	0.9%	—	—	—	—	—	—	—	—	—	—	—	—
Beecher Report	50	7.7%	—	—	—	—	—	—	—	—	—	—	—	—
After Beecher Report until Declaration of the Emergency	86	9.9%	—	—	—	—	—	—	—	—	—	—	—	—
Total before Declaration of the Emergency	144	16.6%	56	30.9%	58	14.5%	23	23.2%	6	4.0%	1	3.1%	—	—
After Declaration of the Emergency until May 1953	275	31.7%	28	15.5%	161	40.3%	34	34.3%	49	32.2%	3	9.4%	—	—
June 1953 and later	15	1.7%	3	1.7%	8	2.0%	4	4.0%	—	—	—	—	—	—
Total after Declaration of the Emergency	290	33.4%	31	17.1%	169	42.3%	38	38.4%	49	32.2%	3	9.4%	—	—
Unknown when oathed	12	1.4%	3	1.7%	6	1.5%	2	2.0%	1	0.7%	—	—	—	—
Total involved	446	51.4%	90	49.7%	233	58.3%	63	63.6%	56	36.8%	4	12.5%	—	—
Total uninvolved	422	48.6%	91	50.3%	167	41.7%	36	36.4%	96	63.2%	28	87.5%	4	100%
Total population	868	100%	181	100%	400	100%	99	100%	152	100%	32	100%	4	100%

Resistance of the Land Poor & Landless

their proceeds to Githunguri, which was close. Nairobi provided roving oath administrators; it did not encourage local men to give the oath. Githunguri relied on local or, at least, proximate help. A man who had taken a second oath could officiate at local events; if no local men were available, men who wanted second oaths went to Githunguri or to other centres. This procedure was followed until the early Emergency when discipline broke down. Individual *mbari* then wanted their own administrators and functionaries, and men barely 18 years old might oath.

Though there is no evidence that oathing centres competed, as there is no evidence that men who had taken oaths at different locations were, in general, hostile to each other, the existence of oathing centres encouraged oath taking by the oathing centre's kin and *ahoi*, particularly the females. Invitations from kin were hard to turn down, whatever one's sympathies.[33] The already shaky correlation between the place of oath taking and which Mau Mau one supported became even less clear, though it remained the only available way to differentiate. By and large, when the 'Beecher' meetings declined and the population was no longer a captive audience at protest meetings, the majority of rural oath takers were more inclined to take a college or Githunguri than a Nairobi oath, just as Nairobi men would take a Nairobi oath.[34]

The oaths of the centres differed. Though more aggressive than before, the Githunguri oath continued to ask first oath takers only for generalized support, money, secrecy and help for Kenyatta. Nairobi oaths demanded obedience, hinted at demands which might be made in the future, and threatened those who neglected to pay or discussed the oath. Local people felt more secure about the Githunguri men behind the oath; they were often familiar and included Kenyatta even though very few could claim to have been oathed by him or Mbiu. Yet he was familiar; he attended some oaths of heavy contributors, but was otherwise often absent on speaking tours and his aides were in charge. He had, however, left strict instructions that he wanted no more conflict with the elders in the area. Some young males, fed up with the control of elders and the slow pace of change, were precisely, therefore, more inclined to seek a Nairobi oath.

Until the Emergency, local centres rarely went beyond the first oath for fear of local action. As it was, many elders were already sufficiently irked by the post-oathing festivities which had become common; they also looked askance at the elaboration of ritual. What saved the centres was that they were not used too frequently and that, until the first months of the Emergency, their volume was low. That the owners of the homesteads were quite unfamiliar with the structure of the organization they served, particularly the Nairobi one, and could not be seen as its front men, diffused the anger of the elders. The men whose homesteads were used, were not then, nor later became leaders; even those who took the second oath had little information. Although many, after 1949/50, again talked about freedom or *weiyathi*, they were not party to any ultimate aims of the organization. The lowly recruits were not told whether this included rising against the colonial government. They were and remained 'men of one goat' who could not be told secrets.

From 1951 until the Declaration of the Emergency

Where 1950 events were remembered clearly by the population, as were the events of the first months after the Declaration of Emergency, much of 1951 and 1952 was a grey area. Only certain events were remembered with clarity.

The danger for Nairobi men increased, as the police lost what control they had had in the locations. Strong-arm tactics of men who claimed to belong to KAU, Mau Mau, a union, or the later *Muhimu* made it unwise to turn down invitations to come to a 'party' and contribute. This encouraged banding together in defence; taking a first oath was almost a necessity. Wise men would seek protection in the informal reference groups which had recourse to men who had taken a second oath. They would form smaller, self-defence groups often composed of oath takers; oaths increased their security, particularly after Kubai and his supporters became more prominent.[35]

No longer content with the help of the unemployed in the labour pool, Nairobi Mau Mau increasingly 'encouraged' employed men to turn out for meetings or accompany buses to rallies at weekends. Like the men from the labour pool, they might have to show approval of speeches and see to it that others, particularly women, did the same. They might have to collect money, heckle a speaker or make sure that he had difficulty being heard.[36]

Nairobi men began to dread requests for the use of their rural homesteads; it increasingly brought conflicts with neighbours and not enough money might be collected to reimburse them for beer and/or meat. *Ahoi* and anyone who used the land of others were particularly reluctant; their land situation was already precarious enough. Yet such requests could be made as Nairobi tried to reinforce its control in the rural area. Nairobi and Githunguri suffered from the sharp dealings of men who had started their own – quite successful – oathing 'business' in locations or the settled area, forcing people, particularly women, to take an oath.[37]

Life in the rural area got steadily worse as fear and anger were mounting. The Beecher oaths had not opened classroom doors; children were being barred from schools because they did not meet the Beecher criteria. Land matters continued to hang fire; coffee had not yet come, security was lost, litigation without decisions continued. Yet the probability that land tenure was going to change motivated members of Gitau, with some members of Chege and Mungai, to file a case for the division of all *mbari* land.[38] No one believed that it had a chance, but it brought fear among the landed as well as among *ahoi*; they would not gain, whatever the decision.[39] It only served to remind the landless – as if they needed it

– that the day of reckoning, when they would lose all, was coming closer.[40]

While the landed hoped that the law would solve their problems, landless and land poor were convinced that the law would only threaten what little they had left. They needed Mau Mau, and they anxiously awaited signs of its power. That Kenyatta was again making speeches about the return of the land was not what they had in mind. They wanted to know what he, or Mau Mau, or perhaps he and Mau Mau, were going to do about 'Beecher', and about giving them land or wages high enough to buy land.

What disturbed all in 1952 was that turmoil and mayhem from Nairobi and the Rift Valley – where murder, the maiming of animals, arson, and the destruction of property seemed to be the order of the day – began to spill over into the rural area. That it was linked to Mau Mau, the only hope of the landless and the land poor, made it doubly distressing; yet it had happened in Gaki as well as in Kiambu. They did not understand why Mau Mau had not found ways to curb the lawlessness, which could only anger the government. They could not afford to see Mau Mau indifference nor could they afford that government destroy it. Yet, when opposition to Mau Mau arose, it did not speak to their condition.

Opposition to Mau Mau in 1952

Authority in Gaki was belatedly making an all-out effort to halt and reverse oathing by trying to make people confess and negate the oath through cleansing. One of the men behind the move was Dr L. S. B. Leakey who, with several other men, had advocated counter-oathing with a modified *kuringa thenge* oath (Appendix VIII/2).

In Kiambu a committee of Europeans and well-to-do land owners, including Chiefs Waruhiu and Kibathi, Harry Thuku, Mbira Githathu, the District Commissioner and L. S. B. Leakey, recommended in May that Kiambu follow a similar approach. It envisioned district-wide meetings with voluntary attendance in the presence of the *githathi* stones.[41] Their sacredness and the fear they inspired would induce confessions; afterwards those who had confessed should go through the *gutahikio* cleansing or purifying ceremony (Appendix VIII/2).[42]

The idea of using sacred oaths horrified Christians and non-Christians, Mau Mau members and non-members alike. However uneasy many elders felt about Mau Mau, however much they thought it a danger to the Kikuyu, they could not ignore that it was a greater threat to the colonial regime. Kikuyu had never hesitated to use colonial rule for their ends; they had reluctantly accepted that it used them for its political and economic ends. But this time they were asked nothing short of allowing that the colonizer use Kikuyu religion and its moral order to uphold colonial political ends. They were asked to condone that the government, backed by Kikuyu opinion, declare that those who had taken oaths were not only seditious, but also moral offenders. The committee's idea that Kikuyu who had taken oaths had contracted *thahu* was a gross overstatement; first oaths would rarely have done so; though there was reason to be concerned about some of the other oaths. Though the government regretfully was in a position to take action against what it considered sedition, whether men or women were *thahu* was not its affair: this could only be decided by senior elders, who also were the only ones allowed to act, had *thahu* been committed. The one redeeming feature in the plan was that participation was not mandatory; people could – and should – stay away. Those who advocated this were 'stumps', men blocking the road, like tree stumps, left behind in a field.

Staying away was precisely what people did; few attended the ceremonies which started in July 1952; the average attendance at the six ceremonies held in Kiambu before the Emergency attracted on average less than 600 people. Attendance at similar ceremonies in the Rift Valley and in Gaki was obligatory.[43]

Local elders, including most church elders and local authority, had talked, preached, and in general agitated during 1952 against Mau Mau oaths, particularly against second oaths and the use of violence, in an effort to keep the resistance within the framework of the Kikuyu moral order. At no time had they called in government aid to do so; unless the government discovered them, oath takers were still safe. Only one local man was rumoured to have betrayed a 'Beecher' meeting as an oath-taking event.[44]

On 22 August 1952, a meeting of church ministers and elders, including Wanyoike and a few other local men, was held at Kambui. Roman Catholic clergymen were invited, but few attended. The meeting published a manifesto; those preparing it would have made sure that they had the backing of traditional elders: the last they needed or wanted, was a split between Christians and Traditionalists.

The manifesto is a remarkable example of the first 'law' of Kikuyu protest, pacification. It appeases the Europeans and makes soothing sounds in their direction, but tells them that they should stay out of Kikuyu affairs. It is also a declaration to Mau Mau leadership that elders are neither willing nor able to continue providing protection for Mau Mau activities, but it makes clear that it only speaks about violent activities. No one among the attenders, nor among the elders outside the Church, was not convinced that the giving and taking of advanced oaths had to stop. Though couched in the language of revivalism, it spoke to all manner of Christians and non Christians.[45]

In 1952 most Protestant Churches contained a number of revivalists; they rejected the use of violence, refused to carry arms, and preferred not to be involved in resistance action, convinced that men and women could be 'saved' and receive temporal and eternal blessing under any regime. They opposed oaths; administering oaths was the work of *Shaitani*, the devil. Mau Mau, with its oaths, could become a greater evil than colonialism. The Churches also contained more militant men, who nevertheless betrayed the background of their conservative missions and genuinely thought that – for all their faults – the Christian Church and the colonial state should be seen as one: a sincere Christian should be loyal to both. The manifesto came, in some ways, dangerously close to accepting, at least not denying, that colonialism was a legitimate system of government. At least some of the attenders wanted to be known as 'the army of Christ'.

The author(s) of the manifesto are not known; no copy was retained locally or at Kambui.

> We will fight this secret and violent organization to the end; we see the way to achieve this is by all men and women of good will cooperating to work together for their just rights.
>
> As true Christians and members of God's family, we will have nothing to do with nor cooperate with Mau Mau, because its teachings are contrary to Christian teachings and our customs.
>
> We are against it because it is against the government which maintains the law and order of the country and thus our safety and happiness.
>
> We oppose Mau Mau because it is retarding the progress of the Africans and also demoralizing them. It is also retarding the general progeess of the country.
>
> We will exclude its followers from our churches, and also expel their children from our schools, lest they infect the others.
>
> We do not fear Mau Mau at all. If the government does not succeed in stamping out the Organisation, we are prepared to fight the Mau Mau adherents even if it is with pangas.[46]

The manifesto probably passed with almost everyone disagreeing with some point or other. The last clause but one echoes missionary language on the female circumcision issue when it threatens the expulsion of church members and holds the schooling of children in pawn for the behaviour of their parents. The last clause probably would not have found favour with revivalist Christians. Yet the most serious problem with the declaration is that, though referring to the 'just rights' of all men, it fails to define which rights and which men are meant. There is no evidence that landless and land poor attended the meeting; that the demise of Mau Mau would also kill what hope they had for any rights is not addressed, and, while a small farmer might not need an alternative to Mau Mau, land poor and landless did need such an alternative; not for nothing were they convinced that Mau Mau was their last hope.

How much the rhetoric was for European consumption is perhaps demonstrated by the fact that – to the best of my knowledge – not a single child was removed from any school, whether a parent had taken an oath or not. The pastoral letter from Bishop Dr John McCarthy, issued one week later, originated with a high Roman Catholic official; it threatened Mau Mau members with excommunication, but did not threaten expulsion of children.[47]

Kenyatta also entered this war of words and denounced Mau Mau in his speeches with increasing directness, particularly after July 1952, sometimes at the request of the government, sometimes without prompting.[48] Yet, like the Kambui manifesto, the speeches make it clear that Kenyatta, while opposing second and more advanced oaths, did not take issue with basic protest oaths and defended Kikuyu rights to the land and their freedom.

In an August 1952 meeting, where he shared a platform with, among others, the local chief, he hinted at 'cursing' Mau Mau; like all Kikuyu, he knew full well that a legitimate act – such as cursing an illegitimate government or its actions – would not rebound on the speaker. But equally, he sounded more than ever like an elder; the admonition to work harder so as to become rich was no consolation to men or women who could only get work which paid less than the cost of their food.

During all this protest against Mau Mau, neither the Churches nor Mau Mau spoke for the landless and the land poor. The Churches spoke about safety and happiness; Kenyatta spoke about hard work bringing riches.[49] The Churches did not speak about those who had neither safety nor happiness, and Kenyatta, with his naïve belief that hard work was sufficient to gain riches, did not speak to those whose work had only maintained poverty. But, although land poor and landless realized that Mau Mau protest did not consider them, they may have been sobered by the condemnation of second oaths and violence. Although they cautiously continued to take oaths, and Mau Mau in Nairobi and the rural area continued to grow, second and other illegitimate oaths, which were the ones the Churches and Kenyatta had attacked, show a marked decline.

In the Beecher year Nairobi had gained 31 first oaths and 15 second oaths; in the period after Beecher but before October 1952, a much longer period, it gained only 51 male first oaths and ten second oaths in spite of the local centres with their easy access to kin. The rural area did not do much better; it gained 50 male first oaths and four second oaths in spite of possibly three local centres (Table 7.2). But many more women began to take oaths: in the rural area, 91 joined for a first and then three for a second oath. Of these women possibly 15 took the oath for Nairobi in a centre run by kinsmen; at least half became treasurers (Table 7.3).

By October 1952 about 41 per cent of the *ahoi* or landless had taken an oath, as had one in four of the land poor, and almost one in three of the small peasants. Oath taking among peasants and small farmers was still negligible (Table 7.4). Females took fewer oaths, but the distribution followed the same pattern (Table 7.5). The rural area, where little if no force was used, had an overall oath level of 17 per cent, but this percentage probably included some Nairobi supporters. In Nairobi, where oaths were needed for protection, almost 50 per cent of the males and most females had taken an oath. It is possible that Mau Mau, experiencing this decline, hoped that a show of force would counteract the relative losses and regain the initiative. Violence in Nairobi continued unabated, raising the question how much of it was Mau Mau, how much ordinary criminal behaviour used or sanctioned by Mau Mau, and how much purely criminal behaviour under the cover of Mau Mau. That violence and crime were also rampant in rural towns, and in the rural area generally, was, according to some, the work of the Nairobi *Muhimu*, sending a message to the rural area that it would brook no interference with its plans.[50] Some pointed to the murder of Senior Chief Waruhiu wa Kungu as a *Muhimu*-inspired act, but others would point out that by this time Nairobi had a number of rural supporters, some holding important rural offices, who wanted Waruhiu out of the way, with or without Nairobi support.

Waruhiu, called 'a tower of strength' in one district report after the other, was one of the early students of Kambui. Possibly more than any other student of that period, and like the fundamentalist mission itself, he had accepted Western values and customs as synonymous with Christianity. He may have believed sincerely that the Gospel gave Christians the right to make decisions according to their beliefs even if they affected non-Christians, however unpopular this might be. Like fundamentalist Christians of this period, he regarded oaths as evil and the use of certain types of oaths as an abomination to be stamped out by any means. He was a keen Church man, probably quite unaware that the Church had become a haven for the well-to-do. As it was, he was the Kiambu chief most loved by Europeans; to him, many of his fellow Kikuyu were breaking moral laws through Mau Mau, and it was his duty to set them right. Kikuyu, on the other hand, revered Koinange Mbiu because he understood their anger, spoke for them, and gave *tha*.[51] In spite of his rejection of oaths, Waruhiu had endorsed most enthusiastically the use of the *githathi* stones; it had not offended him that they were transported between places where confession rituals were held, or that those who did not believe in the rituals should force them on those who did.

He was shot on his return from a case of land litigation and buried with a large number of Europeans in attendance, including the new Governor, Sir Evelyn Baring. As a result of the confession of the gunman, the government arrested John Mbiu Koinange, and later another son and a senior in-law of Koinange Mbiu, as well as Koinange himself as accessories after the fact. Still later, more men were accused, including local Waira Kamau. Eventually most were acquitted, including ex-Senior Chief Koinange Mbiu and Waira Kamau. They were immediately rearrested and detained under Emergency regulations for 'having taken an unlawful oath' prior to the murder.[52]

A few days before Waruhiu's murder a European woman had been killed; after his death, two more attacks on Europeans and strong pressure from Rift Valley Europeans persuaded the government to declare a State of Emergency. One hundred and eighty-three African leaders were arrested within the first days, including Kenyatta.[53]

Notes

1. Compared to the wealth and depth of organizational information in the published literature, information about the resistance in this and the preceding chapter is simple and localized. The local community still lived its own life; what happened elsewhere was of lesser importance. As local alienation had indicated the local date for the start of colonial rule, so Mau Mau was an affair of local men and women, where they lived and worked.
2. This does not negate the continued, strong Kikuyu belief that property was a sign of spiritual righteousness and a validation of power, while poverty was to be shunned, if not despised.
   1992. Berman, Bruce and John Lonsdale, pp. 441ff.
3. There were individual protests; it might take 'some pressure' to get sufficient workers. But there is no evidence of sustained group protest at that time.
4. The LNC could use *gitati* for the building of clinics and agricultural improvements or innovations. In 1933 the administration voiced exception to its use, but it was so entrenched that it was not abolished until 1942, after strong, vocal protest from women who had to terrace the land of others while badly in need of paying jobs.
   1933. R/305 KBU/25.
   1942. AR/314 KBU/33.
5. After the famine land owners had taken more wives than usual to 'bring back' those who had died. They had continued to do so in the early years of alienation, believing that the Europeans would shortly release their land. At the time of the Carter Commission, there were more owner households on the remaining land than land owners deemed in keeping with proper use.
6. Evidence of the twentieth-century survivors of nineteenth-century *ahoi* indicates that they built security by marrying daughters to and from the *mbari* and/or by moving to bought land. Twentieth-century *ahoi* could do neither; older *ahoi*, mostly close kinsmen of *mbari* members, remained secure; no *mbari* member would reduce their allotment below what they needed.
7. Age data based on 1952 call the assertion that Kenyatta was the leader of Mau Mau in doubt. Membership cannot be correlated with having known Kenyatta; age analysis shows that those who had not known Kenyatta were more likely to be members than those who had (Appendix IX/4).
   1960. Corfield Report, *op. cit.*, p. 6.
8. Landless and land-poor informants were rarely literate enough to read the printed word. They depended on word of mouth; they rarely had much information beyond their close surroundings. They might know that Kenyatta wanted the Rift Valley Kikuyu to sign labour contracts, but would not know when and where this had been discussed or promoted. They might know that Kenyatta was for terracing, but would not know when he had made this declaration or where. They were aware that Kenyatta was involved in political activities but had little interest in details which did not affect them. They were convinced that the Koinanges supported him, that by 1948 the old KCA in the Rift Valley and Murang'a were losing faith in him and that he perhaps therefore spent longer periods at Githunguri. By far the most informative account of these years is provided by Spencer, but most of his information would barely have touched local landless and land poor.
   1985. Spencer, John, *op. cit.*, pp. 145ff.
9. That it was proposed to the administration as fund raising for Githunguri College, and that the administration would subsequently regard the mixing of school and Kenyatta funds as fraud, was unavoidable, as it would not have approved collecting funds for Kenyatta. Elders allowed the collections even when they themselves did not give, and banned them only when force was used. Kenyatta may not have had other avenues to get money, as he had no right to assess organizations such as the KCA, the Independent

Schools Association, or KAU.

According to tradition, older *mariika* – or an important member of an older *mariika*, and Kenyatta never doubted his own importance – could demand services or part of the gain of a raid from younger *mariika*. Where Mbiu at an earlier time had tried to do the same, he was at a disadvantage, because his age allowed him to ask from only a few *mariika*. Kenyatta was at an advantage; he was *Mubengi*, subsumed under *Kihiumweri* (1913/14, in other areas 1915/16).

By the 1940s not all males would accept *mariika* membership obligations. It was not uncommon for sons of wealthier parents to be circumcised at birth in hospitals, avoiding all Kikuyu ritual. By the 1930s the communal rites had been dropped. Initiates might still seek a leader, but the number of those who accepted his authority might be small. Nevertheless, many males made a contribution towards the first assessment.
1960. Corfield Report, *op. cit.*, p. 68.
10. How much money was actually collected is difficult to determine. Henry Muoria Mwaniki, the editor of *Mumenyerere*, tried to make the collections into competitions between *mariika*; some data were published in *Mumenyerere*. The Corfield Report mentions different amounts for different periods and indicates that by May 1951 shs 1,000,000 had been collected. While that could have provided all the buildings the college might want, it indicates that contributions were low. The local male population of appropriate age including Nairobi workers was 380; assuming it to be 1 per cent of the appropriate Kiambu population, and a refusal rate of 8,000, 30,000 Kiambu men would have paid. If each paid shs 15/–, Kiambu would have paid shs 450,000, much less than the normal taxes. To reach Corfield's figures, all other regions – the Rift Valley, Murang'a and Gaki – together would have had to pay shs 550,000, which is also low.
1947. *Mumenyerere*, Henry Muoria Mwaniki, editor, 17 November.
1960. Corfield Report, *op. cit.*, pp. 187ff.
11. The post of 'President of all *Mariika*' created in 1947 for Dedan Mugo was an innovation. He combined this job with being the president of the Githunguri Building Committee and travelled to convince the more well-to-do to contribute.
12. The colonial government could take action against what it regarded as unlawful acts and sedition through the Penal Code. Section 62 was directed against administering unlawful oaths or being present when they were administered. Early oaths were ascribed to underground KCA activities until Mau Mau was declared an illegal society on 4 August 1950.
13. More than any other judgments, people resented that early oaths for a number of organizations were lumped together as Mau Mau.
14. Even those who got a trading licence found themselves in financial difficulties. They lacked the capital to acquire sufficient stock, and had too few customers to turn it over in time. Well-to-do customers wanted greater choice; poorer customers could not afford their higher prices.
15. However much land owners in Kiambu were afraid of too much Koinange power, abuse of him by younger males was not acceptable. He had clashed with the KCA during the female circumcision issue, and had been made a subject of attack; and though there was no evidence that the young males were KCA members or supporters, the attacks were regarded as evidence that Nairobi KAU had come under KCA influence, with or without Kenyatta's connivance. Kenyatta retained the image of being a KCA supporter, even though he could not control it.
1947. AR/320/KBU/38.
16. The struggle between the moderate wing of KAU and non-aggressive leaders and radical members as well as union leaders is documented by Spencer.
1985. Spencer, John, *op. cit.*, pp. 202ff.
17. Almost all 32 KAU members in Nairobi took an oath, called the KAU oath: some did so before 1950; most took the oath in 1950. By 1956 some had died, others were detained, and it was no longer possible to find out whether these oaths had differed. All were judged by the 1952/3 screening team to have taken Mau Mau oaths. Most did not show any unusual Mau Mau activity (Appendix IX/1).

18. What Kenyatta thought of this activity, and whether he was even consulted, is not known. During these years Kenyatta's hands were tied; if he were to foster a political base, he could not alienate anyone. He needed political and financial support.
19. The results must have been sobering. According to my data 5.8 per cent (3 out of 52) domestic workers and 11.4 per cent (4 out of 36) mechanical workers, which included taxi drivers, had taken an oath before 1950 (Table 7.1). The strike ordered for taxi drivers in 1949 was somewhat more successful; 16 of the 36 had gone home for at least one day.
20. While second oaths were common, an oath not unlike the *batuni* oath was offered locally in the summer of 1954. The few who took it refused information in 1962.
21. The earliest rumours about a Mau Mau organization reached the local community around 1948; it was located in the Rift Valley. The Director of Intelligence and Security reported the existence of a Mau Mau movement in Naivasha on 21 September 1948. In 1948 a Chief in Fort Hall reports the existence of a secret society called 'Mau Mau'. 1960. Corfield Report *op. cit.*, pp. 78, 81, 84, 85, 88.
22. All through Mau Mau, the promise of land persisted but remained vague. Rural and Nairobi Kikuyu knew that Rift Valley Kikuyu had first right to the land they had worked and that the settled area belonged to specific rural men and their descendants. Nor did they expect to take the land of non-Kikuyu by force. Many, however, firmly believed that Europeans would sell land to the Kikuyu under pressure. The immediate objective therefore was to earn enough to be able to buy.
23. None of the early takers of two oaths had received cuts on his hands to indicate membership, which would have made them conspicuous. That they had become members of a secret society did not bother anyone over much. They had grown up with proscription as a colonial weapon; proscribed or illegal associations were more likely to be good than bad. What mattered was not to get caught.
24. A by-product of the aggressive, defensive organizations was that other ethnic groups shunned locations dominated by Kikuyu. In consequence, Mau Mau may have become equally unattractive. There is no evidence that other ethnic groups betrayed Kikuyu oathing, but they were understandably quite willing to take the jobs Kikuyu abandoned when they were forced out of Nairobi in April 1954.
25. No information was collected about the land ownership of the households of women who took early oaths.
26. It is not known when the Kikuyu settlement in Arusha was established. In December 1953 all Kikuyu in Tanganyika were detained for interrogation and sent back to Kenya.
27. In 1948/9, three women took oaths with their husbands, and five took an oath separately; the husbands of those women did not take oaths. Women who were financially responsible for their households financed their own oaths if needed.
28. Both Dedan Mugo and Waira Kamau had strong Nairobi ties well before they started working for Kenyatta.
29. Mau Mau was proscribed on 4 August 1950; the population had known that their rural oaths were Mau Mau, but they had thought them sufficiently different from other Mau Mau.
30. 1960. Corfield Report, *op. cit.*, p. 85.
31. At least ten men declared in 1956 that they had left Nairobi by 1950 because they felt unsafe.
32. While most males who were clerks or administrators at oathing centres had taken two oaths, women treasurers had often taken only one oath. They were almost always mothers or wives of centre functionaries. The fifteen males who were local chairmen, clerks, guards, or organizers were all under 40; three had paid the first fee for junior eldership. That they became significant in Mau Mau did not count toward local status.
33. The *ithaku* or *mbari* of centres were often their own best clients. In one *mbari* which had a centre, 85.9 per cent of the males and 89.7 per cent of the females took a first oath. Of the males, one in four took a second oath as well. In a roughly comparable *mbari*, without a centre, the figures were 49.5 per cent and 37.3 per cent.
34. Beecher meetings only stopped when the Emergency was declared. In 1952, parents whose children were not admitted to a school they had built in Ngaga chased the teachers

out and installed their own. The government was warned, according to some by a local 'stump', and arrested all involved.
35. In June 1951 three critically important jobs of the Nairobi KAU branch went to union leaders; one was Fred Kubai. The *Muhimu* or Central Committee had been created, according to Spencer, to retain control of oathing and keep it separate from KAU leadership. Spencer gives the most detailed account of the sidelining of Kenyatta and his failure to turn the situation around.
Spencer, John, *op. cit.*; p. 223ff., 227.
36. The request to take a second oath could be made when men took a first oath or years later. In Tables 7.2 and 7.3, the earliest second oath came from men who that year had taken a first oath. Later second oaths may have been recruited from any earlier year.
37. One entrepreneur boasted in 1956 that he had made on average shs 300/- a week; 'much more than the Chief'. The highest paid administrative official at the time earned shs. 7,320/- a year.
38. Had a change in tenure not been afoot, the case might not have been filed. It would have paralysed the economy; litigation might have dragged on for decades without a chance for development. However, the coming new system of tenure would demand that all decisions were irrevocable. For those who believed that communal tenure had been 'the law of the land' this was the last and only change.
39. 1951. Kiambu CNF 17/1951.
40. The local area was gazetted in 1951; larger land owners with private land or undisputed *mbari* land could expect 100 seedlings the following year. Coffee licences would be restricted during the Emergency to those who had not taken an oath; informants remembered that the words 'loyal' and 'loyalist' were already used in 1951 in connection with coffee licences. One of the first recipients was Senior Chief Waruhiu wa Kungu. 1951. KB/42 AR/324.
41. After the Declaration of the Emergency cleansing through a *gutahikio* ceremony was made obligatory in many areas.
1960. Corfield Report, *op cit.*, p. 135.
42. The committee members were predominantly Christians or at least did not practise the Kikuyu religion. The leading force was L. S. B. Leakey, supported by two Christian Kikuyu, who did not believe in the ritual themselves. There is no evidence that Leakey wanted to make it mandatory. The decision did not make a difference between first and subsequent oaths, Leakey may have believed the oath to be such a violation of the Kikuyu moral order that it warranted the serious *githathi* of the *thenge* oaths. Though he probably wanted to ascribe the deleterious effects only to the more serious oaths, his sweeping statement does not give much space for differentiation. He apparently understood the oaths to bring about a state of mind which – unless cured by ritual – made it impossible for the oath takers to refuse orders from the oath organizers on pain of *thahu*, ritual uncleanliness, which could be deadly for their kin as well. Oaths were instigated by evil men 'to create a mass of violent minded, often bewildered people, chained by superstition and fear to the commands of their unscrupulous leaders. In the early days the ritual was primitive but not bestial, its symbolism being sufficiently powerful to bind initiates to the terms of the ghastly oath....' If the powers of the oath were 'supernatural', then punishment alone would be ineffective unless other supernatural powers could free oath takers from their hold, and incidentally make it more likely that they would not take them again. Depending on the oath taker, such power *could* be found in a tribal cleansing ceremony or Christian ritual.
1954. *Report on the Sociological Causes underlying Mau Mau with some Proposals on the Means of Ending It*, Appendix III, secret, mimeographed.
1952. KBU/43 AR/325.
43. There is no report that such ceremonies were held in Nairobi, but it is certain that they were held in the Rift Valley. At one ceremony held on 8 October 1952 close to Nanyuki, 14 'farmers checked off their names against their muster rolls, names of those not attending were noted. So were the names of many Kikuyu who did not take the *githaki* oath.' But even under this pressure the people who were forced managed to register their

opposition, and the *mundu mugo* leading the ceremony had to alter the curse, postponing its consequences for two weeks to give oath takers a chance to confess.
1952. *East African Standard*, 10 October.

44. It was also offensive to the elders that the *githathi* stones were moved around. Although only Chief Waruhiu, who was particularly active in organizing the ceremonies, would be killed, others who might have been sympathetic to counter-oathing or were known opponents of Mau Mau were warned that they would be next. Some spent much of the Emergency under heavy guard.
1952. *East African Standard* Supplement, 10 October.

45. Our data show that, though Mau Mau was growing, it was barely keeping pace with the Beecher year momentum (Table 7.2). Government or CID figures show an almost unbelievably rapid growth in the same period. Official estimates of Mau Mau involvement before and after the Declaration of the Emergency varied widely. No official or unofficial estimates are available for 1950, when Mau Mau was declared illegal, although Corfield reports widespread concern about illegal assemblies and oath taking, particularly from the Rift Valley. In April 1952 the Commissioner of Police estimated the number of involved Kikuyu as less than 10 per cent. However in the middle of that year, the CID estimated that over a quarter of a million Kikuyu were involved, which would be at least 30 per cent of all adults. These figures escalated further; by the Declaration of the Emergency, Corfield reports that the administration believed at least 80 per cent of the Kikuyu had taken Mau Mau oaths.
1960. Corfield Report *op cit.*, pp. 31; 88ff; 130; 182ff; 248.

46. 1952. *East African Standard*, 22 August.

47. 1952. *East African Standard*, 29 August.

48. The government continued to believe that Kenyatta was prevaricating and used the flexibility of the Kikuyu language to say one thing but imply another. Neither Mau Mau leaders nor local men doubted that he was speaking against the direction Mau Mau had taken since 1951, but he did not speak out against the basic oath. This was too much for some Mau Mau leaders; by this time Kenyatta feared assassination, and was accompanied at home and at meetings by a small group of *anake* responsible for his safety. Though the government asked Kenyatta to take a stand against violent Mau Mau, there is no evidence that it opened other political avenues for Kenyatta or provided any protection.

49. Kenyatta exhorted his audience 'to work harder; then trouble would end and when everyone was rich there would be harmony'. A discussion of the attitudes of the Churches to the poor can be found in
1992. Lonsdale, John, 'The moral economy of Mau Mau in Unhappy Valley', *op. cit.*, Book II, pp. 439–45.
1952. *East African Standard*, 29 August.

50. There had already been a number of murders, one of them in September in Kiambu. Although all would be attributed by Corfield to Mau Mau, a number of them no doubt correctly, informants were convinced that some were due to *fatina*, others to ordinary robbers. The violence was possible because neither the Nairobi locations nor the Rift Valley had ever had adequate police protection; rural districts also had to rely on local vigilance.

51. Europeans would praise Koinange Mbiu's honesty and trustworthiness; Kikuyu would praise him for his *tha* and his championship of Kikuyu rights. Waruhiu would be praised by Europeans officials for his fatherly support; he would be faulted by Kikuyu for lack of *tha* and lack of support for matters Kikuyu.

52. The arrests focused strongly on Githunguri and all who could be related directly or indirectly to Githunguri. Some local men held that they should have looked more towards Nairobi; still others maintained that Mau Mau was used as a cover; some wanted him killed before the next Royal Commission. It was widely believed that his murder was to take place the day before, 6 October 1952, when he was a guest of an old elder near Kiambu. Hearing the murderers approach, the old man 'pleaded with them not to kill on his land' and 'that is why they waited till the next day'.

53. The governor signed the orders declaring a State of Emergency on 20 October 1952; it went into effect the next day. It ended in January 1960. On the evening of the 20th and during the following days 183 Kikuyu leaders were arrested and placed under detention orders. The operation was called Jock Scott. Emergency regulations allowed detention without trial. Among the detainees would be ex-Senior Chief Koinange and others who had been accused of Waruhiu's murder, including Waura Kamau. When they were rearrested after having been found not guilty, Waira was returned to Marsabit, where he had been held. In 1954 he and others were transferred to Lamu. He returned home in 1962. Peter Gakabaki, president of the Kikuyu Independent Schools Association, was also held under Emergency regulations. Initially, only 33 independent schools were closed because they were suspected to be oathing centres. On 14 November the two larger independent school councils, KISA and KKEA, were declared unlawful societies in Kiambu. By January 1953, almost all independent schools were closed, affecting more than 13,000 children. Although KAU attempted to separate itself from Mau Mau, it too was proscribed by June 1953.

In the second phase of Jock Scott, which started a few weeks after the Emergency, two other local men were detained; one had returned in 1957, the other by January 1962. Phase Three of Jock Scott consisted of the building of permanent police stations throughout Kikuyu country; the local station was Marige. The stations were manned by one European officer and 25 Africans. The officer in charge was initially seconded from the Kenya Regiment; many of them were young white Kenyans with little or no police experience. When more regular police became available in 1953 and 1954, they were slowly replaced.

The legal system was put on an Emergency footing. Minor cases could be heard before the Magistrate's Courts in the Kikuyu Districts. Capital cases involving arson, possession of arms or consorting with armed terrorists, murder and other acts of violence were referred to the Supreme Court, where they were heard before the Emergency Assize.

1952–60. Marsabit District Annual Report PC/NFD/1/2/5.
1952. *East African Standard*, 14 November.
1955. Education Department, Annual Report, pp. 26, 27.
1960. Corfield Report, *op. cit.*, pp. 84ff.

Eight

The Emergency, Marige & the End of Mau Mau

After months of anxiety and at times horror, after having suffered curfews, suspicion and being accused of crimes because they took oaths, land poor, landless and many landed exploded into joy. The arrest of Nairobi leaders made little impression, but Kenyatta's arrest, charged with being the leader of Mau Mau, changed fear and anger to hope.

The landed had not given him a great deal of credit for leadership; they had seen him more and more as someone trying to become a landed Kiambu elder. Land poor and landless had seen this growth and sadly concluded that he had little to share now and offered even less for the future. No one doubted that he was in favour of resistance and his brand of Mau Mau, but the overwhelming opinion had been that he was not in control of Githunguri, nor of other Mau Mau. If, in spite of what they had thought, he had secretly been in control, outwitting them and the colonial government for years, then he was far more astute than they had given him credit for. The time of secrecy was over; Kenyatta might be arrested, but freedom had never been so close. Those who had, against Kenyatta's will, offered their multiple oaths, should cease to do so and acknowledge him. All people should send Kenyatta a sign that they had understood and would follow: the time for *umoja* was now.

In the short months between the end of October 1952 and the Marige massacre in April, Mau Mau membership soared. In Nairobi, where many had already joined Mau Mau, the increase was not as marked as in the rural area. There, more males joined in these few months than in the whole earlier period, and women's membership more than tripled (Tables 7.2, 7.3, pages 228, 229). The increase covered a much broader economic group. The largest increase came numerically from the land poor but, in relation to the size of their group, small peasants and peasants joined with more eagerness than ever before (Table 7.4, page 232). Shortly before the Marige massacre, 49 per cent of all males and 48 per cent of all females had taken an oath.

Yet even at this time a significant number of males and females did not join. The landed remained mired in land litigation: Gitau and Mwereri were still battling over the land Gitau claimed. According to Gitau, they had owned it since the nineteenth century and Gitau therefore refused to return the land Mwereri had entrusted to them when Mwereri men went to the Rift Valley. Mwereri men claimed that they 'were poor because of Gitau'.

Mungai descendants continued to sue Njau descendants for an inheritance in Njau's private land. Njau descendants refused to yield, because they alleged that Mungai had not helped pay, though he was old enough to have done so. Chege descendants also claimed a part of Njau's private land; according to them Njau had not returned the goats he had borrowed to pay for it. Gitau and Kimani, an adopted son of Njau, had also litigated for an extended period, with Kimani the loser.

Over all these cases hung the hope and fear that land tenure would change and individual ownership would be recognised by title deeds, after which men with four acres or more would be able to apply for coffee permits. Given the many disputed boundaries, whose perspectives would be honoured by the courts? Would they perhaps even listen to Gitau, part of Chege and Mungai, who were propagating that the land should be divided equally among *mbari* members? These fears had fostered more litigation when the courts stopped hearing Igi cases: four new cases had been filed in 1948, seven in 1949.

Some of the landed were still certain that they could leave land for sons; many peasants, however, could leave them at best a subsistence holding. If they could not provide sons with an education which guaranteed a well-paying job – though the Beecher Report had brought improvement, there were, according to peasants, still far too few places in secondary schools – sons would join the large group of subsistence plot owners. Grandsons would have little more than a residential plot. With this as background, most landed were in a difficult position, yet they still had a great deal to lose.

In contrast to the landed, landless and land poor had less to lose, though if a change in land tenure were to come about, many would lose the land they used. Wages were totally inadequate; only a few, whose fathers had held sufficient land, had received enough education to hold a better-paying job.

Wives worked at minimum wages, picking coffee; it was a lucky man who had one son in school, hoping against hope that he would be able to pay school fees until the son sat his Kenya African Preliminary Examination, and was among the few who passed. They had taken their oaths – in contrast to only 7 per cent of the landed, 32.7 per cent of landless, land poor and small peasants had taken one or more oaths – not so much because they, in their heart of hearts, had believed that Kenyatta was Mau Mau, but because there was no other hope. They felt torn between Githunguri and Nairobi, they suffered from Kenyatta's inability to bring them together. The government's arrest of Kenyatta, its declaration that he was *the leader*, renewed their hope and trust and they flocked to the oath-taking centres. Their membership increased to 57.7 per cent (Table 7.4).

Screening

Even if the government had detected the Kikuyu reaction, it is unlikely that it would have changed its mind about Mau Mau or Kenyatta. It saw both as unremitting evil, to be stamped out; Mau Mau had to be destroyed. It therefore instituted a series of measures to flush out Mau Mau members, to deter further recruitment and to punish those who were already involved.

Its prime means was a process of localized screening, in which all adults were to appear before a local committee of men and women who themselves had not taken an oath. This screening team worked under a District Officer; it was empowered to recommend that a non-oath taker be given a 'loyalty certificate' which would allow him or her to work outside the local area or that an oath taker be fined and denied such papers (Appendix IX/6).

Many Nairobi workers consequently had to pay fines and lost jobs and income. In the early months of screening, fines might be as high as shs 100/-; oath takers, many already landless or with very little land, were further liable for a special annual Emergency tax of around shs 20/-.[1] As many households had several oath takers, poverty was severe. Some found local work in *gitati*, which was reinstituted.

The government also mandated that local communities protect themselves and 'fight Mau Mau' by recruiting unpaid Homeguards. By the end of January 1953 a local unit had been recruited from the *ahoi* and *ithaku* of the *mbari*. Many Homeguards had taken Mau Mau oaths; they were allowed to enlist, instead of paying fines (Appendix IX/7). That they were local men did not prevent abuse of power: while most did not misbehave, some became notorious for violence and blackmail. Their strong-arm tactics to get people to appear before the screening committee were particularly resented.

To the dismay of many, most Kiambu areas made cleansing through the *gutahikio* ritual an additional requirement for oath takers. This was itself an oath, in which a guilty party 'vomited' his Mau Mau oath: those who took this oath but did it not 'with a pure heart', or violated it by taking another oath, exposed themselves, their kin and their land to *thahu* (Appendix VIII/2). Many Kikuyu, including those who had taken an oath, would have agreed that oaths beyond the basic or amended commitment oath had to stop. Elders – possibly gladly – would have accepted some government help to bring this about. But the price the government demanded was high and dangerous; the cleansing oath could be a lethal danger, particularly if men who did not want to renounce Mau Mau were forced to be cleansed. This affected mainly Nairobi workers; they had often taken more aggressive Nairobi oaths, which they regarded as binding. They did not want to be cleansed, certainly not by force.

Marige

Most of those involved in what became known as the 'Marige massacre', were local men who worked in Nairobi. They recruited rural men to join them to avenge their forced cleansing in spite of the pleas of the Githunguri local leader who urged them to 'keep their anger in Nairobi'.

They did not follow his advice; they owed no allegiance to Githunguri, and were too angry: they felt that they had been forced to perjure themselves and only revenge would remove the stain. Whether they complained to the *Muhimu* or whether it approached them is uncertain; what is certain is that Nairobi leadership needed to safeguard its interests in the rural area and that those who enforced cleansing were 'stumps' and a threat. Whoever made the decision, it was resolved that the Homeguards who had forced them, had to die.[2] The *Muhimu* provided arms – ten pistols – and promised a reward of shs 100/- for each gang member if the raid was successful.[3]

One of the principals, a Kimani man, was designated leader and assembled a gang of at least thirty local men. The majority were Nairobi migrant labourers, some were from the rural area, some came from neighbouring Kibichoi and Kiratina. Among the gang were at least five who had been forcibly cleansed; there were also several *anake* from the 'Marige boys', who used to pass the time in the Marige market. Most joined without protest; others were pressed into service. Gitau and Kimani were each represented by two, Mwereri by possibly three, men; the *ahoi* in the gang came mainly from local *ithaku*.

The gang was not representative of rural Mau Mau: most rural Mau Mau members were land poor or landless, had little education, and had taken only one oath. But a significant number of the gang members worked in Nairobi; their allegiance was there. Though Nairobi men were often land poor, they had more education and almost all had taken a second oath. Five were *ahoi*, nine were subsistence tract holders (whose land varied from half an acre to almost four), three were small and three large peasants. Several gang members would eventually have had more land, as their fathers were still alive. Educational achievements ranged from illiterate to form IV, and almost all were under 40.

The sense of having been abused, the anger and desire for revenge created an unusual bond among the principals, though their *ithaku* were usually involved in bitter litigation with each other. Unity was 'reinforced' by eating, heavy drinking, and smoking *bangi* while waiting for the signal to move out.[4] During the wait, one of the women who prepared the meal asked them to kill an agricultural assistant; he had fined her and jailed her husband for improper terracing. She lured him into the trap by inviting him to come and see her new efforts; his body was almost certainly used for illegitimate oaths. This increased the gang's solidarity as the use of *murogi* substances gave the leaders an almost unbreakable hold (Appendix IX/6).[5] According to some, the local Githunguri leader visited the gang again around this time, reiterating his request that they go back to Nairobi. According to others, he did not come in person but someone in the gang conveyed his request not to kill. It had little effect; the gang agreed that killing was wrong but then voted that killing Homeguards was different.

When it was almost dark, the gang, intoxicated and disoriented, moved out to find a local headman deeply involved in Homeguard activities. It passed the homestead of a man who had refused to join the gang; afraid that he nevertheless would be suspected, he had asked a Homeguard to stay with him as witness. The two were outside; when they saw the gang approach they ran away, blowing whistles to alert other homesteads that the gang was close. Angry that it failed to catch them, the gang killed his wife and new-born baby.

On their way back, the Kimani gang leader complained that his wife had a problem with the owner of the homestead they were just passing, a Gitau man. The gang decided to avenge their leader; the presence of Kimani and Mwereri men who had recently lost land to Gitau was sufficient to decide the homestead's fate. Whether the Gitau men in the gang agreed in their drunken stupor, or acquiesced under threat, is not certain, but one of them participated in the killing of two children and the serious wounding of the parents and two other children.[6] This was enough: violence and murder dissolved unity and purpose; the gang fled and dispersed.

The following transcripts of the interrogations and court records describe the event and its outcome. This is interspersed with the reports from the *East African Standard*, the local pastor, a participant, and local elders. For clarity's sake the order of the testimony is sometimes changed; words inserted for ease of reading are placed between square brackets. Members of *ithaku* are indicated by the pseudonyms assigned to them in earlier chapters if necessary; other names are indicated by dashes.

Head of the Homeguards

I am in charge of the Homeguards in Marige Location in the Kiambu District....

The following persons who had been forced to be cleansed had said that ... they were going to bring a big gang to attack the people who are anti Mau Mau and therefore we suspected them to be responsible for the attack. They are [there follow six names among them a Kimani and a Gitau member]. All these people had left the Location when they

The Emergency, Marige & the End of Mau Mau

were cleansed and went to Nairobi, but they had promised to attack people in Marige. Before the attack on [name of Gitau victim] I had received information that all these people had held a meeting at [Gitau gang member's] house. This was during the daytime of the same day. I also received information that on the same day [name of Kimani gang leader] had held a meeting in the house of one —. On the same evening I gave instructions to all my Homeguards that they were to arrest any of these people if they met them anywhere.

... On the evening of 5 April 1953 at about 9 pm I was with Headman — and 22 Homeguards in his home. When we were there we heard some people shouting as if they were being attacked. The shouting had come from —'s house. Afterwards we heard two shots fired. I believe they were fired from a pistol. Then we heard the third shot which I believe was fired from a rifle. After that I arranged all the Homeguards and surrounded Headman ... home.[7]

At that time the population still lived in homesteads which were fairly close together. Sound carries far in the late afternoon and at night; the pre-murder feasting was hardly secret, and the population, the Homeguards, and the probable victims were forewarned. The Homeguard did not attempt to arrest the feasting gang, and the security forces were not alerted until the massacre had almost come to an end, possible because the population feared the security forces as much as Mau Mau. Though the head of the Homeguards testified that he heard shots, no other informants nor the security forces mentioned that pistols or rifles were used during the raid. Nor is it likely that gang members used them later to do battle with the security forces; they were preoccupied with finding a place to hide, not with combat. Yet gang members had pistols which had probably been collected by women in Nairobi.

Woman carrier of arms

On Sunday 5 April 1953 at about 1 pm when I was in my house, a woman called — , who lives near my house came to my house. She was carrying a small native basket. She asked me to allow her to keep her basket in my house. I asked her what were the contents of the basket, but she did not tell me, and told me to leave it in my house. Soon — left my house and I took the basket and opened it to see what were the contents. I found that the contents of the basket were ten pistols....[8]

She then relates that the basket was collected after a few hours and that she later went to the homestead of one gang member, where she participated in drinking beer, and saw the woman who had brought the basket to her house distribute guns to at least three men, one of them a Kimani man.

Only three men – one from Kimani, one from Gitau, and one a *muhoi* presumably from Gitau – who had been captured either the day after the raid or later were eventually brought to trial. The Kimani man gave a statement in Kiambu; when his case was brought before the Supreme

The Emergency, Marige & the End of Mau Mau

Court in Nairobi, he retracted it, claiming it had been made under duress.

Part of the Kiambu statement by Kimani gang member

On Thursday, 2nd or 3rd April (I do not remember the exact date) — and — met me at Kariobangi [Nairobi location]. — told me that we would go to Marige on the next Saturday, and that I should stay with — until he returned. — gave him five shillings for food .

On Saturday he returned about 4 pm with four people. — was one but I do not know the other three. — told me that night to go to Mukuyu lodge and await him. I was told to go with the other four. — gave — shs 3/- for food for us all. At 6 pm — brought us all food at Kariobangi. Later he said we should go through the bush and not to go anywhere near houses as otherwise I would be killed. We all except — set off at 7:30. — and — told us that if anyone ran away we would be killed. Went to the Karia river, where we met more than ten people. I recognized — and — whom I had met previously but not the others as it was dark. Went into the school at Komothai. We were told to stop and — said that he would go to — who would show us where to go. We went to —'s house. He saw us and blew a whistle. We all surrounded his house and those who entered the house cut with pangas his wife and children.

Then — and — said let us go. We returned to Komothai. Three men were missing, they had fled. We went to [a Gitau house] and — said he was a local man and we should go in. The house was surrounded and some people entered the house. I stood near the window. He and his family were attacked with pangas. I entered through the window and found all the tables and chairs were thrown down. There were people in each room. I and a youth went off on our own to a farm near the juncture of the Kamiti/Ruiru roads at 5 am where we slept. In the morning we each went our own way.[9]

Before the Supreme Court he explained why others would have wanted to frame him.

... there was recently a land case between him and my brother and that is why he [the Gitau victim] accuses me.... The case was in 1950/1951....

At the same trial the Gitau gang member declared

Gitau [the victim] lies because if I am hanged he will inherit my land as he is my older brother....[10]

Head of Homeguards, continued

About an hour later [i.e., after he had surrounded the homestead of the headman] Chief —'s lorry came to Headman —'s house, the Chief was driving the lorry himself. The Chief collected — and his wife and I was ordered to stay with my Homeguards guarding —'s home, which I did until the following morning.[11]

By this time the chief had already taken the injured to the hospital; he did not encounter hostilities on his act of *tha*. How the security forces were alerted is not known; when they arrived and started to chase the gang, a large part of the Homeguard was employed in guarding an empty homestead.

The Marige aftermath as told by Wanyoike's grandson, in which security forces hunted down the suspects and summarily executed them, conforms substantially to my information, though I was told a number of times that Homeguards did not take part. The brutal torture and murder of the woman who instigated the murder of the agricultural instructor, after she had been found by the security forces, also tallies with my information.[12] The European allegedly involved was given the name *Mbaya*, the evil one. An early administrator of the IBEAC, who was in part thought responsible for one of the bloodiest periods in the European penetration of Kabete, had been given the same name at that time.

Wanyoike Kamawe and Grandson

When members of the security forces arrived on the scene of the attack in the early hours of the morning, a swift operation was carried out to round up the fleeing killers. Many people were caught red-handed, including those who were carrying the bloody weapons or had stains of blood on their clothes. The captives were forced to give the names of others who had managed to get away, and some of these too, were caught that very morning....

Komothai residents began to feel intensely the terrible consequences of the Emergency when they witnessed mass executions without trial of all those who were arrested in connection with the killings. While it was yet dark, all the suspected culprits were driven into the school playground where they were made to stand in a circle as if to be taught a new game. The police stood well behind them, surrounding the victims, while in the centre of the circle fire was opened up from an automatic weapon killing them all instantly. More horror had yet to follow after the break of dawn.[13]

This is followed by a description of the next few days, in which suspects were allegedly forced by a European officer to jump from a moving Landrover and run away, only to be shot in the back.

The perspective of the *East African Standard* is one in which heroic security forces did battle with barbarous Mau Mau; the accounts suggest an armed confrontation although it never says so outright.

East African Standard

Quick police action thwarted another organised Mau Mau attempt to massacre loyal Kikuyu women and their children in the Kiambu Reserve as their menfolk were out patrolling as Homeguards. The gangsters managed to hack five women and children to pieces and seriously wounded another four but the police have already shot and killed 22 of the gangsters. Eleven were shot on the spot and 11 were shot during the chase. The police are still on the trail.

The Emergency, Marige & the End of Mau Mau

The gang was originally estimated to be between 20 and 30 strong. Officials who were on the scene Monday reckoned that the quick action of the police prevented what might have been easily another Uplands massacre....

Main objective of the gang was to 'eliminate' a loyal headman, who had done much for the Homeguard in the area.... But they reckoned without the recently established police post at Marige, personnel of which were on their toes. They heard the gang go into action and the screams and shouts of their victims. In 15 minutes, police patrols were on the scene and had routed the gangsters. Attacking at once, their shots killed 11 and during yesterday afternoon they were still in close contact with the others and are reported to have killed 11 more....

In its 9 April edition the newspaper reports that 12 men have been arrested.[14]

A gang member, who had not wanted to participate, reflects the view of the population and saw only tragedy. The following are extracts from several interviews.

I had joined Mau Mau 'for *umoja*', not for killing. Local members of Mau Mau did not meet together, they were waiting for a *Kiama kia Moscou* which said that it was not going to wait. I cannot tell more about them, [ordinary Mau Mau members] were afraid of them because they could kill you so it was better to know nothing and not to ask. I heard that they also spoke with two sides. I heard that some joined the CID and that is why they called themselves *kia Moscou*....

The Committee in Nairobi told people to kill the Headman and they were giving shs 100/- to each of us.... Because they killed the wrong ones they were not paid.

I do not like killing, even of —, but they found me in the garden....

They killed [Gitau] because he was an enemy of [Kimani, principal leader] they had had litigation. These ... people who wanted to kill came together with about 25 others.... [They] intended to kill the headman and — a Homeguard from Kibichoi who used to beat people like.... They came at [homestead of a Kimani member] and stayecd there until dark.

They were asked by her [his wife] to kill — [an agricultural instructor] because he reported them of not making good terraces. They went for him and they killed him. They then started their journey to [the Headman]. They had asked — to be a watchman. He did not like that. So he called [a] Homeguard ... to stay with him in his house so he could be a witness that he did not take part. [They] heard people coming so [they] ran away and started shouting, using a whistle. They [the gang] got annoyed. They tried to follow him but failed. That is why they went to [his homestead] and killed his wife and child. Then [one of Kimani] told the others that someone of Gitau had been troubling his wife, so ... they went to that [Gitau house] and killed him and his children and wife. But he lived and so did his wife. They then went all away and ran.

He felt caught between the threat of the security forces and the *Muhimu*, which would kill them for not having followed orders.

> ... We all ran away because we thought we are Mau Mau, most of Mau Mau were killed and will be killed if they did something wrong, so we ran away.

The threat from the *Muhimu* was real for all, because it could use local Nairobi men to execute its orders and they had to obey.[15] During most of 1953 and early 1954, the *Muhimu* still had sufficient power to kill in Nairobi and rural areas which it had penetrated.

> ... Already before they [the gang] came from Nairobi [the local Githunguri leader] had told the Nairobi people to stay away but they came nevertheless. This man did not want killing because of *umoja*, but they listened to Nairobi. He told them that they would not succeed. [They] had voted and most said that it was alright to kill — and the Homeguard. That is why [the local Githunguri leader] is the leader of KANU in Komothai, he is *mundu wa tha*, a man of mercy....

Statement of the Kiama:

> The gang was bad and we won't say that they did not do bad things, but they had been given *bangi*.

A smaller group of elders declared:

> What they did was bad, but you must never forget that the *githaku* of — and the — *mbari* have always been bad, with angry people....

The father of a gang member

> My sons were angry with — and even the second generation will not forget how they lost their land.... The anger was right but the deed was wrong because the left hand has now cut the right hand and we are of one *mbari*.

One senior elder summed up the reaction of Mbari ya Igi, when he declared 'The *mbari* has killed itself'.

The raid caused the death of one man, one woman, and three children; others were seriously injured. According to local information, fourteen men were killed by the security forces that same night or the next day. According to the *East African Standard*, 22 gang members were killed in that period; I do not have information about the fate of Kibichoi and Kiratina men.[16] One local woman was killed during interrogation some time later.[17] Three men were hanged, and a number of men and women were detained for shorter or longer periods; three were eventually classified as Hard Core, one of them died at Hola.[18] At least three men and women complained about having been so badly beaten by Homeguards that they were crippled, even though they were neither charged nor arrested.

The Emergency, Marige & the End of Mau Mau

The end of Mau Mau

For the local population and its Nairobi workers, Marige ended Mau Mau. Though the Emergency had barely started and would not be lifted until 12 January 1960, few took an oath after Marige. Twelve males took a first, and three a Nairobi second oath after Marige, but four said that these had been taken for the *Kiama Kia Muingi*, which was organized in 1956 to protest land consolidation.[19] Some first oaths were taken to protest Operation Anvil in April 1954, but as this government action removed Nairobi Mau Mau leadership no more oaths were taken there; the remaining oaths, including second oaths, had been taken in detention (Table 7.2).[20] Two rural women took an oath immediately after Marige out of anger that kinsmen had been killed 'for no reason'.[21] Other female oaths were oriented towards the *Kiama kia Muingi*, Githunguri, or taken in detention (Table 7.3).

When, after Marige, the government imposed villagization on the benumbed population, there was little opposition, despite the cost of building new huts and the unwanted closeness: most people agreed that the gang would not have dared to attack had other people lived closer (Appendix X/2). That the population no longer occupied the land gave an unexpected boost to plans for reform of land tenure, and after Marige few people wanted to protest something so obviously desired by the government. Coffee was an added incentive, because permits would only be given to those who owned undisputed land. When Chief Magugo Waweru asked government permission to reopen the issue and reported that *mbari* members would accept the decisions of a committee of Arbitrators in outstanding litigation, he received permission to go forward. On 18 June 1955, after six days of hearing witnesses, the committee accepted that Njau's land was indeed his alone; it excluded Mungai and denied Chege rights, because the goats his ancestor had lent were paid back. Two other *ithaku* who had helped with the price had rights to a place, because their goats had not been returned.[22]

As to *mbari* land, the idea that it should be divided according to need or strength was not seriously considered; adherents had not been able to marshal support. The feud between Gitau and Mwereri was declared closed; each was given what he had owned after the last court decision. A committee composed of *arumati* of all Igi *ithaku* decided where in Igi each *githaku* would have its land; elders of each *githaku* then decided how it should be divided among the members. Thuita *mbari* remained in the land they had bought. In both Igi and Thuita long-standing *ahoi* were given a quarter of an acre in ownership, although they did not become members of the *mbari*. Their land was not provided by individual *mbari* but from a general land fund, for which each land owner was assessed roughly 0.6 per cent of his holding, which also covered village amenities. Land owners also had to surrender a quarter acre for a village plot on which to live.[23]

The Emergency, Marige & the End of Mau Mau

Apart from these deductions, the overwhelming number of land owners got about as much land as they had before, though title deeds and use often did not cover the same acreage (Appendix X/1).

A number of people who had expected to get coffee licences were in for a rude awakening: as still another punishment, oath takers did not get permits, even if they had the requisite four acres of land. Those with less than four acres did not get coffee, oaths or no oaths.[24]

By 1957, many Nairobi men were allowed to return to Nairobi to seek work. The burden of the Emergency had been extremely heavy, with many people out of work, special taxes for oath takers, detention and fines; many had lost kinsmen to Mau Mau or the security forces.[25]

During this period, people would slowly, first with amazement, then with increasing joy, learn that all their suffering had not been in vain; *weiyathi*, in spite of it all, had not only come closer, but was almost there. By 1957, the population was sure that Kenyatta would be released, and that, once the Emergency was over, Kenya would become independent under his leadership. Much of the burden of bringing this about had been borne by landless and land poor, and they were convinced that, under Kenyatta's leadership, the message they had tried to send would be heard and a solution found, for them and their sons. Kenyatta could not but bring economic relief; freedom from colonialism had to mean land and hope.[26] The Emergency had been caused by Europeans; who had been Mau Mau or who had not, or who had killed Waruhiu, would no longer be important.[27]

The landed were cautiously optimistic; they hoped that Kenyatta would continue to be a Kiambu elder in whatever he did. The only way forward was indeed freedom; freedom under Kiambu Kikuyu leadership was going to be their hope for the future and the certainty of their sons.[28]

All agreed that Mau Mau should become a closed chapter of history for the sake of the future and for peace. This would not be easy, but the past should be laid to rest. Some detainees and some communities felt that some should be compensated: when Waira Kamau returned with the rest of the detainees in 1962, he received lavish gifts. Though harder for some communities than for others, words such as Mau Mau member, Homeguard, or loyalist were to be erased from one's vocabulary.

The Thuita dead had not been killed by members of their own *mbari*, and *mbari* unity had not been harmed. The oneness of Igi had been undermined by Marige, and by the end of the Emergency the *muramati* led all elders in a renewal of the Igi *mbari* oath. This should restore the peace; the population and the land should acknowledge that they were one; its recent history should no longer exist. Thuita *mbari* and the members of Igi planted *matoka* lilies between the different *mbari* to acknowledge their separateness. They planted *mukungugu* between the *ithaku* to indicate their separateness and unity within a *mbari*. Neither Thuita nor Igi marked their boundaries with the settled area: it was their land, and *weiyathi* would see its return.[29]

The Emergency, Marige & the End of Mau Mau

Notes

1. The special tax was instituted by the end of 1953. The government used most of its manpower to hunt 'terrorists' and to protect the European population. This was the impetus for the forming of local Homeguard groups by January 1953, though district officials had pressed for them earlier. The Roman Catholic Church had also encouraged its younger members to form their own defence groups somewhat earlier; these groups were known as *njama* or *athigari*. The Kikuyu Guard saw duty in neighbouring forest areas and their districts. By August 1954 almost 10 per cent of rural males were involved.
   1954. *The Kenya Emergency*, Report of the Kenya War Council, Reference Division of the Central Office of Information, No. R.2940 20/10/54, London. APP.B. Contained detailed breakdown of Emergency statistics.
2. In the last year before and during the Emergency, Kikuyu leaders who were opposed to Mau Mau and therefore seen as 'stumps' were in danger; those who used violence against Mau Mau or betrayed where gangs or arms were hidden were high on Mau Mau lists to be killed. Whether or not they had engaged in violence, all Homeguards were in danger, often because they threatened Mau Mau access to new members, contributions, food or control.
   Not all killings were Mau Mau; it was sometimes made into a scapegoat for impecunious City Council or estate owners to rationalize deaths caused by lack of police protection in locations and 'labour lines', where the atmosphere of anxiety and violence had increased drinking, and fights which easily escalated into killings. One local man deeply involved in Mau Mau was executed for what was termed a Mau Mau killing, though it had involved a 'normal' fight. Two other deaths were attributed to Mau Mau gangs; one involved a Homeguard who had warned his employer about an armed gang or a cache of weapons. The other death was almost certainly personal and not Mau Mau related, though the killers were Mau Mau and the victim a Homeguard. The victim was invited to a beer drink and beheaded when intoxicated.
3. If the *Muhimu* in 1953 could spare ten guns for the control of what was only a small territory, it probably had more arms than Corfield presumed on the testimony of the Arms and Ammunition Investigation Unit, which estimated that the maximum number of precision weapons in terrorist hands would have been 1,030.
   1960. Corfield Report, *op. cit.*, pp. 232ff.
4. Use of the drug was apparently common during Mau Mau. *Bang* or *bangi* was supposed to give a pleasurable sensation of safety and reduce fear. But according to Mau Mau members and others, it also led to loss of judgment and memory. Whether this indeed was the case or whether the combination of alcohol and *bangi* induced temporary amnesia, takers believed that once they had taken *bangi*, they could no longer remember what they had or had not done, and they might have committed all sorts of criminal acts even though they did not remember this. This gave Mau Mau leaders a hold; they could force *bang* users into service by threatening to reveal crimes they had committed on other occasions, whether or not they had done so.
   The marigold flower was called *bangi*. In 1942 a *riika* was called *gicina bangi*, to burn the marigold; male and female initiates had behaved inappropriately and danced together after burning the flowers and seeds.
   The brewing of beer before the raid shows planning; it used the traditional fruit from the *Kigelis Africana*, also known as the sausage tree; during the Emergency brewing beer was a punishable offence.
   1971. Wamweya, J., *Freedom Fighter*, translated from the Kikuyu by Ciia Cerere, Nairobi: East African Publishing House, pp. 58, 59.
5. The first murder involved extensive genital mutilation. Like many other officials, agricultural assistants had to cope with contradictory expectations. Their employer expected them to enforce Western ideas - in this case about proper land use and soil conservation - while the Kikuyu expected them to honour traditional relationships and

260

The Emergency, Marige & the End of Mau Mau

to be aware of what they could or could not do. Unfortunately for agricultural officials, compliance could be seen at a glance and they therefore had to be far more unyielding than other Kikuyu officials, who could hide their non-compliance or compensate the population for onerous duties.

1974. Wanyoike, E. N., *op. cit.*, p. 200.

6. In Kikuyu law, murder between close kinsmen ranks as self-mutilation and is beyond compensation. Perpetrators may however be cursed or forced to leave. Whether the gang had still sufficient awareness to purposely involve Gitau members in the murder of another Gitau member or not, their presence protected the gang and their *ithaku* from demands for compensation.
7. 1953. Supreme Court of Kenya, Nairobi. Emergency Assize Criminal Case no. 38 of 1953. 10-9-1953. Police Case File No. CEF 32/53, 16-6-1953, Marige Police Post.
8. 1953. Supreme Court of Kenya, Nairobi. Emergency Assize Criminal Case no. 38 of 1953. 10-9-1953. Police Case File No. CEF 32/53 27-4-1953, Marige Police Post.
9. 1953. Supreme Court of Kenya, Nairobi. Emergency Assize Criminal Case No. 38 of 1953. 10-9-1953. Statement made before Mr G. F. Sagar, 1st Class Magistrate Kiambu, on Saturday 18 April 1953. 1953 Kiambu No. CEF 32/53 18-4 1953.
10. 1953. Supreme Court of Kenya, Nairobi, Emergency Assize Criminal Case No. 38 of 1953,10-9-1953 with Appendices.
11. 1953. Supreme Court of Kenya, Nairobi. Emergency Assize Criminal Case No. 38 of 1953. 10-9-1953. Police Case File No. CEF 32/53 16-5-1953 Marige Police Post.
12. Security forces as well as Homeguards might act brutally to women connected with Mau Mau activities. The government believed that women, particularly young girls, were forced into Mau Mau from fear that they would otherwise not be marriageable, and that Mau Mau offered a social status to women who had become outcasts in their own society. The president of the East African Women's League was convinced that so many women were involved in Mau Mau that they had become and would remain unsuitable role models for their daughters, and the care and teaching of these Kikuyu girls should be placed in the hands of Anglican or Roman Catholic nuns.

    1953. *Kikuyu Women and Mau Mau*, Office of the District Commissioner, Nyeri, 25 May, cyclostyle.

    1954. *East African Standard*, 3 February. Speech by Lady Sidney Farrar, president, at a council meeting of the East African Women League, Gitgil Country Club.
13. 1974. Wanyoike, E. N., *op. cit.*, pp. 200ff. This part of the Marige events is narrated by Wanyoike's grandson, who helped his grandfather with the manuscript.
14. 1953. *East African Standard* 7 April, 9 April 1953; and

    1953. *East African Standard* Supplement, Friday 10 April.

    According to the Reports *no* guns were used in the attacks, only '*simis* and *pangas*'.
15. Local inhabitants felt threatened by Nairobi Mau Mau but there is evidence that the *Muhimu* used local men for local cases.
16. 1953. *East African Standard*, 10 April.
17. As brutal as Mau Mau was in its methods to force the population to do its bidding, brutality against Mau Mau was equally pervasive and often went unchecked by the authorities. This was one of the reasons for the eventual departure of Sir John Whyatt, Attorney General. I am grateful to Dr Anthony Clayton for the opportunity to look at the papers mentioned below.

    1952. 2 April, Report of I. S. M. Henderson *The Extent of Illegal Oath Taking - Nyeri District.*

    1954. 4 December, Letter DO Mathira Division to District Commissioner Nyeri.

    1954. 17 December, Letter K. P. Haddington, Assistant Commissioner of Police Nyeri to Commissioner of Police Nairobi.

    1954. 23 December, Report by D. Macpherson, Assistant Commissioner of Police (Crime) to the Commissioner of Police, Nairobi.

    1955. 3 January, Letter Sir John Whyatt to Governor of Kenya re: march on Government House as demonstration of protest.

    1956. 22 September, Sir John Whyatt re: intended negotiations with Kenyatta before the Emergency.

The Emergency, Marige & the End of Mau Mau

1956. Extensive Correspondence of Sir John Whyatt, Attorney General with the Governor of Kenya and the reactions of the African Unofficial Members Organisation to his Departure in 1955.

1959. Maxwell, Andrew, and Frank Morris, 'Brutality in Kenya', *Contemporary Issues*, Vol. 10, November–December, pp. 1–9.

18. At least one camp used psychological intimidation. On arrival, detainees would first be classified as 'grey' or 'black', depending on the severity of their suspected involvement and attitude during interrogation. Detainees who refused to cooperate were first segregated and eventually designated 'hard core', and taken to special detention camps such as Lamu, Manyani, or Hola. On 3 March 1959, 85 men in the 'special', i.e., hard core detention camps at Hola had refused to work as they regarded themselves as political prisoners. Though it was initially reported that some of them had died from contaminated water, autopsies showed that 11 had been beaten to death by the guards. This tragic event led to strong protest in England and an official Commission of Inquiry.

1954. *Report on the Sociological Causes Underlying Mau Mau, op. cit.* A Appendix: Memorandum on the Methods Used at Bahati Resistance Movement Center on the Psychological Breaking Down of Mau Mau, pp. 1, 2.

1959. *Report of the Committee on Emergency Detention Camps* (Chairman R. D. Fairn), Nairobi: Government Printer.

1959. Cmnd 778 *Documents Relating to the Death of Eleven Mau Mau Detainees at Hola Camp in Kenya*, London: HMSO, June.

1959. Cmnd 795 *Record of the Proceedings and Evidence in the Inquiry into the Death of Eleven Mau Mau Detainees at Hola Camp in Kenya.* London: HMSO.

1959. Cmnd 816 *Further Documents Relating to the Death of Eleven Mau Mau Detainees at Hola Camp in Kenya*, London: HMSO, July.

19. The *Kiama kia Muingi*, or *Mwangi*, was probably started by ex-detainees in 1956 or 1957. It operated during 1962 under the watchful eye of local KANU officials. Other secret societies in 1962 were also using oaths. Most were small and preoccupied with what should be done to the Europeans after Independence.

20. About 35,000 men were removed from Nairobi by Operation Anvil and Operation Broom in the Thika area. Many males were disturbed that they were punished for oaths taken several years before: they had abandoned Mau Mau, and if they ever had been active they were so no longer. Sixty-two men from the local area were among the detainees; at least forty others were repatriated. When they slowly were allowed to return from 1957 onwards, many found that their Nairobi jobs had been taken by Luo or Akamba.

1954. Official Correspondence, Central Office of Information, London, to G. Sluiter, No. R2940 20/10/54.

21. They denied that their kin had played a part in Marige, yet they were killed or detained.

22. Court of arbitration at the Land Known as Githuya on 15 June 1955, Mbira Githiku, Chairman. Only a few official decisions were available.

23. These became a new source of anger for the land poor, who liked the village no better than those with more land. They had to remain in the village and had to pay a quarter acre of their already small tracts for village land; they argued that a quarter acre could have given sufficient space for a homestead on their land.

24. The required acreage for coffee was in later years reduced to two acres and coffee increased rapidly. By the end of 1957 59 men in Igi were allowed to grow coffee and they had 13,560 trees. Thuita had only seven owners and 1,500 trees. Independence removed the bar against Mau Mau members, and in 1962 Igi had 131 owners with 127,339 trees; Thuita had 94 growers with 41,319 trees.

25. All Kikuyu lost their homesteads, and had to buy the material and provide the work for a new one. At least two women and 19 men lost their lives in anti-Mau Mau actions; one woman, one man, and two children were killed by Mau Mau and others seriously hurt. Fourteen per cent (103 out of 734) of all males were detained for shorter or longer periods, some for as long as eight years; at least 14 women were detained as well. The screening committee assessed 1,034 fines for a total of shs 21,257 which was paid to the

The Emergency, Marige & the End of Mau Mau

ADC. About a quarter of this came back to the local community for local public works and food distribution. In 1955 fines in Kiambu as a whole netted shs 847,000; in 1956 shs 1,809,100. Data for preceding years are not available. Men or women unable to pay their fines had to provide *gitati* or, if unwilling, were detained. On 24 December 1952 an Emergency tax was imposed on all male oath takers over 18; though it was initially for two years only, it was extended year after year. In 1955 the special tax for Komothai yielded shs 21,300; in the first eight months of 1956 shs 17,000. Roughly a quarter of the Komothai special tax would have come from the local area.

Kikuyu who had not taken oaths suffered less, but were often treated badly in spite of their so-called loyalty. They should have prevented the rise of Mau Mau; that they had not made them guilty as well.

Mau Mau members were denied the right to vote in the 1957 election. Votes were given for wealth, age, and government service; a person could have up to three votes. An analysis of local data shows that of 150 male *ahoi*, of whom 51 were allowed to vote, nine did – casting a total of 17 votes. Of the 331 males who owned subsistence tracts, 126 were allowed to vote; 17 voted and cast a total of 27 votes. Of 96 small peasants 31 were allowed to vote; 18 did and cast 23 votes. Of 122 peasants 79 could have voted; 35 did so, casting 71 votes. Of the 29 small farmers 11 were allowed to vote, and cast 22 votes. Of the six farmers four were allowed to vote; two did and cast six votes.

1956. 4 September, Official Correspondence District Commissioner's Office Kiambu to G . Sluiter, Ref . No Fin. 4/2/2/2/398.

1956. KBU/45 AR/331.

MSS Afric.s.839 (1) HOR Kandara Division Fort Hall R .H. L. W. S. Thompson.

26. Kenyatta was convicted of managing Mau Mau on 8 April 1953; he was allowed to return to Kikuyu country on 14 August 1960. He became Prime Minister on 1 June 1963. Kenya became independent on 12 December 1963.

27. Ex-Senior Chief Koinange Mbiu, when very old and detained, first declared that he had never had anything to do with Mau Mau. In 1956 he denounced Mau Mau; in 1957 he admitted that he participated in a committee headed by Jomo Kenyatta. He retracted the statement that he had never had anything to do with Mau Mau, but did not declare the committee of which he was a member to be Mau Mau.

1952–6. Marsabit District Annual Reports PC/N FD1/2/5, Classification Secret.

28. According to D. S. Penwill, District Commissioner of Kiambu during the research period, Kenyatta had been 'made to understand' that land consolidation neither could nor should be undone. 28 July 1962.

29. *Matoka* (*amaryllidaceae*); the darker-coloured variety of this lily was used to mark the boundary of an estate. *Mukungugu* (*commiphora zimmermannii*); shade tree used to mark sub-divisions of an estate.

1977. Leakey, L. S. B., *op. cit.*, Vol. 3, pp. 1306, 1307, 1349.

Appendix I

*Data,
Reliability and Analysis*

1. Method of work

The Preface has described the Emergency restrictions on collecting data and the need for a second period of fieldwork. The bulk of the data were collected in 1956–7; analysis afterwards showed that the economic data were of little value while the lack of dating of Mau Mau oaths prevented proper analysis. The second fieldwork period in the summer of 1962 concentrated on these areas.

During the first period my assistant and I prepared genealogies for loss of life in the late nineteenth-century famine, descent, inheritance of land and present holdings, initiation years and generation. A protocol was drawn up for each household; it was anchored in a questionnaire – changed at least ten times as knowledge grew – which noted family composition, marriages, brideprice, birth and death, education, crops, lifestock and wage income. A special section noted Mau Mau participation and retribution by the government. My assistant or I wrote the information down in the presence of those interviewed; the formal questions were part of a more general conversation. My assistant, or both of us, spoke at least once with one or more adult members of each household. This led to information from 569 households; well over 1,700 men and women, all at least 14 years old at the Declaration of the Emergency, took part. Regular meetings with *arumati* of *mbari* or *ithaku* and the council of elders were part of the process; informal encounters provided as much, if not more information than formally arranged meetings.

Data from Rift Valley repatriates who had returned in or before 1950, and did not intend to return to the Rift Valley, were merged with the general population. Repatriates who had come later and/or intended to return to the Rift Valley were kept distinct. This affected a population of 125 males and 129 females; some of their information is contained in Appendix VI.

The 1956–7 refusal rate was a low of about 2 per cent: those who had opposed Mau Mau saw no reason to hide this fact and many who had put their faith in Mau Mau were eager to explain their oaths to counteract the barrage of anti-Mau Mau propaganda of the government. In 1962 the refusal rate was close to 12 per cent. At that time the incoming Kenyatta government had made it clear that it frowned on the discussion of Mau Mau membership or non-membership. This was welcome to the broad middle range of members – even when they had hoped for compensation of their suffering – but a disappointment to those who had been actively involved in Mau Mau. Most refusals came from those who had not taken oaths; that population may have seen more value in the government's

Appendix I: Data, Reliability and Analysis

decision to 'bury the past' than those who had taken oaths. Because the study had been concerned with those who had participated in Mau Mau, refusals had little influence.

2. Oral traditions

Arumati and ordinary members of *mbari* provided a wealth of information about settlement, land acquisition and transactions. While *mbari* members and *ahoi* might make statements about their own rights or absence of rights, senior males in the *mbari* were the official informants. Individual contributions which were given alone would soon become known and might bring reactions from senior members of other *mbari* or *ithaku*.

Given the nature of the oral traditions, it is not possible to decide which of the many versions provided by men who often disagreed with each other was 'true' in the sense of being most 'factual'. Neither was this their prime role; their function was to provide an account of the past which explained and gave moral and political sanction to the present. Oral histories therefore agreed or conflicted to the degree that men disagreed about the morality and acceptability of the present.

The members of *mbari* and their *ahoi* were survivors of two disastrous famines with great loss of life and European alienation with equally disastrous loss of land. Each generation had handed down that information which validated the survivors; those who received the information would do the same when they gave information to their sons. The vantage points of survivors' traditions would consequently diverge and conflict. The information I received figured largely in land litigation caused by an expanding population, the possibility of commodity production and a dwindling land resource – a contest which had elevated oral histories to arbiters of fact. It is fair to say that conflict was played out in and through oral tradition.

The manuscript outlines only those oral traditions or parts of them which were of help in understanding twentieth-century conflict, some of it in the context of Mau Mau. It excludes most material, conflicting or not, which remained outside that context. The traditions, used or not, were acquired during a number of sessions, often devoted to only one purported set of events. This necessitated combining information from different sessions to create a coherent whole. Some of the shorter accounts cover only one session though the material is translated and edited for the readers. Appendix II provides oral traditions which are relevant to the general history; they are mainly concerned with early Thuita history. It gives insight into the acquisition of land and early history.

3. Oaths

The information about oaths and punishment for oaths is highly reliable. Oath takers were not included on the list of 'loyal Kikuyu' provided by the government; most oaths were common knowledge and screening committees were required to provide written proof of confessions and assessment of fines or detention. I relied on statements of informants and did not ask for written confirmation. In 1956–7 documentation of the screening committees was still classified; in 1962 it had apparently been destroyed.

While information about first and second oaths was easily provided, information about subsequent oaths was not. I accepted without further question the statements

Appendices

of some that they had taken 'more' oaths; I felt it inappropriate to ask about matters which might invoke the fear of *thahu*.

4. Punishments for oaths

Again, I did not ask for written evidence but relied on the statements of informants, who turned out to be highly reliable. Accusations of malfaisance by screening committee members or others were often couched in complaints of having been forced to pay 'without papers', i.e. without evidence. Data for the total fines paid by each village were provided by adding the legal fines. In 1956–7 the District Office had data about fines paid by communities but they were not broken down into smaller units. Such information was no longer available in 1962, either. Nor were data for detention or imprisonment officially available; they too were provided by those involved. Informants rarely used European time to relate their affairs; yet their information about detention was expressed in precise European time: an informant might have been arrested 20 April 1954 and reported 11 September 1956 as his date of release.

5. Time of oath taking

This information, though volunteered by some, was not collected systematically until 1962; for those who had joined in the late 1940s, this was 12–14 years after the event. Reliability therefore cannot be taken for granted.

Though the more educated might date their oath according to European years, many others dated according to Kikuyu events. It was not uncommon that 'when' and 'why' were merged: 'I took the oath when I heard about Beecher.'

European years were a dubious sorting method: few Kikuyu used them to indicate periods in their lives and, if they used years, precision was often lacking. A statement that they had taken an oath in 1951 might mean any time from late 1950 to early 1952. When 'when' and 'why' were merged, this was equally the case. An oath taken 'because of Beecher' had likely been taken in 1950, though it could be later.

I dated by grouping oaths around Kikuyu events; for the local area I chose the Beecher Report, the Declaration of the Emergency (October 1952) and the local Marige attack (April 1953) The periods are of different duration; some are open, others closed. The dating before the Beecher Report is most open, least specific or reliable in European years: the dating after the Beecher Report but before the Emergency is, in so far as I can judge, more or less synonymous with 1951 or 1952 before the Declaration of the Emergency. The period between the Declaration of the Emergency and Marige is closed, short and specific. The period after Marige is open, non-specific and long; it had little local value, as any desire to join Mau Mau after Marige was virtually gone. The period after the Emergency, but before Marige, is closed, specific and short; it has the highest reliability.

6. Dating of oaths and correlation with other factors

While the dating of oaths was important to an understanding of the growth and decline of Mau Mau, correlation of the time of oath taking with economic or other

Appendix I: Data, Reliability and Analysis

factors of that period would have demanded a far broader range of data than I had available or could collect. The Emergency itself brought many economic changes in its wake; many lost income and livelihoods, while some commodity producers gained. Even if one could ignore this, that those who did not take oaths could not be assigned to any period created a significant problem.

For all these reasons causal factors for oath takers and non-takers were standardized at just before (at most a month) the Emergency.

7. Where oaths were taken

These data are broadly reliable, but lack the specificity of other data; they were not collected systematically until 1962. In the early years of oath taking, oaths were geographically distinct, as was the kind of Mau Mau which was joined. Rift Valley oaths were taken there; though they might pledge adherence to Kiambu's Kenyatta, oath takers were under the authority of Rift Valley Mau Mau leaders. In addition to the Rift Valley, there were other 'outside' centres: one of them was Arusha in Tanzania.

The preponderance of local oaths were either Githunguri or Kenyatta oaths and Nairobi oaths; unlike the Rift Valley and the Arusha oaths, by the Emergency the population accepted both as different but valid Mau Mau oaths. Whether Nairobi centres allowed Githunguri oath takers to participate in ritual, I do not know; Githunguri oath takers accepted Nairobi men without demanding that they retake their oath. Informants thought that Kenyatta oaths by and large had been taken only when people were invited and wanted to join; a significant number of Nairobi oath takers had taken them for protection and economic reasons.

Where the place of oath taking initially reflected different loyalties, by 1950/1 this could no longer be assumed without other information. By this time Nairobi expanded its claims into the rural area during the unrest over the Beecher Report. Its oaths were then given in rural homesteads by urban males; rural women carried the revenue to Nairobi. My data do not indicate a similar Kiambu expansion into Nairobi.

8. Age

These data are reliable within their broad categories. Many older and a large number of younger Kikuyu could not give a specific year of birth. It was consequently calculated from their initiation years; the age of initiation for girls – who had to be initiated before the menarche – was set at 13/14. In the late nineteenth and early twentieth century males might be initiated as early as 15 or 16 or as late as their early twenties.

From the 1920s onwards calculation of the year of birth from initiation years became more problematic. Neither girls nor boys might be initiated; boys might be circumcised in hospitals at birth. More individuals could give their age as the number of males and females who had gone to school and had learned their age at home or in school began to rise. When males lacked this information, I assumed that males initiated between the First World War and *Shilling* (1923) were 17 years old at the time of the ritual. Males initiated after *Shilling* but before *Ngigi* (1929/30) were presumed to have been 14 at that time.

Males and females were grouped in five categories on the basis of traditional male categories: those less than 19 (when girls might well be married), youth

Appendices

(19–25), junior elders (26–40), senior elders (41–60) and judicial or religious elders (61 and over).

Age categories are more reliable for younger males and females but are increasingly 'fuzzy' for groups 26 and above. I can only hope that the number of men and women who were classified as 26 and over, but were 24, is matched by the number of individuals who were classified as 24, but were 26. Age has not been correlated with Mau Mau membership; correlation of initiation years and Mau Mau participation is provided in Appendix IX/2.

9. Data on domicile

Domicile of the population was divided into the local area or Nairobi; for Nairobi workers domicile coincided with place of work. This group was overwhelmingly male; they have been regarded as a Nairobi population. Members of their households or other males might live locally and work in the settled area, Kiambu, Ruiru or Githunguri. They returned home daily or at least weekly, and have been regarded as a local population. The local population contained a very small number of men who just before the Emergency worked in Tanganyika. Most were arrested and detained, returning to the local area in 1954 or 1955. Because their number was small and most members of their households were local they have been merged with the local population. Data on domicile were reliable and have been coordinated with Mau Mau membership.

10. Economic classifications

Appendix IV provides many economic data; their source is indicated before the footnotes. Some economic data are more important than others.

Land constituted the major economic variable. During the initial fieldwork period, I had attempted to calculate the yield of each holding according to a fixed formula. To produce land income for an individual, yields were divided in adult or children's shares; when a man lived in Nairobi his share was reduced by a third. The base of these data was weak; even when used for the 1956–7 period, data with their presumption of accuracy were often unreliable. Having decided that oaths had to be correlated with economic conditions at the time of oath taking, multiplied the inherent problem of assessing individual land income.

How to assess the land factor was extensively discussed with an advisory committee of local producers, the *Mbari ya Igi* Agricultural Committee (MAC). It rejected the individual approach as unreliable: commodity producers might perhaps remember how much they had sold and at what prices, but small producers whose land produced most of their subsistence would neither know how much their land had produced, nor how much – domestic – labour had been involved, nor how much produce had been harvested or traded in the local market.

It might be possible to calculate what one acre of land, under different modes of cultivation, ideally could produce during certain periods. This method would ignore most factors related to individual use; it would only take into account whether the land was used for domestic or commodity production, whether it was fallowed, and if so to what extent. It would also consider whether manure was used, how much and at what cost; whether the land was used for monocropping or intercropping. In some cases, particularly in cases of poverty, the density of

Appendix I: Data, Reliability and Analysis

certain crops, such as maize, would be regarded a factor.

If the land was used specifically for commodity production, the cost of labour and marketing was also included. Using these factors, it could be calculated whether an actual plot of land – all things being equal – was potentially able to support an average household or whether it could produce a surplus for sale.

These data have been collected in Appendix IV/8–14; they are extensively discussed in Chapter 5. The Committee could provide information from personal experience for the period just before the Emergency; its memory for the profiles needed for 1939 and before the Carter Commission was more limited. This information was provided by the Kiambu Department of Agriculture and in 1962 by Mr James Mburu, agricultural officer for Kiambu. The pre-Emergency data are highly reliable; the earlier data should be handled with caution though they are valuable in that they show trends.

On the basis of MAC information land owners were divided into six categories, discussed in Chapters 3 and 5. Oath takers and non-takers were regarded as members of households which belonged potentially to a specific category. Those in the categories landless and land poor may have been somewhat better off than data indicate; before land consolidation *ahoi* and land poor were still allowed to use land of owners, though often no more than an acre or so. The data were correlated with oath taking throughout.

11. Information about the size of land holdings

In 1956 land consolidation had recently been completed; the allotment received by owners equalled the sum total of the measured fragments which had made up their earlier possession. All owners had to donate 0.6 per cent of their holding – regardless of the size of their land – for public purposes. They also had to surrender 0.25 acre for their own village plot; government intended that most small holders would continue to live in villages; only large land holders would be allowed to live on their land. Not only the land owners, but also the district office in Kiambu had the relevant data.

The majority of land owners accepted their allocation, although complaints about the location of their new land and allegations of having received inferior land were numerous (Appendix X/1).

Almost everyone knew the size of their land and could extrapolate what they had owned just before the Emergency. Though congruence between the size of the land specified on the certificates was high, as there had been few changes since the Emergency, some owners had pooled their land and registered it in the name of one member, often a senior brother or father, in the hope of being able to grow coffee. In that case one had to enquire which fragments had been used at that time by which *mbari* member. All information was checked with senior members of the *githaku* and *mbari*.

Land used by *ahoi* and poor *mbari* members was not subtracted from the holdings of owners, nor were the users credited with what they used. By the Emergency, usufruct was tenuous and allocations might change from season to season.

12. Wages

Men and women who worked for wages in the local or settled area had often

Appendices

continued in the same job for years; changes in wages had been slow and few. As information from one person could be checked or augmented from others working in similar jobs, with only minor variations in wages, local and settled area data, including data on the employment of women, are more reliable than Nairobi information.

Nairobi workers – but for domestic workers – had changed employers and jobs frequently; they had had long but irregular periods of unemployment. In the early decades of the century the number of Nairobi workers was relatively small; many of these men were in 1956–7 older – if not old – local residents who had long since left Nairobi. While their information for work conditions and life in town might be reliable, their memories of wages and the cost of living in Nairobi were hazy. That relatively few local men had worked in Nairobi under similar conditions made it impossible to standardize Nairobi conditions for that period. Discussions about early Nairobi conditions therefore lack precision; what was available from older local men was augmented by the cited literature.

From the late 1930s and 1940s Nairobi memories are more precise; they could be compared and standardized. Informants were asked in what job and where they had worked just before the Emergency. They were asked what they had earned by day, week or month; an annual mean wage was calculated from reported information; it was based on employment over 10 months of a calendar year. In the early decades few Nairobi men – except for domestic workers – would work that long; periods of work were regularly interspaced with periods of 'rest' at home. By the 1950s many would have liked to work the year round, but only the upper echelons of the clerical and domestic workers would be so employed (Appendix IV/15, 16). Workers were classified according to three specific work areas; type of work was assigned to one of three 'classes'; each class had several sub-classes with a mean wage. The information can only be used to show gross differences between classes of work; the information in Chapters 4 and 5, particularly in so far as it deals with Nairobi employment, can only show broad trends. While correlating sub-classes with Mau Mau involvement is not without merit, correlating sub-classes and Mau Mau involvement is considerably less reliable.

Appendix II

Oral Traditions

1. Oral traditions of Thuita

The settlement got its name around 1870 with the arrival of a large buyer, who had come from a Murang'a ridge called Thuita. Like Igi, its nineteenth-century territory probably included land which in the twentieth century had become part of the settlements of Kibichoi and Kiratina; some Thuita *mbari ithaku* were equally part of those settlements. Nineteenth-century Thuita was thus larger than colonial Thuita which had not been created along *mbari* boundaries.

Two of its twentieth-century *mbari* were formed before *Kirika*; others may have existed at that time as well but left, sold or died out without leaving a record. Several *mbari* were formed after *Kirika*; some of these sold their land and left in the nineteenth century, others in the twentieth. It is likely that some died out in the *Ng'aragu ya Ruraya*.

The 1956-7 data cover 11 *mbari*; two had been formed before *Kirika*, seven in the nineteenth century after *Kirika*, two had been created or were being created in the twentieth century. Igi land had formed Thuita's southern boundary, the Komathi river may have been its northern boundary. In the nineteenth century its land stretched to the confluence of the Komathi and Karia rivers; much of that land was taken during alienation. The traditions were provided by *arumati* and senior *mbari* members; most were obtained during several interviews at different times; some were given in one session. The second part of Appendix II gives some glimpses of oral traditions from Igi relevant to its history and to Kikuyu cultural perceptions.

Pre-Kirika mbari

The first pre-*Kirika mbari* had been created by two 'brothers'; the descendants of one of them left or died some time during the nineteenth century. More 'brothers' had come during that time, but they received only small tracts of land and left eventually. The *mbari* lost much of its large tract when members violated a *kirumi* against sales; it lost additional land – in Kibichoi when it had to pay compensation for a murder by one of its members. He was expelled, he may have become an *muhoi*, or, if he retained some land, Igi's *muthami*. There were other *kirumi* violations; they were blamed for the loss of almost two thirds of the *mbari* population during the *Ng'aragu ya Ruraya*, In the twentieth century the *mbari* lost much of their remaining land land to alienation. A number of survivors went to the Rift Valley, they did not return in the Emergency.

Some violations of *kirumi* resulted in the loss of domicile; the most serious offences meant deprivation of land and all *mbari* rights. Igi was often the refuge of

Appendices

choice; those who had retained land became its *athami*, others its *ahoi*. Yet Igi did not welcome everyone; its tolerance did not extend to *mbari* which had a reputation for fights or aggression, or to those where members had been accused of witchcraft. In keeping with a widely held tolerance for offences committed as a result of drinking, Igi did accept men or women accused of murder or mayhem if such offences had occurred in the heat of an argument or *njohi-ini*, 'in drink'.

The loss of domicile can be illustrated from another pre-*Kirika mbari*.

It had no injunction against land sales and sold frequently to *ahoi*. Land transactions demanded exogamy between buyers and sellers; it was violated when the son of a *muhoi*, who was in the process of buying land from the *mbari*, impregnated a *mbari* girl. The onus was on the selling *mbari* segment; it lost its residence rights but not its land and and took refuge with Igi. Because the *muhoi* was also negotiating with the original owner, the *mwathi*, from whom the girl's *mbari* had bought, he had powerful protection and could continue its negotiations to buy land.

The settlement of Maasai and their integration in Kikuyu society is demonstrated by the following post-*Kirika* tradition.

Between 1840 and 1850 a Maasai who until then had lived with the Ndorobo, founded a *mbari*. He bought, probably at different times, two separate tracts, one in the Thuita–Kibichoi area; the other tract would eventually be lost in alienation. The first tract may have been over two hundred acres; its price was unknown. It had no injunction against sales and probably sold land, until an expanding descent group and a shrinking land base forced it to reserve all land for descendants. It used to be one of the strongest Thuita *mbari* with many *ahoi*. As Kiambu Kikuyu needed some non-Kikuyu for certain rituals, they welcomed such settlers or *ahoi*. This *mbari* produced a famous curer; it also provided leaders in wars with the Maasai.

Prices for acquisitions were not remembered until well after *Kirika*; some were for 'raw' land, some for land which had at least been partially cleared. *Ahoi* habitually bought in Thuita as well as in Igi; some of the buyers became Kikuyu by buying. The following traditions provide some prices for land, illustrate Maasai integration, and show problems of internal *mbari* management.

About five years after the first post-*Kirika mbari* had been formed, another male founded a *mbari* by buying one tract in Thuita and one in Kibichoi. Together they were possibly between fifty and sixty acres; they were paid for in two instalments of thirty and forty goats. The *mbari* could not sell; there is no record that the injunction was violated. It sustained heavy population losses by Maasai attacks and the famine.

Around the same time another man, possibly a *muhoi* of the pre-*Kirika* Maasai *mbari* or of Igi, founded another small *mbari* on possibly fifty acres. It had an injunction against sales and probably adhered to this.

Around 1860 still another *mbari* was formed by *ahoi* of the Maasai *mbari* which had expelled them because the sons frequently got into fights. When the father asked Igi for *muhoi* status, Igi accepted him but refused his sons. The father became a successful herder; wanting to keep his quarrelsome sons apart, he made down payments on two tracts of land in Thuita–Kibichoi and on one tract in Kabete. The sons who got the Kabete land were forced to leave; the remaining sons were allowed to form one *mbari* on the two tracts of Thuita land, but were under a *kirumi* not to live together. Both tracts together were probably around 200 acres; the cost exceeded three hundred goats. It was not fully paid until in the 1950s of the twentieth century when the last twenty goats were handed over.

In spite of the efforts of the father to teach his sons to be less belligerent,

Appendix II: Oral Traditions

the son who lived on the Kibichoi land got into a fight in Kibichoi and was killed. Most of the compensation went to the Kibichoi section of the *mbari*; the Thuita section got a token payment.

Ndorobo who had become Kikuyu often continued to sell land.

Between 1870 and 1880 a member of a Kiratina *mbari* bought about seventy acres in Thuita, retaining his Kiratina rights. According to some informants he paid for it by one payment in stock; according to another version, he gave some stock and a daughter, because the *mwathi*, whose wife had been killed in a Maasai attack, needed another wife. The buyer also gave a daughter to a Ndorobo who had become Kikuyu by taking up agriculture. This Ndorobo Kikuyu slowly sold his land; in the 1930s a descendant sold the last parcel to a *muhoi* of Igi and bought land elsewhere.

The final significant acquisition in the Thuita area was made by a single buyer, who with other kinsmen had been a *muhoi* of a *mbari* which was linked to them by kinship. When this *mbari* was assessed damages because one of its members had impregnated a girl, it asked its *ahoi*-kin for a contribution. The *mbari* could not have asked help from its *ahoi*, but could expect kinsmen to help. The kin-*ahoi* invoked their *ahoi* status and refused. The indignant *mbari* members threatened to seize their stock; the refusers decided to leave before the threat was executed. Most went to Limuru, where excellent agricultural land was available; one became an Igi *muhoi*.

This man's herding skills outranked his political acumen: when *mbari* members remonstrated that he used too much land, he accused them of being too lazy to use it themselves. Igi expelled him, and he became a *muhoi* of a Thuita *mbari* where he started negotiations with the *mwathi* from which his hosts had bought.

This transaction would have demanded exogamy for several generations between him and all others who had bought from the same *mwathi*. Nevertheless, a son of the buyer fell in love with a girl of one of the *mbari* and impregnated her. The *mbari* segment to which the girl belonged lost its residence rights; negotiations for land continued.

The buyer acquired probably more than two hundred acres in two separate tracts, much of it in the south-eastern region. He gave small acreages to distant kinsmen, because of *tha*. He remained an outstanding herder; during his lifetime he paid three hundred goats for the land, bridewealth for seven wives and for a first wife for all his sons. He did not leave an injunction against sales, but his sons put a *kirumi*. Some violated it and died in the *Ng'aragu ya Ruraya*.

Kinsmen of *mbari* members who had not participated in buying the land did not have rights in their kin's *mbari* land; close kin might belong to different *mbari*.

Just before the famine, closely related members of a Kibichoi *mbari* became *ahoi* of two separate Thuita *mbari*. One of them bought from his hosts, probably no more than ten to fifteen acres; the name for his *mbari* differed from his own original *mbari*. His kinsmen remained *ahoi* until well into the twentieth century; they retained their original *mbari* name.

2. Statements about Kikuyu history from Igi elders

Verbatim where possible; they formed part of different discussions about Igi history.

Well before Kirika

'They would break the land and the Ndorobo would come but sometimes he

Appendices

would not come because there was a forest of wild animals between them.'

Decision made by elders of Igi in litigation over one tract of land before land consolidation (23 September 1955), indicating that not all land was paid for:

'The land was originally obtained in the manner known as *kuna* by three persons....'

'Igi was formed by eight men before *Kirika*; Chege was one of them, Gitau may have been another. One of the eight adopted the *mwathi*; they sold their land after *Kirika*. The buyers also became Igi but the sellers left.'

Before or after Kirika

'It was customary in some areas to break the forest first; then the *mwathi* came and wanted goats, then you paid the *mwathi* for what you had cultivated. When you have paid him you can never be deprived of it.'

Probably before Kirika

'When Chege went into the forest, he found a small Ndorobo boy who had been left behind by Ndorobo hunters. Chege took him and provided for him and gave him a wife so he became a *ndungata* of Chege. But he worked very hard and paid Chege the *ruracio* and because he was an excellent herder he took part in the buying of Igi land....'

'These Ndorobo were living in a cave in the forest; they were very poor and stole a cow from Chege. So they were told to move out of the forest so that they could be controlled....'

'Some Ndorobo were living in the bush. They saw a man trying to steal honey ... they threw [a spear?] at him and he fell down and died. They were afraid of being caught and killed by his *mbari* and so they left and stole a cow from Chege who caught them and made them live with him. When one of Chege's sons went to raid the Kamba he found a Kamba boy in the forest. He took him home and later bought a wife for him and gave him a small land.'

After Kirika

'When the *kiama* fined — for adultery, he could not pay and wanted to sell land. There was a *kirumi* not to sell and so the *kiama* told him that he could give a small piece of land to — who was a member of another Igi segment but a *muhoi* in this Igi. This man got the land and — got goats to pay his fine.'

Appendix III

Notes on Kiambu Social Organization

1. Kiambu personalities in the early colonial period

Chege wa Kibiru

He is often mentioned in Mau Mau songs as father of the resistance. Local informants invoked him to explain their philosophy that resistance was initially best served by penetrating European power and utilizing it to strengthen the Kikuyu until they were in a position to shed the yoke.

His prophecy that Kikuyu power would return when a *thingira*, a man's hut, was built at Githunguri, was initially linked with the college which had been built there in 1939.[1] Some informants suggested that Kenyatta therefore chose Githunguri as his centre of activities.

Waiyaki wa Hinga

Having purportedly attacked an officer of the IBEAC while drunk, he was condemned to deportation. According to legend, he ordered that the *anake* should not attempt to liberate him. He died in 1892 in Kibwezi.

During the Mau Mau period he would be heralded as a forerunner of the resistance.[2] Older informants interpreted his order to the *anake* as the wise decision of a nineteenth-century elder and trader who knew that once the *anake* entered the fray, trade contacts built over decades would be lost as well as lives.

In October 1954 a Mau Mau gang abducted Mr and Mrs Gray Arundel Leakey. They died; some thought that their deaths had taken the form of a sacrifice; at least one person saw a connection between this and the death of Waiyaki.[3]

Kinyanyui wa Gathirimu

His father, Mugo, was neither a large land owner nor a member of an important *mbari*. Kinyanyui was initiated during *Nganya* (1884/5); his claim to have headed the 'Acera' is difficult to accept. It is possible that his father was a relatively recent arrival who had not yet decided on a *mbari* name but still used his *muhiriga* (clan) name.

He became a 'friendly' for successive officers of the IBEA at Fort Smith and was gazetted under the Village Headman Ordinance of 1902. His services – which included punitive expeditions against the Kikuyu – were rewarded with political influence and cattle. He was appointed chief over the area south of the Rui Raka, later of the area south of the Chania river. He was gazetted on 18 March 1908.

He may have taken the name Gathirimu at that time or earlier; it is not likely

275

that he could have done so without the consent of this powerful *mbari*. He reportedly sold land to Europeans before the turn of the century. In 1899 he sold the 'occupier's rights' of a tract of land to Patrick Edgar Watcham, who received a Land Certificate for a 99-year lease.

Kinyanyui became paramount chief after the First World War, a position he held until his death in 1929. As late as 1920 local men joined with others in rejecting his ownership of land; they called him a *muhoi*.

He slowly became more active on behalf of the Kikuyu and was willing to support the Kikuyu Association demands for the return of the land. The way he had used his power earlier would create fear among *mbari*; it would harm the work of *Mbiu Koinange* and *mbari* leaders would still be fearful of the centralized control he had represented, decades after Kinyanyui's death.[4]

2. The Kikuyu as a tribe

The concept of a Kikuyu 'tribe' is more colonial and post-colonial than pre-colonial. In the nineteenth century Kikuyu were cognizant that others were Kikuyu and therefore kin, however distant, but they did not form a closed, distinct Kikuyu unit, a recognizable tribe with boundaries and common authority distinct from other similar units.

Kinship created ethnicity; those within the boundaries of kinship – widely drawn – belonged to the same ethnic group. They were bound by the same moral order; they might speak the same language; their primary mode of subsistence was agriculture. Distinct kin might live in Murang'a or Gaki; they should not be attacked 'without cause'. Local Kikuyu derived mainly from Murang'a; Murang'a men remained kin, even though they became enemies when Murang'a elders cursed the Kiambu Kikuyu for refusing to return to Murang'a for crucial ritual.

Kinship was created through common land, through marriage and descent; it was a continuing process in which populations remained with the ethnic group into which they were born or changed to another. It presupposed open boundaries; the Kikuyu did not recognize fixed boundaries in land any more than they recognized fixed boundaries in kin.

Kikuyu could become members of other ethnic groups by marrying those groups' daughters and assuming the lifestyle of the group into which they married. Local *mbari* members had come from different ethnic groups and modes of subsistence; they had joined in buying land and had become agricultural *mbari*. Their ethnic diversity had been immaterial in creating kinship through joint land holdings or intermarriage. They gave daughters in marriage or lost them in raids on other ethnic groups: these women assumed the ethnic group of their husbands. They received daughters from other ethnic groups or raided for them; these women and their children became Kikuyu.

Social and political ties were mainly localized; men might visit and interact more with neighbouring non-Kikuyu than with other Kikuyu. Interaction was most intense within a cluster, frequently composed of a large *mbari* with a number of surrounding smaller ones. Clusters interacted with adjacent Ndorobo and Maasai as well as with other clusters in an ever widening network of clusters. War, peace, marriage, migration and death altered the composition of the clusters and the networks; there were no firm boundaries; they flowed from human relationships and changed with them.

The Kikuyu system of two distinct ritual affiliations has overtones of different

Appendix III: Kiambu Social Organization

ethnic pasts, yet it cannot be described as such. While individuals might belong to the *gikuyu* or the *ukabi* (Maasai) ritual moiety, the *ukabi* moiety was open; Kikuyu of ethnic Kikuyu background could be and were its members, as were those Kikuyu whose ethnic background was not Kikuyu. Ethnic affiliation was therefore kept alive for some, but Kikuyu could choose that affiliation which served them best.

While neither affiliation bestowed political advantage, the *ukabi* moiety gave ritual advantage in that its demands were less stringent. Conditions for ritual cleanliness, *theru*, were lower for *ukabi* than for *gikuyu*; men who were *gikuyu* and were beset by misfortune, might well change to *ukabi*. This change would include their lineal descendants, who, if they so desired, could eventually change back to *gikuyu*. Data for the change from *gikuyu* to *ukabi* abound; I have no data for the reverse.

After colonial policy forbade raiding and later instituted 'reserves' for specific ethnic groups, acquiring wives across boundaries came virtually to a halt as did the change from one ethnic group to another. Intermarriage across ethnic lines became as rare as settling with another ethnic group.

The belief that there had been a 'tribe' became a self-fulfilling prophecy, as boundaries hardened and interaction was stifled. This increased sense of ethnicity fostered the sense of being a closed entity, different and distinct from other entities. Land alienation had affected other ethnic groups as well, but Kikuyu who had lost found it easier to unite with each other than with the Maasai. Education, mission activities, political activism all concentrated on one language, again strengthening the sense of separateness. In towns, men who spoke the same language congregated, separating themselves from those who spoke other languages.

3. Generation and handing over

Little is known about the generation system or the *ituika* (pl. *matuika*) by which one generation 'took over' from another. Information provided by informants varies considerably; where the ritual was held is an example of the diversity of opinion. In 1956 Dr L. S. B. Leakey was convinced that it took place at a mythological birthplace of the Kikuyu, *Mukurue wa Gathanga*, somewhere in Murang'a.[7] In 1938 Hobley had placed the ritual in the Ting'ang'a district in Southern Kikuyu, and described part of it as 'plucking hairs from the tail of the *ndamathia*', a creature somewhere between a crocodile and a snake. Leakey reports this as well.[8] Kenyatta places an *ituika* ritual in Ngenda in Kiambu.[9] In Leakey's 1977 publication, the ritual is put in Ting'ang'a, followed by a ritual for representatives of Kiambu, Murang'a and possibly Gaki in Muthaka in Gatanga, then followed by concluding ritual in Ting'ang'a.[10] Other literature does not provide a clear answer either.[11] Elders' information, though sparse, indicated that the initial rituals were localized, and slowly wound their way to each other, perhaps to a central point in Kiambu. They refused to discuss the frequency of the ritual or the ritual itself, though admitting to an alternating pattern of *Maina* and *Mwangi*.

The first *ituika* of record was one in which a *Mwangi* generation took over from a *Maina* in Murang'a where local men had gone to participate. Just before or during that ritual, a quarrel led to a break with Murang'a, and elders returned to Kiambu to hold or complete the ritual there. Their *Mwangi* generation was called *Iregi*, the protesters or revolters, because of the break.[12] Because no initiations could be held during *matuika*, local candidates 'had to wait a long time'; the first local initiation was Njoroge, which dates the *ituika* as between 1834 and 1839. The *Kirika* famine immediately following these events was associated in the mind of elders with the break with Murang'a and the anger of its elders.

After the break, all rituals – including initiations and the opening and closing of male initiations – became local or Kiambu affairs. Elders' information did not reveal what specific political powers were associated with generational 'rule'. Other information indicates that the ruling generation controlled the sacrifices of the agricultural calendar and the opening or closing of the sequence of initiation years. It therefore controlled the size of the regiments of warriors, and directed the flow of those who could enter into the elders' councils. Those who belonged to the ruling generation paid less in many rituals than those who were not ruling.

The next *ituika* – between 1858 and 1865 – took place in a period of high Kiambu immigration, increasing economic diversification, and probably increased wealth and social differentiation. No memories of special events around this *ituika* when *Maina* took over from *Mwangi* survived.

The next *ituika* from *Maina* to *Mwangi* which took place after the initiation *Mutungu* (about 1893) and before *Kienyeku* (about 1896/7) was clearly remembered. Some elders had been initiated before, others after this event; they mentioned having been ordered to drive some goats to a place 'near by', possibly Ngenda. This had been the last *ituika*: they refused to discuss why no subsequent *matuika* had been held and when they 'should have occurred'.

In a recent publication, Lonsdale suggests a link between the *matuika* and the need to cleanse the land after famines or disasters.[13] Under 'normal' conditions, the ritual would take place when a majority of the 'sitting' elders were elderly or dying; it could then be a ritual in which blessing and strength, as well as the continuity of life, were celebrated. It could also be called for in times of disaster or discontent. When many ritual elders had succumbed in a disaster, or when survivors believed that the spiritual forces had closed their ears to their pleas for help, or a younger generation felt that the 'sitting' elders had not been vigilant enough to prevent a disaster, it might be time to call for an *ituika*. This would reconcile the generations and allow ritual life to resume.

Certainly two of the three *matuika* were clearly associated with disasters, but as far as my data go, in both cases the disasters followed, rather than preceded, the *ituika*. This does not necessarily invalidate the argument as data for disasters are as scarce and difficult to obtain as data for *matuika*. It is quite possible that in both cases, *Kirika* and the *Ngarag'u*, disasters had already started or were threatening and that *matuika* were called to implore the ancestral forces to discontinue their punishment. The *matuika* would then remove the *thahu*, bringing back a state of *theru*. The explanation, however difficult to prove, is also attractive because it would explain the secrecy around *matuika*. As disasters should not be recalled, *matuika* aimed at avoiding them should not be recalled either.

Building on this theory one might argue that subsequent events showed that the last *ituika* had not halted the disasters: the arrival of many Europeans, and the loss of land, had followed. Elders could only conclude that the ancestors and the spiritual forces did not accept the *ituika*, that the atonement had not been sufficient. Proper relations were not – yet – restored; senior elders had to bring this about. All this is speculative, but inner councils, the *ndundu*, may have decided that no *ituika* should take place until they had clear evidence that the spiritual forces were favourable, perhaps evidenced by the return of the land. Independence may have ended the series of misfortunes, but by this time few would have been able to perform the appropriate ritual.

Appendix III: Kiambu Social Organization

Research data casts doubt on the assumption that all males whose fathers belonged to one generation automatically assumed in time the opposite generation. Whatever rights one might have, assumption of rights demanded payment. Those who were not 'paid for' had the right to call themselves members of a generation, but were members only in a symbolic sense: they could not attend meetings, make decisions, or reap any advantages of their status. Only those men, or their fathers, who were wealthy enough could afford the payments.

Wealth was associated with polygyny; the greater the wealth, the greater the chance that males practised serial polygyny and, probably, the greater the number of sons of varied ages. Younger wives – even if the husband had assumed generational authority just before his marriage – would continue to give birth after their husband's generation moved out of office. They might have older sons who might be able to pay for themselves, but the father who moved out of office, had to pay for the younger sons if he wanted them to be real rather than symbolic members of their generation.

He had several options: he could delay the payment and, when the sons were old enough, help them pay to assume their position. If they were very young and did not reach an appropriate age until still another *ituika* assumed office, he might help them pay to 'move down' into that generation.

Only the wealthiest could provide for all their sons; they might even provide posthumously for those born after their death by setting stock apart for this purpose. The data indicate that only the larger land owners could make provision for all their sons; smaller land owners, let alone *ahoi*, could not. Generational membership was consequently significant for some but not for others.

Larger land owners gave their own and their father's generation without a second's thought; small land owners had to think before answering; *ahoi* could rarely give their generation, nor could those who recently had bought land. It is not too far-fetched to venture that *matuika* were connected with land, that they were of great importance to large land owners and their older sons who would inherit the bulk of their estate, but of lesser importance to younger sons who inherited less, and of least importance to landless *ahoi*. This makes even more sense if, following Lonsdale, we look at the *matuika* as at least in part a ritual in which the land was purified; the largest land owners would have had far greater obligations and interest than land poor or landless.

Though my data are limited, questions must be raised about the reported payments of the incoming generation to the outgoing one.[14] The data come from 60 local men who had become *Mwangi* by the end of the nineteenth century. Of them, five said they had paid their own fees; 55 had been paid for by their fathers.[15] Genealogies and other data show that if another *ituika* been held between 1930 and 1935, 119 *Mwangi* men would have been alive; between them they would have had 223 sons waiting to become *Maina*. All these 223 men were certain that, had an *ituika* taken place, they 'would have been paid for': that is, they would have been real, not symbolic members.

Between 1930 and 1935, 119 of these men, slightly more than half, had been initiated; they might have been able to pay their own fees from earning or land. Fathers, however, would have had to pay for the remaining 104 candidates.

Elders refused information about the size of the payment; they were only willing to acknowledge that it varied. Leakey reports that each candidate had to pay three goats or rams.[16] Taking this as base, between 1930 and 1935, 223 *Maina* would have paid 669 goats to 119 *Mwangi* males – if they paid only to local men; if this

Appendices

were divided equally between them, they would each have received five or six goats. Assuming that at least two were used in sacrifices, the others would have been added to Mwangi herds.

However, as *Mwangi* fathers needed to pay for 104 candidates, 312 goats would have come from *Mwangi* herds. These *Mwangi* fathers would have received little more than they paid, while others were in a more advantaged position. What this means in the long run is an open question, because there is still another problem, in that those who paid probably got their payments back within a short time.

Some of the *Mwangi* fathers who had paid for sons were probably old and could be expected to die within the next five years or decade. Their stock would be inherited by *Maina* sons, who had paid from their own herds. Their inheritance might well contain the goats they had paid or their progeny. *Mwangi* fathers – probably younger – who had paid for younger sons received stock in the division of the payments. If they did not have too many sons for whom they had to pay, then they received more than they had paid. The 'payment' turns out to be more symbolic than real.

4. Matuika and Mau Mau

It has been suggested that the failure to perform an *ituika* in the early twentieth century may have played a role in Mau Mau, though such suggestions have also been refuted.[17] The following information provides some data.

If there was a relationship between being denied access to one's generation and Mau Mau, one would expect that the 60 *Mwangi* males still in power in 1956 would have a *lower* than normal pattern of oath taking. The group as a whole, compared with the other local males, has indeed a somewhat lower participation rate (33.3 per cent versus 59.5 per cent). This rate would have been still lower, but for the unusually high rate of oath taking among the Mwangi age group of 26–40 (93 per cent versus 60 per cent). I cannot explain this.

One cannot be certain that the low Mau Mau participation is due to generational advantages. Thirty-eight men of this group were either old or advanced in middle age. Among *Mwangi* men and the male population in general, oath taking after the age of forty is comparatively low, regardless of generation.

If being deprived of an *ituika* created discontent which found an expression in Mau Mau, there were in 1956 223 recognized *Maina* candidates who should have had higher than usual rate of participation in Mau Mau, but do not.

Their rate of 59.6 per cent is only marginally different from the overall male rate of 56.4 per cent for the male population which was not *Maina*. When broken down into age groups they show no deviation from the general patterns; oath taking is highest in the age group between 19 and 25, then tapers off to involve only 11 per cent of a numerically small group over 60.

5. Notes on colonial chiefs

The research area contained only part of one chief's territory; while this does make conclusions hazardous, the relationships in the research area were probably also unusual in that it contained a sizeable part of the chief's own *mbari*.

He was not a newcomer to local power; his grandfather and father had played

Appendix III: Kiambu Social Organization

a role in the late nineteenth-century trade and in early Kikuyu–European relationships. Their wealth and power had allowed them to give abundant *tha* to other *mbari* and *ahoi*; his inherited wealth and the astute management of his land facilitated his work and anchored his power. Members of the same *mbari* held other important local offices; client–patron relationships were common.

All communities had a certain amount of control over their chiefs or headmen; they could accuse them before the administration and endanger their reputation. The literature describes several instances of abuse by office holders; we lack an analysis of the role played by these complaints in local politics. Communities which received sufficient *tha* were more likely to support their office holders. Wealthy chiefs, who could and did provide this, were therefore more secure in their position than poor men, whatever their virtue.

Headmen and chiefs, particularly if they worked well with the *kiama*, could provide *tha*; it might range from protection from the European government to the use of land, shelter, favourable decisions in quarrels, preferential treatment when jobs became available, protection against excessive *gitati* or abusive employers. Chiefs had wide latitude as to how they used the *tha* at their disposal; although no one expected him to ignore the needs of his own *mbari*, he should not provide for it to the exclusion of others.

Discussions about the requirements for 'good' local officials mentioned that one of the key factors was that they be perceived as part of the community, owned by it rather than the administration's men. Whether a community and its Chief had participated in the nineteenth-century trade made a difference, because twentieth-century officials and their populations had then been exposed to strangers and an economy other than their own. In the twentieth century acceptance was more likely if officials had been recruited from a *mbari* which belonged to the leaders and had good working – though not dominant – relationships with the *kiama*. 'A good chief lets the *kiama* do what needs to be done, then people are not angry at him.' A chief who could get this cooperation, would have access to all *mbari* and their *ithaku*.

Chiefs might find themselves in widely different situations. To demand compliance from a population whose land had not been alienated was one thing; asking it from a population which had lost land was another. Chiefs close to settlers or administrative centres faced labour levies; those inland were spared them. On the other hand, populations distant from European areas might have to resort to migrant labour earlier than those who had a source of income close to home, and their problems would differ. Similarly, chiefs whose areas produced surplus faced different problems from those which did not produce sufficient food.

The composition of a chiefly area may have made a difference. Some may have consisted of medium or large *mbari* and their *ahoi*; others might have had a number of small *mbari* but no *ahoi*. Some chiefs had access to mission stations and could encourage education; others were far from schools. Chiefs might bring advantages to their area if they agitated for roads, clinics or manure. Chiefs opposing any new influences might have more stability in the beginning of the twentieth century, but they faced severe problems in later decades.

Kiama, headmen and chiefs suffered a loss of power when they could no longer enforce their decisions. Land became scarcer, even wealthy chiefs could no longer reward or punish by giving or withholding a significant tract of land as *tha*. Yet they were not powerless. They could protect men who were members of unpopular or forbidden organizations; they could influence the hiring policies of government departments and give some help in finding employment.

Appendices

It is not possible to draw conclusions for the acceptance of chiefs and headmen from the Emergency. A crucial factor would probably have been to what degree they could protect Mau Mau or protect the population from some Mau Mau. A cardinal rule for those in authority during the colonial period was that they protect the population from the colonial government as much as possible.

Lonsdale reports that 24 headmen and chiefs had been attacked by early 1952.[18] By the end of 1953, 28 teachers had been killed and 39 had been injured, with 55 schools destroyed.[19] Information which would help to evaluate these data is lacking.

Notes

1. 1938. Kenyatta, Jomo, *Facing Mount Kenya*, London: Secker and Warburg, pp. 41–4.
   1980. Kinyatti, Maina wa, *Thunder from the Mountains*, London: Zed Books, p. 21.
   Forthcoming. Lonsdale, John, *The Prayers of Waiyaki: Political Uses of the Kikuyu Past*, Oxford: James Currey.
2. 1966. Rosberg, Carl G., Jr., and John Nottingham, *The Myth of Mau Mau, Nationalism in Kenya*, Hoover Insitute on War, Revolution and Peace, London: Stanford Praeger, p. 13.
   1974. Muriuki, Godfrey, *A History of the Kikuyu 1500–1900*, London: Oxford University Press, pp. 150–2.
   1977. Leakey, L. S. B., *The Southern Kikuyu before 1903*, Vol. I–III, London: Academic Press, pp. 30, 31; 72–83.
   1980. Kinyatti, Maina wa, *op. cit.*, pp. 13, 25, 29.
   Forthcoming. Lonsdale, John, *op. cit.*
3. Rhodes House Documents MSS Afric. s. 742 (3) Colchester, Trevor Charles, *Note on the Association between the Death of Chief Waiyaki in 1893 and the Leakey Sacrifice during the Mau Mau Emergency*.
4. 1909. AR/15 Ukamba Province Quarterly and Special Report October–December, C. W. Hobley.
   1909. Ukamba Province Land File.
   1970. Thuku, Harry, *An Autobiography*, Nairobi: Oxford University Press, pp. 25–7.
   1974. Muriuki, Godfrey, *op. cit.*, pp. 72 *passim*.
   1974. Wanyoike, E. N., *An African Pastor*, Nairobi: East African Publishing House, p. 96.
5. 1973. Buytenhuys, Robert, *Mau Mau Twenty Years After*, The Hague: Mouton and Co., pp. 113ff.
6. 1977. Lonsdale, John M., 'When did the Gusii (and any other group) become a tribe?', *Kenya Historical Review*, Vol. 5, No. 1.
7. 1956. Leakey, L. S. B., personal communication.
8. 1938. Hobley, C.W., *Bantu Beliefs and Magic*, London: H.F. & G. Witherby, pp. 92ff.
   1977. Leakey, L. S. B., *The Southern Kikuyu before 1903*, Vols I–III, London: Academic Press, pp. 1282ff.
9. 1953. Kenyatta, Jomo, *Facing Mount Kenya*, London: Secker and Warburg, pp. 186ff.
10. 1977. Leakey, L. S. B., *op. cit.*, pp. 1283ff.
11. 1972. Kershaw, Gretha, *The Land is the People*, PhD thesis, University of Chicago, pp. 151ff.
12. From *kurega*, to reject or to refuse. Chapter 1, footnote 33 gives alternative explanations of the name *Iregi*.
13. 1992. Berman, Bruce, and John Lonsdale, *Unhappy Valley, Conflict in Kenya and Africa*, Book II, p. 346.
14. 1977. Leakey, L. S. B., *op. cit.*, pp. 1278 ff.
15. The statement could not be verified. Though the group contained a preponderance of old men, 16 *Mwangi* men had been born well after *Mwangi* took office. Many of the fathers had died.

Appendix III: Kiambu Social Organization

16. 1977. Leakey, L. S. B., *op. cit.*, p. 1284.
17. 1982. Buytenhuys, Rob, *Essays on Mau Mau Contributions to Mau Mau Historiography*, Research Reports No. 17, Leiden, the Netherlands: African Studies Centre, pp. 127ff.
18. 1992. Berman, Bruce, and John Lonsdale, *Unhappy Valley*, Books I and II, *Eastern African Studies*, London: James Currey, p. 440.
19. 1953. *Education Department Annual Report 1953*, Colony and Protectorate of Kenya, Nairobi: Government Printer, p. 27.
20. 1948. KBU/39 Kiambu HOR.

Appendix IV

Economic Data

Though not all data were produced by the local community, no data have been included which were not acceptable to it.

1. Currencies and taxes

The basic currency of the Protectorate was the rupee, divided into 16 annas or 100 cents. By 1906 the rupee was standardized at shs 1/25d: after an interval in which florins were used (1920/1) the standard currency became pounds, shillings and pence. I use shillings throughout.[1] Taxes were imposed under various hut and poll tax ordinances; their implementation might sometimes differ from area to area. In the local area the basic rate for 1901 was shs 1/25d for each occupied hut; the rate doubled in 1902 and tripled in 1906. It remained stable until 1907 when it became shs 7/– rising to shs 16/– by 1921. It dropped to shs 12/– by 1923. In 1956 the basic rate was shs 20/–.

After 1926 the basic rate was increased by levies from the Kiambu LNC; after 1949 locational taxes were added. In 1957 the local tax burden was: poll tax shs 20/–; general levy African District Council shs 17/–; educational levy shs 10/–; locational tax shs 4/–. Mau Mau oath takers also paid a shs 25/– annual punitive tax.

In the early years taxes were collected by elders and headmen, who received first 10, and later 5 per cent of the proceeds, as 'salaries'. For the first two or three years goats could be used for payment, before this was abandoned as discriminatory. Officials tended to demand one goat for each tax liability; sold, a goat might fetch more, from which under-funded colonial offices might receive some help. The flat fee tax was highly regressive; the poor might pay as much as 10 per cent or more of their income while the wealthy might pay as little as 0.1 per cent, if that. This inequality was compounded as taxes financed part of basic services such as education or health, which also demanded user fees. Poor and wealthy paid the tax, but as only the wealthy could afford the user fees the services they used were subsidized by the poor. Efforts by the colonial government to introduce a graduated income tax – which would have run into the difficulty of establishing agricultural income – had been strenuously opposed by district politicians.

2. Cost of goats

Cost depended on age, quality, ancestry, buyer and occasion. 1902 shs 4/20d; 1908 shs 5/60d.; 1910–13 between shs 7/– and shs 9/–; 1913–1917 steady at shs

284

Appendix IV: Economic Data

11/−; 1918 shs 11/−; no price for 1919; 1920 shs 10/−; 1922–25 about shs 12/−; drop to shs 10/−; slow rise afterwards. 1928 shs 12/−; 1929 shs 14/−; 1930 shs 13/−; continued slow rise by small increments; 1956 shs 20/−.

Until 1922 Kiambu District Annual Reports regularly provided prices for stock and produce, presumably for Kiambu station. It is not clear where it was obtained and during what time of the year.[2]

3. Cost of local land[3]

Before *Kĩrĩka* prime forest at about 5,000 feet about 100 acres for forty to fifty goats; one girl paid for half such an area.

After *Kĩrĩka* abandoned land with clearing(s) but possibly clouded ownership one goat.

Prime forest after *Kĩrĩka* 100 acres for forty to fifty goats.

Around 1865 at higher elevation maximum contiguous plots about seventy acres, at least two goats.

Around 1870 at higher elevation maximum contiguous plots about thirty acres; price range between three and four goats.

Around 1870 lower elevation land one goat.
Middle First World War – high status buyer, 1 goat or shs 10/−.
Between First World War I and early 1920s, five goats or shs 50/−.
Late 1920s, high-status buyer, ten goats or shs 150/−.
Before Carter Commission shs 300/−.
About 1939 shs 450/−.
End First World War shs 600/−.
Before Emergency shs 900/−.
After land consolidation shs 1.500/−.
By Independence shs 2.500/−.
Prices higher near Kiambu or Nairobi.

4. Cost of clearing land[4]

Full day of labour for males or female equated with 5–6 hours.

No estimate available for clearing of higher elevation prime forest.

Estimate clearing fallowed higher elevation land, using fire 500 days of predominantly male labour.

Estimate clearing lower elevation virgin land, using fire in some areas, about 500 days of predominantly male labour.

Estimate reclaiming long fallowed lower land, using fire, 400 days of predominantly male labour.

Reclaiming long fallowed land around 1930, no fire, no plough, 400 days of predominantly male labour.

Reclaiming long fallowed land with plough, 200 days.

Reclaiming long fallowed land with tractor and plough between 50 and 100 days (shs 50/− and shs 100/−) depending on growth.

Constructing one acre terraces   1945 shs 500/−.
                                        1950 shs 650/−.

Appendices

5. Minimum wages per day and per annum settled area[5]

Before Carter Commission	shs 0/50*d*	and shs 150/–
About 1939	shs 0/60*d*	and shs 180/–
1945	shs 0/70*d*	and shs 210/–
Before Emergency	shs 0/80*d*	and shs 240/–
1956	shs 1/–	and shs 300/–
1962	shs 2/–	and shs 600/–

6. Piece work[6]

Early piecework per acre: a quarter of annual wage.
1956. One acre beans shs 48/– (sowing, twice weeding, harvesting); one acre maize shs 34/– (sowing, thrice weeding, harvesting); one acre European potatoes shs 95/– (arranging, planting, twice weeding, harvesting). One full-time labourer was expected to care for four acres of monocropped or three acres of intercropped land.

7. Brideprices

Prices refer to the agreed price during marriage negotiations; they do not take into account whether the prices were paid or the value of the additional 'gifts' demanded throughout the marriage. According to the Kikuyu, 'a brideprice never ends'. If a man received an excessively high price for a daughter, his wife's relatives were likely to make additional demands.

Kikuyu maintain that in the nineteenth century a father, with some help from his kinsmen, paid the brideprice for a first wife for all sons before marriage, with sons responsible for brideprice for their subsequent wives. After the First World War many fathers were unable to do so; sons had to make the most of their own payments. By the Second World War only wealthy men paid and payment before marriage was rare. In 1956 only a few church members no longer insisted on receiving bridewealth. Prices cited for younger males often indicated indebtedness rather than payments.

Until the end of the First World War 90–100 per cent of the price was expected in goats; by 1925 it had dropped to 30–40 per cent. By 1935 only 10–20 per cent could be offered in goats, but receivers might ask for cash only, apart from the ceremonial goats.

Before *Kirika*	minimum 25 goats	After First World War	65–70 goats
After *Kirika*	40–50 goats	Before Carter Commission	75 goats
First World War	60–65 goats	About 1940	90 goats
Early 1920s	70 goats	Before Emergency	85 goats

By the end of the Emergency some fathers would argue that an educated girl should fetch a higher brideprice; having educated a son should lower the brideprice because his education served as a guarantee to the bride's family.

8. Production of basic foods: Grade 1, Grade 2 and DARD

The assistance of the *Mbari ya Igi* Agricultural Committee (MAC), which established

Appendix IV: Economic Data

the yields of hypothetical holdings under different conditions and gathered information about prices, is gratefully acknowledged. Data going back as far as 1939 were local prices; earlier prices were obtained from the Department of Agriculture in Kiambu. The data were submitted in 1962 to the Office of Mr James Mburu of the Department of Agriculture in Kiambu, who approved them with minor changes for basic crops but suggested major changes in the estimates for the yield of coffee.

Department of Agriculture Recommended Diet (DARD)
Staple foods per household of five adults per annum: 13¾ bags maize, 4½ bags beans, 10¼ bags potatoes.

Production of basic foods
Prices are given per bag; yields are based on three acres of land. Grade 1 produce is grown on monocropped land which before the Carter Commission was appropriately fallowed; afterwards it was manured at 80 per cent of the Department of Agriculture's recommended rate, the local rate of excellence. Grade 2 produce is grown on intercropped land; before the Carter Commission it was fallowed for half the recommended period; afterwards it was manured at 25 per cent of the local rate of excellence; intercropped land emphasized maize.

Market prices Grade 1 produce
Before Carter: Maize shs 8/50d; beans shs 17/−; E. potatoes shs 6/−.
Around 1939: Maize shs 18/−; beans shs 36/−; E. potatoes shs 8/50d.
Before Declaration of the Emergency: Maize shs 30/−; beans shs 60/−; E. potatoes shs 20/−.
1956: Maize shs 35/−; beans shs 70/−; E. potatoes shs 25/−.

Market prices Grade 2 Produce
Before Carter: Maize 6/50d; beans shs 13/−; E. potatoes shs 4/−.
About 1939: Maize shs 13/−; beans shs 26/−; E. potatoes shs 6/−.
Before Declaration of the Emergency: Maize shs 20/−; beans shs 40/−; E. potatoes shs 14/−.
1956: Maize shs 28/−; beans shs 56/−; E. potatoes shs 19/−.

9. Yield of three acres of land

This model is a simplification and standardization of a much more complex − in a good year a more productive − method of use of three acres of land. Only the three major crops are discussed; no attention is paid to sweet potatoes, millets, peas, bananas or second sowings of maize. It is assumed that all three crops used a full year, from clearing for planting to clearing after harvesting.

Yield before the Carter Commission, Grade 1
10¾ bags maize, 3¾ bags beans, 25 bags E. potatoes. To conform to the DARD, potatoes were sold and maize and beans bought. The cost of the DARD at market prices was shs 254/88d; there was an additional profit of shs 50/25d. The land produced shs 305/13d.

Yield before Carter Commission, Grade 2
23¾ bags maize, 1¼ bag beans, 3 bags E. potatoes. To conform to the DARD,

Appendices

maize was sold and second grade beans and potatoes bought. The cost of the DARD at market prices was shs 188/88*d*; the land produced shs 182/63*d* and shs 6/25*d* had to come from other sources.

Yield about 1939: 80 per cent rate manure, Grade 1
14¾ bags maize, 4¾ bags beans, 34 bags E. potatoes. Though conforming to the DARD, surplus of all crops could be sold. The market value of the DARD was shs 496/63*d*; there was an additional profit of shs 228/88*d*. The land produced shs 725/51*d*.

Yield about 1939: 25 per cent rate manure: Grade 2
29¾ bags maize; 2¾ bags beans, 9 bags E. potatoes. To conform to the DARD maize was sold and beans and potatoes bought. The cost of the DARD at market prices was shs 357/25*d*; there was an additional profit of shs 155/–. The land produced shs 512/25*d*.

Yield just before the Declaration of the Emergency, 80 per cent rate manure: Grade 1
14¾ bags maize, 4¾ bags beans, 34 bags E. pototoes. While conforming to the DARD, surplus of all crops could be sold. The cost of the DARD at market prices was shs 887/50*d*; there was an additional profit of shs 530/–. The land produced shs 1,417/50*d*.

Yield just before the Declaration of the Emergency: 25 per cent rate manure: Grade 2
29¾ bags maize; 2¾ bags beans, 9 bags E. potatoes. To conform to the DARD maize was sold and beans and potatoes bought. The cost of the DARD at market prices was shs 598/50*d*; there was an additional profit of shs 232/50*d*. The land produced shs 831/–.

10. Cost of manure (local data)

Local production from native or high-grade cattle insufficient. One high-grade cow, grazed with additional fodder, produced about 1½ tons, which was not sufficient for her pasture.

Cost manure railhead Nairobi per ton
1939 shs 8/–; 1945 shs 12/–; 1948 shs 18/–; 1950 shs 25/–; stabilized until 1956. Transport to local area doubled cost; in 1945 LNC paid half of transportation cost. Cost to buyers per ton 1939 shs 16/–; 1945 shs 18/–; 1948 shs 27/–; 1956 shs 37/50*d*.

Manuring for Grade 1 produce, 80 per cent of Department recommendation
Intercropped or monocropped potatoes, 30 tons every five years or 6 tons per year. Monocropped maize, 20 tons every five years or 4 tons per year.

Cost manure per year per acre for Grade 1 produce:
Intercropped maize, beans, potatoes or potatoes alone, 1939 shs 96/–; 1945 shs 108/–; 1948 shs 162/–; 1956 shs 225/–.
Maize monocropped 1939 shs 64/–; 1945 shs 72/–; 1948 shs 8/–; 1956 shs 150/–.

Appendix IV: Economic Data

Cost manure per year per acre for Grade 2 produce
25 per cent of local standard of excellence; 7½ tons every five years or 1½ tons per acre per year. Intercropped, maize emphasis.

Cost of manure per year per acre for Grade 2 produce
1939 shs 24/–; 1948 shs 40/50*d*;
1945 shs 27/–; 1956 shs 56/25*d*.

11. Recommended sequence of crop rotation with minimal manure (local conditions)

After application of manure, plant potatoes; follow with beans, maize, cassava, sweet potatoes. Dig in leaves of sweet potatoes for humus; manure again for next sequence of crops.

12. Cost/yield of some auxiliary crops (local data)

Sweet potatoes. Planted as leaves; crop takes 2 seasons to mature. 1956 Cost of labour – after land is prepared, before harvesting shs 85/–. One acre can produce 5 tons, need little or no manure.

Bananas. Tree will produce its first bunch after 2 years. 1956 Cost shs 35/– per tree for planting and first manuring.

Several varieties of *beans* and other pulses grown locally. Unsuitable cash crop because dependence on adequate rainfall and need for high manure. For local consumption beans at least twice as expensive as maize, some pulses more.

13. Production one acre pineapples, 1950 prices

Recurrent costs three seasons before production:
terracing	shs 650/–
planting	shs 60/–
weeding, pruning	shs 100/–

Cost during four productive seasons:
harvesting	shs 600/–
weeding	shs 100/–
transportation	shs 300/–

Total cost of production	shs 1,810/–
Selling price 16,000 fruits @ shs 0/50*d*	*Net profit* shs 6,190/–
Profit per annum	shs 1,768/–

This was the only crop for which the Department of Agriculture had allowed experiments with a fertilizer, sulphate of ammonia; 12 lbs per 100 plants. Cost shs 30/– per cwt; one acre needed 2040 lbs. No manure was used under normal conditions.

Appendices

14. Production one acre onions, 1950 prices

Cost of labour	shs 171/–
Cost manure	shs 300/–
Bagging, transportation	shs 84/–
Total cost of Production	shs 555/–
Selling price 42 bags @ shs 55/– per bag,	total shs 2,310/–
Net profit	shs 1,755/–

15. Minimum wages in settled/local area; compared with general prices and productivity on one acre Grade 2 land[8]

Assumption that worker was employed in settled area for eight tickets and worked an additional 60 days on local land. This gives an inflated income, until well past the Second World War no one, particularly women, was likely to have what amounted to full-time employment.

About 1910
Eight tickets @ shs 8/12*d* and shs 1/– rations. Local work 60 days @ shs 0/20*d*. Total wages shs 84/96*d*. One bag maize shs 3/20*d*. One goat shs 7/–. Brideprice 65 goats.

About 1920
Eight tickets @ shs 10/60*d* and shs 1/50*d* rations. Local work 60 days @ shs 0/30*d*. Total wages shs 114/80*d*. One bag maize shs 4/80*d*. Brideprice 70 goats. One goat shs 10/–. Land shs 125/– and up.

Before Carter Commission
Eight tickets @ shs 13/– and shs 3/–.
Local work 60 days @ shs 0/50*d*. Total wages shs 158/–.
Productivity one acre shs 60/88/–.
One bag maize shs 6/50*d*. One goat shs 13/–. Brideprice 75 goats; land shs 300/–. DARD shs 188/88*d*.

About 1939
Eight tickets @ shs 16/– and shs 4/– rations. Local work 60 days @ shs 0/60*d*. Total wages shs 196/–. Productivity one acre shs 170/75. One bag maize shs 13/–. One goat shs 16/–. Brideprice 80 goats; land shs 450/–. Manure per ton shs 16/–. Manure 1 acre to 25 per cent shs 24/–. DARD shs 357/25*d*.

Before the Declaration of the Emergency
Eight tickets @ 23/– and shs 4/– rations.
Local work 60 days @ shs 0/80*d*. Total wage shs 264/–.
Productivity one acre shs 277/–.
One bag maize shs 20/–. One goat shs 18/00. Brideprice 85 goats; land shs 900/–. Manure per ton shs 37/50*d*. Manure 1 acre to 25% shs 56/25*d*. DARD shs 598/50*d*.

Appendix IV: Economic Data

Buying power from one annual minimum wage in local/settled area
(Grade 2 maize or DARD)

About 1910	26.6 bags
About 1920	23.9 bags
Before Carter Commission	24.3 bags or 83.7 per cent of DARD
About 1939	15.1 bags or 54.9 per cent of DARD
Before Declaration of the Emergency	13.2 bags or 44.1 per cent of DARD

16. Mean wages Nairobi, before Emergency[9]

Casual pool and informal sector	shs 730/–
Military, police, *askaris*	shs 1,370/–
Fundis, artisans, tailors	shs 1,200/–
Mechanics, drivers, technical labour	1,530/–
Domestic personnel	shs 800/– plus housing, food
Self-employed traders, shopkeepers	shs 2,250/–
Clerical and administrative labour	shs 2,150/–

17. Coffee in the settled area in the early twentieth century and its influence on the production of maize

Early decades

By 1904 80 acres under coffee in Kiambu. By the First World War over 5,000 acres; almost tripled during the First World War; after slump reached close to 23,000 acres in 1920, with close to 11,000 acres producing.[10]

Workforce

Forty-five male or female workers for regular maintenance of 100 acres. During picking time – standardized at 2 months – 7 additional workers needed for each 100 trees. Workers also needed for new planting, mulching. For 1920 estimate would be regular force of 10,350 workers, 4,000 planters and about 1,000 pickers for 2 months. All paid cash and 30 lb of *posho* per ticket. Assuming eight tickets for regular workers and planters would have needed slightly over 1,200 tons of maize in 1920 compared to 5 tons in 1904.

18. Local coffee notes

During the First World War a ban was placed on African coffee production because European growers feared that African production would introduce disease.[11] Loss of labour and potential competition played their own roles.

Koinange wa Mbiu had planted coffee early, but pulled his bushes when told that his coffee displeased the settlers.[12] The general African ban was lifted in 1932; by 1934 areas distant from European plantations were licensed but coffee growing in Kikuyu areas remained prohibited.[13] During these years the local population accumulated years of experience with coffee growing in all phases, except for marketing, by working for the settlers.

In the 1930s Koinange was less compliant; when given a tract of coffee land

Appendices

in compensation for what he had lost in alienation, he refused to destroy the coffee.[14] It is not certain when he filed his first official protest; but disjointed notes in one of the few files on land consolidation still available in Kiambu in 1962 indicate that he probably had not pulled up the bushes in the late 1940s or otherwise had replanted them. In 1947 and 1948 he had been prosecuted for illegal coffee growing, was convicted and had lost on appeal.[15] Long before that, the population in the local area honoured him by giving an annual initiation year the name *Kabaka* 'because he brought coffee'.

By 1948 it was known locally that licences were imminent, but not for land under litigation. By late 1948 or early 1949 it was known that men would only be given a licence if they had four or more acres of undisputed private land, could grow their own food and Napier grass, and provide shade. The ban was lifted in 1951, followed by the licensing of the Githunguri district, which contained the local area.[16]

The earliest coffee licences were rewards for 'loyalty', the earliest 100 trees went to Waruhiu.[17] On 3 July 1951 Koinange was found to have 10,000 illegal seedlings for which he was prosecuted.[18] The sentiment of the Kiambu Magistrate's Court was evident in the nominal fine of shs 100/- but he was condemned to uproot the plants. He appealed both sentences; the Nairobi Supreme Court quashed the fine, but it upheld the uprooting of the coffee. In the same decision, part of the *African Grown Coffee Rules G.N.1172/49* was declared to be in conflict with an earlier ordinance and the rules were declared *ultra vires*.[19] It is likely that only some of Koinange's seedlings were uprooted.[20]

Although Koinange was soon arrested and detained, coffee continued to be grown by members of his *githaka* who had remained free. When he, then very old, was released and saw the acres and acres of Kikuyu coffee for the first time, he reportably remarked, 'These are all my children'.

19. Local coffee expectations and production

In 1956 no local men had as yet marketed coffee. Expectations were high. Growers - and hopeful non-growers - calculated the following costs and anticipated returns.

Cost for one acre (540 trees) coffee, 1956 prices

First Year
Cost of labour for terraces	shs 650/-
Cost digging holes, filling with manure, benching, mulching, planting, shading	shs 1,052/-
Cost manure	shs 2,160/-

Three subsequent years
Light mulching, weeding, pruning, disease control	shs 888/-
Picking, twice in fifth year	shs 540/-
Transportation	shs 100/-
Total cost production	shs 5,390/-

MAC producers based their anticipated gains on the 1955 prices of shs 12,160/- per ton; they expected a harvest of 10 cwts dry coffee. Income from first planting would then be shs 6,080/-; net profit in fifth year shs 690/-. The cost in subsequent

Appendix IV: Economic Data

years was estimated at shs 1,600/- per acre. If prices remained stable, profits in subsequent years would be shs 4,480/- per acre.

Small owners and *ahoi* who had thought in terms of 135 trees or one-quarter acre believed that their costs would considerably lower. They expected to use domestic labour and were convinced that a few years of good coffee harvests would provide for many needs. Each tree would yield a minimum of shs 10/- after the fourth year, giving an income of shs 1,350/- for a quarter acre.

The cost would be increased by obligatory membership in a coffee cooperative, which also provided stock from its nurseries. Membership costs were initially shs 50/-. In 1951 the cooperative received a grant from the African District Council (succesor of the LNC) to build a processing plant. Fees were levied on coffee delivered to the plant; after the initial years cost of membership would rise sharply.

By 1962 it was clear that these expectations were far too optimistic.[21] Estimates agreed by and large with the cost of planting but local output was on average only 8 cwts (clean, dry) and prices in 1962 no higher than shs 6,000/- to shs 6,300/- per ton. The gain would be somewhat over a third of 1956 expectations; this might be further depressed because the cost of labour had risen to shs 2/- a day. A labourer by this time could earn more by one year's labour than by a quarter acre of coffee.

Local coffee production and the 1962/1963 slump

In 1956 the local area had 61 growers and about 15,060 trees on 28 acres. In 1962 it had 225 growers, and about 1,686,658 trees on 1,559 acres. Larger land owners had had an early monopoly; the slump in coffee prices came at a time that many small producers marketed their coffee for the first time. With the advent of Independence men who had two acres of land could get coffee licences; before, it was restricted to those with four acres.

20. Costs of living, auxiliary foods and non-food items, based on local information

Rural

Though local land produced basic food, many needed to buy basics as well as other foods. Basic food could be bought from local producers, the *nduka* at Marige or in Kiambu.

Around 1952 the following foods were usually bought; their cost per pound is indicated between brackets. Maize flour (0/30d); *njahi* beans (0/45d); sweet potatoes (0/23d); green bananas (about 30 for 0/90d); peas (0/45d); sugar cane (0/70d for six pieces); sorghum (0/40d); yams (0/36d). Other rootcrops between 0/40d and 0/50d; vegetables, mainly cabbages 0/12d each; onions (0/32d); milk (0/45d per bottle); sugar (0/80d); rice (1/20d); bread (0/55d each); buns (0/12d each); meat (1/10d); tea (5/-); cooking fat (1/95d); salt (0/20d); eggs (0/10d each). Curry powder (shs 3/- per tin).

Non-food: bar soap for laundry (1/80d); facial soap (0/70d); 'blue' (0/20d); kerosene (0/50d). Cigarettes were often sold singly; cost of one packet shs 3/65d. Empty *ndebe* (tin) for carrying water shs 4/-. Blanket (second-hand) or *thuburia* 7/50d; cooking pots shs 4/-; charcoal shs 2/- for a large calabash. The local *nduka* sold scarfs (shs 3/-) and cloth (shs 7/- to shs 12/-); tailors were available; cloth, ready-made and second-hand clothing were available in Nairobi and Kiambu.

Appendices

Nairobi

Migrant workers tried to bring basic food from home but if this was not possible, they had to buy in town. The diet of poorer men was geared towards maize porridge; bread and tea (if milk could be bought) would be luxuries. Beans, which needed extensive cooking, would rarely figure in the diet. Due to long working hours, the absence of affordable transportation (shs 1/50d for the average ride from a location to work) urban tea houses fulfilled a need by providing basic foods, but at a price. A bottle of beer cost shs 1/65d. Transportation from Nairobi to the local area shs 5/- one way.

Unless they lived in housing provided by employers, most workers lived in simple locations which consisted of cement blocks containing 6–8 cubicles. In some locations several blocks shared water and sanitary facilities, in others each block had its own. A cubicle had 'bed spaces', roughly 40 sq. feet; men rented a bed space and shared a cement cooking shelf with others living in the same cubicle. For cooking they needed a charcoal burner, charcoal, matches and a *thuburia*. The charcoal burner also provided heat; light was available only if someone had a 'bed space'. The price of a bed space was on the average shs 7/- per month. Nairobi men who were not 'legitimately employed' could not get a permit for a bed space; they had to get by by 'sleeping rough', hiding in the bazaars or renting a bed space illegally, perhaps for a few hours. Migrant workers needed more clothing than at home; they needed shoes and warm blankets. All Nairobi workers (but for some domestic workers) needed long pants, a shirt and a jacket. A thin mattress for the cement shelf provided as bed space (shs 20/- second-hand) was an indication of wealth.

Other data on the cost of living

The cost of living indices provided in the literature, though useful in general, cannot be used as comparison for data from the local population. They give useful comparisons between years, but rarely provide information about the products and prices included in the base indices. Kitching, using several documents, provides data going back to 1931 and shows that the cost of living index for Africans in Nairobi rose between 1939 and 1949 to 187 and in Mombasa to 207.[22] The Carpenter Report gives some information on which to base a minimum wage for a single male; the needs it assumes are restrictive and unrealistic.[23] Fisher provides an extensive list of prices for domestic and farming needs for the early 1950s in the local area.[24] They are in general higher than I found in 1956.

Notes

1. Data provided by Kiambu District Annual Reports, Chief Magugo Waweru, Tax Collector Gicho Waweru and
    1974. Clayton, Anthony, and Donald C. Savage, *Government and Labour In Kenya 1895–1963*, London: Frank Cass, whose table of conversions I also use.
2. Data before 1922 derive mainly from Kiambu District Annual Reports; later data are from the *Mbari ya Igi* Agricultural Committee. Bibliography gave scattered data.
    1909. *Ukamba Province Quarterly Report*, October–December, Machakos District Political Record Book (Vol. I to 1910, part I).
    1970. Thuku, Harry, *An Autobiography*, Nairobi: Oxford University Press.
    1974. Wanyoike, E. N., *An African Pastor*, Nairobi: East African Publishing House.

Appendix IV: Economic Data

1975. Van Zwanenberg, R. M. A., *Colonial Capitalism and Labour in Kenya 1919–1939*, Nairobi: East African Literature Bureau.
1976. Tignor, Robert, L., *The Colonial Transformation of Kenya*, Princeton: Princeton University Press.
1980. Kitching, Gavin, *Class and Economic Change in Kenya*, New Haven: Yale University Press.
1983. Overton, John David, 'Spatial differentiation in the colonial economy of Kenya', PhD thesis, Cambridge.
3. Price predominantly local; information from elders.
4. Information predominantly local.
5. Information from local sources; confirmed by Kiambu District Annual Report. Local wages slightly lower or on a par with Settled Area.
6. Local information, confirmed by Mbari ya Igi Agricultural Committee.
7. Information local, brideprice of women in each age category totalled and means calculated.
8. Data from Department of Agriculture; later data from local informants and MAC. Dates approximate, earnings for either gender.
9. Mean of wages as declared by local migrant workers.
10. 1915–16. AR/273 KBU/9.
    1918–19. AR/284 KBU/12.
    1919–20. AR/285 KBU/13.
    1920–21. AR/286 KBU/14.
    1938. Salvadori, Max, *La Colonisation Europeene au Kenya*, Paris: La Rose Editeurs. pp. 70ff.
    1956. Hill, M.F., *Planters Progress*, Nairobi: Coffee Board of Kenya, pp. 22ff.
    1976. Tignor, Robert L., *op. cit.*, pp. 151ff.
    1983. Overton, John David, *op. cit.*
11. 1976. Tignor, Robert L., *op. cit.*, pp. 291, 291 note 13.
12. *Ibid.*, note 12.
13. *Ibid.*, pp. 291ff.
14. 1947. Resident Magistrates Court Kiambu (Rex versus Senior Chief Koinange) and
    1948. Appeal from 1st Class Magistrates Court Kiambu, (Koinange Mbiu, Appellate versus Rex).
15. 1963. Bennett, George, *Kenya, a Political History*, London: Oxford University Press, p. 91.
16. 1988. Wamagatta, Evanson N., 'A biography of senior chief Waruhiu wa Kungu of Githunguri, Kiambu District 1890–1952', MA thesis, University of Nairobi, pp. 281, 282.
17. 1970. Thuku, Harry, *op. cit.*, pp. 73.
18. 1951. AR/324 KBU 42.
19. 1951. *Law Reports of Kenya* Vol. 24 (2) K. L. R. Koinange Mbiu (Orig. Crim) versus Rex, Respondent (Orig. Pros). ex Appeal No 406 of 1951; Appeal from 1st Class Mag. Crt. KBU, DO Brummage.
20. 1953. Official Correspondence, 14 November, from Assistant Agricultural Officer Kiambu to District Agricultural Officer Kiambu re *African Coffee in Kiambu District*. JDB/SMT.
21. 1962. 13 November Official Correspondence Agricultural Officer James Mburu, Office of the Department of Agriculture, to G. Kershaw.
22. 1950. Cost of Living Commission Report, 11 November, Colony and Protectorate of Kenya, Government Printer, p. 3, *passim*.
    1980. Kitching, Gavin, *op. cit.*, p. 151.
23. 1954. *Report of the Committee on African Wages* (F. W. Carpenter) (*Carpenter Report*), Colony and Protectorate of Kenya: Government Printer, pp. 55ff.
24. 1955. Fisher, Jeanne, *The Anatomy of Kikuyu Domesticity and Husbandry*. Cambridge: Department of Technical Cooperation, pp. 119ff.

Appendix V

Notes on the Kenya Land Commission Report

However much the Kikuyu had initially hoped that the Kenya Land Commission would return the alienated lands, they were afterwards convinced that the Commission's real task had been to confirm European ownership, accept a few claims as tokens of government goodwill, declare the subject of land alienation closed as far as the previous owners were concerned, and allow continued alienation if land was needed for European needs or missions.[1]

While the Report reflected what had beome official government policy, had the Commission taken evidence in earlier decades, administrative voices against its conclusions might also have been stronger. As late as 1909, when the hey-day of alienation was almost over, C. W. Hobley had had no doubt that the land was bought and therefore owned when he cited the letter of J. E. Henderson of the East Africa Inland Mission with its detailed information about some acquisitions.[2] Local men asserted that before the Europeans had settled, officials from the Protectorate government had accepted that they owned the land. C. W. R. Lane had unquestioningly done so, when he divided the land into districts and asked for taxes. Yet when Europeans wanted Kikuyu land, government had thought it advantageous to side with them. It had then become fashionable as well as profitable to describe the Kikuyu as primitives who did not need all their land; their real problem was bad cultivation practices. That 'primitives' were not held in high regard by the Commission is evident from the question of the Chairman of the Commission to L. S. B. Leakey about the advisability of having land set aside for each ethnic group: 'Do you think it a good thing to have so many private zoos all over the country?'[3]

While Kikuyu had claimed before the Commission that they had bought the land and owned it, the Commission agreed with the Commissioner of Native Lands:

> ... and I wish to record quite definitely that in this case as in every other that I have known on the subject, and my experience covers many tribes totally diverse and widely separated ethnologically and geographically – whatever may be the differences and similarities, there is, in my opinion, one point of absolute certainty. That is that the theory of individual ownership of land is absolutely foreign to the mind of any African until he has begun to absorb the ideas of an alien civilization.... From the beginning to end in this case there is no suggestion of 'ownership' of land as understood in English. The word (or an equivalent) may have crept into the interpreted evidence; if so it is merely as a convenient though inaccurate and hasty synonym for rights of occupation and cultivation'.[4]

Appendix V: Notes on the Kenya Land Commission Report

The Commission rejected much Kikuyu testimony in scathing terms: it was described as often 'wild and extravangant', 'inconsistent' and 'utterly discrepant':

we have no hesitation in characterizing the bulk of it worthless. We go further and say that in our opinion many of the memoranda are deliberately untruthful....

Information provided on prices was 'fantastic and ridiculous'. The land had not been acquired by buying but 'by a process which consisted, as we have seen, partly of alliance and partnership and partly of adoption and chicanery'.[5]

Because the Kikuyu were a 'tribe' which only knew 'tribal ownership', what little compensation was due, could only rarely be given to individuals or even *mbari*; most should be paid to the 'tribe', by adding it to the Native Land Unit (Appendix III/2). Recognition of individual tenure was premature; it would come when the government thought the Kikuyu ready. The Commission Report was the last word; there was to be no reopening of the matter.[6]

Although it was soon evident to administrators in the field that the Commission had underestimated Kikuyu losses, the matter was closed. The tenor of the annual district reports increasingly emphasized the Commission's perspective on Kikuyu culture and society in past and present. There was no real scarcity of land; problems could be solved within the Kikuyu 'tribal' land unit, if the Kikuyu would give up their 'wasteful practices', and if 'individualists' would stop buying up the land of their poorer brethren.[7]

Some Kikuyu testimony would have been understood better by a Kikuyu *kiama* than by the Commission. While some claims were almost certainly fraudulent, almost all aspects of Kikuyu litigation which soon would clog the courts were already present in testimony before the Commission. A *kiama* would have understood that the same tract might be claimed by a Ndorobo or Kikuyu seller who had not yet received the full price and by the buyers, who had made a number of payments. It could even be claimed by a *githaku* or *mbari* member of the owners who felt that he ultimately had more rights than any European who now held the land. A *kiama* would also have understood that a man might claim land which his brother had sold, to Europeans or other Kikuyu, while it should not have been sold; or that a seller himself, beset by misfortune which he attributed to having sold land under *kirumi*, would try to get it back. It would have understood that the hearings before the Commission would become a platform where various Kikuyu and Ndorobo oral traditions were seeking confirmation.

Much of the testimony of Europeans before the Commission had been at pains to promote their preferred version of Kikuyu history; the Commission, while accepting that some European claims might be fraudulent, was oriented towards 'straightforward' European history, couched in terms of surveyors' reports, bills of sale and title deeds. It accepted what was familiar, its moral allegiance – as that of many Europeans – was to an evolutionary history in which Kikuyu society and culture were at a stage which could not have known ownership of land, but had arrived at a stage which could not survive before inevitable change.

The decisions of the Commission continued to create unrest; the slowness with which the government settled the few claims which were accepted, and the speed with which it evicted Kikuyu from land which was to become European, before the owners had been offered other land, brought an angry response. The government kept control over the land it eventually offered as compensation; as befitted guardians of land which was ultimately owned by the Crown, it felt free to regulate the use of the land it provided. Kikuyu who received the land were constantly reminded that they were not the ultimate owners; they were occupiers and tenants.

Appendices

The government disregarded their protest; it had similarly failed to draw conclusions from the anger of the Kiambu Native Council, when the government imposed ordinances for land conservation.[8]

Notes

1. 1967. Sorrenson, M. P. K., *Land Reform in the Kikuyu Country*, Oxford: Oxford University Press, pp. 22ff.
    The Kikuyu also believed that the government had intended the findings and recommendations of the Report to be inaccessible. It was available only in English, all four volumes had to be bought together at the cost of one year's wages to a Nairobi clerk. It was bought by the Kiambu LNC and by Chief Koinange; at least one local claimant had read part of it and had memorized certain phrases.
2. 1909. October–December AR/15 Ukamba Province Quarterly Report, C. W. Hobley, 'Land tenure among the A-Kikuyu'.
3. 1933. Cmnd 4556 *Report of the Kenya Land Commission, Evidence and Memoranda* (KLC), Vols I–IV (Sir Morris Carter, CBE), Vol. I, p. 677.
4. 1933. KLC, *op. cit.*, vol. I, pp. 28ff., 'Memorandum of the Commissioner of Lands on the native claims to land ownership in the Kiambu District'.
5. 1933. KLC, *op. cit.*, Report pp. 79, 81, 85–7, 93.
6. 1967. Sorrenson, M. P. K. *op. cit.*, pp. 25ff, 54.
7. 1941. AR/313 KBU/32 H. E. Lambert Addendum.
    1942. AR/314 KBU/33.
    1945. AR/317 KBU/36.
    1946. AR/318 KBU/37.
8. 1938. AR/310 KBU/29.

Appendix VI

Notes on the Rift Valley

In the early years of the settlement of the Rift Valley, Kikuyu went there only with Europeans; later they went to join relatives, seeking land and work. Permission of the European land owner was sometimes sought. In some areas Europeans had acquired much more land than they could handle; they might discover only slowly, or might not object, to Kikuyu settlements on their land. Until the end of the Second World War even the best-managed farms were strongly labour-dependent. From the earliest settlement onwards, farmers had lacked what was needed to produce sufficient cash for wages. They attracted workers – men, women and sometimes children – with the promise of settlement and use of land. The African population grew rapidly through immigration and polygyny; throughout the European settlement of the Rift Valley, Africans outnumbered Europeans. Shortly after the Second World War, the rate was close to 35 to 1.[1]

Europeans and Kikuyu differentiated between the Rift Valley, sometimes called the White Highlands, and the settled areas outside the Highlands; both were reserved for European ownership. The area considered 'Rift Valley' by the local population was located in the colonial Rift Valley Province and part of Central Province, particularly Nanyuki District which contained Nyeri town and station. Kiambu Kikuyu tended to call this area Ruguru, a term I will use, alternating with Rift Valley. *Ruguru* technically means 'far away'.

Kiambu Kikuyu did not claim Highland land on the basis of previous ownership; they did claim the settled area, which they called *ma-camba*. In a play on words this could mean my *shamba*, my land. Gaki Kikuyu claimed part of the Highlands, particularly the Nanyuki area. Whether they called it *ma-camba* land, I do not know. The land claimed by Gaki Kikuyu in the Highlands was smaller than the settled area land, outside the Highlands, claimed by Kiambu and Murang'a.[2] Alienation had in all cases strongly reduced the number of previous owners; only 6.1 per cent of Kiambu males remained in the Kiambu settled area, as did 5.9 per cent of Murang'a males. The Gaki presence in the land they claimed, was considerably higher: 12.4 per cent.

Kikuyu who had gone to the Rift Valley had settled by preference close to their area of origin, where kinsmen remained. Newcomers to the Highlands preferred land where their kinsmen lived. All tried to avoid – but did not always do so – areas claimed by other Kikuyu. Though Kiambu Kikuyu dominated in many Ruguru districts, Gaki men dominated in the Nanyuki District, and outnumbered other Kikuyu in the Laikipia District of the Rift Valley Province as well. The African population of Nanyuki district, close to and claimed by Gaki, was 68 per

299

Appendices

cent Gaki and only 3 per cent Kiambu.[3] Wherever Kikuyu dominated, one of their three districts was more dominant than others. In Nakuru District 37.2 per cent of the Kikuyu were from Kiambu, 20.4 per cent from Murang'a and only 11.8 per cent from Gaki. In Nakuru town 18.8 per cent came from Kiambu, 17.1 per cent from Murang'a and 6.5 per cent from Gaki. All Kikuyu would avoid areas settled by other ethnic groups, if they went there at all, they would be a minority.

Government information about the early exodus of Kikuyu to the Rift Valley is sparse and biased. Whatever reports do exist, make clear that it was politically unacceptable to consider that land alienation or fear of land scarcity was behind the exodus. This obvious reason is not among the ten mentioned by C. A. G. Lane in 1917/18.[4] Acceptable reasons were the lower price of goats in the Rift Valley, the lower rates of disease, and better grazing. The presumed 'negative' characteristics of the Kikuyu play a significant role: those who went were motivated by crafty selfishness; they sought to escape communal labour and induction into the Carrier Corps. Lane completes the orthodox line by castigating the Kiambu Kikuyu for their wasteful and destructive agriculture which forced them to seek new lands.

Data from the local area show that fear for future lack of land for sons, immediate need for herding land and already existing land scarcity of others, all played a role. Most senior local men initially opposed the migration but ultimately many gave their reluctant consent (Chapter 3). The migration was modelled on fission; senior members of a *nyumba* or *mbari* led the exodus accompanied by junior men from their own and other *ithaku* of the *mbari*; *ahoi* accompanied their patrons. Though none of the *mbari* members were landless, most were land poor. One man left about fifty acres but as he had at least eight sons he would have been unable to provide them with sufficiencies or brideprices.

I did not do fieldwork in Ruguru; the data I have from returnees cannot be verified, nor did informants constitute a sample population. Complete households were rare; part households, with members repatriated to different Kikuyu areas common. They came from areas as distinct as Gilgil and Nakuru, Laikipia and Naivasha. Some had lived in the Rift Valley since its opening and had stayed where they started. Others had changed occupations and farms several times, some were still employed in agricultural or animal husbandry, others were townsmen. Some had graduated to prestigious jobs such as farm headmen, tractor drivers, mechanics, head milkers or higher domestic personnel; others had remained simple daily workers. They had known good and bad times, as had their employers. In some areas the workers had been part of a dominant Kikuyu majority, in others they were a small – often barely tolerated – minority. For obvious reasons the data should be used cautiously if at all for comparisons with Nairobi or the rural area.

1. Return from the Rift Valley

Though many Kikuyu were forcibly repatriated during the Emergency, not all were evicted, and not all who were originally from the local area returned to it.[5] Employers might allow part of a family to stay; unknown to their employers, repatriates sought such opportunities as would make it easier to claim the land once the Europeans had left. Males prohibited from returning to their natal area or area of origin by a *kirumi* went to affinal relatives; wives not affected by such *kirumi* might return to their husband's or their own natal area with their children. Local repatriates had a high rate of incarceration in camps and jails; although

Appendix VI: Notes on the Rift Valley

denied by all, some young males may have been in the forest.

Early repatriates returned by choice. They wanted the land they had left before it might be lost to them in consolidation; they had grown old and wanted to die in land; they might want to find education for children, or escape from the oppression of gangs of Rift Valley *anake*. Some old people with close kin and local land returned as early as 1946/47; they often did not intend to return to the Rift Valley but to leave the Rift Valley claims to their sons. By 1948 this trickle of returnees was becoming a flood. Those who returned voluntarily in or before 1950, and did not intend to return, were merged with the local population. Those who came later and/or intended to return to the Rift Valley were not merged with the general population but classified as Rift Valley repatriates.

Several men and women who had only weak kinship ties outside the Rift Valley, and were not *ahoi* of men whose claims were stronger, or men and women against whom the curse for going to the Rift Valley was never removed, remained in Ruguru until they were forcibly repatriated. Some who had been evicted as early as 1948 had frequently gone to other Rift Valley areas; those evicted by 1952, or later, were not allowed to remain in Ruguru.

Reasons for expulsion were easily found; the Kikuyu might live on a farm with relatives but they themselves lacked permits and were not part of the workforce; they might have refused to be photographed for identity and employment papers, or to sign work contracts. Employers often did not hesitate to interpret any Kikuyu defiance or protest as Mau Mau involvement; evidence was of little concern.

Forced repatriation caused severe hardship; the returning population had contained several older men and women who had died en route or in repatriation centres. Almost everyone had left possessions, including stock and harvests. They arrived without basic necessities to often impoverished kin; nevertheless, kinsmen tried to give what help they could, even if they were themselves hard pressed. Tensions, however, were common.

2. General data on the returnees

At least two males claimed that their employer had given them land outright in lieu of wages, but had not given them 'papers' to prove the land was theirs. In spite of low wages, most males claimed that they had been better off in the Rift Valley than their rural relatives in Kiambu, though they had been insecure, as throughout their Rift Valley occupation employers and government would use the threat of repatriation to enforce compliance.

Using nineteenth- or early twentieth-century standards of well-being, they appear to have had an economic advantage over many rural males, but they lagged in terms of access to twentieth-century opportunities. Their level of polygyny was higher than that of the rural population; they had on average more descendants, more stock and − the use of − more land. The Rift Valley level of polygyny for males unlikely to take more wives because of age was 27.1 per cent; Igi *mbari* members had a rate of 23.9 per cent, Igi *ahoi* 8.9 per cent. No *muhoi* in Igi had after the 1930s been able to use more land than needed for survival; 79 per cent of the Rift Valley males claimed that they had sufficient land for food and trade.

Although they sometimes had been forced to sell to their employers for lower prices than they could have obtained elsewhere, employers did form a secure market. Others had sold to visiting traders or had carried their harvests into town.

Appendices

They often got higher prices, but might not be able to sell all they had, because their harvests and those of others coincided. Eight males reported that they had been independent traders, not otherwise employed though they lived on a farm. Educational attainments were lower than in the rural area: 55.2 per cent of males of 18 or younger had never been to school compared to 16.8 per cent of the male population of Thuita and Igi. The rate of literacy of rural *ahoi* was also much higher; only 23.3 per cent had never been to school. No Rift Valley males or females had held clerical or teaching positions.

The high rate of polygyny in the Rift Valley was tied to the awareness that more women meant a larger workforce and larger harvests; it was also linked to the expectation that the Europeans would leave and that they would be the legal heirs. There is evidence that this belief created tensions between those who had originally 'settled' Ruguru and converted the land from 'bush' to farm land, and those who had come later and found most of the claims already in place. Some of these tensions became apparent during the first years of Rift Valley Mau Mau, when urban youth clashed with rural elders.

As for political participation, 13 males declared that they had been members of the KCA or KAU; they saw no difference between the two. KCA had 'always' asked for oaths; KAU had initially done so to a lesser extent but by 1950 KAU also habitually demanded oaths. Six males claimed to have been long-term KCA members; given that some members had undoubtedly died since the KCA started, KCA membership was probably higher than the data indicate.

How harsh economic conditions had been depended largely on the area and availability of alternative income when Europeans could or would not pay even the small wages they had offered initially. While conditions had been bad from time to time almost everywhere, conditions during and after the Second World War were harsher than usual: threats of expulsion and restrictions on cultivation, herding and trading had been more common and were more frequently enforced. In earlier years such restrictions had been threatened, but enforcement had been spotty and haphazard. Older settlers were rarely affected even then; more recent settlers were, but could still go elsewhere. Enforcement during and after the Second World War extended over larger areas; even employers who would rather have abstained from these measures were forced by the government or the Settlers' Association. Migration to areas where enforcement was lax or absent became more difficult; fines, forfeitures or expulsion were by now a real threat.

Around this time the work load was again increased – with a consequent decrease of what could be produced for sale; those living on farms also needed 'papers', including photographs, to prove that they were legally entitled to residence. Employers reserved the right to evict workers they did not need. This might include *anake* born on the farm; it also involved young males the owner might have wanted as workers, but who did not want that work; they wanted to live there but work in towns.

Younger men were most affected; parents could offer little help. Some went to Nairobi, the Coast or Tanganyika. Others roamed the Rift Valley farming areas, seeking shelter wherever they could. The workforce which stayed was subjected to unusually strict control and harsh measures: because stock had to be kept around the huts at night, owners lost goats to disease and theft. Living quarters were concentrated in 'labour lines'; proximity and squalor created fear and enmity. Soon after the Second World War, farmers who realized the potential for unrest, prowled, heavily armed and with dogs, around the labour lines. When Mau Mau

Appendix VI: Notes on the Rift Valley

took hold, the Kikuyu in the lines knew that they would be the prime suspects if a Mau Mau attack occurred; yet they – unarmed, living in labour lines, possibly surrounded by barbed wire – would not be protected from attacks.[6]

3. Mau Mau membership among Rift Valley repatriates

Local Rift Valley data do not give information about Mau Mau violence. Several males had been incarcerated for allegedly holding Mau Mau office. One young male was killed locally in the aftermath of the Marige massacre, according to his parents because the security forces mistakenly thought that he had that day come from the forest, according to others 'by mistake'. Some certainly came from areas of relatively high Mau Mau anti-European activity, though that does not prove that they participated.

High oath taking among this group is in part related to the strength of the KCA in the Rift Valley – many repatriates would feel that it was the only organization which had shown an interest in their lives – and its attempt to make a comeback after the creation of KAU. They welcomed a movement which promised to speak for them; discontent was high as they were easily dismissed when farmers mechanized or otherwsie declared them and their kinsmen surplus to requirements. Relations between Kikuyu and Europeans, never good, deteriorated further when settlers blamed all Kikuyu for the lawlessness of some of their unemployed young males. It is therefore not surprising that the European Rift Valley screeners used the most inclusive definition of what constituted a Mau Mau oath or Mau Mau behaviour to rid the 'White Highlands' of an unwanted population (Appendix IX/6).

Early detention and expulsion, and the absence of those detained, do not allow for more than cursory observations. Mau Mau was significant in the Rift Valley earlier than elsewhere; undesirable Kikuyu presence or behaviour as Mau Mau do not allow one to conclude whether several movements were an early part or the whole of Mau Mau, and whether Mau Mau – or at least one Mau Mau movement – was born in the Rift Valley. Similarly, though the scant material available on 'advanced' oaths leans heavily on Rift Valley or possibly forest material, there is no evidence that they therefore originated in the Rift Valley or were more prevalent there than elsewhere (Appendix IX/3).[7]

By the time Kenyatta returned 7.2 per cent of the males and 0.8 per cent of the females had taken an oath which screeners later classified as Mau Mau. One of the earliest oaths taken by repatriates was called a 1947 *Kenia* oath; another oath which apparently occurred only in the Rift Valley, was the *United Natives Organization* (1948), reported by one male and one female who lived not too distant from each other.

Though females had been oathed for other organizations, not until 1949 were they oathed for KCA/KAU/Mau Mau on a regular basis; oathing of uninitiated young males remained rare in most areas until 1952; then all ages were oathed.

Forced oath taking, attributed to gangs of *anake* who terrorized labour lines and extracted money, was reported with far greater frequency in the Rift Valley than elsewhere. Some informants reported that every member of their household had to take an oath and that prices could be as high as shs 60/–; administrators defended their price by stating that Rift Valley inhabitants had the most to gain from attempts to drive out the Europeans. In a number of areas early oath taking had more than its share of social banditry.[7]

Appendices

The separation of the Rift Valley Mau Mau from the oaths of the rural area was evident in the lack of recognition for the Rift Valley oath. Rift Valley returnees, whether oathed or not, had to take the rural oath, if they wanted to 'eat and drink' with local Mau Mau. Though at least ten males and females did not take an oath until they came to the rural area, another five 'replaced' their Rift Valley oath with a rural oath according to them and local Mau Mau leaders. Yet they were penalized in that local screeners would accuse them of having taken two oaths.

Though local kin attempted to provide for their returning kin, few were happy that they had come; the full force of their anger, however, was directed at the government. The returns caused hardships; because of its heavy polygyny, Rift Valley goers returned with a large number of descendants. The land they had left was used by kinsmen who had expanded as well; giving it back or sharing it meant poverty – or greater poverty – for all. Repatriates knew that they were not welcome; this sense and the hope that they could claim Rift Valley land caused many to return to the Rift Valley in 1957. By 1962 close to 80 per cent had left, accompanied by 'new' migrants who hoped that European land would become available.

4. Violence and Nanyuki District

By all accounts the Rift Valley was before and during the Emergency an area in which violence was earlier and more extensive than in other areas. Here we only deal with the case of Nanyuki, which contained Nyeri township and environment. Data on general anti-European violence are based on reports in the *East African Standard*.[8] European deaths were analysed from information made available by the British Information Services.[9] No data are available to analyse European anti-Mau Mau actions in the area.

The data suggest significant differences between the three Districts of Central Province: Nanyuki with a strong Gaki population, Nairobi and Thika, both the latter with dense Kiambu or Murang'a populations.

Between 1952 and 1955, Central Province reported 25 European civilian deaths; of these 11, somewhat below half, occurred in Nanyuki District, which was only a small part of Central Province. When considering the broader picture of anti-European attacks, including murder, attempted murder and robbery, Central Province reports 25 instances. Nairobi and Thika Districts record 7 instances; Nanyuki reports 18. The conclusion is inescapable that Nanyuki, effectively alienated from Gaki later than other alienated areas, had a higher level of violence than other areas.

Notes

1. Calculations based on data from
   1950. *African Population of Kenya Colony and Protectorate 1948 Geographical and Tribal Studies*, East African Statistical Department, Nairobi: Government Printer, 15 September (reprinted February 1953).
   1953. *Report on the Census of the Non-Native Population of Kenya Colony and Protectorate, 25 February 1948*, Nairobi: Government Printer.
2. 1975. Dutto, Carl A., *Nyeri Townsmen, Kenya*, Nairobi: East Africa Literature Bureau, pp. 13ff.

Appendix VI: Notes on the Rift Valley

3. Calculations based on data from
   1950. *African Population of Kenya Colony and Protectorate, 1948, op. cit.*
4. 1917/18. Lane, C. A. G., AR/283 Dagoretti Sub-District Report, in AR/281 KBU/ll Kiambu District Annual Reports.
5. Not all Rift Valley areas wanted to get rid of their Kikuyu worker/settlers, nor did all Europeans use any means available to force partial or full Kikuyu repatriation.
6. The *East African Standard* and District Reports in the pre-Emergency years were increasingly filled with incidents of cattle theft, maiming, arson and threatened attacks. Many settlers felt that the unwillingness of Kikuyu to be photographed or to sign labour contracts showed that they were untrustworthy and potentially dangerous, and that given the slowness or lack of action on the part of the government they (the settlers) had to arm themselves in legitimate defence. Some also felt that they should be allowed considerable latitude and that those who held to 'simplistic' ideas of the rule of law did not understand the danger and the need to end Mau Mau terrorism. This attitude comes out clearly in many articles in the *East African Standard*, including letters to the editor. Some documents speaking for or against this have been preserved at Rhodes House in Oxford.
   MSS   Afric. s. 721 Martin, Eric Frank, *Documents concerning Home Guard Duties during Mau Mau in Kenya 1952-1953 and Instructions on Defence of Isolated Homesteads.*
   MSS   Afric. s. 929 contained
   a) 1953 17 April Correspondence between F. G. Cavendish-Bentinck and G. Kinnear, including Schedules of the Movement of the Kikuyu (repatriation, transit camps).
   b) Humphrey Slade-Todd *Selected Papers and Memoranda 1952-1959*, including letter from Humphrey Slade seeking to establish an Emergency Liaison Committee Aberdare Constituency, correspondence between its various members and the District Officer Naivasha, including a critique of the handling of the raid on the Naivasha Police Station.
   c) n.d. anon papers *Photography and All That* and *Employment of Mau Mau Suspects – Penal Settlements*. The Private Papers of Dr Anthony Clayton contained a copy of Correspondence of Sir John Whyatt (Attorney General) and the Governor, defending the obligation to maintain the rule of law, opposition to actions of the security forces and others who impose collective punishments without sufficient cause; a (secret) warning to the Governor that settlers from North Kinangop are being canvassed about a demonstration at Government House against prosecutions of the security forces for actions during the Emergency.
7. 1973. Keller, Edmund J., Jr., 'A twentieth century model: the Mau Mau transformation from social banditry to social rebellion', *Kenya Historical Review*, Vol. 1, No. 2, pp. 189-206.
8. 1952-5. *East African Standard* Friday editions.
9. 19 March 1958. British Information Services, Chicago, to G. Sluiter.

Selected bibliography

1947. Martin, J. H., *The Problem of the Squatter: Economic Survey of Resident Labour in Kenya*, February.
1970. Abuor, C. Ojwando, *White Highlands No More, A Modern Political History of Kenya*, Vol. I, Nairobi: Pan African Researchers.
1972. Wambaa, Rebmann M., and Kenneth King, 'The political economy of the Rift Valley', *Hadith*, Vol. 5, pp. 195-218.
1974. Furedi, F., 'Olenguruone in Mau Mau historiography', paper presented at the University of London Institute of Colonial Studies, 29 March.
1974. Furedi, F., 'The social composition of the Mau Mau movement in the White Highlands', *Journal of Peasant Studies*, Vol. I, No. 4 (July), pp. 486-505.
1975. Furedi, Frank, 'The Kikuyu Squatters in the Rift Valley 1918-1929', *Hadith* Vol. 5,

pp. 177-94.
1977. Kanogo, T. M. J., 'Rift Valley squatters and Mau Mau', *KHR Special Issue: Some Perspectives on the Mau Mau Movement*, W. R. Ochieng and K. K. Janmohammed, eds, Vol. 5, No. 2, pp. 243-53.
1977. Osolo-Nasubo, Ng'weno, *A Socio-Economic Study of the Kenya White Highlands: A Case Study in Uhuru Government*, Washington, DC: UPA.
1977. Tamarkin, M., 'Mau Mau in Nakuru', *KHR Special Issue: Some Perspectives on the Mau Mau Movement*, W. R. Ochieng and K. K. Janmohammed, eds, Vol. 5, No. 2, pp. 225-41.
1978. Tamarkin, M., 'The loyalists in Nakuru during the Mau Mau revolt', *Asian and African Studies*, Vol. 12, No. 2, pp. 247-61.
1981. Omosule, Monone, 'An assessment of the role of the Kenya Land Commission Report in the "Mau Mau" outbreak', paper presented at the Annual Conference of the Historical Association of Kenya, August.
1987. Kanogo, Tabitha, *Squatters and the Roots of Mau Mau 1905-1963*, London: James Currey.
1987. Throup, David W., *Economic and Social Origins of Mau Mau*, London: James Currey.
1989. Furedi, Frank, *The Mau Mau War in Perspective*, London: James Currey.

Appendix VII

Notes on Local Education

There is no history of the local mission station Kambui and little information is available about its educational programmes, the development of its outschools and later primary, intermediate and teacher training education. Apart from Macpherson's contribution, it has been given little attention.[1] This is the more regrettable because it educated several early Kenya leaders such as Waruhiu wa Kungu and Harry Thuku; it created one of the early centres of education around Wanyoike wa Kamawe. He provides the best insight into the operation of the mission, and its conflicts with the local population and Kikuyu culture.[2]

The mission belonged to the Gospel Mission Society, a 'product of the Moody and Sankey revival campaigns in the United States ... set up for the reclamation of men from the power of evil by faith in Christ....'[3] Its predecessor, the Christian Unity Association, was active during the famine through its missionary T. N. Krieger, who had bought 600 acres of land at Thimbigua, not too far from the local area. He was an avid hunter, who liberally shared his bag and earned the name *murata*, friend. He was joined at Thimbigua by W. P. Knapp and his wife, until they were invited to come to the local area by the *mbari ya Gathirimu*, of which Thuku, then a child, was a junior member. The Knapps accepted the offer, together with a medical missionary, Dr J. E. Henderson. They acquired about 100 acres of land, their land grant of May 1903 (L.O. 1064) was for the hill of *Mbui* (Kambui), where they built the mission. The land was equally divided between the mission and the missionaries.

The mission station provided medical aid and education; as far as the population was concerned, its Christian message was of lesser importance than the education it offered.[4] In the first decade, a few years of education, which included a good knowledge of English, gave access to well-paid clerical jobs in Nairobi; graduates were also in demand by chiefs and headmen who wanted teachers for their sons and English-speaking aides for themselves.

The mission had hoped that their more advanced pupils would become teachers and evangelists, but only some did. Mission pay was nominal, and employees needed to combine mission work with care of their land. Some graduates worked in areas where they provided services to the local hierarchy, creating interdependent relationships between the Church, larger land owners, and chiefs. Wanyoike of the *mbari ya Gathirimu* became the right hand of local Chief Waweru. He translated government instructions, helped organize a road-building programme, and, when the Kikuyu Association was formed, served with the chief, who became one of its vice-presidents, on the inner council or *ndundu*. He would later serve with him in the Kiambu LNC.

Appendices

Wanyoike's services brought rewards to the mission; Waweru allowed some of its converts to become *ahoi* on Igi land; its first chance to build an 'outschool' came in 1913 when the chief donated land for a school because he wanted literacy for his sons. The mission intended that the schools should become instruments of conversion; it regarded the three Rs as a way to reach that goal. Students who successfully completed the outschool curriculum, and showed a more than marginal interest in Christianity, could go on to Kambui itself for intermediate instruction.

Early students knew that conversion would be necessary for further education; although the mission in later years reduced the emphasis, in the mind of the population conversion opened the road to education. It therefore became a heuristic device; in 1956 close to 90 per cent of males who had converted in school no longer attended church.

Given the objectives of the mission, it wanted to retain control over the content of education. This did not constitute a problem between itself and the government, as long as the mission itself carried the cost; when more demands were made and government wanted to have significant control over curricula, the stage was set for conflict. Over time the objectives of the government would change with the philosophy of what constituted suitable education for 'natives'; when the Department of Education espoused the view that children should have access to basic intellectual skills, Kambui had few problems because it had from the beginning espoused the value of the three Rs. When the government's emphasis shifted to manual arts, Kambui would run its schools independently of government subsidies. Government and mission united in the conviction that African children – in contrast to European children – needed the 'civilizing influence' only Christianity, as brought by the missions, could provide. Kambui was prepared to devote a good deal of school time to this purpose as it distrusted African family life and culture. The 1956 curriculum for the primary grades still prescribed that half or more of the time in school was used for nature study, handwork, gardening, scripture, and physical education, to the disadvantage of intellectual training.

The difference between parents and mission about what constituted proper education was significant throughout most of the mission's existence. Parents and children perceived education as the royal road to well-paid jobs. While wealthier parents might demand more, or trust that their children would continue into higher education, most parents expected at least basic skills and, above all, literacy and English.

The mission charged no fees until 1917; the earliest fee of shs 0/25d per term was less than 1 per cent of a low-paid rural worker's wage for that period. As sponsoring mission churches became unable to support the sprawling school system, fees increased. Even after the mission accepted government support, the demand for classrooms, teaching materials, and better paid teachers and aid continued to push up fees. In 1956, primary school fees were shs 22/- and intermediate fees shs 45/-; the uniform students were required to wear added shs 10/-. Students had to provide a Bible, which might be used for reading as well as for 'Scripture'. Parents might also be asked to provide labour and materials for the maintenance of grounds, buildings and instructor housing. In spite of all these sources of income, the income of schools was far below their needs.

Parents were initially convinced that three or four years in school should provide their sons with the kind of training which had given the young males, who had gone to the mission stations, well-paying jobs. Outschools were not able to live up to those expectations as conditions at the mission station were radically different

Appendix VII: Notes on Local Education

from the outschools. Mission personnel had been oriented towards teaching, it had material at its disposal. Its teachers did not need to make a living from additional work, even if they sometimes had a few other duties. English had been the medium of daily interaction and instruction, teaching intense and prolonged. Outschool evangelist-teachers had many other mission tasks, including preaching, converting and organizing classes for adults; they had to visit other areas, had little if any help, were poorly paid and would not have been able to provide for their households unless they looked after their own land. Although teachers in outschools were later relieved of some of these duties, throughout the colonial period low pay prevented them from making teaching their primary commitment.

The achievement of the outschool primary schools was further depressed by severe overcrowding when parents realized in the 1920s that not only clerical jobs needed education. As more parents wanted education for more children, many more children attended, but not necessarily regularly. Lack of teaching material, a low level of trained teachers, lack of discipline because too many children did not want to be in school – some had been sent and taken out as many as four times or more – did not give much opportunity for anything beyond rote and recitation work. Yet parents tended to take it for granted that schools adjusted to their situation: they wanted to be able to send their children when they could afford the fees and take them out when this was no longer the case, only to send them back when economic conditions changed again. They thought age or ability an irrelevant factor; as all children could be initiated, so schools should be able to educate them all.

Inefficiency and overcrowding increased when entrance to intermediate school began to demand an examination, failed by almost 90 per cent of the candidates, who promptly returned to school, to make a new attempt the following year. As they occupied the fourth year, the third year could not be promoted and bottlenecks at every level became common.

A student who persisted (and whose parents could afford to pay the fees and exercise enough discipline to keep the child in school in spite of all complaints of boredom) might finally pass the intermediate entry exam. The next hurdle was the Kenya African Preliminary Exam (KAPE); bottlenecks here were equally severe. However, a student who passed KAPE could continue in teacher training or apply to one of the several high schools, available from the late 1920s. Those who sat KAPE, but failed, could apply to teacher training for the lowest grades. The sorting process had more to do with endurance and economics than with intellectual capability; the number of quite bright young males who had dropped out of school under these circumstances was distressingly large. Moreover, the needs of poorer parents, who could use education only intermittently, clashed with those of wealthier parents whose children were unable to advance as they might have done under other circumstances.

By the late 1940s the government, under pressure from parents, employers and the lack of results of African education, attempted a much needed, broad reform of education. Its intent was to provide greater financial aid to African education and to standardize the structure and the curriculum of the schools. It produced the Beecher Report, discussed in Chapter 5.[5]

Appendices

Notes

1. 1970. Macpherson, R., *The Presbyterian Church in Kenya*, Nairobi: Kenya Litho Ltd, pp. 84ff.
2. 1974. Wanyoike, E. N., *An African Pastor*, Nairobi: East African Publishing House.
3. 1970. Macpherson, R., *op. cit.*, pp. 84ff.
4. In July 1912 it claimed 18 converts. Converts sometimes wanted to live closer to the missions and some were given land by *mbari ya Igi* as *ahoi*. In 1946 the GMS and its land became part of the Presbyterian Church of East Africa. In 1956 *mbari ya Igi* had a local church which served the area; records indicated that 44 members of *mbari ya Igi* were communicant members; Thuita *mbari* contributed ten members. Of the *ahoi* of all villages, three were communicant members; of the *athami*, 14. Education had become widely available before Independence for those who could afford it. By 1956 *mbari ya Igi* had an intermediate school leading to the KAPE; Nginduri had a primary school as had Thuita. Girls could receive teacher-training education at Kambui, but they and boys needed to go elsewhere for secondary education.
5. 1948. *A Ten Year Plan for the Development of African Education*, Nairobi: Government Printer.
   1949. *African Education in Kenya: Report of a Committee Appointed to Enquire into the Scope, Content, and Methods of African Education, its Administration and Finance, and to Make Recommendations* (Rev. L. J. Beecher) (Beecher Report), Nairobi: Government Printer.

Some further information is available in:

1925. Cmnd 2373 *Education in East Africa* (Phelps-Stokes Report), (Jones, Jesse T.), Memorandum submitted to the Secretary of State for the Colonies by the Advisory Committee on Native Education in the British Tropical African Dependencies. HCSP, Vol. 21.
1970. Thuku, Harry, *An Autobiography*, Nairobi: Oxford University Press.
1973. Sheffield, James R., *Education in Kenya*, New York: Teachers College Press. This work provides a list of government documents and a basic bibliography.
1976. Tignor, Robert L., *The Colonial Transformation of Kenya*, Princeton, NJ: Princeton University Press, pp. 204ff.

Appendix VIII

Late Nineteenth- and Twentieth-Century Oaths

Twentieth-century oaths share many characteristics with their late nineteenth-century predecessors. Yet in both centuries oaths and their contents had local features, which changed over time. Whatever the changes, legitimacy required that they stayed within certain bounds.

Late nineteenth-century oaths can be divided into commitment, structuring or restructuring, and cursing oaths. Commitment oaths can be taken by older individuals or groups; their clauses indicate a temporary commitment to a new relationship or acceptance of new tasks in an already existing relationship. Although spiritual forces are invoked in the oath, they do not become party to the oath; they function merely as witnesses.

Structuring oaths invoke the decisions of extra-terrestrial forces in creating, recreating, structuring or restructuring relationships intended to be permanent or last a long time. They can be taken by an individual or a group; they must be taken in the presence of others who affirm their legitimacy. Their ritual is complex; they should be avoided by younger males and remain in the hands of senior elders. It may be prudent to ask a specialist to be present or officiate, as such oaths explicitly ask the spiritual forces to be party to the oath.

Cursing oaths invoke evil spiritual forces; they intend to harm, destroy or threaten to destroy relationships. They can be taken by groups or individuals; they do not need witnesses to be effective. They threaten *thahu*, spiritual uncleanliness; some of them belong in the realm of *urogi*, witchcraft, others do not. They may be spoken by individuals, male or female; they can also be inflicted by a specialist in *urogi*.

Kunyua Muuma

Commitment oaths fell in a broad class of oaths, which, referring to the drinking of beer after the oath, were known as *kunyua muuma*, drinking oaths. The oaths were simple, directed at a specific aim or act; they rarely had more than a few clauses. In the nineteenth century they should not be taken by women, children or junior males; yet there are several nineteenth-century incidents in which *anake*, warriors, drank *muuma*.

In the simplest *muuma*, post-oathing festivities were at a minimum; in somewhat more elaborate settings, a post-*muuma* feast might include the meat from a ritually slaughtered *thenge*, male goat, as well as beer. A portion of the beer would, as always when beer was drunk, be poured on the ground for the ancestors.

Appendices

The oaths consisted of clauses, each a clearly delineated promise; after each clause, the person taking the oath invoked supernatural punishment on himself should he break his word. The punishment was acted out by the use of vegetable matter, crushing leaves, breaking twigs or thin branches of trees. If not prohibited by elders for other reasons, such oaths *could* be taken on the land; no *thahu* was involved unless the promises extracted contravened the Kikuyu moral order.

The oaths were of limited duration and extent; most men would regard them as null and void after six seasons. They could also be broken by agreement, by reaching their objective, or by moving to an area away from where the oath had been taken. They could be renewed, but one was not obliged to do so.

The use of vegetable matter during the oath is more indicative of the strength of the oath than the ritual invocation of punishment for non-compliance. The supernatural forces were not seriously concerned in these oaths; an oath taker would be more afraid of the social consequences of breaking them when those who had extracted the oaths felt he had reneged on his promise, than of religious wrath. Some men who had been raised with greater fear of the supernatural than others, might be afraid; they might ask a curer, a *mundu mugo*, to release them through a simple restoration ceremony.

Though within the rank of *muuma*, some commitment oaths carried greater weight; this was indicated by using meat rather than vegetable matter in the ritual. I have called these oaths amended *muuma*; participants in such oaths might touch the raw meat and each other. In still more amended *muuma*, participants might touch the blood of the sacrifical animal, then each other and the leader. The meat would be cooked afterwards; in *muuma* no uncooked meat was eaten.

Whatever the type of *muuma*, the ritual objects held by the oath takers, whether branches, vegetable matter or meat, did not become party to the promises; nor did the invocation of ancestral or other spiritual forces mean that they supported or participated in the *muuma*. None of these oaths were serious enough to warrant cleansing; neither the oath taker, nor his land was defiled. Elders nevertheless discouraged *muuma*, not because they defiled the land, but because they might lead to social tensions.

Commitment oaths were frequent in the nineteenth century; they were taken by young warriors who vowed to stand together against the demands of older warriors and elders for their booty; buyers of land might demand that the person who drove the goats to the seller took the oath as warranty for reasonable care.

Oaths which created, structured or restructured relationships

These oaths dealt with decisions regarding permanent relationships between men, ancestors, spiritual forces and the land. They affected the oath taker, his household, his kinsmen and his land. While humans could speak and be heard as these oaths were public, the opinion of spiritual forces, ancestors and land needed to be read from their actions. It was imperative that they receive sufficient time to signal approval or disapproval. The spiritual forces participated as full members in the oath; the final decision was in the last analysis not made by the human participants but by the spiritual forces.[1]

That the oaths were concerned with long-term, if not permanent relationships

Appendix VIII: Late Nineteenth- and Twentieth-Century Oaths

is shown by the buying of Ndorobo land.[2] In these transactions, land and its ancestors were transferred from the Ndorobo sellers to the Kikuyu, leading to new relationships between them after the sale had been completed. Like all these oaths, the 'adoption' oath was played out over an extended period of time.

The action would start by meetings between seller and buyer; when an agreement was reached, the first part of the oath would spell out the arrangements and the relationship would take effect. The second phase was a waiting period, in which the ancestors – who might need as many as fourteen or more seasons – made their decision known by giving or withholding fertility from a tract of land given by the seller and from the animals (or a girl) given by the buyer. If no evidence of fertility was forthcoming, the proposed transaction was moot. If evidence of fertility – on both sides – was clear, the third stage of the oath was marked by sacrifices, by demarcation of the land and handing over part of the purchase price.

Similar three-part oaths could be used in criminal cases which elders could not solve to the satisfaction of the parties involved. These oaths started with a sacrifice, after which one of the parties made a public statement about the breach in the relationship, perhaps accusing someone of witchcraft or theft. The other party responded; both parties made their statement while holding a part of a sacrifice. Assertions took the form of clauses, each closing with the invocation of the judgment of the spiritual forces. Both sides declared that they were willing to abide by their judgments; the sacrificial animal demonstrated the fate of the man who had committed perjury.

Each party could call witnesses; after all had made their statements, a specified waiting period, commensurate with the matter at issue but no longer than seven or nine seasons, began. In civil cases the spiritual forces spoke through fertility; their medium in criminal cases was death and disaster. During this solemn time all involved, including their animals, might have to observe sexual continence.

Elders would rule for the party least affected by misfortune. Their judgment set the final part of the oath in motion: confession, assessment of damages, purification and sometimes punishment in the form of fines, banishment or death. If a guilty party was willing to confess, if it was a first offence, punishment might be avoided though not payment of damages. Repeat offenders might be banished or put to death, but had to pay damages first. Guilty and innocent had to undergo a cleansing ceremonial, the *gutahikio;* it was itself an oath which was taken facing the symbolic representation of *N'gai* on Mount Kenya. The guilty party ritually removed the crime from his body by vomiting up *tatha*, the stomach content of a slaughtered goat. The end of this ritual indicated that the offender had returned to the community and normal relationships had been restored.

The oaths of the legal system could take several specific forms. The *kuringa thenge* oath demanded that a goat was beaten to death; accuser and accused made their statements while involved in this action. The *thenge* oath graphically displayed the punishment awaiting the guilty; the action of all participants demonstrated their awareness and acceptance, should their guilt be proven. Taking an oath on the *githathi* stone, an atlas bone of an elephant or a stone with seven holes, accentuated and symbolized the presence of the spirits, who would make certain that the guilty did not escape their just deserts. Only a few elders owned a *githathi;* others had to make do with the bone of another animal or a stone. It was kept hidden at all times; if touched by women or the uninitiated, the *githathi* and all involved needed to undergo extensive purification.[3]

Appendices

Cursing oaths

Cursing oaths belonged to the sphere of *kuroga*, witching. They were aimed at the destruction of individuals, their kin, their land, and their relationships. For this purpose they used substances which brought ritual uncleanliness or *thahu*, perhaps semen, menstrual and human blood, or the spilled fluids from suicides. Behind these oaths stood the idea that evil, *thahu*, was always present and could be invoked; remaining *theru*, ritually pure, demanded constant attention and avoidance of what would give the evil forces access to the human community.

Cursing oaths, as part of *urogi*, witchcraft, were taken alone, in darkness and under secrecy. Those cursed might not be aware of what had occurred; fear often accompanied misfortunes: one could not know whether they were due to ordinary circumstances or to a curse. Those who did not want to curse themselves, could pay a *murogi* to do so.

Cursing was not restricted to males; females had the same power, though curses of young people – who should not have cursed to begin with – were considered weak. The older and wealthier the person, the more potent the curse. Reasons for cursing were often personal; anger and jealousy might lead to cursing; envy was one of the most frequently mentioned reasons.

Such cursing was always wrong; those found guilty would be prosecuted before the elders. Witchcraft ranked with murder; it was punishable by death or banishment.

Cursing oaths of a second type were not regarded as witchcraft, though they might involve spilling blood. They were a final resort of people who had been wronged; they might be directed against a *mbari* which refused compensation for the malfeasance of one of its members. A man who felt that he had been convicted unjustly because the opposing party had lied, could curse him. A woman whose children kept dying might single out a kinsman of her husband and accuse him of the killing. Elders could curse in the pursuit of justice; a suspect who refused to take an oath on the *githathi* stones might be cursed, as might individuals who refused the order of elders to give redress, after having been found guilty. A father might curse a son who injured his brother or sold land in spite of a *kirumi*. A curse might be used to prevent or evoke behaviour: one might pay a *murogi* to curse a trespasser on the land; he might demand that stolen goods be returned.

Though legitimate, these curses were dangerous; they could provoke counter curses, unleashing a chain reaction. Legitimate and illegitimate curses would affect the victim; illegitimate curses would also affect those who cursed. This could evoke a flood of evil; one of the prime tasks of elders was to watch against witchcraft and remove it. Secret curses were exceedingly difficult to remove. They might not become known until the curser had long died: a woman whose children died might learn that her husband's grandfather had been cursed and that the curse was only now taking effect. Curses to obtain justice could be diagnosed earlier and easier. They were spoken within the hearing of witnesses; if they used blood – the preferred substance for judicial curses – it was spilled within sight of others.

As long as the curser was alive, and cooperative, elders would do their utmost to solve the problem and bring the parties together in the shortest possible time. If they were successful, all involved would go through a *gutahikio*, a cleansing ritual. If the curser refused, elders had in the final analysis the power to force the issue. This was the only time cleansing could be forced; elders had to be very sure of

Appendix VIII: Late Nineteenth- and Twentieth-Century Oaths

their case because there was a significant chance that the curser would curse the elders, even while submitting to their force.

Even when they had removed their curse, users of *urogi* remained suspect and elders would attempt to ban them for fear that they would repeat their offence. The safest way was to banish them from *mbari* land on pain of death. If they removed the curses they had spoken and left peacefully, they might be given stock to start elsewhere. If they refused to leave, elders – with the cooperation of the curser's kin – could declare that they had been banished; cursers then lost their right to remain with their kin or use their land. The ancestors would no longer protect them. Killing them would not be an offence and 'no case would be held'. If elders were unsuccessful because the curser had already died, those cursed might change their ritual affiliation from the demanding *gikuyu* to the less demanding *ukabi* division. If that did not halt the evil, they might have to abandon their land and start a new life elsewhere: like all oaths, curses were bound by the land of those cursed.

Commitment and structuring oaths in the twentieth century

The legitimacy of oaths depended on the right of the oath administrator to give and oath takers to take them; oaths were also judged on the appropriateness of the clauses and the ritual they used. There was by no means agreement among elders; some of the more conservative and orthodox would demand that everything was done as in the past; others gave more leeway. They attributed 'violations' of nineteenth-century rules to changing times and lack of proper instruction.[4]

Commitment oaths were used widely during the colonial era and were the stock in trade of anti-colonial organizations. When these organizations started to ask for oaths, they would ask ordinary fee-paying members, when they first joined, for a basic commitment oath. Such oaths might be given by men familiar with local conditions, they could vary the clauses to fit local conditions. Recruiters used limited ritual and would avoid conflicts with the owners of the land.

In what was apparently a twentieth-century innovation, leaders or trusted co-workers of leaders frequently offered oaths which not only asked for larger contributions, but also for a more lasting commitment; I have called these oaths of the amended commitment. They were often initiated by leaders, who would invite the chosen to 'come and eat a goat together', the recognized formula for an amended commitment oath, which also was part of structuring oaths. Those invited could come from the ranks of those who had, or had not taken a basic oath.[5] Where basic oaths vary considerably in place and time, the phrases and ritual of the amended commitment of any one leader were less variable: they were rarer and administrators fewer.[6] The oaths might vary considerably between leaders and movements in clauses and ritual because they made direct reference to the objective of the oath and the movement for which it was taken.

Traditional structuring oaths remained common in land transactions and judicial procedures before the elders. In such cases the waiting period – though shorter than before – was enforced. Compared to the nineteenth century, ritual was reduced, yet it always included 'eating a goat together' during and after the rituals. The colonial government used structuring oaths to enforce compliance with its – structuring – rules; the waiting period in such cases was replaced by an invocation of spiritual forces under the tacit assumption that they agreed with the promises to be made. While it allowed Christians to take such an oath on the

Appendices

Bible, others who became members of the *kiama*, the LNC, or the courts had to take a *githathi* oath that they had been and would be 'impartial' in their deliberations.[7]

Named twentieth-century oaths

Many twentieth-century oaths might carry the name of the organization which promoted them or the ideal they were supposed to convey. The immediate purpose of virtually all oaths was to raise money; in the early days some, later almost all, combined this with specific instructions. As more and more such oaths developed during the 1930s and 1940s, the population might call them, by the 1940s, collectively *muuma wa kindu na kindu* or (freely translated) 'oaths for/of many things'.

Oaths given by the same organization might carry different names, depending on place and time; in the late 1930s and the 1940s, when organizations tried to extend their sphere of influence and avoid government restrictions, many organizations had multiple names. Oaths given through and for independent schools might carry the name *Muumbi na Gikuyu;* KCA oaths might be called KCA or *Muumbi na Gikuyu* oaths; the 'College' oath of 1939 became the *Githunguri*, the *Umoja* and the *Muumbi na Gikuyu* oath; the *Mbari* oath was an *Umoja* or a *Muumbi na Gikuyu* oath from the beginning. A 'Beecher' oath might be a KCA oath, a variant of a *Githunguri* oath, a KAU oath, or stand by itself to harness support against the Beecher plan. After the KCA was proscribed, oathing for it continued under several names; in the 1940s some men in the Rift Valley thought that taking an oath for KAU meant taking one for the KCA; others thought that, despite the variety of local names, such as *Kenia*, all were KCA oaths. The degree of support an organization enjoyed cannot be judged by the number of members, nor by the people who were oathed by it: supporters might not be oathed or become members.

While there is no evidence that KAU started out as an oathing organization, around 1948/9 Nairobi KAU did administer KAU oaths but I lack the data to compare this KAU oath with the KCA/KAU oath given in the Rift Valley after Kenyatta had declared that the KCA and KAU were one. I have no overt evidence that Kenyatta himself administered KAU oaths at Githunguri, though he was reputed to have done so in the Rift Valley. Underground KCA leaders administered KCA/KAU or 'pure' KCA oaths at Githunguri; Kenyatta's associates administered *Githunguri*, 'College', *Muumbi na Gikuyu*, or *Umoja* oaths. Some later oaths single out leaders: the 'College', the *Githunguri* and until 1951 possibly the Rift Valley KCA/KAU oath, named Kenyatta and/or Mbiu; there is no such evidence from the Nairobi KAU oaths.

While higher levels of oaths may have developed some similarity of clauses, at the lower level variation persisted. Lower levels of oaths continued to ask for support until the late 1940s; by that time the higher-level oaths had begun to ask for obedience.

The basic oaths of most organizations were commitment oaths, which asked for confidentiality, not to betray fellow Kikuyu, not to sell land, to make contributions, and to support Kenyatta or Mbiu. Takers might also be enjoined not to drink beer, to oppose terracing, or not to greet passing Europeans or their vehicles. Ritual was simple if not absent; there might be a celebration afterwards with beer and meat.

While basic oaths tended to be given locally, most modern organizations also worked through amended commitment oaths for larger contributors and trusted

Appendix VIII: Late Nineteenth- and Twentieth-Century Oaths

aides or spokesmen, which were organized at the headquarters of the organizations. Depending on the size of the movement, the leader or a trusted functionary would officiate; ritual would be more elaborate and include the eating of meat during and after the oath. These higher-level oaths were more likely to ask for obedience than support; they might ask those who took the oath to be willing to accept punishment if they broke the terms of the oath. These oaths might be taken instead of or after a basic commitment oath. During the Emergency still higher levels of oaths developed; their ritual almost always involved material which under ordinary circumstances would only have been part of the cursing oaths, taken by men who felt deprived of justice. These oaths might include hypothetical situations to test the willingness of the taker to obey the movement or its leader; phrases such as 'if ever I be asked to kill my ....' These oaths were only taken by people who had already taken basic commitment oaths and amended commitment oaths. They were rarely offered to women.

Around 1951 names in oaths above the commitment level were supplanted by 'this movement' or 'our movement'. In lower-level oaths Kenyatta had taken pride of place in Githunguri oaths; Nairobi oaths rarely mentioned him, but might mention KAU or the KCA. After his arrest, the Kenyatta name took pride of place.

Legitimacy and illegitimacy of Mau Mau oaths

All Mau Mau oaths must be seen within a framework which rejects the legitimacy of colonial power and European occupation, and in this context allows behaviour which ordinarily would be unacceptable. The dividing line between right and wrong is that what harms Kikuyu land and Kikuyu is wrong.

Though there were changes over time, a great variation from place to place, and sometimes legitimate doubt whether the oath administrator served the resistance, many in the local population in the the last few years before and during the first months of the Emergency became part of a two-tier framework. At the bottom were the largest number of supporters; they had been oathed with a simple commitment oath, which the administration would call a first oath. Men and, somewhat later, women had been inducted; their reasons for joining had varied; but apart from in the Rift Valley very few had been forced. Most were landless or land poor; they had paid even when they could barely afford it, because they hoped that 'the movement' or Kenyatta would bring deliverance. Their oath was not specific, its objectives limited beyond support and secrecy; it was usually binding for three years or less. These oaths might be illegal as far as the Europeans were concerned; they were legitimate within Kikuyu ideology.

What the administration would call a second oath was usually one of two types of oath. Many were re-takes of a first oath – many Nairobi second oaths fell into that category – because the time had lapsed, because the area where they lived during the Emergency did not accept the oath taken elsewhere, or sometimes simply because the movement was running out of money and no longer trusted its constituency. The clauses of such oaths were not much more than a variant on those of the first oath.

A second type of amended commitment oath, which contained 'eating meat together', was used for more important supporters, and taken by a smaller, mostly male group. This oath demanded a greater commitment, involved heavier fees and obedience which was more binding and enduring, though not permanent. It also might contain a number of hypothetical situations such as 'if I ever am called to bring the head of ...'. Taking their example from structuring oaths, they might ask the taker to invoke the wrath of the supernatural forces, should he fail the oath.

Locally these oath takers were often recruited from those who had taken a basic oath, though some wealthier men had not done so. The administration, and consequently the screening teams, called these amended commitment oaths, second oaths; in its eyes the second oath was both later in time and more subversive.

Elders by and large accepted the amended commitment oath, although they came in a bewildering variety. They thought them problematic if the oaths demanded touching blood or when they were administered by younger males, who were not elders as those handling blood should be. They distinguished, however, between wrongful acts and acts which caused *thahu;* under normal conditions, all commitment oaths which used features of structuring or cursing oaths would have been rejected as causing *thahu*. During Mau Mau, elders tended to see such oaths as wrongful acts, which did not need cleansing and were necessitated by the colonial presence.

Many elders preferred that any oaths, even simple commitment oaths, unless they administered them, were not given on *mbari* land. This applied definitely to amended commitment oaths but even more to oaths which went further, the administration's third, fourth or subsequent level oaths. Such oaths used fluids, which harmed the land; their clauses were framed as cursing oaths. They endangered the taker, his kin and the land. They might have been legitimate under extreme circumstances; they had to be aimed at a specific, narrowly defined objective, and to be administered by a ritual specialist. These conditions did not prevail even in the resistance; these oaths were too often used to force Kikuyu into solidarity.[8]

All unacceptable oaths, a few of the second, but all of the consequent oaths, violated the Kikuyu moral order. They were called bi-oaths; oaths which went far, too far.[9] Elders were certain that 'their sons had not taken bi-oaths'; it was not up to them to judge oaths taken elsewhere, unless the takers lived or came to live on *mbari* land. Bi-oaths were a matter for elders of the land where they were taken; those elders knew the special circumstances which might even have made them legitimate. Some might be *muuma wa gutwara tuhii miti*, oaths to give aid and help to males about to be initiated.[10]

Basic oaths did not need cleansing, whether the government had declared the organization for which they were taken, illegal or not.[11] Amended commitment oaths, or second oaths, deserved another look, but given that they were used in the framework of resistance, most were within the range of acceptable oaths. Bi-oaths, some second, but most subsequent oaths, were not likely to be acceptable, though one should only be concerned with those on one's own *mbari* land; those taking these oaths should be offered cleansing.

Though between 1948 and the height of Mau Mau in 1953/4, tolerance for oaths had increased in response to the sweeping condemnation of all oaths by the government, elders continued to reject some oaths. They did not condone the oaths of Dedan Mugo, who was accused in 1950 of using human blood to seal oaths.[12] The oaths taken by participants during a feast before the Marige massacre of April 1953 could not be condoned either, even though the participants were said to have been drunk at the time, which was normally an extenuating circumstance.[13]

My data indicate that the overwhelming number of Mau Mau oaths were legitimate within Kikuyu ideology. Second oaths are difficult to judge; fewer than

Appendix IX: Notes on Mau Mau

20 local men and women went beyond a second oath; the highest known number taken by anyone was four.

Notes

1. The oath has been described as 'fundamentally a procedure by which God is invoked as judge between two litigants when man has failed to determine the issue between them'. This is true for all oaths, but had already become a formality without much significance in nineteenth-century commitment oaths. It is particularly true for judicial oaths, but the presence and active cooperation of the spiritual forces is sought in all structuring oaths (the presence of evil spiritual forces is sought in cursing oaths).
   The quote was part H. E. Lambert's speech, 'Disintegration and reintegration of the Meru tribe'; parts of this speech have been preserved in
   MSS. Afric. s. 424 *Guard Book of Miscellaneous Papers Relating to Africa* (embargoed) papers of Audrey G. M. Mullins and I. R. Gillespie, Rhodes House, Oxford.
2. Though structuring or restructuring oaths were only supposed to be used for intended permanent relationships, they were used in peace treaties with Maasai when 'permanent' was certain to be elastic. Such oaths were nevertheless appropriate as Kikuyu 'never intended to break them' but had to do so, because Maasai did not honour the promises.... Should they be overly concerned, they could ask a *mundu mugo* for a ritual which would set the oath aside.
3. 1924. AR/291/KBU/17.
4. Even the most conservative elder, who felt that the nineteenth century should be the measure of all things, lacked the detailed ritual information surrounding nineteenth-century oathing described by Dr. L. S. B. Leakey's highly ritualized Kikuyu life. It seems likely that this described an 'ideal' structure; under normal conditions ordinary senior elders and a local curer acted according to what knowledge they had. If this failed, they might call in a 'specialist' who then undoubtedly would attribute the failure to ritual commissions and omissions.
   1909. October–December, Ukamba Province Quarterly Report, pp. 5ff.
   1977. Leakey, L. S. B., *The Southern Kikuyu before 1903*, Vols I–III, London: Academic Press. The material on oathing is rich; pp. 98ff. discusses land transactions; p. 1004 deals with judicial oaths, their annulment, punishment for false oaths and purification ritual; p. 1211 provides material on cleansing and purification.
5. There is no agreement what oaths elders took to keep young men from drinking alcoholic beverages in the 1920s.
   1923. AR/290 KBU 16.
6. Such oaths might be given to men who went abroad or were given a political mission.
7. 1926. AR/294 KBU/19.
   1927. HOR/192 KBU/20.
   1950. AR/323 KBU/41.
8. A relatively small number of documents describe the elaboration and proliferation of oaths. All stress the increase in brutality and bestiality of each level. Though they do not give an indication of frequency or other hard data, there is little doubt that they occurred. I regard them as perversions; there is no reason to assume that they were an inevitable consequence of Mau Mau, which should not be judged solely or even principally on these oaths. They were likely situational and rare; they were abhorred by convinced and committed local Mau Mau members.
   The documents generally recognize a hierarchy of seven oaths, with the first oath as least dangerous and a 'brigadier' or 'general's' oath as the most obscene. The second oath already demanded killing; subsequent oaths concentrated on ritual murder and the use of the corpse.
   MSS. Afric. s. 424 *The Guard Book of Miscellaneous Papers Relating to Africa* (embargoed) (Rhodes House, Oxford) contained
   a) n.d. C. J. A. Barnett Papers *Mau Mau Ceremonies as Described by Participants*,

Appendices

Including Several Confessions. It states that the Kikuyu know 70 different oaths; then gives four ascending Mau Mau oaths. In the same file were Papers on *Second and Third Grade Mau Mau Oaths* and *The Mau Mau Oaths Four–Seven.* The first details a *Kiberichia* ceremony, about 45 miles from Nanyuki, attendance about 100. Six participants corroborate eight oaths, a Forest and a Woman's oath. In general oaths are described as increasing in bestiality, with names following military rank.

b) A similar series of oaths is described by the Brodhurst-Hill Report, n.d.

The Private Papers of Dr Anthony Clayton contained

1954. 8 September *Appendix A to Special Branch Summary No 18/54 The Oaths of Mau Mau* which mentions a 1948 first oath at Kiambaa, for 'chosen elders', members of the proscribed KCA, KAU and the Kikuyu Independent Schools Association with Kenyatta, Koinange and Dedan Mugo officiating.

1954. *Report on the Sociological Causes Underlying Mau Mau with some Proposals on the Means of Ending It* contains 'Mau Mau oaths ceremonies', almost certainly prepared by Dr L. S. B. Leakey. Confidential, mimeographed.

1960. Cmnd 1030 *Historical Survey of the Origins and Growth of Mau Mau* (F. D. Corfield) (Corfield Report), pp. 163ff.

9. Kikuyu often designate time and distance with the same word. *Bi* is likely linked to a long drawn out word *bi* which indicates long time or a long distance. According to Benson *bi-i-i* means travelling without stopping A *bi*-oath probably indicated an oath which had overstepped the bounds.

1964. Benson, T. G., *Kikuyu–English Dictionary*, Oxford: Claredon Press, p. 28.

10. In initiation rites relatives provided young males with sticks, *miti*, to compete in mock battles. It can be translated as an oath for younger males, not yet mature enough to be regarded as adults. To translate it as an oath for those who carry arms is rather far-fetched. Buytenhuys has summarized the scant evidence available for Nairobi and Kiambu support for the forest fighter.

1982. Buytenhuys, Rob, *Essays on Mau Mau Contributions to Mau Mau Historiography* (Research Reports No. 17), Leiden, the Netherlands: African Studies Centre, pp. 52ff.

11. 1987. Kanogo, Tabitha, *Squatters and the Roots of Mau Mau 1905–1963*, London: James Currey, pp. 116ff.

12. 1960. Corfield Report, *op. cit.*, p. 85.

13. 1974. Wanyoike, E. N., *An African Pastor*, Nairobi: East African Publishing House, pp. 200ff.

Appendix IX

Notes on Mau Mau

1. The relationship between KAU and Mau Mau[1]

The relationship between KAU membership and Mau Mau can only be tentatively established. Because screening teams (also called committees) considered KAU or KCA oaths as Mau Mau, it is quite possible that a number of men did not admit membership. The raw data I have indicate that 56 out of 61 or 91.8 per cent of KAU/KCA members took a Mau Mau oath, if KAU/KCA oaths were indeed Mau Mau. There was considerable opposition to the classification.

Rift Valley

Many accepted the contention that, after the return of Kenyatta, KCA and KAU were one, with KAU a cover-up for the banned KCA. Among the 125 males, 92, or 73.6 per cent took an oath. Of the 92 oath takers, 13 had been members of the KCA or KAU/KCA and had taken an oath for their organization; the *Kenia* or the 'United Natives' oaths were regarded as KCA oaths. Screening Teams regarded 11 of the 13 oaths or 84.6 per cent of these oaths as Mau Mau. Some protested their classification; the six males who subsequently took a second oath accepted their classification. As oathing in the Rift Valley was interrupted by early detention and dispersion, few conclusions can be drawn.

Rural Area

In the rural area 254 out of 531 men, or 47.8 per cent, had taken an oath. Sixteen males had been members of KAU. In contrast to the Rift Valley, KAU was seen as independent of the KCA. Of the 16, 13 or 81.3 per cent took an oath, which was regarded as a Mau Mau oath by the screening team. Close to half of those designated Mau Mau protested their classification. Two took two oaths; one took more than two oaths. The correlation between KCA/KAU membership and oath taking is high.

Nairobi

Of the 203 males in Nairobi, 167 or 82.3 per cent had been members of Mau Mau. Thirty-two males had belonged to KAU; only four thought that their KAU oath was a KCA oath. Before 1950, seven took an early KAU oath; only three males who were not members of KAU took such an early oath. That several unions before 1950 demanded that their members take a KAU oath *may* have had

Appendices

an influence. By the Declaration of the Emergency, at least 19 additional men who claimed KAU membership had taken an oath; the remaining six KAU members took an oath after 1950. In Nairobi all KAU members took what the screening team regarded as a Mau Mau oath.

Seventeen males took a second oath, four a subsequent oath.

2. Initiation Years and Mau Mau participation

The data cover 725 men from a potential population of 859 males who knew their *riika*. Some years are not represented; some years have multiple names because men were initiated at different locations; sometimes a year in which only females should have been initiated is collapsed with the closest male year. The first number reflects the number of responses; the second Mau Mau involvement. Percentages provided after *Kinyotoku*.

Ngaruya/Gichuru	3/0	
Ngigi/Uhere	5/0	
Kienyeku/Muthura	13/0	
Njege	7/0	
Nyaregi/Manyara	8/2	
Makio	3/1	
Mburu	6/0	
Gichere/Mutungu	8/0	
Kamande	15/4	
Kanyutu	9/2	
Kangei/Kabau	5/2	
Kihiumweri	9/2	
Kinyotoku/Kimiri	42/16	38.1%
Munanda	1/1	100.0%
Chirringi/Nuthu	53/26	49.1%
Muteithia/Munai/Mithuo/Thigu	9/7	77.8%
Gethigo/Sucari	12/9	75.0%
Ndege ya mbere//Ndege ya thutha	47/26	55.3%
Githingithia	2/1	50.0%
Ngigi munyinyi/Ndereche	12/6	50.0%
Mambeleo	5/3	60.0%
Marobo/Karara	17/7	41.2%
Njane Kanini	26/20	76.9%
Ndururu/Mbaca/Wandindi	38/30	78.9%
Kenya Bathi/Kabaka	22/14	63.6%
Japan/Thuhia/Itaka	50/43	86.0%
College/Korenji	18/15	83.3%
Hitira/Kinyara/Bote	35/30	85.7%
Muthua/Mukongo/Kingora	11/9	81.8%
Gichina bangi/Turn-up	13/12	92.3%
Permit/Mwanga/Kamiti	22/21	95.5%
Muomboko	26/21	80.8%
1945/Njata/Muthiro wa Ngui	17/16	94.1%
1946	21/15	71.4%
1947	27/22	81.5%
1948	22/12	54.5%
1949 and later*	86/80	93.0%

* These years include 1952 *Warururungana* (after a type of policeman who cursed people), 1953 *Mwihugo* or *Manjiniti* (Emergency), 1954 *Gotora* (homemade gun), and 1955 *Gicagi* (Villages).

Appendix IX: Notes on Mau Mau

3. Elders' rank and Mau Mau participation: Rift Valley, rural and Nairobi

Many males of appropriate age had in 1956 not paid for elders' status. The first number indicates the total of men in each status category; second number indicates Mau Mau involvement.

No payments	532/372	69.9%
Mburi imwe (1)	50/33	66.0%
Mburi igeri (2)	123/69	56.1%
Mburi ithatu (3)	42/15	35.7%
Mburi inya (4)	48/9	18.8%
Above *mburi inya*	33/0	0.0%

4. Age and Mau Mau membership

When Kenyatta left in 1932 for 14 years, *Njane kanini* had just been or was about to be initiated. If Mau Mau had centred around Kenyatta, one might have expected a higher involvement among those who knew him. The reverse is true.

The *anake* who might have supported him when he left, were by the Emergency (20 years later) at least 40 years old; they belonged to the 41–60 age group in the study and have a 36.6 per cent involvement. Older men who had supported him then might be in the upper range of that age group or older. They do not make a strong showing in Mau Mau, they have a 10.9 per cent involvement.

Those who were at best *anake* when he left but more likely children or even unborn carried the brunt of Mau Mau. In 1952 males who had not yet reached 18 were involved at a rate of 50 per cent; those 18–25 participated 80.7 per cent and those 26–40 participated at a rate of 60 per cent.

5. Resistance and collaboration[2]

The anti-Mau Mau literature of the Emergency period and the pro-Mau Mau literature later were replete with value-laden terminology. Much of the mission literature reflected the idea that Mau Mau was sin, heathenism, or a revival from a dark past in which men lived in terror and fear from evil forces. The belief that Christians and their children were particularly in danger was a common theme. Many Europeans believed it to be primitive and below human standards; the 'Letters to the Editor' of the *East African Standard* speak vociferously to this perspective. Michael Blundel in the Legislative Council called Mau Mau a disease which had to be rooted out; the government's approach that it represented a return to barbarism is documented in speeches and declarations, faithfully reported by that newspaper.[3]

Strongly influenced by L. S. B. Leakey, the Corfield Report, like the pamphlets written by J. G. Carothers, promoted the idea that the Mau Mau rebellion was more than a political movement of insurrection. It was an atavistic and amoral movement as well, in which a primitive people which had stagnated for centuries, too suddenly exposed to modern society, had been exploited by evil leaders.[4] Few, perhaps Christians or older tribal men, perhaps men only out for their own good,

Appendices

had remained outside its fateful influence, and 'loyal' to their colonial leaders.[5]

After Independence there was a significant terminological and attitudinal shift which often expressed itself in the European terminology of the Second World War. The 'thugs', 'criminals', 'barbarians', and 'insurgents' of the *East African Standard* became 'radicals', 'freedom fighters', and 'heroes'. Where 'loyalists' had been praised, they were now more likely to be identified as collaborators, if not traitors and quislings.

Literature written in this framework sees Kikuyu opposition to colonialism growing over decades as aggression – first mainly verbal – from small groups of 'radical politicians' ultimately becomes the armed aggression of the Mau Mau forest fighters, the true heroes and liberators. This scenario is depicted against a backdrop of – mainly older, preferably wealthy – land owners who accommodated colonialism and were its *profiteurs*. These descriptions uncritically use the government's self-serving term 'loyalism' for those who did not take oaths, applying it to all who countered Mau Mau aggression or executed government orders – chiefs, Homeguards, members of screening teams – calling them traitors to the cause. Their motivation is simple; they are the 'wealthy', afraid to lose their advantages, they stayed on the side of the government because of greed.[6]

Both anti- and pro-Mau Mau literature tend to reflect Western ideologies in their acceptance of and often high esteem for physical aggression in the pursuit of approved objectives. They also tacitly support the idea that non-participation in such aggression creates legitimate suspicion about the motives of those who abstain. Even a government servant seemed to have had a sneaking respect for the men who were in the forest and little but disdain for the Kiambu men who were not; 'they are more interested in trade, litigation, corruption, intrigue ... and politics than in wearing the crown of martyrdom'.[7]

The *East African Standard* speaks more to Western imagery than to reality when reporting the Marige massacre. It reflects a world of manly courage with brave Homeguards patrolling their area while debased and cowardly enemies slaughtered wives and children; it describes how watchful security forces undauntedly went to the rescue and slew the murderous barbarians.[8]

In Kikuyu perspectives, heroism and physical aggression have a place and are valid when they can reasonably be expected to bring results at a bearable cost. They are restricted to the young, but are stages a true adult should have left behind in favour of profitable work, when industry, not heroism, is demanded. When faced with an enemy, one fights but hopes for little loss of life; when one takes prisoners, they are incorporated to strengthen the group. When an enemy is too strong, one emulates his achievements, one serves him until strong enough to rout him: if the enemy is wise and sensible, he will know that his hour has come. The ideas attributed to Chege wa Kibiru that the Kikuyu should learn and use the Europeans until they were strong enough for their independence to return, were as valid in the 1950s as in earlier times.

In this perspective, the person who works for or with the government is not a collaborator if he does so to protect his fellow men, to gain strength and share it. A collaborator, on the other hand, might be a person whose single objective is private gain, who does not hesitate to harm his fellow Kikuyu in the process if they can be used to advantage, who does not protect his fellows when he can. The colonial government and Europeans are there to be used; it is right to use them to learn, to take advantage of their capabilities; it is right to use them against Kikuyu who disobey Kikuyu rules and are not amenable to warnings.

Appendix IX: Notes on Mau Mau

To instruct the government in Kikuyu norms was not collaboration, even if government later would use its knowledge to harm the Kikuyu. To give such information with the express intent that government could use it against the Kikuyu, was collaboration. Such behaviour classified one as a 'stump', an enemy on the road. In Mau Mau, non-participation was not collaboration, nor was opposition against oaths which violated Kikuyu norms. Betraying those who were involved in Mau Mau, who had not violated Kikuyu norms, was collaboration; making sure that the government removed those who seriously compromised Kikuyu norms was not.

That local Kikuyu regarded collaboration as relatively rare was borne out by the lack of vengeful actions after Independence, by no means only the result of pervasive directions from above. In 1956 some people had been accused of collaboration. In 1962 no official action had been taken against them, though the accused were well aware of local opinion. They were left to live with fear if and when revenge might be taken; in the meantime they were quietly edged out of any public office.

6. Screening

The government was convinced that the overwhelming number of Kikuyu belonged to Mau Mau, a unitary insurrection movement. Though most were not actively fighting, the oaths they had taken would force them to aid and protect those who were. The population as a whole could safely be assumed to be guilty until proven innocent by screening for oath taking, to which all Kikuyu over about 14 years of age had to submit.

This was to be handled by screening teams, basically *ad hoc* civil courts composed of local males, operating in areas small enough for them to know the people personally. Members were paid between shs 120/– and shs 160/–, the level of junior government clerks. Each team had a clerk, sufficiently proficient in English to prepare weekly reports for the District Officer; he was paid between shs 180/– and shs 200/–. A local team had started operations in January 1953; oath takers were not eligible to serve, even if they had confessed voluntarily prior to being screened.

Initially closely controlled by a European District Officer, the team started out by following the government line that Mau Mau had developed in and from the proscribed KCA, at the end of the 1940s. Mau Mau involvement could therefore be presumed from post-1948 oaths which could be linked to the KCA or any of its presumed front organizations. Oaths after 1950 could be regarded as Mau Mau (proscribed in August 1950), whether taken directly for the movement or for one of its many presumed front organizations. Oaths for KAU were equally suspect.

All inhabitants were required to appear before the team and – with the help of its literate members – fill out written forms detailing membership, the circumstances under which oaths had been taken, the administrator, possible other officials and those present. Those who had not taken oaths received a 'loyalty certificate' which gave exemption from the punitive Emergency tax, and allowed workers to move between their homes and places of work. Men or women who lacked a certificate were Mau Mau members: they were liable for the tax, could work away from home only in exceptional cases, were fined and could be detained. The team imposed the fines; it could recommend that the District Officer give a Detention Order, but could not issue one itself; the District Officer could work together with the CID to impose detention or imprisonment.

In the early months of close supervision the team called those whose involvement was a matter of record or concern; they imposed fines of shs 100/- for one and higher fines for multiple oaths. Though it was supposed to recommend detention orders for oath administrators and active recruiters, knowing that the absence of a breadwinner might punish the household more than the oath taker, it did so only if those involved remained active. It justified its low detention rate by explaining to the District Officer that a high proportion of people had 'sincerely confessed'.

When supervision relaxed, so did the team; detention became even rarer; the fine for one oath was shs 30/- and those who could show hardship might be let off with only a few shillings. Females and males too poor to pay might have to perform unpaid *gitati*; males could also choose to serve in the Homeguard. Poor females, the young, the old and sick might be excused; a chief could 'forgive' fines altogether.

There was no uniformity in the operation or judgment of the screening teams across Kikuyu country or in places where Kikuyu worked. The ideal 'organization' envisioned by the government was often quite different from local organizations.[9]

European-dominated screening teams did not impose fines nor cleansing, while Kikuyu ones did both. Depending on the area, Rift Valley teams, mostly composed of Europeans, used the most inclusive and broad definition of Mau Mau involvement; they relied heavily on detention and eviction. The settled area teams, also European, were slow to start, used detention exceedingly sparingly, but were not likely to rehire those found to be Mau Mau. In Nairobi, employees of the military forces, the police, those working for the government or semi-public institutions were screened early; repatriation, detention and therefore loss of employment was common but fines were rare. After a flurry of early activity, the lack of concentration of the Kikuyu and their mobility hampered the work, as did private employers who refused to let 'their' Kikuyu be screened or expelled.

If Nairobi Mau Mau members were discreet, avoided contact with the police, kept their papers in order, and did not go home where they might be called by their rural team; they could live in Nairobi without detection longer than in any other area. By 1954 Mau Mau was still active when the government on 24 April mounted Operation Anvil; in the first few days 30 per cent of the local Nairobi workers were detained and another 30 per cent were forcibly repatriated. Others soon followed. Many who were arrested and detained had no chance to inform their families or salvage their few possessions; it was not uncommon for a woman to fear that husband or son had died, only to learn months later that they had been detained.

Data on 17 members of local screening teams show that the majority were between 26 and 40 years old and had at least four years of education, while the clerks who prepared reports from the written and oral information received might have eight years of schooling. The majority were among the larger land owners; ten had peasant holdings, one was a small farmer, five were landless and one had only a subsistence plot.

Four identified themselves as having remained true to their Kikuyu religion; two were Revival Christians and the others had become Christians while at school, but had since left the church. Two had taken oaths for Githunguri in 1947; four had been members of KAU. Eight had paid at least one goat for membership in the council of elders.

Appendix IX: Notes on Mau Mau

They were neither the best educated nor the more wealthy members of the community; many with more education earned better wages and could plead financial hardship, as could those with more land because they were engaged in surplus production. They did not need to serve.

7. Homeguards[10]

By 1952 the District Commissioner of Kiambu had suggested that chiefs organize local 'self-protection' groups in locations and sub-locations. Few had taken up the suggestion; although violence was increasing and becoming a daily concern, most Kikuyu did not believe that they were in immediate danger, and vigilante groups – particularly if armed – would only invite attacks. In European areas and on the outskirts of Nairobi, European Homeguard volunteer units were instituted at the time of the Emergency: members served as 'special constables'; they were allowed to carry arms, and had 'rights and powers' similar to that of the regular police. Their activities did not include the protection of the African locations.[11]

A few weeks after the Declaration of the Emergengy, police stations were built in Kikuyu country, one of them at Marige. They were staffed by one or more members of the Kenya Regiment, in charge of a detail of African police. By December of that year Gaki started to organize Homeguards; it spread from there to Kiambu. A local detail was organized by inviting *mbari* and large groups of *ahoi* to provide one or more members.

Groups were loosely organized. A local headman might become a leader of a local guard consisting of between 30 and 50 men. These units might have only spears and *pangas*; later most were provided with firearms, though the number of guards trained in their use was small. Homeguards initially served as guards to chiefs or men thought to be high on Mau Mau's list of 'enemies'; they might enforce curfews and occasionally help the security forces 'sweep' a local area.

However much local areas might be in need of protection, the fears of local authorities that Homeguards would be a mixed blessing were well grounded. Though most local Homeguards remained unaffected by their new-found power, the lack of leadership, training, discipline and supervision allowed a few to use their position for blackmail, extortion and intimidation. More dangerous was their use as enforcers of attendance at screening team meetings and cleansing. Nevertheless, such was the reputation of the security forces, particularly the Kenya Europeans who had enlisted voluntarily, that the local population, for all its fear and criticism, preferred the protection of Homeguards.

Given the economic depression caused by lack of jobs and land, there was no shortage of volunteers. Men who could not pay a fine for oathing could become Homeguards instead; perks might include a small payment but also school fees for one child, food and the right to move about during times of curfews.

Data on 54 Homeguards show that the majority were between 26 and 40 years old. Their rate of literacy was lower than that of members of the screening teams: almost one-third were illiterate; while almost two thirds of the screeners had four or more years of education, less than a third of the Homeguards had reached that level. They were predominantly small land owners; some were landless. Almost half either owned a subsistence plot or were small peasants; slightly above a quarter were peasants. Three out of the 54 were small farmers. Like the screening team

Appendices

members, most were *mbari* members; unlike them, at least half had taken a Mau Mau oath while few had paid fees for membership in the Councils.[12]

8. Cleansing ritual

The government did not encourage the use of traditonal oaths to obtain confessions but, according to elders, 'strongly recommended' that those guilty of oaths submit to a purification or cleansing ritual; it hoped that this would prevent them from retaking oaths.

Ordained clergy of recognized Churches could offer a Christian religious service instead; the Christian Council of Kenya provided guidelines through *Notes for the Guidance of Clergy and others on Cleansing Ceremonies for ex-Mau Mau*. It was only open to members of the Churches or those who had Church relationships, which meant in practice that it was only open to those who had been to school. The CCK recommended service was simple. The person to be cleansed was seated in front of the congregation, and after having been instructed to 'examine yourself before God, and to answer truthfully in the presence of this congregation', he was asked by officiating clergy:

Do you confess that you have taken the Mau Mau oath(s)?

Do you truly repent of this (these) sin(s)?

Do you renounce these oaths and put them from you forever?

Do you seek forgiveness through the blood of Christ our Saviour?

Will you now stand firm with the people of Christ in worship and witness?

Do you affirm that, by the help and grace of God, you will confess the faith of Christ, and fight against the world, the flesh and the devil?

Do you promise to attend regularly further instruction in the Christian faith?

To each of these questions the person was expected to answer 'I do' after which he was given absolution and a blessing.[13] This confession did not mention loyalty to the government, but did call Mau Mau a 'sin'. In the certificate received by those who confessed, loyalty is not mentioned:

To...

This is to certify that ... made public confession in a Christian ceremony on ... that he has repudiated Mau Mau. He has undergone instruction in the Christian faith as indicated on the reverse of this card.

Date...   ... Minister

Wanyoike Kamawe reports a version which links Christianity and the colonial government, which is also evident from the card, received by the one who confessed. In the version he reports, government is mentioned second on the card; but in the actual confession government was mentioned before the Church:[14]

I ... declare before God and these people: I wholeheartedly say that I shall never have any connection with the Mau Mau or any other association which may be against Her Majesty's Government and the good order of the country, or which may stand against Christianity. I shall remain true to this declaration and pray that God may help me to maintain it.

Appendix IX: Notes on Mau Mau

Those who were cleansed in church had been screened and fined in the ordinary way.

Apart from some church members or attenders, the majority of the local population reluctantly chose the *gutahikio*, purification ritual. While elders had regarded screening as a European matter and those who served on such committees as of little importance, the *gutahikio* purification ritual involved a serious oath. Elders therefore made sure that tradition was followed as much as possible; in keeping with this, and to avoid impurity for *mbari* members, those officiating were *ahoi*. Two of the three had reached the highest level of eldership open to *ahoi*.

The ritual was performed on Sunday afternoons at Thuita or Marige; if two men officiated and people were cleansed in twos, thirty could be cleansed at each meeting. That a number of people felt forced into the cleansing oath and retook a Mau Mau oath endangered the community as a whole; when forced cleansing was shown to have played a dominant role in the Marige massacre, the Sunday afternoon ritual was stopped. Individuals who desired to be cleansed had to make their own arrangements.

One goat was needed for two people; it was slaughtered and the intestines removed to a banana leaf where they were mixed with water and soil. The curer added some black powder from his medicine horn; he was willing to reveal only that it was derived from herbs, collected in the forest or from virgin land.

Women and men were required to take off their ornaments; women had to leave their scarves behind; no one could wear shoes or watches. Those to be cleansed knelt, facing Mount Kenya; the curer, with his back to Mount Kenya, faced them.

A small hole was dug at a straight angle to Mount Kenya; the banana leaf with the admixture was placed in it so that its sides remained visible, but only that part of the leaf closest to Mount Kenya could be seen from a distance.

The curer added leaves of the *muthakwa* bush; the men and women about to be cleansed were required to take some of the mixture in their mouth without touching it with their hands.[15] They then were required to spit it out, while the curer intoned *tahika wariga wanganiire mwiri*: 'vomit out of your body [the oath] you took'.

The oath having left the subjects, the curer re-introduced them to the community, chanting three times *chiarai muiuri bururi*: 'be born again from the soil'. He then put two – or if they were small, more – *muthakwa* leaves in the remaining mixture; taking them out and turning to Mount Kenya he called the attention of the spiritual forces to the rebirth of those who had repented, by chanting *gatitika inyukiu*.

Using both hands he dipped the leaves once again in the mixture; taking them out so that each hand held leaves, he crossed and uncrossed his arms until they were wide apart, with the subjects between the outstretched hands. When the mixture had finished dripping on their heads and the soil, the ritual had finished.

9. The unity of Mau Mau, Kiambu and the forest

The government saw Mau Mau as a unitary movement with Kenyatta as leader; local Kikuyu saw various Mau Mau movements, some of which recognized Kenyatta, many of which did not. When he was arrested as leader of all Mau Mau the local population was surprised, but also convinced that the variety of Mau Maus, and the inability of Kenyatta to openly declare his leadership, had blinded them to the underlying unity. Even if there had not been unity as yet, this was the time to show that it was a reality: the case of Kenyatta and the Kikuyu was best served by *umoja*, as Koinange had preached for decades. Mau Mau was ultimately one; 'bad leaders' and different conditions had stood in the way of unity. This should no longer stand in the way: Kenyatta's arrest should unify all behind him.

Kiambu had separated from Murang'a in the nineteenth century; its Rift Valley population was returning and contact between it and the local community had been stressful and at a low ebb since the late 1920s. Contact with Gaki had always been minimal. Though preaching unity, the local population had little chance or interest in pursuing closer contacts; they were convinced, moreover, that their Githunguri version of Mau Mau should be the basis of unity. That this did not fit Nairobi Mau Mau was regrettable, but in time unity would be achieved; the men working in Nairobi were predominantly Kiambu men. They constituted 46.3 per cent of the Nairobi Kikuyu (Murang'a 35.3 per cent, Gaki 18.5 per cent) and had probably been in Nairobi longer than men from the other districts.[16]

Given that the local – perhaps the Kiambu – population regarded their Mau Mau as the standard, their low participation in the Mau Mau of other districts including the forest was not an enigma, but to be expected. That the *muhimu* wanted Kiambu to participate in other districts or the forest, is denied; no informant had been asked or urged to go to the forest from Nairobi.[17]

The local population regarded the forest fighters as a Rift Valley phenomenon, created by the Rift Valley 'land alienations' of the 1940s. The use of the word *komerera*, a word for a parasitic growth, does not indicate disdain; like Mau Mau, it can be used in various ways. It may be used to indicate (positively) that forest fighters sucked the lifeblood out of European power; it may mean (negatively) that they lived on the fear of the people. Locally, the word was not used with either of these extreme meanings.

Though somewhat outside my area of interest, it may be useful to indicate problems with the calculations of the strength of the forest fighters when using Corfield's assertion that by the end of 1956 Mau Mau casualties were slightly above 11,500.[18] There is no evidence that this gives insight into the strength of the forest fighters. During the Emergency anyone killed in an anti-Mau Mau action was automatically counted as a terrorist.

Calculating the contribution of each district on the basis of land confiscated by 1955, is equally fraught with danger.[19] This ignores the contribution of *ahoi* to the forest, moreover: land consolidation had barely started and individual ownership of land confirmed by title deed was still rare. If a 'terrorist' had a share in *mbari* land, any *mbari* threatened with confiscation of that share would have protested that this land did not belong to him and confiscation orders would therefore have been moot. Overall confiscations would have been the exception rather than the rule.[20]

We know a good deal more about the strength of the government's armies than about the forest fighters. By May it included one brigade; sometimes two, sometimes three battalions of British troops; five, sometimes six battalions of the KAR, the Kenya Regiment; an armoured car squadron; an artillery battery; two RAF squadrons of bombers; four Harvards; and nine Lincolns together with radar 'blind' bombing aids. In September 1953 another British brigade was added. The RAF made bombing raids in the forest; they had little military value beyond denying food to the forest fighters; they may even have given them confidence in their superiority.[21]

Appendix IX: Notes on Mau Mau

Notes

1. 1977. Spencer, J., 'Kau and Mau Mau, some connections', *Kenya Historical Review (KHR)*, Vol. 5, No. 2, pp. 201–24.
   1985. Spencer, John, *The Kenya African Union*, London: Routledge and Kegan Paul.
2. Themes concerned with aggression in generation, themes of collaboration and resistance, are discussed in a large number of major and minor general publications, some of them concerned with theoretical implications, others with advocacy, again others with data-based analyses of Mau Mau. Post-Independence literature, notably writers such as Ngugi wa Thiong'o, Maina wa Kinyatti, Samuel Kahiga and others have used these themes in novels and poetry.
3. 1952. 10 July Speech by the Hon. Michael Blundel, ME, MLC in the Legislative Council; reported in part in
   1960. Cmnd 1030 *Historical Survey of the Origins and Growth of Mau Mau* (Corfield Report) (F. D. Corfield), pp. 138, 139.
4. 1954. Carothers, J. C., *The Psychology of Mau Mau*, Nairobi: Government Printer.
   1954. Carothers, J. C., 'Predisposing causes favourable to the rise of Mau Mau', in *Report on the Sociological Causes Underlying Mau Mau with Some Proposals on the Means of Ending It* (secret, mimeographed).
   1960. Corfield Report, *op. cit.* The Report bristles with value statements about the Kikuyu, their backwardness, moral inferiority and low position on the evolutionary ladder.
5. That District Officers did not always subscribe to the theory that 'loyalists' were what they were because of the advantages it provided is expressed in
   1960. HOR June (P. M. Dempster DO to J. D. Lambert DC), p. 68; 'the loyalists should seek their reward in Heaven, they have not received it here'.
6. 1953. Anon., 'History of the Kiambu Guard', CGA, PC, Nyeri, Adm. 28/8a, with appendix by J. D. Campbell, 'Report on the Githunguri Kikuyu Guard, 14 August 1953'; cited in:
   1967. Sorrenson, M. P. K., *Land Reform in Kikuyu Country*, Oxford: Oxford University Press, pp. 107, 108.
   1972. Ogot, Bethwell A., 'Revolt of the elders', *Hadith*, Vol. 4, pp. 134–48.
   1978. Tamarkin, M. 'The Loyalists in Nakuru during the Mau Mau revolt', *Asian and African Studies*, Vol. 12, No. 2 (July), pp. 247–61.
7. 1953. AR/326 KBU/44.
8. 1953. *East African Standard* Supplement Friday, 10 April.
9. 1955. January–April Kiambu HOR/196 Githunguri Division.
10. There is a substantial literature which deals with the behaviour of Homeguards, some of it laudatory, much of it critical. Conflict within the administration, between settlers of certain Rift Valley areas and police, regarding the need to maintain legal safeguards for suspects and accused, and control the security forces as well as the Homeguards, are the subject of correspondence as well as letters to the *East African Standard*, with some defending the right of Homeguards and others 'on the side of the Government' to dole out summary justice and use collective punishments, while others strongly oppose this. Conditions in prisons and detention camps fall outside the scope of this study. In addition to the literature cited in Appendix VIII/5, the following literature portrays Homeguard behaviour and official and unofficial opinions:
    1954. Cmnd 9081 *Report to the Secretary of State for the Colonies by the Parliamentary Delegation to Kenya*, January.
    MSS. Afric. s. 424 *The Guard Book of Miscellaneous Papers Relating to Africa* (embargoed), Rhodes House, Oxford, contained:
    1957. Rutherford, J. A., *History of the Kikuyu Guard Fort Hall*.
    The Private papers of Dr Anthony Clayton contained:
    a) Correspondence of Sir John Whyatt, Attorney General, with the Governor of Kenya

Appendices

regarding the breakdown of law and order in the Conduct of the Emergency, detailing lack of instances of abuse by Homeguards and 'loyalists'.
b) 1954. 23 December An extensive report by D. Macpherson, Assistant Commissioner of Police (Crime) to the Commissioner of Police, Nairobi, listing instances of abuse by Homeguards.
c) 1955. 3 January Letter (secret) from Sir John Whyatt to the Governor of Kenya, warning that settlers in North Kinangop District were being canvassed about the possibility of marching on Government House as demonstration of protest against prosecutions of security forces and 'loyalists'.
d) 1954. 4 December Letter from DO Mathira Division to District Commissioner Nyeri, defending summary justice.
e) 1954. 17 December Letter from K. P. Haddingham, Assistant Commissioner of Police Nyeri area to Commissioner of Police Nairobi against summary justice.
1955. Lavers, Anthony, *The Kikuyu who Fight Mau Mau*, Nairobi: Eagle Press.
11. n.d. MSS. Afric. s. 234, Appleby, J. C., *Woman on Patrol, Home Guard During Mau Mau 1952–1956*, Rhodes House, Oxford, mimeographed. References for European Homeguard organization in the Rift Valley are given in Appendix IV.
12. My data do not confirm that Homeguards came from the landed and wealthy sector of the community as asserted in
1953. J. D. Campbell, 'Report on the Githunguri Kikuyu Guard August 14 1953', Appendix to *History of the Kiambu Guard*, anon, CGA PC Nyeri Adm. 28/8a. Both were quoted in
1967. Sorrenson, M. P. K., *op. cit.*, pp. 107.
13. n.d. *Notes for the Guidance of Clergy and Others on Cleansing*, Nairobi: Christian Council of Kenya.
14. 1974. Wanyoike, E. N., *An African Pastor*, Nairobi: East African Publishing House, p. 195.
15. *Muthakwa* (*vernonia auriculifera*). Leaves of this tree were commonly used in ceremonies affecting single homesteads.
1977. Leakey, L. S. B., *The Southern Kikuyu before 1903*, Vols I–III, London: Academic Press, p. 1081.
16. 1950. *African Population of Kenya Colony and Protectorate 1948 Geograohical and Tribal Studies*, East African Statistical Department, September, (reprinted February 1953), p. 7.
17. This lack of interest may explain why the *baturi* oath, with its forest overtures, was not seen locally until 1954.
1953. Kiambu Annual District Report AR/326 KBU/326.
1982. Buytenhuys, Rob, *Essays on Mau Mau Contributions to Mau Mau Historiography*, pp. 48ff, 190ff.
18. Corfield Report, *op. cit.*, p. 316.
19. 1967. Sorrenson, M. P. K., *op. cit.*, 105ff.
1982. Buytenhuys, Rob, *op. cit.*, p. 55.
20. 1955. Native Land Rights Confiscation Orders, July.
21. 1952. *East African Standard*, 14 November.
1952. KBU/43 AR/325 2/2/53.
1952–1960. Marsabit District Annual Report PC/NFD/1/2/5.
1976. Clayton, Anthony, *Counter-Insurgency in Kenya 1952–1960*, Nairobi: Transafrica Publishers, pp. 23, 24.

Bibliography

Selected general bibliography

1975. Mazrui, Ali A., 'The resurrection of the warrior tradition of African political culture', *Journal of Modern African Studies* Vol. 13, No. 1, p. 67.
1988. Cooper, Frederick, 'Mau Mau and the discourses of colonization', *Journal of African History*, Vol. 29, No 2., pp. 313–20.

Appendix IX: Notes on Mau Mau

Selected bibliography of advocacy materials

1953. Wiseman, E. M., *Kikuyu Martyrs*, London: The Highway Press.
1955. Beecher, L. J., 'After Mau Mau, what?', *International Review of Missions*, Vol. 44, No. 174 (April), pp. 205–11.
1955. Blundell, Sir Michael, 'The present situation in Kenya', *African Affairs*, Vol. 54, No. 215, pp. 99–108.
1958. Phillips, K. N., *From Mau Mau to Christ*, AIM April, Stirling Tract Enterprises.
1959. Osmunson, Rosemarie, *Njoki and the Mau Mau Terror*, Nashville: Southern Publishing Association.
1963. Kariuki, Josiah Mwangi, *Mau Mau Detainee*, Nairobi: Oxford University Press.
1967. Odinga, Oginga, *Not Yet Uhuru*, London: Heinemann, p. 125.
1969. Waciuma, Charity, *Daughter of Muumbi*, Nairobi: East African Publishing House.
1973. Muchai, Karigo, *The Hardcore*, Life Histories from the Revolution; Kenya, Mau Mau No. 1, Richmond: Liberation Support Movement Press.
1973. Kabiro, Ngugi, *Man in the Middle*, Life Histories from the Revolution; Kenya, Mau Mau No. 2, Richmond: Liberation Support Movement Press.
1974. Mohamed, Mathu, *The Urban Guerrilla*, Life Histories from the Revolution; Kenya, Mau Mau No. 3, Richmond: Liberation Support Movement Press.

Selected bibliography of data-based material

1972. Ochieng, William, *Politics and Nationalists in Colonial Kenya*, Nairobi: East African Publishing House.
1972. Ogot, Bethwell A., *op. cit.*
1973. Keller, Edmond J., Jr., 'A twentieth century model: The Mau Mau transformation from social banditry to rebellion', *Kenya Historical Review*, Vol. 1, No. 2, pp. 189–206.
1974. Atieno-Odhiambo, E. S., *The Paradox of Collaboration and Other Essays*, Nairobi: East African Literature Bureau.
1977. Ng'ang'a, Mukaru D., 'Mau Mau, Loyalists and Politics in Murang'a 1952-1970', *Kenya Historical Review*, Vol. 5, No. 2, pp. 365–84.
1978. Tamarkin, M., *op. cit.*
1980. Kipkorir, B. E., (ed.), *Biographical Essays in Imperialism and Collaboration in Colonial Kenya*, Nairobi: Kenya Literature Bureau.

Appendix X

Land Consolidation & Villagization

1. Land consolidation[1]

In 1948, well before the Emergency, leaders in Mbari ya Igi had asked permission to consolidate *mbari* land. Fragmentation prevented effective farming and manuring; an owner of ten acres might have 20 or more plots. Litigation made tenure insecure and prevented investment in development and crops which demanded several years' work and heavy financial investment before producing returns. Because owners could not provide title, banks refused development loans. However sound the reasons, the administration wanted more evidence of popular support, which was not forthcoming.

Elders of several *ithaku* opposed the move. Some were in favour of consolidation in principle, but did not want to embark on it until the principles of the division of land had been spelled out: each faction demanded that its interpretation of oral traditions be used as guide. The opposition of others went deeper: they rightly interpreted land consolidation as a triumph for individual ownership. If consolidation gave *mbari* members individual title, still surviving ideas of communal ownership would have become irrelevant.

Not until the Emergency, when individuals were removed from their homesteads and forced to live in villages, was sufficient agreement reached to convince the administration. Even then, not all agreed: opposition from *mbari* members who adhered to the idea that the land was communally owned, perhaps 5 per cent of the land owners, had continued. *Ahoi* were also opposed; though they had been assured that their rights would be protected to the degree possible, and that they would be represented in all decisions, they knew that they could only lose.[2]

The administration, convinced that a new tenure system would end litigation and herald a period of rural prosperity and progress, was strongly in favour of consolidation; it provided technical knowledge, paid for personnel and carried most of the cost. Consolidation in Igi was rapidly followed in Thuita and other Kiambu areas.

The process started with the settling of outstanding litigation. Locally, this involved a marathon session in which a committee of arbitration settled all conflicts elders had failed to resolve. Its decision was irrevocable.

Owners of land indicated the fragments they regarded as theirs; a committee of the *arumati* of *ithaku* – in other areas a committee of the *arumati* of *mbari* – monitored and approved the claims. After the land was measured, a new acreage was allotted. The government envisaged that all but the wealthiest land owners

Appendix X: Land Consolidation and Villagization

would continue to live in villages, and that even those who lived on their land would need housing for labour. It demanded that land owners acquire at least one quarter-acre plot in the village. They also had to return another 0.6 per cent of their land for rural roads, water, nursery schools, 'community halls' and other village amenities. A title deed was issued for the reduced area.

Where the land was allocated depended on two principles: the land of the same *githaku* or *mbari* should be contiguous and no man should be allocated land which was situated in an area over which he had brought litigation, but had lost. If a man's ancestors had contributed to one acquisition, the land of the *githaku* should be there. If, as in Igi, ancestors had contributed to several acquisitions, one tract contained the principal allocation but at least one member was given land in the other tracts for which contributions had been made. The placement and boundaries of land were a graphic demonstration of what had become official history.[3]

In most cases the actual owner received the acreage and the deed, with significant exceptions. Some men convinced their kinsmen to ask that most of the land be put in their name: this would facilitate loans and perhaps give access to crops. Once the deed had been executed, the kinsmen would redistribute the land without benefit of registration. The administration had promised that the area would be allowed to plant coffee, once tenure was secure. Even before consolidation was set in motion, local men knew that only those with four or more acres of land would get permission to grow coffee. This caused kinsmen to pool their land and register it under one name.

In some cases an old man made himself the owner of all land; in other cases the land was divided so that even very young sons got a share. Ten local wives got their own land and title deed; it would either become their sons' land or remain with the women, with a chance that it would go to their kinsmen. A few put the land in the name of a *mbari* member, long dead.

To avoid new fragmentation, the administration had ruled that land of seven acres or less should not be subdivided on death. This was widely ignored; its potential to cause discord was too great. Better not to register the death; in this, as in many cases, the actual division and the official division were two different things. That title deeds did not reflect local reality was not an important problem for many even if it did create complications when land was bought or sold.[4]

In 1962 the consequences of land consolidation were not yet fully apparent, beyond a massive increase in coffee (Appendix IV/19). There was some indication that this 'flight into coffee' had an adverse effect on the income and decision making of women in small peasant households. Before the planting of coffee these women had grown surplus, which they had sold at Marige market, using the money to augment their incomes and provide for some of the needs of their households. As husbands appropriated any land not needed for household food for coffee, which they regarded as their crop even though women provided a good part of the work, women were left with more work, less income and less decision making.

In 1962 the majority of the population but not the *ahoi* agreed that land consolidation had been a good move. The *ahoi* and others blamed consolidation for the rise in the price of land, which had placed buying outside their reach. These households also complained that food prices had risen more sharply than wages; *ahoi* complained that they had no work and no land.

Size of land and approval or disapproval of land consolidation were closely linked. Large land owners would mention security and the end of litigation as prime advantages; smaller owners would first mention that land was easier to work and manure.[5] Negative reactions were not so much directed at land consolidation itself as at the distribution of the land. Having lost good land and received bad land in return was a prime complaint; having lost permanent crops and trees without compensation ran a close second. The number of men who complained that the land should not have been allocated to individuals, but should have been registered in the name of the *mbari*, was significantly smaller in 1962 than in 1956, indicating that even those who had opposed consolidation *de jure*, accepted it because they had no other choice, and because they too had security in what they had. The number of men who believed that consolidation violated Kikuyu law and order had not changed materially.[6]

2. Villagization

The June 1954 decree of the War Council that all Kikuyu, Embu and Meru were to live in villages resulted in massive population movements, abandonment of housing and loss of building material. By October 1955 1,077,500 Kikuyu and Embu had been moved into 854 villages.[7]

The local population had moved earlier; between May 1953 and and early 1954, all inhabitants of Thuita and Igi had been forced to abandon their homesteads for villages which were laid out on a grid pattern.

Land owners received title to a quarter acre of land in the village; they could share it with kin, labour and/or *ahoi*. Some owners bought an additional plot for sons; others bought more than one plot because they had several wives. That village plots were allocated by *mbari* and *ithaku*, often resulted in wealthier and poorer sections. Villagization also affected Marige market; shops were torn down and boarded up.

When the villages were completed, men who had been spending the night at the Marige Police Post for safety left the police post, which started serving a wider area. The local villages got their own Homeguard post, often stationed at or near the plots of men who were thought to be in danger from Mau Mau. Villages could be permanent or temporary; permanent villages like Igi were provided with some amenities, such as water. They were slow in coming; it took two years before Mbari ya Igi village had one well. Like other villages, Igi had a 'community hall' where the Red Cross or the *Maendeleo wa Wanawake* might arrange for a nursery school. Other villages, not meant to be permanent, lacked most amenities. Local villages were not built as defence posts: they were not stockaded or surrounded by ditches with sharpened sticks. The administration regarded the permanent villages as a step forward; as late as 1962 most of the population disliked them because they provided no privacy and gave rise to gossip, interference and friction.

The government first allowed commercial centres to resume daily operations. By 1955, Marige shops were rebuilt and reopened. Soon after, four-day markets, where women bought and sold small quantities of food, were again allowed.[8] By 1957 people with sufficient arable land were allowed to rebuild their homesteads and move out of the village; rebuilding often involved stone rather than mud and wattle construction. Those who had insufficient land had to stay in the village; those who moved out gave their plots to sons or used them for labour.[9]

Appendix X: Land Consolidation and Villagization

Notes

1. 1956. *A Guide to Consolidation in Kiambu District*. Report of a meeting between the District Commissioner (Lloyd) and Messrs Sutton, Kennedy and Nield, in which district consolidation was revised in the light of experience gained in Mbari ya Igi.
   1956. 'Land consolidation in the Kikuyu areas of Kenya', *Journal of African Administration*, Vol. 8, No. 2 (April), pp. 82–7.
   1961. Simmance, A. J. F., 'Land redemption among the Fort Hall Kikuyu', *Journal of African Law*, Vol. V, No. 2.
   1962. Homan, F. D., 'Consolidation, enclosure and registration of title in Kenya', *Journal of Local Administration Overseas*, Vol. I, No. 1 (January), pp. 4–14.
   1967. Sorrenson, M. P. K., *op. cit.*
   1974. Omosule, M., 'Kiama kia Muingi: Kikuyu and land consolidation', *Transafrican Journal of History*, Vol. 4, Nos 1–2.
2. The *ahoi* were not represented by a *muhoi*, but by a wealthy *muthami*, who, although having no local land, had important holdings elsewhere.
3. It is interesting to note that Gitau got land in all tracts.
4. According to the land consolidation officer, Kiambu owners were given title between 1957 and 1959, when there was as yet no procedure to report the death of a registered holder. When this changed in 1960, 283 deaths were reported between August 1960 and 1962, but only 13 registrations to change title were recorded. He estimated that by 1962 at least 500 title holders had died in Kiambu as a whole without a change in title. He also scorned the habit of registering all land on one deed and one holder; he expected multiple lawsuits in the future, as men disputed the use of land their father had left or a title holder refused to share.
5. As informants could give multiple answers, totals do not reflect the population. Two thirds of the *ahoi* (114 from 150) were negative about land consolidation and saw no redeeming feature. About a third (104 from 341) of the subsistence cultivators were positive but half gave negative evaluations as well. Small peasants and peasants gave positive evaluations at a rate of 44.8 per cent to 52.5 per cent. Small farmers were positive at a rate of 94.7 per cent; farmers were 100 per cent positive. Among *ahoi* and subsistence tract owners the major reason for a negative attitude was that after consolidation land had risen sharply in price and they could not afford to buy.
6. One man thought that it undermined Kikuyu law because one could no longer take an oath on the land, as ancestors of one's *githaku* might not be buried in what one was given. Others had had to move, in spite of a *kirumi* from an ancestor. Some feared that land consolidation would weaken *mbari* authority as members felt free to sell even when the *mbari* had a *kirumi* against it. Igi was an example: in spite of individual ownership and 'papers', its elders refused to allow members to sell. The *kirumi* had also forbidden intermarriage; elders upheld the prohibition. When this was violated repeatedly, the *arumati* of the leading *ithaku* arranged a ceremony in which the *kirumi* was reaffirmed.
7. 1967. Sorrenson, M. P. K., *Land Reform in the Kikuyu Country*, Oxford: Oxford University Press, pp. 110ff.
8. Marige would eventually become an important Kiambu commercial and transportation centre.
9. 1955. *Villages*: Report from the Office of the District Commissioner Kiambu Ref. 17/56/7/5/149, 6 December.
   1955. Hughes, O. E. B., 'Villages in the Kikuyu country', *Journal of African History*, Vol. 7, No. 4, pp. 170–4.
   1957. Shannon, Mary I., 'Rebuilding the social life of the Kikuyu', *African Affairs*, Vol. 56, No. 225 (October), pp. 276–84.

Selected Bibliography

Publisher Abbreviations
CUP Cambridge University Press
EALB East Africa Literature Bureau
EAPH East African Publishing House
KLB Kenya Literature Bureau
LSMP Liberation Support Movement Press
OUP Oxford University Press
PUP Princeton University Press
UCP University of Colorado Press
UMP University of Minnesota Press
UPA University Press of America
UTP University of Toronto Press
YUP Yale University Press

Journal Abbreviations
AA African Affairs
ASR African Studies Review
BJPSC British Journal of Political Science
CJAS Canadian Journal of African Studies
IAI International African Institute
JAA Journal of African Administration
JAH Journal of African History
JAS Journal of African Studies
JLAO Journal of Local Administration Overseas
JMAS Journal of Modern African Studies
JPS Journal of Peasant Studies
JRAI Journal of the Royal Anthropological Institute
KHR Kenya Historical Review
TJH Transafrican Journal of History

Archival sources

Kiambu or other District Reports, Handing Over Reports, Ukamba Province Quarterly Reports and Land Files are not listed separately in the bibliography. The same holds true for Education Annual Reports or Reports of the Department of Agriculture. They were consulted at District offices in Kiambu, Machakos and Githunguri; the microfilm collection of the Seeley Historical Library was also used. As I was unable to use the Kenya National Archives in Nairobi, the references use the designations of *A Guide to the Kenya National Archives* by Robert G. Gregory, Robert M. Maxon and Leon P. Spencer (Syracuse: Program of Eastern African Studies, 1968).

Newspaper reports were consulted from 1950 to the end of the Emergency (*East African Standard, Kenya Weekly News*) in Nairobi where I had access to the archives of the *EAS*; or the Friday editions of the *EAS* at the Collindale Division of the British Museum. I did not have access to *Mumenyerere*; my information came from Mr Henry Muoria Mwaniki and secondary sources. I had access to the archives and publications of the Christian Council of Kenya during the Emergency; I attended several of its meetings and conducted a number of interviews with its secretary and members; I received the Emergency press office handouts regarding community development, detention and rehabilitation. I attended the last two meetings of the Committee to report on the sociological causes underlying Mau Mau.

Selected Bibliography

1. Documents at Rhodes House, Oxford

MSS Afric. s. 234 n.d. Gibson, D. *Mau Mau in Kenya*. n.d. mimeographed, unsigned.
MSS Afric. s. 424 *The Guard Book of Miscellaneous Papers Relating to Africa* (embargoed) contained:
a) 1957 Rutherford, J. A., *History of the Kikuyu Guard Fort Hall.*
b) The C. J. A. Barnett Papers contained
   n.d. *Mau Mau Ceremonies as described by Participants*, including several confessions;
   n.d. *Papers on Second and Third Grade Mau Mau Oaths and the Mau Mau Oaths Four–Seven.*
c) Brodhurst-Hill Report details a similar series of oaths.
d) Papers from Audrey G. M. Mullins and I. R. Gillespie which contained parts of a speech by H. E. Lambert on *Disintegration and Reintegration of the Meru Tribe.*
MSS Afric. s. 663 1925–1954 Gillespie, I. R. Handing Over Reports Kenya Districts.
MSS Afric. s. 721 Martin, Eric Frank. *Documents concerning Homeguard Duties during Mau Mau in Kenya 1952–1953 and Instructions on Defence of Isolated Homesteads.*
MSS Afric. s. 742 (3) Colchester, Trevor Charles. *Note on the Association between the Death of Chief Waiyaki in 1893 and the Leakey Sacrifice during the Mau Mau Emergency.*
MSS Afric. s. 839 (1) HOR Kandara Division Fort Hall RHL W. S. Thompson.
MSS Afric. s. 846 Appleby, J. C. *Woman on Patrol: Home Guard during Mau Mau 1952–1956.*
MSS Afric. s. 929 contained
a) 1953. 17 April Correspondence between F. G. Cavendish-Bentinck and G. Kinnear, includes schedules of the *Movement of the Kikuyu* (repatriation, transit camps).
b) Humprey Slade-Todd *Selected Papers and Memoranda 1952–1959* contained
1952. 14 December Letter from Humphrey Slade to establish Emergency Liaison Committee Aberdare Constituency.
1952. 27 December – 1953. 3 March Correspondence between members from Gilgil, O. I. Kalou, Naivasha, S. Kinangop and the District Officer Naivasha.
n.d. Anon. *Photography and All That* and *Employment of Mau Mau Suspects – Penal Settlements.*
MSS Afric. s. 1741 1937 Maher, A. Colin, *Soil Erosion and Land Utilization in the Kamasia. Njemps and East Suk*, Mimeo. Agricultural Department Nairobi.

2. Private papers

Dr Anthony Clayton allowed access to some of his private papers which contained among others
a) 1952. 2 April. Henderson, I. S. M. *The Extent of Illegal Oath Taking – Nyeri District.*
b) 1954. 8 September. *Appendix A to Special Branch Summary No. 18/54 The Oaths of Mau Mau.*
c) 1954. 4 December. Letter from DO Mathira Division to District Commissioner Nyeri.
d) 1954. 17 December. Letter from K. P. Haddingham, Assistant Commissioner of Police Nyeri area to Commissioner of Police Nairobi.
e) 1954, 23 December. A Report by D. Macpherson, Assistant Commissioner of Police (Crime) to the Commissioner of Police, Nairobi.
f) 1955. 3 January. Letter from Sir John Whyatt to Governor of Kenya re march on Government House as demonstration of protest.
g) Extensive correspondence of Sir John Whyatt, Attorney General with the Governor of Kenya and the reactions of the African Unofficial Members Organization to his departure in 1955.
h) 1956. 22 September. Sir John Whyatt re intended negotiations with Kenyatta before the Emergency.

The *Private Papers of the Hon. W. McLellan-Wilson* contained correspondence from John Ainsworth with regard to Kikuyu land tenure.

3. Official publications

A. UNITED KINGDOM GOVERNMENT:
PARLIAMENTARY PAPERS AND COLONIAL REPORTS:
(Unless otherwise indicated, these are published by HMSO in London.
Names of Chairmen of Commissions are in parentheses.)

1925. Cmnd 2373 *Education in East Africa* Memorandum submitted to the Secretary of State for the Colonies by the Advisory Committee on Native Education in the British

Selected Bibliography

Tropical African Dependencies (Phelps Stokes Report) (Jesse T. Jones), HCSP Vol. 21, London: Edinburgh House Press.
1933. Cmnd 4556 *Report of the Kenya Land Commission. Evidence and Memoranda*, Vols I–IV (Sir Morris Carter CBE).
1934. Cmnd 4580 *Kenya Land Commission: Summary of Conclusions Reached by His Majesty's Government.*
1954. Cmnd 9081 *Report to the Secretary of State for the Colonies by the Parliamentary Delegation to Kenya.* January.
1954. *The Kenya Emergency*, Report by the Kenya War Council. Report of the Reference Division of the Central Office of Information, No R.2940 20/10/54 London. Contains detailed breakdown of Emergency statistics, 1954.
1954. *Cost of Living in East Africa*, The East African Office, September.
1955. Parliamentary Debates (Hansard) *The Situation in Kenya* Vol. 190, No. 19, 10 February.
1955. Cmnd 9475 *East Africa Royal Commission Report 1953–1955* (Sir Hugh Dow).
1959. Cmnd 778 *Documents Relating to the Death of Eleven Mau Mau Detainees at Hola Camp in Kenya.* June.
1959. Cmnd 795 *Record of the Proceedings and Evidence in the Inquiry into the Death of Eleven Mau Mau Detainees at Hola Camp in Kenya.*
1959. Cmnd 816 *Further Documents Relating to the Death of Eleven Mau Mau Detainees at Hola Camp in Kenya.* July.
1960. Cmnd 1030 *Historical Survey of the Origins and Growth of Mau Mau* (F. D. Corfield).

B. KENYA GOVERNMENT PUBLICATIONS

(Unless otherwise indicated, these are published by the government printer in Nairobi. Names of commissions or committee chairmen are in parentheses)

1941. *Report on the Housing of Africans*, Report by the Senior Medical Officer of Health and Municipal Native Affairs Officer, submitted to the Native Affairs Committee of the Municipal Council of Nairobi, 30 April.
1943. *Post-War Employment of Africans*, Report of the Post-War Employment Committee Report and Report of the Sub-Committee on Post-War Employment of Africans.
1945. *Report on Native Tribunals* (Arthur Phillips).
1947. Martin, J. H., *The Problem of the Squatter: Economic Survey of Resident Labour in Kenya*, February.
1948. *A Ten-year Plan for the Development of African Education.*
1949. *African Education in Kenya: Report of a Committee Appointed to Enquire into the Scope, Content, and Methods of African Education, its Administration and Finance, and to Make Recommendations* (Rev. L. J. Beecher).
1950. *African Population of Kenya Colony and Protectorate 1948 Geographical and Tribal Studies*, East African Statistical Department, 15 September. Reprinted February 1953.
1950. *Cost of Living Commission Report*, 11 November.
1950. *Proposals for the Implementation of the Recommendations of the Report on African Education*, Sessional Paper No. 1.
1953. *A Plan to Intensify the Development of African Agriculture in Kenya* AGR. (R. J. M. Swynnerton, OBE, MC) 32/2 14 October.
1953. *Education Department Annual Report 1953.*
1953. *Report on the Census of the Non-Native Population of Kenya Colony and Protectorate*, 25 February 1948.
1954. *Report of the Committee on African Wages* (F. W. Carpenter).
1955. *Education Department Annual Report.*
1958. Native Land Rights Confiscation Orders. July.
1958. *Statistical Abstract.*
1959. *Report of the Committee on Emergency Detention Camps* (R. D. Fairn).
1961. *Commerce and Industry in Kenya.*
1961. *Reported Employment and Wages in Kenya 1948–1960*, East African Statistical Department, August.

C. RESTRICTED AND/OR CONFIDENTIAL REPORTS KENYA GOVERNMENT

1904. *Memorandum to the Land Committee* n.d. Reply J. D. Ainsworth to the Land Committee's

Selected Bibliography

Circular dd. 14 November 1904, 236/3/6.

1904. 'Report of the agricultural conditions obtaining at various homesteads in the Kikuyu District', *East African Quarterly*, July/September. Reproduced in M. F. Hill's *Planters' Progress*, Nairobi: Coffee Board of Kenya, 1956, pp.17ff.

1924. Confidential Records DC Kiambu Chiefs and Headmen (OG 1924, pp. 478 Govt Notice No. 176, 1/5/24).

1937. Maher, C., *Soil Erosion and Land Utilization in the Ukamba (Kitui Reserve)* 2 vols. Mimeographed. Nairobi.

1952–56. Marsabit District Annual Reports PC/NFD/1/2/5 Classification Secret.

1953. Erskine, General George, Commander in Chief, *Report to the Secretary of State for War re The Kenya Emergency*, 23 June (Confidential).

1953. Anon. *History of the Kiambu Guard*, CGAPC. Nyeri Adm. 28/8a with Appendix J. D. Campbell 'Report on the Githunguri Kikuyu Guard', 14 August.

1954. *Kikuyu Women and Mau Mau*, Office of the District Commissioner Nyeri, 2 May. Cyclostyle.

1954. *Report on the Sociological Causes Underlying Mau Mau with some Proposals on the Means of Ending It*, with its appendices, including J. C. Carothers 'Predisposing causes favourable to the rise of Mau Mau' and L. S. B. Leakey, 'Memorandum on Mau Mau oath ceremonies'. (Secret, mimeographed.)

D. KIAMBU DISTRICT REPORTS

1909. Hobley, C. W., *Land Tenure among the A-Kikuyu*. In: AR/15 1909. October – December Ukamba Province Quarterly Report.

1917/1918. Lane, C. A. G., Dagoretti Sub-District Report, AR/283, in AR/281 KBU/11 Kiambu District Reports.

1954. Penwill, D. J., *Provisional Development Policy Kiambu District Appendix A*.

1955. Census Kiambu District, 14 March Ref. ADM: 15/6/1/1958 Office of the District Commissioner Kiambu to Provincial Commissioner, Central Province, Nyeri.

1956. *Villages:* Report from the Office of the District Commissioner Kiambu Ref. 17/56/7/S/149 6 December.

1956. *A Guide to Consolidation in Kiambu District*. Report of a meeting between the District Commissioner (Lloyd) and Messrs Sutton, Kennedy and Nield, in which District Consolidation was revised in the light of experience gained in Mbari ya Igi.

1962. Department of Agriculture Kiambu, James Mburu Agric. Officer
a) *The Minimum Size of an Economic Holding*.
b) Planned 7 acre Holding for Household of 5 adults or 2 adults and 6 children.
c) Planned 4 Acre Holding for Household of 5 adults or adults and 6 children.

E. LEGAL DOCUMENTS, INCLUDING LAND LITIGATION

1935. Govt. Notice No 65 19/1/35 OG.

1947. Resident Magistrate's Court Kiambu (Rex Versus Senior Chief Koinange) and 1948 Appeal from 1st Class Magistrate's Court Kiambu (Koinange Mbiu, Appellate versus Rex).

1948. L 81/48 and *Chief Native Tribunal* Githunguri S/S/08/12/48.

1949. Githunguri L 52/49/MRN0 208526.

1951. Kiambu 1951 17//1951 CNF.

1951. Law Reports of Kenya Vol. 24 (2) KLR *Koinange Mbiu* (Orig. Crim) versus Rex, Respondent (Orig. Pros.) ex Appeal No 406 of 1951; Appeal from 1st Class Mag. Crt. KBU, DO. Brummage

1953. Supreme Court of Kenya, Nairobi. Emergency Assize Criminal Case No. 38 of 1953 10-9-1953, with appendices.

Documents regarding land litigation were provided by litigants.
A certified copy (F. A. Lloyd, DC) dd. 28.6.55 of the *Court of Arbitrators at the Land Known as Githuya on 15 June, 1955* (Mbira Githehu, Chairman).

F. OFFICIAL CORRESPONDENCE

1903. 30 November, Land File Office of the DC Machakos, J. D. Ainsworth to H. H. Horne, 236/3/6.

Selected Bibliography

1953. 14 November, Assistant Agricultural Officer, Kiambu to The District Agricultural Officer Kiambu re *African Coffee Growing in Kiambu District*. JDB/SMT.
1954. Central Office of Information, London, to G. Sluiter, No. R2940 20/10/54.
1956. 4 September, District Commissioner's Office Kiambu to G. Sluiter, Ref. No. Fin. 4/2/2/2/398.
1958. 19 March, British Information Service, Chicago to G. Sluiter. Summarizes European deaths.
1960. 3 October, Chief Conservator of Forests FOR 212/1/6/31.
1962. 13 November, Agricultural Officer James Mburu, Office of the Department of the Agriculture, to G. Kershaw.

Unpublished theses

Clough, M. S., 'Chiefs and politicians: local politics and social change in Kiambu, Kenya, 1918–1936', PhD thesis, Stanford University, 1978.
Kershaw, Gretha, 'The land is the people', PhD thesis, University of Chicago, 1972.
Kovar, M., 'The Kikuyu Independent Schools Association', PhD thesis, University of California, Los Angeles, 1970.
Murray, Jocelyn M., 'The Kikuyu female circumcisions controversy with special reference to the Church Missionary Society's sphere of influence', PhD thesis, University of California, Los Angeles, 1974.
Njonjo, A., 'The Africanization of the "White Highlands" of Kenya: a study in agrarian class struggles in Kenya, 1950–1974', PhD thesis, Princeton University, 1977.
Overton, J., 'Spatial differentiation in the colonial economy of Kenya: Africans, settlers and the state', PhD thesis, Trinity College, Cambridge University, 1983.
Sluiter, G., 'The Kikuyu concepts of land and land kin', MA thesis, University of Chicago, 1960.
Spencer, John, 'The Kenya African Union 1944–1953, a party in search of a constituency', PhD thesis, Columbia University, 1977.
Wamagatta, Evanson N., 'A biography of Senior Chief Waruhiu wa Kungu of Githunguri, Kiambu District 1890–1952', MA thesis, University of Nairobi, 1988.

Unpublished papers, manuscripts and reports

Atieno Odhiambo, 'The production of history in Kenya: the Mau Mau debate'. Fifth International Round Table in Anthropology and History, Paris, July 1986.
Berman, Bruce, and John Lonsdale, 'In the shadows of Mau Mau: the politics of terror in Kenya', unpublished manuscript, 1991.
Christian Council of Kenya 'Notes for the guidance of clergy on "cleansing" ceremonies for ex-Mau Mau', n.d.
Furedi, F. 'Olenguruone in Mau Mau historiography', paper presented at the University of London Institute of Colonial Studies, 9 March 1974.
Makerere College Kikuyu, Embu and Meru Students Association, 'Around Mount Kenya: comment on Corfield', Makerere, Uganda, 1960.
Mburu, James, 'Agriculture in Kiambu Native Reserves', n.d.
Omosule, Monone, 'An assessment of the role of the Kenya Land Commission Report in the "Mau Mau" outbreak', paper presented at the Annual Conference of the Historical Association of Kenya, August 1981.
Throup, David A., 'Kenyatta and the Kenya African Union 1944–1952', unpublished manuscript, n.d.

Other publications

Books and pamphlets

Abuor, C. Ojwando, *White Highlands No More. A Modern Political History of Kenya*, Vol. I., Nairobi: Pan African Researchers, 1970.

Selected Bibliography

Ambler, Charles Hart, *Kenya Communities in the Age of Imperialism*, New Haven: YUP, 1988.
Anderson, David, and David Throup, *Africans and Agricultural Production in Colonial Kenya. The Myth of the War as Watershed* (Cambridge: CUP, 1984).
Atieno-Odhiambo, E. S., *The Paradox of Collaboration and other Essays*, Nairobi: EALP, 1974.
Barnett, Ronald L., and Karairi Njama, *Mau Mau from Within*, London: MacGibbon and Kee, 1966.
Bennett, George, *Kenya, A Political History*, London: OUP, 1963.
Benson, T. G., *Kikuyu–English Dictionary*, Oxford: Clarendon Press, 1964.
Berman, Bruce, *Control and Crisis in Colonial Kenya*, London: James Currey, 1990.
Berman, Bruce, and John Lonsdale, *Unhappy Valley*, Books I and II, Eastern African Studies, London: James Currey, 1992.
Bewes, T. F. C., *Kikuyu Conflict*, London: The Highway Press, 1953.
Brett, E. A., *Colonialism and Underdevelopment in East Africa: The Policies of Economic Change 1919–1939*, London: Heinemann, 1973.
Buytenhuys, Rob, *Essays on Mau Mau. Contributions to Mau Mau Historiography*, Research Reports No. 17, Leiden, the Netherlands: African Studies Center, 1982.
Buytenhuys, Robert, *Mau Mau Twenty Years After*, The Hague: Mouton and Co., 1973.
Carothers, J. C. *The Psychology of Mau Mau*, Nairobi: Government Printer, 1954.
Clayton, Anthony, *Counter-Insurgency in Kenya 1952–1960*, Nairobi: Transafrica Publishers, 1976.
Clayton, Anthony, and Donald C. Savage, *Government and Labour in Kenya 1935–1963*, London: Frank Cass, 1974.
Clough, Marshall S., *Fighting Two Sides: Kenyan Chiefs and Politicians, 1918–1940*, Denver: UCP, 1990.
Dilley, M., *British Policy in Kenya Colony*, Second Edition, London: Frank Cass, 1966.
Dutto, Carl A., *Nyeri Townsmen, Kenya*, Nairobi: EALB, 1975.
Fazan, S. H., *History of the Loyalists*, London: HMSO, 1958.
Fisher, Jeanne, *The Anatomy of Kikuyu Domesticity and Husbandry*, Cambridge: Department of Technical Cooperation, 1955.
Forrester, Marion Wallace, *Kenya To-day*, s'Gravenhage: Mouton and Co., 1962.
Furedi, Frank, *The Mau Mau War in Perspective*, London: James Currey, 1989.
Goldsmith, F. H., John Ainsworth, *Pioneer Kenya Administrator 1864–1946*, London: Macmillan and Co., 1955.
Hake, Andrew, *African Metropolis*, New York: St Martin's Press, 1977.
Hill, M. F., *Planters' Progress*, Nairobi: Coffee Board of Kenya, 1956.
Hobley, C. W., *Kenya from Chartered Company to Crown Colony*, London: H. F. & G. Witherby, 1929.
— *Bantu Beliefs and Magic*, London: H. F. & G. Witherby, 1938.
Hoskin, Fran P., *The Hoskin Report*, Lewington, Mass.: Women's International Network News, 1979.
Iliffe, John, *The Emergence of African Capitalism*, Minneapolis: UMP, 1983.
Itote, W., *Mau Mau General*, Nairobi: EAPH, 1967.
Kabiro, Ngugi, *Man in the Middle*, Life Histories from the Revolution; Kenya, Mau Mau No. 2, Richmond: LSMP, 1973.
Kaggia, Bildad, *Roots of Freedom*, Nairobi: EALB, 1975.
Kanogo, Tabitha, *Squatters and the Roots of Mau Mau 1905–1963*, London: James Currey, 1987.
Kariuki, Josiah Mwangi, *Mau Mau Detainee*, Nairobi: OUP, 1963.
Kenyatta, Jomo, *Facing Mount Kenya*, London: Secker and Warburg, 1938. Reprinted 1953.
Kinyatti, Maina wa, *Thunder from the Mountains*, London: Zed Books, 1980.
Kipkorir, B. E. (ed.), *Biographical Essays in Imperialism and Collaboration in Colonial Kenya*, Nairobi: KLB, 1980.
Kitching, Gavin, *Class and Economic Change in Kenya*, New Haven: YUP, 1980.
Lambert, H. E., *Systems of Land Tenure in the Kikuyu Land Unit*, Cape Town: University of Cape Town, 1950, Communications of School of African Studies, No. 22.
— *Kikuyu Social and Political Institutions* London: OUP, 1956.
Lavers, Anthony, *The Kikuyu who Fight Mau Mau*, Nairobi: Eagle Press, 1955.
Leakey, L. S. B., *Mau Mau and the Kikuyu*, London: Methuen, 1952.
— *Defeating Mau Mau*, London: Methuen, 1954.
— *The Southern Kikuyu before 1903*, Vols I–III, London: Academic Press, 1977.

Selected Bibliography

Lonsdale, John, *The Prayers of Waiyaki, Political Uses of the Kikuyu Past*, forthcoming, James Currey, Oxford.
Lugard, F. J. D., Baron, *The Rise of our East African Empire*, Edinburgh: Blackwood, 1893.
Macpherson, P., *The Presbyterian Church in Kenya*, Nairobi: Kenya Litho Ltd., 1970.
Mathu, Mohamed, *The Urban Guerilla*, Life Histories from the Revolution, Kenya, Mau Mau, No 3., Richmond: LSMP, n.d.
Middleton, John, and Greet Kershaw, *The Kikuyu and Kamba of Kenya*. Ethnographic Survey of Africa, East Central Africa, Part V, London: IAI, 1972).
Miracle, Marvin P., *Economic Change among the Kikuyu 1895–1905*, Nairobi: Institute for Development Studies, University of Nairobi, 1974.
Morgan, W. T. W., *Nairobi, City and Region*, Nairobi: OUP, 1967.
Mosley, P., *The Settler Economies: Studies in the Economic History of Kenya and Southern Rhodesia. 1900–1963*, Cambridge: CUP, 1983.
Muchai, Karigo, *The Hardcore*, Life Histories from the Revolution; Kenya, Mau Mau, No. 1., Richmond: LSMP, 1973.
Mungeam, G. H., *British Rule in Kenya, 1895–1912*, Oxford: Clarendon Press, 1966.
Muriuki, Godfrey, *A History of the Kikuyu 1500–1900*, London: OUP, 1974.
Murray-Brown, Jeremy, *Kenyatta*, London: Allen & Unwin Ltd., 1972.
Ochieng, William, *Politics and Nationalists in Colonial Kenya*, Nairobi: EAPH, 1972.
Odinga, Oginga, *Not yet Uhuru*, London: Heinemann, 1967.
Osmunson, Rosemarie, *Njoki and the Mau Mau Terror*, Nashville: Southern Publishing Association, 1959.
Osolo-Nasubo, Ng'weno, *A Socio-Economic Study of the Kenya Highlands from 1900–1970, A Case Study in Uhuru Government*, Washington DC: UPA, 1977.
Phillips, K. N., *From Mau Mau to Christ*, AIM, April, Stirling Tract Enterprises, 1958.
Presley, Cora Ann, *Kikuyu Women, the Mau Mau Rebellion and Social Change in Kenya*, Boulder: Westview Press, 1992.
Rosberg, Carl G. Jr., and John Nottingham, *The Myth of Mau Mau. Nationalism in Kenya*, Hoover Institute on War, Revolution and Peace, London: Stanford Praeger, 1966.
Routledge, W. S. and K., *With a Prehistoric People*, London: Edward Arnold, 1910.
Salvadori, Max, *La Colonisation Européenne au Kenya*, Paris: La Rose Editeurs, 1938.
Sandbrook, Richard, and Robin Cohen (eds), *The Development of an African Working Class*, Toronto: UTP, 1975.
Sheffield, James R., *Education in Kenya*, New York: Teachers College Press, 1973.
Singh, M., *History of Kenya's Trade Union Movement to 1952*, Nairobi: EAPH, 1969.
Sorrenson, M. P. K., *Land Reform in the Kikuyu Country*, Oxford: OUP, 1967.
— *Origins of European Settlement in Kenya*, Nairobi: OUP, 1968.
Spencer, John, *James Beauttah, Freedom Fighter*, Nairobi: Stellascope Publishing Co. Ltd., 1983.
— *The Kenya African Union*, London: Routledge & Kegan Paul, 1985.
Stigand, C. H., *The Land of Zinj*, London: Cass, 1913.
Swainson, Nicola, *The Development of Corporate Capitalism in Kenya 1918–1977*, London: Heinemann, 1980.
Thomson, Joseph, F. R. G. S., *Through Masai Land*, London: Sampson, Low, Marston, Searle and Rivington, 1885.
Throup, David W., *Economic and Social Origins of Mau Mau, 1945–53*, London: James Currey, 1987.
Thuku, Harry, *An Autobiography*, Nairobi: OUP, 1970.
Thurnwald, Richard C., *Black and White in East Africa*, London, Routledge and Sons, 1935.
Tignor, Robert L., *The Colonial Transformation of Kenya*, Princeton, NJ: PUP, 1976.
Van Zwanenberg, R.M.A., *Colonial Capitalism and Labour in Kenya 1919–39*, Nairobi: EALB, 1975.
Wachanga, H. K., *The Swords of Kirinyaga*, Kampala: EALB, 1975.
Waciuma, Charity, *Daughter of Muumbi*, Nairobi: EAPH, 1969.
Walmsley, R. W., *Nairobi: the Geography of a New City*, Nairobi: Eagle Press, 1957.
Wamweya, J., *Freedom Fighter*, translated from the Kikuyu by Ciira Cerere, Nairobi: EAPH, 1971.
Wanyoike, E. N., *An African Pastor*, Nairobi: EAPH, 1974.
Welbourn, F. B., *East African Rebels*, London: SCM Press, 1961.
Werlin, Herbert H., *Governing an African City*, New York: Africana Publishing Co., 1974.
White, Luise, *The Comforts of Home. Prostitution in Colonial Kenya*, Chicago: University of Chicago Press, 1990.

Selected Bibliography

Wiseman, E. M., *Kikuyu Martyrs*, London: The Highway Press, 1983.

Articles

Anderson, D. M., 'Depression, dust bowl, demography and drought: state attitudes to soil conservation in East Africa 1920–1939', *AA*, Vol. 83, No. 334, 1984, pp. 321–43.

Anderson, David, and David Throup, 'Africans and agricultural production in colonial Kenya: the myth of the war as watershed', *JAH*, Vol. 26, 1985, pp. 327–45.

Beecher, L. J. 'After Mau Mau, what?' *Internal Review of Missions*, Vol. 44, No. 174, April 1955, pp. 205–11.

Bennett, George, 'Settlers and politics in Kenya up to 1945', in V. Harlow *et al.* (eds), *The History of East Africa*, Vol. II, Oxford: Clarendon Press, 1965, pp. 265–332.

Berman, Bruce J., 'Bureaucracy and incumbent violence, administration and the origins of Mau Mau', *BJPSC*, No. 6, April 1976, pp. 143–75.

Blundell, Sir Michael, 'The present situation in Kenya', *AA*, Vol. 54, No. 215, 1955, pp. 99–108.

Breckenridge, J. B. W., 'Up the pipeline', Corona, Vol. II, No. 5, June 1959, pp. 226–8.

Clough, Marshall S., 'Koinange wa Mbiu, Mediator and Patriot', in B. E. Kipkorir (ed.), *Biographical Essays on Imperialism and Collaboration in Colonial Kenya*, Nairobi: KLB, 1980, pp. 57–86.

Cooper, Frederick, 'Mau Mau and the discourses of colonization', *JAH*, Vol. 29, No. 2, 1988, pp. 313–20.

'Current Notes', *Development in Kenya*, Vol. 25, No. 5, 1954, pp. 340–6.

Furedi, Frank, '"The African crowd in Nairobi", popular movements and elite policies', *JAH*, Vol. XIV, No. 2, 1973, pp. 275–290.

— 'The social composition of the Mau Mau movement in the white highlands', *JPS*, Vol. I, No. 4, July 1974, pp. 486–505.

— The Kikuyu squatters in the Rift Valley 1918–29', *Hadith*, Vol. 5, 1975, pp. 177–94.

Gadsden, Fay, 'The African press in Kenya 1945–52', *JAH*, Vol. 21, 1980, pp. 515–35.

Homan, F. D., 'Consolidation, enclosure and registration of title in Kenya', *JLAO*, Vol. I, No. 1, January 1962, pp. 4–14.

Hughes, O. E. B., 'Villages in the Kikuyu Country', *JAH*, Vol. 7, No. 4, 1955, pp.170–4.

Isaacman, Allen, 'Peasants and social protest in Africa', *ASR*, Vol. 33, No. 2, Sept. 1990, pp. 1–119.

Kanogo, T. M. J., 'Rift Valley squatters and Mau Mau', in W. R. Ochieng and K. K. Janohamed (eds), *KHR Special Issue: Some Perspectives on the Mau Mau Movement*, Vol. 5, No. 2, 1977, pp. 243–53.

Keller, Edmund J., Jr., 'A twentieth century model: the Mau Mau transformation from social banditry to social rebellion', *KHR*, Vol. 1, No. 2, 1973, pp. 189–206.

Kershaw, G., 'The changing roles of men and women in the Kikuyu family by sociological strata', *Rural Africana*, No. 29, 1975–76, African Studies Center Michigan SU, pp. 173–95.

— 'Mau Mau from below: fieldwork and experience, 1955–57 and 1962', *CJAS*, Vol. 25, No. 2, 1991, pp. 274–97.

Leakey, L. S. B., 'The Kikuyu problem of the initiation of girls', *JRAI*, Vol. 90, 1931, pp. 277–85.

— 'The economics of Kikuyu tribal life', *East African Economics Review*, Vol. 3, No. 1, 1956, pp. 158–80.

Lonsdale, John M., 'When did the Gusii (and any other group) become a tribe?', *KHR*, Vol. 5, No. 1.

— 'Depression and the Second World War in the transformation of Kenya', in David Killingray and Richard Rathbone (eds), *Africa and the Second World War* (London: Macmillan, 1986), pp. 97–142.

— 'Mau Maus of the mind: making Mau Mau and remaking Kenya', *JAH*, Vol. 31, No. 3, 1990, pp. 393 ff.

— 'The moral economy of Mau Mau: the problem', in Bruce Berman and John Lonsdale, *Unhappy Valley*, Vol. 2, London: James Currey, 1992, pp. 265–314.

— 'The moral economy of Mau Mau: wealth, poverty and civic virtue in Kikuyu political thought', in Bruce Berman and John Lonsdale, *Unhappy Valley*, Vol. 2, London: James

Selected Bibliography

Currey, 1992, pp. 315–504.
Lonsdale, John, and Bruce Berman, 'Coping with the contradictions of the colonial state in Kenya 1895–1914', *JAH*, Vol. 20, 1979, pp. 487–505.
Maxwell, Andrew, and Frank Morris, 'Brutality in Kenya', *Contemporary Issues*, Vol. 10, November–December 1959, pp. 1–9.
Mazrui, Ali A., 'The resurrection of the warrior tradition of African political culture', *JMAS*, Vol. 13, No. 1, 1975, pp. 67–84.
Mboya, Tom, 'Trade unions in Kenya', *Africa South*, Vol. 1, No. 2, January–March 1957, pp. 77–86.
Ng'ang'a, Mukaru D., 'Mau Mau, loyalists and politics in Murang'a 1952–1970', *KHR*, Vol. 5, No. 2, 1977, pp. 365–84.
Ogot, Bethwell A., 'Revolt of the elders', *Hadith*, Vol. 4, 1972, pp. 134–48.
Omosule, M., 'Kiama kia Muingi: Kikuyu and Land Consolidation', *TJH*, Vol. 4, Nos 1–2, 1974, pp. 115–34.
Overton, John, 'War and economic development, settlers in Kenya 1914–1919', *JAH*, Vol. 27, No. 1, 1986, pp.79 ff.
— 'The origins of the Kikuyu land problem: land alienation and land use in Kiambu, Kenya 1895–1920', *ASR*, Vol. 31, No. 2, September 1988, pp. 109–26.
Pedraza, G. J. W., 'Land consolidation in the Kikuyu areas of Kenya', *JAA*, Vol. 8, No. 2, April 1956, pp. 82–7.
Rogers, Peter, 'The British and the Kikuyu 1890–1905, a reassessment', *JAH*, Vol. 20, No. 2, 1979, pp. 255ff.
Santilli, K., 'Kikuyu women in the Mau Mau revolt', *Ufahamu*, Vol. 8, No. 1, 1977/1978, pp. 143–59.
Savage, D. C. and J. Forbes Munro, 'Carrier corps recruitment in the British East African Protectorate 1914–1918', *JAH*, Vol. 7, No. 2, 1966, pp. 313–42.
Shannon, M., 'Rehabilitating the Kikuyu', *AA*, Vol. 54, No. 215, April 1955, pp. 129–37.
Shannon, Mary I., 'Rebuilding the social life of the Kikuyu', *AA*, Vol. 56, No. 225, October 1957, pp. 276–84.
Simmance, A. J. F., 'Land redemption among the Fort Hall Kikuyu', *Journal of African Law*, Vol. V, 1961, No. 2.
Spencer, I. R. G., 'Settler dominance, agricultural production and the Second World War in Kenya', *JAH*, Vol. 21, 1980, pp. 497–514.
Spencer, J., 'KAU and Mau Mau, some connections', *KHR*, Vol. 5, No. 2, 1977, pp. 201–24.
Stichter, Sharon, 'Workers, trade unions and the Mau Mau rebellion', *CJAS*, Vol. 9, No. 2, 1975, pp. 259–75.
— 'The formation of a working class in Kenya', in Richard Sandbrook and Robin Cohen (eds), *The Development of an African Working Class*, Toronto: University of Toronto Press, 1975, pp. 21–49.
Tamarkin, M., 'Mau Mau in Nakuru', *KHR Special Issue: Some Perspectives on the Mau Mau Movement*, W. R. Ochieng and K. K. Janmohammed (eds), Vol. 5, No. 2, 1977, pp. 225–41.
— 'The Loyalists in Nakuru during the Mau Mau revolt', *Asian and African Studies*, Vol. 12, No. 2, July 1978, pp. 247–61.
Throup, D. W., 'The origins of Mau Mau', *AA*, Vol. 84, No. 336, July 1985, pp. 339–43.
Wambaa, Rebmann M., and Kenneth King, 'The political economy of the Rift Valley', *Hadith*, Vol. 5, 1975, pp. 195–218.
Welbourn, F. B., 'Comment on Corfield', *Race*, Vol. 2, May 1961, pp. 7–27.
Wipper, Audrey, 'The Maendeleo ya Wanawake Movement in the colonial period', *Rural Africana*, Audrey Wipper (ed.), Vol. 29, 1975–6, Africa Studies Center, Michigan State University, pp. 195ff.

Index

African District Council, *see* LNC
agendi (sojourners) with Ndorobo, *see* Ndorobo; with Kikuyu, *see mbari*, incorporation
Agriculture, Department of; annual reports 154; anti-fertilizer 158; assistants 161; symbol repression 162, 259; attitude to Kikuyu agriculture 152; condones alienation 161; attitude to small land owners 160, 173; to larger land owners 156ff; soil conservation programme 152, 160, 168; DARD food policy, inadequacy 152, 187; demonstration farms, hidden cost 158, 159, 173; mixed farming 158ff, 169; terracing 160-2, 173; and *gitati* 161; and migrant labourers 173
agricultural policies, clearing land 19, 20, 31, 39, 89, 285; virgin land 23, 39; crop rotation 23, 146; division of labour 19th-C 74, 146; fallowing 23, 78, 112, 146, 153, 164; fragmentation 145; green manure 39, 146, 158; intercropping, monocropping 153; introduction potatoes, improved maize beans 85, 145; LNC-proposed soil conservation, and Dept. of Agriculture 161; manure application 152, 157ff, 158, 288ff; new tools 145
agricultural productivity, DARD 152; DARD Grades 1 and 2 before Carter Commission 154, 155, 287, 288; DARD 1 and 2 around 1939 159, 288; DARD 1 and 2 before Emergency 159, 288; decline domestic, 147; decline gathering 145; division of land 147; female interdependence 156; introduction graded produce 154, 155; local standard of excellence 158; no local standardization 153, 172; production basic food on 3 acres 287; land predominantly maize 155; lower land income 156; male dominance 156; manure 150; reduced fallowing 148; small & large land owners, *ahoi* 156
ahoi 6, 12, 46ff, 77; origin 46; sons of owners 58; affinal relationships 46, 49, 97; bilateral descent groups 46; linking Igi *ithaku* 46, 47, 97; limited Thuita use 47; giving wives, taking daughters 46, 47; access to office 67; small importance as labour 46; collecting stock 47, 48; buying with *mbari* 47, 78; usufruct inherited 56, 78; wide economic range 50; percentage population Igi 47, 72, 84, 98, 114, 212, 213; Thuita 73, 84, 114, 213; *Ruraya* gains 84, 97, losses 74; losses to Rift Valley 92, 97; aging population 97; becoming 20th-C landless 46, 50; decline of senior eldership 214; declining value 9; fear land consolidation 104, 108, 110, 115, 226, 258; lose land to fallowing 148, to divisions of the 1920s 149; sons immigrate 97; lose use of land 100; own fallowing land 151; lose inheritance usufruct 90, 97; lose right to bring in kin 97; no longer desirable affinals 97, 196; land consolidation 334ff
ahoi, tributary, 62, 79; sons leaving for Maasai 62; subjected to raids of *anake* 62; true *igwima* 62

Ainsworth, J. D., *(Njue-ini)* 80; represents *thirikari* 86; defends alienation 86, 111, 176; knowledge of Kikuyu agriculture, productivity 111, 112
Akamba, 19, 44, 48, 50; barter with Kikuyu 63; become Kikuyu settlers 57; caravan middlemen, traders 61, 63; replace Kikuyu on alienated land 87, 88
anake, cost 68-9; duties of herding, defence, right to raid 68-71; must share loot 69; losses of life in raids 82; name initiations 82ff; raids avoiding friendly Kikuyu, Maasai, Akamba 68, 69; raiding important to *ahoi*, small land owners 69; caravans potential booty 63, 68, 69, 64; lawlessness in homesteads 70; Mburu victory 71; commitment oath 71; lawlessness restricted by trading elders 69-71; solidarity broken 70, 71; working as friendlies, porters 70; death toll during *Ruraya*, recovery 86; Mau Mau behaviour 74; threat to attack Europeans 82; decline of herding 120, 121, 123; early migrant labour to escape *gitati* 121
ancestors, 15; giving, withholding blessings 15ff; recruit Ndorobo ancestors when buying land 20-2; ultimate owners of land 13, 15
animal husbandry, browsing on fallow land 146; Kikuyu stock 38; cost goats 284, 285; expansion goats (Fibonacci) 113; grazing 23, 33, 172; meat yield per goat 172; ratio herders to stock 172; Ndeia, Rift Valley 147; cattle replace other stock 147; cattle dips 159, 173; maintenance herd 147; manure production 145, 173
Arthur, Dr J. W. 204
arumati (pl.) see *muramati*
askaris 141
athamaki (pl.) see *muthamaki*
athami (pl.) 77; origin of Igi *athami* 49
athungu (pl.), Europeans, early trading partners 63ff; 20th-C settlers 85, 87; rights of 86
athuri (pl.) *see also* elders 13; 14; 53; 67
atongoria (pl.) 68

Banana Hill, *see* Kiambaa
Bang, bangi, mbang, Indian Hemp, *cannabis sativa* 11; 12; *gicina bangi* 260; in Marige 252, 257, 260
bara bara, see *njira ini*
baraza 93; 102; 191 Kikuyu use of 114; 179
Baring, Sir Evelyn 241
Barlow, Rev. A. R. 181; 204
blessings 15
brideprice 24, 25, 33, 44, 45, 78, 95, 114, 149, 156, 161, 162, 286; composition 113; declining role of livestock 94; decline in parental contribution 94, 149, 162, 286; large land owners continue payment 100, 149; leaving husband angers woman's kin 156; lowering marital age 94, 172; monetization 94 149; Ndorobo dowry to brideprice 38; *ndungata* 59, 60, 79; parents decline brideprice 114; pressure by woman's kin if unpaid 95, 156; sisters' brideprice pays brother's wife 39; woman paying woman 79

347

Index

bururi 81; *bururi wa Agikuyu* 188

cannabis sativa, see *bang*
caravan trade, early 61; Akamba middlemen 62; dislodged 63; intensifiying conflict over control of 70; threat of slavers *(thukumu)* 63, 80; trading goods, payments 62, 63; exchanges for stock 63; exchanges for land and wives 61, 63; end of trade 63
caravans, *anake* clash near Kambui 64, 70; control needed 63–5; 70; friendlies and porters 63–4, 70, 74, 80, 81, 83; choice of headmen 118; camping on Igi herding land 63–4; collection points 63; organization of 62–3; leaders 63; undisciplined, 63–4; size, frequency 63–4; cooperation Mahui, C. W. R. Lane's *thirikari* 64; Igi participation 49, 53, 63; losses, benefits for small *mbari, ahoi* 65, 70
Carter Commission, compensation 102, 296ff; confirms land alienation 102, 296ff; dividing line colonial era 102; evokes *mbari* conflicts 101; impotence of KA 101, 185; KCA and, 101, 185, resistance through economic strength 102, 103; resistance of land poor and landless 103ff; rejected claims 102, 296ff; responsibility to sons 186; phantom claims 101, 102; litigation 101ff
case histories 32, 61, 75, 86, 87, 89, 163–5
Chege Kibachia 218
Chege wa Kibiru 177; 189; 209; 217; 275; 324
chiefs 280ff; local view 118; expectations 176 178; mission graduates as aides of 203; presumed venality 222
Chief Kibathi *xiii*; supporter counter-oathing 237
Chief (Paramount) Kinyanyui wa Gathirimu 60, 70, 85, 275ff; against missions 179; arbitrator Igi land case 60, 61, 79; assumes Gathirimu name 180; attitudes to 179, 202; buying car 172; Harry Thuku translator for 180, 203; damaged by Thuku theft 181; role in KA 179, 180; death of 70
Chief Magugo Waweru *xiii; xiv*, 2, 12, 140, 141; Alliance High School 207; innovations 108; 141; pro land consolidation 108; 258; provides *tha* during Marige 255
Chief Kioi 71, 203; uses Jomo Kenyatta as translator 203
Chief (Senior) Koinange Mbiu 203, 204; aid to Olenguruone victims 206; compared to Waruhiu 241, 246; fighter for coffee 219ff, 263, 392; founder Githunguri Teachers' TC and *Mbari* 187–9; government *kiama* 203; high status Kikuyu, Rift Valley 206, 241, 246; mediator female circumcision 191; opposes mission holding education to ransom 208; and Kenyatta *Mbari* oath 217; opposes KCA replacement Kinyanyui 206; sends son to US 207; supports Olenguruone victims 206, 296; target *mitherigu* 191, 192, 208; target Second World War veterans 222, 243; Waruhiu murder 241; arrested, acquitted, detained Emergency Regulations 241, 247, 263; Mau Mau involvement 263
Chief Waruhiu wa Kungu 85, 118ff; background 241; coffee licence 245; compared to Koinange 241, 246; supports counter-oathing 237, 241; murder 241, 246

Chief Waweru Mahui 85, 118ff, 140, 203; Mburu raid 71; builder roads, bridges 119; extends private land 210; protests alienation 81; raises Igi status 171; reestablishes trade 118; and rural outschool 119; supported by elders 176; vice-president KA 180; member LNC 205; see also elders, *thirikari* period
Christian Council of Kenya (CCK) 1, 328
circumcision, female, see religion, Kambui
ciama (pl.) see elders
Clayton, Anthony; brutality against Mau Mau 261; 332
coffee 167, 290; conditions imposed by Department of Agriculture 108, 168; exclusion land poor, *ahoi* 168, 259; oath takers 245; gazetted 1951 245; income compared to maize 168; local image 167, 291ff; growth until 1960s 262
colonial government, as *thirikari* 86; and *anake* wanting to become friendlies 70; C. W. R. Lane's Kiambu administration 64, 65; proposed tribute 70; retaliatory raids 85; trading relationships with Kikuyu 64; start of 86, 202
collaboration, see resistance
cooperatives 135, 205
Committee on the Sociological Causes Underlying Mau Mau with Some Proposals on the Means of Ending It (secret) 2, 237ff, 245
commodity production, initially little interest 100; need for roads, 120; *posho* for sale to settler coffee producers 126, 148; vegetables 145; comparison Nairobi wages with cash crop production 149; maize, potatoes, 149, 150; *circa* 1939 150, 158; before Emergency 150; Marketing Boards 157; Native Commodities Crop Ordinance 1935 157
communal work, see labour, *gitati*
cost of living, rural area 293ff
Corfield, F. D. 86, 243, 260
Crown Lands Ordinance (1915) 92, 108; *ahoi* use of 179
currency 64, 85, 284

data 5, 165, 187, 264–70
dating, by initiation years 82, 83, 111
diet, in 19th, 20th C 144, 145; DARD auxiliary foods 166, 167, 293ff; cost barrel of honey 171; disparity poor/wealthy 144, 145; introduction potato 145; staples 141; maize staple very poor 166; see also agriculture

East African Standard 2, 246, 252, 253; on Marige 255, 256, 261, 324
East African Institute of Social Research *xiii*
ecology, local area 31, 76
economy, trapping, hunting and foraging 19; hunting, experimental agriculture, some stock 8, 19, 25, 26, 29; agriculture, limited hunting, herding 30, 32, 35; agriculture, stock 61, 62; agriculture with surplus, stock 65, 76; *mbari* 33
education, African in Kenya 1949 (Beecher Report) 169, 249; advantages of higher-income parents 171; attack on African moral standards, intellectual capacities 170ff; closing door on landless and land poor 169, 170, 171, 230; early mission 118, 308; early outschools 118, 308; growth of 119; continued mission control

348

Index

174; mission use of schools 308ff; fees 171; political fall out 230ff; Nyaga school 247; Alliance High School 189; 207; Kikuyu College for Higher Education 189; Kikuyu high school at Githunguri 161, 189; LNC cess for Githunguri high school 161, 189; protest against cess 214; access to intermediate schooling 169; low value of employment for school leavers 128, 129, 189; parental expectations 309; parental protest 189; CCE examination 169, 170; KAPE examinations 169, 249, 308; part-time 128; Kikuyu Karing'a Educational Association (KKEA) 193, 247; Kikuyu Independent Schools Association (KISA) 193, 227, 247; short local history 307–10; Ten Year Plan for the Development of Education (1948) 169; Machakos Technical School 141; Native Industrial Training Depot 141; Jeanes School 142
elders, post-*Kirika* access to eldership 65, 66; divisions, *mbari*, territorial *ciama* 65–8; payments 201; increasing cost 6, 65–8; *tuthuri* 14; verdicts binding 105; *ndundu* membership 66; adjudication inter-*mbari* conflict 66ff; decide intiations 66–8; represent spiritual forces, guard against *thahu* 9, 5, 53, 67, 77, 82, 175, 186; guardians of history 16, 17, 66; restore relationships 105, 176; right to curse, administer ordeal 105; special concerns 42, 78; conflict with *anake*, see *anake*; relations of Mahui, Kimama and Waweru with C. W. R. Lane 64; agree tribute 64, 176; start collecting 85, 176; headman their executive 176; restrain *anake* 86; 177; confront Ainsworth 86, 176; and Kikuyu Association 179–81; 184; resistance, principles of 177, 178; restore stolen land 103, 176; land poor, landless secondary 178; transfer power to more pragmatic sons' generation 102, 185, 186, 206; continued concern for sanctity of land and moral order 186, 196, 202, 237; fewer following concentration of land ownership 196, 214; council payments postponed 196; development economic strength 102ff, 157ff, 185, 197, 202, LNC, use of 186; litigation undermining solidarity 196; and Kenyatta's return 199; Rift Valley repatriates and oath 198, 199; sale eldership rank 201; threat to land 202; *mbari* sovereignty 219; Mau Mau participation 323, against oaths that violate moral order, threaten land 10, 235, 233; *see also athuri*
elections 1957 (Kenyatta elections) 206, 263
Embu 20, 74, 93
Emergency, *see* Mau Mau, Emergency
employment, *see* labour

Fallers, Lloyd A. *xiv*
famine, *Kirika* 30, 31, 38, 45, 51; cause of 16, 36; dating 36; death of people, stock, game 16, 31, 37; land abandoned 37; loss of earlier history 16, 17; Murang'a break 36; selective recall 16, 17; local control 35, 36; Thuita prior acquisitions 29; Igi prior *ithaku* 29–31; post-*Kirika* advantageous land conditions 43; immigration 43; increased herding 43, 44; redistribution of land 43, 44
famine, *Ruraya* 8, 17, 71; *anake* and *Ruraya* 74; antecendent disasters 70ff, 82, 83; comparison *Kirika* 74–6; deaths 37, 71–5, 84; post-*Ruraya* available land 75; change status through inheritance 75; change relationships within *mbari* 75; initiation year 1919/20 shows recovery 172; invasion of game 85; land abandoned for fear of curse 76; loss of *mbari* 75; refugees not returning for fear of curse 76; speculation about causes rejected 76
fatina 246
Fibonacci, *see* animal husbandry
fission, *see mbari*
forest, reputation 20, 25; economy *see* economy, agriculture, hunting, limited herding
friendlies, *see* caravan trade

Gaki 21, 74, 80
Gatabaki, Peter, Chairman KISA 227
genealogies, adjusted 37
generation, *see riika*
Gichuru, James 200, 209; taking *Mbari* oath 206
Gikuyu, *see* moieties
gitati, *see* labour
githaku, see *mbari*, *ithaku*
Githunguri, Teachers' Training College 193–5; trading post 208; Chege wa Kibiru's *thingira* 209; Koinange seeking 'to eat a goat together' with landed 193, 195; oath non-binding, like *Mbari* oath 195; objective to train leaders 193, 194; initiation year 194; Peter Mbiu headmaster 194; elders doubtful suitability, rejected by colonial government 194; fundraising 195; Kenyatta headmaster 217ff; funds for College underscore his status 218; Kenyatta tax 219, 242, 243; selling of elders' rank 201ff, 218; centre of Githunguri Mau Mau 227ff; rejects violence 251ff
Grieves, M. H. Agricultural Officer, Kiambu 157

Hall, Francis *(Wanyahoro)* 80
Henderson, Dr J. E. 207; 296
Highlands, White *see* Rift Valley
history, *mbari* history/oral traditions before *Kirika* 35, 56, 57, 271–3; to be remembered or forgotten 17, 38, 42, 48, 56; European presumptive evolutionary 16, 17, 40, 296; Kikuyu response to European presumptive history 56; Mau Mau to be forgotten 17, 18, 37, 38, 259; *see also* oral traditions and specific periods
Homeguards, 250, 260, 327ff, 331ff; background 327, 332; oath taking 250, 328; recruitment 250; venality 250, 327,332
households, composition 12; definition of 12; Igi, Thuita *mbari* and *ahoi* 72, 73; female heads of households in 1950s 114

Imperial British East African Company (IBEAC) 64, 70, 80; encountered as *thirikari* through C. W. R. Lane 64, 70; changes into Protectorate irrelevant 64; end *thirikari* 86
ideology, of history/loss 15–17, 48; of individual and gender 23–25, 39; of inequality 15, 68, 215; of land 20, 21, 27ff, 213, 214; of wealth and authority 14–16
igwima 26, 62, 74, 77
incorporation, male *see mbari* incorporation

349

Index

Indian merchants 155
informal reference groups 133
inequality, late 19th C 61ff
inheritance, land, *see* land, inheritance of; wives and children 59, 76
Iregi 36
ita ya nyimbo (war of songs) 192
Itara, *see* Thuita
ithaku, see *mbari*, *ithaku*
itoka, see *matoka*
ituika, see *mariika*, generation set system

Kabete 47, 70
Kaggia, Bildad 135, 229
Kambui, attack on caravan 64; *see also* religion, Kambui mission
karinga (purity) 191
Kenya African Union (KAU) *see* political associations
Kenya African National Union (KANU) 18, 257
Kenya Land Commission, *see* Carter Report
Kenyatta, Jomo, on buying Ndorobo land 38, 40; on pre-colonial Kikuyu society 38; on *mariika* 41; member Thuku's YKA 210; Mbiu advocates his return 199, 208ff, 216, presumption of power 216; oaths, for the *Mbari* and KCA 199, 217; popular evaluation of his achievements, 199, 200ff, 217, 218, 226; President KAU 200, 217; headmaster, headquarters Githunguri 199, 200, 217; image of *muthamaki* 11, 200, 230 lacking wealth 199, 200; no legitimate way to raise money 242; raises money by sale of elders' rank 201, 202, 211, 218; raises money through *mariika*, Kenyatta tax 218ff; only moderate return 219, 243; raises money through oathing 231ff; supports Olenguruone 206, 217; denounces Mau Mau, threatens to curse it 240; Kenyatta Mau Mau essentially pacific 230; leadership Mau Mau unlikely according to age data 242, 246, 323; arrest, unifying, bringing hope 241, 248, 330; return Kikuyu country 263; Prime Minister 263; orator, 218, 237; pro-terracing, anti-*gitati* 200; work and wealth 240, 246
kiama, jurisdiction of elders recognized by Native Councils Ordinance (1912) 105, 115; jurisdiction local councils curtailed, establishment African District Councils (1924) 106, 115; Native Divisional Tribunals, with appeals (1943) 106, 115
Kiama kia Mwangi (Muingi) 258, 262
Kiambaa (Banana Hill), Koinange headquarters 187
Kiambu, ritual outpost Murang'a 35ff; break with Murang'a 36; halts caravans 63; organization 64; Kiambu Annual District Report 2; district organization, hardship of 141
Kiambu African District Council, *see* LNC
Kiburi, senior elder, Chief Adviser Law and Custom, Kiambu Court *xiii*, 41, 47
Kimama wa Macharuga, *see also* colonial government, *thirikari* period 84, 85, 111, 118, 176, 202
Kipande 204, 214, 215
Kirika, *see* famine, *Kirika*
Koinange, Peter Mbiu 188, 194, 195, 200, 201, 207-9

Koinange, Charles Karugu 77
komerera 330
Knapp, W. F. Rev. 204; *see also* religion, Kambui
Krieger, T. N. 83
Kubai, Fred 135, 223, 236, 245
kwashiorkor 163

labour, access to jobs 117; labour exchange *(ngwatio)* 84, 111, 116, 120, 146, 154, 156, 168, 200, 218; traditional paid specialists 120, 121, 123, 127; female, 117, 126, 127, 130, 132, 138, 155, 286; *gitati* 120, 141, 159, 175, 200, 214, 217, 242, 250; basic, semi-skilled and skilled (local/settled area) 117, 119ff, 122, 123, 124, 125, 127; clerical and administrative (local) 117-19; safety valves 133-5; unemployment 123; Nairobi 127-35; return veterans 132; strikes, city celebrations 135, 230; vagrancy laws 130, 133, 134; unions 134; summary male employment 131; summary male employment by land 137; Nairobi wages compared with 3 acres land 134, 287ff; buying power minimum wage local/settled area 160, 290-1; mean wages Nairobi before Emergency 291; male clerical wage Nairobi with European female clerical wage 132
Lambert H. E., on pre-colonial society 40; on Kikuyu legal system 318
land, blessing under control of ancestors 13, 15, 16, 53; boundaries, 38, 114, 242, 259, 263; forfeiture of 35, 37, 161; ideology of 15ff, 161; names for 38, 52; conflicts prevent investment 107, create desire for secure tenure 108; inheritance of 8, 32, 38; 58ff, daughter, female 39, 59, non-contributing sons 49, 51
land, acquisition 38; abandoned land 43, 46; *athi*, sellers of 20, 22, 30, 43, 51, 78, 109; compensation 52; *gukuna* 9, 13, 52, 91; from Kikuyu 30; *magatha* 21, 22, 29, 31; Ndorobo, involvement ancestors 20, 21, 31ff; Ndorobo buying 20, 21, 30, 40, 44, 51; options 43, 51, 78; risk buying with girl, accepting *magatha* 78; size acquisitions 22, 29, 44, 50, 51
land, alienation, Ainsworth denying Kikuyu ownership 86; akin to physical attack 177; ancestral anger as cause 176; compensation 87, 88; concept of stolen lands 91; confirmed in Carter Report 102ff, government policy Kikuyu lost only surplus land 14; accepting responsibility 86, 111; protecting buyers 88; losses Igi 89, Thuita 89, measured in plots for basic food 89; memories 85, 89; process of 8, 85-7; settler dependence 88; settler policies to drive Kikuyu away 86, 88; unalienated land in Kikuyu hands depending on use 86; threats of alienation in agricultural policies 112; Nairobi 230, Olenguruone 206; herding land lost, 89ff, 93; settlers fine for trespass 113; *mbari* members aid dispossessed 90ff
land, cost of, pre-*Kirika* 22, 23, 29, 30; post-*Kirika* (19th C) 43, 44, 50, 51, 53, 89; no payment 78; unknown 19th-C 29, 30, 50, 51, 60; women part of 22, 29, 32, 58; higher elevation 44, 49; lower elevation 44; price first colonial period 95, 96; unknown in first colonial period 96; second colonial period 115, 164; influence on status 22, 95

350

Index

land, consolidation, first attempt of 1948 defeated 108ff; increase litigation 109; Department of Agriculture expectations 168, 174; second attempt linked to coffee permits 258; aided by litigation 236; villagization 258, 334ff; binding arbitration outstanding cases 258, 262; victory individual ownership 258, yet *mbari* retained 258; 334ff; procedures 258; title deeds 259; *ahoi* 258, 259, 335, 336; negative, positive opinions 334, 335

land, ownership, categories and potential 98–100; 148, 149ff; 213, 214; buying land by *ahoi*, owners first colonial period 96ff; second colonial period 104; divisions of the 1920s and 1930s 148ff; fallowing land for small land owners 151; landless, land poor 216, 240; return stolen lands irrelevant for *ahoi* by mid-1930s 215; protest privileges landed 214

land tenure, European image 28, 40, 102, 108, 110, 180, 296ff; European attitudes to Kikuyu 111, 112, 152, 160, 173; Kiambu 26ff; Murang'a 19, 46; Murang'a redemption 19; government recognition owners and *ahoi* have different rights 180

Lane, C. W. R., institutes tribute system 64, 85; organizes Kiambu 64, rejects initiation year as 'friendlies' 70

Leakey, Canon 203, 204; unable to get more mission land 193

Leakey, Gray Arundel 81, 275

Leakey, L. S. B. *xiv*, 2, 319; differences with 41; on *ahoi* and *athami* 77; on buying Ndorobo land 38, 78; on *mbari* 40; on nature Kikuyu culture and society 41, 80; on political organization 81; on counter-oathing 237, 245

Limuru 47, 70

Local Native Council (LNC), established 173, 205; defender *mbari* sovereignty 103; organization larger land owners 103; female circumcision 191ff; economic role boosted by Carter Commission 169, 171; Githunguri High School 190, 214; cess for, 214; providing health care 205; manure, importation and subsidies 158, 288; providing health care 205; soil conservation 161; conflict with government over soil conservation 161; use of *gitati* 161, 214, 242, 249

Lonsdale, John *xiv*, on *matuika* 42, 70; on use of fire 39; on *mihiriga* 40

loyalism 238, 260, 251, 324; *see also* Mau Mau, resistance and collaboration, 323ff

Maasai 19, 21, 44, 48; hosts to poor and immigrants 57, 62, 69; barter with Kikuyu 63; warfare with Kikuyu late 19th C (Mburu battle) 71; agricultural settlers 82; treaties with Europeans, freeing land 91, 112, 113; selling manure 158, 228

Mahui wa Ihuthia 63, 64

Makwa 31

Maendeleo ya Wanawake 136

Mathu, Eliud, attending Alliance 206; winning nominated seat over Mbiu 188, 197; taking *Mbari* oath 188, 206; taking Mau Mau oath 206, 207

Marige market, bus station, *ndukas* 122, 123, 155, 157; land owners diversifying 155; police station under Jock Scott 3

mariika, generation system alternating Maina/Mwangi 31, 36, 42, 59, 71; change over at *ituika* 42, 36, 277ff; failure to perform an *ituika* and Mau Mau 280

mariika, initiation years, *see also anake* rough dating 82, 111; organization of names 64, 70, 68, 70, 82; attacking caravans 64, 70; early, later cost 35, 69; curbing power 69, 70, 82; friendlies 70, 81; split along property lines 69; Mau Mau behaviour during *Ruraya* 74; change *anake* into labourers 120ff; ritual cohesion lost 243; significance 20th C 135; used by Kenyatta to raise money 69, 218, 219, 243; Mau Mau participation 322

mariika, regiment system 82

marriage, raiding for brides 25; Ndorobo bride's husband receiving *magatha* 36; Ndorobo changing from *magatha* to brideprice 38 (*see also* brideprice); rights of affines 17, wives 24; lowering age of marriage 94, 130; monogamy 25, 45, 76, 207; polygyny, extent of 78, increasing chance survival in forest economy 25, 45; increase after *Kirika*, *Ruraya*, except for *ahoi* 45, 97, 98, 148; high level in Rift Valley 23, 25, 44, 59, 76, 78, 114, 197; serial 149; problems church and 190ff

matoka 38, 114, 259, 263

matuika (pl.) *see ituika* in *mariika*, generation system

Mau Mau, name of 83, 208

Mau Mau, pre-Emergency, anti-Mau Mau movements, Army of Christ 239; counter-oathing 237; 238; Kambui Manifesto 1952, threat to bar children from school 239; Pastoral Letter 239; Kenyatta denunciation, threat of curse 240

Mau Mau, perceived as separate movements by population 9, 220, 230, 234; Githunguri/rural 220; 226–30; Nairobi 221–6, 236; Rift Valley 197ff, 220, 303–5; Tanganyika 209, 210, 227, 244; Beecher Report conflict between Nairobi and rural Githunguri 230, 231, 240; oathing as private enterprise 236, 245; oathing centres competing 233, 235; oathing of kin 244; personnel centres 244; local organization 256

Mau Mau, by Declaration of Emergency 10, 225, 228, 229, 232, 234; increase Kenyatta boon 10, 248; growth Nairobi membership by gender, occupation and period 225; comparison growth Nairobi, rural Githunguri 228; females 229; growth Mau Mau membership by period and land position, male 232, female 234

Mau Mau activities, unions and Mau Mau 222, 223; KAU and Mau Mau 221–3, 321, 322; oaths deemed illegal 220, 221, 223, 224, 226, 227, 230, 231, 233, 235, 236, 315–17, 318; multiple oaths 228, 229, 319; legitimate or illegitimate 317–18; *batuni* oath, associated with RV and forest, not available until 1954 244

Mau Mau, government acts against 12, 243; perceived as illegal society 4, 220; criteria for illegal oaths 220; Declaration Emergency 1, 111, 246; Penal Code enforced 220; obligatory screening 221; Operation Jock Scott 247; Operation Anvil 258, 262; Operation Broom 262; Emergency ended 246, 258; background local screening team 326, 327; civil committee

351

Index

250, 326, 327; local operations 220, 325–27, 250, 325; operations in other areas 326; imposing punishments 326; imposing cleansing Christian confession service 11, 328; *gutahikio* ritual 250, 326, 327–9; certificates of loyalty 238, 251, 260; forced confessions, cleansing 251, 329

Mau Mau, Marige, arms from *Muhimu* 251, 260; abuse of *bang* and beer 11, 252, 260; forced recruitment 251; Githunguri objections 251, 252, 257; wrong people killed 256; forewarned population 252; murder of agricultural instructor 252, 260, 261; other victims 252, 256; role of Gitau–Mwereri–Kimani litigation 252; victims taken to hospital, act of *tha* 255; security forces aftermath 255, 256; may have killed innocent victims 258, 262; toll, including court death sentences 257, 258, 261; *East African Standard* reports 255, 256, 261; reaction elders 257; oaths after Marige, end of Mau Mau 258

Mau Mau, punishments 221, 250; all lost homestead 269; death 12; death during interrogation 255; detention camps 262; fines 250, 262, 263; *gitati* if too poor to pay 263; detention 262; special tax 263; loss of urban jobs after Anvil 258, 262; lifted 259; no vote in 1957 election 263; no coffee permits 245, 262; Athi River 262; Hola 257; 262

Mau Mau, and age 221, 250, 323; elders' rank 223; initiation years 322; *Kiama kia Moscou* 256; *Muhimu*, 241, 245, 251, 257, 260, 26

Mau Mau, non-participation 323–5; 'stumps' 238; certificate of loyalty 221, 250; loyalism 245, 251, 263, 332ff

Mau Mau, Kiambu 329ff

Mau Mau, and women 260–1

mbari, origins, autonomy and sovereignty 103; 174; 176, 180, 186, 219; buyers of land 18, 30, 31, 51–3, 54, 114; group of brothers 20, 30, 45; closely related kinsmen 2, 29, 45; joint buying, kin or no kin 47, 49, 50, 107; private land 28, 50, 51, 108; ritual land 51, 77, 108; incorporating *agendi* 26ff, 31–3, 42, 46, 59; exogamy between buyers, sellers 45, 47; kin with the sellers, 21, 38; kinship between buyers 21, 49; *kirumi* on affinal terms between members 55, 108, 113; rights and duties of members 18, 27, 28, 55, 56; rules in *mbari* oath 51, 54, 77, 107, 259; *kirumi* on sales 50; violation of *kirumi* 50, 51; spiritual forces ultimate owners 15, 27, 65

mbari, expansion, fission procedures 34, 36, fission authorized, unauthorized 36, 37, 90–2; *ithaku* formation 18, 45, 50, 53 kinsmen incorporated in *ithaku* 45, 77, 78, 273, 274; new members from *ahoi* 47, 50, 53, 54, 78; others 48; unequal contributions to new acquisitions 60, 61; evidence unequal contributions 53

mbari, names 18; Igi purported name 62; name Thuita 77; population strength Igi 72, 98; Thuita 73, 74, 98 Igi location 77; Thuita location 12, 271

mbari, Igi acquisitions of land 49, 50; *mbari* solidarity through oaths, affinity through *ahoi* 47, 49, 97, 107; *ithaku* different strength 54, 107 *muramati* 51; participation buying land unequal 19, 52, 53, 60, 107; participation, leadership role caravan trade 49; private land 49, 50, 51, 55; 96; 104; price land 60, 61; price disputed 78; price private land 96, 104 regional centre of power 68, 77; refuge *ahoi, athami* 272; use of Igi herding land 47, 49, 62, 97

mbari, Igi oral traditions, Chege 29–31, 36, 41, 42, 50–3, 78; Gitau 30, 52; Kimani 31, 51, 64, 109; Kungu 29, 30, 50, 51, 78; Mungai 31, 51; Mwereri 29, 30, 52; Njau 29–31; 36, 42, 50, 51, 56, 77, 78

mbari, Igi society, increased polygyny after *Kirika*, *Ruraya* 44, 98; losses land alienation 89; mid-1920s *ahoi* insufficient, small *ithaku* relying on larger *ahoi* 98; divisions of 1920s 97, 98, 102; strong increase subsistence plots second colonial period 99; land *ahoi* dwindling 100; start serious conflicts 115; communal versus individual ownership of land 236, 245, 249; communal ownership 27ff, 54, 108, 110, 249; individual ownership (ritual unity) 14, 26–8, 31–3, 53–6, 78, 79, 90, 108; conflicts between *ithaku*, parts of 9, 53, 108, 110; Gitau versus Mwereri 49, 50, 53, 90, 93, 109–11, 249, 252ff, 258; Gitau versus Kimani 109, 249, 251, 252ff, 256; Gitau versus large part Igi 52, 54, 109, 236; Njau versus Mungai 43, 51, 53, 109, 111, 249, 258; Njau versus part Chege 48, 53, 54, 78, 109, 111, 249, 258; court decisions 109ff

mbari, Thuita, comparison Igi 106ff; dependence on Igi 50, 272; land scarcity late 19th C 13, 48, 49; oral traditions 13, 29, 271–93; losses in *Ruraya* 73; in alienation 89; to Rift Valley 92; land buying 96, 104; sales 20th C 96ff, 104; prices 96

Mbaya, *see* Perkiss, G.

Mburu, James 287

McCarthy, Bishop John 239

Mihiriga (pl.) *see muhiriga*

Mitherigu (pl.), shaming songs 192, 208

missions, *see* religion

Miti ya Kenya 184, 205

moieties, *ukabi, gikuyu* 277

monetization 93; brideprice increase 94; currency replacing goats 94; land prices rising 95; stock reduction 93

Morrison, Stanley S. *xiii*

mugendi, see *agendi*

Mugo, Dedan Mugo Kimani, Kenyatta aide 201; giving first, second oaths outside Githunguri 202, 210, 227; rejected by elders 210, 233; president of the *mariika* 243; strong Nairobi ties 244

muhiriga 40

muhoi, see *ahoi*

Muigwithania 210

Mumenyerere 243, promoter Kenyatta 210; Kenyatta tax 216, 219, 243

mundu mugo 250, 312ff

Mungai, J. M. 217

muramati 51, 60, 62–4, 77, 95

Murang'a, early ritual control over Kiambu settlements 19, 21, 35, 36, 51; *see also mariika*, generation set systems

murica 82

muthamaki 64, 68, 81

muthami, see *athami*

mutherigu (sing.) *see mitherigu*

352

Index

muthungu (sing.) *see athungu*, Europeans
muthuri (sing.) *see athuri*, elders
mutongoria (sing.) *see atongoria*
Muumbi na Gikuyu, *mbari* of 175, 180
mwanake, see *anake*
mwangi, see *mariika*, generation set systems
Mwaniki, Henry Muoria 243

Nairobi, city charter 230
Native Industrial Training Depot 141
Ndorobo, accepting *agendi* 9; 25; 21, 29–31; *athi* 19th C 20, 78; *athi* 20th C 77, 104; ancestors recruited by Kikuyu 21, 48; barter with Kikuyu 63; conflicts 78; culture destroyed 38; intermarriage 19, 22, 29, 38; landed 8, 19, 44, 50, 57; landless 20, 29; *magatha* dowry 19, 21, 30; merging with other populations, 38, 44, 57; price, sales policies 22, 46, 60ff; price additions 60, 61; rude to refer to Ndorobo background 49, 89; shift to agriculture, Kikuyu 39, 44, 48, 157; shift to brideprice 38
nduka 165
ndungata 59, 60, 79
ngwatio, see labour, exchange
njira-ini or *bara bara* 114
Nyakeru, mbari ya 209
Nyeri, see Gaki

oaths, cleansing 313, 314; government illegal 220; Kikuyu legitimate, illegitimate 237, 245; *kunyua muuma*, commitment or amended commitment 183, 184, 344ff; structuring, restructuring 183, 312ff; to curse, warn, use in ordeal or judgment 34, 42, 68, 77, 313ff; under control of elders, to avoid *thahu* 312–15, 318ff; *kuringa thenge*, in presence of *githathi* 237, 238, 246, 313ff; commitment oaths common for higher echelons 315, 316; various commitment oaths within political organizations 315; commitment oath in higher echelons, East African Association 183; amended commitment oaths in early Kikuyu Central Association (KCA), for higher contributors 184; amended commitment oath, KCA after proscription ('goat oaths') 196, 217; commitment oath, preparation for Githunguri, 'to eat a goat together' 193; advanced commitment oath for money carriers, Githunguri 219; commitment oath for larger contributors, Githunguri 194; commitment/advanced commitment oaths after Kenyatta speeches 201; KCA oath given at Githunguri 195; Olenguru-one, amended commitment oath, later KCA, dealing with perceived land alienation 206, 296ff; provincial organization women allowed to take oaths, later all oaths accessible unless they mentioned land specifically 195; proliferation of 201, 316; government use of structuring oaths 204, 315; government use of structuring oaths to combat Mau Mau 237, 245; Kenyatta threat of cursing oath to combat Mau Mau 240
Ogot, Bethwell A. 202
oral traditions, selective 19, not a matter of choice 28; evolving 37; official, unofficial 48; Igi 30–1, 48–50, 273, 274; Thuita 29, 48; 271–3; *see also* history

pacification, *see* elders, resistance of
Pastoral Letter 239
Penal Code 220, 243
Penwill, D. S., District Commissioner Kiambu 263
Perkiss, George (Mbaya) 80
political organizations, pre-colonial, *see* elders
political organizations, Kikuyu Association (KA), council of elders, not party or chiefs, no fees 179, 180, 204; mission influence 180; nudging to become party 181; objection diluting land issues 181; opposition Koinange, driving force 180, 181; influence declining 184, 185; revival during Carter Commission 185; virtual dissolution 185, 186
political organizations, Young Kikuyu Association, becoming East African Association, party 181; issues 181; fees, local participation 183; opposition from KA, fear of diluting land issue, Murang'a 181; theft of memorandum 181; organization with two/three tiered base, like later KCA, 'men of one goat' 67, 182; higher echelon 'eating goat together' 183; flexible but unstable 182; oaths to solve organizational problems 183; Thuku conspicuous consumption 183, 205; arrest, disbanded 183, 184
political organizations, Kikuyu Central Association (KCA), founding, limited oathing 184; Carter Commission, representation and losses 185; conflict with KA 185; conflict with missions 191; legitimated after Carter Commission 186, 187; Murang'a KCA hostile 187; strong in Rift Valley 187; proscribed under Penal Code 220; identified with Githunguri 195
political organizations, Koinange creates *Mbari* 187ff; return of stolen land, end alienation 187; moral unity 188; *Mbari* oath symbol of political legitimacy 188
political organizations, Kikuyu Provincial Organization, incorporates women 195
political organizations, Kenya African Union (KAU) 134; involvement local elders 196, 209; KAU Nairobi attack unions 223; conflict between Kenyatta and Nairobi KAU 223; Nairobi attempts to involve rural area 222; status Nairobi unions' leaders 243; struggle between KCA and KAU 243; Nairobi union men in control of KAU 245; proscribed 247
political organizations, growing awareness of after Second World War 222; fees too high for landless, land poor 215
population, estimate before *Kirika* 35; increase after *Kirika* 43ff; first decades after *Ruraya* 97; until Emergency, Igi 72, 74; Thuita 73, 74; around 1955, Igi, Thuita 12
posho 126, 148, 172
poverty 19th C 68; households below/above poverty line 165–7; solutions seen by poor 167

raiding, punitive, confiscating stock 177; economic significance of 65–70; obligations of raiding parties 69; raiding for girls 25, 68
railway 63, 111
rape, ceremonial after initiation 82
Regeneration, *see* ideology, of individual and gender
religion, Ng'ai supreme being living in Mt Kenya,

353

Index

other mountains 205; with spiritual forces controls blessings 15, 16, 23, 27; *uhoro wa Ng'ai*, beyond human understanding 16, 75; religion essentially ethical, concerned with *theru, thahu* 176, 177

religion, Kambui mission (Gospel Missionary Society), buying land 118, 180; conversion prime object, literacy to maintain it 118; medical aid 205; outschools, Wanyoike teacher/minister 118ff; opposed to polygyny, female circumcision 190ff; need to reestablish control after LNC Githunguri school attempts 190; KCA attacks 191; Kambui losing support of parents 192; end of its close association with new élite 193

religion, growth of church, 310; mission becoming Presbyterian Church of East Africa 119; Revival 136; providing *tha* 136; refusal to carry arms 238

repatriation, from Rift Valley 197

reserves 93

resistance, of the elders, duty to 9, 177; principles of 9ff, 175ff; return of stolen lands central to 177; resistance through strength 186ff

resistance, of land poor, landless 9, 186ff, 212ff

resistance, and collaboration 323–5

Rift Valley (Ruguru) 111, 299; approved, unapproved fission 91, 300; argument for going 71; according to government 300; argument against going 91; cursing unapproved fission 91, 113, 197; losses of Igi, Thuita 92, 93, 97; general data 299–303; Mau Mau among population 303–4; Rift Valley oaths not propagated nor accepted 188, 304

riika, see *mariika*

ritual affiliation, *see* moieties

ritual speech 17

ritual specialist, *see mundu mugo*

robbers, *see thabari*

rugongo 65–8

Scott Agricultural Laboratory 52

settled area *(macamba)*, continued Kikuyu grazing 87; early productivity settlers 112; estimate Kikuyu population on alienated land 86; importation non-Kikuyu resident labour 87, 96; need for maize flour 126; settlers demanding payment for grazing 87

slave raids 63, 80

Sorrenson, M. P. K., on early European productivity 112; on colonial land policy 114

Spencer, John, on struggle between KCA and KAU, 243

strikes, Mombasa 1947 134; Nairobi 1950 135; settled area 1947, 1951 135; upland 1947 218

sufficiencies 57, 78, 95, 98, 100, 114, 147, 153, 159, 163, 168, 215

taxes, imposed late 19th C, not collected 176; flat rate system 9, 64, 85, 165, 284; use of 120

taxis 110, 118

tha 14, 15, 37, 75, 77, 109, 110; *kuigua tha*, to provide *tha* 37; *tha* given 14, 42, 45, 46, 52, 56, 80, 96, 100, 107, 126, 135, 147, 148, 153, 156, 162, 163, 200, 205, 215; *tha, mundu wa* 257; *tha* provided by Mandeleo and women of Revival 136

thabari 20, 26, 32, 56, 57, 77

thahu 42, 177, 186, 250

theru 42

thingira 184, 189, 209, 217

Thuku, Harry 204, claimed *Matiba* 207, supporter of counter-oathing 237; *see also* political organizations, EAA

thukumu 63

Tigoni 206

trade, with Ndorobo, Kamba, Maasai 63, restoration early 20th C 148; with settlers, Indian merchants 172; *see also* caravan trade

transportation 110

tribal allegiance, change of 2, 21, 48

tribal attitude, hindrance to education 169

tribe, concept of 93, 108, 276ff

tribute, demanded by settlers 86, 87

unions, Nairobi African Taxi Drivers Union 217; Kenya African Road Transport and Mechanics Union, orders oath taking for KAU 223; Kenya Houseboys Organization, orders oath taking for KAU 223; significance for low-paid workers 134; strikes, *see* strikes; *see also* labour

Unuthi (Nubians) 63

urogi, see witchcraft

usufruct 86

vagrancy, 1949 Nairobi Vagrancy (Amendment) Bill 133; 1950 Voluntary Unemployed Persons Ordinance 134

veterans (Second World War) 132, 196, 221ff; background 221; expectations 222; become members Kiambu African District Council (LNC) 222; follow KCA tactics 222; blame chiefs for lack of permits 222; vilefy Koinange 222, 243; discontented urban element 222

villagization 1, 12, 111, 258, 336ff; larger land owners allowed to return to own land 258, 266

Waira Kamau *xiii*; background 210; Kenyatta coworker 199, 201, 210; strong Nairobi ties 244; arrested for Waruhiu murder 241; guilty, detained 241

Waiyaki wa Hinga 64, 80, 177

Wanyoike Kamawe, Kambui student 202; claims Matiba 207; teacher outschool 119; local preacher, aide to Chief 118; building bridges, roads 118; treasurer KA 180; member LNC 191; attempt to mediate female circumcision issue 191; moderator Chania Presbytery 119

weiyathi, wiathi, wiyathi 235, 259

witchcraft *(urogi)* 35, 39, 65, 314; elders charged with control of 27, 39, 65, 314

women, contributor to husband's lineage, natal lineage 24; ideology of role 23ff; obligation to provide basic, auxiliary food 126; right to sufficient land 126; right to inherit land 39, 59; oath, after Provincial Association 195; no *Mbari* oath 187; oath taking 138; 225; 229; 234; security forces' brutality against 261; status before Emergency 24ff, 47, 157

www.ingramcontent.com/pod-product-compliance
Lightning Source LLC
Chambersburg PA
CBHW031230290426
44109CB00012B/231